Oxford
School
Thesaurus

Chief Editor: Andrew Delahunty

Al

D1494229

OXFORD
UNIVERSITY PRESS

OXFORD
UNIVERSITY PRESS

Great Clarendon Street, Oxford OX2 6DP

Oxford University Press is a department of the University of Oxford.
It furthers the University's objective of excellence in research,
scholarship, and education by publishing worldwide in

Oxford New York

Auckland Cape Town Dar es Salaam Hong Kong Karachi
Kuala Lumpur Madrid Melbourne Mexico City Nairobi
New Delhi Shanghai Taipei Toronto

With offices in

Argentina Austria Brazil Chile Czech Republic France Greece
Guatemala Hungary Italy Japan Poland Portugal Singapore
South Korea Switzerland Thailand Turkey Ukraine Vietnam

Oxford is a registered trade mark of Oxford University Press
in the UK and in certain other countries

© Copyright Oxford University Press 2016

Database right Oxford University Press (maker)

• First published 2005 • Second edition 2007 • First published as *Oxford School Thesaurus*
in pocket-sized paperback 2012 • This edition 2016

British Library Cataloguing in Publication Data

Data available

ISBN-13: 978-0-19-274711-2

10 9 8 7 6 5

Printed in China by Leo Paper Products Ltd.

Paper used in the production of this book is a natural,
recyclable product made from wood grown in sustainable forests.
The manufacturing process conforms to the environmental
regulations of the country of origin.

Oxford
OWL

For school
Discover eBooks, inspirational
resources, advice and support

For home
Helping your child's learning
with free eBooks, essential
tips and fun activities

www.oxfordowl.co.uk

Contents

Preface

The *Oxford School Thesaurus* has been specially written for students aged 10 and above. It is particularly useful for students who are about to start secondary school and who need an up-to-date, student-friendly reference tool that they can consult at home or at school.

This thesaurus is easy to use and understand. The vocabulary has been carefully selected and covers school curriculum topics ranging from English Language and Science and Technology to Sports and Music in order to support students in their writing assignments and homework.

The *Oxford School Thesaurus* gives all the information that students need for exam success in a simple and accessible format. Use of the thesaurus will help students develop the best English language skills and equip them with excellent writing and speaking skills for years to come.

The *Oxford School Thesaurus* can also be used very effectively in conjunction with the *Oxford School Dictionary*, which offers further support with reading, writing and vocabulary building.

The publisher and editors are indebted to all the advisors, consultants and teachers who were involved in planning and compiling this thesaurus.

Introduction
– how a thesaurus can help you

A thesaurus gives you alternatives – often more interesting and colourful ones – to the words you already know and use; these are known as **synonyms**. In some cases it also gives you the opposites of words, which are known as **antonyms**. Using a thesaurus regularly will extend your vocabulary and help you to be more accurate and imaginative in the way that you express yourself.

➤ When you are preparing for a presentation, writing and redrafting, a thesaurus can be very useful in helping you to avoid such things as overused words or words that are too general to have any impact. For example, *nice* is a perfectly acceptable word in conversation, but a thesaurus will allow you to replace it with more interesting words like *pleasant*, *agreeable*, *enjoyable*, *likeable* or *friendly*.

➤ When you are writing or giving a presentation at school, you need to think about such things as whether your language should be formal or colloquial. A word that is 'right' for one audience might not be for another. An important role for a thesaurus is to provide you with more choices of words for different situations. For example, *kill* is a word for general use, whereas *slay* is mostly found in stories and dramas; *little* is a much more affectionate and intimate word than its more neutral **synonym** *small* (compare a *small child* and a *little child*).

The difference between a dictionary and a thesaurus

Dictionaries and thesauruses help you in different ways with using language. A dictionary tells you mostly about what words mean whereas a thesaurus helps you to find alternative words to the ones you know and so helps you to put more words into use. When you are writing you might want to look up a word in a dictionary to check its exact meaning or spelling, but you use a thesaurus when you want to find a better, more interesting or more exact way of expressing your ideas.

Finding a better word

When you are writing a first draft, you quite often put down the first appropriate word that comes to mind. Using a thesaurus might help you to come up with one that makes a different impact on the reader. In the sentences below, they all mean the same thing but one is more formal, one less formal, and one uses a metaphor. Which sentence is the best for you will depend on the purpose of your writing.

> ➤ *The new school uniform rules made me **lose my temper***.
> ➤ *The new school uniform rules made me **freak out***.
> ➤ *The new school uniform rules made me **see red***.

Finding a more interesting word

There are nearly always different ways of expressing the same idea. In your writing you will often need to think of different ways of saying the same thing. For example, suppose you are writing a letter of complaint about *non-stop noise*. You can say *non-stop* the first time, but a thesaurus will help you describe the noise as *continuous, constant, endless, unending* or *ceaseless*.

Special panels

Special panels give extra help or more information for certain words.

➤ The **OVERUSED WORD** panels offer more interesting alternatives for common words like *bad, good, happy* and *sad*.

➤ The **WORD WEBS** list words which are related to a particular topic, such as *football, music* and *space*. Some **WORD WEBS** list words which belong to a particular category, such as *collective noun, dog* or *phobia*.

➤ Some thesaurus entries feature **WRITING TIPS**, which give help for descriptive writing. For example, at the entry for *weather* there is a panel on describing the weather and at *colour* on describing colours.

Young Writer's Toolkit

This thesaurus contains a section called the **Young Writer's Toolkit**, where you will find useful tips on how to improve your writing skills.

➤ It covers key skills such as using sentences and paragraphs effectively and choosing the right language for formal and informal writing.

➤ It also offers advice on how to avoid some common mistakes in punctuation and spelling, and on how to make your writing more interesting by being creative with language.

WORD WEB

- accommodation
- aircraft
- amphibian
- animal
- anniversary
- armed services
- art
- artist
- athletics
- bee
- bell
- bicycle
- bird
- blue
- boat
- body
- bone
- book
- bridge
- brown
- building
- camel
- car
- castle
- cat
- chess
- clock
- clothes
- coin
- collective noun
- communication
- computer
- cook
- cricket
- criminal
- crustacean
- cutlery
- dance
- dinosaur
- dog
- drama
- earthquake
- electricity
- eye
- fabric
- family
- film
- finger
- fish
- flower
- foot
- football
- frog
- fruit
- fuel
- furniture
- gem
- green
- hat
- herb
- horse
- ice
- illness
- injury
- insect
- jewellery
- light
- mammal
- mathematics
- meal
- measure
- meat
- medicine
- metal
- moon
- music
- musician
- nut
- occupation
- ocean
- paper
- pattern
- phobia
- pink
- planet
- plant
- poetry
- politics
- pottery
- prehistoric
- punctuation
- purple
- red
- religion
- reptile
- restaurant
- rock
- rodent
- room
- royalty
- ruler
- science
- sea
- shape
- shellfish
- shoes
- shop
- snake
- song
- space
- spice
- sport
- swim
- temperature
- tennis
- textiles
- time
- tooth
- tree
- vegetable
- vehicle
- volcano
- weapon
- writer
- yellow
- zodiac

OVERUSED WORDS

- all right
- bad
- beautiful
- big
- bit
- eat
- funny
- good
- happy
- hard
- hit
- like
- little
- look
- lovely
- move
- nice
- old
- sad
- say
- small
- strong
- walk

WRITING TIPS

- animal
- bird
- body
- building
- clothes
- colour
- crime
- face
- fantasy
- hair
- historical
- horror
- landscape
- light
- science fiction
- smell
- sound
- sport
- spy
- taste
- texture
- weather

How to use this thesaurus

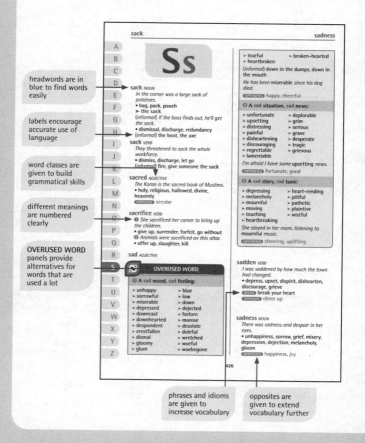

headwords are in blue to find words easily

labels encourage accurate use of language

word classes are given to build grammatical skills

different meanings are numbered clearly

OVERUSED WORD panels provide alternatives for words that are used a lot

phrases and idioms are given to increase vocabulary

opposites are given to extend vocabulary further

---

sack · sadness

Ss

sack NOUN
In the corner was a large sack of potatoes.
• bag, pack, pouch
▶ **the sack**
(informal) If the boss finds out, he'll get the sack.
• dismissal, discharge, redundancy
(informal) the boot, the axe

sack VERB
They threatened to sack the whole workforce.
• dismiss, discharge, let go
(informal) fire, give someone the sack

sacred ADJECTIVE
The Koran is the sacred book of Muslims.
• holy, religious, hallowed, divine, heavenly
OPPOSITES secular

sacrifice VERB
❶ She sacrificed her career to bring up the children.
• give up, surrender, forfeit, go without
❷ Animals were sacrificed on this altar.
• offer up, slaughter, kill

sad ADJECTIVE

OVERUSED WORD

❶ A sad mood, sad feeling:
▶ unhappy	▶ blue
▶ sorrowful	▶ low
▶ miserable	▶ down
▶ depressed	▶ dejected
▶ downcast	▶ forlorn
▶ downhearted	▶ morose
▶ despondent	▶ desolate
▶ crestfallen	▶ doleful
▶ dismal	▶ wretched
▶ gloomy	▶ woeful
▶ glum	▶ woebegone

▶ tearful	▶ broken-hearted
▶ heartbroken	

(informal) down in the dumps, down in the mouth
He has been miserable since his dog died.
OPPOSITES happy, cheerful

❷ A sad situation, sad news:
▶ unfortunate	▶ deplorable
▶ upsetting	▶ grim
▶ distressing	▶ serious
▶ painful	▶ grave
▶ disheartening	▶ desperate
▶ discouraging	▶ tragic
▶ regrettable	▶ grievous
▶ lamentable	

I'm afraid I have some upsetting news.
OPPOSITES fortunate, good

❸ A sad story, sad tune:
▶ depressing	▶ heart-rending
▶ melancholy	▶ pitiful
▶ mournful	▶ pathetic
▶ moving	▶ plaintive
▶ touching	▶ wistful
▶ heartbreaking	

She stayed in her room, listening to mournful music.
OPPOSITES cheering, uplifting

sadden VERB
I was saddened by how much the town had changed.
• depress, upset, dispirit, dishearten, discourage, grieve
IDIOM break your heart
OPPOSITES cheer up

sadness NOUN
There was sadness and despair in her eyes.
• unhappiness, sorrow, grief, misery, depression, dejection, melancholy, gloom
OPPOSITES happiness, joy

426

---

x

synonyms are given in appropriate order

scent   science fiction

scent NOUN
There was an overpowering scent of vanilla.
• smell, fragrance, perfume, aroma, odour
SEE ALSO: **smell**

sceptical ADJECTIVE
At first, I was sceptical about these results.
• disbelieving, doubtful, doubting, dubious, incredulous, unconvinced, suspicious
OPPOSITES certain, convinced

schedule NOUN
We have a busy training schedule.
• programme, timetable, plan, calendar, diary
– A schedule for a meeting is an **agenda**.
– A schedule of places to visit is an **itinerary**.

scheme NOUN
They worked out a scheme to raise more money.
• plan, proposal, project, strategy, tactic, method, procedure, system

scheme VERB
She felt they were all scheming against her.
• plot, conspire, intrigue

school NOUN
He goes to a school for international students.
• academy, college, institute

science NOUN
He is an expert in the science of genetics.
• discipline, subject, field of study, branch of knowledge

⚙ WORD WEB

Some branches of science:
- aeronautics
- anatomy
- astronomy
- biochemistry
- biology
- botany
- chemistry
- computer science
- earth science
- ecology
- electronics
- engineering
- environmental science
- food science
- forensic science
- genetics
- geography
- geology
- information technology
- mathematics
- mechanical engineering
- medical science
- meteorology
- nuclear science
- oceanography
- pathology
- physics
- psychology
- robotics
- space technology
- veterinary science
- zoology

context is given to explain how to use particular synonyms

science fiction NOUN

Ⓦ WRITING TIPS

WRITING SCIENCE FICTION

Characters:
- alien life-form
- android
- artificial life-form
- astronaut
- cyborg
- robot
- space traveller
- time traveller

Setting:
- alien planet
- deep space
- mother ship
- outer space
- parallel universe
- space colony
- spacecraft
- spaceship
- space shuttle
- space station
- starship
- time machine

Useful words and phrases:
- bionic
- black hole
- extraterrestrial
- force field
- futuristic
- galactic
- home planet
- humanoid
- hyperspace
- intelligent life
- inter-galactic
- inter-planetary
- inter-stellar
- light year
- orbit
- portal
- post-apocalyptic
- spacesuit
- space-time continuum
- space walk
- suspended animation
- telepathic

WRITING TIPS give useful words for creative writing

up-to-date example sentences and phrases show how words are used in context

WORD WEBS give extra vocabulary around topic words

431

xi

aback *ADVERB*
➤ **taken aback**
He was clearly taken aback by my question.
• surprised, astonished, startled, shocked, disconcerted, dumbfounded

abandon *VERB*
❶ *He abandoned his family and went off to Australia.*
• desert, leave, leave behind, strand (*informal*) dump, ditch (*old use*) forsake
IDIOM turn your back on
❷ *The search for the missing climbers was abandoned after two days.*
• give up, scrap, drop, cancel, abort, discard, renounce

abbreviate *VERB*
Saint is often abbreviated to St.
• shorten, reduce, abridge, contract

abdomen *NOUN*
see stomach

abduct *VERB*
He claims he was abducted by aliens.
• kidnap, seize, capture, carry off (*informal*) snatch

ability *NOUN*
❶ *Tiredness affects your ability to concentrate.*
• capability, capacity, power, facility, means
❷ *She is a player of exceptional ability.*
• talent, skill, aptitude, competence, expertise, proficiency

able *ADJECTIVE*
Penguins are very able swimmers.
• competent, capable, accomplished, expert, skilful, proficient, talented, gifted
OPPOSITE incompetent

➤ **able to**
Will you be able to play on Saturday?
• capable of, in a position to, up to, fit to, allowed to, permitted to
OPPOSITE unable to

abnormal *ADJECTIVE*
It is abnormal weather for this time of year.
• unusual, uncommon, atypical, extraordinary, exceptional, peculiar, odd, strange, weird, bizarre, unnatural, freak
OPPOSITES normal, typical

abolish *VERB*
Slavery was abolished in Britain in 1807.
• get rid of, do away with, put an end to, eliminate, eradicate, stamp out
OPPOSITE create

about *PREPOSITION*
❶ *The tour takes about an hour.*
• approximately, roughly, close to, around, in the region of
❷ *He was reading a book about the solar system.*
• regarding, relating to, on the subject of, on
➤ **be about something**
The film is about a teenage spy.
• concern, deal with, involve, relate to

about *ADVERB*
❶ *Rats were scurrying about in the attic.*
• around, here and there, in all directions
❷ *There were not many people about.*
• near, nearby, around, hereabouts

above *PREPOSITION*
❶ *There was a window above the door.*
• over, higher than
❷ *The temperature was just above freezing.*
• more than, larger than, over

abroad *ADVERB*
We spent a year abroad.
• overseas, in a foreign country

abrupt *ADJECTIVE*
❶ *The riders came to an abrupt halt.*
• sudden, hurried, hasty, quick, rapid,

a
b
c
d
e
f
g
h
i
j
k
l
m
n
o
p
q
r
s
t
u
v
w
x
y
z

1

unexpected
OPPOSITE gradual
❷ *I was put off by his abrupt manner.*
• curt, blunt, rude, brusque, terse, short, brisk, sharp, impolite, uncivil
OPPOSITE polite

absence NOUN
❶ *No one noticed his absence.*
• non-attendance, being away, leave
OPPOSITE presence
❷ *Outside there was a complete absence of birdsong.*
• lack, want, non-existence, deficit, shortage, dearth
OPPOSITE presence

absent ADJECTIVE
She was absent from school yesterday.
• away, missing
– To be absent from school without a good reason is to **play truant**.
– Someone who is absent is an **absentee**.
OPPOSITE present

absent-minded ADJECTIVE
I'm sure Dad is getting more absent-minded.
• forgetful, inattentive, distracted, scatterbrained
IDIOM with a memory like a sieve

absolute ADJECTIVE
There was a look of absolute terror on her face.
• complete, total, utter, outright, pure, sheer

absolutely ADVERB
The stench was absolutely disgusting.
• completely, totally, utterly, thoroughly, wholly, entirely, quite

absorb VERB
Let the rice absorb all the water.
• soak up, suck up, take in, draw in, mop up

absorbed ADJECTIVE
➤ be absorbed in
I was so absorbed in my book that I forgot the time.
• be engrossed in, be interested in, be preoccupied with, be immersed in, concentrate on, focus on

absorbing ADJECTIVE
It is an absorbing book.
• interesting, fascinating, intriguing, gripping, enthralling, engrossing, captivating, riveting, spellbinding

abstain VERB
➤ abstain from
I'm abstaining from junk food for a month.
• go without, give up, forgo, refrain from, avoid, reject, renounce, deny yourself, desist from
OPPOSITE indulge in

abstract ADJECTIVE
Beauty and truth are abstract ideas.
• theoretical, intellectual, philosophical
OPPOSITE concrete

absurd ADJECTIVE
That's an absurd idea!
• ridiculous, ludicrous, nonsensical, senseless, irrational, illogical, preposterous, stupid, foolish, silly, laughable
(*informal*) daft
OPPOSITES sensible, reasonable

abundance NOUN
There was an abundance of food and drink.
• plenty, profusion, plethora
OPPOSITES scarcity, lack, shortage

abundant ADJECTIVE
The birds have an abundant supply of food.
• ample, plentiful, generous, profuse, lavish, liberal
OPPOSITES meagre, scarce

abuse VERB
❶ *The dog had been abused by its owner.*
• mistreat, maltreat, ill-treat, hurt, injure, beat
❷ *He was booked for abusing the referee.*
• insult, be rude to, swear at
IDIOM call someone names

abuse NOUN
❶ *They campaigned against the abuse of animals.*
• mistreatment, maltreatment, ill-treatment, harm, injury
❷ *A spectator was yelling abuse at the referee.*
• insults, name-calling, swear words, expletives

abusive ADJECTIVE
He was thrown out for using abusive language.
• insulting, rude, offensive, derogatory, hurtful, impolite, slanderous, libellous
OPPOSITE polite

abysmal ADJECTIVE
The service in the restaurant was abysmal.
• poor, very bad, awful, appalling, dreadful, disgraceful, terrible, worthless, woeful
(*informal*) rotten, dire

abyss NOUN
I felt as if I were falling into an abyss.
• chasm, pit, void, gulf, crater, rift, fissure

academy NOUN
He attended an academy of music and drama.
• college, school, university, institute, conservatory, conservatoire

accelerate VERB
The bus accelerated to its top speed.
• go faster, speed up, pick up speed
OPPOSITES decelerate, slow down

accent NOUN
❶ *She speaks with a slight Welsh accent.*
• pronunciation, intonation, tone
❷ *The accent is on the first syllable.*
• beat, stress, emphasis, rhythm, pulse

accept VERB
❶ *Will you accept my apology?*
• take, receive, welcome
OPPOSITES reject, refuse

❷ *Do you accept responsibility for the damage?*
• admit, acknowledge, recognize, face up to
❸ *He accepted my decision as final.*
• go along with, abide by, defer to, put up with, resign yourself to

acceptable ADJECTIVE
She said my handwriting was not acceptable.
• satisfactory, adequate, good enough, sufficient, suitable, tolerable, passable
OPPOSITE unacceptable

access NOUN
The access to the house is through the garden.
• entrance, entry, way in, approach

access VERB
Can I access my email on this computer?
• get at, obtain, reach, make use of

accident NOUN
❶ *He was injured in a climbing accident.*
• misfortune, mishap, disaster, calamity, catastrophe
– Someone who is always having accidents is **accident-prone**.
❷ *A motorway accident is causing traffic delays.*
• crash, collision, smash
– An accident involving a lot of vehicles is a **pile-up**.
– A railway accident may involve a **derailment**.
➤ **by accident**
I found the letter by accident.
• by chance, accidentally, coincidentally, unintentionally

accidental ADJECTIVE
❶ *The damage to the window was accidental.*
• unintentional, unintended, unwitting, incidental
❷ *We made an accidental discovery.*
• unexpected, unforeseen, unplanned, chance, fortuitous
OPPOSITES deliberate, intentional

3

A
B
C
D
E
F
G
H
I
J
K
L
M
N
O
P
Q
R
S
T
U
V
W
X
Y
Z

acclaim VERB
Her latest film has been acclaimed by the critics.
• praise, applaud, commend, cheer, welcome

accommodate VERB
❶ *The tent can accommodate two people.*
• house, shelter, lodge, put up, take in, hold, sleep, have room for
❷ *The staff tried to accommodate our needs.*
• serve, assist, help, cater for, oblige, supply, satisfy

accommodation NOUN
The price includes food and accommodation.
• housing, lodging, living quarters, residence, dwelling, shelter, home
IDIOM a roof over your head

 WORD WEB

Some types of accommodation:

➤ apartment	➤ hostel
➤ barracks	➤ hotel
➤ bed and	➤ house
breakfast	➤ inn
➤ bedsit	➤ motel
➤ boarding house	➤ (*informal*) pad
➤ chalet	➤ studio
➤ (*informal*) digs	➤ timeshare
➤ flat	➤ villa
➤ guest house	➤ youth hostel
➤ hall of residence	

SEE ALSO building

accompany VERB
❶ *I'll accompany you to the door.*
• escort, go with, show, conduct, usher, attend
IDIOM keep someone company
❷ *You can have a free drink to accompany your meal.*
• go along with, complement, partner

accomplish VERB
The team had accomplished their mission.
• achieve, fulfil, complete, finish, succeed in, realize, attain, carry out, perform

accomplishment NOUN
Reaching the Moon was a remarkable accomplishment.
• achievement, feat, success, effort, exploit

account NOUN
❶ *She wrote a vivid account of her childhood in Russia.*
• report, record, description, history, narrative, story, chronicle, log (*informal*) write-up
❷ *Your opinion is of no account to me.*
• importance, significance, consequence, interest, value
➤ on account of
He gave up work on account of ill health.
• because of, owing to, due to

account VERB
➤ account for
How do you account for the missing money?
• explain, give reasons for, justify, make excuses for

accumulate VERB
❶ *He had accumulated a fortune by the age of twenty.*
• collect, gather, amass, assemble, heap up, pile up, hoard
OPPOSITES disperse, lose
❷ *Dust had accumulated on the mantelpiece.*
• build up, grow, increase, multiply, accrue
OPPOSITE decrease

accuracy NOUN
Can we trust the accuracy of these figures?
• correctness, precision, exactness, validity, reliability

accurate *ADJECTIVE*
❶ *Make sure you take accurate measurements of the room.*
• exact, precise, correct, careful, meticulous
OPPOSITES inexact, rough
❷ *Is this an accurate account of what happened?*
• faithful, true, reliable, truthful, factual, authentic
OPPOSITES inaccurate, false

accusation *NOUN*
There were several false accusations of witchcraft.
• allegation, charge, indictment, claim

accuse *VERB*
➤ accuse of
Two contestants were accused of cheating.
• charge with, blame for, condemn for, denounce for
OPPOSITE defend

accustomed *ADJECTIVE*
➤ accustomed to
He was clearly not accustomed to being laughed at.
• used to, familiar with
OPPOSITE unaccustomed to

ache *NOUN*
The ache in my tooth was getting worse.
• pain, soreness, throbbing, discomfort, pang, twinge

ache *VERB*
Our legs ached from the long walk.
• hurt, be painful, be sore, throb, pound, smart

achieve *VERB*
❶ *She achieved her ambition to run a marathon.*
• accomplish, attain, succeed in, carry out, fulfil
❷ *He achieved the highest score in the test.*
• acquire, win, gain, earn, get, score

achievement *NOUN*
Winning the title was a fantastic achievement.
• accomplishment, attainment, success, feat, triumph

acknowledge *VERB*
❶ *Do you acknowledge that there is a problem?*
• admit, accept, concede, grant, allow, recognize
OPPOSITE deny
❷ *She didn't even acknowledge my email.*
• answer, reply to, respond to
OPPOSITE ignore

acquaintance *NOUN*
He was an old acquaintance of mine.
• associate, contact, colleague

acquainted *ADJECTIVE*
➤ acquainted with
I'm not acquainted with the area myself.
• familiar with, aware of, knowledgeable about
OPPOSITE ignorant of

acquire *VERB*
Her family acquired the land years ago.
• get, get hold of, obtain, come by, gain, secure
IDIOM get your hands on
OPPOSITE lose

across *PREPOSITION*
They live in the house across the road.
• on the other side of, over

act *NOUN*
❶ *It was an act of great courage.*
• action, deed, feat, exploit, operation, gesture
❷ *His friendliness was just an act.*
• pretence, show, pose, charade, masquerade
❸ *They opened the show with a song-and-dance act.*
• performance, sketch, turn, routine, number

act VERB
  ❶ *She had only a second in which to act.*
  • do something, take action, make a move
  ❷ *Just try to act normally.*
  • behave, conduct yourself, react
  ❸ *The beaver's tail acts as a rudder.*
  • function, operate, serve, work
  ❹ *Have you acted in a musical before?*
  • perform, play, appear

action NOUN
  ❶ *The rocks have been worn smooth by the action of the waves.*
  • operation, working, effect, mechanism
  ❷ *The driver's action prevented an accident.*
  • deed, act, effort, exploit, feat, undertaking, measure, step
  ❸ *The film was packed with action.*
  • drama, excitement, activity, liveliness
  ❹ *He was killed in action in the First World War.*
  • battle, fighting, combat

activate VERB
  Press any key to activate the screen.
  • switch on, turn on, start, trigger, set off
  OPPOSITES deactivate, switch off

active ADJECTIVE
  ❶ *She is very active for her age.*
  • energetic, lively, busy, vigorous, dynamic
  IDIOM (informal) on the go
  OPPOSITE inactive
  ❷ *He is an active member of the drama group.*
  • hard-working, dedicated, tireless, industrious
  ❸ *Is this email account still active?*
  • functioning, working, operational, in operation, live
  IDIOM up and running
  OPPOSITES inactive, dormant

activity NOUN
  ❶ *The streets were full of activity.*
  • action, life, liveliness, excitement, movement, animation
  IDIOM hustle and bustle
  ❷ *She enjoys activities such as hillwalking and horse riding.*
  • hobby, interest, pastime, pursuit, recreation, occupation, task

actor, actress NOUN
  A number of well-known actors trained at this drama school.
  • performer, player
  – The main actor in a play or film is the **lead** or **star**.
  – The other actors are the **supporting actors**.
  – All the actors in a play or film are the **cast** or the **company**.

actual ADJECTIVE
  This photograph shows the actual size.
  • real, true, genuine, authentic
  OPPOSITES imaginary, supposed

actually ADVERB
  Just tell me what actually happened.
  • really, truly, definitely, in fact, in reality, for real
  IDIOM as a matter of fact

acute ADJECTIVE
  ❶ *She felt an acute pain in her leg.*
  • intense, strong, piercing, agonizing, searing
  OPPOSITES mild, slight
  ❷ *There is an acute shortage of food.*
  • severe, serious, urgent, critical
  ❸ *Dogs have an acute sense of smell.*
  • keen, sharp, perceptive
  OPPOSITE dull

adapt VERB
  ❶ *The play has been adapted for television.*
  • modify, adjust, change, alter, convert, customize
  ❷ *They adapted quickly to their new surroundings.*
  • become accustomed, adjust, acclimatize

add VERB
  She has added an extra line in the last verse of the poem.
  • attach, join on, append, tack on, insert

➤ **add to**
The sound effects add to the atmosphere.
• increase, enhance, intensify, heighten, deepen

➤ **add up**
❶ *Can you add up these figures for me?*
• count up, find the sum of
(*informal*) tot up
❷ (*informal*) *His story just doesn't add up.*
• be convincing, make sense

➤ **add up to**
The angles in a triangle add up to 180°.
• total, amount to, come to, run to, make

addition NOUN
The waiter said there was an addition to the menu.
• add-on, supplement, adjunct, extra, appendage

➤ **in addition**
In addition, I would like to say thanks.
• also, as well, too, moreover, furthermore

➤ **in addition to**
In addition to fiction, she also wrote poetry.
• as well as, besides, apart from, on top of, over and above

additional ADJECTIVE
You should bring an additional change of clothes.
• extra, further, added, supplementary, spare

address NOUN
❶ *Is this your usual address?*
• home, residence, dwelling
❷ *In 1863 Lincoln gave his famous address at Gettysburg.*
• speech, lecture, talk, presentation, sermon

address VERB
She stood up to address the crowd.
• speak to, talk to, make a speech to, lecture to

adequate ADJECTIVE
❶ *The room was barely adequate for one person.*
• enough, sufficient
❷ *The work must be of an adequate standard.*
• satisfactory, acceptable, tolerable, passable, competent
OPPOSITE inadequate

adjacent ADJECTIVE
I waited in an adjacent room.
• adjoining, connecting, neighbouring, next-door

➤ **adjacent to**
The playing fields are adjacent to the school.
• next to, next door to, beside, alongside, bordering

adjust VERB
You may need to adjust the height of your seat.
• modify, alter, change, customize, rearrange, regulate, tune, set
(*informal*) tweak

➤ **adjust to**
It took a moment for her eyes to adjust to the dark.
• adapt to, get used to, get accustomed to, become acclimatized to, come to terms with

adjustment NOUN
We had to make some minor adjustments to the script.
• change, alteration, modification, amendment, edit
(*informal*) tweak

administer VERB
❶ *The island is administered by its own council.*
• manage, run, regulate, govern, direct, preside over, control, supervise, command, oversee
❷ *She is learning how to administer first aid.*
• dispense, distribute, give out, hand out, issue, provide, supply, dole out, deal out

7

admirable *ADJECTIVE*
Your plan is admirable, but will it work?
• commendable, praiseworthy, laudable, creditable, exemplary, worthy, honourable, deserving, pleasing
OPPOSITE deplorable

admiration *NOUN*
I'm full of admiration for her music.
• respect, appreciation, approval, high regard, esteem
OPPOSITES contempt, scorn

admire *VERB*
❶ *I admire your honesty.*
• respect, think highly of, look up to, have a high opinion of, hold in high regard, applaud, approve of, esteem
OPPOSITE despise
❷ *We stopped to admire the view.*
• enjoy, appreciate, be delighted by

admirer *NOUN*
He is a great admirer of Steven Spielberg.
• fan, devotee, enthusiast, follower, supporter

admission *NOUN*
❶ *It was an admission of guilt.*
• confession, declaration, acknowledgement, acceptance
OPPOSITE denial
❷ *Admission to the show is by ticket only.*
• entrance, entry, access, admittance

admit *VERB*
❶ *He was admitted to hospital last night.*
• take in, receive, accept, allow in, let in
OPPOSITE exclude
❷ *I admit that I was wrong.*
• acknowledge, confess, concede, accept, grant, own up
OPPOSITE deny

admittance *NOUN*
There is no admittance to the park after dark.
• entry, entrance, admission, access

adopt *VERB*
❶ *We have adopted a stray kitten.*
• foster, take in
❷ *They had to adopt new methods of working.*
• take on, take up, choose, follow, accept, embrace, assume

adorable *ADJECTIVE*
What an adorable kitten!
• lovable, delightful, charming, appealing, enchanting
(*informal*) cute

adore *VERB*
❶ *She adored both her grandchildren.*
• love, be devoted to, dote on, cherish, treasure, worship
IDIOM think the world of
❷ (*informal*) *I simply adore chocolate ice cream.*
• love, like, enjoy
OPPOSITES hate, detest

adult *ADJECTIVE*
He found himself face to face with an adult gorilla.
• grown-up, mature, full-size, fully grown
OPPOSITES young, immature

advance *NOUN*
❶ *You can't stop the advance of science.*
• progress, development, growth, evolution
❷ *The programme discusses some of the latest advances in medicine.*
• improvement, breakthrough, step forward
➤ **in advance**
We knew about the test in advance.
• beforehand, ahead of time

advance *VERB*
❶ *The army advanced towards the capital.*
• move forward, go forward, proceed, press on, make progress, gain ground, make headway
OPPOSITE retreat

❷ *Computer animation has advanced rapidly.*
• progress, develop, grow, improve, evolve

advantage NOUN
One of the advantages of living in the country is the fresh air.
• benefit, strong point, asset, blessing, plus, bonus, boon
OPPOSITES disadvantage, drawback, downside

advent NOUN
These calculations were made before the advent of computers.
• arrival, appearance, emergence, invention

adventure NOUN
❶ *She's been telling me about her adventures on holiday.*
• exploit, venture, escapade
❷ *He travelled the world in search of adventure.*
• excitement, thrills, action

adventurous ADJECTIVE
❶ *She's more adventurous than her brother.*
• bold, daring, enterprising, intrepid
❷ *He has led an adventurous life.*
• exciting, eventful, challenging, risky
OPPOSITE unadventurous

advertise VERB
He designed a poster to advertise the concert.
• publicize, promote, announce, make known
(*informal*) plug

advertisement NOUN
We put an advertisement in the local paper.
• announcement, notice, promotion, commercial
(*informal*) ad, advert, plug

advice NOUN
The website offers advice on coping with exam nerves.
• guidance, help, directions,

recommendations, suggestions, tips, hints, pointers

advise VERB
❶ *He advised her to go to the police.*
• recommend, counsel, encourage, urge
❷ *The doctor advised a period of rest.*
• suggest, prescribe, urge, advocate

aeroplane NOUN
see aircraft

affair NOUN
Dinner time was a gloomy affair.
• event, incident, happening, occasion, occurrence, episode
➤ **affairs**
I don't discuss my private affairs on the phone.
• business, matters, concerns, questions, subjects, topics, activities

affect VERB
❶ *The area was badly affected by the drought.*
• influence, have an effect on, have an impact on, change, modify, alter
❷ *Her story affected me deeply.*
• move, touch, make an impression on, disturb, upset, concern, trouble, distress

affection NOUN
They clearly have feelings of affection for one another.
• fondness, liking, love, friendship, friendliness, attachment, devotion, warmth
OPPOSITE dislike

affectionate ADJECTIVE
She gave him an affectionate kiss.
• loving, tender, caring, fond, friendly, warm
OPPOSITES unfriendly, cold

affirm VERB
The police affirmed that they had a suspect.
• declare, confirm, assert, state, pronounce
OPPOSITE deny

A
B
C
D
E
F
G
H
I
J
K
L
M
N
O
P
Q
R
S
T
U
V
W
X
Y
Z

affirmative ADJECTIVE
He was hoping for an affirmative answer.
• positive
OPPOSITE negative

affluent ADJECTIVE
This is an affluent neighbourhood.
• prosperous, wealthy, rich, well off, well-to-do
(*informal*) flush, well-heeled
OPPOSITES poor, impoverished

afford VERB
❶ *I can't afford a new phone.*
• have enough money for, pay for, run to
❷ *How much time can you afford?*
• spare, allow

afraid ADJECTIVE
❶ *She was too afraid to move.*
• frightened, scared, terrified, petrified, alarmed, fearful, intimidated, cowardly
IDIOMS frightened out of your wits, scared to death, scared stiff
❷ *Don't be afraid to ask.*
• hesitant, reluctant, unwilling, shy
➤ **be afraid of**
I used to be afraid of the dark.
• be frightened of, be scared of, fear, dread

afterwards ADVERB
Shortly afterwards, the phone rang.
• later, later on, subsequently, in due course, thereafter

again ADVERB
Can I see you again next week?
• another time, once more, once again, over again, afresh

against PREPOSITION
❶ *A bike was leaning against the wall.*
• touching, up against, in contact with
❷ *We started a campaign against bullying.*
• in opposition to, opposed to, hostile to, averse to

age NOUN
The book is set in the age of the Vikings.
• period, time, era, epoch, days

age VERB
❶ *Dogs age faster than humans.*
• become older, grow old
❷ *The cheese is left to age for six months.*
• mature, mellow, ripen

agency NOUN
My brother works for a travel agency.
• office, business, department, service, bureau

agenda NOUN
What's on the agenda for today?
• programme, plan, schedule, timetable

agent NOUN
❶ *When she became a writer she needed an agent.*
• representative, spokesperson, negotiator, intermediary, mediator
❷ *The main character is a CIA agent.*
• spy, secret agent, operative
For tips on writing spy fiction see **spy**.

aggression NOUN
The attack was an act of mindless aggression.
• hostility, violence, aggressiveness, confrontation, militancy, belligerence

aggressive ADJECTIVE
Why are you in such an aggressive mood?
• hostile, violent, confrontational, antagonistic, argumentative, quarrelsome, bullying, warlike, belligerent
OPPOSITES friendly, peaceful, peaceable

agile ADJECTIVE
She is as agile as a mountain goat.
• nimble, graceful, sure-footed, sprightly, acrobatic, supple, lithe
OPPOSITES clumsy, stiff

agitated ADJECTIVE
As time passed, I grew more and more agitated.
• upset, nervous, anxious, flustered, unsettled, edgy, restless, disturbed, ruffled
OPPOSITES calm, cool

agonizing ADJECTIVE
It was an agonizing decision.
• painful, excruciating, torturous, harrowing, distressing

agony NOUN
The creature writhed in agony.
• pain, suffering, torture, torment, anguish, distress

agree VERB
❶ *I'm glad that we agree.*
• concur, think the same, be unanimous
IDIOM see eye to eye
OPPOSITE disagree
❷ *I agree that you are right.*
• accept, acknowledge, admit, grant, allow, assent
OPPOSITE deny
❸ *I agreed to pay my share.*
• consent, promise, be willing, undertake, acquiesce
OPPOSITE refuse
❹ *The two stories don't agree.*
• match, correspond, tally
(*informal*) square
➤ **agree on**
Can we agree on a price?
• decide, fix, settle, choose, establish
➤ **agree with**
❶ *I don't agree with this decision.*
• support, advocate, defend, back
❷ *Spicy food doesn't agree with me.*
• suit

agreement NOUN
❶ *Everyone nodded their heads in agreement.*
• accord, consensus, assent, consent, unanimity, harmony
OPPOSITE disagreement
❷ *Eventually the two sides reached an agreement.*
• settlement, deal, bargain, pact, treaty, contract, understanding
– An agreement to end fighting is an **armistice** or **truce**.

ahead ADVERB
❶ *A messenger was sent ahead with the news.*
• in advance, in front, before

❷ *Keep looking straight ahead.*
• forwards, to the front

aid NOUN
❶ *She walks with the aid of a stick.*
• help, support, assistance, backing, cooperation
❷ *The government is increasing aid for the victims of the earthquake.*
• relief, support, funding, subsidy, donations, contributions

aid VERB
They were accused of aiding him in his escape.
• help, assist, support, back, collaborate with, cooperate with
IDIOM lend a hand to

aim NOUN
What is the aim of the experiment?
• objective, purpose, object, goal, intention, end, target, ambition, wish, dream, hope

aim VERB
❶ *He aimed his gun at her.*
• point, direct, train, line up, focus, take aim
❷ *The book is aimed at teenagers.*
• target, direct, design, tailor, pitch
❸ *She aims to go to drama school.*
• intend, mean, plan, propose, want, wish, seek

air NOUN
❶ *We shouldn't pollute the air we breathe.*
• atmosphere
– The word **aerial** means 'in or from the air', as in **aerial photograph**.
❷ *Open the window and let some air in.*
• fresh air, ventilation, draught, breeze
❸ *The words are set to a traditional air.*
• song, tune, melody
❹ *The castle had an air of menace about it.*
• appearance, look, atmosphere, aura, impression, mood, tone, feeling

air VERB
❶ *He opened the window to air the room.*
• ventilate, freshen, refresh

A
B
C
D
E
F
G
H
I
J
K
L
M
N
O
P
Q
R
S
T
U
V
W
X
Y
Z

❷ *This is an opportunity to air your views.*
• express, voice, make known, make public, articulate, declare, state

aircraft NOUN

WORD WEB

Some types of aircraft:

➤ aeroplane (*North American* airplane)
➤ airliner
➤ air ambulance
➤ airship
➤ biplane
➤ bomber
➤ delta wing
➤ fighter
➤ glider
➤ hang-glider
➤ helicopter
➤ hot-air balloon
➤ jet
➤ jumbo jet
➤ microlight
➤ monoplane
➤ seaplane
➤ spy plane
➤ (*historical*) Zeppelin

Parts of an aircraft:

➤ cabin
➤ cargo hold
➤ cockpit
➤ engine
➤ fin
➤ flap
➤ flight deck
➤ fuselage
➤ joystick
➤ passenger cabin
➤ propeller
➤ rotor
➤ rudder
➤ tail
➤ tailplane
➤ undercarriage
➤ wing

- The flying of aircraft is **aviation**.
- A person who flies aircraft is a **pilot** or **aviator**.
- The pilot of a hot-air balloon is a **balloonist**.
- The study of aircraft and aviation is **aeronautics**.

airy ADJECTIVE
The room I was given was light and airy.
• well-ventilated, fresh, breezy, cool
OPPOSITES airless, stuffy

aisle NOUN
I had a seat next to the aisle.
• passageway, passage, gangway, lane

alarm NOUN
❶ *Something set off the burglar alarm.*
• signal, warning, alert, siren
❷ *Her eyes widened in alarm.*
• fear, fright, panic, anxiety, apprehension, distress, terror

alarm VERB
The sudden noise alarmed the horses.
• frighten, scare, panic, agitate, upset, distress, unnerve, startle, shock
OPPOSITE reassure

alarming ADJECTIVE
We have just received some alarming news.
• frightening, terrifying, shocking, startling, disturbing
(*informal*) scary
OPPOSITE reassuring

alert NOUN
➤ be on the alert
Police are warning residents to be on the alert.
• be vigilant, be on your guard, be on the lookout
IDIOMS stay on your toes, keep your eyes peeled

alert ADJECTIVE
Security guards need to be alert at all times.
• vigilant, watchful, attentive, observant, wide awake, on the alert, on the lookout
IDIOM (*informal*) on the ball
OPPOSITE inattentive

alert VERB
We alerted them to the danger.
• warn, notify, inform, make aware, forewarn
(*informal*) tip off

alien NOUN
I wrote a story about aliens who invade the Earth.
• extraterrestrial, alien life form
For tips on writing science fiction see **science fiction**.

alien ADJECTIVE
❶ *The dry desert landscape looked*

alien to us.
• foreign, strange, unfamiliar, exotic
OPPOSITES native, familiar
❷ *Scientists are searching for alien life.*
• extraterrestrial

alight ADJECTIVE
One of the sparks set the grass alight.
• burning, on fire, in flames, blazing,
ablaze

align VERB
Align the text with the left-hand margin.
• line up, even up, straighten up

alike ADJECTIVE
The twins look exactly alike.
• similar, the same, identical,
indistinguishable, uniform
OPPOSITES dissimilar, different

alive ADJECTIVE
Do you think that cactus is still alive?
• living, live, existing, in existence,
surviving, flourishing
OPPOSITE dead
➤ **alive to**
She has always been alive to new ideas.
• receptive to, open to, alert to, aware
of, conscious of
OPPOSITE unaware of

allege VERB
He alleged that I had cheated.
• claim, assert, contend, maintain,
accuse, charge

allegiance NOUN
*They pledged an oath of allegiance to
the king.*
• loyalty, faithfulness, obedience,
fidelity, devotion
OPPOSITES disloyalty, treachery

alley NOUN
*He disappeared around a corner into an
alley.*
• passage, passageway, lane, backstreet

alliance NOUN
The two countries formed an alliance.
• partnership, association, union,
confederation, league

– An alliance between political parties is
a **coalition**.

allocate VERB
*A sum of money has been allocated to
each project.*
• allot, assign, set aside, reserve,
earmark

allow VERB
❶ *Do you allow calculators in the exam?*
• permit, let, authorize, approve of,
consent to, agree to, give permission
for, put up with, stand, tolerate
OPPOSITE forbid
❷ *We've allowed three hours for the
journey.*
• allocate, set aside, assign, allot,
designate, earmark

alloy NOUN
Brass is an alloy of copper and zinc.
• blend, combination, composite,
compound, amalgam, fusion, mixture

all right ADJECTIVE

OVERUSED WORD

❶ **Saying that something is all right:**

➤ satisfactory	➤ passable
➤ acceptable	➤ tolerable
➤ adequate	➤ not bad
➤ reasonable	

(informal) OK or okay

*The food on the plane was **tolerable**.*

OPPOSITES unsatisfactory,
unacceptable, below standard

❷ **Being all right to do something:**

➤ permissible	➤ acceptable
➤ permitted	➤ allowed

*Taking photographs here is not
permitted.*

❸ **Feeling, looking all right:**

➤ well	➤ unharmed
➤ unhurt	➤ uninjured

a
b
c
d
e
f
g
h
i
j
k
l
m
n
o
p
q
r
s
t
u
v
w
x
y
z

13

> ➤ in good health   ➤ fine
> ➤ safe
> **IDIOM** in one piece
> *The stunt man was uninjured, apart
> from a few bruises.*

ally NOUN
The two countries work together as allies.
• friend, partner
OPPOSITE enemy

almost ADVERB
I've almost finished my homework.
• nearly, practically, just about, virtually,
all but, well-nigh, as good as, not quite

alone ADVERB
Did you go to the party alone?
• on your own, by yourself,
unaccompanied

alone ADJECTIVE
She had no friends and felt very alone.
• lonely, friendless, isolated, solitary,
lonesome

also ADVERB
*We need some bread and also some
butter.*
• in addition, besides, too, additionally,
furthermore, further, moreover, to boot

alter VERB
*We had to alter our plans for the
weekend.*
• change, adjust, adapt, modify, amend,
revise, redo, work, transform, vary

alternate ADJECTIVE
The club meets on alternate Tuesdays.
• every other, every second

alternative ADJECTIVE
Do you have an alternative plan?
• different, other, second, substitute,
standby, reserve, backup, fallback

alternative NOUN
I had no alternative but to pay the fine.
• choice, option, substitute, replacement

altogether ADVERB
❶ *I have six cousins altogether.*
• in all, in total, all told
❷ *I'm not altogether convinced.*
• completely, entirely, absolutely, quite,
totally, utterly, wholly, fully, perfectly,
thoroughly, one hundred per cent

always ADVERB
❶ *The planets are always in motion.*
• continually, continuously, constantly,
endlessly, all the time, day and night,
unceasingly, perpetually, eternally, for
ever
❷ *My bus is always late.*
• consistently, invariably, persistently,
regularly, repeatedly, habitually,
unfailingly, without fail, every time

amateur NOUN
All the players in the team are amateurs.
• non-professional
OPPOSITE professional

amaze VERB
*It amazes me that anyone could be so
stupid.*
• astonish, astound, surprise, stun,
stagger, dumbfound, startle, shock
(*informal*) flabbergast, bowl over
IDIOM (*informal*) knock for six

amazed ADJECTIVE
*I was amazed by the number of people in
the audience.*
• astonished, astounded, stunned,
surprised, dumbfounded, speechless,
staggered, thunderstruck, at a loss for
words
(*informal*) flabbergasted

amazing ADJECTIVE
98 per cent is an amazing score!
• astonishing, astounding, staggering,
stunning, extraordinary, remarkable,
incredible, unbelievable, breathtaking,
awesome, phenomenal, sensational,
stupendous, tremendous, wonderful
(*informal*) mind-boggling,
jaw-dropping
(*literary*) wondrous

ambition NOUN
❶ At that age, he was full of
ambition.
• drive, determination, enthusiasm,
enterprise, initiative, motivation
❷ Her ambition is to go to art college.
• goal, aim, dream, desire, intention,
objective, target, wish, hope,
aspiration

ambitious ADJECTIVE
❶ She is a very ambitious young woman.
• enterprising, determined, motivated,
purposeful, committed, keen
(informal) go-ahead, go-getting
OPPOSITES unambitious, laid-back
❷ I think your plan is too ambitious.
• demanding, challenging, formidable,
difficult, grand, large-scale
OPPOSITES modest, low-key

ambush VERB
Highwaymen used to ambush wealthy
travellers.
• waylay, pounce on, surprise

amend VERB
I amended the last paragraph to make it
clearer.
• revise, change, alter, adjust, modify,
adapt, edit, rewrite, reword

amends PLURAL NOUN
➤ make amends for
He's trying to make amends for what he
did.
• make up for, atone for

among PREPOSITION
We spotted a deer among the trees.
• amid, in the middle of, surrounded by,
in, between

amount NOUN
❶ A computer can store a huge amount
of information.
• quantity, measure, supply, volume,
mass, bulk
❷ He wrote out a cheque for the full
amount.
• sum, total, lot, quantity, number

amount VERB
➤ amount to
The bill amounted to 40 euros.
• add up to, come to, run to, total, equal,
make

amphibian NOUN

WORD WEB

Some animals which are amphibians:

➤ bullfrog   ➤ salamander
➤ frog   ➤ toad
➤ natterjack toad   ➤ tree frog
➤ newt

ample ADJECTIVE
❶ There is ample space for parking.
• enough, sufficient, adequate, plenty
of, lots of, more than enough
(informal) loads of
OPPOSITES insufficient, inadequate
❷ We had an ample supply of water.
• plentiful, abundant, copious, profuse,
generous, lavish, liberal
OPPOSITES meagre, scanty

amuse VERB
❶ I think this story will amuse you.
• make you laugh, entertain, please,
divert, cheer up
(informal) tickle
OPPOSITE bore
❷ We were left to amuse ourselves.
• entertain, occupy, busy, engage

amusement NOUN
❶ Our favourite amusement was
catching tadpoles.
• pastime, activity, recreation,
entertainment, diversion, game, hobby,
interest, sport
❷ a source of much amusement
• mirth, merriment, hilarity, laughter,
glee
❸ He built the boat for his own
amusement.
• entertainment, pleasure, enjoyment,
fun, delight

a
b
c
d
e
f
g
h
i
j
k
l
m
n
o
p
q
r
s
t
u
v
w
x
y
z

A
B
C
D
E
F
G
H
I
J
K
L
M
N
O
P
Q
R
S
T
U
V
W
X
Y
Z

amusing ADJECTIVE
It is an amusing story about a pig who can talk.
• funny, humorous, comical, witty, hilarious, diverting, entertaining, droll
OPPOSITES solemn, serious

analyse VERB
We then analysed the results of the experiment.
• examine, study, inspect, investigate, scrutinize, evaluate, interpret

analysis NOUN
Here is an analysis of the data.
• examination, study, inspection, investigation, scrutiny, evaluation, interpretation

ancestor NOUN
His ancestors came from Russia.
• forebear, forefather, predecessor, antecedent
OPPOSITE descendant

ancestry NOUN
Sofia was proud of her Polish ancestry.
• descent, origins, heredity, heritage, lineage, extraction, roots, blood

ancient ADJECTIVE
❶ *In ancient times, our ancestors were hunters.*
• early, prehistoric, primitive, olden
OPPOSITE modern
❷ *Honey is an ancient remedy for wounds.*
• old, age-old, archaic, time-honoured
OPPOSITES new, recent
❸ *That old computer game looks ancient now.*
• antiquated, old-fashioned, dated, archaic
OPPOSITES contemporary, up to date

anecdote NOUN
They swapped anecdotes about their childhood.
• story, tale, narrative, reminiscence
(*informal*) yarn

angelic ADJECTIVE
She has an angelic smile.
• innocent, virtuous, pure, saintly, cherubic
OPPOSITES devilish, demonic

anger NOUN
She was filled with anger.
• rage, fury, rancour, indignation, vexation, outrage
(*literary*) ire, wrath
– An outburst of anger is a **tantrum** or a **fit of temper**.

anger VERB
I was angered by his reply.
• enrage, infuriate, incense, inflame, madden, outrage, annoy, vex, irk, exasperate, antagonize, provoke
IDIOMS make your blood boil, make you see red
OPPOSITE pacify

angle NOUN
❶ *A cupboard is built into the angle between the two walls.*
• corner, point, nook
❷ *She wore a beret set at a slight angle.*
• slope, slant, tilt, gradient
❸ *Let's look at the problem from a different angle.*
• perspective, point of view, viewpoint, standpoint, view, outlook, aspect, approach, slant, tack

angry ADJECTIVE
He was angry at his parents for lying to him.
• cross, furious, irate, enraged, infuriated, incensed, outraged, annoyed, exasperated, in a temper, fuming, indignant, raging, seething
(*informal*) mad, livid
IDIOMS up in arms, foaming at the mouth, seeing red
OPPOSITE calm
➤ **get angry**
She turns purple when she gets angry.
• lose your temper, fly into a rage, go berserk
IDIOMS (*informal*) blow a fuse, blow your top, flip your lid, fly off the handle,

hit the roof, lose your rag, go off the deep end

anguish NOUN
He let out a cry of anguish.
• agony, pain, distress, torment, suffering, misery, woe, sorrow, heartache

animal NOUN
Wild animals roam freely in the safari park.
• creature, beast
– A word for wild animals in general is **wildlife**.
– The animals of a particular place or time are its **fauna**.

⊕ **WORD WEB**

Types of animal:

➤ amphibian	➤ mammal
➤ arachnid	➤ marsupial
➤ bird	➤ mollusc
➤ fish	➤ reptile
➤ insect	➤ rodent

– Animals with a backbone are **vertebrates** and those without a backbone are **invertebrates**.
– Animals that eat meat are **carnivores** and those that eat plants are **herbivores**.
– Animals that eat both meat and plants are **omnivores**.
– Animals that are kept by people are **domestic animals** and those kept on a farm are **livestock**.
– Animals that sleep most of the winter are **hibernating** animals.
– Animals that are active at night are **nocturnal** animals.
– The scientific study of animals is **zoology**.
– The study of plants and animals is **natural history** and a person who studies them is a **naturalist**.
– The medical treatment of animals is **veterinary medicine**.

(SEE ALSO) amphibian, bird, cat, dog, fish, horse, insect, reptile, rodent
For groups of animals see collective noun.

W **WRITING TIPS**

DESCRIBING ANIMALS
Body parts:

➤ antler	➤ horn
➤ coat	➤ mane
➤ fang	➤ muzzle
➤ fin	➤ paw
➤ fleece	➤ pelt
➤ flipper	➤ snout
➤ fluke	➤ tail
➤ foreleg	➤ tentacle
➤ forelimbs	➤ trotter
➤ fur	➤ trunk
➤ hide	➤ tusk
➤ hind leg	➤ whisker
➤ hoof	

Skin or coat:

➤ camouflaged	➤ scaly
➤ coarse	➤ shaggy
➤ drab	➤ shiny
➤ furry	➤ silky
➤ glossy	➤ sleek
➤ hairy	➤ slimy
➤ leathery	➤ smooth
➤ matted	➤ spiky
➤ mottled	➤ spotted
➤ patchy	➤ striped
➤ piebald	➤ wiry
➤ prickly	➤ woolly

Movement:

➤ bound	➤ paw
➤ canter	➤ pounce
➤ crouch	➤ range
➤ dart	➤ roam
➤ gallop	➤ scuttle
➤ gambol	➤ skip
➤ leap	➤ skulk
➤ lumber	➤ slink
➤ nuzzle	➤ slither
➤ pad	➤ spring

> stalk
> stamp
> stampede
> trot

Sounds:

> bark
> bay
> bellow
> bleat
> bray
> buzz
> cluck
> croak
> gabble
> growl
> grunt
> hiss
> howl
> jabber
> low
> mew
> neigh
> pipe
> purr
> roar
> snap
> snarl
> snort
> snuffle
> squeak
> trumpet
> whimper
> whine
> whinny
> yap
> yelp
> yowl

animated ADJECTIVE
We had an animated discussion about our favourite films.
• lively, spirited, energetic, enthusiastic, vibrant, vivacious, exuberant, perky
OPPOSITES lifeless, lethargic

annihilate VERB
They threatened to annihilate the whole population of the planet.
• destroy, wipe out, eradicate, obliterate

anniversary NOUN

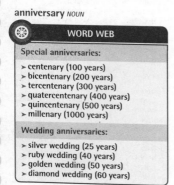

WORD WEB

Special anniversaries:

> centenary (100 years)
> bicentenary (200 years)
> tercentenary (300 years)
> quatercentenary (400 years)
> quincentenary (500 years)
> millenary (1000 years)

Wedding anniversaries:

> silver wedding (25 years)
> ruby wedding (40 years)
> golden wedding (50 years)
> diamond wedding (60 years)

announce VERB
I will now announce the winner of the competition.
• make known, make public, declare, state, report, present, proclaim, give out, broadcast, release

announcement NOUN
Ladies and gentlemen, I'd like to make an announcement.
• statement, declaration, pronouncement, proclamation, bulletin

annoy VERB
❶ The comments had clearly annoyed her.
• irritate, displease, exasperate, anger, antagonize, upset, vex, irk, nettle
(informal) rile, aggravate
OPPOSITES please, gratify
❷ Please don't annoy me while I'm working.
• pester, bother, trouble, harass, badger, nag, plague
(informal) bug, hassle

annoyance NOUN
❶ Much to my annoyance, the DVD was scratched.
• irritation, exasperation, indignation, anger, vexation, displeasure
❷ Junk mail is a constant annoyance.
• nuisance, bother, trouble, worry

annoyed ADJECTIVE
He sounded quite annoyed on the phone.
• irritated, exasperated, vexed, irked, nettled
(informal) riled, aggravated, put out

annoying ADJECTIVE
My brother has a lot of annoying habits.
• irritating, exasperating, maddening, provoking, tiresome, trying, vexing, irksome, troublesome, bothersome

anonymous ADJECTIVE
❶ It was an anonymous donation.
• unnamed, nameless, unidentified, unknown
❷ I received an anonymous letter today.
• unsigned

answer NOUN
❶ Did you get an answer to your letter?
• reply, response, acknowledgement, reaction
– A quick or angry answer is a **retort**.
❷ The answers to the quiz are on the next page.
• solution, explanation
OPPOSITE question

answer VERB
❶ You haven't answered my question.
• reply to, respond to, react to, acknowledge, give an answer to
❷ 'I don't know,' she answered.
• reply, respond, return
– To answer quickly or angrily is to **retort**.

anthology NOUN
I'm reading an anthology of ghost stories.
• collection, compilation, selection, compendium, miscellany

anticipate VERB
❶ No one anticipated that the harvest would fail.
• expect, predict, foresee, foretell, bargain on
❷ We are eagerly anticipating their arrival.
• look forward to, await, long for

anticlimax NOUN
After all the hype, the match was an anticlimax.
• let-down, disappointment
(informal) washout

antiquated ADJECTIVE
He still uses an antiquated typewriter.
• out of date, outdated, outmoded, old-fashioned, ancient, obsolete
OPPOSITES modern, up to date

antique ADJECTIVE
The palace is full of antique furniture.
• old, vintage, antiquarian
OPPOSITES modern, contemporary

antisocial ADJECTIVE
❶ Neighbours complained about his antisocial behaviour.
• objectionable, offensive, disruptive, disorderly, discourteous
❷ I'm feeling a bit antisocial today.
• unsociable, unfriendly
OPPOSITES sociable, gregarious

anxiety NOUN
We waited for news with a growing sense of anxiety.
• apprehension, concern, worry, fear, dread, nervousness, nerves, unease, disquiet
(informal) the jitters
OPPOSITES calmness, confidence

anxious ADJECTIVE
❶ We are all anxious about what will happen next.
• nervous, worried, apprehensive, concerned, uneasy, fearful, edgy, fraught, tense, troubled
(informal) uptight, jittery
OPPOSITES calm, confident
❷ I'm anxious to do my best.
• eager, keen, enthusiastic, willing, impatient, itching

apart ADVERB
➤ apart from
No one knows, apart from us.
• except for, aside from, besides, other than, excepting, with the exception of

apartment NOUN
He lives in an apartment in the centre of town.
• flat, suite, rooms

apologetic ADJECTIVE
An apologetic email arrived the next day.
• sorry, repentant, remorseful, regretful, penitent, contrite
OPPOSITE unrepentant

apologize VERB
She apologized for her mistake.
• say you are sorry, repent, be penitent

A B C D E F G H I J K L M N O P Q R S T U V W X Y Z

appal VERB
We were appalled by the number of casualties.
• horrify, shock, dismay, distress, outrage, scandalize, revolt, disgust, sicken

appalling ADJECTIVE
❶ *Some of the children live in appalling conditions.*
• shocking, horrifying, horrific, dreadful, horrendous, atrocious, horrible, terrible, distressing, sickening, revolting
❷ (*informal*) *My handwriting is appalling.*
• very bad, awful, terrible, deplorable, disgraceful
(*informal*) abysmal

apparatus NOUN
This apparatus is for breathing underwater.
• equipment, tackle
(*informal*) gear

apparent ADJECTIVE
❶ *She quit her job for no apparent reason.*
• obvious, evident, clear, noticeable, detectable, perceptible, recognizable, conspicuous, visible
OPPOSITE unclear
❷ *I could not understand his apparent lack of interest.*
• seeming, outward, ostensible

apparently ADVERB
Apparently you did not receive my email.
• evidently, seemingly, ostensibly

appeal VERB
Police are appealing for information.
• ask, request, call, entreat, plead, beg, implore
➤ **appeal to**
That kind of film doesn't appeal to me.
• attract, interest, please, fascinate, tempt, draw in

appeal NOUN
❶ *We have launched an appeal for donations to the charity.*
• request, call, cry, entreaty

– *An appeal signed by a lot of people is a* **petition**.
❷ *Baby animals always have great appeal.*
• attraction, interest, fascination, allure, charm, attractiveness

appear VERB
❶ *Cracks started to appear on the surface.*
• become visible, come into view, emerge, develop, occur, show up, surface, arise, crop up, spring up
❷ *Our visitors didn't appear until midnight.*
• arrive, come, turn up
(*informal*) show up
❸ *At first, the room appeared to be empty.*
• seem, look
❹ *She appears in two new films this week.*
• act, perform, take part, feature

appearance NOUN
❶ *Her sudden appearance in the doorway startled me.*
• approach, arrival, entrance, entry
❷ *I apologize for my rather scruffy appearance.*
• look, air, aspect, bearing
❸ *He gave every appearance of enjoying himself.*
• impression, air, semblance, show

appetite NOUN
❶ *I've lost my appetite.*
• hunger
❷ *She had a great appetite for adventure.*
• desire, eagerness, enthusiasm, passion, keenness, wish, urge, taste, thirst, longing, yearning, craving, lust, zest

appetizing ADJECTIVE
The appetizing smell of baking filled the house.
• delicious, tasty, tempting, mouth-watering

applaud VERB
❶ *The spectators applauded loudly.*
• clap, cheer
OPPOSITE boo
❷ *I applaud your honesty.*
• praise, commend, admire, welcome
OPPOSITES condemn, criticize

applause NOUN
The audience burst into applause.
• clapping, cheering, ovation

appliance NOUN
The shop sells and repairs kitchen appliances.
• device, machine, gadget, instrument, apparatus, contraption
(*informal*) gizmo

application NOUN
❶ *Thank you for your application for a refund.*
• request, claim, appeal, petition
❷ *The job needs patience and application.*
• effort, hard work, diligence, commitment, dedication, perseverance, persistence, devotion

apply VERB
❶ *She applied lipstick to her mouth.*
• put on, lay on, spread
❷ *You will need to apply all your skill and concentration.*
• use, employ, exercise, utilize
❸ *I applied for a place on the course.*
• make an application for, ask for, request, bid, petition
➤ **apply to**
Answer all the questions that apply to you.
• be relevant to, relate to, refer to, concern, affect, cover

appoint VERB
We have appointed a new team captain.
• choose, select, elect, vote for, decide on, settle on

appointment NOUN
❶ *I have an appointment to see the doctor.*
• arrangement, engagement, date

❷ *The team are waiting for the appointment of a new coach.*
• nomination, naming, selection, choice, choosing, election
❸ *My uncle has got a new appointment at the university.*
• job, post, position, situation, office

appreciate VERB
❶ *He appreciates good music.*
• enjoy, like, love, admire, respect, esteem
OPPOSITES disparage, disdain
❷ *I appreciate your help with this.*
• value, be grateful for, be glad of
❸ *I appreciate that this is a difficult time.*
• recognize, realize, understand, comprehend, be aware
❹ *Antique jewellery will appreciate in value.*
• grow, increase, go up, mount, rise
OPPOSITES depreciate, decrease

appreciation NOUN
❶ *She had a keen appreciation of poetry.*
• enjoyment, love, admiration
OPPOSITES disparagement, disdain (for)
❷ *Please accept this small token of our appreciation.*
• gratitude, thanks
❸ *They had no appreciation of the danger.*
• recognition, acknowledgement, realization, awareness

appreciative ADJECTIVE
They were an appreciative audience.
• admiring, enthusiastic, approving, complimentary

apprehend VERB
Police have apprehended a third suspect.
• arrest, capture, detain, seize
OPPOSITE release

apprehension NOUN
His mouth was dry with apprehension.
• anxiety, worry, concern, unease, disquiet, nervousness, trepidation

A B C D E F G H I J K L M N O P Q R S T U V W X Y Z

apprehensive ADJECTIVE
She gave an apprehensive glance over her shoulder.
• anxious, worried, nervous, tense, agitated, edgy, uneasy, unsettled, troubled, frightened, fearful
OPPOSITES calm, untroubled

apprentice NOUN
His first job was as a plumber's apprentice.
• trainee, learner, novice, probationer
(*informal*) rookie

approach VERB
❶ *She approached the door on tiptoe.*
• move towards, draw near to, come near to, near, advance on, close in on, gain on
❷ *They approached me with an offer to join the squad.*
• speak to, talk to, go to, contact, sound out
❸ *What is the best way to approach this problem?*
• tackle, undertake, set about, go about, embark on, address

approach NOUN
❶ *We could hear the approach of footsteps.*
• arrival, advance, coming
❷ *They made an approach to the bank for a loan.*
• application, appeal, proposal, submission, request
❸ *He brought a fresh approach to filmmaking.*
• attitude, manner, style, method, system, way
❹ *Two soldiers guarded the approach to the bridge.*
• access, entry, entrance, way in

approachable ADJECTIVE
The staff are always very approachable.
• friendly, pleasant, agreeable, welcoming, sympathetic
OPPOSITES unapproachable, aloof

appropriate ADJECTIVE
Jeans are not appropriate for a formal party.
• suitable, proper, fitting, apt, right, well-judged, relevant, pertinent
OPPOSITE inappropriate

approval NOUN
❶ *The head gave her approval to our plan.*
• agreement, consent, support, acceptance, assent, permission, authorization, go-ahead, blessing
OPPOSITE refusal
❷ *He looked at them with approval.*
• appreciation, admiration, praise, high regard, acclaim, respect, support, liking
OPPOSITE disapproval

approve VERB
A majority voted to approve the plan.
• agree to, consent to, authorize, allow, accept, pass, permit, support, back
IDIOMS give the green light to, give the thumbs-up to
OPPOSITES refuse, give the thumbs-down to
➤ **approve of**
Her family did not approve of the marriage.
• agree with, be in favour of, favour, welcome, support, endorse, like, think well of, take kindly to, admire, commend, applaud
OPPOSITE condemn

approximate ADJECTIVE
All the measurements are approximate.
• estimated, rough, broad, loose, inexact
(*informal*) ballpark
OPPOSITE exact

approximately ADVERB
The film finishes at approximately five o'clock.
• roughly, about, around, round about, close to, nearly, more or less
OPPOSITE precisely

apt ADJECTIVE
❶ *He is apt to forget things.*
• inclined, likely, liable, prone, given

❷ *Each chapter begins with an apt quotation.*
• **appropriate, suitable, proper, fitting, right, well-judged, relevant, pertinent** (*informal*) **spot on**
OPPOSITE **inappropriate**

aptitude NOUN
She has a remarkable aptitude for music.
• **talent, gift, ability, skill, flair, expertise, bent**

arbitrary ADJECTIVE
It was an apparently arbitrary decision.
• **illogical, irrational, random, subjective, capricious**
OPPOSITE **rational**

arc NOUN
I could see the arc of a rainbow.
• **arch, bow, curve, crescent**

arch NOUN
They waited under the arch of the bridge.
• **curve, arc, bow, crescent**

arch VERB
The cat arched its back and hissed.
• **curve, bend, bow, hunch**

archive NOUN
The library contains the family archives.
• **records, annals, history**

arduous ADJECTIVE
It was an arduous climb to the summit.
• **tough, difficult, hard, laborious, strenuous, taxing, demanding, challenging, gruelling, punishing**

area NOUN
❶ *From the plane we saw a vast area of desert.*
• **expanse, stretch, tract, space**
– A small area is a **patch**.
– An area of water or ice is a **sheet**.
❷ *They live in an inner-city area.*
• **district, locality, neighbourhood, region, zone, vicinity**
❸ *This is a fascinating area of study.*
• **field, sphere, province, domain**

arena NOUN
A new indoor sports arena will open next year.
• **stadium, amphitheatre, ground, park**

argue VERB
❶ *Those two are always arguing about something.*
• **quarrel, disagree, fight, have an argument, squabble, wrangle, bicker**
IDIOMS **cross swords, lock horns**
– To argue about the price of something is to **haggle**.
OPPOSITE **agree**
❷ *I argued that it was my turn to use the computer.*
• **claim, assert, maintain, contend, reason, allege**

argument NOUN
❶ *There was an argument over who should pay for the meal.*
• **disagreement, quarrel, dispute, row, clash, fight, squabble, altercation**
❷ *There are strong arguments both for and against this decision.*
• **reasoning, justification, evidence, case**

arid ADJECTIVE
It is an arid landscape.
• **dry, barren, parched, waterless, lifeless, infertile, sterile, unproductive**
OPPOSITES **fertile, lush**

arise VERB
❶ *Let me know if any problems arise.*
• **occur, emerge, develop, ensue, appear, come about, come up, crop up, happen, come to light, surface**
❷ (*old use*) *Arise, Sir Francis.*
• **stand up, get up**

aristocrat NOUN
The house belongs to a Spanish aristocrat.
• **noble, nobleman or noblewoman, peer**
OPPOSITE **commoner**

aristocratic ADJECTIVE
She comes from an aristocratic family.
• **noble, titled, upper-class, blue-blooded**

a b c d e f g h i j k l m n o p q r s t u v w x y z

arm VERB

The men were armed with heavy sticks.
• equip, supply, provide, furnish, fit out

armed services PLURAL NOUN

⚙ WORD WEB

The main armed services:

➤ air force	➤ navy
➤ army	

– Men and women in the services are **troops**.

– A new serviceman or servicewoman is a **recruit**.

– A young person training to be in the armed services is a **cadet**.

Various groups in the armed services:

➤ battalion	➤ legion
➤ brigade	➤ patrol
➤ company	➤ platoon
➤ corps	➤ regiment
➤ fleet	➤ squad
➤ garrison	➤ squadron

Servicemen and servicewomen:

➤ aircraftman	➤ paratrooper
➤ aircraftwoman	➤ sailor
➤ commando	➤ soldier
➤ marine	

SEE ALSO **soldier**

armour NOUN

The illustration shows a knight in armour.
• chain-mail
– An outfit of armour is a **suit of armour**.
– Something fitted with armour is **armoured** or **armour-plated**.

arms PLURAL NOUN

The two armies laid down their arms and made peace.
• weapons, weaponry, guns, firearms, armaments, fire-power
– A store of arms is an **armoury** or **arsenal**.

army NOUN

❶ *He served with the army in France.*
• armed force, military, militia, troops, infantry
– A country's army, navy and air force are its **armed services**.
❷ *An army of servants was working in the kitchen.*
• mass, horde, mob, swarm, throng

aroma NOUN

The aroma of fresh coffee filled the room.
• smell, scent, odour, fragrance, perfume

around PREPOSITION

❶ *She wore a silver necklace around her neck.*
• about, round, encircling, surrounding
❷ *There were around a hundred people in the audience.*
• about, approximately, roughly, more or less

arouse VERB

I had to get into the house without arousing suspicion.
• cause, generate, lead to, evoke, produce, provoke, set off, excite, stimulate, incite, stir up, whip up
OPPOSITES calm, quell

arrange VERB

❶ *The books are arranged in alphabetical order.*
• sort, order, organize, set out, lay out, display, group, categorize, classify, collate
❷ *We're arranging a surprise party for Mum.*
• plan, organize, prepare, set up, fix up, see to

arrangement NOUN

❶ *I don't like the arrangement of the furniture.*
• layout, positioning, organization, grouping, display, design
❷ *I said I'd deal with the arrangements for our holiday.*
• plan, preparation, planning
❸ *We have an arrangement to share*

A
B
C
D
E
F
G
H
I
J
K
L
M
N
O
P
Q
R
S
T
U
V
W
X
Y
Z

the costs.
• agreement, deal, bargain, contract

array NOUN
There was an array of dials on the control panel.
• range, display, line-up, arrangement

arrest VERB
❶ *A man has been arrested for murder.*
• seize, capture, apprehend, detain, take prisoner
(*informal*) nick
❷ *Doctors are trying to arrest the spread of the disease.*
• stop, halt, check, curb, block, prevent, obstruct

arrival NOUN
We awaited the arrival of our guests.
• coming, appearance, entrance, approach

arrive VERB
When is the train due to arrive?
• come, appear, turn up, get in
(*informal*) show up
➤ **arrive at**
❶ *We arrived at our hotel before noon.*
• get to, reach
❷ *Have you arrived at a decision?*
• make, reach, settle on, decide on

arrogant ADJECTIVE
His arrogant manner annoys me.
• boastful, conceited, proud, haughty, self-important, pompous, superior, bumptious
(*informal*) big-headed, cocky
IDIOMS full of yourself, (*informal*) too big for your boots
OPPOSITE modest

arrow NOUN
She shot an arrow into the middle of the target.
– The spine of an arrow is the **shaft**.
– The point of an arrow is the **arrowhead**.
– Arrows are shot using a **bow**.
– A holder for several arrows is a **quiver**.

– The sport of shooting arrows at a target is **archery**.
– Someone who practises archery is an **archer**.

art NOUN
❶ *She took a course in art and design.*
• visual arts, fine art
❷ *The art of writing letters is disappearing.*
• skill, craft, technique, talent, knack, trick

WORD WEB

Terms used in art, craft and design:

➤ 2D	➤ life form
➤ 3D	➤ materials
➤ abstract	➤ media
➤ applied art	➤ modelling
➤ artist	➤ montage
➤ artwork	➤ painter
➤ ceramics	➤ painting
➤ collage	➤ pattern
➤ composition	➤ plastic arts
➤ crafts	➤ portrait
➤ craftsperson	➤ pottery
➤ design	➤ printmaking
➤ designer	➤ process
➤ drawing	➤ modern
➤ fine art	➤ sculptor
➤ form	➤ sculpture
➤ graphic design	➤ shape
➤ illustration	➤ technique
➤ image	➤ textile art
➤ installation	➤ textiles
➤ jewellery	➤ texture
➤ landscape	➤ visual arts

article NOUN
❶ *On the table were various articles for sale.*
• item, object, thing
❷ *I wrote an article for the school magazine.*
• essay, report, piece, feature

articulate ADJECTIVE
He is certainly an articulate speaker.
• fluent, eloquent, lucid
OPPOSITE inarticulate

artificial ADJECTIVE
❶ *On the shelf was a vase of artificial flowers.*
• man-made, synthetic, imitation, unreal, unnatural, manufactured, fake, false
OPPOSITES real, natural
❷ *She gave us an artificial smile.*
• pretended, sham, affected, assumed, simulated
(*informal*) put on
OPPOSITES genuine, natural

artist NOUN

🎡 **WORD WEB**

Some artists and craftspeople:

➤ animator   ➤ illustrator
➤ blacksmith   ➤ knitter
➤ carpenter   ➤ mason
➤ cartoonist   ➤ painter
➤ designer   ➤ photographer
➤ draughtsman   ➤ potter
➤ draughtswoman   ➤ printer
➤ embroiderer   ➤ quilter
➤ engraver   ➤ sculptor
➤ goldsmith   ➤ silversmith
➤ graphic designer ➤ weaver

artistic ADJECTIVE
The room was decorated in an artistic style.
• creative, imaginative, aesthetic, attractive, tasteful
(*informal*) arty

ascend VERB
❶ *He slowly ascended the staircase.*
• climb, go up, mount, move up, scale
❷ *A kite ascended into the air.*
• fly up, rise, soar, lift off, take off
OPPOSITE descend

ascent NOUN
❶ *Next year they will attempt the ascent of Everest.*
• climbing, mounting, scaling
❷ *The trail follows a steep ascent.*
• slope, gradient, incline, rise
OPPOSITES descent, drop

ashamed ADJECTIVE
He felt ashamed of what he had done.
• sorry, remorseful, regretful, repentant, shamefaced, embarrassed, contrite, mortified, penitent
(*informal*) red-faced
OPPOSITES unashamed, unrepentant

ask VERB
❶ *She asked us to be quiet.*
• request, entreat, appeal to, beg, implore
❷ *I asked him where he came from.*
• enquire, demand, query, question
❸ *Who are you asking to the party?*
• invite
(*formal*) request the pleasure of your company
➤ ask for
❶ *I asked for their advice.*
• request, appeal for, call for, seek, solicit
❷ *They were asking for trouble!*
• encourage, attract, cause, provoke, stir up

asleep ADJECTIVE
My brother is still fast asleep.
• sleeping, dozing, having a nap, napping
(*informal*) snoozing
(*formal*) slumbering
IDIOMS (*informal*) dead to the world, (*humorous*) in the land of Nod
– An animal asleep for the winter is hibernating.
OPPOSITE awake
➤ fall asleep
I fell asleep on the couch.
• go to sleep, doze, drop off, nod off
– To fall asleep quickly is to **go out like a light**.

aspect NOUN
❶ *The writer covers most aspects of life on a submarine.*
• part, feature, element, angle, detail, side, facet

❷ *The ruined tower had a grim aspect.*
• appearance, look, manner, air, expression, face, countenance
❸ *The front room has a southern aspect.*
• outlook, view, prospect

aspire VERB
➤ **aspire to**
He aspires to be Olympic champion.
• aim for, hope for, dream of, long for, desire, seek
IDIOMS set your heart on, set your sights on

assault NOUN
She was the victim of a serious assault.
• attack, mugging

assault VERB
He was charged with assaulting a police officer.
• attack, strike, hit, beat up, mug

assemble VERB
❶ *A crowd assembled to watch the rescue.*
• gather, come together, congregate, convene, converge, meet, rally
OPPOSITE disperse
❷ *We assembled our luggage in the hall.*
• collect, gather, bring together, put together, round up, marshal, muster
❸ *The machine is now ready to be assembled.*
• construct, build, put together, fit together

assembly NOUN
❶ *There was a large assembly of people in the market square.*
• gathering, meeting, convention, congregation, crowd
(*informal*) get-together
– An assembly to show support for something, often out of doors, is a **rally**.
– An assembly to discuss political matters is a **council** or **parliament**.
❷ *The bookcase is now ready for assembly.*
• construction, building, fabrication, manufacture

assent NOUN
She has already given us her assent.
• agreement, approval, consent, go-ahead, permission
OPPOSITE refusal

assert VERB
❶ *The prisoner asserts that he is innocent.*
• state, claim, contend, declare, argue, maintain, proclaim, insist
❷ *Mary asserted her claim to the English throne.*
• insist on, stand up for, uphold, defend

assertive ADJECTIVE
You should try to be more assertive.
• confident, self-confident, bold, forceful, insistent, commanding

assess VERB
People came out of their houses to assess the damage.
• evaluate, determine, judge, rate, appraise, measure, gauge, estimate, calculate, work out, value, weigh up
(*informal*) size up

assessment NOUN
What is your assessment of the situation?
• judgement, estimation, rating, appraisal, valuation

asset NOUN
She has proved a real asset to the team.
• advantage, benefit, blessing, help, strength, good point
OPPOSITE liability

assign VERB
❶ *I was assigned the job of guarding the door.*
• allocate, allot, give, consign, hand over, delegate, charge with, entrust with
❷ *An experienced detective was assigned to the case.*
• appoint, nominate

a
b
c
d
e
f
g
h
i
j
k
l
m
n
o
p
q
r
s
t
u
v
w
x
y
z

assignment NOUN
I have a homework assignment to finish.
• task, project, exercise, piece of work, job, mission, undertaking

assist VERB
Your job is to assist the crew with their duties.
• help, aid, support, back up, cooperate with, collaborate with
IDIOM lend a hand to
OPPOSITE hinder

assistance NOUN
Can I be of any assistance?
• help, aid, support, backing, cooperation, collaboration, reinforcement
IDIOM a helping hand

assistant NOUN
The team leader has three assistants.
• helper, aide, partner, colleague, associate, supporter

associate VERB
➤ associate with
❶ *Black cats are often associated with witchcraft.*
• connect with, identify with, link with, relate to
❷ *He used to associate with members of the band.*
• be friends with, go about with, mix with

association NOUN
❶ *We have started a junior tennis association.*
• club, society, organization, group, league, fellowship, partnership, union, alliance
– A political association is a **party**.
❷ *Our association goes back a long way.*
• relationship, partnership, friendship, relation, connection, link, bond

assorted ADJECTIVE
There are assorted flavours of ice cream on the menu.
• various, different, mixed, diverse, miscellaneous, several, sundry

assortment NOUN
There is an assortment of sandwiches to choose from.
• variety, selection, mixture, array, choice, collection, medley, miscellany

assume VERB
❶ *I assume that you agree with me.*
• presume, suppose, take for granted, believe, fancy, think, understand, gather
❷ *This is my fault and I assume full responsibility for it.*
• accept, take on, undertake, shoulder, bear
❸ *He assumed an air of wide-eyed innocence.*
• adopt, put on, feign, affect

assumed ADJECTIVE
She writes under an an assumed name.
• false, fake, fictitious, bogus, invented, made-up

assumption NOUN
The assumption is that prices will stay the same.
• belief, presumption, supposition, theory, hypothesis

assurance NOUN
❶ *You have my assurance that I will be there.*
• promise, guarantee, pledge, vow
❷ *She had an air of calm assurance.*
• confidence, self-confidence, self-assurance, self-possession

assure VERB
❶ *He assured us that he was telling the truth.*
• promise, reassure, give your word to, vow to
❷ *We worked hard to assure the success of the mission.*
• ensure, make certain of, secure, guarantee

assured ADJECTIVE
Her voice was calm and assured.
• confident, self-confident, self-assured, poised, composed
(*informal*) unflappable

astonish VERB
They were astonished at the size of the crater.
• amaze, astound, surprise, stagger, shock, dumbfound, startle, stun, take aback, take by surprise (*informal*) flabbergast
IDIOMS leave you speechless, take your breath away, bowl you over, (*informal*) knock you for six

astonishing ADJECTIVE
It was an astonishing result.
• amazing, astounding, staggering, stunning, remarkable, surprising, extraordinary, incredible, breathtaking, phenomenal, sensational, stupendous, tremendous, dazzling (*informal*) mind-boggling

astound VERB
see **astonish**

astounding ADJECTIVE
see **astonishing**

astrology NOUN
see **zodiac**

astronomy NOUN
For terms used in astronomy see **space**.

astute ADJECTIVE
He made some very astute comments.
• shrewd, sharp, acute, smart, clever, canny

ate
past tense see **eat**

athletic ADJECTIVE
He is tall with an athletic build.
• muscular, fit, strong, sturdy, powerful, strapping, well-built, brawny, burly (*informal*) sporty
OPPOSITES puny, weedy

athletics PLURAL NOUN

WORD WEB

Some athletic events:

➤ cross-country	➤ pentathlon
➤ decathlon	➤ pole vault
➤ discus	➤ relay
➤ heptathlon	➤ shot put
➤ high jump	➤ sprint
➤ hurdles	➤ steeplechase
➤ javelin	➤ triathlon
➤ long jump	➤ triple jump
➤ marathon	

For tips on writing about sport see **sport**.

atmosphere NOUN
❶ *The atmosphere on Mars is unbreathable.*
• air, sky
❷ *There was a relaxed atmosphere at the end of term.*
• feeling, feel, mood, spirit, air, ambience, aura (*informal*) vibe

atrocious ADJECTIVE
❶ *He committed a series of atrocious murders.*
• wicked, brutal, barbaric, cruel, vicious, savage, monstrous, inhuman, vile, fiendish, horrifying, abominable, terrible, dreadful
❷ *The weather has been atrocious.*
• very bad, terrible, dreadful, awful

attach VERB
❶ *Attach this label to the parcel.*
• fasten, fix, join, tie, bind, secure, connect, link, couple, stick, affix, add, append
OPPOSITE detach
❷ *She attaches great importance to punctuality.*
• ascribe, assign, give

a
b
c
d
e
f
g
h
i
j
k
l
m
n
o
p
q
r
s
t
u
v
w
x
y
z

attached ADJECTIVE
➤ attached to
Some people get very attached to their pets.
• fond of, close to, devoted to, keen on, loyal to, affectionate towards, friendly towards

attack NOUN
❶ *The enemy attack took them by surprise.*
• assault, strike, charge, raid, ambush, invasion, onslaught, offensive
– An attack from the air is an **air raid** or **blitz** and a continuous attack with guns or missiles is a **bombardment**.
❷ *She was upset by this attack on her character.*
• criticism, censure, condemnation, outburst, tirade
❸ *I had an attack of coughing.*
• bout, fit, spasm, episode
(*informal*) turn

attack VERB
❶ *They were attacked by a mob armed with sticks.*
• assault, set on, beat up, mug, charge, pounce on, assail, raid, storm, bombard
– To attack someone from a hidden place is to **ambush** them.
– If an animal attacks you, it might **savage** you.
❷ *A number of articles attacked the author's reputation.*
• criticize, censure, denounce, condemn
(*informal*) knock
OPPOSITE defend

attacker NOUN
He managed to escape his attacker.
• assailant, mugger, raider, invader
OPPOSITE defender

attain VERB
This is the highest speed ever attained on the sea.
• achieve, obtain, reach, get, accomplish, gain, secure

attempt VERB
She will attempt to beat the world record.
• try, endeavour, strive, seek, aim, venture, make an effort, have a go at
(*informal*) have a shot at, have a bash at

attempt NOUN
This is my first attempt at writing a novel.
• try, effort, go
(*informal*) shot, bash

attend VERB
Over a hundred people attended the rally.
• be present at, go to, appear at, take part in, turn up at
(*informal*) show up at
➤ attend to
❶ *Excuse me, I have some business to attend to.*
• deal with, see to, take care of, look after
❷ *A nurse attended to the injured.*
• take care of, care for, look after, help, tend, mind, treat
❸ *Please attend to what I say.*
• listen to, pay attention to, follow, heed, mark, mind, note

attendance NOUN
❶ *Attendance at these classes is not compulsory.*
• presence, appearance, participation
OPPOSITE non-attendance
❷ *The attendance was low because of the rain.*
• audience, turnout, gate, crowd

attendant NOUN
She was the personal attendant of Queen Victoria.
• assistant, aide, companion, escort, retainer, servant

attention NOUN
❶ *Please give this task your full attention.*
• concentration, consideration, study, focus, observation, scrutiny, thought, awareness
– To **pay heed to something** or take

heed of it is to pay careful attention to something.
❷ The survivors needed urgent medical attention.
• treatment, care

attentive ADJECTIVE
Thank you for being such an attentive audience.
• alert, paying attention, observant, watchful, aware, vigilant, on the alert, on the lookout

attic NOUN
We have a lot of boxes stored in the attic.
• loft, garret

attitude NOUN
She now has a more positive attitude to life.
• outlook, approach, stance, position, view, manner, disposition, frame of mind

attract VERB
The show continues to attract a wide audience.
• interest, appeal to, captivate, charm, entice, lure, draw in, pull in
OPPOSITES repel, put off

attraction NOUN
❶ I can't see the attraction of living in the countryside.
• appeal, desirability, charm, allure, pull
OPPOSITE repulsion
❷ The Eiffel Tower is one of Paris's main tourist attractions.
• place of interest, sight, draw

attractive ADJECTIVE
❶ She is an attractive young woman.
• beautiful, pretty, good-looking, handsome, gorgeous, glamorous, striking, fetching, fascinating, captivating, enchanting, arresting
OPPOSITES unattractive, ugly, repulsive
❷ It was an attractive offer.
• appealing, interesting, agreeable, desirable, pleasing, tempting, inviting
OPPOSITES unattractive, uninviting

attribute VERB
The quote is sometimes attributed to Shakespeare.
• ascribe, assign, credit

attribute NOUN
He has all the attributes of a top striker.
• quality, characteristic, trait, property, feature, element, aspect, mark, hallmark

audible ADJECTIVE
Her voice was barely audible.
• perceptible, detectable, discernible, distinct
OPPOSITE inaudible

audience NOUN
Some members of the audience cheered.
• crowd, spectators
– The audience for a TV programme is the **viewers**.
– The audience for a radio programme is the **listeners**.

authentic ADJECTIVE
❶ This is an authentic Roman coin.
• genuine, real, actual
OPPOSITES imitation, fake
❷ His diary is an authentic account of life at sea.
• accurate, truthful, reliable, true, honest, dependable, factual
OPPOSITES false, inaccurate

author NOUN
My copy of the book is signed by the author.
• writer, novelist, poet, playwright

authority NOUN
❶ I need your authority to read these files.
• permission, authorization, consent, approval, clearance
❷ They dared to challenge the authority of the king.
• power, command, control, domination, rule, charge
❸ She is a leading authority on handwriting.
• expert, specialist, pundit, connoisseur

a
b
c
d
e
f
g
h
i
j
k
l
m
n
o
p
q
r
s
t
u
v
w
x
y
z

authorize VERB
Has this payment been authorized?
• approve, agree to, consent to, sanction, clear, allow

automatic ADJECTIVE
❶ *We took our car through the automatic car wash.*
• automated, mechanical, programmed, computerized
❷ *His reaction was automatic.*
• instinctive, involuntary, impulsive, spontaneous, reflex, unconscious, unthinking

auxiliary ADJECTIVE
Fortunately we have an auxiliary power supply.
• supplementary, secondary, reserve, back-up
OPPOSITE primary

available ADJECTIVE
❶ *Is the Internet available in the library?*
• accessible, obtainable, at hand, within reach
OPPOSITES unavailable, inaccessible
❷ *There are no more seats available.*
• unoccupied, unsold, free
(*informal*) up for grabs
OPPOSITES unavailable, taken

average ADJECTIVE
It was just an average day at school.
• ordinary, normal, typical, standard, usual, regular, everyday, commonplace
OPPOSITES unusual, extraordinary

averse ADJECTIVE
➤ averse to
I'm not averse to the idea.
• against, opposed to, hostile to
OPPOSITES keen on, for

aversion NOUN
➤ aversion to
She had an aversion to water and soap.
• dislike of, distaste for, antipathy to, hostility to
OPPOSITE liking for

avert VERB
❶ *He averted his eyes from the glare.*
• turn away, turn aside
❷ *We must take steps to avert a disaster.*
• prevent, avoid, ward off, stave off, pre-empt, forestall

avid ADJECTIVE
My sister is an avid reader.
• keen, eager, enthusiastic, passionate, ardent, fervent

avoid VERB
❶ *I swerved to avoid the lamp post.*
• get out of the way of, keep clear of, steer clear of, dodge, fend off
❷ *We narrowly avoided defeat.*
• prevent, preclude, avert, pre-empt, forestall
❸ *I've been avoiding getting down to work all day.*
• get out of, evade, dodge, shirk

await VERB
We are awaiting further instructions.
• wait for, look out for, expect, look forward to, anticipate

awake VERB
Our guests awoke early.
• wake up, wake, awaken, rise, stir

awake ADJECTIVE
She lay awake all night worrying.
• wide awake, sleepless, restless, conscious, astir
– Not being able to sleep is to be suffering from **insomnia**.
OPPOSITE asleep

awaken VERB
❶ *I was awakened by birds singing.*
• wake up, waken, wake, rouse
❷ *The song awakened memories of her youth.*
• arouse, stir up, stimulate, evoke, kindle, revive

award VERB
They awarded her the Nobel Peace Prize.
• give, grant, accord, bestow on, confer on, present to

award NOUN
He won the award for best singer.
• prize, trophy, medal

aware ADJECTIVE
➤ aware of
Were you aware of the danger?
• acquainted with, conscious of, familiar with, informed about
OPPOSITE ignorant of

awe NOUN
The audience listened in awe.
• wonder, amazement, admiration, reverence

awesome ADJECTIVE
The mountains were an awesome sight.
• awe-inspiring, amazing, breathtaking, spectacular, stunning, staggering, formidable

awful ADJECTIVE
❶ *The weather was awful last weekend.*
• very bad, dreadful, terrible, dire, appalling, abysmal
(*informal*) rubbish, lousy
❷ *The whole country was shocked by this awful crime.*
• horrifying, shocking, appalling, atrocious, abominable
❸ *What an awful thing to say!*
• unpleasant, disagreeable, nasty, horrid, detestable
❹ *I feel awful about forgetting your birthday.*
• sorry, ashamed, embarrassed, guilty, remorseful

awkward ADJECTIVE
❶ *The box isn't heavy, but it's awkward to carry.*
• difficult, cumbersome, unmanageable, unwieldy
(*informal*) fiddly
OPPOSITES easy, handy
❷ *You've arrived at an awkward time.*
• inconvenient, inappropriate, inopportune, difficult
OPPOSITES convenient, opportune
❸ *There was then an awkward silence.*
• uncomfortable, embarrassing, uneasy, tense
OPPOSITES comfortable, relaxed
❹ *I often feel awkward in a group of people.*
• embarrassed, uncomfortable, uneasy, out of place
OPPOSITES comfortable, at ease
❺ *Why are you being so awkward?*
• uncooperative, unhelpful, unreasonable, stubborn, obstinate
OPPOSITE cooperative
❻ *He runs in an awkward way.*
• clumsy, graceless, unskilful, ungainly, inept, blundering
OPPOSITES graceful, skilful, dexterous

axe NOUN
He has an axe for splitting wood.
• hatchet, cleaver, chopper

axe VERB
The company is going to axe thousands of jobs.
• terminate, discontinue, abolish, cancel, get rid of, cut, drop, scrap

a
b
c
d
e
f
g
h
i
j
k
l
m
n
o
p
q
r
s
t
u
v
w
x
y
z

Bb

babble *VERB*
What was that man babbling about?
• chatter, prattle, gabble, jabber, burble
(*informal*) witter

baby *NOUN*
The woman was holding a baby.
• infant, child, newborn
(*poetic*) babe
– A baby just learning to walk is a **toddler**.
– The time when someone is a baby is their **babyhood**.

babyish *ADJECTIVE*
She is too old for such babyish toys.
• childish, immature, infantile
OPPOSITES grown-up, mature

back *NOUN*
❶ *We always sit at the back of the bus.*
• rear, end, tail end
– The back end of an animal is its **hindquarters**, **rear** or **rump**.
– The back of a ship is the **stern**.
OPPOSITES front, head
❷ *I wrote a shopping list on the back of an envelope.*
• reverse, underside
OPPOSITES front, face

back *ADJECTIVE*
The back door of the house was unlocked.
• rear, rearmost
– The back legs of an animal are its **hind** legs.
OPPOSITE front

back *VERB*
❶ *I began backing towards the door.*
• go backwards, reverse, retreat, step back, draw back
OPPOSITE advance

❷ *The government is backing the city's bid to host the Games.*
• support, endorse, favour, advocate, sponsor
IDIOMS give your blessing to, throw your weight behind
OPPOSITE oppose
❸ *Which horse did you back?*
• bet on, put money on
➤ **back down**
We've come too far to back down now.
• give in, surrender, concede defeat
➤ **back off**
The men backed off at the sight of the dog.
• retreat, withdraw, retire, recoil, give way
➤ **back out of**
They now want to back out of the deal.
• withdraw from, pull out of, drop out of
➤ **back up**
❶ *I'll back you up if you need help.*
• support, stand by, second
❷ *The new evidence backs up his story.*
• confirm, substantiate, corroborate, bear out

backfire *VERB*
His plan backfired spectacularly.
• fail, go wrong, go awry
IDIOM blow up in your face

background *NOUN*
❶ *You can see a steeple in the background.*
• backdrop, setting, distance
OPPOSITE foreground
❷ *The first chapter deals with the background to the war.*
• circumstances surrounding, lead-up to, history of
❸ *There are people from many different backgrounds living here.*
• family circumstances, environment, upbringing, tradition, culture, class

backing *NOUN*
The new manager has the backing of the players.
• support, endorsement, approval, blessing

backward ADJECTIVE

❶ She walked off without a backward glance.
• towards the rear, rearward
OPPOSITE forward

❷ It is an economically backward country.
• underdeveloped, undeveloped
OPPOSITES advanced, progressive

bad ADJECTIVE

 OVERUSED WORD

❶ Bad in quality, bad at doing something:

> poor
> inferior
> unsatisfactory
> substandard
> second-rate
> inadequate
> weak
> incompetent
> imperfect
> awful
> hopeless
> terrible
> dreadful
> useless
> worthless
> abysmal
> woeful
> pathetic
> shoddy
> slipshod

(informal) rubbish, lousy, duff

The film was spoilt by the incompetent acting.
OPPOSITES excellent, fine

❷ A bad experience, bad news:

> unpleasant
> unwelcome
> disagreeable
> upsetting
> horrific
> horrendous
> disastrous
> horrible
> awful
> terrible
> dreadful
> appalling
> shocking
> hideous
> ghastly
> frightful
> abominable

– Another word for a bad experience is an ordeal.

Some patients experienced unwelcome side effects.
OPPOSITES good, excellent

❸ A bad accident, bad illness:

> severe
> serious
> grave
> profound
> critical
> acute

She sometimes suffers from severe headaches.
OPPOSITES minor, slight

❹ A bad habit, something that is bad for you:

> harmful
> damaging
> detrimental
> dangerous
> hazardous
> injurious

The sun's rays are damaging to your eyes.

❺ A bad smell, bad taste:

> disgusting
> revolting
> repulsive
> sickening
> nauseating
> repugnant
> foul
> loathsome
> offensive
> vile

A nauseating smell invaded our nostrils.
OPPOSITES pleasant, appetizing

❻ Bad timing, a bad moment:

> inconvenient
> unsuitable
> unfortunate
> inappropriate
> inopportune

Is this an inconvenient time to call?
OPPOSITES convenient, opportune

❼ Bad weather, a bad reception:

> harsh
> hostile
> unfavourable
> adverse
> miserable

(formal) inclement

The adverse weather is forecast to continue.
OPPOSITES fine, favourable

❽ A bad person, bad deed:

> wicked
> evil
> malevolent
> malicious
> villainous
> cruel
> vicious
> corrupt
> sinful
> nefarious
> monstrous
> diabolical
> immoral
> detestable

a
b
c
d
e
f
g
h
i
j
k
l
m
n
o
p
q
r
s
t
u
v
w
x
y
z

A
B
C
D
E
F
G
H
I
J
K
L
M
N
O
P
Q
R
S
T
U
V
W
X
Y
Z

> hateful ➤ nasty
> mean

– A bad person is a **scoundrel**, **rogue** or **rascal**. A bad character in a story or film is a **villain** or (*informal*) **baddy**.

*He plays a **monstrous villain** in the film.*

OPPOSITES good, virtuous

⑨ A bad mood, bad temper:

> angry ➤ foul
> ill-humoured

*She arrived in a **foul** temper.*

OPPOSITE good-humoured

⑩ Bad behaviour:

> disobedient ➤ undisciplined
> naughty ➤ wayward
> mischievous ➤ disgraceful
> unruly ➤ deplorable

*A player has been suspended for **unruly** conduct.*

OPPOSITES exemplary, angelic

⑪ Feeling bad about something:

> guilty ➤ remorseful
> ashamed ➤ repentant
> sorry

*Claudius feels **guilty** about murdering King Hamlet.*

OPPOSITES unashamed, unrepentant

⑫ Food going bad:

> mouldy ➤ sour
> rotten ➤ spoiled
> off ➤ rancid
> decayed ➤ putrid

*Eat the bananas before they go **mouldy**.*

OPPOSITE fresh

⑬ Not bad:

> acceptable ➤ passable
> adequate ➤ tolerable
> reasonable ➤ all right

*The prices are **reasonable** if you book early.*

badly ADVERB

❶ *The wall was badly painted.*
• not well, poorly, unsatisfactorily, inadequately, incorrectly, shoddily
OPPOSITES well, properly

❷ *These animals have been badly treated.*
• ill, unkindly, harshly, cruelly, unfairly
OPPOSITES well, humanely, fairly

❸ *A rescue worker has been badly injured.*
• seriously, severely, gravely, critically
OPPOSITE slightly

❹ *She badly wanted to win.*
• very much, desperately

bad-tempered ADJECTIVE

She is always bad-tempered when she gets up.
• cross, grumpy, grouchy, irritable, moody, quarrelsome, fractious, ill-tempered, short-tempered, cantankerous, crotchety, curmudgeonly, snappy, testy, tetchy, sullen, peevish
OPPOSITES good-humoured, affable

baffle VERB

The instructions baffled me completely.
• puzzle, confuse, perplex, bewilder, mystify, stump
(*informal*) flummox, fox, flabbergast, bamboozle

bag NOUN

I put my wet clothes in a plastic bag.
• sack, carrier, holdall, satchel, handbag, shoulder bag
– A bag you carry on your back is a **backpack** or **rucksack**.

baggage NOUN

We loaded our baggage onto a trolley.
• luggage, bags, cases, suitcases, belongings, things
(*informal*) gear, stuff

baggy *ADJECTIVE*
He was wearing a pair of baggy jeans.
• loose, loose-fitting, roomy

bait *NOUN*
Some people fell for the bait and answered the email.
• lure, enticement, trap, decoy, inducement

bake *VERB*
The hot sun was baking the earth.
• scorch, burn, parch, sear

balance *NOUN*
She lost her balance and fell to the ground.
• stability, equilibrium, footing

balance *VERB*
The waiter arrived, balancing a tray on each hand.
• steady, keep balanced, stabilize, poise

bald *ADJECTIVE*
Uncle Ted has a bald patch on the top of his head.
• bare, hairless
OPPOSITE hairy

ball *NOUN*
Wind the string into a ball.
• sphere, globe, orb
– A small ball of something is a **pellet** or **globule**.

ballot *NOUN*
The club held a secret ballot to choose a new president.
• vote, poll, election, referendum

ban *VERB*
❶ *Mobile phones are banned in school.*
• forbid, prohibit, bar, veto, proscribe, exclude, outlaw, banish
OPPOSITES allow, permit
❷ *The sprinter has been banned from international competition.*
• exclude, bar, banish, outlaw, expel
OPPOSITE admit

banal *ADJECTIVE*
a disappointingly banal ending
• unoriginal, commonplace, predictable, hackneyed, trite, unimaginative, uninspiring

band *NOUN*
❶ *The captain wears a red arm band.*
• strip, stripe, ring, line, belt, hoop
❷ *They were captured by a band of outlaws.*
• gang, group, company, party, body, troop, crew, mob, team, set
(*informal*) bunch
❸ *A jazz band was playing in the town square.*
• group, ensemble, orchestra

bandage *NOUN*
You need a bandage round that knee.
• dressing, plaster, gauze, lint

bandit *NOUN*
Bandits used to live in these mountains.
• robber, brigand, thief, outlaw, desperado, highwayman, pirate

bang *NOUN*
❶ *Suddenly there was a loud bang.*
• blast, boom, crash, crack, thud, thump, pop, explosion, report
❷ *He got a bang on the head from the low ceiling.*
• bump, knock, blow, hit, bash, thump, punch, smack, crack
(*informal*) whack, wallop, clout

bang *VERB*
She banged her fist on the table.
• hit, strike, beat, bash, thump, knock, hammer, pound, rap, slam
(*informal*) whack, wallop

banish *VERB*
❶ *He was banished from the kingdom forever.*
• exile, expel, deport, send away, eject
❷ *She struggled to banish these fears.*
• dispel, remove, dismiss, allay, drive away

bank NOUN

❶ *The temple was built on the banks of the River Nile.*
• edge, side, shore, embankment, margin, verge, brink
❷ *We ran down the steep grassy bank.*
• slope, mound, ridge, rise, knoll
❸ *Below the screen was a bank of dials and switches.*
• array, row, line, series

banner NOUN

❶ *The turrets were decorated with colourful banners.*
• flag, standard, streamer, pennant
❷ *Demonstrators marched past, carrying banners.*
• placard, sign, notice, poster

banquet NOUN

There was a state banquet in their honour.
• dinner, feast
(*informal*) spread

bar NOUN

❶ *There were bars across the window.*
• rod, rail, spar, strut, beam, pole
❷ *I bought a bar of chocolate.*
• block, slab, wedge, tablet, cake
– A bar of gold or silver is an **ingot**.

bar VERB

❶ *The door had been barred on the inside.*
• bolt, fasten, secure, barricade
❷ *A fallen tree barred the way ahead.*
• block, hinder, impede, obstruct, stop, check
❸ *She has been barred from entering the country.*
• ban, prohibit, forbid, exclude, keep out

barbaric ADJECTIVE

the barbaric treatment of slaves
• cruel, brutal, inhuman, inhumane, barbarous, savage, brutish

bare ADJECTIVE

❶ *I put suncream on my bare arms and legs.*
• naked, nude, exposed, uncovered, unclothed, undressed
OPPOSITES clothed, covered
❷ *We looked out on a bare landscape.*
• barren, bleak, desolate, treeless, leafless
OPPOSITES fertile, lush
❸ *The room was bare except for a single bed.*
• empty, clear, unfurnished, undecorated
OPPOSITE furnished
❹ *Here are the bare facts of the case.*
• plain, simple, unembellished, bald, stark
❺ *Only pack the bare essentials.*
• basic, minimum

barely ADVERB

We barely had time to get changed.
• hardly, scarcely, only just

bargain NOUN

❶ *I'll make a bargain with you.*
• deal, agreement, arrangement, promise, contract, pact
❷ *We went looking for bargains in the sales.*
• good buy, special offer
(*informal*) snip, steal

bargain VERB

I am not going to bargain with you.
• haggle, do a deal, negotiate
➤ **bargain on**
I hadn't bargained on sleeping in a tent.
• expect, anticipate, envisage, foresee, count on, reckon on, allow for

barge VERB

➤ **barge into**
❶ *People were running around and barging into each other.*
• bump into, collide with, veer into
❷ *Don't just barge into my room without knocking.*
• push into, rush into, storm into

bark VERB

Dogs barked from behind the fence.
• woof, yap, yelp, growl

barrage NOUN
  ❶ *a tidal barrage*
  • dam, weir, barrier
  ❷ *a heavy artillery barrage*
  • bombardment, volley, gunfire
  ❸ *facing a barrage of questions*
  • mass, stream, flood, torrent, deluge, onslaught, avalanche

barrel NOUN
  He hid in an empty beer barrel.
  • cask, drum, tub, keg, butt

barren ADJECTIVE
  The surface of the planet was a barren landscape.
  • arid, dry, bare, infertile, sterile, unproductive, unfruitful
  OPPOSITES fertile, lush

barricade NOUN
  They built a barricade of sandbags.
  • barrier, blockade, obstacle, obstruction

barrier NOUN
  ❶ *Spectators must stay behind the barrier.*
  • fence, railing, barricade, blockade
  – A barrier across a road is a **roadblock**.
  ❷ *Lack of confidence can be a barrier to success.*
  • obstacle, obstruction, bar, hindrance, impediment, hurdle, stumbling block

base NOUN
  ❶ *We stood at the base of the pyramid.*
  • bottom, foot, foundation, support, stand
  – A base under a statue is a **pedestal** or **plinth**.
  ❷ *The decimal system has 10 as its base.*
  • basis, foundation, root, starting point
  ❸ *The lifeboat crew returned to base safely.*
  • headquarters, camp, station, post, depot

base VERB
  ❶ *She based the story on an event in her own childhood.*
  • found, build, construct, establish, ground

  ❷ *The company is based in Wales.*
  • locate, site, situate, position

basement NOUN
  Steps led down to the basement.
  • cellar, vault
  – A room underneath a church is a **crypt**.
  – An underground cell in a castle is a **dungeon**.

bashful ADJECTIVE
  He was too bashful to ask for a dance.
  • shy, reserved, timid, diffident

basic ADJECTIVE
  ❶ *The basic ingredients of bread are flour, yeast and water.*
  • fundamental, essential, main, primary, principal, chief, key, central, crucial
  OPPOSITES secondary, extra
  ❷ *The campsite has very basic facilities.*
  • plain, simple, minimal, rudimentary, elementary, limited, unsophisticated
  OPPOSITES elaborate, advanced

basically ADVERB
  Basically, I think you're right.
  • fundamentally, essentially, in essence, at heart, at bottom

basics PLURAL NOUN
  That week I learnt the basics of fishing.
  • fundamentals, essentials, first principles, foundations, groundwork
  IDIOM nuts and bolts

basin NOUN
  Fill a basin with soapy water.
  • sink, bowl, dish

basis NOUN
  What is the basis of your argument?
  • base, foundation, grounds

basket NOUN
  She was carrying a basket of fruit.
  – A basket of food is a **hamper**.
  – A basket on a bicycle is a **pannier**.
  – A small basket of fruit is a **punnet**.

a
b
c
d
e
f
g
h
i
j
k
l
m
n
o
p
q
r
s
t
u
v
w
x
y
z

bass *ADJECTIVE*

He sang in a loud, bass voice.
• low, deep
OPPOSITES high-pitched, high

bat *NOUN*

a heavy, wooden bat
• club, stick

batch *NOUN*

She made a fresh batch of pancakes for us.
• group, quantity, set, lot, bunch, bundle

bathe *VERB*

❶ It was too cold to bathe in the sea.
• swim, go swimming, take a dip
– To walk about in shallow water is to **paddle**.
❷ You should bathe the wound carefully.
• clean, wash, rinse, cleanse

batter *VERB*

Huge waves battered the rocks.
• beat, pound, thump, pummel, buffet

battle *NOUN*

❶ The battle took place a few miles north of the city.
• fight, conflict, action, engagement, hostilities, skirmish, armed struggle
– A place where a battle takes place is a **battlefield**, **battleground** or **field of battle**.
❷ The legal battle lasted several years.
• argument, dispute, struggle, clash, conflict

bawl *VERB*

❶ I heard someone bawl out my name.
• shout, cry, yell, roar, bellow, bark (informal) holler
❷ A baby was bawling in the next room.
• cry, wail, howl, sob

bay *NOUN*

The ship was anchored in a sheltered bay.
• cove, inlet, gulf, sound

be *VERB*

❶ I'll be at home all morning.
• stay, continue, remain
❷ The concert will be in March.
• take place, happen, come about, occur
❸ She wants to be a famous writer.
• become, develop into

beach *NOUN*

In front of the hotel is a sandy beach.
• sands, seashore, seaside, shore, strand

bead *NOUN*

He stopped to wipe beads of sweat from his brow.
• drop, droplet, drip, blob, pearl

beam *NOUN*

❶ Wooden beams ran across the ceiling.
• bar, timber, plank, post, joist, rafter, boom, spar, strut, support
❷ A beam of sunlight entered the cave.
• ray, shaft, stream, streak, gleam
❸ A huge beam spread across her face.
• smile, grin

beam *VERB*

❶ In the photo, we are all beaming at the camera.
• smile, grin
❷ The satellite will beam a signal back to Earth.
• transmit, send out, broadcast, emit

bear *VERB*

❶ The rope won't bear my weight.
• support, hold, take, sustain
❷ A messenger arrived, bearing news.
• carry, bring, convey, transport, take, transfer
❸ The gravestone bears an old inscription.
• display, show, exhibit, carry, have
❹ I can't bear all this noise.
• endure, tolerate, put up with, stand, withstand, cope with, abide, stomach
❺ Queen Victoria bore nine children.
• give birth to, have, produce
❻ Several trees in the garden bear fruit.
• produce, yield, give, supply

➤ **bear out**
This bears out everything I said.
• confirm, support, substantiate, corroborate, back up

➤ **bear with**
Please bear with me a little longer.
• be patient with, put up with, tolerate

bearable ADJECTIVE
The pain was only just bearable.
• tolerable, endurable, acceptable
OPPOSITE unbearable

bearings PLURAL NOUN
We lost our bearings in the fog.
• sense of direction, orientation, position, whereabouts

beast NOUN
They could hear the roars of wild beasts.
• animal, creature, brute

beat VERB
❶ *The man was beating a dog with a stick.*
• hit, strike, thrash, thump, batter, whip, lash, flog, lay into, rain blows on (*informal*) whack, wallop
❷ *Spain beat Germany in the final.*
• defeat, conquer, win against, vanquish, get the better of, overcome, overwhelm, rout, trounce, thrash (*informal*) hammer, lick
❸ *Beat the eggs, milk and sugar together.*
• whisk, whip, blend, mix, stir
❹ *Her heart was beating with excitement.*
• pound, thump, palpitate

➤ **beat someone up**
They threatened to beat us up.
• assault, attack (*informal*) rough up

beat NOUN
❶ *Can you feel the beat of your heart?*
• pulse, throb, palpitation, pounding, thumping
❷ *The music has a strong beat.*
• rhythm, accent, stress

beautiful ADJECTIVE

> **OVERUSED WORD**

❶ A beautiful **person**:

➤ attractive   ➤ elegant
➤ good-looking   ➤ enchanting
➤ pretty   ➤ dazzling
➤ gorgeous   ➤ stunning
➤ glamorous   ➤ magnificent
➤ radiant   ➤ resplendent

(*Scottish*) bonny

The queen looked radiant *in a red silk gown.*

– A man who is pleasing to look at is good-looking or handsome.
OPPOSITES ugly, unattractive

❷ A beautiful **day**, beautiful **weather**:

➤ fine   ➤ sunny
➤ excellent   ➤ superb
➤ glorious   ➤ splendid
➤ marvellous   ➤ wonderful

We are hoping for fine *weather tomorrow.*
OPPOSITES dull, gloomy, drab

❸ A beautiful **sight**, beautiful **view**:

➤ picturesque   ➤ splendid
➤ scenic   ➤ glorious
➤ charming   ➤ magnificent
➤ delightful   ➤ spectacular

I chose a postcard with a scenic *view of the Alps.*

❹ A beautiful **sound**, beautiful **voice**:

➤ harmonious   ➤ melodious
➤ mellifluous   ➤ sweet-sounding

The nightingale has a sweet-sounding *song.*
OPPOSITES grating, harsh

beauty NOUN
The film star was famous for her beauty.
• attractiveness, prettiness, loveliness,

a b c d e f g h i j k l m n o p q r s t u v w x y z

charm, allure, magnificence, radiance, splendour
OPPOSITE ugliness

because CONJUNCTION
I came here because I was invited.
• since, as, seeing that, in view of the fact that
➤ **because of**
Play was stopped because of bad light.
• as a result of, on account of, thanks to, owing to, due to, by virtue of

beckon VERB
The old man beckoned me to come forward.
• gesture, signal, motion, wave, gesticulate

become VERB
❶ *Women's football is becoming more popular.*
• begin to be, turn, get
❷ *Eventually, the tadpoles will become frogs.*
• grow into, change into, develop into, turn into
❸ *Short hair really becomes you.*
• suit, flatter, look good on
➤ **become of**
Whatever became of your plan to go abroad?
• happen to, come of

bed NOUN
❶ *The room has a double bed.*
• bunk, mattress
– A bed for a baby is a **cot**, **cradle** or **crib**.
– A bed on a ship or train is a **berth**.
❷ *We planted daffodils in the flower bed.*
• plot, patch, border
❸ *These creatures feed on the bed of the ocean.*
• bottom, floor
OPPOSITE surface
➤ **go to bed**
Is it time to go to bed yet?
• retire, turn in
IDIOM (informal) hit the sack

bedraggled ADJECTIVE
We carried the wet and bedraggled kitten into the house.
• dishevelled, disordered, untidy, unkempt, scruffy
OPPOSITES smart, spruce

bee NOUN

WORD WEB

Some types of bee:
➤ bumblebee
➤ drone
➤ honeybee
➤ queen
➤ worker
– A young bee after it hatches is a **larva**.
– A group of bees is a **swarm** or a **colony**.
– A place where bees live is a **hive**.
– A person who keeps bees is an **apiarist**.

before ADVERB
❶ *Those people were before us in the queue.*
• in front of, ahead of, in advance of
OPPOSITES after, behind
❷ *Please switch off the lights before you leave.*
• prior to, previous to, earlier than, preparatory to
OPPOSITE after
❸ *Have you seen this film before?*
• previously, in the past, earlier, sooner
OPPOSITE later

beg VERB
❶ *The prisoners begged for mercy.*
• ask, plead, call
❷ *They begged her not to leave.*
• implore, plead with, entreat, beseech, appeal to

begin VERB
❶ *The builders began work yesterday.*
• start, commence, embark on, set about
OPPOSITES end, finish, conclude
❷ *When did the trouble begin?*
• appear, arise, emerge, originate, start,

commence, spring up
OPPOSITES end, stop, cease

beginner NOUN
This swimming class is for beginners.
• learner, starter, novice
(informal) rookie
– A beginner in a trade or a job is an
apprentice or **trainee**.
– A beginner in the police or armed
services is a **cadet** or **recruit**.

beginning NOUN
❶ I missed the beginning of the film.
• start, opening, commencement,
introduction, preamble
– A piece of writing at the beginning of
a book is an **introduction**, **preface** or
prologue.
– A piece of music at the beginning
of a musical or opera is a **prelude** or
overture.
OPPOSITES end, conclusion
❷ The programme is about the beginning
of life on Earth.
• starting point, origin, inception,
genesis, onset, establishment,
foundation, emergence, birth, launch,
dawn

behave VERB
❶ Our neighbour is behaving very oddly.
• act, conduct yourself, react, perform
❷ My little brother promised to behave.
• be good, be on your best behaviour,
behave yourself
OPPOSITE misbehave

behaviour NOUN
I apologize for my behaviour yesterday.
• conduct, manners, actions,
performance

being NOUN
They looked like beings from another
planet.
• creature, individual, person, entity

belch VERB
The chimney belched clouds of black
smoke.
• discharge, emit, give out, send out,
gush, spew

belief NOUN
❶ She is a woman of strong religious
beliefs.
• faith, principle, creed, doctrine
❷ It is my belief is that he stole the
money.
• opinion, view, conviction, feeling,
notion, theory

believable ADJECTIVE
Few of the characters in the book are
believable.
• credible, plausible
OPPOSITES unbelievable, implausible

believe VERB
❶ I don't believe anything he says.
• accept, have faith in, have confidence
in, rely on, trust
OPPOSITES disbelieve, doubt
❷ I believe you know my parents.
• think, understand, assume, presume,
gather
(informal) reckon

bell NOUN
I can hear the bell.
• chime, alarm, carillon, knell, peal

WORD WEB

Words for how a bell sounds:
➤ chime   ➤ peal
➤ clang   ➤ ring
➤ jangle   ➤ tinkle
➤ jingle   ➤ toll

bellow VERB
He started to bellow out orders.
• shout, roar, bawl, yell, bark, boom,
thunder

belong VERB
❶ This ring belonged to my
grandmother.
• be owned by, be the property of,
be in the hands of
❷ Do you belong to a sports club?
• be a member of, be in, be associated
with

a
b
c
d
e
f
g
h
i
j
k
l
m
n
o
p
q
r
s
t
u
v
w
x
y
z

❸ *I never felt that I really belonged in my old school.*
• fit in, be suited to, feel welcome, be at home

belongings PLURAL NOUN
Put any personal belongings in a locker.
• possessions, property, goods, things, effects, bits and pieces
(*informal*) gear, stuff

beloved ADJECTIVE
She finally returned to her beloved homeland.
• much loved, adored, dear, darling, cherished, treasured, precious
OPPOSITE hated

below PREPOSITION
❶ *Fish were swimming just below the surface.*
• under, underneath, beneath
OPPOSITE above
❷ *The temperature never fell below 20 degrees.*
• less than, lower than
OPPOSITES above, over

belt NOUN
❶ *He wore a black leather belt.*
• girdle, sash, strap, band
– A broad sash worn round the waist is a **cummerbund**.
❷ *We drove through a belt of thick fog.*
• band, strip, line, stretch, zone, area

bench NOUN
We sat on a bench in the park.
• seat, form
(*North American*) bleacher
– A long seat in a church is a **pew**.

bend VERB
❶ *The fire had bent the railings out of shape.*
• curve, curl, coil, loop, hook, twist, crook, angle, flex, arch, warp
– Things which bend easily are **flexible** or **pliable**.
OPPOSITE straighten
❷ *I bent down to tie my shoelaces.*
• stoop, bow, crouch, lean over

❸ *Just ahead the road bends to the right.*
• turn, swing, veer, wind

bend NOUN
We came to a sharp bend in the road.
• curve, turn, angle, corner, twist, kink

beneath PREPOSITION
She was sitting beneath a cherry tree.
• under, underneath, below, at the foot of
OPPOSITES above, on top of

beneficial ADJECTIVE
Eating fruit is beneficial to health.
• favourable, advantageous, helpful, useful, valuable, salutary
OPPOSITES harmful, detrimental

benefit NOUN
She always talks about the benefits of regular exercise.
• advantage, reward, gain, good point, blessing, boon
(*informal*) perk
OPPOSITES disadvantage, drawback

benefit VERB
The rainy weather will benefit gardeners.
• be good for, be of service to, help, aid, assist, serve, profit
OPPOSITES hinder, harm

benevolent ADJECTIVE
She greeted everyone with a benevolent smile.
• kind, kindly, friendly, warm-hearted, kind-hearted, good-natured, sympathetic, charitable, caring, benign
OPPOSITES malevolent, unkind

benign ADJECTIVE
❶ *There was a benign expression on her face.*
• kindly, friendly, kind-hearted, good-natured, genial, sympathetic, well-disposed, benevolent
OPPOSITES unfriendly, hostile
❷ *The island has a benign climate.*
• mild, temperate, balmy, favourable
OPPOSITE hostile

bent ADJECTIVE

❶ *After the crash, the car was a mass of bent metal.*
• curved, twisted, coiled, looped, buckled, crooked, warped, misshapen, out of shape, deformed, contorted
OPPOSITE straight

❷ *The old man had a bent back and walked with a stick.*
• crooked, hunched, curved, arched, bowed
OPPOSITE straight

➤ **bent on**
Are you still bent on going?
• intent on, determined on, set on

bent NOUN

She has a definite artistic bent.
• talent, gift, flair, aptitude, inclination

berserk ADJECTIVE

➤ **go berserk**
The crowd went berserk when the band appeared.
• go mad, go crazy, go wild
IDIOMS (*informal*) go off your head, go bananas, freak out

beside PREPOSITION

They sat beside each other on the bus.
• next to, alongside, abreast of, adjacent to, next door to, close to, near, by

➤ **beside the point**
The fact that I'm a girl is beside the point.
• irrelevant, unimportant, neither here nor there

besides PREPOSITION

No one knows the password, besides you and me.
• as well as, in addition to, apart from, other than, aside from

besides ADVERB

Besides, it's too late to phone now.
• also, in addition, furthermore, moreover

besiege VERB

❶ *The Greeks besieged the city of Troy for ten years.*
• blockade, lay siege to

❷ *Fans besieged the singer after the concert.*
• surround, mob, harass, plague

best ADJECTIVE

❶ *She is our best player.*
• finest, foremost, greatest, leading, top, premier, supreme, pre-eminent, outstanding, unequalled, unrivalled, second to none
(*informal*) star, top-drawer
OPPOSITE worst

❷ *I did what I thought was best.*
• most suitable, most appropriate, most advisable

best ADVERB

Which song did you like best?
• most, the most
OPPOSITE least

bestow VERB

➤ **bestow on**
The ring is said to bestow power on the wearer.
• confer on, give to, grant to, present with

bet NOUN

I had a bet that they would win.
• wager, gamble, stake
(*informal*) flutter

bet VERB

❶ *Do you ever bet on the lottery?*
• wager, gamble, stake
(*informal*) have a flutter

❷ (*informal*) *I bet I'm right.*
• feel sure, be certain, be convinced, expect, predict

betray VERB

❶ *He was betrayed by one of his own men.*
• be disloyal to, be unfaithful to, inform on, conspire against, double-cross
IDIOMS stab someone in the back, sell someone down the river
– Someone who betrays you is a **traitor**.
– To betray your country is to commit **treason**.

❷ *Her face betrayed no emotion.*
• reveal, show, indicate, disclose, divulge, expose, tell

A
B
C
D
E
F
G
H
I
J
K
L
M
N
O
P
Q
R
S
T
U
V
W
X
Y
Z

better *ADJECTIVE*
❶ *This computer is much better than my old one.*
• superior, finer, preferable
IDIOM a cut above
OPPOSITES worse, inferior
❷ *I hope you feel better soon.*
• recovered, cured, healed, well, fitter, stronger
OPPOSITE worse

between *PREPOSITION*
❶ *There is a path between the house and the garden.*
• connecting, joining, linking
❷ *We divided the food between us.*
• among, amongst

beware *VERB*
Beware! There are thieves about.
• be careful, watch out, look out, take care, be on your guard
➤ beware of
Beware of the bull.
• watch out for, avoid, mind, heed, keep clear of

bewilder *VERB*
We were bewildered by the directions on the map.
• puzzle, confuse, perplex, mystify, baffle, bemuse
(*informal*) flummox, fox, flabbergast

beyond *PREPOSITION*
The village lies just beyond those hills.
• past, after, behind, the other side of, further away than
OPPOSITES in front of, before

bias *NOUN*
Does the author show signs of bias?
• prejudice, partiality, one-sidedness, favouritism, discrimination, unfairness, imbalance
OPPOSITE impartiality

biased *ADJECTIVE*
The referee was clearly biased.
• prejudiced, partial, one-sided, partisan, discriminatory, bigoted, unbalanced
OPPOSITE impartial

bicycle *NOUN*
There is a rack outside for parking bicycles.
• push bike
(*informal*) bike
– A person who rides a bicycle is a **cyclist**.

WORD WEB

Types of bicycle:

➤ BMX bike
➤ mountain bike
➤ racing bicycle
➤ reclining or recumbent bicycle
➤ road bicycle
➤ tandem
➤ trailer bike
➤ touring bicycle
➤ track bicycle
➤ (*historical*) penny-farthing

– A cycle with one wheel is a **unicycle**.
– A cycle with three wheels is a **tricycle** or (*informal*) **trike**.
– A cycle without pedals is a **scooter**.
– An arena for track cycling is a **velodrome**.

bid *NOUN*
❶ *The painting attracted bids of thousands of dollars.*
• offer, tender, proposal
❷ *His bid to beat the world record failed.*
• attempt, effort, try, go, endeavour

bid *VERB*
Someone bid $2 million for the painting.
• offer, tender, propose, put up

big *ADJECTIVE*

OVERUSED WORD

❶ **Big in size, scale:**

➤ large
➤ huge
➤ great
➤ massive
➤ immense
➤ enormous
➤ gigantic
➤ giant
➤ colossal
➤ mammoth
➤ monstrous
➤ monumental
➤ titanic

(*informal*) whopping, mega

(*literary*) **gargantuan**

Our class made a giant model of a human ear.

OPPOSITES small, little, tiny

❷ Big in area, distance:

> vast
> immense
> expansive
> considerable
> sweeping

Some day spaceships will be able to travel vast distances.

❸ Big inside:

> spacious
> roomy
> capacious
> extensive
> sizeable
> palatial
> cavernous

Inside, the car is surprisingly roomy.

OPPOSITES cramped, confined, poky

❹ Big and heavy, awkward:

> bulky
> cumbersome
> weighty
> hefty

What could be inside that bulky envelope?

❺ Big and strong, tall:

> well built
> hulking
> hefty
> strapping
> burly
> beefy
> brawny
> sturdy
> mighty
> towering
> mountainous
> giant

His strapping physique is perfect for an action hero.

❻ A big part, big portion:

> ample
> considerable
> substantial
> sizeable
> generous
> lavish
> bumper

Each character gets an ample share of the treasure.

OPPOSITES meagre, paltry

❼ A big **decision**, big **moment**:

> important
> serious
> grave
> weighty
> significant
> key
> momentous
> historic
> far-reaching
> crucial
> vital
> major

This year's final promises to be a momentous occasion.

OPPOSITES insignificant, minor

bill NOUN
❶ *Please send us the bill by email.*
• account, invoice, statement, charges
❷ *The first act on the bill was a comedian.*
• programme, line-up

billow VERB
❶ *Smoke was billowing from the chimney.*
• pour, swirl, spiral, roll
❷ *The huge sail billowed in the wind.*
• swell, fill out, puff out, bulge, balloon

bind VERB
❶ *We bound the sticks together with some rope.*
• tie, fasten, secure, join, clamp, lash
❷ *The leaves can be used to bind wounds.*
• bandage, wrap, strap up
OPPOSITES untie, unwrap
❸ *They were bound by ties of friendship.*
• unite, connect, join, attach
OPPOSITE separate

bird NOUN

⊛ WORD WEB

Some common british birds:

> blackbird
> blue tit
> bullfinch
> bunting
> chaffinch
> crow
> cuckoo
> dove
> finch
> great tit
> greenfinch
> jackdaw
> jay
> linnet

a
b
c
d
e
f
g
h
i
j
k
l
m
n
o
p
q
r
s
t
u
v
w
x
y
z

- magpie
- martin
- nightingale
- pigeon
- raven
- robin
- rook
- skylark
- sparrow
- starling
- swallow
- swift
- thrush
- wagtail
- woodpecker
- wren

Birds of prey:

- buzzard
- eagle
- falcon
- hawk
- kestrel
- kite
- merlin
- osprey
- owl
- sparrowhawk
- vulture

Farm and game birds:

- chicken
- duck
- goose
- grouse
- guinea fowl
- partridge
- pheasant
- quail
- turkey

- Birds kept by farmers are called poultry.

Sea-birds and water birds:

- albatross
- auk
- bittern
- coot
- cormorant
- crane
- curlew
- duck
- gannet
- goose
- guillemot
- gull
- heron
- kingfisher
- kittiwake
- lapwing
- mallard
- moorhen
- oystercatcher
- peewit
- pelican
- penguin
- puffin
- seagull
- snipe
- stork
- swan
- teal

Birds from other countries:

- bird of paradise
- budgerigar
- canary
- cockatoo
- flamingo
- humming bird
- ibis
- kookaburra
- macaw
- mynah bird
- parakeet
- parrot

- peacock or peafowl
- toucan

Birds which cannot fly:

- emu
- kiwi
- ostrich
- penguin

- A female bird is a **hen** and a male bird is a **cock**.
- A young bird is a **chick, fledgling** or **nestling** and a family of chicks is a **brood**.
- A group of birds is a **colony** or **flock** and a group of flying birds is a **flight** or **skein**.
- The scientific study of birds is **ornithology**.
- A person who observes birds in their natural habitat is a **birdwatcher**.

WRITING TIPS

DESCRIBING BIRDS
Body parts:

- beak
- bill
- breast
- claw
- comb
- crest
- crop
- feathers
- plumage
- tail
- talon
- wattle
- wing

Plumage:

- bedraggled
- downy
- drab
- feathery
- fluffy
- ruffled
- speckled
- spotted

Movement:

- circle
- dart
- flap
- flit
- flutter
- fly
- glide
- perch
- soar
- swoop
- waddle
- wheel

Sounds:

- caw
- chirp

- cluck
- coo
- gabble
- honk
- hoot
- quack
- screech
- squawk
- trill
- twitter
- warble

bit NOUN

OVERUSED WORD

❶ A bit of a whole:

- piece
- part
- section
- portion
- fraction
- share
- segment
- slice

The first section of the film is shot in black and white.

❷ A large, heavy bit:

- chunk
- lump
- hunk
- wedge
- slab
- brick

Saturn's rings are made of lumps of ice and rock.

❸ A small bit:

- fragment
- scrap
- shaving
- shred
- sliver
- snippet
- chip
- speck
- spot
- particle
- atom
- mite
- jot
- modicum
- pinch
- touch
- dab
- daub
- trace
- hint
- suggestion

(informal) smidgen, tad

The map was drawn on a scrap of old paper.

❹ A bit of food:

- morsel
- crumb
- bite
- nibble
- taste
- mouthful
- soupçon

We ate every last morsel of breakfast.

❺ A bit of liquid:

- drop
- dash
- dribble
- drizzle
- dollop
- blob
- splash

(informal) swig

Add a dash of lemon juice to the sauce.

❻ A bit:

- slightly
- rather
- fairly
- somewhat
- quite
- vaguely
- faintly
- a little
- a shade

I found the whole evening slightly dull.

❼ To bits:

- to pieces

(informal) to smithereens

The raft will surely be pounded to pieces.

bite VERB

❶ *I bit a chunk out of my apple.*
• munch, nibble, chew, crunch, gnaw
(informal) chomp
❷ *I've been bitten all over by midges.*
• nip, pinch, sting, pierce, wound, snap at
– A fierce animal **mauls** or **savages** its prey.

bite NOUN

❶ *Can I have a bite of your sandwich?*
• mouthful, nibble, taste, morsel
❷ *She was covered in mosquito bites.*
• nip, sting, wound

biting ADJECTIVE

❶ *There was a biting wind outside.*
• freezing, bitter, piercing, raw, wintry, icy
(informal) perishing
❷ *He faced biting criticism.*
• sharp, critical, scathing, cutting, savage, caustic

a
b
c
d
e
f
g
h
i
j
k
l
m
n
o
p
q
r
s
t
u
v
w
x
y
z

49

A
B
C
D
E
F
G
H
I
J
K
L
M
N
O
P
Q
R
S
T
U
V
W
X
Y
Z

bitter ADJECTIVE
❶ *The medicine has a bitter taste.*
• sour, sharp, acid, acrid, tart
OPPOSITE sweet
❷ *I still feel bitter about what happened.*
• resentful, embittered, disgruntled, aggrieved
OPPOSITE contented
❸ *The decision was a bitter disappointment.*
• upsetting, hurtful, distressing, cruel
OPPOSITES mild, slight
❹ *A bitter wind was blowing in from the sea.*
• freezing, biting, piercing, raw, wintry, icy
(*informal*) perishing

bizarre ADJECTIVE
It was a bizarre coincidence.
• strange, odd, peculiar, weird, uncanny, extraordinary, outlandish
(*informal*) freaky

black ADJECTIVE
❶ *The horse had a shiny black coat.*
• jet-black, pitch-black, ebony, inky, raven, charcoal, sooty
For tips on describing colours see colour.
❷ *He arrived in a black mood.*
• bad-tempered, ill-humoured, angry, foul
OPPOSITES bright, cheerful

blame VERB
Nobody blames you for what happened.
• hold responsible, accuse, condemn, reproach, scold
➤ **to blame**
Who do you think was most to blame?
• responsible, culpable, guilty, at fault, in the wrong

blame NOUN
They were cleared of all blame for the accident.
• responsibility, culpability, guilt, fault

bland ADJECTIVE
❶ *The cheese has a bland flavour.*
• mild, weak, insipid, flavourless, tasteless
OPPOSITES strong, pungent

❷ *He has a bland style of writing.*
• dull, uninteresting, unexciting, lacklustre, monotonous, boring
(*informal*) wishy-washy
OPPOSITES exciting, thrilling

blank ADJECTIVE
❶ *On the desk was a blank sheet of paper.*
• empty, bare, clean, plain, unmarked, unused
❷ *The assistant at the counter gave me a blank look.*
• expressionless, vacant, stony, impassive, deadpan

blank NOUN
Fill in the blanks to complete the sentence.
• space, break, gap

blanket NOUN
❶ *The baby was wrapped in a woollen blanket.*
• cover, sheet, quilt, rug, throw
❷ *A blanket of snow covered the ground.*
• covering, layer, film, sheet, carpet, mantle

blast NOUN
❶ *A blast of cold air came through the door.*
• gust, rush, draught, burst
❷ *The referee gave a long blast on his whistle.*
• blare, honk, toot, peep
❸ *Several people were injured in the blast.*
• explosion, detonation, shock

blast VERB
❶ *Dynamite was used to blast through the rock.*
• explode, blow up, burst
❷ *Music was blasting out of the speakers.*
• blare, boom

blatant ADJECTIVE
It was a blatant lie.
• obvious, flagrant, glaring, shameless, barefaced, brazen, unabashed

blaze NOUN
❶ *Firefighters fought the blaze for hours.*
• fire, flames, inferno
❷ *She was dazzled by the sudden blaze of light.*
• glare, burst, flare, flash

blaze VERB
❶ *Soon the campfire was blazing.*
• burn, flare up, be alight, be in flames
❷ *Lights blazed from the top floor.*
• shine, beam, flare, flash, gleam

bleach VERB
In the old days, linen was bleached in the sun.
• turn white, whiten, blanch, make pale

bleak ADJECTIVE
❶ *Ahead was a bleak mountainside.*
• bare, barren, desolate, empty, exposed, stark
❷ *The future looks bleak for the club.*
• gloomy, hopeless, depressing, dismal, grim, miserable
OPPOSITES bright, promising

blemish NOUN
This peach has a slight blemish on the skin.
• flaw, defect, imperfection, mark, spot, stain

blend VERB
❶ *Blend the ingredients together.*
• mix, combine, stir, whisk
❷ *The colours blend well with each other.*
• go together, match, fit, be compatible, harmonize, coordinate
OPPOSITE clash

blend NOUN
The book is a blend of action, history and horror.
• mixture, mix, combination, compound, amalgam, fusion

blessing NOUN
❶ *The author has given the film her blessing.*
• approval, backing, support, consent, permission
OPPOSITE disapproval
❷ *Having an open fire is a blessing in*

the winter.
• benefit, advantage, plus, bonus, boon, godsend
OPPOSITES curse, evil

blew
past tense see **blow**

blight NOUN
That tower block is a blight on the landscape.
• curse, affliction, nuisance, menace, plague
OPPOSITES blessing, boon

blight VERB
Knee injuries have blighted his career.
• afflict, plague, menace, curse, ruin, spoil, mar

blind ADJECTIVE
Polar bear cubs are born blind.
• sightless, unsighted, unseeing, visually impaired
OPPOSITES sighted, seeing
➤ **blind to**
They remained blind to the danger around them.
• ignorant of, unaware of, oblivious to, indifferent to, heedless of
OPPOSITES aware of, mindful of

bliss NOUN
The poem is about the sheer bliss of being in love.
• joy, delight, pleasure, happiness, heaven, ecstasy
OPPOSITE misery

blissful ADJECTIVE
We have enjoyed a blissful week of sunshine.
• joyful, delightful, pleasurable, heavenly, ecstatic
OPPOSITE miserable

blob NOUN
There was a blob of glue on the table.
• drop, lump, spot, dollop, daub, globule

block NOUN
❶ *A block of ice fell from the glacier.*
• chunk, hunk, lump, piece, wedge, slab, brick

a b c d e f g h i j k l m n o p q r s t u v w x y z

② *There must be a block in the drainpipe.*
• blockage, jam, obstacle, obstruction, impediment

block VERB
① *A mass of leaves had blocked the drain.*
• clog, choke, jam, plug, stop up, congest
(*informal*) bung up
OPPOSITE clear
② *The new building will block our view.*
• obstruct, interfere with, hamper, hinder, impede

blockage NOUN
The main pipe has a blockage.
• block, jam, obstruction, congestion

blond or **blonde** ADJECTIVE
She was wearing a blonde wig.
• fair-haired, fair, golden, flaxen
OPPOSITE dark

blood NOUN
Do you have any Spanish blood?
• ancestry, family, lineage, roots, descent, parentage

bloodshed NOUN
In ancient times, this was a scene of bloodshed.
• killing, massacre, slaughter, butchery, carnage

bloodthirsty ADJECTIVE
Outside we could hear the bloodthirsty cries of an angry mob.
• murderous, vicious, barbaric, savage, brutal

bloody ADJECTIVE
① *He handed back the bloody handkerchief.*
• bloodstained, blood-soaked, gory
② *It was the bloodiest battle of the war.*
• gory, bloodthirsty, brutal, barbaric, savage, murderous

bloom NOUN
The pear tree was covered in white blooms.
• flower, blossom, bud

bloom VERB
① *The daffodils bloomed early this year.*
• blossom, flower, open
OPPOSITES fade, wither
② *New ideas began to bloom.*
• develop, grow, flourish, thrive, burgeon

blossom NOUN
I love to see the cherry blossom in spring.
• blooms, buds, flowers

blossom VERB
① *The seeds we've sown will blossom next year.*
• bloom, flower, open
OPPOSITES fade, wither
② *She has blossomed into a fine young actress.*
• develop, grow, mature, progress, evolve

blot NOUN
The page was covered with ink blots.
• spot, blotch, mark, blob, splodge, smudge, smear, stain

blot VERB
➤ **blot out**
A huge dark cloud blotted out the sun.
• block out, hide, mask, conceal, obscure, obliterate

blotch NOUN
There were damp blotches on the walls.
• patch, blot, spot, mark, blob, splodge, splash, stain

blow VERB
① *The wind was blowing from the east.*
• blast, gust, bluster, puff, fan
② *Leaves were blowing across the road.*
• drift, flutter, waft, float, glide, whirl, swirl
③ *The wind nearly blew my hat off.*
• sweep, force, drive, carry, toss
④ *Cars blew their horns.*
• sound, play, blast, honk, hoot
➤ **blow out**
I blew out all the candles on the cake.
• extinguish, put out, snuff
➤ **blow something up**
① *I need to blow up the tyres on my bike.*
• inflate, pump up, swell, fill out, expand

❷ *A small group of soldiers were sent to blow up the bridge.*
• blast, bomb, destroy
❸ *Do you think you could blow up this photograph?*
• enlarge, magnify

blow NOUN
❶ *He received a painful blow on the head.*
• knock, bang, bash, hit, punch, clout, slap, smack, swipe, thump
(*informal*) wallop, whack
❷ *Losing the match was a terrible blow.*
• shock, upset, setback, disappointment, catastrophe, misfortune, disaster, calamity

blue ADJECTIVE & NOUN

WORD WEB

Some shades of blue:

> aquamarine   > lapis
> azure   > navy
> baby blue   > sapphire
> cobalt   > sky blue
> cyan   > turquoise
> indigo   > ultramarine

For tips on describing colours see colour.

bluff VERB
He tried to bluff his way through the interview.
• deceive, trick, fake, fool, hoodwink
(*informal*) con, kid

blunder NOUN
I spotted a few blunders in the spelling.
• mistake, error, fault, slip, slip-up, gaffe, faux pas
(*informal*) howler

blunder VERB
❶ *The goalkeeper blundered again and let in a second goal.*
• make a mistake, err, miscalculate, slip up
❷ *I could hear someone blundering about in the dark.*
• stumble, stagger, founder, lurch

blunt ADJECTIVE
❶ *I had to use a blunt pencil.*
• dull, worn, unsharpened
OPPOSITES sharp, pointed
❷ *Her reply to my question was very blunt.*
• abrupt, frank, candid, plain-spoken, direct, brusque, curt

blur VERB
The steam had blurred her glasses.
• cloud, fog, obscure, dim, smudge
OPPOSITES sharpen, focus

blurred ADJECTIVE
The old photo was blurred at the edges.
• indistinct, hazy, fuzzy, unclear, vague, out of focus
OPPOSITES sharp, clear

blush VERB
He felt his face start to blush.
• flush, redden, go red, colour, burn

blustery ADJECTIVE
It was a blustery day in autumn.
• gusty, windy, blowy, stormy, squally, wild
OPPOSITES calm, still

board NOUN
❶ *The table top was made from a wooden board.*
• plank, panel, beam, timber
❷ *The board of directors meet every month.*
• committee, panel, council

board VERB
Passengers may now board the aircraft.
• get on, go on board, enter, embark

boast VERB
❶ *My father never boasted about his success.*
• brag, show off, crow, gloat, swagger
IDIOM blow your own trumpet
❷ *The film boasts an impressive cast.*
• feature, possess, have, enjoy

boastful ADJECTIVE
I tried not to sound too boastful.
• arrogant, big-headed, conceited, vain, bumptious

a
b
c
d
e
f
g
h
i
j
k
l
m
n
o
p
q
r
s
t
u
v
w
x
y
z

(*informal*) cocky, big-mouted, full of oneself, swanky

OPPOSITES modest, humble

boat NOUN

Several fishing boats were moored in the harbour.
• ship, craft, vessel

WORD WEB

Some types of boat or ship:

➤ barge	➤ lifeboat
➤ canoe	➤ motor boat
➤ catamaran	➤ oil tanker
➤ cruise liner	➤ punt
➤ dhow	➤ raft
➤ dinghy	➤ rowing boat
➤ dugout	➤ schooner
➤ ferry	➤ skiff
➤ freighter	➤ speedboat
➤ gondola	➤ steamship
➤ hovercraft	➤ tanker
➤ hydrofoil	➤ trawler
➤ junk	➤ tug
➤ kayak	➤ yacht
➤ launch	

Military boats or ships:

➤ aircraft carrier	➤ gunboat
➤ battleship	➤ minesweeper
➤ destroyer	➤ submarine
➤ frigate	➤ warship

Some boats used in the past:

➤ brigantine	➤ man-of-war
➤ clipper	➤ paddle steamer
➤ coracle	➤ schooner
➤ cutter	➤ trireme
➤ galleon	➤ windjammer
➤ galley	

Parts of a boat or ship:

➤ boom	➤ fo'c'sle or
➤ bridge	forecastle
➤ bulwark	➤ funnel
➤ cabin	➤ galley
➤ crow's nest	➤ helm
➤ deck	➤ hull
➤ engine room	➤ keel
➤ mast	➤ rigging
➤ poop	➤ rudder
➤ porthole	➤ sail
➤ propeller	➤ tiller
➤ quarterdeck	

- The front part of a boat is the **bow** or **prow** and the back part is the **stern**.

- The left-hand side of a boat when you are facing forward is called **port** and the right-hand side is called **starboard**.

bob VERB

Little boats bobbed up and down in the water.
• bounce, toss, dance, wobble, jiggle

body NOUN

WORD WEB

Outer parts of the human body:

➤ abdomen	➤ instep
➤ ankle	➤ jaw
➤ arm	➤ knee
➤ armpit	➤ kneecap
➤ breast	➤ knuckle
➤ buttocks	➤ leg
➤ calf	➤ lip
➤ cheek	➤ mouth
➤ chest	➤ navel
➤ chin	➤ neck
➤ ear	➤ nipple
➤ elbow	➤ nose
➤ eye	➤ pores
➤ finger	➤ shin
➤ foot	➤ shoulder
➤ forehead	➤ skin
➤ genitals	➤ stomach
➤ groin	➤ temple
➤ hand	➤ thigh
➤ head	➤ throat
➤ heel	➤ waist
➤ hip	➤ wrist

Inner parts of the human body:

➤ arteries	➤ brain
➤ bladder	➤ eardrum
➤ bowels	➤ glands

- gullet
- gums
- guts
- heart
- intestines
- kidneys
- larynx
- liver
- lungs
- muscles
- nerves
- ovaries
- pancreas
- prostate
- sinews
- stomach
- tendons
- tongue
- tonsils
- tooth
- uterus
- veins
- windpipe
- womb

- The study of the human body is **anatomy**.
- The main part of your body except your head, arms and legs is your **trunk** or **torso**.
- The shape of your body is your **build**, **figure** or **physique**.
- The dead body of a person is a **corpse** and the dead body of an animal is a **carcass**.

WRITING TIPS

DESCRIBING PEOPLE'S BODIES
Big or strong:

- athletic
- beefy
- brawny
- bulky
- burly
- hefty
- hulking
- muscular
- sinewy
- statuesque
- tall
- wiry

Overweight:

- chubby
- corpulent
- dumpy
- fat
- flabby
- heavyset
- obese
- plump
- podgy
- portly
- rotund
- round
- stocky
- stout
- tubby
- well-rounded

Small or thin:

- bony
- diminutive
- gangling or gangly

- gaunt
- lanky
- lean
- petite
- puny
- scraggy
- scrawny
- short
- skeletal
- skinny
- slender
- slight
- spindly
- squat
- svelte
- thin
- trim
- weedy
- willowy

bog NOUN
We felt out boots sinking into the bog.
• swamp, marsh, mire, quagmire, wetland, fen

bogus ADJECTIVE
The man had given a bogus address.
• fake, false, spurious, fraudulent, counterfeit, sham
(*informal*) phoney
OPPOSITES genuine, authentic

boil VERB
Let the water boil before you add the pasta.
• bubble, simmer, seethe, steam

boisterous ADJECTIVE
A group of boisterous children were playing on the beach.
• lively, high-spirited, noisy, rowdy, unruly, wild, exuberant, uproarious, riotous
OPPOSITES restrained, calm

bold ADJECTIVE
❶ *It was a bold move to attack with such a small army.*
• brave, courageous, daring, heroic, adventurous, audacious, fearless, dauntless, valiant, intrepid, plucky, daredevil
OPPOSITES timid, cowardly
❷ *The picture is painted in bold colours.*
• striking, strong, vivid, bright, eye-catching, prominent, showy, loud, gaudy, garish
OPPOSITES pale, subtle

bolt NOUN

The fence panels were held together with metal bolts.
• pin, bar, peg, rivet

bolt VERB

❶ *Did you remember to bolt the door?*
• fasten, bar, latch, lock, secure
❷ *He saw us coming and bolted out of the shop.*
• run away, dash away, flee, fly, rush off, dart off, escape
❸ *I just had time to bolt down a sandwich.*
• gobble, gulp, guzzle, wolf down (*informal*) scoff

bombard VERB

❶ *Enemy ships bombarded the harbour.*
• shell, pound, bomb, blast, blitz
❷ *When she finished speaking she was bombarded with questions.*
• overwhelm, besiege, inundate, swamp, flood, snow under

bond NOUN

❶ *There is a special bond between our countries.*
• relationship, association, connection, tie, link
❷ *The prisoner tried to escape from his bonds.*
• rope, restraint, chain, fetter, shackle

bone NOUN

WORD WEB

Some bones in the human body:

> backbone or spine
> collarbone
> cranium or skull
> pelvis
> ribs
> shoulder blade
> vertebrae

- The bones of your body are your skeleton.

bonus NOUN

❶ *Every member of staff received a Christmas bonus.*
• handout, supplement, reward, gratuity, tip

❷ *The climate here is certainly a bonus.*
• advantage, benefit, strong point, plus, blessing

OPPOSITES disadvantage, downside

bony ADJECTIVE

He stretched out his long bony arms.
• skinny, lean, skeletal, emaciated, gaunt

book NOUN

WORD WEB

Parts of a book:

> binding
> cover
> jacket
> spine
> contents
> design
> layout
> illustrations
> typeface
> title page
> preface
> introduction
> chapter
> epilogue
> appendix
> prelims
> appendices
> index
> end pages
> blurb

Some types of book:

> album
> annual
> anthology
> atlas
> audiobook
> diary
> dictionary
> directory
> e-book
> encyclopedia
> graphic novel
> fiction
> guidebook
> manual
> novel
> non-fiction
> picture book
> reading book
> reference book
> story book
> textbook
> thesaurus

- A book with hard covers is a hardback.
- A book with soft covers is a paperback.
- A book which is typed or handwritten but not printed is a manuscript.
- A thin book in paper covers is a booklet, leaflet or pamphlet.
- A book which is part of a set is a volume.
- A large, heavy book is a tome.

book VERB
❶ *Have you booked a seat on the train?*
• order, reserve
❷ *I've booked the disco for the party.*
• arrange, engage, organize, lay on, line up
➤ **book in**
You need to book in at the front desk.
• register, check in, enrol

boom VERB
❶ *A voice boomed along the corridor.*
• roar, bellow, shout, blast, thunder, resound, reverberate
❷ *Business was booming in the restaurant.*
• flourish, thrive, prosper, do well, expand, progress

boom NOUN
❶ *A loud boom shook the building.*
• blast, roar, rumble, thunder, reverberation, resonance
❷ *There has been a recent boom in teenage fiction.*
• growth, increase, escalation, expansion, upsurge
OPPOSITE slump

boost VERB
Being in the drama group has really boosted his confidence.
• increase, enhance, improve, strengthen, bolster, help, encourage, raise, uplift
OPPOSITES lower, dampen

boost NOUN
❶ *We have recently had a boost in sales.*
• increase, growth, rise, upsurge, upturn
❷ *Winning that game gave my confidence a great boost.*
• lift, uplift, encouragement, spur

boot NOUN
He wore a pair of leather boots.
For tips on describing clothes see clothes.

boot VERB
The goalkeeper booted the ball to midfield.
• kick, strike, drive, punt

booth NOUN
Is there a photo booth in the station?
• cubicle, kiosk, stall, stand, compartment

border NOUN
❶ *The town is on the border between France and Germany.*
• boundary, frontier
❷ *The tablecloth is white with a blue border.*
• edge, margin, perimeter, rim, fringe, verge

border VERB
Their orchard was bordered by a stone wall.
• surround, enclose, encircle, edge, fringe, bound

bore VERB
❶ *Computer games like this bore me now.*
• weary, tire, pall on
IDIOM send you to sleep
OPPOSITE thrill
❷ *The thieves bored a hole through the wall.*
• drill, pierce, perforate, puncture, burrow, tunnel, sink

bore NOUN
Filling in forms is such a bore.
• bother, nuisance, pest, trial
(*informal*) drag, hassle
OPPOSITE thrill

bored ADJECTIVE
I sat at home feeling bored.
• weary, uninterested, uninspired
(*informal*) fed up

boring ADJECTIVE
The film was so boring I fell asleep.
• dull, dreary, tedious, unexciting, uninteresting, dry, monotonous, uninspiring, insipid, unimaginative, uneventful, humdrum, tiresome
OPPOSITES interesting, exciting

borrow VERB
Can I borrow some money?
• get on loan, have use of

A
B
C
D
E
F
G
H
I
J
K
L
M
N
O
P
Q
R
S
T
U
V
W
X
Y
Z

(*informal*) scrounge, cadge
OPPOSITE lend

boss NOUN
He was the boss of a film studio.
• head, chief, manager, leader, director, chair, president

bossy ADJECTIVE
The new receptionist is a bit bossy.
• domineering, bullying, overbearing, officious, imperious, pushy

bother VERB
❶ Would it bother you if I played some music?
• disturb, trouble, inconvenience, annoy, irritate, pester, vex, exasperate
(*informal*) bug, hassle
❷ I can see that something is bothering you.
• worry, trouble, concern, perturb
IDIOM prey on your mind
❸ Don't bother to phone tonight.
• make an effort, take trouble, concern yourself, care, mind

bother NOUN
❶ It's such a bother to remember the password.
• nuisance, annoyance, irritation, inconvenience, pest, trouble, difficulty, problem
(*informal*) hassle, drag
❷ I went to a lot of bother to get your present.
• trouble, fuss, effort, care

bottle NOUN
Bring a bottle of water with you.
• flask, flagon, jar, pitcher
– A bottle for serving water or wine is a **carafe** or **decanter**.
– A small bottle for perfume or medicine is a **phial**.

bottle VERB
➤ bottle something up
It's not good to keep your feelings bottled up.
• hold in, cover up, conceal, suppress
OPPOSITES show, express

bottom NOUN
❶ We camped at the bottom of the mountain.
• foot, base, foundation
OPPOSITES top, peak
❷ The divers found a wreck at the bottom of the sea.
• bed, floor
OPPOSITE surface
❸ We have a shed at the bottom of the garden.
• end, far end, extremity
❹ A wasp stung me on the bottom.
• buttocks, rear, rump, seat
(*informal*) behind, backside, bum

bottom ADJECTIVE
I keep my paints on the bottom shelf.
• lowest, last, bottommost
OPPOSITES top, highest

bough NOUN
The robin perched on the bough of a tree.
• branch, limb

bought
past tense see buy

bounce VERB
❶ The ball bounced twice before it reached the net.
• rebound, ricochet
❷ The children were bouncing on their beds.
• jump, spring, leap, bound, bob, prance

bound VERB
❶ She came bounding down the stairs.
• leap, bounce, jump, spring, vault, skip, hop, prance
❷ Their land is bounded by the river.
• border, edge, hem in, enclose, surround, encircle

bound NOUN
A kangaroo can cover 10 metres in a single bound.
• leap, jump, spring, vault, skip, hop

bound ADJECTIVE
➤ bound for
The ship was bound for the West Indies.
• going to, heading for, making for, travelling towards, off to

bound ADJECTIVE

❶ *It's bound to rain at the weekend.*
• certain, sure, destined, fated

❷ *I felt bound to invite them to the party.*
• obliged, duty-bound, committed, compelled, forced, required

boundary NOUN

Some animals use scent to mark the boundary of their territory.
• border, frontier, edge, end, limit, perimeter, dividing line

bouquet NOUN

She was holding a bouquet of flowers.
• bunch, posy, sprig, spray

bout NOUN

❶ *She's recovering from a bout of flu.*
• attack, fit, dose, spasm

❷ *He challenged me to a fencing bout.*
• contest, match, round, fight, encounter

bow VERB

❶ *The man bowed his head.*
• lower, bend, incline, duck

❷ *In the end they had to bow to pressure.*
• give in, submit, yield, succumb, surrender

bow NOUN

❶ *She greeted me with a slight bow of her head.*
• nod, bend, lowering, dip, duck, stoop

❷ *We stood at the bow of the ship.*
• front, prow, nose, head

bowl NOUN

There was a bowl of fresh fruit on the table.
• basin, dish, pot, vessel
– A large bowl for serving soup is a **tureen**.

bowl VERB

He ran up to bowl the last ball of the match.
• throw, pitch, fling, hurl, toss

box NOUN

In the corner was a box full of junk.
• case, chest, carton, packet, crate, trunk, casket

boy NOUN

He was a boy of ten or eleven.
• lad, youngster, youth
(*informal*) kid

brag VERB

My brother was still bragging about the goal he scored.
• boast, gloat, crow, show off
IDIOM blow your own trumpet
– A person who is always bragging is a **braggart**.

brain NOUN

I racked my brain, trying to remember.
• mind, reason, sense, wit, intellect, intelligence, brainpower
IDIOM (*humorous*) grey matter

brainy (*informal*) ADJECTIVE

She is the brainy one in the family.
• clever, intelligent, bright, smart

branch NOUN

❶ *A robin perched on a branch of the tree.*
• bough, limb, arm

❷ *I've joined the local branch of the Kennel Club.*
• section, division, department, wing

branch VERB

Follow the road until it branches into two.
• divide, fork, split

brand NOUN

Which brand of ice cream do you like?
• make, kind, sort, type, variety, label
– The sign of a particular brand of goods is a **trademark**.

brandish VERB

The men leapt out of the boat, brandishing their swords.
• flourish, wield, wave, flaunt

a
b
c
d
e
f
g
h
i
j
k
l
m
n
o
p
q
r
s
t
u
v
w
x
y
z

brave ADJECTIVE
They put up a brave fight.
• courageous, heroic, valiant, bold, fearless, daring, gallant, intrepid, plucky
OPPOSITE cowardly

bravery NOUN
She was awarded a medal for bravery.
• courage, heroism, valour, fearlessness, daring, nerve, gallantry, grit, pluck
(*informal*) guts, bottle
OPPOSITE cowardice

brawl NOUN
We could hear a brawl on the street outside.
• fight, quarrel, skirmish, scuffle, tussle
(*informal*) scrap

brawny ADJECTIVE
The guard stepped forward, a big, brawny man.
• muscular, athletic, well built, strapping, burly, beefy, hulking
OPPOSITES puny, scrawny

breach NOUN
❶ *Handling the ball is a breach of the rules.*
• breaking, violation, infringement, offence (against)
❷ *The storm caused a breach in the sea wall.*
• break, rupture, split, crack, opening, fracture, fissure

breach VERB
They finally breached the castle walls.
• break through, burst, rupture

break VERB
❶ *Break the chocolate bar into small pieces.*
• divide, split, snap, crack
❷ *The vase fell off the shelf and broke.*
• smash, shatter, burst, fracture, crack, split, splinter, snap, chip
(*informal*) bust
❸ *The flash on my camera has broken again.*
• stop working, go wrong, malfunction, fail, crash, break down
(*informal*) pack in, conk out

❹ *If you do that you will be breaking the law.*
• disobey, contravene, violate, breach, infringe, flout
❺ *In the final, she broke the world record.*
• beat, better, exceed, surpass, top, outdo
➤ break down
❶ *Our car broke down on the motorway.*
• stop working, go wrong, malfunction, fail
(*informal*) pack in, conk out
❷ *The peace talks have broken down.*
• fail, fall through, collapse, founder
➤ break in
❶ *Thieves broke in during the night.*
• force your way in
❷ *Excuse me for breaking into your conversation.*
• interrupt, cut in, butt in
(*informal*) chip in
➤ break off
Let's break off for lunch.
• have a rest, pause, stop
➤ break out
A flu epidemic broke out last winter.
• begin, spread, start
➤ break out of
Two prisoners managed to break out of the jail.
• escape from, break loose from, abscond from
➤ break up
❶ *After the speeches, the crowd began to break up.*
• disperse, scatter, disband
❷ *The couple broke up after only two years.*
• separate, split up

break NOUN
❶ *Can you see any breaks in the chain?*
• breach, crack, hole, gap, opening, split, rift, rupture, fracture, fissure
❷ *Let's take a break for lunch.*
• interval, pause, rest, lull, time-out
(*informal*) breather
❸ *The prisoners made a break for freedom.*
• escape, dash, bid

breakable ADJECTIVE
Does the parcel contain anything breakable?
• fragile, delicate, brittle, frail
OPPOSITE unbreakable

breakdown NOUN
❶ *There has been a breakdown in the peace talks.*
• failure, collapse
❷ *Can you give me a breakdown of the figures?*
• analysis

break-in NOUN
There was a break-in at the local bank.
• burglary, robbery, theft, raid

breakthrough NOUN
Scientists believe this is a major breakthrough in cancer research.
• advance, leap forward, discovery, development, revolution, progress, innovation
OPPOSITE setback

breast NOUN
The painting shows a baby at its mother's breast.
• bosom, bust, chest

breath NOUN
❶ *Take a deep breath.*
• inhalation
OPPOSITE exhalation
❷ *There wasn't a breath of wind in the air.*
• breeze, puff, waft, whiff, whisper, sigh

breathe VERB
❶ *The doctor asked me to breathe in and out.*
– To breathe in is to **inhale** and to breathe out is to **exhale**.
– The formal word for breathing is **respiration**.
– To breathe heavily is to **pant** or **puff**.
– To breathe with difficulty is to **gasp** or **wheeze**.
❷ *Don't breathe a word of this to anyone.*
• speak, say, relate, pass on

breathless ADJECTIVE
I was breathless after running for the bus.
• out of breath, gasping, panting, puffing, wheezing

breathtaking ADJECTIVE
The view from the summit is breathtaking.
• spectacular, stunning, staggering, astonishing, amazing, overwhelming, awe-inspiring, awesome

breed VERB
❶ *Salmon swim upstream to breed every year.*
• reproduce, have young, procreate, multiply, spawn
❷ *I was born and bred in the city.*
• bring up, rear, raise, nurture
❸ *Bad hygiene breeds disease.*
• cause, produce, generate, encourage, promote, cultivate, induce

breed NOUN
What breed of dog is that?
• variety, type, kind, sort, class, strain

breeze NOUN
A cool breeze was coming in from the sea.
• wind, breath of air, gust, draught

breezy ADJECTIVE
❶ *It was a bright and breezy morning.*
• windy, blowy, blustery, gusty, fresh, brisk
❷ *He had a breezy manner.*
• cheerful, cheery, carefree, jaunty (*informal*) upbeat

brew VERB
❶ *I'm just going to brew some tea.*
• make, prepare, infuse
– When you brew beer it **ferments**.
❷ *It looks like a storm is brewing.*
• develop, form, loom, build up, gather, threaten

brew NOUN
The witches concocted an evil-smelling brew.
• mixture, mix, concoction, blend, cocktail

a
b
c
d
e
f
g
h
i
j
k
l
m
n
o
p
q
r
s
t
u
v
w
x
y
z

61

A
B
C
D
E
F
G
H
I
J
K
L
M
N
O
P
Q
R
S
T
U
V
W
X
Y
Z

bridge NOUN

WORD WEB

Some types of bridge:

➤ cantilever bridge
➤ flyover
➤ footbridge
➤ pontoon bridge
➤ rope bridge
➤ suspension bridge
➤ swing bridge

– A bridge to carry water is an **aqueduct** and a long bridge carrying a road or railway is a **viaduct**.

brief ADJECTIVE

❶ *We paid a brief visit to our cousins on the way home.*
• **short, quick, hasty, fleeting, flying, short-lived, temporary, cursory**
❷ *She gave us a brief account of what happened.*
• **concise, succinct, short, abbreviated, condensed, compact, potted, pithy**
OPPOSITES **long, lengthy**

bright ADJECTIVE

❶ *We saw the bright lights of the town in the distance.*
• **shining, brilliant, blazing, dazzling, glaring, gleaming**
OPPOSITES **dim, weak**
❷ *The day was cold, but bright.*
• **sunny, fine, fair, clear, cloudless**
OPPOSITES **dull, cloudy, overcast**
❸ *Her shoes were a bright shade of pink.*
• **strong, intense, vivid, vibrant, bold, lurid, garish**
– Colours that glow in the dark are **luminous** colours.
OPPOSITES **dull, faded, muted**
❹ *She was a bright student.*
• **clever, intelligent, sharp, quick-witted, smart**
(*informal*) **brainy**
OPPOSITES **stupid, dull-witted**
❺ *He gave me a bright smile.*
• **cheerful, happy, lively, merry, jolly, radiant**
OPPOSITES **sad, gloomy**

brighten VERB

Her eyes brightened and she began to smile.
• **light up, lighten, become bright**
➤ **brighten something up**
A new coat of paint will brighten up the place.
• **cheer up, perk up, light up, enliven**

brilliant ADJECTIVE

❶ *The fireworks burned with a brilliant light.*
• **bright, blazing, dazzling, glaring, gleaming, glittering, glorious, shining, splendid, vivid**
OPPOSITES **dim, dull**
❷ *Brunel was a brilliant engineer.*
• **clever, exceptional, outstanding, gifted, talented**
OPPOSITES **incompetent, talentless**
❸ (*informal*) *I saw a brilliant film last week.*
• **excellent, marvellous, outstanding, wonderful, superb**
(*informal*) **fantastic, fabulous**

brim NOUN

My glass was full to the brim.
• **rim, edge, brink, lip**

bring VERB

❶ *Did you remember to bring the sandwiches?*
• **carry, bear, deliver, transport, fetch**
❷ *You can bring a friend to the party.*
• **invite, escort, accompany, conduct, lead, guide**
❸ *This road will bring you to the centre of town.*
• **lead, take, conduct**
❹ *The drought brought famine and disease.*
• **cause, produce, lead to, result in, give rise to, generate**
➤ **bring something about**
They are campaigning to bring about a change in the law.
• **cause, effect, achieve, create, engineer**
➤ **bring something off**
The author manages to bring off a surprise ending.
• **accomplish, carry out, pull off, achieve**

> **bring someone up**
It is a story about a boy who is brought up by wolves.
• rear, raise, care for, foster, look after, nurture
> **bring something up**
Why did you have to bring up the subject of money?
• mention, raise, introduce, broach, air

brink NOUN
❶ *They stood on the brink of a deep crater.*
• edge, lip, rim, verge, brim
❷ *We were on the brink of a great discovery.*
• verge, threshold, point

brisk ADJECTIVE
❶ *The runners set off at a brisk pace.*
• quick, fast, rapid, swift, energetic, invigorating, vigorous, refreshing
OPPOSITES slow, leisurely
❷ *A brisk, business-like voice answered the phone.*
• curt, abrupt, blunt, short, terse, brusque
❸ *The shops do a brisk trade in the summer.*
• busy, lively, bustling, hectic
OPPOSITES quiet, slack, slow

bristle NOUN
Shrimps have fine bristles on their legs.
• hair, whisker, spine, pickle, barb, quill
– Short hairs that grow on a person's chin are **stubble**.

bristle VERB
❶ *She bristled at the idea of being left behind.*
• take offence, bridle, take umbrage
❷ *The room bristled with computer screens.*
• be full of, be packed with, abound in, overflow with

brittle ADJECTIVE
The bones of the skeleton were dry and brittle.
• breakable, fragile, crisp, crumbly
OPPOSITE flexible

broach VERB
He seemed unwilling to broach the subject.
• mention, bring up, raise, introduce, air

broad ADJECTIVE
❶ *Above the hills was a broad expanse of blue sky.*
• wide, extensive, vast, open, large, spacious, expansive, sweeping
OPPOSITE narrow
❷ *Give me a broad outline of the plot.*
• general, rough, vague, loose, indefinite, imprecise
OPPOSITES specific, detailed
❸ *She spoke with a broad Australian accent.*
• strong, distinct, marked, obvious
OPPOSITE slight

broadcast VERB
The concert will be broadcast live on TV.
• transmit, relay, beam, air, screen, show, televise

broaden VERB
❶ *You need to broaden your interests.*
• expand, increase, enlarge, extend, develop, diversify
❷ *The river broadens as it nears the ocean.*
• widen, expand, open out, spread out, stretch out

brochure NOUN
We've been looking at holiday brochures.
• leaflet, pamphlet, booklet, catalogue
– A brochure advertising a school or university is a **prospectus**.

broke
past tense see **break**

broken ADJECTIVE
❶ *I started to pick up the pieces of the broken vase.*
• smashed, shattered, cracked, splintered, in pieces, in bits
(*informal*) in smithereens
OPPOSITES intact, whole

a
b
c
d
e
f
g
h
i
j
k
l
m
n
o
p
q
r
s
t
u
v
w
x
y
z

② *Which of these computers is broken?*
• faulty, defective, malfunctioning, damaged, out of order
OPPOSITE working
③ *I had a night of broken sleep.*
• disturbed, interrupted, fitful, restless
④ *From that day on, he was broken in spirit.*
• crushed, defeated, beaten, shattered

brood VERB
Are you still brooding over what I said?
• worry, fret, mope, dwell on, agonize over

brother NOUN
I have an elder brother.
– A formal name for a brother or sister is a **sibling**.
For other members of a family see family.

brought
past tense see bring

brown ADJECTIVE & NOUN

WORD WEB

Some shades of brown:
➤ beige
➤ bronze
➤ buff
➤ caramel
➤ chestnut
➤ chocolate
➤ coffee
➤ dun
➤ fawn
➤ hazel
➤ khaki
➤ mahogany
➤ russet
➤ sandy
➤ sepia
➤ tan
➤ tawny

For tips on describing colours see colour.

browse VERB
I was just browsing through a magazine.
• look through, leaf through, scan, skim, peruse

bruise NOUN
He had a bruise on his leg.
• swelling, bump, contusion

bruise VERB
I fell and bruised my knee.
• mark, discolour, hurt, injure

brush VERB
① *Wait while I brush my hair.*
• groom, comb, tidy, smooth
② *I'll just brush my teeth.*
• scrub, clean, polish
③ *He brushed a few crumbs off the table.*
• sweep, flick
④ *Something soft brushed against my cheek.*
• touch, stroke, graze, scrape, sweep
➤ **brush aside**
My question was just brushed aside.
• dismiss, disregard, shrug off, make light of
➤ **brush up**
I have two weeks to brush up my French.
• revise, improve, go over, refresh your memory of
(*informal*) mug up on, swot up on

brutal ADJECTIVE
He committed a series of brutal murders.
• savage, vicious, violent, cruel, barbaric, ferocious, bloodthirsty, inhuman, merciless, pitiless, ruthless, callous, sadistic
OPPOSITES gentle, humane

bubble NOUN
The water was full of soap bubbles.
• lather, suds, foam, froth
– The bubbles in a fizzy drink are called **effervescence**.

bubble VERB
Heat the water until it starts to bubble.
• boil, seethe, gurgle, froth, foam

bubbly ADJECTIVE
  ❶ *I like bubbly drinks.*
  • fizzy, sparkling, effervescent, carbonated, gassy
  ❷ *She has a bright and bubbly personality.*
  • cheerful, lively, vivacious, bouncy, high-spirited, spirited, animated

bucket NOUN
  He was carrying a bucket of water.
  • pail, can

buckle NOUN
  He wore a belt with a large silver buckle.
  • clasp, fastener, fastening, clip, catch

buckle VERB
  ❶ *Please buckle your seat belts.*
  • fasten, secure, clasp, clip, do up, hook up
  ❷ *The bridge buckled under our weight.*
  • bend, warp, twist, crumple, cave in, collapse

bud NOUN
  Buds are appearing on the apple trees.
  • shoot, sprout

budding ADJECTIVE
  She is a budding actress.
  • aspiring, promising, potential, would-be, up-and-coming, rising

budge VERB
  The window was stuck and wouldn't budge.
  • move, shift, give way, stir

budget NOUN
  I have a budget of £50 to spend on clothes.
  • allowance, allocation, funds, resources

budget VERB
  How much have you budgeted for the holidays?
  • allocate, set aside, allow, allot, earmark

buffet VERB
  The coast was buffeted by strong winds all day.
  • batter, pound, beat, lash, pummel

bug NOUN
  ❶ *I spent the morning collecting bugs from the garden.*
  • insect, minibeast
  (*informal*) creepy-crawly
  ❷ *There are still a few bugs in the computer program.*
  • fault, error, defect, flaw
  (*informal*) glitch, gremlin
  ❸ (*informal*) *I can't get rid of this stomach bug.*
  • infection, virus, disease, germ, illness
  ❹ *Someone had planted a bug in the room.*
  • hidden microphone, wire, tap
  For words to do with writing spy fiction see spy.

bug VERB
  ❶ *Our conversations were being bugged.*
  • tap, record, monitor, intercept, listen in to
  ❷ (*informal*) *Please stop bugging me with questions.*
  • bother, annoy, pester, trouble, harass

build VERB
  ❶ *Dad is going to build a shed in the garden.*
  • construct, erect, put together, put up, set up, assemble
  ❷ *Traffic has been building steadily.*
  • increase, accumulate, grow, build up
  ➤ **build up**
  Tension was building up in the crowd.
  • increase, intensify, grow, rise, mount, escalate
  ➤ **build something up**
  ❶ *You need to build up your strength.*
  • increase, improve, strengthen, develop, boost
  ❷ *He has built up a reputation for getting results.*
  • establish, develop, create, amass, accumulate, assemble, collect, put together

build NOUN
  She was a woman of slender build.
  • body, form, frame, figure, physique

a
b
c
d
e
f
g
h
i
j
k
l
m
n
o
p
q
r
s
t
u
v
w
x
y
z

A
B
C
D
E
F
G
H
I
J
K
L
M
N
O
P
Q
R
S
T
U
V
W
X
Y
Z

building NOUN

It is one of the tallest buildings in New York.

• construction, structure, dwelling
– A person who designs buildings is an **architect** and the process of designing buildings is **architecture**.

WORD WEB

Some types of building:

➤ apartment block	➤ school
➤ bungalow	➤ shed
➤ cabin	➤ shop
➤ castle	➤ skyscraper
➤ cinema	➤ stadium
➤ cottage	➤ tenement
➤ factory	➤ terrace
➤ fort	➤ theatre
➤ hut	➤ tower
➤ lighthouse	➤ tower block
➤ mansion	➤ townhouse
➤ mill	➤ villa
➤ observatory	➤ warehouse
➤ palace	

For religious buildings see religion.

WRITING TIPS

DESCRIBING BUILDINGS
Parts of a building:

➤ arch	➤ gutter
➤ balcony	➤ masonry
➤ balustrade	➤ parapet
➤ bay window	➤ pediment
➤ bow window	➤ pillar
➤ buttress	➤ pipes
➤ chimney	➤ porch
➤ colonnade	➤ quadrangle
➤ column	➤ roof
➤ courtyard	➤ shutter
➤ cupola	➤ spire
➤ dome	➤ storey
➤ dormer window	➤ terrace
➤ drainpipe	➤ tower
➤ eaves	➤ turret
➤ foundations	➤ vault
➤ gable	➤ veranda

➤ wall	➤ windowsill
➤ window	➤ wing

Parts you might find inside a building:

➤ attic	➤ gallery
➤ basement	➤ garret
➤ ceiling	➤ lobby
➤ cellar	➤ mezzanine
➤ conservatory	➤ room (*old use*
➤ corridor	chamber)
➤ crypt	➤ staircase
➤ dungeon	➤ stairwell
➤ foyer	

Adjectives:

➤ airy	➤ run-down
➤ compact	➤ solid
➤ cramped	➤ spacious
➤ crumbling	➤ sprawling
➤ forbidding	➤ squalid
➤ grand	➤ stark
➤ imposing	➤ stately
➤ ramshackle	➤ towering
➤ rickety	➤ tumbledown
➤ ruined	

bulge NOUN

Asian elephants have two bulges on their foreheads.

• bump, hump, lump, swelling, protuberance

bulge VERB

His eyes bulged with excitement.

• stick out, swell, protrude, balloon, curve outwards

bulk NOUN

❶ *The sheer bulk of a blue whale is staggering.*

• size, dimensions, magnitude, mass, largeness

❷ *We did the bulk of the work ourselves.*

• main part, most part, majority

IDIOM the lion's share

OPPOSITE minority

bulky ADJECTIVE

The parcel is too bulky to post.

• unwieldy, cumbersome, awkward,

unmanageable, hefty
OPPOSITE compact

bulletin NOUN
❶ We listened to the news bulletin.
• report, announcement, broadcast
❷ The society publishes a quarterly bulletin.
• newsletter, review, magazine, gazette

bully VERB
Some of the other children used to bully him.
• persecute, intimidate, torment, terrorize
(informal) push around

bump VERB
❶ He bumped his head on the low ceiling.
• hit, strike, knock, bang
❷ My bicycle was bumping up and down over the cobbles.
• bounce, shake, jerk, jolt
➤ **bump into**
❶ I nearly bumped into a lamp post.
• collide with, bang into, run into, crash into
❷ We bumped into some friends in town.
• meet, come across, run into

bump NOUN
❶ We felt a bump as the plane landed.
• thud, thump, bang, blow, knock
❷ How did you get that bump on your head?
• lump, swelling, bulge, protuberance

bumpy ADJECTIVE
❶ The car jolted up and down on the bumpy road.
• rough, uneven, irregular, lumpy
OPPOSITES smooth, even
❷ We had a bumpy ride in the back of a truck.
• bouncy, jerky, jolting, jarring, lurching, choppy

bunch NOUN
❶ He handed me a bunch of keys.
• bundle, collection, set, cluster, clump
❷ She picked a bunch of flowers.
• bouquet, posy, spray
❸ (informal) They're a friendly bunch of people.
• group, set, circle, band, gang, crowd

bundle NOUN
I found a bundle of old newspapers.
• bunch, batch, pile, stack, collection, pack, bale

bundle VERB
❶ I quickly bundled up the papers that were on the desk.
• pack, tie, fasten, bind, wrap, roll
❷ They bundled him into the back of a taxi.
• shove, push, jostle, thrust, manhandle

burden NOUN
❶ Each mule was carrying a heavy burden.
• load, weight, cargo
❷ We should share the burden of all the work that needs doing.
• responsibility, obligation, duty, pressure, stress, trouble, worry

burden VERB
❶ She staggered in, burdened with shopping.
• load, weigh down, encumber, lumber
❷ I won't burden you with my problems.
• bother, worry, trouble, distress, afflict, oppress
(informal) saddle

burglar NOUN
The burglars got in through the window.
• robber, thief, housebreaker

burglary NOUN
There have been reports of burglaries in the area.
• robbery, theft, break-in, stealing

burly ADJECTIVE
Two burly security guards appeared.
• well built, strapping, sturdy, muscular, beefy

A
B
C
D
E
F
G
H
I
J
K
L
M
N
O
P
Q
R
S
T
U
V
W
X
Y
Z

burn VERB

❶ *Forest fires are burning out of control.*
• be alight, be on fire, blaze, flame, flare
– To burn without flames is to **glow** or **smoulder**.

❷ *He burnt the letters in the fire.*
• set fire to, incinerate, reduce to ashes
– To start something burning is to **ignite**, **kindle** or **light** it.
– To burn a dead body is to **cremate** it.

❸ *The match had burnt a hole in the carpet.*
• scorch, singe, sear, char, blacken
– To burn yourself with hot liquid is to **scald** yourself.
– To burn a mark on an animal is to **brand** it.

burning ADJECTIVE

He has a burning ambition to become an actor.
• strong, intense, extreme, acute, eager, fervent, passionate

burrow NOUN

The field was full of rabbit burrows.
• hole, tunnel
– A piece of ground with many burrows is a **warren**.
– A fox's burrow is called an **earth**.
– A badger's burrow is called an **earth** or a **set**.

burrow VERB

Rabbits had burrowed under the fence.
• tunnel, dig, excavate, mine, bore

burst VERB

❶ *People started bursting the balloons.*
• break, rupture, split, tear, pop
(informal) **bust**

❷ *The dam burst under the weight of water.*
• break apart, split apart, fall to pieces, give way, rupture, explode

❸ *A man suddenly burst into the room.*
• charge, barge, rush, dash, hurtle, plunge

burst NOUN

There was a short burst of gunfire.
• outbreak, outburst, rush, wave, explosion

bury VERB

❶ *They were buried in an unmarked grave.*
• inter, entomb
OPPOSITES disinter, exhume, unearth

❷ *The letter was buried under a pile of papers.*
• cover, conceal, hide, secrete

bush NOUN

The ball was caught up in a bush.
• shrub, thicket, undergrowth

bushy ADJECTIVE

He has bushy eyebrows.
• thick, dense, hairy, shaggy, bristly

business NOUN

❶ *What kind of business are you in?*
• trade, trading, commerce, industry, work, occupation

❷ *She wants to run her own business.*
• company, firm, organization, enterprise

❸ *The whole business was a mystery to me.*
• matter, issue, affair, point, concern, question

bustle VERB

The square was full of people bustling about.
• rush, dash, hurry, scurry, scuttle
(informal) **buzz**

busy ADJECTIVE

❶ *I've been busy all afternoon.*
• occupied, engaged, employed, working, hard-pressed
(informal) **hard at it**
IDIOMS up to your eyes, run off your feet
OPPOSITE idle

❷ *We've got a busy day ahead of us.*
• hectic, active, full, eventful, frantic
OPPOSITES quiet, restful

❸ *The town is always busy on Saturdays.*
• crowded, bustling, lively, teeming
OPPOSITES quiet, peaceful

but CONJUNCTION

It was morning but it was still dark.
• however, nevertheless

but *PREPOSITION*
  No one spoke but me.
  • except, except for, other than

butt *VERB*
  The ship had to butt its way through the ice.
  • ram, shove, push, thrust, bump, knock
  ➤ butt in
  Please don't butt in when I'm talking.
  • interrupt, cut in, break in
  (*informal*) chip in
  IDIOM (*informal*) put your oar in

buy *VERB*
  Where did you buy your trainers?
  • purchase, pay for, obtain, acquire
  OPPOSITE sell

buzz *NOUN*
  ❶ *The buzz of conversation suddenly stopped.*
  • hum, drone
  ❷ (*informal*) *I always get a buzz from going to the cinema.*
  • thrill, excitement, tingle
  (*informal*) kick

Cc

cabin NOUN
❶ He lived in a log cabin in the woods.
• hut, shack, shed, lodge, chalet, shelter
❷ The crew assembled in the captain's cabin.
• berth, compartment, quarters

cable NOUN
❶ The tent was held down with strong cables.
• rope, cord, line, chain
❷ Don't trip over the computer cable.
• flex, lead, wire, cord

cadet NOUN
She is a cadet in the police force.
• recruit, trainee

cafe NOUN
We had lunch at a local cafe.
• snack bar, cafeteria, coffee shop, tea-room, bistro, brasserie

cage NOUN
I put the hamster back into its cage.
• enclosure, pen, pound, hutch
– A large cage or enclosure for birds is an **aviary**.
– A cage or enclosure for poultry is a **coop**.

cake NOUN
❶ Would you like a piece of birthday cake?
• sponge, flan, gateau, pastry
❷ I unwrapped a fresh cake of soap.
• bar, block, tablet, slab

caked ADJECTIVE
My boots were caked with mud.
• coated, covered, plastered, encrusted

calamity NOUN
The earthquake was a national calamity.
• disaster, catastrophe, tragedy, misfortune, mishap, blow

calculate VERB
❶ I calculated that it would take an hour to walk home.
• compute, work out, reckon, add up, count up, tally, total
(informal) tot up
– To calculate something roughly is to **estimate**.
❷ Her remarks were clearly calculated to hurt me.
• intend, mean, design

call VERB
❶ 'Stop that infernal noise!' I called.
• cry out, shout, yell, exclaim
(informal) holler
❷ I'll call you tonight.
• phone, ring, telephone, give someone a call
(informal) give someone a ring
❸ The website is called 'News4U'.
• name, dub, title, entitle, term
❹ She called us all for a meeting.
• summon, send for, order
❺ The doctor called to see if I was feeling better.
• visit, pay a visit, drop in, drop by
➤ **call for**
❶ This calls for a celebration.
• require, need, necessitate, justify, warrant, be grounds for
❷ They are calling for a ban on fireworks.
• request, demand, appeal for, ask for, seek
➤ **call something off**
The race was called off at the last minute.
• cancel, abandon, scrap
(informal) scrub

call NOUN
❶ We heard a call for help from the upstairs window.
• cry, shout, yell, exclamation
❷ I'll give you a call at the weekend.
• phone call
(informal) ring, buzz, bell
❸ I need to pay a quick call on grandma.
• visit, stop
❹ There has been a call for action on climate change.
• demand, request, appeal, plea

⑤ There's no call for that kind of language.
• need, necessity, reason, justification

callous ADJECTIVE
It was a callous and mindless attack.
• cold-hearted, hard-hearted, heartless, unfeeling, insensitive, unsympathetic
OPPOSITES compassionate, kind

calm ADJECTIVE
① Please try to stay calm.
• composed, cool, level-headed, relaxed, serene, sedate, unruffled, unflustered, unperturbed, unemotional, unexcitable
OPPOSITES anxious, nervous
② It was a calm sunny day.
• still, quiet, peaceful, tranquil, windless
OPPOSITES stormy, windy
③ The sea was calm that morning.
• smooth, still, flat, motionless, tranquil
OPPOSITES rough, choppy

came
past tense see come

camel NOUN

WORD WEB

- A **dromedary** camel has one hump and a **Bactrian** camel has two humps.

camouflage VERB
We used branches to camouflage our tent.
• disguise, mask, screen, cover up, conceal

camp NOUN
We could see a camp in the field below us.
• campsite, camping ground, base
- A military camp is an **encampment**.

campaign NOUN
① He planned each military campaign with great care.
• operation, offensive, action, war

② She joined the campaign to end child poverty.
• movement, crusade, drive, fight, effort, struggle

campaign VERB
They are campaigning to save the rainforests.
• fight, battle, push, lobby, agitate

cancel VERB
① We had to cancel the race because of the weather.
• call off, abandon, scrap, drop
(informal) scrub, ditch, axe
- To cancel something after it has already begun is to **abort** it.
- To put something off until later is to **postpone** it.
② They agreed to cancel the debt.
• revoke, annul, rescind, erase, retract, withdraw

candid ADJECTIVE
Thank you for that candid answer.
• frank, direct, open, honest, straightforward, forthright
(informal) upfront
OPPOSITE guarded

candidate NOUN
They interviewed four candidates for the job.
• applicant, contender, entrant

canopy NOUN
The trees formed a canopy overhead.
• covering, awning, shade

cap NOUN
Who left the cap off the toothpaste?
• lid, top, cover, stopper

cap VERB
The mountains were capped with snow.
• top, crown, cover, tip

capable ADJECTIVE
She is a very capable student.
• competent, able, accomplished, proficient, skilful, talented, gifted
OPPOSITE incompetent

a b c d e f g h i j k l m n o p q r s t u v w x y z

➤ be capable of
Do you think he is capable of murder?
• be able to do, be equal to, be up to
OPPOSITE be incapable of

capacity NOUN
① *What is the capacity of this glass?*
• size, volume, space, extent, room
② *He has a great capacity for making friends.*
• ability, capability, power, potential, aptitude, competence, skill
③ *She spoke in her capacity as team captain.*
• position, function, role, office

cape NOUN
① *She wore a black cape.*
• cloak, shawl, wrap, robe
(old use) mantle
② *Gibraltar is situated on a narrow cape.*
• headland, promontory, point, head

capital NOUN
① *Kingston is the capital of Jamaica.*
• capital city
② *In three years he had enough capital to start his own business.*
• funds, money, finance, cash, assets, means, resources

capsize VERB
The boat struck a rock and capsized.
• overturn, tip over, turn over, keel over
IDIOM turn turtle

capsule NOUN
① *The medicine is taken in the form of capsules.*
• pill, tablet, lozenge, pastille
② *The space capsule was designed to carry astronauts.*
• module, craft, pod

captain NOUN
① *The ship's captain made an announcement.*
• commander, commanding officer, master
(informal) skipper

② *She has been the team captain for two years.*
• leader, head, chief
(informal) skipper

caption NOUN
Write a caption for the picture.
• title, heading, legend, description

captive NOUN
The gunmen agreed to release their captives.
• prisoner, convict, detainee
– A person who is held captive until a demand is met is a **hostage**.

captive ADJECTIVE
They were held captive for ten days.
• imprisoned, captured, in captivity, arrested, detained, jailed
IDIOM behind bars
OPPOSITES free, released

captivity NOUN
He was held in captivity for three years.
• imprisonment, confinement, detention, incarceration
OPPOSITE freedom

capture VERB
① *He was captured boarding a ship for France.*
• catch, arrest, apprehend, seize, take prisoner
(informal) nab
② *Rome was captured in 410.*
• occupy, seize, take, conquer

car NOUN
Our car is parked round the corner.
• motor car, motor, vehicle
(North American) automobile
– An informal name for an old, noisy car is a **banger**.

⊛	WORD WEB

Some types of car:

➤ convertible
➤ coupé
➤ electric car
➤ estate

➤ four-wheel drive or four-by-four
➤ hatchback

> limousine (*informal* limo)
> MPV (multi-purpose vehicle)
> people carrier
> racing car
> saloon
> sports car
> SUV (sports utility vehicle)

- Very early cars are veteran or vintage cars.

Parts of a car:

> accelerator
> bonnet
> brake
> boot (*North American* trunk)
> bumper (*North American* fender)
> chassis
> choke
> clutch
> doors
> engine
> exhaust pipe
> fuel tank
> gearbox
> gear lever
> handbrake
> headlamps
> ignition
> lights
> mirrors
> mudguards
> roof
> steering wheel
> tyres
> undercarriage
> wheels
> windscreen
> windscreen wipers
> wings

SEE ALSO vehicle

carcass NOUN
The lions fed on the carcass of an antelope.
• dead body, corpse, remains
(*formal*) cadaver

care NOUN
❶ *I took great care with my handwriting.*
• attention, concentration, thoroughness, thought, meticulousness
OPPOSITE carelessness
❷ *Please choose your words with care.*
• caution, discretion, thought, consideration, regard, sensitivity
OPPOSITE disregard
❸ *We left our cat in the care of a neighbour.*
• charge, keeping, protection, safe keeping, supervision
❹ *The old woman's face was full of care.*
• worry, anxiety, trouble, concern, burden, responsibility, sorrow, stress

> take care
Please take care crossing the road.
• be careful, be on your guard, look out, watch out
> take care of
Who will take care of my plants?
• care for, look after, mind, watch over, attend to, tend

care VERB
I don't care which film we see.
• mind, bother, be interested, be bothered, be worried
> care about
He really cares about the environment.
• be concerned about, be interested in, be worried about, be bothered about
> care for
❶ *The veterinary hospital cares for sick animals.*
• look after, take care of, attend to, tend, nurse
❷ *They obviously care for each other.*
• love, be fond of, cherish, adore, hold dear, dote on
IDIOM think the world of
❸ *I don't really care for broccoli.*
• like, be fond of, be keen on, be partial to

career NOUN
He had a long career as a teacher.
• job, occupation, profession, trade, business, employment, calling

carefree ADJECTIVE
He looked happy and carefree.
• unworried, untroubled, easy-going, light-hearted, relaxed
(*informal*) laid-back
OPPOSITE anxious

careful ADJECTIVE
❶ *We kept a careful watch on the bonfire.*
• attentive, cautious, watchful, alert, wary, vigilant
OPPOSITES careless, inattentive
❷ *You must be more careful with your spelling.*
• diligent, conscientious, thoughtful, meticulous, painstaking, thorough, precise

a b c d e f g h i j k l m n o p q r s t u v w x y z

OPPOSITES careless, negligent
➤ be careful
Please be careful with those scissors.
• take care, be on your guard, look out, watch out

careless ADJECTIVE
❶ *This is a careless piece of work.*
• messy, untidy, thoughtless, inaccurate, slapdash, shoddy, scrappy, sloppy, slovenly, slipshod
OPPOSITES careful, thoughtful
❷ *I was careless and cut my finger.*
• inattentive, thoughtless, absent-minded, heedless, irresponsible, negligent, reckless
OPPOSITES careful, attentive

caress VERB
The woman gently caressed her baby.
• stroke, touch, fondle, pet

cargo NOUN
The plane was carrying cargo rather than passengers.
• goods, freight, merchandise

carnival NOUN
The town was holding its annual carnival.
• festival, fair, fête, gala, parade, procession, pageant

carpenter NOUN
Next door was a carpenter's workshop.
• woodworker, joiner, cabinetmaker

carriage NOUN
a horse-drawn carriage
• cab, hansom cab, stagecoach, coach, trap, wagon

carry VERB
❶ *I'll help you carry the shopping to the car.*
• take, transfer, convey, move, bring, fetch, lift
(*informal*) cart, lug
❷ *These ships carry both passengers and freight.*
• transport, convey, handle, ferry, ship
❸ *Most of these cables carry electricity.*
• transmit, conduct, relay, convey, send
❹ *The road bridge has to carry a lot*

of traffic.
• bear, support, hold up
❺ *Her voice carried to the back of the hall.*
• be audible, be heard, reach, travel
❻ *The vote was carried by a huge majority.*
• approve, accept, pass, endorse, ratify
➤ carry on
We carried on in spite of the rain.
• continue, go on, persevere, persist, keep on
(*informal*) stick with it, stick at it
➤ carry something out
Did you carry out my instructions?
• perform, execute, accomplish, achieve, complete, finish

cart NOUN
The fruit was taken to the barns in carts.
• barrow, wheelbarrow, handcart, trolley

carton NOUN
I bought a carton of ice cream.
• box, pack, packet, package, case, container

cartoon NOUN
❶ *The kids were watching a Bugs Bunny cartoon.*
• animation, animated film
❷ *Batman first appeared in a cartoon.*
• cartoon strip, comic strip, comic, graphic novel
❸ *On the cover was a cartoon of the Prime Minister.*
• caricature

carve VERB
❶ *The statue was carved out of marble.*
• sculpt, chisel, hew, shape, fashion
❷ *She had carved her initials on the tree.*
• engrave, incise, score, cut
❸ *Mum started to carve the chicken.*
• cut up, slice

cascade NOUN
Cascades of water tumbled down the rock face.
• torrent, waterfall, fall

case NOUN

❶ Put your cases on the trolley.
• suitcase, bag, trunk, holdall, baggage, luggage
❷ The camera comes with its own case.
• box, container, holder, covering, casing, canister, carton, casket
❸ It was a clear case of mistaken identity.
• instance, example, occurrence, illustration
❹ The film is based on a famous murder case.
• inquiry, investigation
❺ She put forward a good case for equality.
• argument, line of reasoning, thesis

cash NOUN

❶ Can I pay by cash?
• currency, change, coins, notes
❷ They have plenty of cash in the bank.
• money, finance, funds

cast VERB

❶ He cast a coin into the fountain.
• throw, toss, pitch, fling, sling, lob
❷ The light from the candle cast her shadow on the wall.
• emit, send out, give off, shed
❸ I cast a glance backwards.
• direct, send, shoot
❹ The statue is cast in bronze.
• form, mould, shape, fashion

castle NOUN

These are the remains of a twelfth-century castle.
• fortress, fort, fortification, citadel, chateau, stronghold

WORD WEB

Parts of a castle:

➤ bailey	➤ dungeon
➤ barbican	➤ gate
➤ battlements	➤ gateway
➤ buttress	➤ keep
➤ courtyard	➤ magazine
➤ donjon	➤ moat
➤ drawbridge	➤ motte

➤ parapet	➤ tower
➤ portcullis	➤ turret
➤ postern	➤ wall
➤ rampart	➤ watchtower

casual ADJECTIVE

❶ It was just a casual remark.
• unthinking, off-hand, unconsidered, impromptu, throwaway, chance (*informal*) off-the-cuff
OPPOSITES considered, thoughtful
❷ The restaurant had a casual atmosphere.
• easy-going, informal, relaxed (*informal*) laid-back, chilled-out, chilled
OPPOSITE formal
❸ He has a casual approach to life.
• relaxed, nonchalant, carefree, easy-going, slack (*informal*) laid-back
❹ She had changed into casual clothes.
• informal, everyday, leisure
OPPOSITE formal

casualty NOUN

There are reports of heavy casualties.
• victim, sufferer, death, injury, loss, fatality

cat NOUN

Our cat has very long whiskers.
• (*informal*) puss, pussy cat, kitty, moggy

WORD WEB

Some breeds of domestic cat:

➤ Abyssinian	➤ Manx
➤ Burmese	➤ Persian
➤ chinchilla	➤ Siamese

- A male cat is a **tom** or **tomcat**.
- A young cat is a **kitten**.
- A cat with streaks in its fur is a **tabby**.
- A cat with mottled brown fur is a **tortoiseshell**.
- A word meaning 'to do with cats' is **feline**.

a b c d e f g h i j k l m n o p q r s t u v w x y z

For tips on describing animals see animal.

Wild animals of the cat family:

➤ bobcat	➤ mountain lion
➤ cheetah	➤ ocelot
➤ cougar	➤ panther
➤ jaguar	➤ puma
➤ leopard	➤ tiger
➤ lion	➤ wild cat
➤ lynx	

catalogue NOUN
❶ I checked the library catalogue.
• list, listing, index, register, directory, inventory, archive
❷ Look in our Christmas catalogue.
• brochure, pamphlet, leaflet

catastrophe NOUN
The floods were a catastrophe for the area.
• disaster, calamity, tragedy, cataclysm, debacle

catch VERB
❶ I leapt up to catch the ball.
• seize, grab, grasp, grip, clutch, snatch, receive, intercept, get
OPPOSITES drop, miss
❷ They didn't catch many fish that day.
• hook, net, trap
❸ The police have caught the culprits.
• capture, apprehend, arrest, seize, take prisoner
(informal) nab, collar
OPPOSITE release
❹ I think I've caught a cold.
• contract, pick up, get, develop, be taken ill with
(informal) go down with, come down with
❺ I caught my brother listening at the door.
• discover, surprise, find out
❻ You must hurry if you want to catch the bus.
• be in time for, get on, get
❼ I caught my foot in the stirrup.
• get stuck, snag, jam, wedge, lodge
➤ catch on

❶ E-books soon caught on.
• become popular, do well, succeed, thrive, flourish
(informal) take off
❷ It took me a while to catch on.
• understand, comprehend
(informal) cotton on, latch on

catch NOUN
❶ The fishermen returned with a large catch of salmon.
• haul, yield, net
❷ It looks like a good offer, but there must be a catch.
• disadvantage, drawback, snag, hitch, problem, trap, trick
❸ All the windows are fitted with safety catches.
• fastening, latch, lock, bolt, clasp

catching ADJECTIVE
Chickenpox is catching.
• infectious, contagious, communicable
OPPOSITE non-infectious

catchy ADJECTIVE
It's a very catchy tune.
• memorable, unforgettable, appealing

category NOUN
He won first prize in the under-16s category.
• class, group, grouping, section, division, set, grade, rank

cater VERB
➤ cater for
❶ The hotel can cater for a hundred wedding guests.
• cook for, provide food for, feed, serve
❷ The school caters for children of all abilities.
• provide for, serve, accommodate, meet the needs of

cattle PLURAL NOUN
Cattle were grazing in the meadow.
• cows, herd, livestock
– Male cattle are **bulls**, **steers** or **oxen**.
– Young male cattle are **calves** or **bullocks**.
– Young female cattle are **calves** or **heifers**.

– A word meaning 'to do with cattle' is
bovine.

caught
past tense see catch

cause NOUN
❶ *The cause of the accident is a mystery.*
• source, root, origin, starting point
❷ *There is no cause for alarm.*
• reason, grounds, need, justification,
call
❸ *They are raising money for a good
cause.*
• purpose, object, aim, objective

cause VERB
A single spark caused the fire.
• bring about, give rise to, lead to, result
in, create, generate, engender, produce,
prompt, induce, provoke, trigger

caution NOUN
❶ *Drivers were advised to proceed with
caution.*
• care, attention, alertness,
watchfulness, wariness, vigilance,
discretion, prudence
❷ *He received a caution from the police.*
• warning, reprimand, admonishment,
rebuke
(*informal*) telling-off

cautious ADJECTIVE
My grandad is a cautious driver.
• careful, attentive, alert, watchful,
wary, vigilant, prudent
OPPOSITES careless, reckless

cave NOUN
There are caves at the foot of the cliffs.
• cavern, pothole, chamber
– A man-made cave with decorative
walls is a **grotto**.
– The entrance to a cave is the **mouth**.
– The hobby of exploring caves is **caving**
or **potholing**.

cave VERB
➤ cave in
❶ *The whole roof had caved in.*
• collapse, fall in
❷ *She finally caved in and agreed that*

he could go.
• give in, yield, surrender

cavity NOUN
There is a hidden cavity in the wall.
• hole, hollow, space, chamber,
pocket, gap

cease VERB
❶ *The fighting ceased at midnight.*
• come to an end, end, finish, stop, halt,
conclude
OPPOSITES begin, resume, continue
❷ *The firm ceased trading last year.*
• bring to an end, stop, discontinue,
terminate, suspend, wind up

celebrate VERB
❶ *Let's celebrate!*
• enjoy yourself, have fun, have a good
time
(*informal*) party
❷ *The couple celebrate their silver
wedding anniversary last week.*
• commemorate, observe, mark, keep,
honour

celebrated ADJECTIVE
She is now a celebrated author.
• famous, well-known, acclaimed,
renowned, eminent, notable, prominent,
esteemed
OPPOSITES little-known, obscure

celebration NOUN
❶ *We had a big celebration for his
birthday.*
• party, function, festivity, festival,
jamboree
❷ *Her triumph was a cause for
celebration.*
• festivities, merrymaking, enjoying
yourself, partying

celebrity NOUN
❶ *He never really enjoyed his celebrity.*
• fame, renown, stardom, popularity,
prominence
❷ *The award is usually presented by a TV
celebrity.*
• famous person, personality, VIP, star,
superstar, idol, big name
(*informal*) celeb

cellar NOUN

We keep our bikes in the cellar.
• basement, vault
– A room underneath a church is a **crypt**.

cemetery NOUN

Some famous people are buried in the local cemetery.
• graveyard, burial ground, churchyard
– A place where dead people are cremated is a **crematorium**.

central ADJECTIVE

❶ We were looking at a map of central Europe.
• middle, core, inner, innermost, interior
OPPOSITE outer
❷ The film's central character is a fifteen-year-old girl.
• main, chief, principal, major, primary, foremost, key, core, essential, vital, fundamental
OPPOSITES minor, lesser

centre NOUN

The burial chamber is in the centre of the pyramid.
• middle, heart, core, hub
– The edible part in the centre of a nut is the **kernel**.
– The central part of an atom or cell is the **nucleus**.
– The centre of a storm or hurricane is the **eye**.
OPPOSITES edge, periphery

ceremony NOUN

❶ We watched the opening ceremony of the Olympic Games.
• rite, ritual, formalities, service, observance
– A ceremony to celebrate something new is an **inauguration** or **opening**.
– A ceremony to remember a dead person or a past event is a **commemoration**.
– A ceremony where someone is given a special honour is an **investiture**.
❷ The presentation was made with a great deal of ceremony.
• formality, pomp, pageantry, spectacle

certain ADJECTIVE

❶ I'm certain we'll get tickets.
• confident, convinced, positive, sure, determined
OPPOSITE uncertain
❷ We have certain proof that the painting is a forgery.
• definite, clear, convincing, absolute, unquestionable, reliable, trustworthy, undeniable, infallible, genuine, valid
OPPOSITE unreliable
❸ They were facing certain disaster.
• inevitable, unavoidable
OPPOSITE possible
❹ It is certain to be a success.
• bound, sure
➤ for certain
I'll give you the money tomorrow for certain.
• certainly, definitely, for sure, without doubt
➤ make certain
Please make certain that you switch off the lights.
• make sure, ensure

certainly ADVERB

I'd certainly like to meet her.
• definitely, undoubtedly, unquestionably, assuredly, without a doubt

certainty NOUN

❶ We may never know the answer with certainty.
• confidence, conviction, assurance, sureness
OPPOSITE doubt
❷ They are a certainty to win the title.
• inevitability, foregone conclusion (informal) sure thing, dead cert
OPPOSITE possibility

certificate NOUN

At the end of the course, you will receive a certificate.
• diploma, document, licence, guarantee

chain NOUN

❶ The police formed a chain to keep the crowd back.
• line, row, cordon

❷ *It was an unfortunate chain of events.*
• series, sequence, succession, string

chain VERB
He chained his bike up outside.
• secure, fasten, tie, hitch, tether, shackle, fetter

chair NOUN
see seat

challenge NOUN
❶ *The role will be the biggest challenge of his acting career.*
• test, trial
❷ *Do you accept my challenge?*
• dare

challenge VERB
❶ *I challenge you not to eat chips for a week.*
• dare, defy
IDIOM throw down the gauntlet to
❷ *This job doesn't really challenge me.*
• test, stretch, tax, make demands on
❸ *We will have to challenge the decision.*
• question, dispute, call into question

challenging ADJECTIVE
She has a challenging new job.
• demanding, testing, taxing, exacting
OPPOSITE undemanding

champion NOUN
❶ *She is the current Paralympic champion.*
• title-holder, prizewinner, victor, winner, conqueror
(*informal*) champ
❷ *Martin Luther King was a champion of civil rights.*
• supporter, advocate, defender, proponent, promoter, upholder, backer, patron

champion VERB
The charity champions the rights of children.
• advocate, support, promote, uphold, defend, back, espouse, stand up for

championship NOUN
Sixteen schools took part in the hockey championship.
• competition, contest, tournament

chance NOUN
❶ *There's a chance of rain later.*
• possibility, prospect, likelihood, probability, danger, threat, risk
OPPOSITE certainty
❷ *Give me a chance to answer.*
• opportunity, time, occasion, opening, turn
❸ *Are you prepared to take a chance?*
• gamble, risk
(*informal*) punt
IDIOM leap in the dark
➤ **by chance**
We found the place purely by chance.
• by accident, accidentally, unintentionally, fortuitously, by coincidence
OPPOSITE intentionally

change VERB
❶ *We will have to change all our plans.*
• alter, modify, rearrange, reorganize, adjust, adapt, amend, revise, transform, vary
OPPOSITES preserve, retain
❷ *The town has changed a lot since Victorian times.*
• alter, become different, develop, evolve, move on, metamorphose
❸ *Could I change this shirt for a larger size?*
• exchange, replace, switch, substitute
(*informal*) swap
➤ **change into**
Tadpoles change into frogs.
• become, turn into, metamorphose into, be transformed into

change NOUN
❶ *There has been a last-minute change of plan.*
• alteration, modification, variation, revision, amendment, adjustment, adaptation, metamorphosis
❷ *Have you brought a change of clothes?*
• exchange, replacement, switch, substitution
(*informal*) swap

changeable ADJECTIVE
The weather has been changeable today.
• variable, unsettled, unpredictable,

a
b
c
d
e
f
g
h
i
j
k
l
m
n
o
p
q
r
s
t
u
v
w
x
y
z

unreliable, inconsistent, erratic, unstable
– If your loyalty is changeable you are
fickle.
OPPOSITE steady

channel NOUN
❶ *The rainwater runs along this channel.*
• duct, conduit, gutter, drain, ditch,
trough, sluice
❷ *How many TV channels do you get?*
• station

chaos NOUN
*After the earthquake, the city was in
chaos.*
• disorder, confusion, mayhem, turmoil,
tumult, pandemonium, disorganization,
anarchy, lawlessness, bedlam, muddle,
a shambles
OPPOSITES order, orderliness

chaotic ADJECTIVE
*At first the music seemed to be a chaotic
jumble of sounds.*
• disorderly, disorganized, confused,
muddled, topsy-turvy, in turmoil,
anarchic, unruly, riotous
(*informal*) shambolic
OPPOSITES orderly, organized

chapter NOUN
❶ *I read the opening chapter last night.*
• section, part, division
❷ *This was to be a new chapter in my
life.*
• period, phase, stage, era

character NOUN
❶ *She was a woman with a strong
character.*
• personality, temperament, nature,
disposition, mentality, make-up,
manner, spirit, identity
❷ *He's a bit of an odd character.*
• person, individual, figure, personality,
creature
❸ *Who is your favourite character in the
play?*
• part, role
❹ *The sign was written in Chinese
characters.*
• letter, figure, symbol, hieroglyph

characteristic NOUN
*The building has some interesting
characteristics.*
• feature, attribute, trait, property,
quality, peculiarity, idiosyncrasy, quirk

characteristic ADJECTIVE
*Windmills are a characteristic feature of
this area.*
• typical, distinctive, recognizable,
representative, particular, special,
peculiar, idiosyncratic, singular

charge NOUN
❶ *The admission charge is six euros.*
• price, payment, fee, rate, tariff,
levy
– The charge made for a ride on public
transport is the **fare**.
– A charge made to join a club is a **fee**
or **subscription**.
– A charge made for certain things by
the government is a **duty** or **tax**.
– A charge made to use a private road,
bridge or tunnel is a **toll**.
❷ *He is facing three charges of burglary.*
• accusation, allegation, indictment
❸ *The infantry suffered heavy casualties
in the charge.*
• attack, assault, offensive, onslaught,
drive, push
❹ *We are leaving the house in your
charge.*
• care, keeping, protection, custody,
trust
➤ be in charge of
*She was now in charge of the
expedition.*
• manage, supervise, oversee, direct,
lead, command, run
(*informal*) head up

charge VERB
❶ *How much do you charge for lessons?*
• ask for, make someone pay, invoice
❷ *The men have been charged with
attempted robbery.*
• accuse (of), indict
❸ *The bull put its head down and
charged.*
• attack, storm, rush, drive, stampede,
go headlong

charitable ADJECTIVE
Let's be charitable and assume she just made a mistake.
• generous, magnanimous, considerate, compassionate, unselfish, benevolent, humanitarian, philanthropic

charity NOUN
Show some charity towards those in need.
• compassion, generosity, kindness, benevolence, consideration, caring, goodwill
OPPOSITE selfishness

charm NOUN
❶ *He was a man of great charm.*
• appeal, attractiveness, allure, charisma
❷ *The sorcerer recited a magic charm.*
• spell, incantation
❸ *She carried special coin as a lucky charm.*
• talisman, mascot, amulet, trinket

charm VERB
She charmed the audience with her humour and wit.
• delight, please, captivate, enchant, entrance, fascinate, beguile, bewitch, win over

charming ADJECTIVE
We drove through some charming scenery.
• delightful, endearing, appealing, likeable, pleasing, attractive, captivating

chart NOUN
❶ *This chart shows the average monthly rainfall.*
• diagram, graph, table
❷ *The captain consulted a chart of the Pacific.*
• map

charter VERB
We can charter an aircraft over the mountains.
• hire, lease, rent

chase VERB
My dog likes chasing rabbits.
• pursue, run after, follow, track, trail, hunt

chasm NOUN
Below the bridge was a deep chasm.
• opening, gulf, fissure, rift, ravine, crevasse, canyon, gorge, pit, abyss

chat NOUN
Do you have time for a quick chat?
• talk, conversation, gossip
(*informal*) natter, chinwag

chat VERB
They spend hours chatting on the phone.
• talk, converse, gossip
(*informal*) natter, have a chinwag

chatter VERB
❶ *They chattered away happily for a while.*
• prattle, babble, chat
(*informal*) natter, rabbit on
❷ *My teeth were chattering with the cold.*
• rattle, jangle

chatter NOUN
I don't engage in idle chatter.
• prattle, babble
(*informal*) chit-chat, nattering

chatty ADJECTIVE
She seemed to be in a chatty mood.
• talkative, communicative, garrulous
OPPOSITES uncommunicative, taciturn

cheap ADJECTIVE
❶ *We got a cheap flight to Paris.*
• inexpensive, low-priced, low-cost, affordable, reasonable, economical, budget, bargain, cut-price, discount
❷ *These tyres are made from cheap rubber.*
• inferior, poor-quality, second-rate, substandard, shoddy, trashy
(*informal*) rubbishy, cheapo, tacky
OPPOSITES superior, good-quality

a b c d e f g h i j k l m n o p q r s t u v w x y z

cheat *VERB*
The bank is accused of cheating its customers.
• deceive, defraud, trick, swindle, dupe, double-cross, hoodwink
(*informal*) con, diddle, fleece, rip off, sucker

cheat *NOUN*
Are you calling me a cheat?
• cheater, deceiver, swindler, fraudster, fraud, charlatan

check *VERB*
❶ *Remember to check your spelling.*
• examine, inspect, look over, scrutinize
IDIOM (*informal*) give the once-over
❷ *I'll just check that the door is locked.*
• make sure, confirm, verify
❸ *Firebreaks are used to check the spread of forest fires.*
• halt, stop, arrest, block, obstruct, curb, hold back, hamper, hinder, slow, slow down

check *NOUN*
❶ *I need to run some checks on my computer.*
• test, examination, inspection, check-up, study, scrutiny, perusal
❷ *Parliament acts as a check on the power of the sovereign.*
• control, curb, limitation, restraint, restriction, constraint

cheeky *ADJECTIVE*
My little sister has a cheeky answer for everything!
• impudent, impertinent, insolent, disrespectful, rude, irreverent, flippant
OPPOSITE respectful

cheer *NOUN*
There was a loud cheer from the crowd.
• applause, ovation, hurray, hurrah, whoop

cheer *VERB*
❶ *We'll be there to cheer when you win.*
• applaud, clap, shout, yell
OPPOSITES jeer, boo
❷ *The good news cheered them a good deal.*
• comfort, console, gladden, delight, please, encourage, uplift

OPPOSITE sadden
➤ **cheer up**
Everyone had cheered up by the afternoon.
• brighten up, perk up, rally, revive, take heart, bounce back
(*informal*) buck up
➤ **cheer someone up**
What can I do to cheer you up?
• raise your spirits, brighten, hearten, gladden, uplift, buoy up, perk up
(*informal*) buck up
OPPOSITES sadden, depress

cheerful *ADJECTIVE*
❶ *We set out in a cheerful mood.*
• happy, good-humoured, cheery, merry, jolly, joyful, light-hearted, sunny, chirpy, perky, lively, animated, elated, buoyant, jovial, gleeful
(*informal*) upbeat
IDIOM full of beans
OPPOSITES sad, gloomy
❷ *It was a sunny and cheerful room.*
• pleasant, agreeable, attractive, bright, welcoming, friendly
OPPOSITES dark, dismal

chemist *NOUN*
I bought some skin cream from the chemist.
• pharmacist
(*old use*) apothecary, alchemist
– A chemist's shop is a **dispensary** or **pharmacy**.

chequered *ADJECTIVE*
The tablecloth had a chequered pattern.
• check, criss-cross
– Scottish cloth with a chequered pattern is **tartan**.

cherish *VERB*
❶ *I shall cherish this gift all my life.*
• treasure, prize, value, hold dear, care for, keep safe
❷ *We have lost a dear and cherished friend.*
• love, adore, dote on, be devoted to, revere
IDIOM think the world of

chess NOUN

WORD WEB

Names of chess pieces:

➤ bishop	➤ knight
➤ castle or rook	➤ pawn
➤ king	➤ queen

Other terms used in chess:

➤ castling	➤ mate
➤ check	➤ move
➤ checkmate	➤ opening
➤ chessboard	➤ queening
➤ endgame	➤ sacrifice
➤ gambit	➤ stalemate
➤ grandmaster	➤ tournament

chest NOUN

❶ *The bullet hit him in the chest.*
• breast, torso, ribcage, front
❷ *I found a chest full of old clothes.*
• box, crate, case, trunk, casket, coffer

chew VERB

He is always chewing a piece of gum.
• munch, gnaw, chomp

chicken NOUN

A few chickens scratched around in the yard.
– A female chicken is a **hen.**
– A male chicken is a **rooster.**
– A young chicken is a **chick.**
– A group of chickens is a **brood.**
– A farm which keeps chickens is a **poultry farm.**

chief NOUN

❶ *Sitting Bull was chief of the Lakota.*
• leader, ruler, commander, captain, chieftain, master
❷ *He is the chief of NASA.*
• head, chief executive, director, president, governor, principal, CEO
(*informal*) boss

chief ADJECTIVE

❶ *The chief ingredients are butter and icing sugar.*
• main, principal, primary, prime, major, foremost, key, central, basic, essential,
vital, fundamental, predominant, prominent
OPPOSITES minor, secondary
❷ *She became the chief editor of the magazine.*
• head, senior, top, leading, principal, supreme, highest
OPPOSITE subordinate

chiefly ADVERB

Kangaroos are found chiefly in Australia.
• mainly, mostly, primarily, principally, predominantly, generally, usually, typically, in the main, on the whole

child NOUN

❶ *The book festival is aimed especially at children.*
• boy or girl, infant, juvenile, youngster, youth, lad or lass
(*informal*) kid, tot, nipper
❷ *How many children do you have?*
• son or daughter, descendant, offspring
– A child whose parents are dead is an **orphan.**
– A child looked after by a guardian is a **ward.**

childhood NOUN

He spent much of his childhood by the sea.
• boyhood or girlhood, youth, early life, infancy
– The time when someone is a baby is their **babyhood.**
– The time when someone is a teenager is their **adolescence** or **teens.**
OPPOSITE adulthood

childish ADJECTIVE

Don't be so childish!
• immature, babyish, juvenile, infantile, puerile
OPPOSITE mature

chill NOUN

We felt a distinct chill in the air.
• coldness, chilliness, coolness, nip

a b c d e f g h i j k l m n o p q r s t u v w x y z

83

chill VERB

❶ *Chill the pudding before serving it.*
• cool, refrigerate, freeze
OPPOSITES warm, heat
❷ *The look in his eyes chilled me to my core.*
• frighten, scare, terrify, petrify
IDIOMS make your blood run cold, give you goosebumps
➤ **chill out**
(*informal*) *We've been chilling out in front of the TV.*
• relax, unwind, take it easy
(*informal*) chill
IDIOM put your feet up

chilly ADJECTIVE

❶ *It was a chilly evening.*
• cold, cool, frosty, icy, crisp, fresh, raw, wintry
(*informal*) nippy
OPPOSITE warm
❷ *They gave us a very chilly reception.*
• unfriendly, unwelcoming, cold, cool, frosty
OPPOSITES friendly, warm

chime VERB

The hall clock chimes every hour.
• ring, sound, strike, peal, toll

chimney NOUN

I could see smoke coming from the chimney.
– A chimney on a ship or steam engine is a **funnel**.
– A pipe to take away smoke and fumes is a **flue**.

china NOUN

There were pieces of broken china on the floor.
• crockery, dishes, plates, tableware, cups and saucers, porcelain

chink NOUN

❶ *I looked through a small chink in the wall.*
• gap, space, crack, crevice, hole, opening, aperture, fissure, split, slit, rift, cleft
❷ *There was a chink of coins as the money changed hands.*
• clink, jingle, jangle, tinkle

chip NOUN

❶ *There were chips of broken glass on the pavement.*
• bit, piece, fragment, scrap, sliver, splinter, flake, shaving
❷ *This teapot has a chip on the lid.*
• crack, nick, notch, flaw

chip VERB

Someone has chipped my favourite mug.
• crack, nick, notch

choice NOUN

❶ *I'm afraid you have no choice.*
• alternative, option
❷ *There is now a wide choice of TV channels.*
• range, selection, variety, assortment, array
❸ *She wouldn't be my choice as team captain.*
• selection, preference, choosing, pick

choice ADJECTIVE

We use only choice ingredients.
• superior, first-class, first-rate, top-quality, best, finest, prime, premier, select, prize
(*informal*) top-notch
OPPOSITES inferior, second-rate

choke VERB

❶ *The fumes were nearly choking them.*
• suffocate, smother, stifle, asphyxiate, throttle
❷ *She was choking on a fish bone.*
• gag, cough, retch
❸ *The drain is choked with leaves.*
• block, clog, obstruct, congest, bung up, stop up

choose VERB

❶ *It has not been easy to choose this year's winner.*
• select, decide on, pick out, opt for, plump for, settle on, vote for, elect
❷ *I would never choose to live there.*
• decide, determine, prefer, resolve

chop VERB
He was outside, chopping wood for the fire.
• cut, split, hew, hack, slash, cleave
– To chop down a tree is to **fell** it.
➤ **chop something off**
We chopped off the lower branches.
• cut off, lop off, sever, shear
– To chop off an arm or a leg is to **amputate** it.
➤ **chop something up**
Help me chop up some vegetables.
• cut up, cube, dice, mince

chronicle NOUN
At the front is a chronicle of her early life.
• story, history, narrative, account, record, journal, annals, saga

chubby ADJECTIVE
He was a chubby little baby.
• plump, tubby, podgy, round, dumpy

chuck (*informal*) VERB
Just chuck your bag on the floor.
• throw, fling, sling, toss, hurl, pitch, cast
(*informal*) bung, dump

chuckle VERB
He was chuckling as he left the room.
• laugh, giggle, snigger, chortle, titter

chunk NOUN
I bit a chunk out of my apple.
• piece, portion, lump, block, hunk, slab, wedge
(*informal*) wodge

church NOUN
I could see the spire of an old parish church.
• chapel, cathedral, minster, abbey
For other religious buildings see **religion**.

churn VERB
Vast crowds had churned the field into a sea of mud.
• agitate, disturb, stir up

circle NOUN
❶ *We arranged the chairs in a circle.*
• ring, round, hoop, loop, band, circlet
– A flat, solid circle is a **disc**.
– A three-dimensional round shape is a **sphere**.
– An egg shape is an **oval** or **ellipse**.
– The distance round a circle is the **circumference**.
– The distance across a circle is the **diameter**.
– The distance from the centre to the circumference is the **radius**.
– A circular movement is a **revolution** or **rotation**.
– A circular trip round the world is a **circumnavigation**.
– A circular trip of a satellite round a planet is an **orbit**.
❷ *She has a wide circle of friends.*
• group, set, crowd
(*informal*) gang, bunch

circle VERB
❶ *Vultures were circling overhead.*
• go round, wheel, revolve, rotate, whirl, spiral
❷ *Satellites circle the earth.*
• go round, orbit, circumnavigate, revolve round

circuit NOUN
We have to complete two circuits of the race track.
• lap, round, circle, revolution, orbit

circular ADJECTIVE
Most of Saturn's rings are circular.
• round, ring-shaped, disc-shaped

circulate VERB
❶ *Blood circulates in the body.*
• pass round, go round, move round
❷ *I asked friends to circulate our newsletter.*
• distribute, send round, broadcast, communicate, publicize, disseminate

circumference NOUN
  There is a path around the circumference of the lake.
  • perimeter, edge, rim, border, boundary

circumstances PLURAL NOUN
  The police pieced together the circumstances surrounding the murder.
  • situation, conditions, background, context, state of affairs, factors, particulars, details

citizen NOUN
  ❶ *The citizens of New York are proud of their city.*
  • resident, inhabitant, city-dweller, townsman or townswoman
  (*formal*) denizen
  ❷ *She is an Australian citizen.*
  • national, passport holder, subject

city NOUN
  Nairobi is a city in Kenya.
  – The chief city of a country or region is the **metropolis**.
  – An area of houses outside the central part of a city is the **suburbs**.
  – Words meaning 'to do with a city' are **urban**, **civic** and **metropolitan**.
  SEE ALSO town

civil ADJECTIVE
  ❶ *Please try to be civil.*
  • polite, courteous, well-behaved, well-mannered
  OPPOSITES uncivil, rude
  ❷ *He is good at recognizing civil aircraft.*
  • civilian, non-military
  OPPOSITE military

civilization NOUN
  We are studying the civilization of ancient Egypt.
  • culture, society, way of life

civilized ADJECTIVE
  Try to behave in a civilized manner.
  • polite, courteous, well-behaved, well-mannered, civil, sophisticated, cultured, polished, refined
  OPPOSITES uncivilized, rude

claim VERB
  ❶ *You can claim a refund at the office.*
  • ask for, apply for, request, demand
  ❷ *He claims that he can speak Russian.*
  • declare, assert, allege, maintain, contend, argue, insist

clamber VERB
  It was dangerous clambering over the rocks.
  • climb, scramble, crawl, move awkwardly

clammy ADJECTIVE
  The walls of the dungeon were cold and clammy.
  • damp, moist, dank, slimy, sticky

clamp VERB
  The rack is clamped onto the car roof.
  • fasten, attach, fix, secure, screw, bolt

clap VERB
  ❶ *The audience clapped loudly at the end of the concert.*
  • applaud, cheer, give a round of applause
  IDIOMS give a big hand (to), put your hands together (for)
  ❷ *Suddenly, a hand clapped me on the shoulder.*
  • slap, hit, pat, smack

clarify VERB
  Can you clarify the situation for me?
  • explain, make clear, elucidate, illuminate
  IDIOMS throw light on, spell out
  OPPOSITE confuse

clarity NOUN
  She explained everything with great clarity.
  • clearness, coherence, lucidity, transparency, precision
  OPPOSITE confusion

clash VERB
  ❶ *We heard the sound of cymbals clashing.*
  • crash, resound

❷ *Demonstrators clashed with the police.*
• argue, fight, contend, squabble
IDIOMS come to blows, lock horns
❸ *The film clashes with the football highlights.*
• coincide, happen at the same time, conflict
❹ *Do these colours clash?*
• conflict, jar, be incompatible
IDIOM be at odds
OPPOSITES harmonize, go together

clash NOUN
❶ *The clash of cymbals made me jump.*
• crash, bang, ringing
❷ *There was a clash between rival supporters.*
• fight, confrontation, argument, conflict, scuffle
(*informal*) scrap

clasp VERB
❶ *The little boy clasped his mother's hand.*
• grasp, grip, hold, squeeze, clutch
❷ *She clasped him in her arms.*
• embrace, hug, hold, cling to

clasp NOUN
The cloak was held in place by a gold clasp.
• clip, pin, fastener, brooch, buckle

class NOUN
❶ *There are 24 children in our class.*
• form, set, stream
– The other pupils in your class are your **classmates**.
❷ *There are many different classes of plants.*
• category, group, classification, division, grade, set, sort, type, kind, species
❸ *He appeals to people from all classes of society.*
• level, rank, status, stratum

class VERB
Our books are classed according to size.
• classify, categorize, group, rank, grade, designate

classic ADJECTIVE
❶ *That was a classic tennis final this year.*
• outstanding, exceptional, excellent, first-class, first-rate, fine, great, admirable, masterly
(*informal*) top-notch
OPPOSITES ordinary, second-rate
❷ *It was a classic case of overconfidence.*
• typical, representative, characteristic, perfect, textbook, model, archetypal, quintessential
OPPOSITE atypical

classify VERB
All living things can be classified into species.
• categorize, class, group, grade, rank, sort, order, bracket

claw NOUN
❶ *Lions have very sharp claws.*
• talon, nail
❷ *The crab had something in one of its claws.*
• pincer

claw VERB
We could hear the bear clawing at the door.
• scratch, scrape, tear, rip

clean ADJECTIVE
❶ *He found a clean pair of socks.*
• washed, cleaned, laundered, scrubbed, swept, tidy, immaculate, spotless, unstained, unsullied, hygienic, sanitary
OPPOSITE dirty
❷ *You need to keep the wound clean.*
• sterile, sterilized, disinfected, uninfected
OPPOSITES infected, septic
❸ *I love the clean air of the mountains.*
• pure, clear, fresh, unpolluted, uncontaminated
OPPOSITES polluted, contaminated
❹ *I started the story on a clean page.*
• blank, unused, unmarked, empty, bare, fresh, new, pristine
OPPOSITES used, marked

⑤ *The referee said he wanted a clean fight.*
• fair, honest, honourable, sporting, sportsmanlike
OPPOSITES unfair, dirty

clean VERB

① *We cleaned the house from top to bottom.*
• wash, wipe, mop, swab, sponge, scour, scrub, dust, sweep, vacuum, shampoo, swill
– To clean clothes is to **launder** them.
OPPOSITES dirty, mess up

② *The nurse cleaned the wound with antiseptic.*
• cleanse, bathe, disinfect, sterilize, sanitize
OPPOSITES infect, contaminate

clear ADJECTIVE

① *We saw fish swimming in the clear pool.*
• clean, pure, transparent, translucent
OPPOSITES opaque, muddy

② *It was a beautiful clear day.*
• bright, sunny, cloudless, unclouded
– A clear night is a **moonlit** or **starlit** night.
OPPOSITES cloudy, overcast

③ *The address on the envelope is not clear.*
• legible, recognizable, visible
OPPOSITE illegible

④ *Your camera takes very clear pictures.*
• sharp, well defined, focused
OPPOSITE blurred

⑤ *He spoke in a clear voice.*
• distinct, audible
OPPOSITES indistinct, muffled

⑥ *I gave you clear instructions.*
• understandable, intelligible, comprehensible, lucid, coherent, plain, explicit, straightforward, unambiguous
OPPOSITES ambiguous, confusing

⑦ *It was a clear case of mistaken identity.*
• definite, unambiguous, indisputable, unmistakable, evident, obvious, patent, manifest, noticeable, distinct, conspicuous, perceptible, pronounced, glaring
OPPOSITE imperceptible

⑧ *Is the road clear ahead?*
• open, unobstructed, passable, empty, free
OPPOSITES blocked, obstructed

⑨ *My conscience is clear.*
• innocent, untroubled, blameless
OPPOSITE guilty

clear VERB

① *I cleared the weeds from the path.*
• get rid of, remove, eliminate, strip

② *The plumber came to clear the blocked drain.*
• unblock, unclog, unstop, open up
– To clear a channel is to **dredge** it.

③ *If the alarm goes, clear the building by the nearest exit.*
• evacuate, empty

④ *The fog cleared slowly.*
• disappear, go away, vanish, evaporate, disperse, dissipate, shift, lift, melt away, fade

⑤ *He was cleared of all the charges against him.*
• acquit, free, absolve, exonerate, (informal) let off

⑥ *All the runners cleared the first hurdle.*
• go over, get over, jump over, pass over, vault

➤ clear up
① *The weather should clear up by the afternoon.*
• become clear, brighten, brighten up

② *The symptoms often clear up by themselves.*
• heal, get better, recover, mend

➤ clear something up
① *I'll clear up the mess later.*
• clean up, tidy up, put right, put straight, put in order

② *Thank you for clearing up that little mystery.*
• explain, answer, solve, resolve
IDIOM get to the bottom of

clearly ADVERB

① *Speak slowly and clearly.*
• distinctly, plainly, intelligibly, audibly, legibly

② *Clearly, we need to talk.*
• obviously, evidently, plainly, patently,

undoubtedly, unquestionably, without question

clench VERB
❶ *He clenched his teeth in anger.*
• close tightly, squeeze together, grit, clamp
❷ *She clenched the coin tightly in her hand.*
• grip, clasp, grasp, hold

clergyman or **clergywoman** NOUN
see religion

clever ADJECTIVE
❶ *He was an exceptionally clever student.*
• intelligent, bright, smart, quick-witted, astute, able, capable, competent, gifted, talented
(*informal*) brainy
OPPOSITE unintelligent
❷ *They came up with a clever scheme to make money.*
• ingenious, crafty, cunning, canny, shrewd, smart, artful, wily
OPPOSITE stupid
❸ *She has always been clever with her hands.*
• skilful, dexterous, adroit, nimble, deft, adept, handy
OPPOSITES unskilful, clumsy

client NOUN
The firm has a number of overseas clients.
• customer, user, consumer, buyer, shopper

cliff NOUN
The village is perched on the top of a cliff.
• crag, rock face, precipice, ridge, bluff, escarpment, scar

climate NOUN
She has studied the effects of pollution on our climate.
• weather conditions, weather patterns
SEE ALSO weather

climax NOUN
The climax of the film is a stunning car chase.
• high point, highlight, height, culmination, peak, pinnacle
OPPOSITE anticlimax

climb VERB
❶ *It took us several hours to climb the mountain.*
• ascend, go up, scale, mount, clamber up
OPPOSITE descend
❷ *We watched the balloons climb into the sky.*
• rise, soar, ascend, mount, rocket
❸ *The road climbs steeply up to the village.*
• go uphill, rise, slope, incline
➤ **climb down**
❶ *I carefully climbed down from the roof.*
• descend, go down, get down
❷ *You'll never get him to climb down.*
• back down, give in, surrender, admit defeat
IDIOMS eat your words, do a U-turn

climb NOUN
It's a steep climb to the cave entrance.
• ascent, rise, slope, gradient, incline

clinch VERB
A late goal clinched the victory for the home team.
• secure, seal, settle, decide, confirm, conclude, finalize, close
(*informal*) sew up

cling VERB
❶ *She clung to the rope with all her strength.*
• clasp, clutch, grasp, hold on
❷ *Ivy clings to the wall.*
• stick, adhere, fasten on

clip NOUN
❶ *She undid the clip and opened the case.*
• fastener, clasp, catch, hook
❷ *They showed a clip from his latest film.*
• extract, excerpt, snippet, trailer

a
b
c
d
e
f
g
h
i
j
k
l
m
n
o
p
q
r
s
t
u
v
w
x
y
z

clip VERB

❶ *The two sheets were clipped together.*
• pin, staple, fasten, attach
❷ *Dad was clipping the hedge in the back garden.*
• cut, trim, prune, crop
❸ *The back wheel just clipped the kerb.*
• hit, strike, scrape, nudge

cloak NOUN

She wrapped her cloak tightly around herself.
• cape, coat, wrap
(*old use*) mantle

clock NOUN

WORD WEB

Instruments used to measure time:

> atomic clock   > quartz clock
> chronograph   > stopwatch
> cuckoo clock   > sundial
> digital clock   > water clock
> hourglass   > wristwatch
> pocket watch

– The study of clocks and timekeeping is **horology**.

– A person who makes clocks or watches is a **clockmaker** or **watchmaker**.

clog VERB

Dead leaves are clogging the drain.
• block, choke, congest, obstruct, bung up, stop up, jam, plug

close ADJECTIVE

❶ *Our house is close to the shops.*
• near, nearby, not far (from)
– To be actually by the side of something is to be **adjacent** to it.
OPPOSITES far, distant
❷ *She is one of my closest friends.*
• intimate, dear, devoted, firm, faithful, inseparable, bosom, close-knit
OPPOSITES distant, casual
❸ *The police made a close examination of the stolen car.*
• careful, detailed, thorough, painstaking, minute, meticulous, rigorous
OPPOSITES casual, cursory
❹ *He bears a close resemblance to the prime minister.*
• strong, firm, distinct, marked, noticeable, unmistakable
OPPOSITES slight, passing
❺ *It was a very close race.*
• equal, even, level, well-matched
IDIOM neck and neck
OPPOSITE one-sided
❻ *The air is very close in this room.*
• humid, muggy, stuffy, clammy, heavy, airless, stifling, sticky, sultry
OPPOSITES fresh, airy

close VERB

❶ *Don't forget to close the lid.*
• shut, fasten, seal, secure
❷ *The road is now closed to traffic.*
• block, seal off, barricade, obstruct
❸ *They closed the concert with my favourite song.*
• finish, end, conclude, stop, terminate, complete
(*informal*) wind up

close NOUN

What was the score at the close of play?
• finish, end, stop, conclusion, termination, completion

clot VERB

Blood will clot when exposed to the air.
• coagulate, solidify, thicken, congeal

cloth NOUN

❶ *The curtains were made of striped cotton cloth.*
• fabric, material, textile
For types of cloth see fabric.
❷ *Use a cloth to wipe the windows.*
• rag, duster, flannel, wipe

clothe VERB

➤ be clothed in
He was clothed in green from head to toe.
• be dressed in, be wearing, be clad in, be decked in, be fitted out in

clothes PLURAL NOUN

What clothes are you taking on holiday?

• clothing, garments, outfits, dress, attire, garb, finery

(*informal*) gear, get-up, togs

– A set of clothes to wear is a **costume**, **outfit** or **suit**.

– An official set of clothes worn for school or work is a **uniform**.

– A collection of clothes or costumes is a **wardrobe**.

WORD WEB

Some items of clothing:

- anorak
- apron
- ball gown
- bandanna
- bikini
- blazer
- blouse
- bow tie
- boxer shorts (*informal* boxers)
- bra
- briefs
- cagoule
- camisole
- cape
- cardigan
- cloak
- coat
- cowl
- cravat
- cummerbund
- dinner jacket (*North American* tuxedo)
- dress
- dressing gown
- dungarees
- gloves
- gown
- Hawaiian shirt
- headscarf
- hoody
- jacket
- jeans
- jersey

- jodhpurs
- jumper
- kaftan
- kilt
- knickerbockers
- knickers
- leggings
- leotard
- mackintosh (*informal* mac)
- mini skirt
- mittens
- nightdress (*informal* nightie)
- overalls
- overcoat
- petticoat
- pinafore
- plus-fours
- polo shirt
- pullover
- pyjamas
- raincoat
- robe
- rugby shirt
- sari
- sarong
- scarf
- shawl
- shirt
- shorts
- shrug
- skirt
- slip

- socks
- stockings
- stole
- suit
- sweater
- sweatshirt
- swimsuit
- tails
- tank top
- three-piece suit
- tie
- tights
- top
- tracksuit

- trousers (*North American* pants)
- trunks
- T-shirt
- tunic
- twinset
- underpants
- underwear (*informal* undies)
- veil
- vest
- waistcoat
- wetsuit
- wrap

SEE ALSO hat

For clothes worn in the past see historical.

WRITING TIPS

DESCRIBING CLOTHES
Parts and accessories:

- belt
- bodice
- braces (*North American* suspenders)
- braid
- buckle
- buttons
- collar
- cuff
- flounce
- frill
- fringe
- hem

- hood
- lapel
- leg
- lining
- pintucks
- pocket
- ruffle
- seam
- sleeve
- trim
- turn-ups
- waist
- waistband
- zip

Adjectives:

- baggy
- casual
- chic
- creased
- crumpled
- dapper
- designer
- dingy
- drab

- elegant
- fashionable
- frayed
- frilly
- frumpy
- grubby
- ill-fitting
- in good or bad repair

a
b
c
d
e
f
g
h
i
j
k
l
m
n
o
p
q
r
s
t
u
v
w
x
y
z

> patched
> printed
> ragged
> scruffy
> shabby
> slovenly
> sporty
> stylish

> tailored
> tattered
> tatty
> threadbare
> unfashionable
> waterproof
> windproof
> worn

– Someone who wears smart clothes is well dressed or well groomed.

cloud NOUN
A cloud of steam billowed from the kettle.
• billow, puff, haze, mist

cloud VERB
Don't let anger cloud your judgement.
• obscure, confuse, muddle

cloudy ADJECTIVE
❶ It was a cold and cloudy day.
• overcast, dull, grey, dark, dismal, gloomy, sunless, leaden
OPPOSITES cloudless, clear
❷ The pond water was cloudy.
• muddy, murky, milky, dirty
OPPOSITES clear, transparent

club NOUN
❶ He brandished a wooden club.
• stick, bat, baton, truncheon, cudgel
❷ She belonged to a book club.
• group, society, association, organization, circle, union

club VERB
The victim was clubbed over the head with a blunt instrument.
• hit, strike, beat, batter, bludgeon (informal) clout, clobber

clue NOUN
❶ Can you give me a clue?
• hint, suggestion, indication, pointer, tip, idea
❷ The police are still looking for clues.
• piece of evidence, lead

clump NOUN
The owl flew into a clump of trees.
• group, thicket, cluster, mass
– A clump of grass or hair is a **tuft**.

clumsy ADJECTIVE
❶ My fingers were clumsy with the cold.
• awkward, graceless, ungainly, inelegant, lumbering
OPPOSITE graceful
❷ He apologized for his clumsy handling of the situation.
• unskilful, inept, incompetent
OPPOSITE skilful

cluster NOUN
There was a cluster of buildings at the top of the hill.
• bunch, group, clump, mass, knot, collection, gathering, crowd

cluster VERB
We all clustered around the computer screen.
• crowd, huddle, gather, collect, group

clutch VERB
In her hand, she clutched a handkerchief.
• grip, grasp, clasp, cling to, hang on to, hold on to

clutches PLURAL NOUN
At last he was free from their clutches.
• grasp, power, control

clutter NOUN
It's difficult to work with all this clutter around.
• mess, muddle, disorder, untidiness, junk, litter, rubbish

coach NOUN
❶ We will travel there by coach.
• bus
❷ The football team has a new coach.
• trainer, instructor, teacher, tutor

coach VERB
He was coached by a former champion.
• train, teach, instruct, drill

coarse ADJECTIVE
❶ *All he had on his bed was a coarse woollen blanket.*
• rough, harsh, scratchy, bristly, hairy
OPPOSITES soft, fine
❷ *We were shocked by their coarse table manners.*
• rude, impolite, uncouth, improper, crude, vulgar
OPPOSITES polite, refined

coast NOUN
We walked along the coast for three miles.
• shore, coastline, shoreline, seaside, seashore

coast VERB
I coasted downhill on my bike.
• cruise, freewheel, glide

coat NOUN
❶ *Put on a coat if you go out.*
• overcoat, jacket
❷ *The fox had a reddish-brown coat.*
• hair, fur, hide, pelt, skin
– A sheep's coat is a **fleece**.
❸ *The front door needs a new coat of paint.*
• layer, coating, covering, film, skin

coat VERB
I bought a packet of raisins coated with chocolate.
• cover, spread, smear, plaster, daub, glaze

coax VERB
A woman was trying to coax a kitten out of a tree.
• persuade, cajole, wheedle, tempt, entice

code NOUN
❶ *The message was written in a secret code.*
• cipher
– To put a message in code is to **encode** or **encrypt** it.
– To understand a message in code is to **decode**, **decipher** or (*informal*) **crack** it.

❷ *There is a strict code of conduct for using the pool.*
• rules, regulations, laws

coil NOUN
He passed me a coil of rope.
• spiral, twist, curl, twirl, screw, corkscrew, whirl, whorl, roll, scroll
– A coil of wool or thread is a **skein**.

coil VERB
The snake coiled itself round a branch.
• curl, loop, wind, wrap, roll, twist, twirl, twine, spiral

coin NOUN
Do you have a pound coin?
• piece, bit

✺ WORD WEB

Some coins used in the past:

- denarius
- doubloon
- ducat
- farthing
- florin
- groat
- guinea
- halfpenny
- shilling
- sixpence
- sovereign

– A series of coins used for currency is **coinage**.
– The making of coins for currency is **minting**.
– The study of coins is **numismatics** and a person who studies or collects coins is a **numismatist**.

---

coin VERB
The word 'robot' was coined by a Czech writer.
• invent, make up, think up, dream up, conceive, create, devise

coincide VERB
❶ *This year, half-term coincides with my birthday.*
• co-occur, fall together, happen together, clash
❷ *Our opinions rarely coincide.*
• agree, correspond, tally, accord, be in accord, be compatible, match up

a b c d e f g h i j k l m n o p q r s t u v w x y z

coincidence NOUN

By a strange coincidence, we have the same birthday.
• chance, accident, luck, fortune, fluke, happenstance

cold ADJECTIVE

❶ *We can expect a spell of cold weather.*
• chilly, chill, frosty, freezing, icy, raw, arctic, bitter, cool, crisp, snowy, wintry
(*informal*) perishing, nippy
OPPOSITES hot, warm
❷ *I was feeling cold.*
• chilled, chilly, frozen, freezing, shivering, shivery
– Someone with an abnormally low body temperature is suffering from **hypothermia**.
❸ *She gave me a cold stare.*
• unfriendly, unkind, unfeeling, distant, cool, indifferent, stony, uncaring, unemotional, unsympathetic
OPPOSITES warm, friendly

collaborate VERB

❶ *Several zoos collaborated on the rhino project.*
• work together, cooperate, join forces, pool resources
❷ *They were accused of collaborating with the enemy.*
• cooperate, collude, consort, fraternize

collapse VERB

❶ *Many buildings collapsed in the earthquake.*
• fall down, fall in, cave in, give way, crumple, buckle, disintegrate, tumble down
❷ *Some of the runners collapsed in the heat.*
• faint, pass out, black out, fall over, keel over

colleague NOUN

He said he would discuss the case with his colleagues.
• co-worker, workmate, teammate, partner, associate, collaborator

collect VERB

❶ *My brother and I were collecting shells on the beach.*
• gather, accumulate, amass, hoard, pile up, store up, stockpile
❷ *We are collecting money for charity.*
• raise, take in
❸ *I need to collect a parcel from the post office.*
• fetch, pick up, get, call for
OPPOSITES drop off, hand in
❹ *A crowd collected at the stage door.*
• assemble, gather, come together, congregate, convene, converge, muster
OPPOSITES scatter, disperse

collection NOUN

She has a wonderful collection of old photographs.
• hoard, store, stock, pile, accumulation, set, assortment, array
– A collection of books is a **library**.
– A collection of stories or poems is an **anthology**.

collective ADJECTIVE

It was a collective decision.
• common, shared, joint, group, mutual, communal, combined

collective noun NOUN

WORD WEB

- an **army** or a **colony** of ants
- a **flock** of birds
- a **herd** of cattle
- a **brood** of chicks
- a **pod** of dolphins
- a **herd** of elephants
- a **shoal** of fish
- a **gaggle** or **skein** of geese
- a **band** of gorillas
- a **swarm** of insects
- a **troop** of kangaroos
- a **pride** of lions
- a **troop** of monkeys

- a **colony** of penguins
- a **litter** of piglets or kittens or puppies
- a **pack** of rats
- a **flock** of sheep
- a **school** of whales
- a **pack** of wolves

college NOUN
He studied at a music college.
• academy, school, university, institute

collide VERB
➤ **collide with**
The car collided head-on with the van.
• crash into, smash into, bump into, run into, hit, strike

collision NOUN
He had to brake hard to avoid a collision with the car in front.
• crash, accident, smash, bump, knock
– A collision involving a lot of vehicles is a **pile-up**.

colloquial ADJECTIVE
Her books are written in a colloquial style.
• informal, conversational, casual, everyday, idiomatic, vernacular
OPPOSITE formal

colony NOUN
Australia and New Zealand were once British colonies.
• territory, dependency, protectorate, settlement

colossal ADJECTIVE
A colossal statue towered above us.
• huge, enormous, gigantic, immense, massive, giant, mammoth, monumental, towering, vast
OPPOSITES small, tiny

colour NOUN
These T-shirts are available in a range of colours.
• hue, shade, tint, tone, tinge

WRITING TIPS

DESCRIBING COLOURS
Light colours:
➤ delicate
➤ faded
➤ muted
➤ neutral
➤ pale
➤ pastel
➤ soft
➤ subtle
➤ washed-out

Dark or strong colours:
➤ bold
➤ bright
➤ deep
➤ fiery
➤ flaming
➤ fluorescent
➤ garish
➤ gaudy
➤ intense
➤ iridescent
➤ (informal) jazzy
➤ loud
➤ luminous
➤ lurid
➤ neon
➤ radiant
➤ vibrant
➤ vivid
➤ (informal) zingy

- The colours red, blue and yellow are known as **primary colours**.
- A colour made by mixing two primary colours is a **secondary colour**.
- The pattern of colours seen in a rainbow is called a **spectrum**.

colour VERB
❶ *She decided to colour her hair green.*
• tint, dye, stain, tinge, paint
❷ *The experience coloured his whole childhood.*
• affect, influence, have an impact on, skew

colourful ADJECTIVE
❶ *The poster has a very colourful design.*
• multicoloured, vibrant, vivid, bright, showy, garish, gaudy
(informal) jazzy
OPPOSITE colourless
❷ *She gave a colourful account of her trip.*
• vivid, lively, interesting, exciting, striking, rich, picturesque
OPPOSITE dull

colourless ADJECTIVE

❶ The flask contained a colourless liquid.
• uncoloured, clear, transparent, neutral
– Something which has lost its colour is **bleached** or **faded**.

❷ All the characters in the book are colourless.
• dull, boring, uninteresting, unexciting, drab, dreary, lacklustre
OPPOSITES colourful, interesting

column NOUN

❶ The roof of the temple was supported by stone columns.
• pillar, post, support, upright, shaft, pile

❷ She writes a column in the local newspaper.
• article, piece, report, feature

❸ The troops marched in three columns.
• line, file, procession, row, convoy

comb VERB

❶ I'm just combing my hair.
• groom, brush, tidy, arrange, untangle

❷ The police combed the crime scene for evidence.
• search, scour, sweep, ransack, rummage through

combat NOUN

In the square is a memorial for soldiers killed in combat.
• battle, war, warfare, fighting, action, hostilities

combat VERB

There is a new campaign to combat crime in the city.
• fight, oppose, counter, resist, stand up to, tackle, battle against, grapple with

combination NOUN

He succeeded through a combination of talent and hard work.
• mixture, mix, union, fusion, blend, merger, amalgamation, synthesis

combine VERB

❶ Combine all the ingredients in a saucepan.
• mix, blend, fuse, bind, merge, marry, integrate, amalgamate
OPPOSITES separate, divide

❷ Three schools combined to stage the event.
• unite, join forces, get together

come VERB

❶ My parents will be coming tomorrow.
• arrive, appear, visit, turn up
(informal) show up
OPPOSITES leave, go

❷ Summer is coming at last.
• advance, draw near

❸ How did you come to write the novel?
• happen, chance

➤ come about
How did the accident come about?
• happen, occur, take place, arise, result

➤ come across
I came across an old friend of mine.
• find, discover, chance upon, meet, bump into

➤ come from
Where does your family come from?
• originate from, hail from, be from

➤ come round or to
How long did it take to come round after the operation?
• become conscious, revive, wake up

➤ come to
❶ We came to the end of the road.
• reach, get to, arrive at

❷ The hotel bill came to a hundred euros.
• add up to, amount to, total

comfort NOUN

❶ He tried to offer a few words of comfort.
• consolation, support, encouragement, sympathy, condolence

❷ They had enough money to live in comfort.
• ease, contentment, well-being, prosperity, luxury, affluence
OPPOSITES hardship, discomfort

comfort VERB

She went upstairs to comfort the baby.
• console, soothe, calm, reassure, cheer up, hearten
OPPOSITES distress, upset

comfortable ADJECTIVE
❶ *It is a very comfortable sofa.*
• cosy, snug, relaxing, soft, roomy, padded, plush
(*informal*) comfy
OPPOSITE uncomfortable
❷ *Wear comfortable clothes for travelling.*
• casual, informal, loose-fitting
OPPOSITES restrictive, tight-fitting
❸ *Our cat leads a comfortable life.*
• contented, pleasant, agreeable, well-off, prosperous, luxurious, affluent
OPPOSITE hard

comic ADJECTIVE
The act opens with a comic scene.
• humorous, funny, amusing, comical, light-hearted
OPPOSITES serious, tragic

comical ADJECTIVE
Her impersonation of the queen is quite comical.
• funny, amusing, humorous, hilarious, witty, droll
– To be comical in a cheeky way is to be **facetious**.
– To be comical in a silly way is to be **absurd**, **farcical**, **ludicrous** or **ridiculous**.
– To be comical in a hurtful way is to be **sarcastic**.

command NOUN
❶ *The general gave the command to attack.*
• order, instruction, direction, commandment, edict
❷ *Who has command of the ship?*
• control, charge, authority, dominion, jurisdiction, leadership, management, supervision, power
❸ *The job requires a good command of German.*
• knowledge, mastery, grasp, understanding, comprehension, ability (in)

command VERB
❶ *The officer commanded his troops to fire.*
• order, instruct, direct, tell, bid

❷ *Nelson commanded the British fleet.*
• be in charge of, control, direct, govern, head, lead, manage, supervise, oversee
(*informal*) head up

commander NOUN
He was the commander of the Roman fleet.
• leader, head, chief, officer-in-charge, commanding officer

commemorate VERB
A plaque on the wall commemorates the battle.
• celebrate, remember, mark, observe, pay tribute to, be a memorial to, honour, salute

commence VERB
Let the battle commence.
• begin, start, get going, get under way
(*informal*) kick off
IDIOM get off the ground

commend VERB
My photo was commended in the under-18 category.
• praise, compliment, congratulate, applaud
OPPOSITE criticize

comment NOUN
❶ *He was always making sarcastic comments.*
• remark, statement, observation, opinion, pronouncement, mention
– A hostile comment is a **criticism**.
❷ *She wrote a few comments in the margin.*
• note, annotation, footnote, gloss, reference

comment VERB
➤ comment on
Several people commented on my dress.
• remark on, mention, make mention of, notice, discuss, talk about

commentary NOUN
We were listening to the match commentary.
• narration, description, report, voice-over, review

a
b
c
d
e
f
g
h
i
j
k
l
m
n
o
p
q
r
s
t
u
v
w
x
y
z

commerce NOUN
The port became a centre of commerce.
• business, trade, trading, dealing

commit VERB
❶ It is still a mystery who committed the murder.
• carry out, do, perform, execute, accomplish, perpetrate
(informal) pull off
❷ She committed a lot of time and energy to the project.
• devote, allocate, dedicate, make available, assign, consign, pledge

commitment NOUN
❶ No one can doubt her total commitment to her sport.
• dedication, devotion, allegiance, loyalty, passion
❷ I have made a commitment to finish the job by next week.
• promise, pledge, vow, undertaking, resolution

committee NOUN
The club is run by a committee of volunteers.
• board, panel, council, body

common ADJECTIVE
❶ Colds are a common complaint in winter.
• commonplace, everyday, frequent, normal, ordinary, familiar, well known, regular, widespread
OPPOSITE rare
❷ 'Good morning' is a common way to greet people.
• typical, usual, regular, standard, routine, customary, conventional, habitual, popular
OPPOSITE uncommon
❸ Humans and apes share a common ancestor.
• shared, mutual, joint, communal, collective

commonplace ADJECTIVE
It is a city where cycling is commonplace.
• common, everyday, regular, routine,

normal, ordinary, frequent, familiar, usual
OPPOSITES rare, unusual

commotion NOUN
Someone was causing a commotion in the street.
• disturbance, row, uproar, racket, rumpus, fuss, stir, unrest, disorder, furore, fracas, hullabaloo, brouhaha, pandemonium, bedlam

communal ADJECTIVE
There is a communal kitchen at the end of the corridor.
• shared, joint, public, common, collective
OPPOSITES private, individual

communicate VERB
❶ Someone has to communicate the bad news to her.
• convey, relay, transmit, relate, pass on, report, tell, impart, express
❷ We usually communicate by email.
• contact each other, correspond, be in touch, liaise
❸ Malaria is communicated by mosquitoes.
• transmit, transfer, pass on, spread

communication NOUN
❶ Dolphins use sound for communication.
• communicating, contact, dialogue, conversation
❷ I have received an urgent communication.
• message, dispatch, statement, announcement, letter, report

WORD WEB

Some forms of communication:
- advertising
- blog
- body language
- Braille
- broadcast
- bulletin board
- chat
- email
- fax
- instant messaging
- junk mail
- letter
- mailshot

> memo or memorandum
> mobile phone
> Morse code
> newspaper
> podcast
> postcard
> radio
> satellite
> semaphore
> sign language or signing
> smartphone
> social networking
> telegram
> telepathy
> telephone
> television
> texting
> video conference
> videophone
> webcast
> website
> wiki

communicative ADJECTIVE
I'm not feeling very communicative today.
• talkative, expressive, vocal, chatty, forthcoming
OPPOSITES uncommunicative, taciturn

community NOUN
He grew up in a small farming community.
• society, population, people, residents, inhabitants, neighbourhood, district, region, locality

compact ADJECTIVE
❶ The camera is light and compact.
• small, portable, handy, neat, petite
OPPOSITE bulky
❷ The fabric has a compact weave.
• dense, tight, close, firm, solid, compressed
OPPOSITE loose

companion NOUN
He turned to speak to his companions.
• friend, associate, partner, comrade (informal) mate, pal, buddy, chum

company NOUN
❶ She works for a computer company.
• firm, business, corporation, organization, establishment, enterprise, agency, office
❷ He missed the company of his friends.
• fellowship, companionship, society, friendship

compare VERB
We have been comparing the two sets of figures.
• contrast, juxtapose, set side by side, weigh up
➤ **compare with something**
It doesn't compare with the original version.
• be as good as, rival, emulate, equal, match up to, come close to, be on a par with

comparison NOUN
❶ We put the signatures side by side for comparison.
• comparing, contrast, juxtaposition
❷ There's no comparison between their team and ours.
• resemblance, similarity, likeness, correspondence

compartment NOUN
The money was hidden in a secret compartment.
• section, division, pocket, space, cubicle

compassion NOUN
He feels compassion for these victims of war.
• sympathy, empathy, fellow feeling, concern, consideration, understanding, kindness, charity
OPPOSITE indifference

compatible ADJECTIVE
The couple were never really compatible.
• well-suited, well matched, like-minded
IDIOMS on the same wavelength, in tune
OPPOSITE incompatible

compel VERB
Villagers were compelled to leave their homes.
• force, make, press, push
(informal) lean on

compelling ADJECTIVE
❶ She has written a compelling story of love and revenge.
• captivating, enthralling, absorbing, gripping, riveting, spellbinding, mesmerizing

❷ *It is a compelling argument.*
• convincing, persuasive, powerful, strong, irresistible

compensate VERB
They promised to compensate him for his loss of earnings.
• recompense, repay, reimburse, remunerate
➤ **compensate for**
This victory compensates for our earlier defeats.
• make up for, offset, counteract, balance out, cancel out

compensation NOUN
She put in a claim for compensation.
• recompense, repayment, reimbursement, remuneration, damages

compete VERB
Eight schools will be competing in the hockey tournament.
• participate, take part, enter, play, go in (for)
➤ **compete against**
We are competing against a strong team this week.
• oppose, play against, contend with, vie with, challenge
IDIOM go head to head with

competent ADJECTIVE
You have to be a competent swimmer to join the club.
• able, capable, skilful, skilled, accomplished, proficient, expert
OPPOSITE incompetent

competition NOUN
❶ *He won first prize in a poetry competition.*
• contest, quiz, championship, tournament, match, game, trial, race
❷ *There was fierce competition for the job.*
• rivalry, competitiveness
❸ *I stood on the starting line, eyeing up the competition.*
• opposition, rivals, opponents, other side

competitor NOUN
❶ *The competitors lined up for the start of the race.*
• contestant, contender, participant, player, entrant
❷ *Who are your main competitors?*
• rival, opponent, challenger

compile VERB
She has compiled a collection of children's poems.
• assemble, put together, make up, compose, organize, gather, collect, collate, edit

complacent ADJECTIVE
We've done well so far but we mustn't become complacent.
• self-satisfied, smug, overconfident

complain VERB
My brother spent most of the weekend complaining.
• protest, grumble, grouse, carp, bleat, whine, make a fuss
(informal) gripe, moan, whinge
➤ **complain about something**
The neighbours complained about the noise.
• protest about, object to, criticize, find fault with
OPPOSITE praise

complaint NOUN
❶ *They received hundreds of complaints about the programme.*
• criticism, objection, protest, grievance, grouse, grumble
(informal) gripe, whinge
❷ *I had a nasty stomach complaint.*
• disease, illness, ailment, sickness, disorder, infection, condition, problem, upset

complement NOUN
❶ *The music is a perfect complement to the film.*
• accompaniment, accessory, supplement, companion, partner
OPPOSITES contrast, foil

❷ *We had our full complement of players for the match.*
• quota, contingent, amount, allowance, capacity

complement *VERB*
That shade of green complements your eyes.
• accompany, go with, suit, set off, enhance
OPPOSITES contrast with, clash with

complete *ADJECTIVE*
❶ *I have collected the complete set of cards.*
• whole, entire, full, intact
OPPOSITES incomplete, partial
❷ *The new building is not yet complete.*
• finished, completed, ended, concluded
OPPOSITE unfinished
❸ *My audition was a complete disaster.*
• total, absolute, thorough, utter, pure, sheer, downright, unqualified, unmitigated, out-and-out

complete *VERB*
❶ *She has another year to complete her training.*
• finish, end, conclude, finalize
(*informal*) wind up, wrap up
❷ *I only need one more card to complete the set.*
• finish off, round off, top off, crown, cap

completely *ADVERB*
I'm not completely convinced.
• totally, wholly, entirely, thoroughly, utterly, fully, absolutely

complex *ADJECTIVE*
Defusing a bomb is a complex task.
• complicated, intricate, difficult, elaborate, detailed, involved
(*informal*) fiddly
OPPOSITES simple, straightforward

complexion *NOUN*
The girl had red hair and a pale complexion.
• skin, skin tone, colour, colouring

complicated *ADJECTIVE*
❶ *It is a complicated task.*
• complex, intricate, difficult
(*informal*) fiddly
OPPOSITES simple, straightforward
❷ *The film has a very complicated plot.*
• involved, elaborate, convoluted

compliment *NOUN*
She blushed at the unexpected compliment.
• commendation, tribute, accolade
IDIOM pat on the back
OPPOSITES criticism, insult
➤ **compliments**
I'm not used to receiving compliments about my cooking.
• praise, acclaim, admiration, appreciation, congratulations

complimentary *ADJECTIVE*
❶ *The comments were all complimentary.*
• appreciative, approving, admiring, positive, favourable, flattering, congratulatory
OPPOSITES critical, insulting, negative
❷ *We were given complimentary tickets for the film.*
• free, gratis, courtesy
IDIOM on the house

component *NOUN*
The factory makes components for computers.
• part, piece, bit, element, ingredient, constituent, module

compose *VERB*
Beethoven composed nine symphonies.
• create, devise, write, pen, produce, make up, think up, invent

➤ **be composed of**
Water is composed of hydrogen and oxygen.
• be made of, consist of, comprise

composition *NOUN*
❶ *Is the song your own composition?*
• creation, work, piece, study
(*formal*) opus

a
b
c
d
e
f
g
h
i
j
k
l
m
n
o
p
q
r
s
t
u
v
w
x
y
z

❷ *Scientists have studied the composition of the soil.*
• make-up, structure, formation, constitution

compound NOUN
Steel is a compound of iron and carbon.
• amalgam, alloy, mixture, mix, blend

comprehend VERB
The crowd couldn't comprehend what was happening.
• understand, make sense of, grasp, appreciate, perceive, follow, fathom, take in
(*informal*) figure out, get

comprehension NOUN
She spoke in a dialect that was beyond my comprehension.
• understanding, knowledge, awareness, conception, grasp, mastery
OPPOSITE ignorance

comprehensive ADJECTIVE
She gave us a comprehensive account of her travels.
• complete, full, thorough, detailed, extensive, exhaustive, inclusive, all-inclusive, all-embracing, wide-ranging, encyclopedic, sweeping, wholesale
(*informal*) blow-by-blow
OPPOSITES selective, partial

compress VERB
I tried to compress all my clothes into one bag.
• press, squeeze, squash, crush, jam, flatten

comprise VERB
The team comprised athletes from several countries.
• be composed of, consist of, be made up of, include, contain

compromise VERB
Neither side was willing to compromise.
• come to an understanding, make a deal, make concessions
IDIOMS meet each other halfway, find a happy medium

compulsive ADJECTIVE
❶ *Suddenly, I felt a compulsive urge to laugh.*
• irresistible, uncontrollable, compelling, overwhelming, overpowering
❷ *She is a compulsive liar.*
• obsessive, habitual, chronic, incurable, persistent

compulsory ADJECTIVE
The wearing of seat belts is compulsory.
• obligatory, mandatory, required, necessary
OPPOSITE optional

computer NOUN

WORD WEB

Some types of computer:

➤ desktop	➤ notebook
➤ handheld	➤ palmtop
➤ laptop	➤ PC
➤ mainframe	➤ server
➤ netbook	➤ tablet

Parts of a computer system:

➤ CD-ROM drive	➤ motherboard
➤ DVD drive	➤ mouse
➤ hard disk	➤ processor
➤ hub	➤ router
➤ keyboard	➤ screen
➤ memory stick	➤ terminal
➤ microchip	➤ touchpad
➤ microprocessor	➤ USB port
➤ modem	➤ webcam
➤ monitor	

Other terms used in computing:

➤ back-up	➤ email
➤ bit	➤ firewall
➤ broadband	➤ gigabyte
➤ browser	➤ hacker
➤ bug	➤ hardware
➤ byte	➤ ICT
➤ cursor	➤ input
➤ data	➤ interface
➤ database	➤ Internet
➤ digital	(*informal* Net)
➤ download	➤ malware

➤ megabyte	➤ software
➤ memory	➤ spam
➤ menu	➤ spreadsheet
➤ network	➤ start-up
➤ offline	➤ surfing
➤ online	➤ upload
➤ operating	➤ virus
system	➤ Web
➤ peripheral	➤ wi-fi
➤ printout	➤ window
➤ program	➤ wireless
➤ reboot	➤ word processor

concave ADJECTIVE
a concave lens
• diverging
OPPOSITES convex, converging

conceal VERB
❶ *The prisoners concealed the entrance to the tunnel.*
• hide, cover up, screen, disguise, mask, camouflage
OPPOSITES uncover, reveal
❷ *He managed to conceal the truth for years.*
• keep quiet about, keep secret, hush up, suppress
IDIOM keep a lid on
OPPOSITES disclose, confess

conceited ADJECTIVE
What a conceited man you are!
• arrogant, proud, vain, self-satisfied, self-important, boastful
(*informal*) big-headed, cocky
IDIOMS full of yourself, (*informal*) too big for your boots
OPPOSITES modest, self-effacing

conceive VERB
❶ *Who conceived this silly plan?*
• think up, originate, devise, invent, formulate, design, develop
(*informal*) dream up
❷ *I can't conceive what it must have been like for them.*
• imagine, envisage, see, visualize, grasp

concentrate VERB
❶ *Be quiet! I'm trying to concentrate.*
• think hard, focus, pay attention

❷ *This term, we are concentrating on the First World War.*
• focus, centre
❸ *The shops are concentrated in the centre of town.*
• collect, gather, cluster, mass, converge

concept NOUN
I find the concept of time travel fascinating.
• idea, thought, notion, theory

concern VERB
❶ *This conversation doesn't concern you, so go away.*
• affect, involve, be relevant to, apply to, be important to, matter to, relate to
❷ *The melting of the ice caps concerns me deeply.*
• worry, trouble, disturb, distress, upset, bother
❸ *The story concerns a group of rabbits.*
• be about, deal with, relate to, pertain to

concern NOUN
❶ *People are too wrapped up in their own concerns.*
• affair, business, responsibility, interest
❷ *A new virus is causing concern among beekeepers.*
• anxiety, worry, apprehension, unease, disquiet, fear
❸ *She's the head of a large banking concern.*
• company, business, firm, enterprise, establishment, corporation

concerned ADJECTIVE
❶ *Many scientists are concerned about global warming.*
• worried, anxious, troubled, upset, distressed, bothered
❷ *We will be emailing all those concerned.*
• involved, affected, interested, implicated

concerning PREPOSITION
The head spoke to me concerning my future.
• about, regarding, relating to, with

concert NOUN
Tonight there's a concert of jazz music at the town hall.
• recital, performance, show

concise ADJECTIVE
His diary entry gives a concise account of what happened.
• brief, short, condensed, succinct, abridged, abbreviated, compact, pithy
– A concise account of something is a **précis** or **summary**.
OPPOSITES lengthy, expanded

conclude VERB
❶ *This concludes our tour of the library.*
• bring to an end, complete, close, finish, terminate, round off, wind up
(*informal*) wrap up
❷ *The festival concluded with some fireworks.*
• come to an end, finish, close, terminate, culminate, draw to a close
❸ *The jury concluded that she was guilty.*
• decide, judge, deduce, infer, gather

conclusion NOUN
❶ *The conclusion of the book was disappointing.*
• end, ending, close, finale, finish, completion, culmination
❷ *It took the jury some time to reach a conclusion.*
• decision, judgement, opinion, verdict, deduction

concrete ADJECTIVE
The police did not have much concrete evidence.
• real, actual, definite, conclusive, firm, solid, substantial, physical, material, tangible
OPPOSITE abstract

condemn VERB
❶ *The manager condemned the behaviour of the players.*
• criticize, censure, denounce, deplore, disapprove of

OPPOSITES praise, condone
❷ *The two men were condemned to death.*
• sentence, punish

condense VERB
Try to condense the story into a hundred words.
• shorten, abridge, reduce, compress, abbreviate, summarize, edit
OPPOSITE expand

condescending ADJECTIVE
She has a very condescending manner.
• superior, patronizing, disdainful, snobbish
(*informal*) snooty, stuck-up

condition NOUN
❶ *Is the guitar in good condition?*
• state, order, repair, shape, form, fitness
❷ *These people are living in overcrowded conditions.*
• circumstances, environment, situation
❸ *There are strict conditions for using this information.*
• requirement, obligation, term, proviso
➤ **on condition that**
You can come on condition that you keep quiet.
• provided, providing that, on the understanding that, only if

condone VERB
We do not condone this sort of behaviour.
• accept, allow, disregard, let pass, pardon, excuse, tolerate
IDIOM turn a blind eye to
OPPOSITE condemn

conduct VERB
❶ *She conducted a series of important experiments.*
• organize, administer, run, carry out, coordinate, manage, preside over, direct, control, supervise, handle
❷ *A guide conducted us round the site.*
• guide, lead, escort, accompany, usher, take

> ➤ conduct yourself

They conducted themselves with dignity.
• behave, act, acquit yourself

conduct NOUN
The referee sent him off for violent conduct.
• behaviour, manners, actions, deeds

confer VERB
❶ *You are allowed to confer with your teammates.*
• consult, have a discussion, converse, deliberate, talk things over
❷ *Thank you for conferring this honour upon me.*
• bestow (on), award (to), grant (to), present (to)

conference NOUN
He was invited to give a speech at a scientific conference.
• meeting, congress, convention, forum, summit, discussion

confess VERB
❶ *She confessed that she had stolen the money.*
• admit, own up, acknowledge, reveal, divulge
(*informal*) come clean
OPPOSITE deny
❷ *I confess I don't know the answer.*
• acknowledge, admit, concede, grant, allow

confide VERB
He was afraid to confide the secret to anyone.
• reveal, disclose, tell, divulge, confess

confidence NOUN
❶ *The team had lost all confidence in the manager.*
• trust, faith, belief
❷ *We can face the future with confidence.*
• hope, optimism, faith
❸ *I wish I had her confidence.*
• self-assurance, self-confidence, assertiveness, boldness, conviction

confident ADJECTIVE
❶ *I am confident that we will win.*
• certain, sure, positive, hopeful, optimistic, convinced, satisfied, in no doubt
OPPOSITE doubtful
❷ *She is more confident than her sister.*
• self-assured, self-confident, bold, fearless, assertive

confidential ADJECTIVE
The details of the plan are confidential.
• private, secret, classified, restricted
(*informal*) hush-hush
OPPOSITE public

confine VERB
❶ *They confined their discussion to the weather.*
• limit, restrict, keep
❷ *Our chickens are not confined indoors.*
• enclose, shut in, coop up, incarcerate

confirm VERB
❶ *His guilty expression confirmed my suspicions.*
• prove, substantiate, corroborate, justify, verify, vindicate, bear out, back up
OPPOSITE disprove
❷ *Please phone to confirm your booking.*
• verify, make official
OPPOSITE cancel

confiscate VERB
One of the teachers confiscated my phone.
• take possession of, seize, impound

conflict NOUN
❶ *There's a lot of conflict in their family.*
• disagreement, quarrelling, hostility, friction, antagonism, opposition, discord, strife, unrest
❷ *Both countries wanted to avoid a military conflict.*
• war, warfare, combat, fighting, engagement, hostilities

conflict VERB
➤ conflict with
Her statement conflicts with the evidence.
• disagree with, differ from, contradict, contrast with, clash with, be at odds with

conflicting ADJECTIVE
My brother and I have conflicting tastes in music.
• contrasting, incompatible, contradictory, opposite, contrary, irreconcilable

conform VERB
➤ conform to or with
The building does not conform with safety regulations.
• comply with, follow, keep to, obey, observe, abide by, fit in with, submit to
OPPOSITES disobey, flout

confront VERB
❶ *I decided to confront her and demand an apology.*
• challenge, stand up to, face up to, take on, tackle
❷ *He was confronted with a very difficult decision.*
• face, stand in your way, threaten

confuse VERB
❶ *I was confused by her message.*
• puzzle, bewilder, mystify, baffle, perplex, bemuse
(*informal*) flummox, fox
❷ *You must be confusing me with someone else.*
• mix up, muddle

confusing ADJECTIVE
These instructions are confusing.
• puzzling, perplexing, baffling, bewildering, unclear, misleading, ambiguous
OPPOSITES clear, unambiguous

confusion NOUN
❶ *There was a look of confusion on his face.*
• bewilderment, perplexity, bafflement, puzzlement
OPPOSITES certainty, clarity
❷ *It was a scene of utter confusion.*
• chaos, disorder, disarray, mayhem, pandemonium, bedlam
OPPOSITES order, calm

congested ADJECTIVE
The roads are congested during the rush hour.
• blocked, jammed, choked, clogged, obstructed, crowded
(*informal*) snarled up, jam-packed, gridlocked
OPPOSITE clear

congratulate VERB
We congratulated the winners.
• praise, applaud, compliment, pay tribute to, salute
IDIOMS pat someone on the back, take your hat off to
OPPOSITE criticize

congregate VERB
The guests congregated in the hall.
• gather, assemble, collect, convene, come together, muster, cluster
OPPOSITE disperse

connect VERB
❶ *Have you connected the printer to the computer?*
• join, attach, fasten, link, couple, fix together, tie together
OPPOSITE separate
❷ *Police believe the two murders could be connected.*
• associate, link, relate, couple, bracket together

connection NOUN
There is a connection between the Moon and the tides.
• relationship, link, association, interconnection, bond, tie

conquer VERB
❶ *The Romans used people they had conquered as slaves.*
• defeat, beat, vanquish, subjugate, overcome, overwhelm, crush
❷ *Alexander the Great conquered Egypt*

in 332 BC.
• seize, capture, take, win, occupy, possess
❸ *She's trying to conquer her fear of flying.*
• overcome, suppress, master, control, curb, get the better of

conquest *NOUN*
Next week's programme is about the Mongol conquest of China.
• capture, seizure, invasion, occupation, possession, takeover

conscientious *ADJECTIVE*
She is a conscientious student.
• hard-working, diligent, industrious, careful, attentive, meticulous, painstaking, thorough, dedicated, dutiful, responsible
OPPOSITES careless, irresponsible

conscious *ADJECTIVE*
❶ *The patient was conscious throughout the operation.*
• awake, alert, aware
OPPOSITES unconscious, unaware
❷ *We are making a conscious effort to save energy.*
• deliberate, intentional, planned, calculated, premeditated
OPPOSITES accidental, unintentional

consecutive *ADJECTIVE*
It rained for three consecutive days.
• successive, succeeding, running, straight, in a row, in succession
IDIOM (*informal*) on the trot
You can say *three days straight* or *three straight days* but only *three days running*.

consent *NOUN*
You can only go on the trip if your parents give their consent.
• agreement, assent, permission, authorization, approval, acceptance
(*informal*) go-ahead

consent *VERB*
➤ consent to
The head has consented to our request.
• agree to, grant, allow, approve of,

authorize, go along with
IDIOM give the green light to
OPPOSITE refuse

consequence *NOUN*
❶ *He drove too fast, with tragic consequences.*
• result, effect, outcome, upshot, repercussion
OPPOSITE cause
❷ *Her wealth was of no consequence to him.*
• importance, significance, concern, account, value

conservation *NOUN*
Our group supports the conservation of wildlife.
• preservation, protection, maintenance, upkeep
OPPOSITE destruction

conservative *ADJECTIVE*
❶ *My dad has a very conservative taste in music.*
• old-fashioned, conventional, unadventurous, traditional, restrained
OPPOSITES progressive, up-to-date
❷ *At a conservative estimate, the work will take six months.*
• cautious, moderate, modest, reasonable
OPPOSITE extreme

conserve *VERB*
You can conserve electricity by switching off lights.
• save, preserve, be sparing with, safeguard, look after, protect, sustain
OPPOSITE waste

consider *VERB*
❶ *She paused to consider all the options.*
• think about, examine, contemplate, ponder on, reflect on, study, evaluate, meditate on, weigh up, mull over
(*informal*) size up
❷ *His first novel is considered to be his best.*
• reckon, judge, deem, regard as, rate

a
b
c
d
e
f
g
h
i
j
k
l
m
n
o
p
q
r
s
t
u
v
w
x
y
z

considerable ADJECTIVE
1000 dollars is a considerable sum of money.
• large, sizeable, substantial, significant
OPPOSITE negligible

considerate ADJECTIVE
How considerate of you to offer me a lift.
• thoughtful, kind, helpful, obliging, unselfish, neighbourly
OPPOSITE selfish

consist VERB
➤ consist of
A comet consists largely of ice and dust.
• be made up of, be composed of, comprise, contain, include, involve

consistency NOUN
The mixture had the consistency of porridge.
• texture, thickness, density

consistent ADJECTIVE
The greenhouse is kept at a consistent temperature.
• steady, constant, regular, stable, even, unchanging, uniform
OPPOSITES variable, fluctuating
➤ be consistent with
The injuries are consistent with a crocodile attack.
• be compatible with, be in keeping with, be in line with
OPPOSITE be inconsistent with

consolation NOUN
A late goal provided some consolation for the losers.
• comfort, solace, sympathy, commiseration, support

console VERB
I tried everything I could to console her.
• comfort, sympathize with, commiserate with, support, soothe, cheer up

conspicuous ADJECTIVE
The clock tower is a conspicuous landmark.
• noticeable, prominent, obvious, clear, unmistakable, eye-catching, visible, evident, apparent, glaring
OPPOSITE inconspicuous

conspiracy NOUN
They were involved in a conspiracy to overthrow the government.
• plot, intrigue, scheme, ploy, plan

constant ADJECTIVE
❶ *We have to put up with the constant noise of traffic outside.*
• continual, continuous, non-stop, ceaseless, incessant, persistent, perpetual, interminable, endless, unending, never-ending, everlasting, permanent
OPPOSITE intermittent
❷ *The wheel should turn at a constant speed.*
• steady, consistent, regular, stable, even, unchanging, uniform
OPPOSITE variable
❸ *She proved to be a constant friend.*
• faithful, loyal, devoted, dependable, reliable, firm, true, trustworthy
OPPOSITE unreliable

constitute VERB
❶ *Eleven players constitute a hockey team.*
• make up, compose, comprise, form
❷ *The oil spill constitutes a danger to wildlife.*
• amount to, represent, be equivalent to, be tantamount to

construct VERB
When was the bridge constructed?
• build, erect, assemble, put together, put up, set up
OPPOSITE demolish

construction NOUN
❶ *He was put in charge of the construction of the emperor's palace.*
• building, erecting, erection, assembly, setting-up
❷ *The bridge is a temporary construction.*
• structure, edifice, building

consult VERB

❶ *You should consult a doctor first.*
• seek advice from, speak to, ask, talk things over with
❷ *If you don't know how to spell a word, consult your dictionary.*
• refer to, check, look something up in

consume VERB

❶ *An adult penguin consumes up to 500g of fish a day.*
• eat, devour, swallow
❷ *Refrigerators consume a vast amount of energy.*
• use up, go through, spend, exhaust, deplete
❸ *The building was consumed by fire.*
• destroy, devastate, lay waste, gut, raze
➤ **be consumed with**
The king was consumed with jealousy.
• be filled with, be overwhelmed by, be gripped by

contact VERB

I'll contact you when I have some news.
• get in touch with, communicate with, notify, speak to, talk to, correspond with, write to, call, phone, ring

contact NOUN

❶ *Rugby is a sport which involves physical contact.*
• touch, touching, handling
❷ *Have you had any contact with him lately?*
• communication, correspondence, connection, dealings

contagious ADJECTIVE

Measles is a very contagious disease.
• infectious, communicable, (*informal*) catching
OPPOSITE non-infectious

contain VERB

❶ *The box contains various odds and ends.*
• have inside, hold, accommodate
❷ *This book contains a great deal of information.*
• include, incorporate, comprise, consist of
❸ *I tried hard to contain my impatience.*
• restrain, hold back, suppress, control, curb, rein in, bottle up

container NOUN

Put the leftover sauce in a container.
• receptacle, vessel, holder, repository, box, case, canister, carton, pot, tub, tin

contaminate VERB

The drinking water may have become contaminated.
• pollute, poison, defile, taint, soil
OPPOSITE purify

contemplate VERB

❶ *She contemplated herself in the mirror.*
• look at, view, regard, observe, gaze at, stare at, survey, study
❷ *I am contemplating what to do next.*
• think about, consider, ponder, reflect on, meditate on, weigh up, mull over

contemporary ADJECTIVE

The gallery is putting on an exhibition of contemporary art.
• modern, current, recent, present-day, the latest, up-to-date, fashionable

contempt NOUN

She gave a snort of contempt.
• scorn, disdain, derision, disrespect
OPPOSITES admiration, respect

contemptuous ADJECTIVE

He gave me a contemptuous look.
• scornful, disdainful, derisive, disrespectful
OPPOSITES admiring, respectful

contend VERB

❶ *The witness contends that he heard a noise.*
• assert, declare, claim, maintain, argue, insist
❷ *Four teams are contending for a place in the final.*
• compete, vie, battle, strive, struggle
➤ **contend with**
We had to contend with bad weather

a b c d e f g h i j k l m n o p q r s t u v w x y z

and midges!
• cope with, deal with, put up with, grapple with, face, confront, take on

content ADJECTIVE
I was content to sit and wait.
• happy, contented, satisfied, pleased, willing
OPPOSITE unwilling

contented ADJECTIVE
She sank into the armchair with a contented sigh.
• happy, pleased, content, satisfied, fulfilled, serene, peaceful, relaxed, comfortable, tranquil, untroubled
OPPOSITE discontented

contents PLURAL NOUN
Try to guess the contents of the mystery parcel.
• constituents, components, ingredients, elements

contest NOUN
The final was an exciting contest.
• competition, challenge, tournament, match, game, encounter, bout, fight, battle, struggle, tussle

contest VERB
❶ Six parties will be contesting the election.
• compete for, fight for, contend for, vie for
❷ No one contested the referee's decision.
• challenge, disagree with, object to, dispute, oppose, call into question

contestant NOUN
She was once a contestant on a TV quiz show.
• competitor, participant, contender, player, entrant

continual ADJECTIVE
It was a day of continual interruptions.
• recurrent, repeated, constant, frequent, perpetual
OPPOSITE occasional
The words continual and continuous are not synonyms. Continual noises happen

repeatedly, whereas a continuous noise never stops.

continue VERB
❶ We continued our search until it got dark.
• keep up, prolong, sustain, persevere with, pursue
(informal) stick at
❷ This rain can't continue for long.
• carry on, last, persist, endure, extend, keep on, go on, linger, drag on
❸ We'll continue the lesson after lunch.
• resume, carry on with, proceed with, return to, pick up

continuous ADJECTIVE
She has continuous pain in her ankle.
• persistent, uninterrupted, unbroken, never-ending, non-stop, incessant, unceasing
– An illness which continues for a long time is a **chronic** illness.
OPPOSITE intermittent
SEE ALSO continual

contract NOUN
The actress has signed a contract for a new film.
• agreement, deal, compact, bargain, undertaking
– A contract between two countries is an **alliance** or **treaty**.
– A contract to end a dispute about money is a **settlement**.

contract VERB
❶ Metal contracts when it gets colder.
• shrink, constrict, tighten, draw in, reduce, lessen
OPPOSITE expand
❷ The crew contracted a mysterious disease.
• catch, pick up, get, develop
(informal) go down with, come down with

contradict VERB
❶ No one dared to contradict the boss.
• challenge, disagree with, speak against, oppose

❷ *The two stories contradict each other.*
• go against, be at odds with, counter, dispute

contraption NOUN
The room was full of weird contraptions.
• machine, device, gadget, invention, apparatus, contrivance, mechanism
(*informal*) gizmo

contrary ADJECTIVE
❶ *She had always been a contrary child.*
• awkward, difficult, stubborn, disobedient, obstinate, uncooperative, unhelpful, wilful, perverse
OPPOSITE cooperative
❷ *Other people may take a contrary view.*
• opposite, opposing, conflicting, contradictory, different
OPPOSITE similar
➤ contrary to
Contrary to popular belief, snakes are not slimy.
• in opposition to, at odds with, differing from

contrast NOUN
There is a sharp contrast between the two paintings.
• difference, distinction, dissimilarity, disparity, variance
OPPOSITE similarity

contrast VERB
❶ *We were asked to contrast two of our favourite poems.*
• compare, juxtapose, distinguish between, differentiate
❷ *The title of the book contrasts with its theme.*
• differ (from), conflict, be at variance, be at odds, clash, disagree
OPPOSITES match, suit

contribute VERB
Many people contributed blankets and clothing.
• donate, give, provide, supply, grant
(*informal*) chip in

➤ contribute to
The good weather contributed to the success of the occasion.
• add to, enhance, help, play a part in

contrive VERB
➤ contrive to
She contrived to get away without anyone seeing her.
• manage to, find a way to, succeed in

control VERB
❶ *The government controls the country's affairs.*
• be in control of, be in charge of, run, direct, command, manage, lead, guide, govern, administer, regulate, rule, superintend, supervise
❷ *Please try to control your temper.*
• restrain, contain, hold back, check, curb

control NOUN
❶ *Spain once had control over a rich empire.*
• authority, power, command, rule, government, management, direction, leadership, dominance
❷ *The government imposed tighter controls on the import of live animals.*
• restriction, limit, restraint, regulation, curb, check

controversial ADJECTIVE
It was a controversial decision by the umpire.
• debatable, questionable, arguable, contentious

controversy NOUN
There is much controversy about the election results.
• disagreement, dispute, debate, argument, quarrelling, contention, storm
(*informal*) row

convalescence VERB
She needed a month's convalescence after the operation.
• recovery, recuperation, rehabilitation

convenient ADJECTIVE
❶ I'll call back at a more convenient time.
• suitable, appropriate, fitting, favourable, opportune, timely
OPPOSITE inconvenient
❷ A bike is often more convenient than a car in towns.
• practical, useful, helpful, handy, labour-saving

convention NOUN
❶ We have many social conventions, such as shaking hands.
• custom, tradition, practice, norm
❷ He attended a convention of leading scientists.
• conference, congress, meeting, forum

conventional ADJECTIVE
This is the conventional way of cooking a turkey.
• customary, traditional, usual, accepted, common, normal, ordinary, everyday, routine, standard, regular, habitual, orthodox
OPPOSITES unconventional, unorthodox

converge VERB
The two rivers converge at this point.
• come together, join, meet, merge, combine, coincide
OPPOSITE divide

conversation NOUN
My mum overheard our conversation.
• discussion, talk, chat, gossip
– Conversation in a play, film or novel is **dialogue**.

convert VERB
❶ They converted their attic into a bedroom.
• adapt, turn, change, alter, transform, modify
❷ My sister converted me into becoming a vegetarian.
• win over, reform, persuade

convex ADJECTIVE
a convex lens
• converging
OPPOSITES concave, diverging

convey VERB
❶ The craft was designed to convey astronauts to the Moon.
• transport, carry, bring, deliver, take, fetch, bear, transfer
– To convey something by sea is to **ferry** or **ship** it.
❷ The tone of his voice conveyed his disgust.
• communicate, indicate, impart, signify, relay, pass on, carry, tell, relate, mean

convict VERB
Three of the men were convicted of fraud.
• find guilty, condemn, sentence
OPPOSITE acquit

convict NOUN
Police are looking for two escaped convicts.
• prisoner, inmate, criminal, offender

convince VERB
How can I convince you that I am not lying?
• persuade, assure, satisfy, prove to, win over

convincing ADJECTIVE
❶ I tried to think of a convincing excuse.
• believable, credible, plausible, likely
❷ He saved his most convincing argument until the end.
• persuasive, powerful, strong, compelling, telling, conclusive

cook VERB
Who's going to cook lunch?
• prepare, make
(informal) rustle up
– The art or skill of cooking is **cookery**.
– To cook food for guests or customers is to **cater** for them.

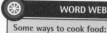

WORD WEB

Some ways to cook food:
- bake
- barbecue
- boil
- braise
- brew
- broil
- casserole
- chargrill

- deep-fry
- fry
- grill
- microwave
- poach
- roast
- sauté
- scramble
- sear
- simmer
- steam
- stew
- stir-fry
- toast

Other ways to prepare food:

- baste
- blend
- chop
- dice
- grate
- grind
- infuse
- knead
- liquidize
- marinade
- mince
- mix
- peel
- purée
- sieve
- sift
- stir
- whisk

Equipment used in cooking:

- baking tin
- blender
- casserole
- chopping board
- colander
- food mixer
- food processor
- frying pan
- grill
- ladle
- liquidizer
- microwave
- mincer
- oven
- roasting tin
- rolling pin
- saucepan
- sieve
- skewer
- spatula
- tandoor
- whisk
- wok

Measurements used in cooking:

- cup or cupful
- dessertspoon
- pinch
- spoonful
- teaspoon
- tablespoon

cook NOUN
He trained as a ship's cook.
- The chief cook in a restaurant or hotel is the **chef**.
- A person who cooks food as a business is a **caterer**.

cool ADJECTIVE
❶ *There was a cool breeze outside.*
• chilly, coldish, fresh, bracing
(*informal*) **nippy**
OPPOSITE warm

❷ *I'd like a cool glass of lemonade.*
• chilled, iced, refreshing
❸ *She remained cool when everyone else panicked.*
• calm, composed, collected, level-headed, relaxed, at ease, unflustered, unruffled, unflappable
(*informal*) laid-back
❹ *We got a cool reception.*
• unfriendly, unwelcoming, distant, remote, aloof, frosty, chilly
(*informal*) stand-offish
OPPOSITE warm
❺ *There was a cool response to my idea.*
• unenthusiastic, half-hearted, indifferent, lukewarm, tepid
OPPOSITE enthusiastic
❻ (*informal*) *Your new shoes are really cool!*
• impressive, fashionable, chic, smart
(*informal*) trendy

cool VERB
Cool the mixture in the fridge overnight.
• chill, refrigerate, freeze
OPPOSITES warm, heat up

cooperate VERB
➤ cooperate with
Local people refused to cooperate with the authorities.
• work with, collaborate with, aid, assist, support, be of service to
IDIOM (*informal*) play ball with

cooperation NOUN
The game was developed with the cooperation of NASA.
• collaboration, assistance, participation, teamwork

cooperative ADJECTIVE
I found him surprisingly cooperative.
• supportive, helpful, obliging, accommodating, willing
OPPOSITE uncooperative

cope VERB
Shall I help you or can you cope on your own?
• manage, carry on, get by, make do, survive

➤ **cope with**
I can't cope with all this homework!
• deal with, handle, manage, tackle, face
IDIOM get to grips with

copy NOUN
That isn't the original painting–it's a copy.
• replica, reproduction, duplicate, imitation, likeness
– A copy made to deceive someone is a **fake**, **forgery** or **counterfeit**.
– A living organism which is identical to another is a **clone**.

copy VERB
❶ *I copied the message into my notebook.*
• duplicate, reproduce, replicate
– To copy something in order to deceive is to **fake**, **forge** or **counterfeit** it.
❷ *Lots of bands tried to copy the Beatles.*
• imitate, mimic, impersonate, emulate

cord NOUN
He pulled the cord to open his parachute.
• string, rope, cable, thread, twine, flex

core NOUN
❶ *It is extremely hot at the Earth's core.*
• centre, interior, middle, heart, nucleus
❷ *This is the core of the problem.*
• essence, heart, basis, nub, crux
(*informal*) nitty-gritty

corn NOUN
The farmer was growing corn in the field.
• grain, cereal, cereal crop, wheat

corner NOUN
❶ *I'll meet you at the corner of the road.*
• turn, turning, bend, curve, junction, intersection
– The place where two lines meet is an **angle**.
❷ *I sat in a quiet corner and read her letter.*
• alcove, recess, nook

corny ADJECTIVE
What a corny joke!
• overused, clichéd, stale, banal, trite, hackneyed, feeble

corpse NOUN
Police found the corpse under the floorboards.
• dead body, body, remains, carcass
(*formal*) cadaver

correct ADJECTIVE
❶ *Your answers are all correct.*
• right, accurate, true, exact, precise, faultless, perfect
❷ *What is the correct way to address this letter?*
• proper, right, acceptable, accepted, regular, appropriate, suitable

correct VERB
❶ *She quickly corrected a couple of spelling mistakes.*
• rectify, amend, put right, remedy, repair, fix, sort
❷ *Most of the teachers were busy correcting exam papers.*
• mark

correspond VERB
➤ **correspond to**
Each symbol corresponds to a sound.
• equate to, relate to, be equivalent to, match
➤ **correspond with**
❶ *The paint doesn't correspond with the colour on the tin.*
• agree with, match, be similar to, be consistent with, tally with
❷ *I correspond regularly with a friend in Paris.*
• write to, communicate with, send letters to

corrode VERB
This acid will corrode metal.
• eat away, erode, rot, rust

corrupt ADJECTIVE
Corrupt officials had accepted millions of pounds in bribes.
• dishonest, criminal, unethical, unscrupulous, untrustworthy

(*informal*) bent, crooked
OPPOSITES honest, ethical

cost NOUN
❶ *The bill shows the total cost.*
• price, charge, payment, fee, amount, figure, tariff, fare, toll, levy, outlay, expense, expenditure, spend
(*humorous*) damage
❷ *The cost in human lives was too great.*
• loss, sacrifice, toll, penalty, damage

cost VERB
How much did your camera cost?
• sell for, go for, come to, amount to
(*informal*) set you back

costly ADJECTIVE
Buying new furniture may prove too costly.
• dear, expensive, high-cost
(*informal*) pricey
OPPOSITE cheap

costume NOUN
The guards wear the Greek national costume.
• outfit, dress, clothing, suit, attire, garment, garb
(*informal*) get-up
– A costume you dress up in for a party is fancy dress.
– An official set of clothes worn for school or work is a uniform.

cosy ADJECTIVE
They lived in a cosy little house.
• snug, comfortable, warm
(*informal*) comfy
OPPOSITE uncomfortable

couch NOUN
The cat sat next to me on the couch.
• settee, sofa

council NOUN
They are both members of the school council.
• committee, board, panel

counsel VERB
His advisors counselled him to surrender.
• advise, guide, direct, recommend, urge, warn, caution

count VERB
❶ *I am counting the days until the end of term.*
• add up, calculate, compute, estimate, reckon, figure out, work out, total
❷ *It's playing well that counts, not winning.*
• matter, be important, be significant, carry weight
❸ *I would count it an honour to be asked.*
• regard, consider, judge, deem, rate
➤ count on
You can count on my support.
• depend on, rely on, trust, bank on, be sure of

countless ADJECTIVE
He has appeared in countless TV programmes.
• innumerable, numerous, numberless, untold
OPPOSITE finite

country NOUN
❶ *England and Wales are separate countries.*
• nation, state, land, territory
– A country ruled by a king or queen is a kingdom, monarchy or realm.
– A country governed by leaders elected by the people is a democracy.
– A democratic country with a president is a republic.
❷ *They bought a house in the country.*
• countryside, provinces, outdoors
(*informal*) the sticks
– A word meaning 'to do with the country' is rural and its opposite is urban.
OPPOSITES town, city
❸ *You drive through lovely open country.*
• terrain, countryside, territory, landscape, environment, scenery, surroundings

a b c d e f g h i j k l m n o p q r s t u v w x y z

coupon NOUN
You can exchange this coupon for a free sandwich.
• voucher, token, ticket

courage NOUN
He showed great courage and determination.
• bravery, valour, fearlessness, boldness, daring, audacity, heroism, gallantry, nerve, pluck, grit
(informal) guts
OPPOSITE cowardice

courageous ADJECTIVE
It was a courageous decision.
• brave, valiant, fearless, bold, daring, audacious, heroic, gallant, intrepid, plucky
OPPOSITE cowardly

course NOUN
❶ The spacecraft could drift off its course.
• route, path, track, way, trajectory, bearing, direction
❷ The best course is to wait and watch.
• plan of action, procedure, approach, strategy
❸ Some changes have been made to the geography course.
• syllabus, programme, curriculum
➤ of course
Of course you can come to my party.
• naturally, certainly, definitely, undoubtedly, needless to say, it goes without saying

courteous ADJECTIVE
I received a courteous reply to my letter.
• polite, respectful, well-mannered, civil, gracious, considerate
OPPOSITES rude, impolite

cover VERB
❶ Cover the chicken with foil.
• envelop, enclose, protect, overlay
❷ A rug covered the hole in the carpet.
• conceal, obscure, disguise, hide, mask, blot out
❸ Wear goggles to cover your eyes.
• shield, screen, protect, shade, veil

❹ My new shoes were covered with mud.
• cake, coat, plaster, encrust
❺ The book covers all aspects of photography.
• deal with, include, incorporate, take in, embrace
❻ The cyclists will cover 150 km over two days.
• progress, travel

cover NOUN
❶ Leave the cover of the jar loose.
• lid, top, cap
❷ The cover of the book was torn.
• wrapper, binding, jacket, envelope
❸ On the bare hillside, there was no cover from the storm.
• shelter, protection, shield, refuge, sanctuary

covering NOUN
There was a light covering of snow on the hills.
• coating, coat, layer, blanket, carpet, film, veneer, skin, sheet, veil, shroud

cowardly ADJECTIVE
They made a cowardly retreat.
• faint-hearted, spineless, lily-livered, craven, timid, fearful
(informal) gutless, yellow, chicken
OPPOSITES brave, courageous

cower VERB
A tiny creature was cowering in the corner.
• cringe, shrink, crouch, flinch, quail

crack NOUN
❶ There's a crack in this cup.
• break, chip, fracture, flaw, chink, split
❷ She peered through a crack in the rock.
• gap, space, opening, crevice, fissure, rift, cleft, cranny
❸ I heard the crack of a pistol shot.
• bang, explosion, report, pop
❹ In the scuffle I got a crack on the head.
• blow, knock, hit, bash, bang, thump, smack
(informal) whack, wallop, clout

crack VERB

❶ *I dropped the vase and cracked it.*
• break, fracture, chip, split, rupture, shatter, splinter
❷ *He was beginning to crack under the strain.*
• break down, lose control
(*informal*) lose it
IDIOM go to pieces
❸ (*informal*) *The code proved difficult to crack.*
• decipher, decode, interpret, solve, break

craft NOUN

❶ *I'd like to learn the craft of weaving.*
• art, skill, technique, expertise, handicraft
– A person who is skilled in a particular craft is a **craftsman** or **craftswoman**.
For terms used in art, craft and design see **art**.
❷ *All sorts of craft were in the harbour.*
• vessels, boats, ships

crafty ADJECTIVE

We came up with a crafty plan.
• cunning, shrewd, canny, artful, devious, sly, tricky, wily, scheming

cram VERB

❶ *I managed to cram all my clothes into one bag.*
• stuff, pack, squeeze, squash, force, jam, thrust, push, shove, compress, crush
❷ *We all crammed into the back of the car.*
• crowd, push, pile, squeeze, squash
❸ *My sister is cramming for an exam.*
• revise, study
(*informal*) swot

cramped ADJECTIVE

The seating on the plane was cramped.
• confined, restricted, tight, narrow, uncomfortable, crowded
(*informal*) poky
OPPOSITE roomy

crash NOUN

❶ *There was a loud crash from the kitchen.*
• bang, clash, clatter, racket
– A crash of thunder is a **peal**.
For tips on describing sound see **sound**.
❷ *We saw a nasty crash on the motorway.*
• collision, accident, smash, bump
– A crash involving a lot of vehicles is a **pile-up**.
– A train crash may involve a **derailment**.

crash VERB

❶ *Their car crashed into the back of a lorry.*
• bump, smash, collide, knock, plough
❷ *The satellite may crash to Earth soon.*
• fall, drop, plunge, plummet, dive, tumble

crate NOUN

We packed all our belongings into crates.
• box, case, chest, packing case, container

crater NOUN

The surface of the Moon is full of craters.
• pit, hollow, hole, dip, depression, bowl, basin, cavity

craving NOUN

I often have a craving for chocolate.
• desire, longing, yearning, hankering, hunger, appetite, thirst

crawl VERB

I watched a caterpillar crawling along a leaf.
• creep, edge, inch, slither, wriggle

craze NOUN

These shoes are the latest craze in footwear.
• fad, trend, vogue, fashion, obsession, mania, rage
(*informal*) thing

crazy ADJECTIVE

❶ *It's enough to drive you crazy!*
• mad, insane, demented, deranged, unbalanced, hysterical, frantic, frenzied, wild, berserk

a b c d e f g h i j k l m n o p q r s t u v w x y z

(*informal*) nuts, bonkers, loopy, crackers
IDIOMS (*informal*) off your head, round
the bend, round the twist
OPPOSITE sane
❷ *Everyone told me it was a crazy idea.*
• absurd, ridiculous, ludicrous, idiotic,
senseless, silly, stupid, foolhardy,
preposterous, hare-brained, half-baked
(*informal*) crackpot, cockeyed, wacky,
zany, daft, barmy
OPPOSITE sensible
❸ (*informal*) *She is crazy about
football.*
• fanatical, enthusiastic, passionate,
fervent, wild
(*informal*) mad, nuts

creamy ADJECTIVE
That ice cream is really creamy.
• rich, smooth, thick, velvety

crease NOUN
*Can you iron the creases out of this
shirt?*
• wrinkle, crinkle, pucker, fold, furrow,
line, ridge, groove
– A crease made deliberately in a
garment is a **pleat**.

crease VERB
Try not to crease the paper.
• wrinkle, crinkle, crumple, crush,
pucker, scrunch up

create VERB
❶ *You have created a beautiful work of
art there.*
• make, produce, generate, originate,
fashion, build, construct, compose,
devise, design
OPPOSITE destroy
❷ *We have created a website for our
chess club.*
• establish, set up, start up, launch,
institute, initiate, found
OPPOSITE abolish
❸ *The bad weather created huge
problems for us.*
• cause, bring about, lead to, produce,
give rise to, prompt

creation NOUN
❶ *The TV series is about the creation of
life on earth.*
• beginning, origin, birth, generation,
initiation
❷ *They raised money for the creation of
a sports centre.*
• establishment, foundation, institution,
setting up, construction
❸ *This pasta sauce is my own creation.*
• work, invention, concoction, concept
(*informal*) brainchild

creative ADJECTIVE
He is a writer with a very creative mind.
• imaginative, inventive, innovative,
original, experimental, artistic, inspired
OPPOSITE unimaginative

creator NOUN
*Walt Disney was the creator of Mickey
Mouse.*
• inventor, maker, originator, producer,
designer, deviser, author, architect

creature NOUN
*A hideous creature emerged from the
swamp.*
• animal, beast, being, brute
For mythological creatures see **fantasy**.

credible ADJECTIVE
Did you find the plot credible?
• believable, plausible, conceivable,
likely, possible, probable, reasonable,
persuasive, convincing
OPPOSITES incredible, implausible

credit NOUN
*She is finally getting the credit she
deserves.*
• recognition, honour, praise,
distinction, fame, glory, reputation
OPPOSITE dishonour

credit VERB
❶ *It's hard to credit that they are
brother and sister.*
• believe, accept, have faith in, give
credence to, trust
(*informal*) swallow, buy
OPPOSITE doubt

❷ *Edison is credited with inventing the light bulb.*
• recognize, attribute, identify

creed NOUN
Pupils of all races and creeds attend the school.
• faith, religion, belief, ideology, principle

creep VERB
❶ *The snail crept halfway out of its shell.*
• crawl, edge, inch, slither, wriggle
❷ *I crept out of bed without waking the others.*
• tiptoe, sneak, slip, slink, steal

creepy (*informal*) ADJECTIVE
The graveyard was creepy at night.
• frightening, eerie, ghostly, sinister, uncanny, unearthly, weird
(*informal*) spooky, scary

crest NOUN
❶ *The bird had a large red crest on its head.*
• comb, crown, plume, tuft
❷ *There was a wonderful view from the crest of the hill.*
• summit, top, peak, crown, ridge, head, brow
❸ *On the wall was a carving of the family crest.*
• emblem, insignia, coat of arms, regalia, badge

crevice NOUN
Moss was growing in the crevices in the rock.
• crack, split, gap, fissure, rift, cleft, chink, cranny
– A deep crack in a glacier is a **crevasse**.

crew NOUN
❶ *None of the passengers or crew were injured.*
• company, corps, squad, hands
❷ *A film crew was setting up outside.*
• team, unit, party, band, gang

cricket NOUN

WORD WEB

Terms used in cricket:
➤ bails	➤ LBW
➤ batsman	➤ leg spin
➤ batting average	➤ maiden over
➤ boundary	➤ not out
➤ bowler	➤ over
➤ century	➤ run
➤ crease	➤ six
➤ cricketer	➤ spin bowler
➤ declaration	➤ stump
➤ dismissal	➤ test match
➤ duck	➤ umpire
➤ fielder	➤ wicket
➤ googly	➤ wicketkeeper
➤ innings	

crime NOUN
❶ *Blackmail is a serious crime.*
• offence, misdemeanour, felony
❷ *Police have announced a crackdown on petty crime.*
• lawbreaking, wrongdoing, criminality, illegality

WRITING TIPS

WRITING CRIME FICTION
Characters:
➤ criminologist	➤ pathologist
➤ detective	➤ police officer
➤ forensic scientist	➤ private detective
	➤ private eye
➤ master criminal	➤ sleuth
➤ murderer	➤ toxicologist

Useful words and phrases:
➤ accessory	➤ corroborate
➤ accomplice	➤ crime scene
➤ alibi	➤ cross-examine
➤ bloodstain	➤ CSI
➤ case history	➤ deduction
➤ circumstantial evidence	➤ DNA sample
➤ clue	➤ dusting for fingerprints
➤ confession	➤ evidence

> examination
> expert witness
> false identity
> fingerprint analysis
> forensics
> forgery
> homicide
> hunch
> hypothesis
> incriminate
> in custody
> inquiry
> investigation
> lead
> line of enquiry
> manhunt
> morgue
> motive
> perpetrator
> post-mortem
> prime suspect
> profiling
> proof
> reconstruction
> questioning
> sequence of events
> statement
> suspect
> testimony
> (informal) tip-off
> whodunnit
> witness
> victim

criminal NOUN

These men are dangerous criminals.
• lawbreaker, offender, felon, wrongdoer
(informal) crook
– A criminal who has been sent to prison is a **convict**.

WORD WEB

Some types of criminal:

> assassin
> bandit
> blackmailer
> burglar
> cat burglar
> (informal) con man
> cybercriminal
> forger
> gangster
> hacker
> highwayman
> hijacker
> identity thief
> kidnapper
> money launderer
> mugger
> murderer
> outlaw
> pickpocket
> pirate
> poacher
> robber
> shoplifter
> smuggler
> terrorist
> thief
> thug
> vandal

criminal ADJECTIVE

Police have uncovered a criminal network.
• illegal, unlawful, corrupt, dishonest

(informal) crooked
OPPOSITES lawful, honest, above board

cringe VERB

The eerie sound made him cringe in fear.
• shrink, flinch, wince, cower

cripple VERB

❶ The fall may have crippled the horse.
• disable, handicap, maim, lame
❷ The country was nearly crippled by war and famine.
• ruin, destroy, crush, wreck, damage, weaken, paralyse, incapacitate

crisis NOUN

The country was facing a financial crisis.
• emergency, calamity, catastrophe, disaster, predicament, meltdown

crisp ADJECTIVE

❶ These sweets have a crisp coating of chocolate.
• crunchy, crispy, brittle, hard
OPPOSITES soft, soggy
❷ It was a crisp winter morning.
• fresh, brisk, bracing, refreshing, invigorating

critic NOUN

❶ She is the newspaper's film critic.
• reviewer, commentator, columnist, analyst, pundit, expert
❷ He is a major critic of government policy.
• opponent, attacker, detractor

critical ADJECTIVE

❶ Why do you always have to be so critical?
• negative, disapproving, derogatory, uncomplimentary, unfavourable, scathing, disparaging, censorious
OPPOSITES complimentary, positive
❷ Fortunately, he ducked his head at the critical moment.
• crucial, important, vital, essential, pivotal, key, paramount, decisive
OPPOSITE unimportant
❸ The patient is in a critical condition.
• serious, grave, dangerous, precarious

criticism NOUN

❶ *The team has received a lot of criticism recently.*
• condemnation, censure, fault-finding, disparagement, disapproval, reproach
(*informal*) flak
OPPOSITE praise

❷ *He wrote many works of literary criticism.*
• analysis, evaluation, assessment, appraisal, commentary

criticize VERB

The film has been criticized for its poor script.
• condemn, find fault with, censure, attack, denigrate, disparage, reproach, berate
(*informal*) knock, pan, slam, slate
OPPOSITE praise

crockery NOUN

The top shelf was full of crockery.
• china, dishes, plates

crooked ADJECTIVE

❶ *She put a crooked finger to her lips.*
• bent, twisted, warped, contorted, misshapen, deformed, gnarled
OPPOSITE straight

❷ (*informal*) *Several crooked lawyers made money from the case.*
• criminal, dishonest, corrupt
OPPOSITE honest

crop NOUN

We had a good crop of apples this year.
• harvest, yield, produce

crop VERB

I need to crop the edges of the picture.
• cut, trim, clip, snip, shear, shave, chop
➤ **crop up**
Several problems have cropped up.
• arise, occur, appear, emerge, surface, come up, turn up, pop up
IDIOM come to light

cross VERB

❶ *Cross the road at the traffic lights.*
• go across, travel across, pass over, traverse, span
– To cross a river or stream is to **ford** it.

❷ *The two sets of footprints cross here.*
• intersect, meet, join, connect
– To form a pattern of crossing lines is to **criss-cross**.
➤ **cross out**
My name had been crossed out on the list.
• delete, score out, strike out, cancel

cross ADJECTIVE

The coach will be cross if we miss training.
• angry, annoyed, irate, upset, vexed, irked, bad-tempered, ill-tempered, irritable, grumpy, testy, surly, snappy
OPPOSITE pleased

crossroads NOUN

Turn left at the crossroads.
• intersection, junction
– A junction of two motorways is an **interchange**.

crouch VERB

I waited outside, crouching behind a bush.
• squat, stoop, duck, bend, bob down, hunch, cower

crowd NOUN

❶ *A crowd formed outside the gates.*
• gathering, assembly, throng, multitude, horde, swarm, mob, mass, crush, rabble

❷ *The show attracted a huge crowd.*
• audience, spectators, gate, attendance

crowd VERB

❶ *People crowded outside to watch the fireworks.*
• gather, collect, cluster, assemble, congregate, mass, flock, throng, muster

❷ *Hundreds of people crowded into the hall.*
• push, pile, squeeze, pack, cram, crush, jam, bundle, herd

crowded ADJECTIVE

The shops are always crowded at the weekend.
• full, packed, busy, teeming, swarming, overflowing, jammed, congested
(*informal*) chock-a-block, jam-packed
OPPOSITES empty, deserted

a b c d e f g h i j k l m n o p q r s t u v w x y z

crown NOUN

The Queen wore a crown of solid gold.
• coronet, circlet, diadem, tiara

crown VERB

❶ *Queen Victoria was crowned in 1837.*
– A ceremony at which a monarch is crowned is a **coronation**.
❷ *The mountain peaks were crowned with snow.*
• top, cap, tip, surmount
❸ *They crowned a remarkable season with yet another win.*
• round off, cap, complete

crucial ADJECTIVE

Copernicus made a crucial discovery about the universe.
• important, critical, decisive, vital, pivotal, key, momentous, all-important
OPPOSITE unimportant

crude ADJECTIVE

❶ *The refinery processes crude oil.*
• raw, natural, unprocessed, unrefined, untreated
OPPOSITES refined, treated
❷ *It was a crude carving of a horse.*
• rough, clumsy, makeshift, primitive, rudimentary, rough and ready
OPPOSITES skilful, sophisticated
❸ *He tells a lot of crude jokes.*
• rude, obscene, indecent, dirty, smutty, vulgar, coarse, lewd
OPPOSITE clean

cruel ADJECTIVE

❶ *I detest people who are cruel to animals.*
• brutal, savage, inhumane, barbaric, barbarous, heartless, ruthless, merciless, callous
OPPOSITES compassionate, humane
❷ *This was a cruel blow to all our hopes.*
• severe, harsh, bitter, painful, agonizing

cruelty NOUN

He has campaigned against cruelty to animals.
• brutality, inhumanity, heartlessness, ruthlessness, barbarity, savagery
OPPOSITES compassion, humanity

crumb NOUN

There were only a few cake crumbs on the plate.
• bit, fragment, scrap, morsel, particle

crumble VERB

❶ *The castle walls were beginning to crumble.*
• disintegrate, break up, fall apart, fall to pieces, collapse, decay, decompose
❷ *Crumble the dried leaves between your fingers.*
• crush, grind, pulverize

crumpled ADJECTIVE

Your shirt is crumpled.
• creased, wrinkled, crinkled, rumpled, crushed

crunch VERB

❶ *The dog was crunching on a bone.*
• chew, munch, chomp, grind
❷ *I could hear footsteps crunching through the snow.*
• crush, grind, pound, smash

crush VERB

❶ *I crushed my jumper into my school bag.*
• squash, squeeze, mangle, pound, press, bruise, crunch, scrunch
– To crush something into a soft mess is to **mash** or **pulp** it.
– To crush something into a powder is to **grind** or **pulverize** it.
– To crush something out of shape is to **crumple** or **smash** it.
❷ *The army soon crushed the rebellion.*
• defeat, conquer, vanquish, overcome, overwhelm, quash, trounce, rout

crush NOUN

There was a crush of people at the front gates.
• crowd, throng, mob, press, jam, congestion

crust NOUN

The liquid rock cooled to form a crust.
• skin, shell, coating, film, exterior
– A crust that forms over a cut or graze is a **scab**.

crustacean NOUN

WORD WEB

Some animals which are crustaceans:

➤ barnacle   ➤ prawn
➤ crab   ➤ sea slater
➤ crayfish   ➤ shrimp
➤ langoustine   ➤ woodlouse
➤ lobster

cry NOUN
Someone let out a cry of pain.
• call, shout, yell, roar, howl,
exclamation, bellow, scream, screech,
shriek, yelp

cry VERB
❶ She looked like she was going to cry.
• weep, sob, shed tears, wail, whimper,
snivel
(informal) blubber
– When someone starts to cry, their eyes
well up with tears.
❷ We heard someone crying for help.
• call, shout, yell, exclaim, roar, bawl,
bellow, scream, screech, shriek
(informal) holler

cuddle VERB
My little brother cuddles a teddy bear
in bed.
• hug, clasp, embrace, caress, fondle,
nestle against, snuggle against

cue NOUN
When I nod, that is your cue to speak.
• signal, sign, prompt, reminder

culminate VERB
➤ culminate in
The film culminates in a tense
shoot-out.
• finish with, conclude with, close with,
build up to, lead up to

culprit NOUN
Police are still searching for the
culprits.
• offender, wrongdoer, criminal,
felon

cultivate VERB
❶ Farmers have cultivated this land for
centuries.
• farm, work, till, plough, grow crops on
❷ We need to cultivate good training
habits.
• develop, encourage, promote, further,
foster, nurture

cultural ADJECTIVE
The city has a rich cultural life.
• artistic, intellectual, aesthetic, creative

culture NOUN
❶ She is a woman of culture.
• refinement, taste, sophistication
❷ He is an expert on the culture of
ancient Greece.
• civilization, society, traditions,
customs, heritage

cunning ADJECTIVE
❶ He was as cunning a criminal as you'll
ever meet.
• crafty, devious, artful, scheming, sly,
tricky, wily, sneaky
❷ I came up with a cunning plan.
• clever, shrewd, ingenious, inventive,
creative, inspired, brilliant

cup NOUN
He handed me a cup and saucer.
– A tall cup with straight sides is a **mug**.
– A tall cup without a handle is a **beaker**
or **tumbler**.
– A decorative drinking cup is a **goblet**
or **chalice**.

cupboard NOUN
There are some spare pillows in the
cupboard.
• cabinet, dresser, sideboard
– A cupboard for food is a **larder**.

curb VERB
I tried hard to curb my anger.
• control, restrain, hold back, suppress,
contain, check, limit, restrict, rein in,
keep in check
IDIOM keep a lid on

a
b
c
d
e
f
g
h
i
j
k
l
m
n
o
p
q
r
s
t
u
v
w
x
y
z

cure VERB

❶ *A good night's rest will cure your headache.*
• heal, ease, improve, make better, relieve

OPPOSITE aggravate

❷ *He finally cured the rattling noise in his car.*
• remedy, put right, sort, solve, repair, mend, fix, put an end to, eliminate

cure NOUN

Scientists continue to search for a cure for cancer.
• remedy, treatment, antidote, therapy, medicine, medication
– A cure for all kinds of diseases or troubles is a **panacea**.

curiosity NOUN

Babies are full of curiosity about the world.
• inquisitiveness, interest
– Uncomplimentary words are **nosiness**, **prying** and **snooping**.

curious ADJECTIVE

❶ *We were all curious about the visitors.*
• intrigued, interested (in), agog, inquisitive
– An uncomplimentary word is **nosy**.

OPPOSITES uninterested (in), indifferent (to)

❷ *What is that curious smell?*
• odd, strange, peculiar, abnormal, unusual, extraordinary, funny, mysterious, puzzling, weird, bizarre

curl NOUN

❶ *Her hair was a mass of golden curls.*
• wave, ringlet, lock

❷ *A curl of smoke rose up from the fire.*
• coil, twist, scroll, spiral, swirl

curl VERB

❶ *The snake curled itself around a branch.*
• wind, twist, loop, coil, wrap, twine

❷ *Smoke curled upwards from the chimney.*
• coil, spiral, twirl, swirl, furl, snake, writhe, ripple

curly ADJECTIVE

The boy had curly black hair.
• wavy, curled, curling, frizzy, crinkly, ringleted

OPPOSITE straight

current ADJECTIVE

❶ *The shop sells all the current teenage fashions.*
• modern, contemporary, present-day, up to date, topical, prevailing, prevalent

OPPOSITES past, old-fashioned

❷ *Have you got a current passport?*
• valid, usable, up to date

OPPOSITE out of date

❸ *Who is the current prime minister?*
• present, existing, incumbent, reigning

OPPOSITES past, former

current NOUN

The raft was drifting along with the current.
• flow, tide, stream
– A current of air is a **draught**.

curse NOUN

❶ *According to legend, there is a curse on the family.*
• jinx, hex

❷ *I could hear him muttering curses.*
• swear word, oath, expletive, profanity

cursed ADJECTIVE

It seemed to me that our voyage was cursed.
• doomed, damned, jinxed, ill-fated, ill-starred

curt ADJECTIVE

I received a very curt reply.
• abrupt, terse, blunt, brusque, short

curve NOUN

He looked out on the gentle curve of the bay.
• bend, turn, loop, arch, arc, bow, bulge
– A curve in the shape of a new moon is a **crescent**.
– A curve on a road surface is a **camber**.

curve VERB

The road ahead curves round to the right.
• bend, turn, wind, loop, curl, arc, arch, swerve, veer, snake, meander

curved ADJECTIVE

The wall was painted with a pattern of curved lines.
• curving, curvy, bent, looped, arched, bowed, bulging, winding, meandering, serpentine, undulating
– A surface curved like the inside of a circle is **concave** and one curved like the outside of a circle is **convex**.

cushion VERB

The mat will cushion your fall.
• soften, reduce the effect of, lessen, alleviate, absorb, deaden, dampen, muffle

custody NOUN

> in custody
Two men are being held in custody.
• in jail, in prison
(informal) inside
IDIOMS under lock and key, behind bars

custom NOUN

❶ *When did the custom of giving presents at Christmas begin?*
• tradition, practice, convention, habit, routine, observance, ritual
❷ *We need to attract more custom.*
• customers, buyers, clients, trade, business

customary ADJECTIVE

It is customary to leave the waiter a tip.
• traditional, conventional, usual, normal, common, typical, expected, habitual, routine, regular, everyday, ordinary, prevailing, prevalent
OPPOSITE unusual

customer NOUN

There was a queue of angry customers.
• buyer, shopper, client, purchaser, consumer

cut VERB

❶ *Cut the vegetables into chunks.*
• chop, slice, carve, split, slit, sever, cleave
– To cut food into cubes is to **dice** it.
– To cut something up to examine it is to **dissect** it.
– To cut down a tree is to **fell** it.
❷ *A name had been cut into the stone.*
• carve, score, incise, engrave, notch, chisel, chip
❸ *You've had your hair cut!*
• trim, clip, crop, snip, shave
– To cut grass is to **mow** it.
– To cut twigs off a growing plant is to **prune** it.
– To cut wool off a sheep is to **shear** it.
– To cut corn is to **harvest** or **reap** it.
❹ *He fell and cut his knee.*
• gash, slash, wound, lacerate, scratch, graze, nick
❺ *I had to cut my essay to make it fit the page.*
• shorten, condense, edit, abbreviate, abridge
❻ *We are cutting our prices by 10%.*
• lower, reduce, decrease, drop, slash
– If you cut something by half, you **halve** it.
> cut something off
❶ *Help me cut off the lower branches.*
• chop off, lop, sever
– To cut off a limb is to **amputate** it.
❷ *They threatened to cut off the electricity.*
• discontinue, disconnect, shut off, suspend

cut NOUN

❶ *Make a small cut in the fabric.*
• slash, slit, incision, snip, nick, gash
❷ *I got a nasty cut on my forehead.*
• gash, wound, injury, scratch, graze, laceration
❸ *There has been a cut in the price of fuel.*
• fall, reduction, decrease, lowering, drop

cutlery NOUN

WORD WEB

Some items of cutlery:

- bread knife
- butter knife
- carving knife
- cheese knife
- chopsticks
- dessert spoon
- fish knife
- fork
- knife
- ladle
- spoon
- steak knife
- tablespoon
- teaspoon

cutting ADJECTIVE

He made a cutting remark about my tie.
• hurtful, wounding, scathing, biting, caustic, barbed

cycle NOUN

This ancient myth is about the cycle of the seasons.
• round, circle, rotation, succession, sequence, pattern

Dd

dab *NOUN*
a little dab of glue
• spot, drop, bit, blob, daub, dollop

dab *VERB*
She dabbed her eyes with a handkerchief.
• pat, touch, press, wipe, daub

daily *ADJECTIVE*
a daily exercise routine
• everyday, day-to-day, regular

daily *ADVERB*
The rooms are cleaned daily.
• every day, each day, once a day

dainty *ADJECTIVE*
a dainty little ribbon
• delicate, neat, charming, elegant, fine,
exquisite, bijou
(*informal*) cute, dinky
OPPOSITE clumsy

dam *NOUN*
a dam built by beavers
• barrage, barrier, embankment, dyke,
weir

damage *NOUN*
The floods caused a lot of damage.
• harm, destruction, devastation, injury,
ruin

damage *VERB*
Many paintings were damaged in the
fire.
• harm, spoil, mar, break, impair,
weaken, disfigure, deface, mutilate, scar
– To damage something beyond repair is
to **destroy**, **ruin** or **wreck** it.
– To damage something deliberately is to
sabotage or **vandalize** it.

damp *ADJECTIVE*
❶ These clothes are still damp.
• moist, dank, soggy, clammy
OPPOSITE dry
❷ It was a cold and damp morning.
• drizzly, foggy, misty, rainy, wet

– Weather which is both damp and warm
is **humid** or **muggy**.

dampen *VERB*
❶ Dampen the cloth with a little water.
• moisten, wet
❷ Nothing could dampen my
enthusiasm.
• lessen, decrease, diminish, reduce,
stifle, suppress

dance *VERB*
I could have danced for joy.
• caper, cavort, skip, prance, gambol,
leap, hop, whirl, twirl, gyrate, pirouette

dance *NOUN*

WORD WEB

Some kinds of dance or dancing:

➤ ballet	➤ jive dancing
➤ ballroom dancing	➤ limbo dancing
	➤ line dancing
➤ barn dance	➤ mazurka
➤ belly dancing	➤ morris dance
➤ bolero	➤ quadrille
➤ breakdancing	➤ reel
➤ cancan	➤ rumba
➤ disco	➤ samba
➤ flamenco	➤ Scottish country dancing
➤ folk dance	
➤ Highland dancing	➤ square dance
	➤ step dancing
➤ hornpipe	➤ street dance
➤ jazz dance	➤ tap dancing
➤ jig	➤ tarantella

Some ballroom dances:

➤ foxtrot	➤ quickstep
➤ minuet	➤ tango
➤ polka	➤ waltz

– A person who writes the steps for a
dance is a **choreographer**.

danger *NOUN*
❶ Is the crew in any danger?
• peril, jeopardy, menace, threat,
trouble, crisis
OPPOSITE safety

a
b
c
d
e
f
g
h
i
j
k
l
m
n
o
p
q
r
s
t
u
v
w
x
y
z

❷ *The article explains the dangers of sunbathing.*
• risk, hazard, problem, pitfall, trap
❸ *There is a danger that the volcano may erupt.*
• chance, possibility, risk

dangerous ADJECTIVE
❶ *Finding and removing landmines is dangerous work.*
• hazardous, perilous, risky, unsafe, precarious, treacherous
(*informal*) hairy, dicey
❷ *She was arrested for dangerous driving.*
• careless, reckless
❸ *It is a highly dangerous chemical.*
• harmful, destructive, poisonous, deadly, toxic
OPPOSITES harmless, safe

dangle VERB
There was a bunch of keys dangling from the chain.
• hang, swing, sway, wave, droop, flap, trail

dare VERB
❶ *Who dares to enter the Mummy's Tomb?*
• have the courage, be brave enough, have the nerve, venture
❷ *My friends dared me to ring the doorbell.*
• challenge, defy, provoke, goad

daring ADJECTIVE
He began to plan a daring escape.
• bold, brave, courageous, audacious, fearless, valiant, intrepid, plucky
(*informal*) gutsy
– A daring person is a **daredevil**.
OPPOSITES timid, cowardly

dark ADJECTIVE
❶ *It was a dark winter night.*
• black, murky, dim, gloomy, dingy, inky, shadowy
OPPOSITE bright
❷ *He wore a dark blue coat.*
OPPOSITES pale, light

❸ *She has long dark hair.*
• black, brunette, raven, ebony
(*literary*) sable
OPPOSITE fair
❹ *It was a dark period of my life.*
• bleak, unhappy, miserable, grim, gloomy, dismal, negative
OPPOSITE happy
❺ *This peaceful island holds a dark secret.*
• mysterious, sinister, ominous, disturbing

dark NOUN
❶ *I can't see you in the dark.*
• darkness, blackout, gloom
OPPOSITES light, brightness
❷ *No one was allowed out after dark.*
• nightfall, night-time
OPPOSITES daytime, daybreak

darken VERB
Suddenly, the sky darkened.
• grow dark, become overcast, blacken, cloud over
OPPOSITES brighten, lighten

dart VERB
A rabbit darted out of the bushes.
• run, dash, race, sprint, speed, rush, tear, pelt, scurry, scamper

dash VERB
❶ *We dashed home as soon as we could.*
• hurry, run, rush, race, hasten, speed, sprint, tear, fly, zoom
❷ *She dashed her cup against the wall.*
• throw, hurl, fling, toss, smash
(*informal*) sling, chuck
❸ *Injury dashed his hopes of winning a medal.*
• destroy, wreck, ruin, shatter, scotch
(*informal*) scupper
IDIOM put paid to

dash NOUN
❶ *We made a dash for shelter.*
• run, rush, race, sprint, bolt, charge
❷ *Add a dash of milk.*
• drop, splash, spot, swig, dribble, drizzle

data NOUN
I entered all the data into the computer.
• information, details, facts, figures, statistics

date NOUN
When is your lunch date?
• meeting, appointment, engagement

date VERB
❶ *Some films never seem to date.*
• age, become dated, show its age
❷ *(informal) Is she dating someone just now?*
• go out with, see, be involved with

dated ADJECTIVE
The special effects look dated now.
• old-fashioned, outdated, outmoded, antiquated, behind the times
(informal) old hat
IDIOM out of the ark
OPPOSITES modern, cutting-edge

daunting ADJECTIVE
An audition can be a daunting prospect.
• formidable, challenging, forbidding, unnerving, discouraging, off-putting

dawdle VERB
Don't dawdle—we haven't got all day!
• linger, dally, drag your feet, delay, lag behind, straggle
(informal) dilly-dally
OPPOSITE hurry

dawn NOUN
❶ *We were woken at dawn by birdsong.*
• daybreak, sunrise, first light
OPPOSITES dusk, sunset
❷ *It was the dawn of a new era.*
• beginning, start, birth, origin, genesis, onset, rise

dawn VERB
A new era in medicine is dawning.
• begin, start, emerge, arise, develop, unfold
OPPOSITE end
➤ **dawn on someone**
The truth was beginning to dawn on me.
• become clear to, occur to, register with, strike, hit

day NOUN
❶ *Badgers sleep during the day.*
• daytime, daylight
OPPOSITES night, night-time
❷ *Things were different in my grandfather's day.*
• age, era, time, period, epoch

daze VERB
She was dazed by the news.
• stun, shock, stupefy, stagger, bewilder, perplex, take aback

dazzle VERB
❶ *My eyes were dazzled by the light.*
• blind, daze
❷ *She dazzled the audience with her performance.*
• amaze, astonish, stun, impress, overwhelm, awe
(informal) bowl over, blow away, knock out

dead ADJECTIVE
❶ *Both her parents were dead.*
• deceased, departed, lifeless
– You can describe a person who is recently dead as **the late**. *a tribute to the late actor*
– A dead body is a **corpse**.
– The dead body of an animal is a **carcass**.
OPPOSITES alive, living
❷ *The town centre is dead at this time of night.*
• quiet, dull, boring, lifeless, sleepy, flat, slow
OPPOSITES lively, animated
❸ *Suddenly the phone went dead.*
• not working, broken, inoperative, defective, worn out
– A battery which is dead is **flat**.
❹ *Latin is a dead language.*
• extinct, obsolete, defunct, disused
OPPOSITE living

deaden VERB
❶ *The doctor gave me an injection to deaden the pain.*
• anaesthetize, lessen, reduce, suppress
OPPOSITE increase

❷ *Double glazing deadens the noise of traffic.*
• dampen, muffle, quieten
OPPOSITE amplify

deadly ADJECTIVE
❶ *the deadly sting of a scorpion*
• lethal, fatal, mortal, life-threatening
OPPOSITE harmless
❷ *A deadly hush descended on the room.*
• complete, total, absolute, utter

deafening ADJECTIVE
There was a deafening roar from the crowd.
• loud, blaring, booming, thunderous, ear-splitting, penetrating

deal VERB
❶ *Who is going to deal the cards?*
• give out, distribute, share out, hand out, pass round, dispense
❷ *He deals in scrap metal.*
• do business, trade
➤ **deal with something**
❶ *I'll deal with the washing-up.*
• cope with, sort out, attend to, see to, handle, manage, look after, take charge of, take in hand
❷ *This chapter deals with whales and dolphins.*
• be concerned with, cover, discuss, explore, examine

deal NOUN
This year she signed a deal with a record company.
• agreement, contract, bargain, settlement, arrangement
➤ **a good deal** or **a great deal**
It is a good deal colder than last year.
• a lot, considerably, markedly, substantially

dear ADJECTIVE
❶ *She is a very dear friend of mine.*
• close, loved, beloved, valued, cherished, treasured
OPPOSITE distant
❷ *Their shoes are far too dear for me.*
• expensive, costly, high-priced, exorbitant

(*informal*) **pricey**
OPPOSITE cheap

death NOUN
❶ *He vowed to avenge the death of his friend.*
• dying, end, passing, decease
– A death caused by an accident or war is a **fatality**.
❷ *The news meant the death of all their dreams.*
• end, extinction, destruction

debate NOUN
We had a debate about animal rights.
• discussion, argument, dispute
– Something which people argue about a lot is a **controversy**.

debate VERB
❶ *We debated whether it is right to kill animals for food.*
• discuss, argue about, talk through, thrash out
❷ *I was debating whether to go or not.*
• consider, ponder, deliberate, weigh up, reflect on, mull over

debris NOUN
Debris from the shipwreck was scattered over a large area.
• remains, wreckage, fragments, flotsam and jetsam

decay VERB
❶ *Dead leaves fall to the ground and decay.*
• decompose, rot, disintegrate, putrefy, spoil, perish
❷ *Ancient Greek civilization eventually decayed.*
• decline, deteriorate, degenerate
IDIOM go downhill

deceit NOUN
I saw through his lies and deceit.
• deception, trickery, dishonesty, fraud, duplicity, double-dealing, pretence, bluff, cheating, deceitfulness, lying
OPPOSITE honesty

deceitful ADJECTIVE
Foxes are often portrayed as deceitful in stories.
• dishonest, underhand, insincere, duplicitous, untruthful, false, cheating, hypocritical, lying, treacherous, two-faced, sneaky
OPPOSITE honest

deceive VERB
She had been deceiving all of us for years.
• fool, trick, delude, dupe, hoodwink, cheat, double-cross, mislead, swindle *(informal)* con, take in
IDIOMS pull the wool over your eyes, take you for a ride

decent ADJECTIVE
❶ *I did the decent thing and owned up.*
• honourable, honest, proper
❷ *Mum didn't think my dress was decent.*
• proper, appropriate, respectable, modest, seemly
OPPOSITES indecent, improper
❸ *I haven't had a decent night's sleep for ages.*
• satisfactory, adequate, sufficient, reasonable, tolerable, acceptable, fair
OPPOSITE inadequate

deception NOUN
see deceit

deceptive ADJECTIVE
The blurb on the back of the book is deceptive.
• misleading, unreliable, false

decide VERB
❶ *Have you decided what to wear yet?*
• choose, make a decision, make up your mind, opt, elect, resolve
❷ *The umpire decided that the ball was in play.*
• conclude, judge, rule, adjudicate
❸ *There will be a play-off to decide the medals.*
• determine, settle

decision NOUN
We are waiting for the judges' decision.
• judgement, verdict, ruling, conclusion, findings

decisive ADJECTIVE
❶ *The knife was a decisive piece of evidence.*
• conclusive, deciding, irrefutable, critical, key
❷ *A referee needs to be decisive.*
• firm, forceful, strong-minded, resolute
OPPOSITES indecisive, hesitant

declare VERB
❶ *She declared her intention to retire next year.*
• announce, make known, state, express, reveal, voice, proclaim
❷ *He declared that he was innocent.*
• assert, affirm, profess, state, maintain, contend, insist

decline VERB
❶ *She declined his offer of help.*
• refuse, reject, rebuff, turn down, say no to, pass up
OPPOSITE accept
❷ *The band's popularity declined rapidly.*
• decrease, diminish, lessen, dwindle, wane, shrink, subside, tail off
OPPOSITE increase

decline NOUN
❶ *There has been a sharp decline in sales.*
• fall, drop, lowering, decrease, reduction, downturn, slump
❷ *The region fell into a decline after the mines closed.*
• descent, slide, fall, degeneration

decode VERB
see code

decorate VERB
❶ *We decorated the tree with tinsel.*
• adorn, ornament, beautify, prettify, deck, festoon, garnish
❷ *Here are some ideas for decorating your bedroom.*
• refurbish, renovate, paint, wallpaper *(informal)* do up, make over

a
b
c
d
e
f
g
h
i
j
k
l
m
n
o
p
q
r
s
t
u
v
w
x
y
z

❸ *Several firefighters were decorated for bravery.*
• award a medal to, honour, reward

decoration NOUN
❶ *We've been putting up the Christmas decorations.*
• ornament, bauble, garland, trinket, knick-knack
❷ *Look at the rich decoration inside the dome.*
• ornamentation, embellishment, adornment, furnishing
❸ *a decoration for bravery*
• medal, award

decorative ADJECTIVE
The book had a decorative design on the cover.
• ornamental, elaborate, fancy, ornate, colourful, attractive, pretty
OPPOSITES plain, functional

decrease VERB
❶ *Our enthusiasm decreased as the day went on.*
• decline, diminish, lessen, weaken, dwindle, flag, wane, shrink, subside, tail off
OPPOSITE increase
❷ *The jet decreased its speed.*
• reduce, cut, lower, lessen, minimize (*informal*) slash
OPPOSITE increase

decrease NOUN
There has been a decrease in the use of plastic bags.
• decline, drop, fall, cut, reduction, downturn
OPPOSITE increase

decree VERB
The king decreed that the day would be a holiday.
• order, command, declare, pronounce, proclaim, ordain

dedicate VERB
She dedicated her whole life to helping others.
• commit, devote, set aside, sacrifice

dedicated ADJECTIVE
The band have hundreds of dedicated fans.
• committed, devoted, keen, enthusiastic, faithful, staunch, firm

dedication NOUN
It requires years of dedication to master kung fu.
• commitment, devotion, application, resolve, effort

deduce VERB
From her name I deduced that she was Russian.
• conclude, work out, infer, reason, gather

deduct VERB
Points are deducted for each incorrect answer.
• subtract, take away, take off, knock off, debit
OPPOSITE add

deed NOUN
There are many stories of his heroic deeds.
• act, action, feat, exploit, effort, achievement

deep ADJECTIVE
❶ *Loch Ness is deep, dark and murky.*
– A very deep pit or lake may be described as **bottomless**.
OPPOSITE shallow
❷ *a deep feeling of unease*
• intense, strong, extreme, profound, deep-seated
OPPOSITE slight
❸ *The letter expressed his deep regret.*
• wholehearted, earnest, genuine, sincere, heartfelt
OPPOSITE superficial
❹ *She fell into a deep sleep.*
• heavy, sound, profound
OPPOSITE light
❺ *A deep voice answered the phone.*
• low, low-pitched, bass, resonant
OPPOSITE high

> **deep in**
They were deep in conversation.
• absorbed in, immersed in, preoccupied by, lost in

deer NOUN
a herd of red deer
– A male deer is a **buck, hart, roebuck** or **stag.**
– A female deer is a **doe** or **hind.**
– A young deer is a **fawn.**
– Deer's flesh used as food is **venison.**

defeat VERB
Hannibal defeated the Roman army at Cannae.
• beat, conquer, vanquish, triumph over, get the better of, overcome, overpower, crush, rout, trounce
(*informal*) lick

defeat NOUN
It's our first defeat of the season.
• conquest, loss, rout, trouncing
(*informal*) drubbing
OPPOSITE victory

defect NOUN
He will need surgery to correct a heart defect.
• fault, flaw, imperfection, deformity, shortcoming, failure, weakness
– A defect in a computer program is a **bug.**

defective ADJECTIVE
The disease is caused by a defective gene.
• faulty, flawed, imperfect, unsound, malfunctioning, damaged, out of order
OPPOSITES perfect, intact

defence NOUN
❶ *The castle was built as a defence against enemy attack.*
• protection, barricade, fortification, shield, guard, safeguard
❷ *He stood up to speak in defence of his friend.*
• support, justification, vindication, excuse, explanation, argument, case

defend VERB
❶ *We will defend ourselves against enemy attack.*
• protect, guard, fortify, shield, secure, safeguard, keep safe
OPPOSITE attack
❷ *He gave a speech defending his actions.*
• justify, vindicate, support, back, stand up for, make a case for
OPPOSITE accuse

defensive ADJECTIVE
The Roman army took up a defensive position.
• protective, defending
OPPOSITES offensive, attacking

defer VERB
We deferred our departure until the weekend.
• delay, put off, put back, postpone

defiant ADJECTIVE
The prisoner gave a defiant answer.
• rebellious, uncooperative, obstinate, mutinous, insubordinate
OPPOSITES cooperative, compliant

deficiency NOUN
a vitamin deficiency
• lack, shortage, want, inadequacy, insufficiency
OPPOSITE sufficiency

deficient ADJECTIVE
Their diet is deficient in vitamins.
• lacking (in), short (of), wanting, inadequate, insufficient, unsatisfactory
OPPOSITE sufficient

define VERB
How would you define this word?
• explain, give the meaning of, interpret, clarify

definite ADJECTIVE
❶ *Have you made a definite decision?*
• certain, sure, fixed, settled, decided
OPPOSITES uncertain, undecided
❷ *She is showing definite signs of improvement.*
• clear, distinct, noticeable, obvious,

a
b
c
d
e
f
g
h
i
j
k
l
m
n
o
p
q
r
s
t
u
v
w
x
y
z

marked, positive, pronounced, unmistakable
OPPOSITES indistinct, vague

definitely ADVERB
That is definitely the paw print of a bear.
• certainly, for certain, surely, unquestionably, undoubtedly, absolutely, positively, without doubt, without fail

definition NOUN
❶ Give a definition of the following words.
• explanation, interpretation, meaning, sense
❷ The face in the photograph lacks definition.
• clarity, focus, sharpness, resolution

deflect VERB
He deflected the blow with his shield.
• divert, turn aside, parry, avert, fend off, ward off, stave off

deft ADJECTIVE
With a few deft strokes she painted a fish.
• skilful, agile, nimble, dexterous, expert, proficient, adept
(informal) nifty
OPPOSITE clumsy

defy VERB
❶ They continued to defy the law.
• disobey, resist, flout, violate, contravene, breach, challenge
OPPOSITE obey
❷ I defy you to come up with a better idea.
• challenge, dare
❸ The door defied all efforts to open it.
• resist, withstand, defeat, prevent, frustrate

degrading ADJECTIVE
His parents thought that any kind of manual labour was degrading.
• shameful, humiliating, demeaning, undignified

degree NOUN
Playing the oboe requires a high degree of skill.
• level, standard, grade, measure, extent, amount

dejected ADJECTIVE
I felt dejected after we lost the game.
• depressed, dispirited, disheartened, downhearted, downcast, despondent, disconsolate, crestfallen, miserable, forlorn
IDIOMS (informal) down in the mouth, down in the dumps
OPPOSITES cheerful, upbeat
SEE ALSO sad

delay VERB
❶ My bus was delayed again this morning.
• detain, hold up, keep waiting, make late, hinder, slow down
❷ They had to delay the start of the race.
• postpone, put off, defer, hold over
❸ We cannot delay any longer.
• hesitate, hold back, dawdle, shilly-shally, stall, linger, loiter
(informal) dilly-dally
IDIOM drag your feet

delay NOUN
There has been an unexpected delay.
• hold-up, wait, stoppage, postponement

delete VERB
I deleted your email by mistake.
• remove, erase, cancel, cross out, strike out, cut
OPPOSITES add, insert

deliberate ADJECTIVE
❶ It was a deliberate attempt to sink the ship.
• intentional, planned, calculated, conscious, premeditated
OPPOSITES accidental, unintentional
❷ She walked slowly, taking small, deliberate steps.
• careful, steady, cautious, unhurried, measured
OPPOSITES hasty, careless

deliberately VERB
Are you ignoring me deliberately?
• on purpose, intentionally, knowingly
OPPOSITES accidentally, unintentionally

delicate ADJECTIVE
❶ *The blouse has delicate embroidery on the cuffs.*
• fine, dainty, intricate, exquisite
OPPOSITES coarse, crude
❷ *He carefully picked up one of the delicate glass ornaments.*
• fragile, frail, flimsy
OPPOSITE sturdy
❸ *Her scarf was a delicate shade of lilac.*
• subtle, soft, muted, pale, light
OPPOSITES garish, lurid
❹ *The child was born with a delicate constitution.*
• frail, weak, feeble, sickly, unhealthy, tender
OPPOSITES strong, hardy, robust
❺ *I admired his delicate handling of the situation.*
• tactful, sensitive, careful, considerate, discreet, diplomatic
OPPOSITE insensitive
❻ *This is rather a delicate issue.*
• awkward, embarrassing, tricky, ticklish
❼ *Listen to her delicate playing of the piano concerto.*
• sensitive, gentle, light, soft
OPPOSITE clumsy

delicious ADJECTIVE
This soup is delicious.
• tasty, appetizing, mouth-watering, delectable, flavoursome
(*informal*) scrumptious, yummy, moreish
OPPOSITE unappetizing
For tips on describing taste see **taste**.

delight VERB
The magic of this book never fails to delight me.
• please, charm, amuse, divert, entertain, enchant, entrance, fascinate, captivate, thrill
OPPOSITE dismay

➤ **delight in**
He delights in playing tricks on people.
• enjoy, get pleasure from, relish, savour, lap up, revel in

delight NOUN
Her eyes lit up with delight.
• happiness, joy, pleasure, enjoyment, bliss, ecstasy
OPPOSITE displeasure

delighted ADJECTIVE
My friend was delighted with her present.
• pleased, happy, glad, joyful, thrilled, ecstatic, overjoyed, elated, exultant

delightful ADJECTIVE
What a delightful surprise!
• lovely, pleasant, pleasing, enjoyable, appealing, attractive, charming

delirious ADJECTIVE
He was raving in his sleep, as if delirious.
• feverish, frenzied, frantic, deranged, mad, crazy, wild, beside yourself
OPPOSITE calm

deliver VERB
❶ *The postman delivered a parcel this morning.*
• convey, carry, transport, hand over, present, supply, distribute, dispatch, ship
❷ *She stood up to deliver her speech.*
• give, make, read out, pronounce, utter, broadcast
❸ *He raised his sword to deliver the final blow.*
• strike, deal, administer, inflict, give
(*informal*) land

delude VERB
You're deluding yourself if you think that.
• deceive, fool, trick, mislead, hoax, bluff
(*informal*) con

delusion NOUN
People were under the delusion that the Earth was flat.
• misconception, misapprehension, false impression, fantasy, self-deception

135

demand VERB
❶ *I demanded a refund for my ticket.*
• insist on, claim, call for, seek, request
❷ *'What do you want?' a voice demanded.*
• ask, enquire
❸ *Archery demands skill and concentration.*
• require, need, call for, involve, entail

demand NOUN
❶ *King John agreed to the demands of his barons.*
• request, requirement, call, claim
❷ *There was a great demand for tickets.*
• desire, call, need, appetite, market

demanding ADJECTIVE
❶ *Nursing is a demanding profession.*
• difficult, challenging, exhausting, hard, tough, testing, taxing, onerous, arduous
OPPOSITE easy
❷ *Toddlers can be very demanding.*
• difficult, trying, tiresome, insistent

demolish VERB
❶ *The building was demolished in the 1960s.*
• knock down, pull down, tear down, flatten, level, destroy, bulldoze
OPPOSITES build, construct
❷ *She demolished his argument in one sentence.*
• destroy, pull apart, tear to pieces, ruin, wreck, overturn

demonstrate VERB
❶ *These results demonstrate that our theory is correct.*
• prove, indicate, verify, establish, confirm
❷ *The crew demonstrated how to use a life jacket.*
• show, exhibit, illustrate, exemplify
❸ *Campaigners were demonstrating in the street.*
• protest, march, parade

demonstration NOUN
❶ *I watched a demonstration of the new software.*
• show, display, presentation
❷ *Thousands joined the demonstration against world poverty.*
• protest, rally, march, parade (informal) demo

demote VERB
After this defeat, the head of the army was demoted.
• downgrade, put down, relegate
OPPOSITE promote

den NOUN
❶ *the winter den of a polar bear*
• lair, burrow, hole
❷ *This room is my private den.*
• hideout, shelter, hiding place

denote VERB
What does this symbol denote?
• indicate, signify, stand for, mean, express, symbolize, represent

denounce VERB
They denounced him as a spy.
• attack, condemn, censure, criticize, disparage, condemn, accuse, expose

dense ADJECTIVE
❶ *a blanket of dense fog*
• thick, heavy
❷ *a rainforest with dense undergrowth*
• compact, thick, impenetrable, solid, packed, crowded
❸ (informal) *I'm being rather dense today!*
• stupid, slow, foolish, simple-minded (informal) dim, thick

dent NOUN
There was a large dent in the car door.
• indentation, depression, hollow, dip, dimple

dent VERB
A football hit the door and dented it.
• make a dent in, knock in, push in

dentist NOUN
a check-up at the dentist
– A dentist who specializes in straightening teeth is an **orthodontist**.
– A dental assistant who helps you look after your teeth is a **hygienist**.

deny *VERB*
❶ *The boy denied that he had stolen the money.*
• repudiate, contradict, refute, dispute, challenge, contest
OPPOSITES admit, confirm
❷ *He denied our request for an interview.*
• refuse, reject, rebuff, decline, dismiss, turn down
OPPOSITES accept, agree to, allow

depart *VERB*
Our guests departed after breakfast.
• leave, set off, get going, set out, go away, exit, withdraw
IDIOM make tracks
OPPOSITES arrive, get in

department *NOUN*
Mr Lloyd works in the sales department.
• section, branch, division, sector, unit, office, agency

departure *NOUN*
The weather delayed our departure.
• leaving, leave-taking, going, exit, withdrawal
OPPOSITES arrival, entrance

depend *VERB*
➤ depend on someone
You can depend on me.
• rely on, count on, bank on, trust
➤ depend on something
Good health depends on many different things.
• be decided by, be determined by, be dependent on, rest on, hinge on

dependable *ADJECTIVE*
Are these friends of yours dependable?
• reliable, trustworthy, loyal, faithful, trusty, honest, sound, steady
OPPOSITE unreliable

dependent *ADJECTIVE*
➤ dependent on
Our plans are dependent on the weather.
• determined by, decided by, subject to, controlled by, reliant on

depict *VERB*
❶ *The painting depicts a village in winter.*
• portray, illustrate, picture, represent, reproduce, paint, draw, sketch
❷ *The film depicts the horror of war.*
• describe, present, show, outline, detail, relate, set forth

deplorable *ADJECTIVE*
Their rudeness was deplorable.
• disgraceful, shameful, scandalous, shocking, unforgivable, lamentable, reprehensible, inexcusable
OPPOSITE admirable

deplore *VERB*
We all deplore cruelty to animals.
• condemn, denounce, disapprove of, frown on
(*formal*) abhor

depose *VERB*
The last Roman emperor was deposed in 476 AD.
• overthrow, dethrone, unseat, topple, oust

deposit *NOUN*
❶ *Today we paid the deposit on a new computer.*
• down payment, first instalment, prepayment
❷ *The country has large deposits of oil and natural gas.*
• layer, seam, vein, stratum, sediment

deposit *VERB*
❶ *She deposited a pile of papers on the desk.*
• put down, set down, place, rest, drop
(*informal*) dump, plonk
❷ *The flood water deposited layers of mud.*
• leave behind, cast up, wash up

depress *VERB*
The long, dark nights were depressing me.
• sadden, dispirit, dishearten, demoralize, get you down, weigh down on you
OPPOSITE cheer

depressed *ADJECTIVE*
The argument left me feeling depressed.
• downhearted, dispirited, disheartened, unhappy, sad, miserable, gloomy, glum, melancholy, morose, despondent, dejected, desolate, downcast, low, down, blue
IDIOMS (*informal*) down in the dumps, down in the mouth
OPPOSITE cheerful

depressing *ADJECTIVE*
I found the ending of the book depressing.
• disheartening, dispiriting, gloomy, sad, dismal, dreary, sombre, bleak, cheerless
OPPOSITE cheerful

depression *NOUN*
❶ *She sank into a state of depression.*
• despair, sadness, gloom, unhappiness, low spirits, melancholy, misery, dejection, despondency
OPPOSITE cheerfulness
❷ *the Great Depression of the 1930s*
• recession, slump, downturn
OPPOSITE boom
❸ *The rain had collected in several depressions in the ground.*
• hollow, indentation, dent, dip, pit, cavity, crater, basin, bowl

deprive *VERB*
➤ to deprive someone of something
The prisoners were deprived of food.
• deny, refuse, strip of, rob
OPPOSITE provide with

deprived *ADJECTIVE*
The charity tries to help deprived families.
• poor, needy, underprivileged, disadvantaged, destitute
OPPOSITES wealthy, privileged

depth *NOUN*
➤ in depth
Let's examine the poem in depth.
• in detail, thoroughly, comprehensively
OPPOSITE superficially

deputy *NOUN*
The Sheriff's Office has two deputies.
• second-in-command, assistant, aide, stand-in, substitute, reserve
The prefix vice- can also be used to mean a deputy, for example a *vice-captain* or a *vice-president*.

derelict *ADJECTIVE*
They plan to pull down those derelict buildings.
• dilapidated, run-down, neglected, disused, deserted, abandoned, ramshackle

derision *NOUN*
His idea was greeted with shouts of derision.
• scorn, ridicule, mockery, disdain, taunts, jeers

derive *VERB*
❶ *Bill derives a lot of pleasure from his garden.*
• get, gain, obtain, receive
❷ *She derives many of her plots from news stories.*
• borrow, draw, pick up, acquire, take, extract
(*informal*) lift

derogatory *ADJECTIVE*
His email was full of derogatory remarks.
• critical, uncomplimentary, insulting, disparaging, scornful, pejorative, negative
OPPOSITES complimentary, positive

descend *VERB*
❶ *She descended the stairs slowly.*
• go down, come down, climb down, move down
– To descend through the air is to **drop** or **fall**.
– To descend through water is to **sink**.
OPPOSITES ascend, climb
❷ *The road descends gradually into the valley.*
• drop, fall, slope, slant, incline, dip, sink
OPPOSITES ascend, climb

> ➤ **be descended from**
Humans are descended from apes.
• come from, originate from, be related to, spring from, stem from

descendant NOUN
the descendants of Queen Victoria
• successor, heir
OPPOSITE ancestor

descent NOUN
❶ *The path makes a steep descent into the valley.*
• drop, fall, dip, incline, gradient, slide
OPPOSITE ascent
❷ *a family of Polish descent*
• ancestry, lineage, origin, extraction, roots, stock, blood

describe VERB
❶ *Can you describe what you saw?*
• report, recount, relate, tell about, narrate, outline
❷ *Friends described him as a modest man.*
• portray, characterize, represent, present, depict, label

description NOUN
❶ *An eyewitness was able to give a detailed description of what happened.*
• report, account, narrative, story
❷ *Write a description of your favourite character.*
• portrait, portrayal, characterization, representation, sketch
❸ *We sell antiques of every description.*
• kind, type, sort, variety

descriptive ADJECTIVE
The author writes in a very descriptive style.
• expressive, colourful, detailed, graphic, vivid

desert NOUN
The surface of Mars is a cold and dry desert.
• wasteland, wilderness, wastes

desert VERB
He deserted his friends when they needed him most.
• abandon, leave
(*informal*) walk out on, ditch
(*old use*) forsake
IDIOMS leave high and dry, leave in the lurch
– To leave someone in a place from which they cannot escape is to **maroon** or **strand** them.

deserted ADJECTIVE
By midnight, the streets were deserted.
• empty, unoccupied, uninhabited, vacant, desolate, abandoned
OPPOSITES crowded, inhabited

deserve VERB
You deserve a break after all your hard work.
• be entitled to, be worthy of, have earned, merit, warrant

design NOUN
❶ *This is the winning design for the new art gallery.*
• plan, drawing, outline, blueprint, sketch
– A first version of something, from which others are made, is a **prototype**.
❷ *Do you like the design of this wallpaper?*
• style, pattern, motif, arrangement, composition, layout

design VERB
❶ *Ada Lovelace designed the first computer language.*
• create, develop, invent, devise, conceive, think up
❷ *The course is designed for beginners.*
• intend, plan, devise, aim (at), mean

desirable ADJECTIVE
❶ *The house has many desirable features.*
• appealing, attractive, sought-after, tempting
(*informal*) must-have
OPPOSITE unappealing
❷ *It is desirable to phone in advance.*
• advisable, sensible, prudent, wise,

recommended, preferable
OPPOSITE unwise

desire *NOUN*
She had a burning desire to visit China.
• **wish, want, longing, yearning, craving, ambition, aspiration, fancy, hankering, yen, urge, hunger, itch**

desire *VERB*
I will grant you whatever your heart desires.
• **wish for, long for, want, aspire to, crave, fancy, hanker after, yearn for, pine for, have a yen for, hunger for**
IDIOM **set your heart on**

desolate *ADJECTIVE*
❶ *He felt desolate and utterly alone.*
• **depressed, dejected, miserable, sad, melancholy, hopeless, wretched, forlorn**
OPPOSITE cheerful
❷ *It was a desolate landscape.*
• **bleak, barren, stark, bare, deserted, uninhabited, inhospitable, godforsaken, dismal, cheerless**
OPPOSITE pleasant

despair *NOUN*
He threw his hands up in despair.
• **desperation, anguish, wretchedness, hopelessness, misery, despondency, unhappiness, gloom**
OPPOSITE hope

despair *VERB*
There are many reasons not to despair.
• **lose hope, be discouraged, be despondent, lose heart**
OPPOSITE hope

despatch *NOUN & VERB*
see **dispatch**

desperate *ADJECTIVE*
❶ *The crew were in a desperate situation.*
• **difficult, critical, grave, serious, severe, drastic, dire, urgent, extreme**
❷ *We were desperate for news.*
• **anxious, frantic, eager, impatient, longing, itching**
❸ *a band of desperate outlaws*
• **dangerous, reckless, rash, impetuous**

despicable *ADJECTIVE*
They were known for despicable acts of cruelty.
• **disgraceful, hateful, shameful, contemptible, loathsome, vile**

despise *VERB*
I despise people who cheat.
• **hate, loathe, deplore, disdain, feel contempt for, have a low opinion of, look down on, scorn, sneer at**
(*formal*) **abhor**
OPPOSITES admire, respect

despite *PREPOSITION*
We went for a walk despite the rain.
• **in spite of, regardless of, notwithstanding**
OPPOSITE because of

dessert *NOUN*
There is plum crumble for dessert.
• **pudding, sweet**
(*informal*) **afters**

destination *NOUN*
The train arrived at its destination five minutes early.
• **terminus, stop, objective**
IDIOM **journey's end**

destined *ADJECTIVE*
❶ *They felt they were destined to win.*
• **fated, doomed, preordained, intended, meant, certain**
❷ *The ship was destined for Australia.*
• **bound, headed, intended, directed**

destiny *NOUN*
She felt that it was her destiny to be a great singer.
• **fate, fortune, future, doom, lot**

destroy *VERB*
❶ *An avalanche destroyed the village.*
• **demolish, devastate, crush, smash, shatter, flatten, level, knock down, sweep away**
❷ *The injury has destroyed her chances of a medal.*
• **ruin, wreck, spoil, sabotage, thwart, undo**

destruction NOUN
❶ *The hurricane caused widespread destruction.*
• devastation, damage, demolition, ruin, wreckage, havoc
OPPOSITE creation
❷ *The species is threatened by the destruction of its habitat.*
• eradication, obliteration, elimination, annihilation, extermination, extinction
OPPOSITES preservation, conservation

destructive ADJECTIVE
Tornadoes have a great destructive power.
• damaging, devastating, catastrophic, disastrous, harmful, injurious, ruinous, violent

detach VERB
The camera lens can be detached for cleaning.
• remove, separate, disconnect, take off, split off, release, undo, unfasten, part
– To detach a trailer from a vehicle is to **unhitch** it.
– To detach railway carriages is to **uncouple** them.
OPPOSITE attach

detail NOUN
Her account was accurate in every detail.
• fact, particular, feature, characteristic, aspect, respect, element, item, point, specific

detailed ADJECTIVE
The novel gives a detailed description of Victorian London.
• precise, exact, specific, full, thorough, elaborate, comprehensive, exhaustive, minute
OPPOSITES rough, vague

detain VERB
❶ *I'll try not to detain you for long.*
• delay, hold up, keep, keep waiting
❷ *Police have detained two suspects.*
• hold, arrest, apprehend, imprison, confine, take into custody
OPPOSITE release

detect VERB
❶ *I could detect a note of fear in her voice.*
• perceive, discern, be aware of, notice, spot, recognize, make out, catch
❷ *They have detected evidence of snow on Mars.*
• discover, find, uncover, unearth, reveal, identify, track down

detective NOUN
Hercule Poirot is a fictional detective.
• investigator, sleuth
(*informal*) private eye
For tips on writing crime fiction see **crime**.

deter VERB
How can we deter slugs from eating our vegetables?
• discourage, dissuade, prevent, stop, avert, put off, scare off
OPPOSITE encourage

deteriorate VERB
Her sight has begun to deteriorate.
• worsen, decline, fail, degenerate, get worse
IDIOM go downhill
OPPOSITES improve, get better

determination NOUN
All of the players showed great determination.
• resolve, commitment, will-power, courage, dedication, drive, grit, perseverance, persistence, spirit
(*informal*) guts

determine VERB
❶ *I determined to follow their advice.*
• resolve, decide, make up your mind
❷ *Your genes determine your body size.*
• dictate, decide, control, regulate, govern
❸ *Can you determine the height of the mountain?*
• calculate, compute, establish, ascertain, work out, figure out

a b c **d** e f g h i j k l m n o p q r s t u v w x y z

determined ADJECTIVE

❶ *My grandmother was a very determined woman.*
• resolute, decisive, purposeful, strong-minded, persistent, tenacious, adamant
OPPOSITES weak-minded, irresolute
❷ *She was determined to finish the race.*
• resolved, committed, dogged
OPPOSITES feeble, half-hearted

detest VERB

I detest the smell of boiled cabbage.
• dislike, hate, loathe, despise
(*informal*) can't bear, can't stand
(*formal*) abhor
OPPOSITES love, adore

detour NOUN

We wasted time by taking a detour.
• diversion, indirect route, roundabout route

detrimental ADJECTIVE

Too much water can be detrimental to plants.
• damaging, harmful, destructive, adverse
OPPOSITE beneficial

devastate VERB

❶ *The tsunami devastated the island.*
• destroy, wreck, ruin, demolish, flatten, level, lay waste
❷ *We were devastated by the news.*
• shock, stun, daze, overwhelm, shatter

develop VERB

❶ *The zoo is developing its education programme.*
• expand, extend, enlarge, build up, enhance, improve, broaden, diversify
❷ *Their fan base has developed over the years.*
• grow, spread, expand, flourish, build up
❸ *The symptoms developed quickly.*
• emerge, arise, break out, grow, spread
❹ *Her piano playing has developed this year.*
• improve, progress, evolve, get better, advance, refine, mature

❺ *They soon developed bad habits.*
• get, acquire, pick up, cultivate

development NOUN

❶ *We are pleased with the development of our website.*
• growth, evolution, expansion, improvement, progress, spread
❷ *Have there been any further developments?*
• event, happening, occurrence, incident, change

deviate VERB

We were forced to deviate from our original plan.
• diverge, differ, vary, depart, digress, stray

device NOUN

The TV comes with a remote control device.
• tool, implement, instrument, appliance, apparatus, gadget, contraption
(*informal*) gizmo

devious ADJECTIVE

❶ *He got rich by devious means.*
• deceitful, underhand, dishonest, furtive, scheming, cunning, sly, sneaky, treacherous, wily
❷ *The bus took a devious route.*
• indirect, roundabout, winding, meandering, circuitous
OPPOSITE direct

devise VERB

Between them they devised a plan to escape.
• conceive, form, invent, contrive, formulate, make up, come up with, plan, prepare, map out, think out, think up

devote VERB

She devotes her spare time to the garden.
• dedicate, allocate, set aside, allot, assign, commit

devoted ADJECTIVE
The band has many devoted fans.
• loyal, faithful, dedicated, committed, staunch, steadfast

devotion NOUN
It is the story of a dog's devotion to his master.
• loyalty, fidelity, commitment, dedication, attachment, fondness, allegiance

devour VERB
He devoured a whole plateful of sandwiches.
• eat, consume, gobble up, bolt down, gulp down, swallow
(informal) guzzle, scoff, wolf down
SEE ALSO **eat**

devout ADJECTIVE
a devout Catholic
• dutiful, committed, loyal, pious, sincere, reverent

diagnose VERB
No one could diagnose the cause of her illness.
• identify, determine, detect, recognize, name, pinpoint

diagram NOUN
This is a diagram of the digestive system.
• chart, plan, sketch, drawing, representation, outline

dialogue NOUN
The play consists of a series of dialogues.
• conversation, talk, discussion, exchange, debate, chat

diary NOUN
She kept a diary from the age of nine.
• journal, chronicle, record, memoir
– A diary describing a voyage or mission is a **log** or **logbook**.
– A diary published on a website is a **blog**.

dictate VERB
➤ dictate to someone
You have no right to dictate to me!
• order about, give orders to, command,

bully
(informal) boss about, push around
IDIOM lord it over

dictator NOUN
Hitler became a ruthless dictator.
• autocrat, absolute ruler, tyrant, despot

die VERB
❶ *She died in 2002 at the age of 94.*
• expire, perish, pass away, pass on
(informal) snuff it, croak
IDIOM give up the ghost
IDIOMS *(informal)* kick the bucket, pop your clogs
– To die of hunger is to **starve**.
❷ *My computer has died on me again.*
• fail, crash, break down, malfunction
(informal) pack up, conk out
➤ die down
The wind should die down soon.
• lessen, decrease, decline, subside, abate, ease off, let up, peter out, wane, ebb
➤ die out
When did the dinosaurs die out?
• become extinct, cease to exist, disappear, vanish

diet NOUN
You should include plenty of fruit and vegetables in your diet.
• food, nourishment, nutrition
– A diet which does not include meat is a **vegetarian** diet.
– A diet which does not include any animal products is a **vegan** diet.
SEE ALSO **food**

differ VERB
The statements differ on a number of points.
• disagree, conflict, clash, contradict each other
IDIOM be at odds
OPPOSITE agree
➤ differ from
How do the poems differ from each other?
• be different from, contrast with, vary from, run counter to
OPPOSITE resemble

difference NOUN

❶ Can you see any difference between these two colours?
• contrast, distinction, dissimilarity, disparity, variation, divergence
OPPOSITE similarity

❷ This money will make a difference to their lives.
• change, alteration, modification, improvement

❸ We've had our differences in the past.
• disagreement, argument, quarrel, dispute

different ADJECTIVE

❶ The twins have very different personalities.
• dissimilar, unlike, differing, contrasting, varying, disparate
IDIOMS like chalk and cheese, poles apart
OPPOSITES identical, similar

❷ Every person's handwriting is different.
• distinct, distinctive, distinguishable, individual, unique, special

❸ Birds have beaks of different shapes and sizes.
• various, assorted, several, diverse, numerous

❹ Your hair looks different today.
• changed, altered, unfamiliar

❺ Let's do something different this weekend.
• unusual, original, fresh, new, novel, out of the ordinary

difficult ADJECTIVE

❶ This is a really difficult crossword puzzle.
• hard, complicated, complex, involved, intricate, baffling, perplexing, puzzling, tricky
(informal) thorny, knotty
OPPOSITE simple

❷ It is a difficult climb to the top of the hill.
• challenging, arduous, demanding, taxing, exhausting, formidable, gruelling, laborious, strenuous, tough
OPPOSITE easy

❸ Mum says I was a difficult child.
• troublesome, awkward, demanding, uncooperative, obstinate, stubborn, trying, tiresome
OPPOSITES cooperative, accommodating

difficulty NOUN

❶ One of the climbers got into real difficulty.
• trouble, adversity, hardship, distress, problems, challenges
(informal) hassle

❷ We ran into one difficulty after another.
• problem, complication, hitch, obstacle, snag, stumbling block

dig VERB

❶ We spent the afternoon digging the garden.
• cultivate, fork over, turn over

❷ Rabbits dig holes in the ground.
• burrow, excavate, tunnel, bore, gouge out, hollow out, scoop out

❸ I felt someone dig me in the ribs.
• poke, prod, jab, stab

➤ **dig up**
Can you dig up some more information?
• discover, uncover, find, reveal, expose, turn up

dignified ADJECTIVE

He rose to his feet in a calm and dignified manner.
• stately, distinguished, grand, noble, majestic, august, imposing, formal, solemn, sedate
OPPOSITE undignified

dignity NOUN

❶ The joke spoilt the dignity of the occasion.
• formality, seriousness, solemnity, propriety, decorum

❷ She faced her death with great dignity.
• calmness, poise, self-control

dilemma NOUN
I now faced the dilemma of whether to stay or go.
• quandary, predicament
IDIOM catch-22

diligent ADJECTIVE
❶ *She is a diligent student.*
• hard-working, conscientious, industrious
❷ *Police made a diligent search of the crime scene.*
• careful, attentive, painstaking, meticulous, rigorous, thorough

dilute VERB
Dilute the juice before serving.
• thin, water down, weaken
OPPOSITE concentrate

dim ADJECTIVE
❶ *the dim light of a single candle*
• faint, muted, subdued
OPPOSITE bright
❷ *a long, dim corridor*
• dark, dull, dingy, murky, gloomy, badly lit
OPPOSITE bright
❸ *I have only a dim memory of the plot.*
• vague, indistinct, faint, blurred, fuzzy, hazy, sketchy
OPPOSITE clear

dimension NOUN
First we need to measure the dimensions of the room.
• measurements, size, extent, capacity
SEE ALSO measurement

diminish VERB
❶ *The bad news did not diminish her enthusiasm.*
• lessen, reduce, decrease, minimize, curtail
❷ *Our water supply was diminishing rapidly.*
• become less, decrease, decline, subside, dwindle, wane
OPPOSITE increase

din NOUN
I can't hear above that din!
• noise, racket, row, clatter, commotion, uproar, hullabaloo, hubbub, cacophony

dine VERB
We will be dining at eight o'clock.
• eat, have dinner, have lunch

dingy ADJECTIVE
How can we brighten up this dingy room?
• dull, drab, dreary, dowdy, colourless, dismal, gloomy, murky
OPPOSITE bright

dinosaur NOUN

WORD WEB

Some types of dinosaur:
➤ apatosaurus
➤ archaeopteryx
➤ brachiosaurus
➤ diplodocus
➤ gallimimus
➤ iguanodon
➤ megalosaurus
➤ pterodactylus
➤ stegosaurus
➤ triceratops
➤ tyranno-saurus rex
➤ velociraptor
– The study of dinosaurs and other fossils is palaeontology.
SEE ALSO prehistoric

dip VERB
❶ *I dipped my hand in the water.*
• immerse, lower, submerge, plunge, dunk
❷ *The road dips down into the valley.*
• descend, go down, slope down, drop down, fall away, sink

dip NOUN
❶ *There's a dip in the road ahead.*
• slope, slide, decline, hollow, depression
❷ *It was hot so we took a dip in the sea.*
• swim, bathe, paddle

dire ADJECTIVE
❶ *They warned us of dire consequences.*
• dreadful, terrible, awful, appalling, severe, grave

a b c d e f g h i j k l m n o p q r s t u v w x y z

❷ The ground is in dire need of rain.
• urgent, desperate, drastic, extreme, pressing

direct ADJECTIVE
❶ Which is the most direct route?
• straight, short, quick
OPPOSITES indirect, roundabout
❷ Please give me a direct answer.
• straightforward, frank, honest, sincere, blunt, plain, candid, unambiguous, unequivocal
OPPOSITE evasive
❸ She is a shy girl but her sister is the direct opposite.
• exact, complete

direct VERB
❶ Can you direct me to the station?
• guide, point, show the way, give directions to
❷ The advert is directed at young people.
• aim, target, point
❸ Dr Knox will direct the experiment.
• manage, run, be in charge of, control, administer, govern, superintend, supervise, take charge of
– To direct an orchestra is to **conduct** it.
❹ Officers directed the crowd to move back.
• instruct, command, order, tell

direction NOUN
Which direction did they go in?
• way, route, course, path, bearing
➤ **directions**
Follow the directions on the packet.
• instructions, guidance, guidelines

director NOUN
She is the director of the town's new art gallery.
• manager, head, chief, chief executive, leader, president
(informal) boss

dirt NOUN
❶ The floor was covered in dirt.
• filth, grime, mess, muck, mud, dust
❷ Chickens were scratching about in the dirt.
• earth, soil, clay, ground

dirty ADJECTIVE
❶ There's a pile of dirty washing to do.
• unclean, unwashed, soiled, stained, grimy, grubby, filthy, messy, mucky, muddy, squalid
(informal) manky, grotty
OPPOSITE clean
❷ It's dangerous to drink dirty water.
• impure, polluted, foul, contaminated
OPPOSITE pure
❸ That was a dirty trick!
• unfair, dishonest, underhand, mean, unsporting
OPPOSITE honest
❹ He was telling dirty jokes.
• rude, obscene, indecent, coarse, crude, smutty, filthy
OPPOSITE decent

disability NOUN
The Paralympics are open to athletes with disabilities.
• handicap, incapacity, impairment, infirmity

disabled ADJECTIVE
He has been disabled since the accident.
• handicapped, incapacitated
– An animal which is injured and cannot walk is **lame**.
– A person who cannot move part of their body is **paralysed**.
OPPOSITE able-bodied

disadvantage NOUN
Being short is a disadvantage for basketball players.
• drawback, handicap, hindrance, inconvenience, downside, snag, catch
OPPOSITES advantage, plus

disagree VERB
We often disagree about music.
• argue, differ, clash, quarrel, be of a different opinion
IDIOMS be at odds, be at loggerheads
OPPOSITE agree
➤ **disagree with**
❶ He disagrees with everything I say.
• argue with, contradict, oppose, object to, dispute, contest, challenge, take issue with

② *Onions disagree with me.*
• make you ill, upset your stomach, have a bad effect on you

disagreeable *ADJECTIVE*
What a disagreeable man!
• unpleasant, nasty, horrible, offensive, revolting, repellent, repulsive, obnoxious
OPPOSITE pleasant

disagreement *NOUN*
There was some disagreement over the bill.
• argument, dispute, difference of opinion, conflict, discord, quarrel, row, clash, squabble
OPPOSITE agreement

disappear *VERB*
① *The scar has nearly disappeared.*
• vanish, fade away, melt away, clear
OPPOSITE appear
② *It is a way of life that has almost disappeared.*
• die out, cease to exist, come to an end, vanish, pass away
OPPOSITES emerge, arise

disappoint *VERB*
The announcement will disappoint some fans.
• let down, fail, dissatisfy, displease, dismay, upset, sadden
OPPOSITES please, satisfy

disappointed *ADJECTIVE*
I was disappointed with my score.
• displeased, unhappy, upset, unsatisfied, saddened, downhearted, disheartened, discouraged, let down
(*informal*) gutted
OPPOSITES pleased, satisfied

disapprove *VERB*
➤ **disapprove of**
Her family disapproved of her marriage.
• object to, take exception to, dislike, deplore, condemn, criticize, denounce, frown on
IDIOM take a dim view of
OPPOSITE approve of

disaster *NOUN*
① *The country was rocked by a series of disasters.*
• catastrophe, calamity, tragedy, misfortune, blow
– Events such as earthquakes, hurricanes and floods are called **natural disasters**.
② *The show was a complete disaster.*
• failure, fiasco, shambles
(*informal*) flop, wash-out

disastrous *ADJECTIVE*
This mistake had disastrous results.
• catastrophic, devastating, calamitous, destructive, dire, dreadful, terrible, ruinous

disbelief *NOUN*
We stared at the TV screen in disbelief.
• incredulity, doubt, distrust, mistrust, scepticism

disc *NOUN*
the disc of the full moon
see **circle**

discard *VERB*
It's time to discard some of these old clothes.
• get rid of, throw away, throw out, reject, cast off, dispose of, dump, scrap, toss out
(*informal*) ditch, bin

discharge *VERB*
① *He was found not guilty and discharged.*
• free, release, let go, liberate
② *The chimneys were discharging thick smoke.*
• emit, expel, eject, give out, give off, produce

disciple *NOUN*
Confucius had many disciples.
• follower, supporter, adherent, admirer, devotee
– In Christianity, the disciples of Jesus are called the **apostles**.

a
b
c
d
e
f
g
h
i
j
k
l
m
n
o
p
q
r
s
t
u
v
w
x
y
z

A
B
C
D
E
F
G
H
I
J
K
L
M
N
O
P
Q
R
S
T
U
V
W
X
Y
Z

discipline NOUN
❶ *Discipline is important in the army.*
• control, order, good behaviour, obedience
❷ *Genetics is a relatively new discipline.*
• field, subject, area of study, speciality

disclose VERB
Someone has been disclosing top-secret information.
• reveal, divulge, make known, pass on, tell, impart, make public
OPPOSITE conceal

discomfort NOUN
❶ *Is your tooth still giving you discomfort?*
• pain, soreness, aching
❷ *I could sense her discomfort at my question.*
• uneasiness, unease, embarrassment, awkwardness, distress

disconnect VERB
First you need to disconnect the computer cable.
• detach, unplug, unhook, cut off, disable

discontented ADJECTIVE
She was feeling discontented with life.
• dissatisfied, disgruntled, displeased, unhappy, miserable
(*informal*) fed up
OPPOSITES contented, satisfied

discount NOUN
They are offering a discount of 20 per cent.
• reduction, deduction, cut, concession, markdown

discount VERB
We cannot discount that possibility.
• ignore, dismiss, disregard, pay no attention to, overlook
OPPOSITE acknowledge

discourage VERB
❶ *Don't let her words discourage you.*
• dishearten, demoralize, depress, unnerve
OPPOSITE encourage

❷ *The burglar alarm will discourage thieves.*
• deter, dissuade, prevent, restrain, hinder
(*informal*) put you off

discover VERB
❶ *I discovered some old games in the attic.*
• find, come across, spot, stumble across, track down, uncover, unearth
❷ *We discovered the truth years later.*
• find out, learn, realize, recognize, ascertain, work out

discovery NOUN
This drug was an important discovery in the history of medicine.
• find, breakthrough, innovation

discreet ADJECTIVE
I made a few discreet enquiries.
• tactful, sensitive, delicate, careful, cautious, diplomatic
OPPOSITE tactless

discretion NOUN
❶ *You can count on my discretion.*
• tact, sensitivity, delicacy, diplomacy
OPPOSITE tactlessness
❷ *Marks are awarded at the discretion of the judges.*
• option, choice, preference, inclination, will

discriminate VERB
It's sometimes hard to discriminate between fact and fiction.
• distinguish, differentiate, tell the difference, tell apart, draw a distinction
➤ **discriminate against**
It's wrong to discriminate against people because of their age.
• be biased against, be prejudiced against, treat unfairly, victimize

discrimination NOUN
❶ *The school has a policy against any form of discrimination.*
• prejudice, bias, intolerance, bigotry, unfairness, favouritism
– Discrimination against people because of their sex is **sexism**.

– Discrimination against people because of their race is **racism**.
❷ She shows discrimination in her choice of music.
• good taste, good judgement

discuss VERB
❶ I discussed the idea with my friends.
• talk about, confer about, debate
❷ This topic is discussed in the next chapter.
• examine, explore, deal with, analyse, consider, tackle

discussion NOUN
We had a lively discussion about Internet safety.
• conversation, talk, dialogue, exchange of views
– A formal discussion is a **conference** or **debate**.

disease NOUN
He was suffering from a serious disease.
• illness, sickness, ailment, disorder, complaint, affliction, condition
(informal) bug
– An outbreak of disease that spreads quickly is an **epidemic**.
　SEE ALSO　illness

diseased ADJECTIVE
Gardeners throw away diseased plants.
• unhealthy, sickly, ailing, infected
　OPPOSITE　healthy

disgrace NOUN
❶ He never got over the disgrace of being caught cheating.
• humiliation, shame, dishonour, scandal, ignominy, disrepute
　IDIOM　loss of face
❷ The litter on the streets is a disgrace.
• outrage, scandal

disgraceful ADJECTIVE
We were shocked by her disgraceful behaviour.
• shameful, shocking, appalling, outrageous, scandalous, reprehensible
　OPPOSITES　honourable, admirable

disguise VERB
❶ She disguised herself as a boy.
• dress up, be in disguise, pretend to be, pose as
❷ I tried to disguise my feelings.
• conceal, hide, cover up, camouflage, mask
　OPPOSITES　reveal, expose

disguise NOUN
I wore a wig as a disguise.
• costume, camouflage, mask

disgust NOUN
She wrinkled her nose in disgust at the smell.
• revulsion, repugnance, repulsion, abhorrence, distaste, dislike, loathing, detestation
　OPPOSITES　delight, liking

disgust VERB
The sight of blood disgusts me.
• repel, revolt, repulse, sicken, appal, offend, distress, horrify
　IDIOM　turn your stomach
　OPPOSITES　delight, please

disgusting ADJECTIVE
What a disgusting smell!
• repulsive, revolting, horrible, nasty, loathsome, repellent, repugnant, offensive, sickening, nauseating, stomach-turning
(informal) yucky, icky, gross
　OPPOSITES　delightful, pleasing

dish NOUN
❶ He tipped the pasta into a dish.
• bowl, basin, plate, platter
– A dish to serve soup from is a **tureen**.
❷ What's your favourite dish?
• food, recipe, meal, course

dish VERB
➤ dish out
Mr Elliot began dishing out sheets of paper.
• distribute, hand out, dole out, dispense, allocate

dishevelled ADJECTIVE
He arrived looking flushed and dishevelled.
• messy, untidy, scruffy, unkempt,

a b c **d** e f g h i j k l m n o p q r s t u v w x y z

bedraggled, slovenly, ruffled
OPPOSITES neat, tidy

dishonest ADJECTIVE
❶ They were taken in by a dishonest salesman.
• deceitful, corrupt, untrustworthy, immoral, disreputable, cheating, lying, swindling, thieving
(informal) bent, crooked, dodgy, shady
❷ The website makes some dishonest claims.
• false, fraudulent, misleading, untruthful
OPPOSITE honest

dishonesty NOUN
She accused him of dishonesty.
• deceit, cheating, lying, insincerity, fraud, corruption
(informal) crookedness
OPPOSITE honesty

disinfect VERB
The nurse disinfected my wound.
• cleanse, sterilize
– To disinfect an infected place is to decontaminate it.
– To disinfect a room with fumes is to fumigate it.
OPPOSITE infect

disintegrate VERB
The fuel tank exploded and the spacecraft started to disintegrate.
• break up, fall apart, break into pieces, crumble, decay, decompose

disinterested ADJECTIVE
Referees have to remain disinterested.
• impartial, neutral, unbiased, unprejudiced, detached, fair
OPPOSITE biased
The word uninterested is not a synonym of disinterested. A disinterested referee is unbiased, but an uninterested referee is bored.

dislike NOUN
She had already taken a dislike to him.
• hatred, loathing, detestation, antipathy, distaste, disgust, disapproval, revulsion
OPPOSITE liking

dislike VERB
I dislike people who lie to me.
• hate, loathe, detest, disapprove of, object to, take exception to
OPPOSITE like

dislodge VERB
The wind dislodged some tiles on the roof.
• displace, move, shift, disturb

disloyal ADJECTIVE
They were accused of being disloyal to the king.
• unfaithful, treacherous, faithless, false, unreliable, untrustworthy
OPPOSITES loyal, faithful

dismal ADJECTIVE
❶ She led him into a dismal little room.
• dull, drab, dreary, mournful, dingy, colourless, cheerless, gloomy, murky
OPPOSITES bright, cheerful
❷ (informal) It was a dismal performance by our team.
• dreadful, awful, terrible, feeble, useless, hopeless
(informal) pathetic

dismantle VERB
We were busy dismantling the bunk beds.
• take apart, take down, break up
– To dismantle a group of tents is to strike camp.
OPPOSITES assemble, put together

dismay NOUN
We watched the news reports with dismay.
• distress, alarm, shock, concern, anxiety, consternation

dismayed ADJECTIVE
We were dismayed by the recent news.
• distressed, disturbed, discouraged, disconcerted, depressed, taken aback, shocked, alarmed
OPPOSITES pleased, encouraged

dismiss VERB
❶ Mrs Owen dismissed her class.
• send away, discharge, free, let go, release

❷ *The firm dismissed ten workers.*
• sack, give the sack to, discharge, let go, give notice to, make redundant (*informal*) fire
❸ *I dismissed the idea as nonsense.*
• discard, drop, reject, banish, set aside, brush aside, wave aside, put out of your mind

disobedient ADJECTIVE
She said she had never known such a disobedient child.
• badly behaved, naughty, insubordinate, undisciplined, uncontrollable, unmanageable, unruly, troublesome, defiant, disruptive, rebellious, mutinous
OPPOSITE obedient

disobey VERB
❶ *He was too frightened to disobey her.*
• be disobedient to, defy, rebel against
– To refuse to obey orders from a commanding officer is to **mutiny**.
OPPOSITE obey
❷ *You will be penalized if you disobey the rules.*
• break, disregard, ignore, violate, infringe, flout

disorder NOUN
❶ *She stared at the disorder of her desk.*
• untidiness, mess, muddle, chaos, confusion, clutter, jumble
OPPOSITE order
❷ *The meeting broke up in disorder.*
• disturbance, uproar, commotion, quarrelling, rioting, brawling, fighting, lawlessness, anarchy
❸ *The patient was suffering from an eating disorder.*
• disease, condition, complaint, affliction, illness, ailment, sickness

disorderly ADJECTIVE
❶ *Books were arranged on the shelves in a disorderly fashion.*
• untidy, disorganized, chaotic, messy, in disarray
(*informal*) higgledy-piggledy
OPPOSITE orderly

❷ *The class were behaving in a disorderly manner.*
• disobedient, unruly, uncontrollable, undisciplined, ungovernable, unmanageable

dispatch VERB
The parcel has already been dispatched.
• post, send, transmit, forward

dispatch NOUN
A messenger brought a dispatch from headquarters.
• message, communication, report, letter, bulletin

dispense VERB
❶ *Waiters were there to dispense drinks.*
• distribute, hand out, dole out, pass round, supply, provide
❷ *He was like a feudal lord dispensing justice.*
• administer, issue, deliver, deal out, mete out
➤ dispense with
We are dispensing with fees altogether.
• get rid of, dispose of, do without, forego, waive, drop, omit
IDIOM (*informal*) give something a miss

disperse VERB
❶ *Dandelion seeds are dispersed by the wind.*
• scatter, spread, distribute, disseminate
❷ *The crowd dispersed quickly after the match.*
• break up, scatter, disband, separate, split up, go in different directions
OPPOSITE gather
❸ *The morning fog soon dispersed.*
• dissipate, dissolve, melt away, vanish, clear, lift

displace VERB
❶ *The gales displaced some roof tiles.*
• dislodge, put out of place, shift
OPPOSITE replace
❷ *Last year she displaced him as captain.*
• replace, take the place of, succeed, supersede, supplant

display VERB
❶ *The students' work was displayed in the foyer.*
• exhibit, present, show, set out, put on show, show off, parade, showcase
– To display something boastfully is to **flaunt** it.
❷ *They displayed great courage.*
• show, demonstrate, reveal, show evidence of

display NOUN
We set out a display of our recent art work.
• exhibition, show, presentation, demonstration, parade, spectacle, showcase

displease VERB
I must have done something to displease her.
• annoy, irritate, upset, put out, anger, irk, exasperate, vex

dispose VERB
➤ dispose of something
Please dispose of all your rubbish.
• get rid of, discard, throw away, throw out, jettison, scrap
(*informal*) dump
➤ be disposed to do something
No one seems disposed to help us.
• be willing to, be inclined to, be ready to, be likely to

disposition NOUN
Our dog has a very friendly disposition.
• temperament, nature, character, make-up, personality, mentality

disprove VERB
There is no evidence to disprove her story.
• refute, rebut, prove false, demolish, debunk
IDIOM shoot full of holes
OPPOSITE prove

dispute VERB
Some disputed her claim to the throne.
• disagree with, object to, challenge, contest, call into question, take issue with

dispute NOUN
There was a dispute over who should pay.
• argument, disagreement, debate, controversy, difference of opinion, quarrel, row, squabble, clash

disregard VERB
I disregarded the doctor's advice.
• ignore, pay no attention to, take no notice of, discount, reject, brush aside, shrug off
IDIOM turn a blind eye to
OPPOSITE heed

disrespectful ADJECTIVE
It's disrespectful to walk on someone's grave.
• rude, bad-mannered, insulting, impolite, insolent, cheeky
OPPOSITE respectful

disrupt VERB
The roadworks are disrupting bus services.
• interrupt, disturb, upset, unsettle, interfere with, play havoc with, throw into confusion

dissatisfied ADJECTIVE
I felt dissatisfied with my score.
• displeased, discontented, disappointed, disgruntled, unhappy, frustrated
OPPOSITES satisfied, contented

dissolve VERB
Stir the mixture until the sugar dissolves.
• disperse, disintegrate, melt

dissuade VERB
➤ dissuade someone from
I tried to dissuade her from leaving.
• discourage from, persuade not to, talk out of, deter from, warn against
OPPOSITES persuade to, encourage to

distance NOUN
What is the distance from the Earth to the Sun?
• measurement, space, extent, reach, mileage
– The distance across something is the **breadth** or **width**.

– The distance along something is the **length**.
– The distance between two points is a **gap** or **interval**.
SEE ALSO measurement

distant ADJECTIVE
❶ *She was always travelling to distant countries.*
• faraway, far-off, remote, out-of-the-way
OPPOSITES nearby, close
❷ *His distant manner puts me off.*
• unfriendly, unapproachable, formal, reserved, withdrawn, cool, haughty, aloof
OPPOSITES friendly, warm

distinct ADJECTIVE
❶ *I can see a distinct improvement.*
• definite, evident, noticeable, obvious, perceptible
OPPOSITE imperceptible
❷ *The image is quite distinct.*
• clear, well defined, distinguishable, recognizable, sharp, unmistakable, visible, plain to see
OPPOSITE indistinct
❸ *The country is divided into three distinct regions.*
• separate, discrete, different, individual

distinction NOUN
❶ *What is the distinction between reptiles and amphibians?*
• difference, contrast, distinctiveness, differentiation
❷ *He had the distinction of being the youngest ever captain of the team.*
• honour, glory, merit, credit, prestige

distinctive ADJECTIVE
She has a very distinctive laugh.
• characteristic, recognizable, unmistakable, particular, special, peculiar, unique

distinguish VERB
❶ *It was impossible to distinguish one twin from the other.*
• tell apart, tell, differentiate, tell the difference between, discriminate between
❷ *I was too far away to distinguish what they were saying.*
• make out, identify, recognize, tell, determine, discern, perceive

distinguished ADJECTIVE
❶ *The school has a distinguished academic record.*
• excellent, first-rate, outstanding, exceptional
OPPOSITE ordinary
❷ *He is a distinguished Hollywood actor.*
• famous, celebrated, well-known, eminent, notable, prominent, renowned, acclaimed
OPPOSITES unknown, obscure

distort VERB
❶ *The crash distorted the front wheel.*
• bend, buckle, twist, warp, contort, deform, put out of shape
❷ *The newspaper distorted the facts of the story.*
• misrepresent, twist, slant, garble

distract VERB
Don't distract the bus driver.
• divert the attention of, disturb, put off, sidetrack

distress NOUN
She let out a cry of distress.
• suffering, torment, anguish, pain, misery, dismay, anxiety, grief, sadness, sorrow, wretchedness

distress VERB
I could see that my words distressed him.
• upset, disturb, trouble, worry, dismay, perturb, alarm, agitate, torment, pain
OPPOSITE comfort

distribute VERB
❶ *They spent the day distributing leaflets.*
• give out, hand round, circulate, dispense, issue, deal out, share out, dole out, dish out
❷ *Distribute the seeds evenly.*
• scatter, spread, disperse

district NOUN

a mountainous district of Nepal
• area, region, territory, locality, vicinity, neighbourhood, quarter, sector, zone

distrust VERB

I distrusted him from the moment I met him.
• doubt, mistrust, be suspicious of, be wary of, question, suspect, be sceptical about, have misgivings about
OPPOSITE trust

disturb VERB

❶ *Please don't let me disturb you.*
• interrupt, intrude on, disrupt, bother, pester, trouble, distract
❷ *Some of the pictures may disturb you.*
• distress, trouble, upset, unsettle, worry, perturb
❸ *Someone had disturbed the papers on my desk.*
• rearrange, move around, mix up, muddle up, mess up

disused ADJECTIVE

They turned the disused railway line into a cycle track.
• abandoned, unused, neglected, obsolete, closed down

ditch NOUN

He slipped and fell into a muddy ditch.
• trench, channel, drain, gutter, gully

dither VERB

I'm still dithering over what to do.
• hesitate, waver, be in two minds, vacillate
(*informal*) shilly-shally

dive VERB

❶ *A group of penguins dived into the water.*
• plunge, jump, leap
– A dive in which you land flat on your front is a **bellyflop**.
❷ *The eagle dived towards its prey.*
• swoop, plummet, plunge, drop, fall, pitch, nosedive

diverse ADJECTIVE

People from many diverse cultures live in the area.
• varied, mixed, assorted, miscellaneous, various, different, differing, varying

diversion NOUN

❶ *The police had set up a traffic diversion.*
• detour, alternative route, deviation
❷ *There were lots of diversions on offer at the theme park.*
• entertainment, amusement, recreation

divert VERB

❶ *Our plane was diverted to another airport.*
• redirect, re-route, switch
❷ *She diverted herself by browsing the Internet.*
• entertain, amuse, occupy, interest, distract, keep happy

divide VERB

❶ *We divided the class into two teams.*
• separate, split, split up, break up, part, partition
OPPOSITE combine
❷ *We divided the chocolate between us.*
• distribute, share out, ration, give out, deal out, dish out, dispense
❸ *The river divides into several channels.*
• diverge, branch off, fork, split, part
OPPOSITE converge

divine ADJECTIVE

❶ *The temple is used for divine worship.*
• religious, sacred, holy, spiritual
❷ *The Greeks believed divine beings lived on Mount Olympus.*
• godly, godlike, immortal, heavenly
❸ (*informal*) *These muffins taste divine!*
• excellent, wonderful, superb

division NOUN

❶ *The map shows the division of Europe after the war.*
• dividing, splitting, break-up, separation, partition, dividing up, carving up

❷ *There were deep divisions within the government.*
• disunity, disagreement, discord, conflict, split, feud
❸ *She has a job in the sales division.*
• branch, department, section, arm, unit

divulge VERB
He refused to divulge any more details.
• disclose, make known, reveal, tell, impart, pass on, give away

dizzy ADJECTIVE
When she looked down she felt dizzy.
• light-headed, giddy, dazed, faint, reeling, unsteady, wobbly
(*informal*) woozy

do VERB
❶ *She didn't know what to do.*
• act, behave, conduct yourself
❷ *I have a lot of work to do this morning.*
• attend to, cope with, deal with, handle, look after, perform, undertake
❸ *It took half an hour to do the washing-up.*
• accomplish, achieve, carry out, complete, execute, finish
❹ *I need to do all of these sums.*
• answer, puzzle out, solve, work out
❺ *Sunbathing can do damage to your skin.*
• bring about, cause, produce, result in
❻ *If you don't have milk, water will do.*
• be acceptable, be enough, be satisfactory, be sufficient, serve
➤ **do away with**
I wish our school would do away with homework.
• get rid of, abolish, eliminate, end, put an end to
(*informal*) scrap
➤ **do something up**
❶ *He bent down to do up his shoelaces.*
• fasten, tie, lace
❷ *We're doing up the spare room.*
• redecorate, make over, refurbish, renovate, restore

docile ADJECTIVE
Our dog is quite docile.
• tame, gentle, meek, obedient, manageable, submissive
OPPOSITE fierce

dock NOUN
The ferry was pulling in to the dock.
• harbour, quay, jetty, wharf, landing stage, dockyard, pier, port, marina

dock VERB
❶ *The ferry docks at 8 a.m.*
• moor, berth, tie up, anchor
❷ *I am going to dock ten points from your final score.*
• deduct, take away, subtract, remove, cut

doctor NOUN
She needs to see a doctor.
• physician, general practitioner, GP, consultant
(*informal*) doc, medic
SEE ALSO medicine

document NOUN
He found a box containing old documents.
• paper, record, file, certificate, deed, report

dodge VERB
❶ *I just managed to dodge the snowball.*
• avoid, evade, sidestep
❷ *She tried to dodge the question.*
• avoid, evade, sidestep, duck
❸ *He dodged in and out of the line of cars.*
• dart, dive, slip, duck, wriggle

dog NOUN
Our dog has a very shaggy coat.
• hound
(*informal*) mutt, pooch
– An uncomplimentary word for a dog is cur.

WORD WEB

Some breeds of dog:
➤ Afghan hound   ➤ Alsatian

- basset hound
- beagle
- bloodhound
- boxer
- bulldog
- bull terrier
- cairn terrier
- chihuahua
- cocker spaniel
- collie
- corgi
- dachshund
- Dalmatian
- Dobermann
- fox terrier
- golden retriever
- Great Dane
- greyhound
- husky
- Irish setter
- Labrador
- mastiff
- Pekinese or Pekingese
- Pomeranian
- pointer
- poodle
- pug
- retriever
- Rottweiler
- St Bernard
- Schnauzer
- setter
- sheepdog
- spaniel
- terrier
- Weimaraner
- West Highland terrier
- whippet
- wolfhound
- Yorkshire terrier (*informal* Yorkie)

- A female dog is a **bitch**.
- A young dog is a **pup, puppy** or **whelp**.
- A dog of pure breed with known ancestors has a **pedigree**.
- A dog of mixed breeds is a **mongrel**.
- A word meaning 'to do with dogs' is **canine**.

For tips on describing animals see **animal**.

dole VERB
➤ **dole out**
She started doling out cartons of fruit juice.
• give out, distribute, dispense, hand out, dish out, deal out

domestic ADJECTIVE
❶ *At weekends I do various domestic chores.*
• household, family
❷ *Cats and dogs are domestic animals.*
• domesticated, tame, pet
OPPOSITE wild

dominant ADJECTIVE
❶ *Arabic is the dominant language of*
the Middle East.
• leading, main, primary, chief, major, foremost, principal, powerful, important, influential
OPPOSITE minor
❷ *The castle is a dominant feature of the landscape.*
• conspicuous, prominent, obvious, large, imposing, eye-catching
OPPOSITE insignificant

dominate VERB
❶ *Their team dominated the first half.*
• control, direct, monopolize, govern, take control of, take over
❷ *The mountain dominates the whole landscape.*
• tower over, loom over, overlook, command, dwarf

donate VERB
She donates a lot of money to charity.
• give, contribute, grant, present

donation NOUN
We rely on donations from the public.
• contribution, gift, grant, offering

done ADJECTIVE
❶ *My thank-you letters are all done now.*
• finished, complete, over
❷ *The cake will be brown on top when it's done.*
• cooked, ready

donor NOUN
The money was a gift of an anonymous donor.
• benefactor, contributor, sponsor, patron, backer

doomed ADJECTIVE
The mission was doomed from the start.
• ill-fated, ill-starred, fated, cursed, jinxed, damned

door NOUN
She walked out through the door.
• entrance, exit, doorway, portal
– A door in a floor or ceiling is a **hatch** or **trapdoor**.
– The plank or stone underneath a door is the **threshold**.

– The beam or stone above a door is the
lintel.

dose NOUN
a dose of medicine
• measure, dosage, portion

dot NOUN
There were dots of paint on the carpet.
• spot, speck, fleck, point, mark, speckle
➤ **on the dot**
(*informal*) *The bus leaves at nine on the
dot.*
• exactly, precisely, on time

dot VERB
The hillside was dotted with sheep.
• spot, fleck, mark, spatter, scatter,
sprinkle, pepper

dote VERB
➤ **dote on someone**
She dotes on her grandchildren.
• adore, be devoted to, love dearly,
worship, idolize, cherish, treasure

double ADJECTIVE
*You enter the room through a double set
of doors.*
• dual, twofold, paired, twin, matching,
duplicate

double NOUN
Anna is the double of her sister.
• twin, duplicate, lookalike
IDIOMS spitting image, dead ringer
– A living organism created as an exact
copy of another one is a **clone**.

doubt NOUN
❶ *Have you any doubt about his story?*
• distrust, suspicion, mistrust,
hesitation, reservation, scepticism,
wariness, misgivings
OPPOSITE confidence
❷ *There is no doubt that you will pass
your exam.*
• question, uncertainty, ambiguity,
controversy, confusion
OPPOSITE certainty

doubt VERB
There is no reason to doubt his story.
• distrust, feel uncertain about, feel
unsure about, question, disbelieve,
mistrust, suspect, be sceptical about,
be suspicious of, be wary of, have
misgivings about
OPPOSITE trust

doubtful ADJECTIVE
❶ *I was doubtful about the idea at first.*
• unsure, uncertain, unconvinced,
hesitant, distrustful, sceptical,
suspicious, wary
IDIOM in two minds
OPPOSITE certain
❷ *Our plans for the weekend are looking
doubtful.*
• unlikely, improbable, in doubt
❸ *It was a doubtful decision by the
referee.*
• questionable, debatable, arguable,
open to question
(*informal*) iffy

downfall NOUN
His enemies began to plot his downfall.
• ruin, fall, collapse, overthrow, failure,
undoing

downward ADJECTIVE
*We took the downward path into the
valley.*
• downhill, descending
OPPOSITE upward

doze VERB
He began to doze by the fire.
• rest, sleep, nap, nod off
(*informal*) drop off, have a snooze
IDIOM (*informal*) have forty winks

drab ADJECTIVE
The room was painted in drab colours.
• dull, dingy, dreary, cheerless,
colourless, dismal, gloomy, sombre
OPPOSITES bright, cheerful

draft NOUN
I wrote a first draft of my story.
• outline, plan, sketch, rough version

draft VERB
I began to draft my first chapter.
• outline, plan, prepare, sketch, work out

a
b
c
d
e
f
g
h
i
j
k
l
m
n
o
p
q
r
s
t
u
v
w
x
y
z

drag VERB

He came in, dragging a suitcase behind him.
• pull, tow, haul, draw, tug, trail, heave, lug
OPPOSITE push

dragon NOUN

For creatures found in fantasy fiction see fantasy.

drain NOUN

Surplus water runs away along a drain.
• ditch, channel, drainpipe, gutter, pipe, sewer

drain VERB

❶ *If they drain the marsh, lots of water birds will die.*
• dry out, empty out, remove water from
❷ *You need to drain oil from the engine.*
• draw off, empty, extract, siphon off, bleed
❸ *The water slowly drained away.*
• flow, stream, trickle, seep, leak, ooze
❹ *The tough climb drained my energy.*
• use up, consume, exhaust, deplete, expend, sap
❺ *I waited till everyone had drained their glass.*
• drink up, empty, swallow, quaff (*informal*) knock back, swig

drama NOUN

❶ *a television drama*
• play, dramatization
❷ *She is studying drama at college.*
• acting, the theatre, the stage, stagecraft
❸ *We were witnessing the drama of a real robbery.*
• action, excitement, suspense, spectacle

⊛ **WORD WEB**

Some types of drama:

➤ ballet	➤ dance theatre
➤ comedy	➤ improvisation
➤ comic sketch	➤ melodrama

➤ mime	➤ review
➤ musical	➤ situation comedy (*informal* sitcom)
➤ music theatre	
➤ mystery play	
➤ one-act play	
➤ opera	➤ soap opera (*informal* soap)
➤ pantomime (*informal* panto)	➤ tragedy

Parts of a play:

➤ act	➤ script or playscript
➤ scene	
➤ prologue	➤ dialogue
➤ intermission	➤ monologue
➤ finale	➤ soliloquy

Parts of a theatre:

➤ apron	➤ front of house
➤ auditorium	➤ green room
➤ balcony or circle	➤ orchestra pit
➤ box office	➤ proscenium
➤ curtain	➤ stage
➤ dressing room	➤ stalls
➤ foyer	➤ wings

People involved in drama:

➤ actor (*formal* thespian)	➤ dramatist or playwright
➤ actress	➤ producer
➤ audience	➤ prompter
➤ cast	➤ set designer
➤ director	➤ stagehand
➤ dramatis personae	➤ stage manager
	➤ voice coach

Other terms relating to drama:

➤ acting	➤ ensemble
➤ amphitheatre	➤ entrance
➤ aside	➤ exit
➤ audition	➤ lines
➤ backdrop	➤ off-stage
➤ backstage	➤ on-stage
➤ blocking	➤ premiere
➤ casting	➤ props
➤ characters	➤ protagonist
➤ chorus	➤ read-through
➤ cue	➤ rehearsal
➤ downstage	➤ scenery
➤ dress rehearsal	➤ set design

> stage directions   > theatre in the
> stage set   round
> tableau   > upstage

dramatic ADJECTIVE
❶ She is a member of the local dramatic society.
• theatrical, stage
❷ The ending of the film is very dramatic.
• exciting, thrilling, action-packed, sensational, spectacular, eventful, gripping, riveting
❸ The next day saw a dramatic change in the weather.
• noticeable, considerable, substantial, remarkable, marked, extreme

drank
past tense see **drink**

drastic ADJECTIVE
It was time to take drastic action.
• desperate, extreme, radical, harsh, severe, serious, far-reaching
OPPOSITE moderate

draught NOUN
I could feel a cold draught from the window.
• breeze, current of air, gust, puff

draw VERB
❶ My brother is good at drawing animals.
• sketch, trace, doodle, outline, illustrate, depict, portray
❷ She drew her chair up to the table.
• pull, drag, haul, tow, tug, lug, heave
❸ The train drew slowly into the station.
• move, progress, proceed, roll, inch, cruise, glide
❹ The samurai warrior drew his sword.
• pull out, take out, withdraw, unsheathe
❺ The fair drew large crowds.
• attract, bring in, pull in
❻ The two teams drew 1–1.
• finish equal, tie
❼ Where did you draw your information from?
• take, extract, derive

> draw near
A shadowy figure drew near us.
• approach, advance, come near
> draw something up
The lawyers will draw up a new contract.
• compose, write out, formulate, prepare, draft, devise, design

draw NOUN
❶ The game ended in a draw.
• tie, dead heat
❷ I won a television in the prize draw.
• lottery, raffle

drawback NOUN
The only real drawback is the cost.
• disadvantage, downside, difficulty, handicap, obstacle, inconvenience, hindrance, snag, catch
IDIOM fly in the ointment
OPPOSITES advantage, plus

drawing NOUN
There was a drawing of a bowl of fruit on the wall.
• sketch, illustration, picture, design, study, cartoon, doodle, scribble

dread NOUN
The thought of entering the cave filled me with dread.
• fear, terror, trepidation, alarm, apprehension, anxiety

dread VERB
She was dreading the exam results.
• fear, be afraid of, worry about, be anxious about
OPPOSITE look forward to

dreadful ADJECTIVE
❶ There has been a dreadful accident at sea.
• terrible, appalling, horrendous, horrible, distressing, shocking, upsetting, tragic, grim
❷ I thought the acting was dreadful.
• bad, awful, terrible, abysmal, atrocious, abominable, dire (informal) rotten, rubbish, lousy
OPPOSITES good, excellent

a b c d e f g h i j k l m n o p q r s t u v w x y z

dream NOUN

❶ *I was woken by a bad dream.*
– A bad dream is a **nightmare**.
– A dreamlike experience you have while awake is a **daydream**, **fantasy** or **reverie**.
– Something you see in a dream or daydream is a **vision**.
– The dreamlike state when you are hypnotized is a **trance**.
– Something you think you see that is not real is a **hallucination** or an **illusion**.
❷ *Her dream is to be on the stage.*
• ambition, hope, wish, desire, longing, yearning, aspiration, goal

dream VERB

I dreamed I was lost in a maze.
• imagine, fancy, fantasize, daydream
➤ **dream of**
I've always dreamt of being an astronomer.
• wish to, hope to, aspire to, long to, yearn to, hanker after

dreary ADJECTIVE

❶ *The coach driver had a very dreary voice.*
• dull, boring, tedious, flat, monotonous, unexciting, uninteresting
OPPOSITE lively
❷ *When will this dreary weather end?*
• dull, dismal, depressing, gloomy, cheerless, murky, overcast
OPPOSITES bright, sunny

drench VERB

The rain drenched me to the skin.
• soak, saturate, wet through, steep, douse, drown

dress NOUN

❶ *She wore a beautiful red dress.*
• frock, gown, robe
❷ *The invitation said to wear casual dress.*
• clothes, clothing, attire, outfit, costume, garments, wear
SEE ALSO clothes

dress VERB

❶ *I woke and dressed quickly.*
• get dressed, put clothes on
OPPOSITE undress

❷ *She was dressed in a smart suit.*
• clothe, attire, deck out, garb
❸ *A nurse dressed my wound.*
• bandage, bind, wrap, put a dressing on

dressing NOUN

The nurse put a dressing on the wound.
• bandage, plaster

drew

past tense see **draw**

dribble VERB

❶ *The baby was dribbling down its chin.*
• drool, slobber
❷ *Water dribbled out of the tap.*
• drip, trickle, drizzle, leak, ooze, seep

drift VERB

❶ *The boat began to drift downstream.*
• float, be carried, be borne, glide, waft
❷ *People started to drift out of the hall.*
• wander, stray, meander

drift NOUN

❶ *The car was stuck in a snow drift.*
• bank, heap, mound, pile, ridge
❷ *I'm afraid I don't get your drift.*
• meaning, point, gist, sense

drill NOUN

❶ *There was a fire drill at school today.*
• practice, training
❷ *You all know the drill by now.*
• procedure, routine, system

drill VERB

It took a long time to drill through the wall.
• bore, penetrate, pierce, puncture

drink VERB

I drank the potion in one go.
• swallow, gulp, quaff, drain, sip, slurp
(*informal*) swig, glug, knock back, down

drink NOUN

❶ *They sell a selection of soft drinks.*
• beverage
❷ *He took a long drink from his flask.*
• swallow, draught, gulp, sip
(*informal*) swig, slug, glug

❸ *We listened to a talk on the dangers of drink.*
• alcohol, liquor, spirits
(*informal*) booze

drip VERB
Water was dripping from the ceiling.
• drop, dribble, splash, trickle, leak

drip NOUN
He found a bucket to catch the drips of water.
• drop, dribble, spot, splash, trickle

drive VERB
❶ *Can you drive a tractor?*
• control, operate, handle, manage, steer, work
❷ *She offered to drive us to the station.*
• run, give someone a lift, take, transport, convey, ferry
❸ *The engine is driven by wind power.*
• power, propel, move, push
❹ *The dogs drove the sheep into the field.*
• direct, guide, herd
❺ *Hunger drove them to steal.*
• compel, lead, force, oblige, prompt, spur
❻ *He drove a nail into the wall.*
• push, thrust, plunge, sink, ram, hammer
➤ **drive someone out**
Many people were driven out of their homes.
• eject, throw out, expel, evict
– To drive people out of their country is to **banish** or **exile** them.

drive NOUN
❶ *We went for a drive in the country.*
• ride, trip, journey, outing, excursion, jaunt
(*informal*) spin
❷ *She definitely has the drive to succeed.*
• ambition, determination, commitment, motivation, keenness, energy, zeal

driver NOUN
Many drivers go too fast.
• motorist
– A person who drives someone's car as a job is a **chauffeur**.

droop VERB
The roses have begun to droop.
• wilt, sag, hang down, bend, flop, slump

drop NOUN
❶ *Large drops of rain began to fall.*
• drip, droplet, spot, bead, blob, globule
❷ *Add a drop or two of milk.*
• dash, dribble, splash, trickle, spot
❸ *Experts predict a drop in the price of oil.*
• decrease, reduction, cut, fall, slump
❹ *There's a drop of two metres on the other side of the wall.*
• descent, drop, plunge

drop VERB
❶ *Suddenly a hawk dropped out of the sky.*
• descend, dive, swoop, dip, plunge, plummet
❷ *I dropped to the ground exhausted.*
• collapse, fall, sink, subside, slump, tumble
❸ *Harry dropped the ball and ran.*
• let fall, let go of, release, lose your grip on
❹ *Temperatures have dropped sharply.*
• decrease, decline, reduce, fall, dip, slump
❺ *Let's drop the idea altogether.*
• abandon, discard, reject, give up, scrap, dispense with
(*informal*) ditch, dump
❻ *He's been dropped from the team.*
• omit, eliminate, exclude, leave out
➤ **drop in**
Do drop in on your way home.
• visit, call, pay a call
➤ **drop off**
I felt myself starting to drop off.
• fall asleep, doze off, drift off
(*informal*) nod off
➤ **drop out**
Three contestants have now dropped out.
• withdraw, back out, pull out
(*informal*) quit

a
b
c
d
e
f
g
h
i
j
k
l
m
n
o
p
q
r
s
t
u
v
w
x
y
z

drove
past tense see **drive**

drown VERB
The music from upstairs drowned our conversation.
• overwhelm, overpower, drown out

drowsy ADJECTIVE
By midnight, I was starting to feel drowsy.
• sleepy, tired, weary

drug NOUN
a new drug for cancer
• medicine, remedy, treatment
– A drug which relieves pain is an **analgesic** or a **painkiller**.
– A drug which calms you down is a **sedative** or **tranquillizer**.
– Drugs which make you more active are **stimulants**.

drum NOUN
For musical instruments see **music**.

dry ADJECTIVE
❶ Nothing will grow in this dry soil.
• arid, parched, waterless, moistureless, dehydrated, desiccated, barren, shrivelled
OPPOSITES wet, moist
❷ He gave rather a dry speech.
• dull, boring, uninteresting, dreary, tedious, unimaginative, uninspiring
OPPOSITES interesting, lively
❸ She has a dry sense of humour.
• ironic, wry, subtle

dry VERB
❶ If it's sunny, I'll hang the clothes out to dry.
• get dry, dry out
❷ The earth had been dried by the desert sun.
• parch, scorch, dehydrate, desiccate, shrivel, wither

dual ADJECTIVE
This building has a dual purpose.
• double, twofold, twin, combined

dubious ADJECTIVE
❶ I'm a bit dubious about the idea.
• doubtful, uncertain, unsure, hesitant, sceptical, suspicious
OPPOSITES certain, sure
❷ The firm has a dubious reputation.
• unreliable, untrustworthy, questionable, suspect
(informal) shady, dodgy

duck NOUN
a yellow-billed duck
– A male duck is a **drake**.
– A young duck is a **duckling**.

duck VERB
❶ I ducked to avoid the snowball.
• bend down, bob down, crouch, stoop
❷ They threatened to duck me in the pool.
• dip, immerse, plunge, submerge
❸ Stop trying to duck the question.
• avoid, evade, dodge, shirk, sidestep

due ADJECTIVE
❶ The train is due in five minutes.
• expected, anticipated, scheduled for
❷ Your subscription is now due.
• owed, owing, payable, outstanding, unpaid
❸ We should treat animals with due respect.
• proper, suitable, appropriate, fitting, adequate, sufficient, deserved

dug
past tense see **dig**

dull ADJECTIVE
❶ The walls were a dull shade of green.
• drab, dingy, dreary, sombre, muted, subdued
OPPOSITE bright
❷ It was a dull morning.
• cloudy, overcast, grey, sunless, murky, dreary
OPPOSITE clear
❸ The film was so dull that I fell asleep.
• uninteresting, boring, tedious, unexciting, unimaginative, monotonous, flat, lacklustre, lifeless, uneventful
OPPOSITE interesting

❹ I heard a dull thud from upstairs.
• indistinct, muffled, muted
OPPOSITES distinct, sharp
❺ He's rather a dull student.
• stupid, slow, unintelligent, unimaginative, obtuse
(informal) dim, dense
OPPOSITES clever, bright

dumb ADJECTIVE
❶ We were all struck dumb with amazement.
• silent, mute, speechless, tongue-tied
IDIOM at a loss for words
❷ (informal) What a dumb question!
• stupid, silly, unintelligent, brainless, idiotic
(informal) daft

dumbfounded ADJECTIVE
I was dumbfounded when I heard the news.
• amazed, astonished, astounded, stunned, staggered, thunderstruck, speechless, struck dumb
(informal) flabbergasted
(British informal) gobsmacked

dump NOUN
❶ a rubbish dump
• tip, dumping ground, scrapheap
❷ (informal) This place is a bit of a dump.
• tip, hovel, pigsty, mess
(informal) hole

dump VERB
❶ An old mattress had been dumped at the side of the road.
• get rid of, throw away, throw out, discard, dispose of, scrap
❷ Just dump your things in the bedroom.
• put down, set down, place, drop, deposit, throw down
(informal) plonk, bung

duplicate NOUN
This is an exact duplicate of the letter.
• copy, reproduction, replica
– An exact copy of a document is a **facsimile**.
– A person who looks exactly like you is your **double** or **twin**.

– A living organism which is a duplicate of another one is a **clone**.

durable ADJECTIVE
Denim is a very durable material.
• hard-wearing, lasting, strong, tough, robust
OPPOSITE flimsy

duration NOUN
We'll be away for the duration of the holidays.
• length, period, extent, span

dusk NOUN
Bats begin to emerge at dusk.
• twilight, nightfall, sunset, sundown, close of day
(poetic) gloaming
OPPOSITE dawn

dust NOUN
The furniture was covered in dust.
• dirt, grime, particles, powder, grit

dust VERB
❶ I dusted the bookshelves.
• wipe, clean, brush, sweep
❷ Now dust the top of the cake with icing sugar.
• sprinkle, sift, powder

dusty ADJECTIVE
In the attic were piles of dusty old books.
• dirty, grimy, grubby
OPPOSITE clean

dutiful ADJECTIVE
She had always been a dutiful daughter.
• faithful, loyal, obedient, devoted, conscientious, reliable, responsible, trustworthy
OPPOSITES irresponsible, lazy

duty NOUN
❶ It's our duty to help those in need.
• responsibility, obligation, mission
❷ Here is a list of your daily duties on board the boat.
• job, task, assignment, chore
❸ The government is increasing the duty on petrol.
• tax, charge

dwell *VERB*
➤ dwell on
Try not to dwell on the past.
• keep thinking about, worry about, brood over

dwelling *NOUN*
see house

dwindle *VERB*
Our supplies are dwindling fast.
• diminish, decrease, decline, lessen, shrink, subside, wane
OPPOSITE increase

dye *VERB*
My sister has dyed her hair red.
• colour, tint, stain

dynamic *ADJECTIVE*
The team has a dynamic new captain.
• energetic, lively, spirited, enthusiastic, vigorous, forceful, active
OPPOSITES apathetic, laid-back

Ee

eager *ADJECTIVE*
Vicky is always eager to help.
• keen, enthusiastic, anxious, impatient, desperate, willing
(*informal*) itching
OPPOSITE unenthusiastic

early *ADJECTIVE*
❶ *The bus was early today.*
• ahead of time, ahead of schedule
OPPOSITE late
❷ *the early attempts at manned flight*
• first, initial, preliminary, advance
OPPOSITES recent, latest
❸ *an example of early cave painting*
• old, primitive, ancient
OPPOSITES modern, later

earn *VERB*
❶ *How much do you earn each week?*
• be paid, receive, get, make, bring in
OPPOSITE lose
❷ *She trained hard and earned her success.*
• deserve, merit, warrant, justify, be worthy of

earnest *ADJECTIVE*
He's a terribly earnest young man.
• serious, sincere, solemn, thoughtful, grave, sober
OPPOSITES casual, flippant

earth *NOUN*
❶ *Four-fifths of the Earth's surface is covered by water.*
• world, globe, planet
❷ *an area of hard, parched earth*
• ground, land, soil, dirt, clay
– Rich, fertile earth is **loam**.
– The top layer of fertile earth is **topsoil**.
– Rich earth consisting of decayed plants is **humus**.

earthquake *NOUN*

WORD WEB

– When there is an earthquake, you feel a shock or **tremor**.
– A word meaning 'to do with earthquakes' is **seismic**.
– The scientific study of earthquakes is **seismology**.

ease *NOUN*
❶ *She can swim ten lengths of the pool with ease.*
• effortlessness, no trouble, no difficulty, simplicity
OPPOSITE difficulty
❷ *Wealthy Romans led lives of ease.*
• comfort, contentment, leisure, relaxation, rest, tranquillity
OPPOSITE stress

ease *VERB*
❶ *The doctor gave her some pills to ease the pain.*
• relieve, lessen, reduce, soothe, alleviate, moderate
OPPOSITE aggravate
❷ *My headache slowly began to ease.*
• decrease, lessen, abate, subside, let up, die down, slacken
OPPOSITES increase, intensify
❸ *We eased the piano into position.*
• edge, guide, manoeuvre, inch, slide, slip

easily *ADVERB*
The rules of the game are easily understood.
• without difficulty, with ease, effortlessly, comfortably, readily
OPPOSITE with difficulty

east *NOUN, ADJECTIVE & ADVERB*
Queensland is in the east of Australia.
– The parts of a country or continent in the east are the **eastern** parts.
– To travel towards the east is to travel **eastward** or **eastwards**.
– A wind from the east is an **easterly** wind.

– In the past, the countries of east Asia were called **oriental** countries.

easy ADJECTIVE
❶ *Tonight's homework is really easy.*
• undemanding, effortless, light (*informal*) a cinch, a doddle
IDIOMS a piece of cake, plain sailing
❷ *The instructions were easy to understand.*
• simple, straightforward, uncomplicated, clear, plain, elementary
❸ *Our cat has an easy life.*
• carefree, comfortable, peaceful, relaxed, leisurely, restful, tranquil, untroubled
OPPOSITES difficult, hard

eat VERB
❶ *Seals eat their own weight in fish every day.*
• consume, devour, swallow, feed on, dine on
(*informal*) put away
❷ *Let's eat out tonight.*
• have a meal, have dinner, dine, feed
The synonyms feed and feed on are used mainly about animals: *Bats typically feed around dusk and dawn..*
➤ **eat away at** or **eat into**
Salt water had eaten away at the timbers.
• corrode, erode, wear away, decay, rot

S   **OVERUSED WORD**

❶ To eat **quickly, greedily:**

➤ bolt down   ➤ gobble
➤ demolish   ➤ gulp
(*informal*) guzzle, scoff, wolf down
Todd and his friends demolished a whole pizza each.

❷ To eat **noisily:**

➤ chomp   ➤ gnaw
➤ crunch   ➤ munch
➤ gnash   ➤ slurp
The contestants were dared to munch live insects.

---

❸ To eat **large amounts:**

➤ feast   ➤ gorge
IDIOM eat like a horse
The guests gorged themselves on roasted meats.

❹ To eat **too much:**

➤ overeat
(*informal*) stuff yourself, make a pig of yourself
Uncle Amos had overeaten and had to lie down.

❺ To eat **small amounts:**

➤ nibble   ➤ pick away at
➤ peck   ➤ snack on
➤ pick at   ➤ taste
Nicole nibbled nervously on a cracker.

❻ To eat **something completely:**

➤ eat up   ➤ gobble up
(*informal*) polish off
I ate up every last crumb on my plate.

❼ To eat **with pleasure:**

➤ relish   ➤ savour
(*informal*) tuck into, get stuck into
The cheese is best eaten slowly to savour the taste.

SEE ALSO bite, chew

---

ebb VERB
❶ *The fishermen waited for the tide to ebb.*
• recede, go out, retreat, flow back
❷ *She felt her strength began to ebb.*
• decline, weaken, lessen, diminish, dwindle, fade, wane

eccentric ADJECTIVE
He had an eccentric style of dress.
• odd, peculiar, strange, weird, bizarre, abnormal, unusual, curious, unconventional, unorthodox, outlandish, quirky, zany

(*informal*) **way-out, dotty**
OPPOSITES conventional, orthodox

echo *VERB*
❶ *The sound echoed across the valley.*
• resound, reverberate, ring
❷ *Her words echoed my own feelings.*
• repeat, reproduce, restate, imitate, mimic, parrot

ecological *ADJECTIVE*
an ecological campaigner
• environmental, green, conservation, eco-
SEE ALSO environment

economic *ADJECTIVE*
❶ *a global economic crisis*
• financial, fiscal, monetary, budgetary
❷ *The theatre is no longer economic to run.*
• profitable, lucrative, fruitful, productive
OPPOSITE unprofitable

economical *ADJECTIVE*
❶ *You need to be economical with your money.*
• careful, prudent, thrifty, frugal
– If you are economical with money in a selfish way, you are **mean, miserly** or **parsimonious**.
OPPOSITES wasteful, profligate
❷ *This car is economical to run.*
• cheap, inexpensive, low-cost, reasonable
OPPOSITES expensive, costly

ecstatic *ADJECTIVE*
I was ecstatic when I was told that I had won.
• elated, delighted, overjoyed, gleeful, joyful, blissful, rapturous, euphoric, exultant
IDIOMS (*informal*) **over the moon, tickled pink**

edge *NOUN*
❶ *a house on the edge of a lake*
• border, margin, side, fringe, brink, verge, perimeter, boundary
❷ *The edge of this cup is chipped.*
• brim, rim, lip

❸ *Her voice had an edge to it.*
• sharpness, keenness, intensity, bite

edge *VERB*
❶ *He edged slowly away from the door.*
• creep, inch, work your way, sidle, steal, slink
❷ *Her bonnet was edged with black lace.*
• trim, hem

edgy *ADJECTIVE*
Sitting there all alone, I began to feel edgy.
• nervous, restless, anxious, agitated, excitable, tense, jumpy, fidgety
(*informal*) jittery, uptight
OPPOSITE calm

edible *ADJECTIVE*
Are these berries edible?
• safe to eat, fit to eat, non-poisonous
OPPOSITE poisonous
The words **edible** and **eatable** do not mean the same thing. An **edible** mushroom is safe to eat, whereas an **eatable** mushroom is in a good enough condition to be eaten.

edit *VERB*
The letters were edited before they were published.
• revise, correct, adapt, modify, rework, rewrite, rephrase

edition *NOUN*
a special Christmas edition of the magazine
• issue, number, version

educate *VERB*
The job of a school is to educate young people.
• teach, train, inform, instruct, tutor, school

educated *ADJECTIVE*
She is an educated woman.
• knowledgeable, learned, literate, well informed, well read, cultivated, cultured, intellectual, scholarly

education *NOUN*
a school for the education of local children
• schooling, teaching, training,

a
b
c
d
e
f
g
h
i
j
k
l
m
n
o
p
q
r
s
t
u
v
w
x
y
z

instruction, tuition, tutoring, coaching
– A programme of education is a
curriculum or **syllabus**.

eerie ADJECTIVE
There was an eerie silence in the hall.
• weird, uncanny, sinister, ghostly,
unearthly, other-worldly
(*informal*) scary, spooky, creepy

effect NOUN
❶ *the harmful effects of the sun's rays*
• result, consequence, outcome, sequel,
upshot
❷ *The music had a strange effect on me.*
• impact, influence
❸ *The lighting gives an effect of warmth.*
• feeling, impression, sense, illusion

effective ADJECTIVE
❶ *an effective treatment for spots*
• successful, powerful, potent
OPPOSITES ineffective, weak
❷ *He presented an effective argument
against hunting.*
• convincing, persuasive, compelling,
impressive, strong, powerful, telling
OPPOSITE unconvincing

efficient ADJECTIVE
❶ *Hyenas are supremely efficient
hunters.*
• competent, capable, able, proficient,
skilled, effective, productive
❷ *an efficient method of transport*
• economic, cost-effective, streamlined,
organized, orderly
OPPOSITE inefficient

effort NOUN
❶ *A lot of effort went into making the
film.*
• work, trouble, exertion, application,
industry, labour, toil
❷ *I made an effort to be friends with
her.*
• attempt, try, endeavour, go
(*informal*) shot, stab, bash

eject VERB
❶ *Lava is ejected from volcanoes.*
• discharge, emit, send out, vent, belch,
spew out

❷ *The protesters were ejected from the
meeting.*
• remove, expel, evict, banish, throw
out, turn out
(*informal*) kick out

elaborate ADJECTIVE
*It is a clever story with an elaborate
plot.*
• complicated, complex, detailed,
intricate, involved, convoluted
OPPOSITE simple

elated ADJECTIVE
We were elated when we won the match.
• delighted, pleased, thrilled, joyful,
ecstatic, gleeful, exultant, delirious
IDIOMS (*informal*) over the moon,
tickled pink

elbow VERB
*He elbowed his way to the front of the
queue.*
• push, shove, nudge, jostle

elder ADJECTIVE
My elder brother is at college now.
• older, big
OPPOSITE younger

elderly ADJECTIVE
I helped an elderly lady onto the bus.
• aged, ageing, old, senior
OPPOSITE young

elect VERB
We elected a new team captain.
• vote for, vote in, appoint, choose, pick,
select

election NOUN
*We had an election to choose a new
captain.*
• vote, ballot, poll

electricity NOUN
*The electricity went off in the middle of
the thunderstorm.*
• power, power supply, current
– Someone whose job is to fit and repair
electrical equipment is an **electrician**.

WORD WEB

- A flow of electricity is called a **current**.
- An electrical **circuit** is a complete path that an electric current can flow around.
- The units used to measure electric current are called **amps** or **amperes**.
- **Volts** are a measure of the energy of a flow of electricity.
- **Watts** are a measure of electrical power.

elegant *ADJECTIVE*
She always wears elegant clothes.
• graceful, stylish, fashionable, chic, smart, tasteful, sophisticated
OPPOSITE inelegant

element *NOUN*
We discussed various elements of the play.
• part, feature, aspect, factor, facet, component, ingredient, strand
➤ **be in your element**
Owen is in his element on stage.
• be at home, be comfortable, be happy, enjoy yourself

elementary *ADJECTIVE*
a course in elementary maths
• basic, simple, easy, fundamental, rudimentary, straightforward
OPPOSITES advanced, complex

eligible *ADJECTIVE*
Children under twelve are not eligible to enter.
• qualified, allowed, authorized, permitted, entitled
OPPOSITE ineligible

eliminate *VERB*
a spray to eliminate bad odours
• get rid of, put an end to, do away with, stamp out
– To be eliminated from a competition is to be **knocked out**.

eloquent *ADJECTIVE*
The winning author gave an eloquent speech.
• articulate, fluent, well expressed, expressive, powerful

elude *VERB*
He eluded his pursuers with ease.
• avoid, evade, escape from, get away from, dodge, shake off

embark *VERB*
Passengers may embark at any port.
• board, go aboard
OPPOSITE disembark
➤ **embark on something**
They were about to embark on a dangerous mission.
• begin, start, commence, undertake, set out on

embarrass *VERB*
I didn't mean to embarrass you in front of your friends.
• humiliate, shame, mortify, make you blush

embarrassed *ADJECTIVE*
I feel embarrassed when I speak in public.
• humiliated, ashamed, awkward, uncomfortable, bashful, mortified, self-conscious, red-faced

embarrassing *ADJECTIVE*
The show was so bad it was embarrassing.
• humiliating, mortifying, shameful *(informal)* cringe-making, toe-curling

emblem *NOUN*
The dove is an emblem of peace.
• symbol, sign, representation, image, mark, badge, crest

embrace *VERB*
❶ *The old man got up and embraced his son.*
• hug, clasp, cuddle, hold
❷ *The exhibition embraces both modern and traditional art.*
• include, incorporate, take in, cover

a
b
c
d
e
f
g
h
i
j
k
l
m
n
o
p
q
r
s
t
u
v
w
x
y
z

❸ *She's always ready to embrace new ideas.*
• welcome, accept, adopt, take up
IDIOM take on board

emerge VERB
❶ *Zak emerged gingerly from his hiding place.*
• appear, issue, come out, come into view
❷ *Gradually more details began to emerge.*
• become known, be revealed, come out, come to light, unfold

emergency NOUN
Try to keep calm in an emergency.
• crisis, disaster, catastrophe, calamity

emigrate VERB
Thousands were forced to emigrate to America.
• leave the country, move abroad, relocate, resettle
OPPOSITE immigrate

eminent ADJECTIVE
a group of eminent scientists
• renowned, celebrated, famous, great, well known, distinguished, notable, prominent, respected, acclaimed, esteemed, illustrious
OPPOSITE unknown

emit VERB
❶ *The chimney was now emitting clouds of smoke.*
• discharge, expel, belch, blow out, give off
❷ *The satellite emits radio signals.*
• transmit, broadcast, give out, send out
OPPOSITE receive

emotion NOUN
His voice was full of emotion.
• feeling, passion, sentiment, heart, fervour, strength of feeling

emotional ADJECTIVE
❶ *He gave an emotional farewell speech.*
• moving, touching, stirring, affecting, poignant

❷ *She's a very emotional woman.*
• passionate, intense, excitable, sensitive, temperamental
OPPOSITES unemotional, cold

emphasis NOUN
❶ *This term we will give more emphasis to creative writing.*
• importance, prominence, weight, attention, priority
❷ *Put the emphasis on the first syllable.*
• stress, accent, weight, beat

emphasize VERB
Let me emphasize the need to stay calm.
• highlight, stress, focus on, draw attention to, spotlight, underline

employ VERB
❶ *The new centre will employ 100 workers.*
• hire, recruit, engage, take on, sign up, appoint
❷ *They employed a variety of methods to collect the information.*
• use, utilize, make use of, apply

employee NOUN
100 employees will work at the new centre.
• worker, member of staff
– All the employees of an organization are its **staff**, **personnel** or **workforce**.

employment NOUN
She is still looking for suitable employment.
• work, a job, an occupation, a profession, a trade
SEE ALSO job

empty ADJECTIVE
❶ *This bottle is empty.*
OPPOSITE full
❷ *The building has been empty for years.*
• unoccupied, uninhabited, vacant, deserted
OPPOSITE occupied
❸ *There's an empty space in the corner.*
• free, clear, blank, bare, unused
❹ *These warnings were not just empty threats.*
• meaningless, idle, hollow, ineffectual

empty VERB

❶ *Empty the dirty water from the sink.*
• drain, pour out, tip out, remove, extract
OPPOSITE fill
❷ *She emptied her handbag onto the table.*
• unload, unpack
❸ *The building emptied when the alarm went off.*
• clear, evacuate, vacate

enable VERB

❶ *The money will enable us to build a sports centre.*
• allow, make it possible for
❷ *A passport enables you to travel abroad.*
• permit, allow, entitle, authorize, qualify
OPPOSITE prevent (from)

enchanting ADJECTIVE

Sirens were said to lure sailors with their enchanting voices.
• captivating, charming, delightful, attractive, appealing, engaging, bewitching, spellbinding

enchantment NOUN

❶ *The island had an air of enchantment.*
• magic, wonder, delight, pleasure
❷ *a book of ancient enchantments*
• spell, incantation

enclose VERB

❶ *The garden was enclosed by a high wall.*
• surround, encircle, bound, close in, fence in, shut in
❷ *The documents were enclosed in a brown envelope.*
• contain, insert, wrap, bind, sheathe

enclosure NOUN

the new chimpanzee enclosure at the zoo
• compound, pen, cage
– An enclosure for chickens is a **coop** or **run**.
– An enclosure for horses is a **paddock**.
– An enclosure for sheep is a **fold**.

encounter VERB

❶ *He had never encountered a creature like this before.*
• meet, come across, run into, come face to face with
(*informal*) bump into
❷ *The space crew encountered some problems.*
• experience, come upon, confront, be faced with

encourage VERB

❶ *We went along to encourage our team.*
• support, motivate, inspire, cheer, spur on, egg on
❷ *She encouraged me to try the audition.*
• persuade, urge, press, coax
❸ *The scheme is designed to encourage new research.*
• stimulate, promote, boost, further, strengthen, foster, nurture, cultivate
OPPOSITE discourage

encouragement NOUN

My coach gave me a lot of encouragement.
• support, inspiration, motivation, morale boosting, incitement, stimulation, urging, incentive, stimulus, reassurance

encouraging ADJECTIVE

The results of the tests were encouraging.
• hopeful, positive, promising, reassuring, optimistic, cheering, favourable

end NOUN

❶ *There is a surprise twist at the end of the film.*
• ending, finish, close, conclusion, culmination, termination, finale
– A section added at the end of a letter is a **postscript**.
– A section added at the end of a story is an **epilogue**.
OPPOSITES start, beginning

a b c d e f g h i j k l m n o p q r s t u v w x y z

② *At last we had reached the end of our journey.*
• termination, destination
③ *The fence marks the end of the garden.*
• boundary, limit, extremity, bottom
OPPOSITE top
④ *We found ourselves at the end of the queue.*
• back, rear, tail
OPPOSITE head
⑤ *What end did you have in mind?*
• aim, purpose, intention, objective, plan, outcome, result

end VERB
① *The concert ended with a firework display.*
• close, conclude, come to an end, finish, stop, cease, terminate, culminate
(*informal*) round off, wind up
② *Britain ended its slave trade in 1807.*
• abolish, do away with, get rid of, put an end to, discontinue, terminate, eliminate, cancel

endanger VERB
Bad driving endangers other people.
• put at risk, put in danger, jeopardize, threaten, imperil
OPPOSITES protect, safeguard

endeavour VERB
We will endeavour to respond within 24 hours.
• try, attempt, aim, seek, strive, make an effort

endeavour NOUN
Despite our best endeavours, things can go wrong.
• attempt, effort, try, bid

ending NOUN
The ending of the film was the best part.
• end, finish, close, conclusion, culmination, finale

endless ADJECTIVE
① *Teachers need endless patience.*
• unending, limitless, infinite, inexhaustible, unlimited

② *There's an endless procession of cars along the main road.*
• continual, continuous, constant, incessant, interminable, perpetual, unbroken, uninterrupted, everlasting, ceaseless

endurance NOUN
The climb was a test of our endurance.
• perseverance, persistence, determination, resolution, stamina, fortitude, staying power

endure VERB
① *Many mill workers endured harsh conditions.*
• bear, stand, suffer, cope with, experience, go through, put up with, tolerate, face, undergo
② *These traditions have endured for centuries.*
• survive, continue, last, persist, abide, carry on, live on, keep going

enemy NOUN
They used to be friends but now they are bitter enemies.
• opponent, antagonist, adversary, rival
(*literary*) foe
OPPOSITES friend, ally

energetic ADJECTIVE
① *My mum has always been an energetic person.*
• dynamic, active, animated, spirited, tireless, indefatigable
IDIOM full of beans
OPPOSITES inactive, lethargic
② *It is a very energetic dance.*
• lively, vigorous, brisk, fast, quick moving, strenuous
OPPOSITES slow-paced, sluggish

energy NOUN
① *The dancers had tremendous energy.*
• liveliness, vitality, spirit, vigour, life, drive, zest, verve, gusto, enthusiasm, dynamism
(*informal*) get-up-and-go, zip, oomph
OPPOSITE lethargy

❷ *Wind power is a renewable source of energy.*
• power, fuel

enforce VERB
The umpire's job is to enforce the rules.
• impose, apply, administer, carry out, implement, put into effect, insist on

engage VERB
❶ *The plot failed to engage my attention.*
• capture, catch, grab, gain, hold, arrest, grip, absorb, occupy
❷ *It was a mistake to engage in conversation with him.*
• take part, participate, partake, join
❸ *We engaged the enemy at dawn.*
• attack, encounter, clash with, do battle with, take on, fight
❹ *The store always engages extra staff for Christmas.*
• employ, hire, recruit, take on, appoint

engaged ADJECTIVE
❶ *I'll be engaged all afternoon.*
• busy, occupied, employed, immersed (in), preoccupied (with)
(*informal*) tied up
❷ *I tried phoning but the line was engaged.*
• busy, being used, unavailable
OPPOSITES free, available

engagement NOUN
a business engagement
• meeting, appointment, commitment, date

engine NOUN
a wind-powered engine
• motor, mechanism, turbine
– A railway engine is a **locomotive**.

engrave VERB
The following words were engraved on the tombstone.
• carve, cut, etch, inscribe

engrossed ADJECTIVE
He was still engrossed in his book.
• absorbed, busy, occupied, preoccupied, engaged, immersed

engulf VERB
The tsunami engulfed several villages.
• flood, swamp, drown, immerse, inundate, overwhelm, submerge, swallow up

enhance VERB
The award will enhance the author's reputation.
• improve, strengthen, boost, further, increase, heighten

enjoy VERB
I enjoyed the film very much.
• like, love, be fond of, be keen on, relish, revel in, delight in, take pleasure in
(*informal*) get a kick out of
OPPOSITES dislike, hate
➤ **enjoy yourself**
We all enjoyed ourselves at the party.
• have fun, have a good time, celebrate
(*informal*) have a ball

enjoyable ADJECTIVE
I hope you find the show enjoyable.
• pleasant, agreeable, entertaining, amusing, pleasing, delightful, pleasurable, satisfying
OPPOSITE unpleasant

enlarge VERB
The zoo is enlarging its lion enclosure.
• expand, extend, develop, make bigger, broaden, widen, elongate, stretch
– To make something seem larger is to **magnify** it.
OPPOSITE reduce

enormous ADJECTIVE
Enormous waves battered the ship.
• huge, gigantic, immense, colossal, massive, monstrous, monumental, mountainous, towering, tremendous, vast, mighty, mammoth
(*informal*) whopping, humongous
(*literary*) gargantuan
OPPOSITES small, tiny

enough DETERMINER
We have enough food for thirty guests.
• sufficient, adequate, ample

enquire VERB
➤ **enquire about**
I enquired about train times to York.
• ask for, make enquiries about, request

enquiry NOUN
Please send your enquiries by email.
• question, query, request

enrage VERB
I was enraged by their stupidity.
• anger, infuriate, madden, incense, exasperate, provoke
IDIOMS make you see red, make your blood boil
OPPOSITES placate, pacify

enrol VERB
She enrolled at the local art school.
• join, sign up, register, put your name down, apply

ensure VERB
Please ensure that you lock the door.
• make certain, make sure, guarantee, see to it

enter VERB
❶ *Silence fell as she entered the room.*
• come in, walk in, go into
IDIOM set foot in
OPPOSITE leave
❷ *The bullet entered his left shoulder.*
• go into, penetrate, pierce, puncture
❸ *Please enter your details on the form.*
• insert, record, register, log, put down, set down, sign, write
OPPOSITE cancel
❹ *Four teams are entering the competition.*
• take part in, enrol in, sign up for, go in for, join in, participate in, compete in
OPPOSITE withdraw from

enterprise NOUN
❶ *Deep-sea diving is still a hazardous enterprise.*
• undertaking, activity, venture, task, business, exercise, project, scheme, mission

❷ *All the contestants showed enterprise and enthusiasm.*
• resourcefulness, initiative, drive, ambition, imagination

enterprising ADJECTIVE
The website was created by an enterprising group of students.
• resourceful, imaginative, creative, ambitious, entrepreneurial, intrepid, bold, adventurous, industrious
(*informal*) go-ahead

entertain VERB
❶ *We entertained ourselves by telling ghost stories.*
• amuse, divert, keep amused, interest, occupy
OPPOSITE bore
❷ *You can entertain guests in the private dining room.*
• receive, welcome, cater for, give hospitality to
❸ *She would never entertain such a foolish idea.*
• consider, contemplate, countenance, accept, hear of, think of

entertainer NOUN
For musicians and other performing artists see **music**, **performance**.

entertainment NOUN
Gladiators fought for the entertainment of huge crowds.
• amusement, recreation, diversion, enjoyment, fun

enthusiasm NOUN
We ran onto the pitch full of enthusiasm.
• keenness, commitment, drive, passion, fervour, zeal, zest, energy, vigour, gusto
OPPOSITE apathy

enthusiast NOUN
My brother is a motor racing enthusiast.
• fan, fanatic, devotee, lover, supporter, admirer, addict
(*informal*) freak, nut

enthusiastic ADJECTIVE
  ❶ *She has been an enthusiastic supporter of the club for years.*
• keen, passionate, avid, devoted, energetic, fervent, zealous
  OPPOSITE apathetic
  ❷ *The crowd burst into enthusiastic applause.*
• eager, excited, lively, vigorous, exuberant, hearty

entire ADJECTIVE
My brother spent the entire morning in bed.
• whole, complete, total, full

entirely ADVERB
I'm not entirely sure that I agree with you.
• completely, absolutely, totally, wholly, utterly, fully, perfectly, quite

entitle VERB
  ❶ *This coupon entitles you to a free ticket.*
• permit, allow, enable, authorize, qualify
  ❷ *The story is entitled 'The Return of Dracula'.*
• name, title, call, designate

entrance NOUN
  ❶ *Please pay at the main entrance.*
• entry, way in, access, approach, door, gate, portal
– The entrance to a cave is the **mouth**.
– An entrance hall is a **foyer** or **lobby**.
– When you go through the entrance to a building, you cross the **threshold**.
  OPPOSITE exit
  ❷ *Entrance to the museum is free.*
• admission, access, entry, admittance
  ❸ *My aunt made a dramatic entrance.*
• entry, arrival, appearance

entrant NOUN
A prize will be awarded to the winning entrant.
• contestant, competitor, contender, candidate, participant

entry NOUN
  ❶ *A van was blocking the entry to the school.*
• entrance, way in, access, approach, door, gate
  ❷ *We were refused entry.*
• admission, access, entrance, admittance
  ❸ *Every evening I write an entry in my diary.*
• item, note, memo, record, log

envelop VERB
A thick mist enveloped the whole city.
• cover, surround, hide, mask, conceal, cloak, shroud, veil

envious ADJECTIVE
He was envious of his brother's success.
• jealous, resentful, grudging
  IDIOM green with envy (at)

environment NOUN
The team study gorillas in their natural environment.
• habitat, surroundings, setting, conditions, situation
➤ **the environment**
the impact of humans on the environment
• the natural world, nature, the earth, the world

envy NOUN
He was consumed with envy and rage.
• jealousy, resentment, bitterness

envy VERB
She had never envied her sister's fame.
• be jealous of, begrudge, grudge, resent

episode NOUN
  ❶ *It was so embarrassing and I want to forget the whole episode.*
• event, incident, occurrence, occasion, experience
  ❷ *the first episode of the new series*
• instalment, part, programme, show, section

equal ADJECTIVE
  ❶ *Give everyone an equal amount.*
• equivalent, identical, matching,

corresponding, uniform, the same
❷ *The scores were equal at half-time.*
• even, level, tied, drawn
IDIOMS all square, level pegging, neck and neck
– To make the scores equal is to **equalize**.

equal VERB
❶ *Six plus five equals eleven.*
• be equal to, come to, add up to, total, amount to, make
❷ *Her time equals the Olympic record.*
• match, be level with, be the same as

equip VERB
Each classroom is equipped with a computer.
• provide, supply, furnish
– To equip soldiers with weapons is to **arm** them.

equipment NOUN
The shed is full of gardening equipment.
• apparatus, tools, implements, materials, machinery, gadgetry, hardware, paraphernalia, tackle, kit (*informal*) gear

equivalent ADJECTIVE
A metre is equivalent to a hundred centimetres.
• matching, the same as, identical, corresponding, parallel, similar

era NOUN
Shakespeare lived in the Elizabethan era.
• age, period, time, epoch

erase VERB
Someone had erased the message.
• delete, remove, rub out, wipe out, obliterate

erect ADJECTIVE
The dog sat up with its ears erect.
• upright, vertical, perpendicular, bristling, standing on end

erect VERB
The town hall was erected in 1890.
• build, construct, raise, put up, set up
– To erect a tent is to **pitch** it.
OPPOSITE demolish

erode VERB
Rainwater has eroded the soil.
• wear away, eat away, grind down

errand NOUN
I went on an errand to the corner shop.
• task, job, assignment, mission, trip, journey

erratic ADJECTIVE
The team's performance has been erratic this season.
• inconsistent, irregular, uneven, variable, changeable, fluctuating, unpredictable, unreliable, unstable
OPPOSITE consistent

error NOUN
❶ *a grammatical error*
• mistake, fault, lapse, blunder, slip, slip-up
❷ *I think there is an error in your argument.*
• flaw, inaccuracy, misunderstanding, inconsistency

erupt VERB
Ash continued to erupt from the volcano.
• be discharged, be emitted, pour out, issue, spout, gush, spurt, belch

escape VERB
❶ *They must have had help to escape from prison.*
• get away, run away, break free, break out, slip away, make a getaway
❷ *The driver narrowly escaped injury.*
• avoid, sidestep
IDIOM steer clear of
❸ *Oil was escaping from a crack in the hull.*
• leak, seep, ooze, drain, spill out, run out

escape NOUN
❶ *The prisoner's escape was filmed by security cameras.*
• getaway, breakout, flight
❷ *The explosion was caused by an escape of gas.*
• leak, leakage, spill, seepage, discharge

escort NOUN
The mayor always travels with a police escort.
• bodyguard, guard, convoy, entourage, minder

escort VERB
An usher will escort you to your seat.
• accompany, conduct, take, lead, guide, usher

especially ADVERB
I love shopping, especially for clothes.
• above all, chiefly, particularly, primarily, most of all

espionage NOUN
see spy

essential ADJECTIVE
Fruit and vegetables are an essential part of our diet.
• important, necessary, crucial, basic, vital, fundamental, key, intrinsic, all-important, indispensable
OPPOSITES unimportant, trivial

establish VERB
❶ *She plans to establish a new children's hospital.*
• set up, start, create, found, initiate, institute, inaugurate, launch
❷ *The police have not managed to establish his guilt.*
• prove, demonstrate, determine, confirm, verify

estate NOUN
❶ *a new housing estate*
• area, development, scheme
❷ *The castle is sited on a large estate.*
• land, grounds, park
❸ *The millionaire left his estate to charity.*
• property, fortune, wealth, possessions

estimate NOUN
an estimate of the age of the universe
• assessment, calculation, evaluation, guess, judgement, opinion
– An estimate of the value of something is a **valuation**.

– An estimate of what a job is going to cost is a **quotation** or **tender**.

estimate VERB
Scientists estimate that the Earth is 4.5 billion years old.
• calculate, assess, work out, compute, count up, evaluate, judge, reckon

eternal ADJECTIVE
❶ *The magic fountain was believed to give eternal life.*
• everlasting, unending, never-ending, permanent, perpetual, infinite, undying
OPPOSITES transitory, transient
❷ *(informal) I'm tired of her eternal complaining.*
• constant, continual, continuous, never-ending, non-stop, perpetual, endless, persistent, incessant, unbroken, uninterrupted
IDIOM round the clock
OPPOSITES occasional, intermittent

evacuate VERB
❶ *Hundreds of residents were evacuated.*
• remove, send away, move out
❷ *We were told to evacuate the building.*
• leave, vacate, abandon, withdraw from, clear, empty, quit

evade VERB
❶ *They managed to evade capture for six months.*
• elude, avoid, escape, steer clear of, fend off
❷ *Stop trying to evade my question!*
• avoid, dodge, bypass, sidestep, skirt around, shirk
(informal) duck
OPPOSITES confront, tackle

even ADJECTIVE
❶ *You need an even surface for ice-skating.*
• level, flat, smooth, plane
OPPOSITE uneven
❷ *The runners kept up an even pace.*
• regular, steady, unvarying, constant, uniform
OPPOSITE irregular

❸ *The scores were even at half time.*
• equal, level, tied, drawn
IDIOMS all square, level pegging, neck and neck

❹ *2, 4 and 6 are even numbers.*
OPPOSITE odd

❺ *She has a very even temperament.*
• calm, cool, placid, unexcitable
OPPOSITE excitable

even VERB
➤ **even something up**
We need another player to even up the numbers.
• equalize, balance, match, level out, square up

evening NOUN
By evening, the temperature had dropped.
• dusk, nightfall, sunset, twilight
(*North American*) sundown

event NOUN
❶ *The biography gives the main events of her life.*
• happening, incident, occurrence
❷ *We are holding a couple of events to mark the bicentenary.*
• function, occasion, ceremony, reception
❸ *a major sporting event*
• competition, contest, fixture, game, match, tournament

eventful ADJECTIVE
It has been an eventful two weeks.
• interesting, exciting, busy, action-packed, lively, hectic
OPPOSITES uneventful, dull

eventual ADJECTIVE
Who was the eventual winner?
• final, ultimate, overall, resulting, ensuing

eventually ADVERB
The bus eventually arrived.
• finally, in the end, at last, ultimately

evergreen ADJECTIVE
Most pine trees are evergreen.
OPPOSITE deciduous
SEE ALSO tree

everlasting ADJECTIVE
Peter Pan has an everlasting childhood.
• never-ending, unending, endless, ceaseless, eternal, infinite, perpetual, undying
– Everlasting life is **immortality.**
OPPOSITES transitory, transient

everyday ADJECTIVE
Just wear your everyday clothes.
• ordinary, normal, day-to-day, usual, regular, standard, customary, routine, commonplace, run-of-the-mill

evict VERB
Thousands were evicted from their farms.
• expel, eject, remove, throw out, turn out, put out

evidence NOUN
This letter is evidence of his guilt.
• proof, confirmation, verification
– Evidence given in a law court is a **testimony.**
– To give evidence in court is to **testify.**

evident ADJECTIVE
It was evident that he didn't like her.
• clear, obvious, apparent, plain, certain, unmistakable, undeniable, noticeable, conspicuous

evidently ADVERB
The woman was evidently upset.
• clearly, obviously, plainly, undoubtedly, unmistakably, patently

evil ADJECTIVE
❶ *The charm was used to ward off evil spirits.*
• malevolent, malign, sinister, fiendish, diabolical
OPPOSITES good, benign
❷ *Who would do such an evil deed?*
• wicked, immoral, cruel, sinful, villainous, malicious, foul, hateful, vile
OPPOSITES good, virtuous

evil NOUN

❶ *The message of the film is that good triumphs over evil.*
• wickedness, malevolence, badness, wrongdoing, sin, immorality, villainy, malice, the dark side
OPPOSITE good

❷ *the twin evils of famine and drought*
• disaster, misfortune, suffering, pain, affliction, curse, woe

evolve VERB

Life evolved on Earth over millions of years.
• develop, grow, progress, emerge, mature

exact ADJECTIVE

❶ *I can't tell you the exact number of people who are coming.*
• accurate, precise, correct, definite
OPPOSITES inaccurate, rough

❷ *She gave us exact instructions.*
• specific, clear, detailed, meticulous, strict
OPPOSITE vague

exactly ADVERB

❶ *The room was exactly as I remembered it.*
• precisely, strictly, in every respect, absolutely, just
OPPOSITES roughly, more or less

❷ *The bus leaves at 9 a.m. exactly.*
• specifically, precisely, strictly
IDIOM on the dot

❸ *I copied down her words exactly.*
• accurately, correctly, perfectly, faithfully, literally
IDIOM word for word

exaggerate VERB

He tends to exaggerate his problems.
• magnify, inflate, overstate, make too much of
IDIOM blow out of all proportion
OPPOSITES minimize, understate

examination NOUN

❶ *We sit our examinations in June.*
• test, assessment
(*informal*) exam

❷ *I have an appointment for an eye examination.*
• check-up, test
– A medical examination of a dead person is a **post-mortem**.

❸ *The judge made a thorough examination of the evidence.*
• investigation, inspection, scrutiny, study, analysis, survey, review, appraisal

examine VERB

❶ *Detectives examined all the evidence.*
• inspect, study, investigate, analyse, look closely at, pore over, scrutinize, probe, survey, review, weigh up, sift

❷ *You will be examined on your chosen subject.*
• question, interrogate, quiz
– To examine someone rigorously is to **grill** them.

example NOUN

❶ *Give me an example of what you mean.*
• instance, illustration, sample, specimen, case

❷ *Her courage is an example to us all.*
• model, ideal, standard, benchmark

exasperate VERB

All these delays were beginning to exasperate us.
• annoy, irritate, upset, frustrate, anger, infuriate, madden, vex

exceed VERB

The amount we raised exceeded all our expectations.
• surpass, better, outdo, go beyond, beat, top

excel VERB

She's a good all-round athlete, but she excels at sprinting.
• do best, stand out, shine
IDIOM be second to none

excellent ADJECTIVE

What an excellent idea!
• outstanding, exceptional, tremendous, marvellous, wonderful, superb, great, fine, superior, superlative, top-notch, first-class, first-rate

a b c d e f g h i j k l m n o p q r s t u v w x y z

(*informal*) brilliant, fantastic, terrific, fabulous, sensational, super
OPPOSITES bad, awful, second-rate
SEE ALSO good

except PREPOSITION
Everyone knew the answer except me.
• apart from, aside from, other than, with the exception of, excluding, not counting, barring, bar, but

exception NOUN
It is an exception to the usual spelling rule.
• oddity, peculiarity, deviation, special case, anomaly
➤ **take exception to something**
I took exception to what he said.
• dislike, object to, complain about, disapprove of, take issue with

exceptional ADJECTIVE
❶ *It is exceptional to have such cold weather in June.*
• unusual, uncommon, abnormal, unexpected, unprecedented, unheard-of, surprising
OPPOSITES normal, usual
❷ *He showed exceptional talent for art when he was young.*
• extraordinary, outstanding, phenomenal, amazing, rare, special, uncommon, remarkable, prodigious
OPPOSITE average

excerpt NOUN
He read an excerpt from his new novel.
• extract, passage, quotation, section
– An excerpt from a film is a **clip**.

excess NOUN
They have an excess of fat in their diet.
• surplus, surfeit, glut
➤ **in excess of**
speeds in excess of 60 mph
• more than, greater than, over, beyond

excessive ADJECTIVE
❶ *I find their prices excessive.*
• too great, too high, outrageous, extortionate, exorbitant, extravagant, unreasonable
IDIOM (*informal*) over the top

❷ *Police were accused of using excessive force.*
• extreme, superfluous, unreasonable, disproportionate

exchange VERB
The shop will exchange faulty goods.
• change, replace, substitute, swap, switch, trade
– To exchange goods for other goods without using money is to **barter**.

excite VERB
The prospect of seeing a whale excited him.
• thrill, enthuse, exhilarate, elate, stimulate, enliven, rouse, electrify
OPPOSITE calm

excited ADJECTIVE
I was too excited to sleep.
• agitated, lively, enthusiastic, exuberant, thrilled, elated, eager, animated
OPPOSITE calm

excitement NOUN
I could hardly bear the excitement.
• suspense, tension, drama, thrill, eagerness, anticipation
(*informal*) buzz

exciting ADJECTIVE
The last ten minutes of the match were the most exciting.
• dramatic, eventful, thrilling, gripping, compelling, sensational, stirring, rousing, stimulating, electrifying, exhilarating
OPPOSITES dull, boring

exclaim VERB
❶ *'Run for your lives!' he exclaimed.*
• call, shout, cry out, yell
SEE ALSO say

exclamation NOUN
He let out a sudden exclamation of pain.
• cry, shout, yell

exclude VERB
❶ *Adults are excluded from our club.*
• ban, bar, reject, keep out, banish,

prohibit
OPPOSITE admit (to)
❷ *She had to exclude dairy products from her diet.*
• leave out, omit, rule out
OPPOSITE include

excluding *PREPOSITION*
The zoo is open every day excluding Christmas.
• except, except for, with the exception of, apart from, aside from, other than, barring, bar, but

exclusive *ADJECTIVE*
❶ *They stayed at a very exclusive hotel.*
• select, upmarket, high-class, elite
(*informal*) posh, fancy, swish, classy
OPPOSITE downmarket
❷ *The room is for your exclusive use.*
• private, personal, individual, sole
OPPOSITES shared, joint

excursion *NOUN*
We went on an excursion to the seaside.
• trip, journey, outing, expedition, jaunt, day out

excuse *VERB*
I can't excuse his behaviour.
• forgive, overlook, disregard, pardon, condone, justify
OPPOSITE condemn
➤ be excused
May I be excused swimming?
• be exempt from, be let off, be relieved from

excuse *NOUN*
I had a perfect excuse for being late.
• reason, explanation, defence, justification, pretext

execute *VERB*
❶ *The tsar and his family were executed in 1918.*
• put to death
– Someone who executes people is an **executioner**.
– To execute someone unofficially without a proper trial is to **lynch** them.

❷ *She executed a perfect dive.*
• perform, carry out, implement, complete, accomplish, bring off

exempt *ADJECTIVE*
➤ exempt from
Some students will be exempt from fees.
• free from, not liable to, not subject to
OPPOSITES subject to, liable to

exercise *NOUN*
❶ *Regular exercise helps to keep you fit.*
• physical activity, working out, workouts, keep-fit, training
❷ *Doing guitar exercises will improve your playing.*
• drill, practice, lesson, task

exercise *VERB*
❶ *If you exercise regularly, you will keep fit.*
• do exercises, work out, train
❷ *I sometimes exercise our neighbour's dog.*
• take for a walk, take out, walk
❸ *You need to exercise more patience.*
• use, make use of, employ, practise, apply

exert *VERB*
He exerted a huge influence on younger artists.
• bring to bear, exercise, apply, use, employ

exertion *NOUN*
He was tired from the exertion of climbing the hill.
• effort, hard work, labour, toil

exhale *VERB*
Please exhale slowly.
• breathe out
OPPOSITE inhale

exhaust *VERB*
❶ *Walking in the midday heat had exhausted me.*
• tire, tire out, wear out, fatigue, weary, drain, take it out of you
(*informal*) do you in

❷ *Within three days they had exhausted their supply of food.*
• use up, go through, consume, deplete, drain

exhausted ADJECTIVE
The climb had left us all exhausted.
• tired, weary, worn out, fatigued, breathless, gasping, panting
(*informal*) all in, done in, bushed, zonked

exhausting ADJECTIVE
Digging the garden is exhausting work.
• tiring, demanding, hard, laborious, strenuous, difficult, gruelling, wearisome
OPPOSITE easy

exhaustion NOUN
He was overcome by sheer exhaustion.
• tiredness, fatigue, weariness, weakness

exhibit VERB
❶ *Her paintings are currently being exhibited in the local gallery.*
• display, show, present, put on display
❷ *The patient is exhibiting signs of anxiety.*
• show, demonstrate, display, reveal
OPPOSITE hide

exhibition NOUN
an exhibition of Japanese art
• display, show

exile VERB
Thousands were exiled from their own country.
• banish, expel, deport, eject, drive out

exile NOUN
❶ *The poet is returning to his country after years in exile.*
• banishment, expulsion, deportation
❷ *the return of political exiles*
• refugee, deportee, displaced person

exist VERB
❶ *Do you think that vampires really exist?*
• be real, be found, occur

❷ *Plants cannot exist without sunlight.*
• live, stay alive, survive, subsist, keep going, last, continue, endure

existence NOUN
❶ *Do you believe in the existence of life on other planets?*
• occurrence, reality
❷ *For several years he led a lonely existence.*
• life, way of life, lifestyle
➤ **in existence**
This is the oldest human skeleton in existence.
• existing, surviving, remaining, living, alive

existing ADJECTIVE
❶ *There are two existing species of elephants.*
• surviving, living, remaining
❷ *Next year the existing rules will be replaced by new ones.*
• present, current

exit NOUN
❶ *I'll wait for you by the exit.*
• door, way out, doorway, gate, barrier
OPPOSITE entrance
❷ *The robbers made a hurried exit.*
• departure, escape, retreat, withdrawal, exodus
OPPOSITES entrance, arrival

exit VERB
Please exit by the main door.
• go out, leave, depart, withdraw
OPPOSITE enter

exotic ADJECTIVE
❶ *The marketplace was filled with exotic sights and smells.*
• unusual, unfamiliar, alien, exciting, romantic
OPPOSITES familiar, commonplace
❷ *an exotic holiday destination*
• faraway, far-off, far-flung, remote, distant
OPPOSITE nearby

expand VERB
❶ *Wood expands when it gets wet.*
• swell, enlarge, extend, stretch,

lengthen, broaden, widen, thicken, fill out
OPPOSITE contract

❷ *Their business is expanding rapidly.*
• increase, enlarge, grow, build up, develop, branch out
OPPOSITES decrease, reduce

expanse NOUN
They crossed a vast expanse of desert.
• area, stretch, tract
– An expanse of water or ice is a **sheet**.

expect VERB
❶ *I expect you'd like something to eat.*
• suppose, presume, imagine, assume
(*informal*) guess, reckon
❷ *They are expecting a lot of visitors to the exhibition.*
• anticipate, envisage, predict, foresee, look forward to
❸ *She expects me to do everything for her!*
• require, want, count on, insist on, demand

expedition NOUN
a scientific expedition to Antarctica
• voyage, exploration, mission, quest
– An expedition to worship at a holy place is a **pilgrimage**.
– An expedition to watch or hunt wild animals is a **safari**.

expel VERB
❶ *Whales expel air through their blowholes.*
• send out, force out, eject
❷ *The entire team was expelled from the tournament.*
• dismiss, throw out, send away, ban, evict, deport, banish, exile

expense NOUN
She was worried about the expense of staying in a hotel.
• cost, price, charges, expenditure, outlay

expensive ADJECTIVE
an expensive pair of trainers
• dear, costly, high-priced, exorbitant, extortionate, overpriced

(*informal*) pricey
OPPOSITE cheap

experience NOUN
❶ *Have you had any experience of singing in a choir?*
• practice, involvement, participation, knowledge, know-how, track record
❷ *It was the most terrifying experience of my life.*
• happening, event, occurrence, incident
– An exciting experience is an **adventure**.
– An unpleasant experience is an **ordeal**.

experienced ADJECTIVE
He is an experienced stage actor.
• skilled, qualified, expert, knowledgeable, trained, professional, seasoned, practised
OPPOSITE inexperienced

experiment NOUN
We carried out a scientific experiment.
• test, trial, examination, investigation, observation, research

experiment VERB
➤ experiment with
I need to experiment with the camera's different settings.
• try out, test out, trial, sample
(*informal*) check out

expert NOUN
She's an expert in web design.
• specialist, authority, genius, ace, wizard, master, maestro
(*informal*) whizz, dab hand

expert ADJECTIVE
He's an expert cook.
• skilful, skilled, capable, experienced, knowledgeable, professional, proficient, qualified, trained
OPPOSITES amateur, unskilful

expertise NOUN
I don't have much expertise in tying knots.
• skill, competence, knowledge, ability, know-how, proficiency, prowess

a b c d e f g h i j k l m n o p q r s t u v w x y z

183

expire VERB
❶ *Your library card has expired.*
• run out, come to an end, become invalid, lapse
❷ *I felt as if I was about to expire from the heat.*
• die, pass away

explain VERB
❶ *My teacher explained how to tune a guitar.*
• make clear, describe, clarify
IDIOMS throw light on, spell out
❷ *Your theory does not explain the footprints.*
• account for, give reasons for, excuse, justify

explanation NOUN
❶ *She gave a brief explanation of how her invention works.*
• account, description, demonstration, clarification
❷ *They found no explanation for the accident.*
• reason, excuse, justification

explode VERB
❶ *The firework exploded with a bang.*
• blow up, go off, make an explosion, detonate, burst
❷ *They exploded the dynamite in the tunnel.*
• detonate, set off, let off

exploit NOUN
The book records the exploits of a teenage spy.
• adventure, deed, feat, act, escapade

exploit VERB
❶ *They plan to exploit the area as a tourist attraction.*
• make use of, make the most of, capitalize on, develop, profit by (*informal*) cash in on
❷ *The company is accused of exploiting its workers.*
• take advantage of, abuse, misuse, ill-treat

explore VERB
❶ *The vehicle will explore the surface of Mars.*
• travel through, survey, inspect, search, probe
❷ *We must explore all the possibilities.*
• examine, investigate, look into, research, analyse, scrutinize

explorer NOUN
a team of undersea explorers
• voyager, traveller, discoverer, researcher

explosion NOUN
The explosion rattled the windows.
• blast, bang, boom, detonation
– An explosion of laughter is an **outburst**.
– The sound of a gun going off is a **report**.

export VERB
China exports many of its goods to the US.
• sell abroad, send abroad, ship overseas
OPPOSITE import

expose VERB
❶ *The creature snarled, exposing its fangs.*
• uncover, reveal, lay bare
❷ *The truth about his past was exposed in the newspaper.*
• make known, publish, reveal, disclose

express VERB
He's always quick to express his opinions.
• voice, state, convey, communicate, air, put into words, put across, give vent to

expression NOUN
❶ *An expression of horror flooded his face.*
• look, face, appearance, countenance
For facial expressions see face.
❷ *'Cheesed off' is a colloquial expression.*
• phrase, saying, idiom, term
– An expression that people use too much is a **cliché**.

❸ *She plays the piano with great expression.*
• feeling, emotion, passion, intensity

expressive *ADJECTIVE*
❶ *My sister gave me an expressive nudge.*
• meaningful, significant, revealing, telling
❷ *Try to be more expressive in your playing.*
• passionate, emotional, moving, stirring
OPPOSITES expressionless, flat

exquisite *ADJECTIVE*
Notice the exquisite stitching on the quilt.
• beautiful, fine, delicate, intricate, dainty

extend *VERB*
❶ *He sat back and extended his legs.*
• stretch out, hold out, put out, reach out, stick out
OPPOSITES pull back, withdraw
❷ *We extended our visit by a couple of days.*
• lengthen, prolong, delay, draw out, spin out
OPPOSITES shorten, cut
❸ *The company plans to extend its range of products.*
• enlarge, expand, increase, build up, develop, enhance, add to, widen the scope of
OPPOSITES reduce, cut back
❹ *We extended a warm welcome to the visitors.*
• give, offer, proffer
❺ *The road extends as far as the border.*
• continue, carry on, reach, stretch

extension *NOUN*
They are building an extension to the school.
• addition, annex, add-on

extensive *ADJECTIVE*
❶ *The rainforest covers an extensive area.*
• large, great, substantial, considerable, vast, broad, wide, spread out
OPPOSITE small
❷ *My brother has an extensive knowledge of the film business.*
• wide, wide-ranging, comprehensive, thorough, broad
OPPOSITE narrow

extent *NOUN*
❶ *The map shows the extent of the island.*
• area, expanse, spread, breadth, length, dimensions, proportions, measurement
❷ *No one guessed the full extent of the damage.*
• amount, degree, level, size, scope, magnitude, range

exterior *ADJECTIVE*
an exterior wall
• outside, external, outer, outward, outermost
OPPOSITE interior

exterior *NOUN*
The exterior of the house has been repainted.
• outside, external surface
OPPOSITE interior

exterminate *VERB*
They used poison to exterminate the rats.
• destroy, kill, get rid of, annihilate, wipe out

external *ADJECTIVE*
In external appearance, the house was shabby.
• exterior, outside, outer, outward, outermost
OPPOSITE internal

extinct *ADJECTIVE*
Dodos became extinct in the seventeenth century.
– An extinct species is one that has **died out**, **vanished** or been **wiped out**.
– An extinct volcano is an **inactive** volcano.

a
b
c
d
e
f
g
h
i
j
k
l
m
n
o
p
q
r
s
t
u
v
w
x
y
z

A
B
C
D
E
F
G
H
I
J
K
L
M
N
O
P
Q
R
S
T
U
V
W
X
Y
Z

extinguish VERB
Extinguish all fires before leaving the campsite.
• put out, quench, douse, smother, snuff out, stamp out
OPPOSITE ignite

extra ADJECTIVE
❶ There is an extra charge for taking your bike on the train.
• additional, further, added, supplementary, excess
❷ We brought extra clothes just in case.
• more, spare, surplus, reserve

extract VERB
❶ The dentist extracted my tooth.
• take out, remove, pull out, draw out, withdraw
(informal) whip out
❷ It was difficult to extract any names from him.
• obtain, wrest, draw, glean, derive, gather

extract NOUN
There's an extract from her latest novel in the magazine.
• excerpt, quotation, citation, passage, section
– An extract from a newspaper is a **cutting**.
– An extract from a film is a **clip**.

extraordinary ADJECTIVE
an ordinary woman who led an extraordinary life
• amazing, astonishing, astounding, remarkable, exceptional, incredible, outstanding, phenomenal, sensational, marvellous, miraculous, rare, special, unheard of, unusual
OPPOSITE ordinary

extravagant ADJECTIVE
They planned a large and extravagant wedding.
• lavish, expensive, showy, ostentatious, fancy
(informal) flashy
– Someone who spends money in an

extravagant way is a **spendthrift**.
OPPOSITES modest, low-key

extreme ADJECTIVE
❶ Polar bears can withstand extreme cold.
• great, intense, severe, acute, exceptional, excessive, utmost, maximum
OPPOSITE slight
❷ an island in the extreme north of Canada
• farthest, furthest, remotest
OPPOSITE near
❸ He holds extreme views on religion.
• radical, immoderate, extremist, fanatical
OPPOSITE moderate

extremely ADVERB
Crows are extremely intelligent birds.
• very, exceptionally, especially, highly, extraordinarily, immensely, hugely, tremendously, supremely
(informal) awfully, terribly

eye NOUN

WORD WEB

Parts of an eye:
➤ cornea   ➤ iris
➤ eyeball   ➤ lens
➤ eyebrow   ➤ pupil
➤ eyelash   ➤ retina
➤ eyelid

– Words meaning 'to do with eyes' are ocular, optic and optical.
– A person who tests your eyesight is an optician.

For tips on describing faces see face.

eye VERB
The two strangers eyed each other warily.
• look at, regard, watch, observe, scrutinize, view, survey, gaze at, stare at, contemplate

fable NOUN
the fable of the Tortoise and the Hare
• legend, story, tale, parable
SEE ALSO **fiction**

fabric NOUN
His jacket is made of windproof fabric.
• cloth, material, textile

☀ WORD WEB

Some types of fabric:

➤ calico	➤ (*trademark*)
➤ canvas	Lycra
➤ cheesecloth	➤ moleskin
➤ chiffon	➤ muslin
➤ chintz	➤ nylon
➤ corduroy	➤ organdie
➤ cotton	➤ organza
➤ crepe	➤ polyester
➤ damask	➤ rayon
➤ denim	➤ satin
➤ felt	➤ serge
➤ fleece	➤ silk
➤ flannel	➤ taffeta
➤ gabardine	➤ tulle
➤ gingham	➤ tweed
➤ hessian	➤ velour
➤ jersey	➤ velvet
➤ linen	➤ velveteen
➤ (*trademark*)	➤ vinyl
Lurex	➤ wool

fabulous ADJECTIVE
❶ (*informal*) *Thank you for a fabulous weekend!*
• excellent, first-class, outstanding, wonderful, tremendous, marvellous, splendid, superb
(*informal*) fantastic, terrific, brilliant, smashing
❷ *Dragons are fabulous creatures.*
• fictitious, imaginary, legendary, mythical

face NOUN
❶ *Donna's face flushed with anger.*
• countenance, features, visage
(*informal*) mug
(*formal*) physiognomy
– A side view of someone's face is their **profile**.
❷ *Why are you making that funny face?*
• expression, look, appearance
❸ *a clock face*
• front, facade, cover
OPPOSITE **back**
❹ *the north face of the Eiger*
• side, surface, plane

Ⓦ WRITING TIPS

DESCRIBING FACES
Facial features:

➤ beauty spot	➤ jawline
➤ bloom	➤ jowl
➤ brow	➤ laugh-lines
➤ cheekbones	➤ lower lip
➤ complexion	➤ mole
➤ crow's feet	➤ pimple
➤ dimple	➤ scar
➤ double chin	➤ spot
➤ ear lobes	➤ temples
➤ forehead	➤ upper lip
➤ freckles	➤ wrinkles

Facial expressions:

➤ beam	➤ pout
➤ frown	➤ scowl
➤ glare	➤ smile
➤ glower	➤ smirk
➤ grimace	➤ sneer
➤ grin	➤ wince
➤ leer	➤ yawn

Adjectives:

➤ bloated	➤ freckled
➤ chinless	➤ gaunt
➤ chiselled	➤ haggard
➤ clean-shaven	➤ heart-shaped
➤ craggy	➤ heavy
➤ drawn	➤ lined
➤ fine-boned	➤ livid
➤ florid	➤ olive
➤ flushed	➤ pallid

a b c d e f g h i j k l m n o p q r s t u v w x y z

➤ pasty	➤ sunburned
➤ pimply	➤ tanned
➤ pinched	➤ unshaven
➤ pockmarked	➤ wan
➤ rosy	➤ wasted
➤ ruddy	➤ weather-beaten
➤ sallow	➤ weathered
➤ scarred	➤ wizened
➤ spotless	➤ wrinkled
➤ spotty	

Chin:

➤ jutting	➤ square
➤ lantern	➤ stubbly
➤ pointed	➤ weak

Ears:

➤ earringed	➤ pierced
➤ flappy	➤ sticking-out
➤ lobed	(*informal* jug)
➤ pendulous	

Eyebrows:

➤ arched	➤ shaggy
➤ beetling	➤ tufted
➤ bushy	➤ unruly
➤ knitted	

Eyes:

➤ baggy	➤ hollow
➤ beady	➤ hooded
➤ bleary	➤ piercing
➤ bloodshot	➤ protuberant
➤ bulging	➤ puffy
➤ close-set	➤ steely
➤ cross-eyed	➤ sunken
➤ deep-set	➤ swollen
➤ downcast	➤ tearful
➤ glassy	➤ twinkling
➤ heavy-lidded	➤ watery

Lips:

➤ full	➤ pursed
➤ pouting	➤ thin
➤ puckered	

Nose:

➤ aquiline	➤ bulbous
➤ beaked	➤ button

➤ classical	➤ hooked
➤ crooked	➤ Roman

SEE ALSO **hair**

face VERB
❶ *She turned to face me.*
• be opposite to, look towards
❷ *We had to face some tough questions.*
• stand up to, face up to, deal with, cope with, tackle, meet, encounter, confront
OPPOSITE avoid

facet NOUN
❶ *Each facet of the gem shone as it caught the light.*
• side, surface, plane, face
❷ *the many facets of Indian culture*
• aspect, feature, element, dimension, strand, component

fact NOUN
It is a fact that dodos are now extinct.
• reality, truth, certainty
OPPOSITE fiction
➤ **the facts**
Let us consider the facts of the case.
• details, particulars, information, data, evidence
➤ **in fact**
In fact, rhubarb is not a fruit.
• actually, as a matter of fact, in reality

factor NOUN
Many factors affect the climate.
• element, component, feature, aspect, dimension

factory NOUN
an old tyre factory
• works, plant, mill

factual ADJECTIVE
a factual account of life in China
• true, truthful, accurate, authentic, faithful, genuine, correct, exact
OPPOSITES fictitious, made-up

fad NOUN
the latest fad in computer games
• craze, trend, vogue, fashion

fade VERB
❶ *The colours will fade over time.*
• become paler, become dim, bleach, blanch
OPPOSITE brighten
❷ *Gradually the afternoon light began to fade.*
• weaken, decline, diminish, dwindle, die away, wane, ebb
OPPOSITE grow

fail VERB
❶ *Their first attempt to climb Everest failed.*
• be unsuccessful, go wrong, fall through, founder, come unstuck, come to grief, miscarry
(*informal*) flop, bomb
OPPOSITE succeed
❷ *The rocket engine failed before take-off.*
• break down, stop working, cut out, malfunction
(*informal*) pack in, conk out
❸ *By late afternoon, the light was failing.*
• weaken, decline, diminish, dwindle, fade, deteriorate, peter out
OPPOSITE improve
❹ *You failed to warn us of the danger.*
• neglect, forget, omit
OPPOSITE remember
❺ *My brother failed his driving test.*
• be unsuccessful in
(*informal*) flunk
OPPOSITE pass

fail NOUN
➤ **without fail**
Deliver this message without fail.
• for certain, assuredly, without exception

failing NOUN
Vanity is one of his failings.
• fault, flaw, imperfection, weakness, defect
OPPOSITES strength, strong point

failure NOUN
❶ *The storm caused a power failure.*
• breakdown, fault, malfunction, crash, loss, collapse, stoppage
❷ *Our first experiment was a failure.*
• defeat, disappointment, disaster, fiasco
(*informal*) flop, wash-out
OPPOSITE success

faint ADJECTIVE
❶ *a faint line*
• indistinct, unclear, dim, vague, faded, blurred, hazy, pale, shadowy, misty
OPPOSITES clear, distinct
❷ *a faint smell of burning*
• delicate, slight
OPPOSITE strong
❸ *a faint cry for help*
• weak, feeble, muted, subdued, muffled, hushed, soft, low, distant
OPPOSITE loud
❹ *Are you feeling faint?*
• dizzy, giddy, light-headed, unsteady, weak, feeble
(*informal*) woozy

faint VERB
I nearly fainted in the midday heat.
• become unconscious, collapse, pass out, black out, keel over
(*old use*) swoon

faintly ADVERB
❶ *Lights glimmered faintly in the distance.*
• indistinctly, unclearly, dimly, hazily, weakly
OPPOSITES clearly, distinctly
❷ *His face seemed faintly familiar.*
• slightly, vaguely, somewhat, a little, a bit

fair ADJECTIVE
❶ *a fair trial*
• just, equitable, even-handed, impartial, unbiased, honest, honourable, fair-minded, unprejudiced, disinterested
OPPOSITE unfair
❷ *a boy with fair hair*
• blond, blonde, light, golden, yellow, flaxen
OPPOSITE dark
❸ *The forecast is for fair weather.*
• fine, dry, sunny, bright, clear, cloudless
OPPOSITE inclement

a
b
c
d
e
f
g
h
i
j
k
l
m
n
o
p
q
r
s
t
u
v
w
x
y
z

❹ *We have a fair chance of winning.*
• reasonable, moderate, average, acceptable, satisfactory, passable, respectable, tolerable
OPPOSITE poor

fair NOUN
❶ *a village fair*
• fête, gala, funfair, festival, carnival
❷ *a book fair*
• show, exhibition, display, market, bazaar

fairly ADVERB
❶ *The competition will be judged fairly.*
• justly, impartially, honestly, properly
IDIOM fair and square
OPPOSITE unfairly
❷ *The stew is fairly spicy.*
• quite, rather, somewhat, slightly, moderately
❸ *I'm fairly certain he's lying.*
• reasonably, up to a point, tolerably, passably, adequately

fairy NOUN
Tinker Bell is a mischievous fairy.
• pixie, elf, imp, brownie, sprite, leprechaun
SEE ALSO fantasy

faith NOUN
❶ *I have complete faith in my teammates.*
• trust, belief, confidence, conviction
OPPOSITES doubt, mistrust
❷ *people of many faiths*
• religion, belief, creed, doctrine
SEE ALSO religion

faithful ADJECTIVE
❶ *a faithful friend*
• loyal, constant, devoted, true, reliable, dependable, firm, staunch, steadfast, trusty
OPPOSITE disloyal
❷ *a faithful copy of the original painting*
• accurate, exact, precise, true
OPPOSITE inaccurate

fake NOUN
❶ *It's not a real Leonardo: it's a fake.*
• imitation, copy, forgery, replica, reproduction
❷ *That fortune-teller was a fake.*
• charlatan, fraud, impostor

fake ADJECTIVE
❶ *a fake passport*
• false, forged, counterfeit, bogus (informal) phoney, dud
❷ *a fake diamond*
• imitation, artificial, pretend, simulated, mock, sham
OPPOSITES real, genuine, authentic

fake VERB
❶ *Someone managed to fake my signature.*
• forge, copy, counterfeit, fabricate, falsify, imitate, reproduce
❷ *I tried to fake interest in what she was saying.*
• feign, pretend, put on, simulate, affect

fall VERB
❶ *Thousands of meteorites fall to Earth each year.*
• drop, descend, come down, plunge, plummet, nosedive
❷ *The athlete fell and sprained her ankle.*
• tumble, topple, trip, stumble
❸ *The temperature fell to below freezing.*
• go down, become lower, decrease, decline, lessen, diminish, dwindle
❹ *Sea levels have fallen dramatically.*
• go down, subside, recede, sink, ebb
❺ *Edinburgh fell to the Jacobites without any fighting.*
• give in, surrender, yield, capitulate
❻ *a memorial to those who fell in the war*
• die, be killed, perish
(old use) be slain
❼ *My birthday falls on a Saturday this year.*
• happen, occur, take place
➤ **fall apart**
The paper fell apart in my hands.
• break up, go to pieces, disintegrate, shatter
➤ **fall in**
The roof fell in during the storm.
• collapse, cave in, give way
➤ **fall out**
Those two are always falling out.
• argue, disagree, quarrel, squabble,

bicker, fight
➤ **fall through**
Our holiday plans have fallen through.
• fail, come to nothing, collapse, founder

fall NOUN
❶ *a fall from a great height*
• tumble, topple, trip, plunge, dive, descent
❷ *a sharp fall in temperature*
• drop, lowering
OPPOSITE rise
❸ *a fall in the number of pupils*
• decrease, reduction, decline, slump
OPPOSITE increase
❹ *a story about the fall of Troy*
• downfall, defeat, overthrow, surrender

false ADJECTIVE
❶ *We were given false information.*
• wrong, incorrect, untrue, inaccurate, mistaken, erroneous, faulty, invalid, misleading, deceptive
OPPOSITE correct
❷ *He was travelling under a false identity.*
• fake, bogus, sham, counterfeit, forged
OPPOSITES genuine, authentic
❸ *wearing false eyelashes*
• artificial, imitation, synthetic, simulated, fake, mock, pretend
OPPOSITES real, natural
❹ *a false friend*
• unfaithful, disloyal, unreliable, untrustworthy, deceitful, dishonest, treacherous
OPPOSITES faithful, loyal

falter VERB
❶ *The actor faltered slightly over his lines.*
• hesitate, stumble, pause, waver, vacillate, stammer, stutter
❷ *Her courage began to falter.*
• weaken, diminish, flag, wane

fame NOUN
His plays brought him international fame.
• celebrity, stardom, renown, glory, reputation, name, standing, stature, prominence

– Fame that you get for doing something bad is **notoriety**.

familiar ADJECTIVE
❶ *Bicycles are a familiar sight in Beijing.*
• common, everyday, normal, ordinary, usual, regular, customary, frequent, mundane, routine
OPPOSITE rare
❷ *Don't be too familiar with the customers.*
• informal, friendly, intimate, relaxed, close
OPPOSITES formal, unfriendly
➤ **be familiar with**
Are you familiar with the story of Frankenstein?
• be acquainted with, be aware of, know

familiarity NOUN
❶ *There was an air of familiarity between them.*
• friendship, closeness, intimacy, friendliness
❷ *I have some familiarity with her music.*
• knowledge of, acquaintance with, experience of, understanding of

family NOUN
Most of her family live in South Africa.
• relations, relatives, kin, clan
IDIOMS flesh and blood, kith and kin

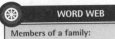

WORD WEB

Members of a family:

➤ ancestor	➤ sister
➤ forebear	➤ sibling
➤ forefather	➤ aunt
➤ descendant	➤ uncle
(*literary* scion)	➤ nephew
➤ father	➤ niece
➤ mother	➤ cousin
➤ husband	➤ second cousin
➤ wife	➤ grandparent
➤ spouse	➤ great-grand-
➤ parent	parent
➤ child	➤ grandfather
➤ daughter	➤ grandmother
➤ son	➤ granddaughter
➤ brother	➤ grandson

> great-aunt
> great-uncle
> father-in-law
> mother-in-law
> daughter-in-law
> son-in-law
> brother-in-law
> sister-in-law
> stepfather
> stepmother
> stepchild
> stepdaughter
> stepson
> stepbrother
> stepsister
> half-brother
> half-sister
> foster-parent
> foster-child

- The study of family history and ancestors is **genealogy**. A family tree is a diagram which shows how people in a family are related.

SEE ALSO father, mother

famine NOUN
years of drought and famine
• starvation, hunger

famous ADJECTIVE
J K Rowling is a famous author.
• well-known, celebrated, renowned, acclaimed, distinguished, revered, eminent, illustrious, noted, notable
– A **notorious** person or place is famous for a bad reason. *a notorious accident blackspot.*
OPPOSITES unknown, obscure
The word infamous is not the opposite of famous. An infamous person has a bad reputation: *Blackbeard was an infamous pirate.*

fan NOUN
a football fan
• enthusiast, admirer, devotee, follower, supporter

fanatic NOUN
a fitness fanatic
• enthusiast, addict, devotee
(*informal*) freak, nut

fanatical ADJECTIVE
Josh is fanatical about football.
• enthusiastic, passionate, obsessive, extreme, fervent, over-enthusiastic, rabid, zealous
OPPOSITE moderate

fanciful ADJECTIVE
a fanciful tale set in ancient Japan
• imaginary, fictitious, made-up, fantastic, fabulous, whimsical
OPPOSITE realistic

fancy VERB
❶ (*informal*) *Which film do you fancy seeing?*
• feel like, want, wish for, desire, prefer
❷ *I fancied I heard a noise upstairs.*
• imagine, think, believe, suppose
(*informal*) reckon

fancy ADJECTIVE
The guitarist wore a fancy waistcoat.
• elaborate, decorative, ornate, ornamented, showy
(*informal*) flashy, snazzy
OPPOSITE plain

fancy NOUN
❶ *Painting is much more than a passing fancy for her.*
• whim, urge, desire, caprice
❷ *The author is given to strange flights of fancy.*
• imagination, fantasy, dreaming, creativity

fantastic ADJECTIVE
❶ *The rock had been carved into fantastic shapes.*
• fanciful, extraordinary, strange, odd, weird, outlandish, incredible, imaginative, far-fetched
OPPOSITE realistic
❷ (*informal*) *We had a fantastic time on holiday.*
• excellent, outstanding, superb, splendid, wonderful, tremendous, marvellous
(*informal*) brilliant, fabulous, smashing

fantasy NOUN
❶ *She has a fantasy about being a movie star.*
• dream, daydream, delusion, wish, hope
❷ *The book is a mixture of science fiction and fantasy.*
• make-believe, invention, imagination, fancy

WRITING TIPS

WRITING FANTASY FICTION
Characters:

➤ alchemist	➤ shape-shifter
➤ apprentice	➤ soothsayer
➤ changeling	➤ sorcerer
➤ druid	➤ sorceress
➤ enchanter	➤ warlock
➤ enchantress	➤ witch
➤ magus	➤ witchfinder
➤ seer	➤ wizard
➤ shaman	

Creatures:

➤ banshee	➤ gorgon
➤ basilisk	➤ gryphon
➤ centaur	➤ harpie
➤ chimera	➤ kelpie
➤ cyclops	➤ mermaid
➤ dragon	➤ merman
➤ dwarf	➤ ogre
➤ elf	➤ phoenix
➤ fairy	➤ selkie
➤ faun	➤ sphinx
➤ genie	➤ troll
➤ giant	➤ unicorn
➤ goblin	➤ yeti

Setting:

➤ castle	➤ island
➤ cave or cavern	➤ kingdom
➤ den	➤ labyrinth
➤ dungeon	➤ lair
➤ empire	➤ maze
➤ enchanted	➤ realm
forest	➤ stronghold
➤ fortress	➤ underworld

Useful words and phrases:

➤ amulet	➤ dark arts
➤ augury	➤ divination
➤ bewitch	➤ elixir
➤ charm	➤ enchantment
➤ chronicle	➤ hex
➤ clairvoyance	➤ immortality
➤ coven	➤ incantation
➤ crucible	➤ invisibility
➤ curse	➤ legend

➤ lore	➤ sorcery
➤ mace	➤ spell
➤ magic	➤ spirit guide
➤ nemesis	➤ spirit quest
➤ omen	➤ staff
➤ oracle	➤ superhuman
➤ portal	➤ talisman
➤ potion	➤ vision
➤ prophecy	➤ wand
➤ quest	➤ witchcraft
➤ riddle	➤ wizardry
➤ rune	

far ADJECTIVE
❶ *They live in the far north of Canada.*
• distant, faraway, far-off, far-flung, remote, outlying
❷ *We rowed to the far side of the lake.*
• opposite, other
OPPOSITE near
➤ **by far**
They are by far the best team.
• far and away, easily
IDIOMS by a long shot, by a mile

far ADVERB
❶ *We were still far from sight of land.*
• far away, a long way, at a distance (*informal*) miles
❷ *The road is far more dangerous in winter.*
• much, considerably, significantly, markedly, decidedly, greatly, a good deal

fare NOUN
How much is the train fare?
• charge, cost, price, fee, payment

far-fetched ADJECTIVE
Her story sounds far-fetched to me.
• unbelievable, unlikely, improbable, unconvincing, unrealistic, incredible, dubious, fanciful
OPPOSITES likely, believable

farm NOUN
a sheep farm
• farmstead, holding, ranch
(*Australia & New Zealand*) station

farm VERB
This land has been farmed for centuries.
• cultivate, work, till, plough

farming NOUN
organic methods of farming
• agriculture, cultivation, husbandry

fascinate VERB
Wells was fascinated by the idea of time travel.
• interest (in), captivate, enthral, engross, absorb, attract, beguile, entrance, charm, enchant
OPPOSITES bore, repel

fascinating ADJECTIVE
I found the programme fascinating.
• interesting, absorbing, enthralling, captivating, engrossing, riveting, gripping, entertaining, intriguing, diverting, engaging, stimulating
OPPOSITES boring, dull

fashion NOUN
❶ *She was behaving in a very odd fashion.*
• manner, way, style
❷ *This is the latest fashion in footwear.*
• trend, vogue, craze, fad, style, look

fashionable ADJECTIVE
a fashionable new hairstyle
• stylish, chic, up-to-date, popular, elegant, smart
(*informal*) trendy, hip, in
IDIOM all the rage
OPPOSITES unfashionable, out-of-date

fast ADJECTIVE
❶ *a fast lap around the track*
• quick, rapid, speedy, swift, brisk, hurried, hasty, high-speed, headlong, breakneck
(*informal*) nippy
OPPOSITES slow, unhurried
❷ *Be sure to make the rope fast.*
• secure, fastened, firm, tight
OPPOSITE loose

fast ADVERB
❶ *A boy was running very fast across the field.*
• quickly, speedily, swiftly, rapidly, briskly
(*informal*) flat out
IDIOMS at full tilt, like a shot, like the wind
❷ *The jeep was stuck fast in the mud.*
• firmly, securely, tightly
❸ *By now he was fast asleep.*
• deeply, sound, completely

fasten VERB
❶ *They fastened their ropes to the rock face.*
• tie, fix, attach, connect, join, link, bind, hitch, tether, clamp, pin, clip, tack, stick
OPPOSITES unfasten, untie
❷ *Please fasten your seat belts.*
• secure, lock, bolt, make fast, seal
OPPOSITES unfasten, release

fat ADJECTIVE
❶ *Eating too much sugary food will make you fat.*
• overweight, obese, plump, chubby, podgy, dumpy, tubby, round, rotund, portly, stout, heavy, beefy, corpulent, flabby
– Someone with a fat stomach is **pot-bellied**.
OPPOSITES thin, skinny
For tips on describing people's bodies see body.
❷ *a large fat envelope*
• thick, bulky, chunky, weighty, substantial
(*informal*) stuffed
OPPOSITE thin

fatal ADJECTIVE
❶ *a fatal wound*
• deadly, lethal, mortal
❷ *a fatal disease*
• incurable, terminal
❸ *a fatal error*
• disastrous, catastrophic, dreadful, calamitous

A B C D E F G H I J K L M N O P Q R S T U V W X Y Z

fate NOUN
❶ *I didn't know what fate had in store for me.*
• fortune, destiny, providence, chance, luck, future, lot
IDIOM the lap of the gods
❷ *Each of the crew met with a grisly fate.*
• death, demise, end, doom

father NOUN
❶ *My father grew up in South Africa.*
• (*informal*) dad, daddy, pa, old man (*North American informal*) pop
– A word meaning 'to do with a father' is **paternal**.
For other members of a family see **family**.
❷ *Galileo is considered the father of astronomy.*
• founder, originator, inventor, creator, architect

fatigue NOUN
Some of the runners were overcome with fatigue.
• exhaustion, tiredness, weariness, weakness

fatty ADJECTIVE
Try to cut down on fatty foods.
• fat, greasy, oily
OPPOSITE lean

fault NOUN
❶ *a fault in the electrical wiring*
• defect, flaw, malfunction, snag, problem, weakness (*informal*) glitch, bug
❷ *It's not my fault that you overslept.*
• responsibility, liability
➤ **at fault**
Both the drivers were at fault.
• to blame, guilty, responsible, culpable

faultless ADJECTIVE
a faultless performance
• perfect, flawless, immaculate, impeccable
OPPOSITES imperfect, flawed

faulty ADJECTIVE
a faulty DVD
• broken, not working, malfunctioning, defective, out of order, unusable, damaged
IDIOM (*informal*) on the blink
OPPOSITES working, in good order

favour NOUN
❶ *Would you do me a favour?*
• good turn, good deed, kindness, service, courtesy
❷ *The idea found favour with the public.*
• approval, support, liking, goodwill
➤ **be in favour of**
Hands up all those who are in favour of longer holidays.
• approve of, support, be on the side of, be for, be pro
OPPOSITES be against, disapprove of

favour VERB
I favour the second explanation.
• approve of, support, back, advocate, choose, like, opt for, prefer (*informal*) fancy, go for
OPPOSITE oppose

favourable ADJECTIVE
❶ *The weather is favourable for flying.*
• advantageous, beneficial, helpful, good, suitable, encouraging
OPPOSITE unfavourable
❷ *The film received favourable reviews.*
• positive, complimentary, good, glowing, approving, agreeable, enthusiastic, sympathetic (*informal*) rave
OPPOSITES critical, hostile, negative

favourite ADJECTIVE
What's your favourite book?
• preferred, best-loved, favoured, treasured, dearest, special, top

fear NOUN
❶ *He was shaking with fear.*
• fright, terror, horror, alarm, panic, dread, anxiety, apprehension, trepidation
OPPOSITE courage
SEE ALSO afraid
❷ *a fear of snakes and spiders*
• phobia, dread
For special types of fear see **phobia**.

fear VERB
❶ *As a child, I used to fear the dark.*
• be frightened of, be afraid of, be scared of, dread
❷ *I fear we may be too late.*
• suspect, expect, anticipate

fearful ADJECTIVE
❶ *She was fearful of being left behind.*
• frightened, afraid, scared, terrified, petrified, nervous, apprehensive, anxious, timid, panicky
❷ *We came across a fearful sight.*
• frightening, terrifying, shocking, ghastly, dreadful, appalling, terrible, awful, frightful, fearsome, gruesome

fearless ADJECTIVE
The fearless explorers entered the dark cave.
• brave, courageous, daring, bold, heroic, valiant, intrepid, plucky, unafraid
OPPOSITES cowardly, timid

fearsome ADJECTIVE
The dragon yawned, revealing a fearsome set of teeth.
• frightening, fearful, horrifying, terrifying, dreadful, awesome
(*informal*) scary

feasible ADJECTIVE
Is it feasible to fly there and back in a day?
• possible, practicable, practical, achievable, realistic, workable, viable
(*informal*) doable
OPPOSITES impractical, impossible

feast NOUN
❶ *a wedding feast*
• banquet, dinner
(*informal*) spread
❷ *the feast of Saint Valentine*
• festival, holiday

feast VERB
a band of hyenas feasting on their prey
• gorge, feed, dine

feat NOUN
The Channel Tunnel was an incredible feat of engineering.
• act, action, deed, exploit, achievement, undertaking, performance

feather NOUN
a goose feather
• plume, quill
– All the feathers on a bird are its **plumage**.
– Soft, fluffy feathers are **down**.

feature NOUN
❶ *The room has several unusual features.*
• characteristic, attribute, property, aspect, quality, peculiarity, trait, facet, element, hallmark
❷ *a feature in the school magazine*
• article, report, story, item, piece, column
➤ features
a tall, thin man with fine features
• face, countenance, visage
(*formal*) physiognomy
For tips on describing faces see face.

feature VERB
❶ *The film features some stunning special effects.*
• present, show off, highlight, spotlight, showcase
❷ *Holmes features in over fifty short stories.*
• appear, participate, take part, figure, star

fed up (*informal*) ADJECTIVE
She looked tired and fed up.
• depressed, dispirited, dejected, unhappy, bored
(*informal*) cheesed off, hacked off
➤ be fed up with
I'm fed up with doing all the work.
• be tired of, be sick of, have had enough of
(*informal*) be sick and tired of

fee NOUN
an annual membership fee
• charge, cost, payment, price

feeble ADJECTIVE

❶ The king was growing old and feeble.
• weak, frail, infirm, poorly, sickly, puny, weedy
OPPOSITES strong, powerful

❷ I made a feeble attempt to catch the ball.
• weak, poor, ineffective, inadequate, unconvincing, lame, flimsy

feed VERB

❶ There's enough food to feed everyone.
• provide for, cater for, give food to, nourish, sustain

❷ Bats usually feed at night.
• eat, take food

➤ **feed on**
Chameleons feed on a variety of insects.
• eat, consume, devour, live on

feel VERB

❶ Feel how soft this material is.
• touch, stroke, caress, fondle, handle
SEE ALSO texture

❷ In the dark I felt my way along the landing.
• grope, fumble

❸ The animal won't feel any pain.
• experience, undergo, endure, suffer from

❹ I usually don't feel the cold.
• perceive, sense, notice, detect, be aware of, be conscious of

❺ I feel that I've met you before.
• think, believe, consider, maintain
(informal) reckon

❻ It feels warmer today.
• appear, seem, strike you as

➤ **feel for**
I feel for the people who live there.
• sympathize with, pity

➤ **feel like**
Do you feel like something to eat?
• fancy, want, desire, wish for

feel NOUN
the feel of sand between your toes
• feeling, sensation, touch, texture

feeling NOUN

❶ She had lost all feeling in her toes.
• sense of touch, sensation, sensitivity

❷ I didn't mean to hurt your feelings.
• emotion, passion, sentiment

❸ I had a feeling that something was wrong.
• suspicion, notion, inkling, idea, impression, intuition, hunch

❹ the strength of public feeling
• opinion, belief, view, attitude, mood

fell
past tense see fall

fellow NOUN
an odd-looking fellow with a squint
• man, person, character, individual
(informal) guy
(British informal) bloke, chap

female ADJECTIVE
a female friend
OPPOSITE male
For female animals see animal.

feminine ADJECTIVE
a feminine style of dress
• womanly, ladylike, girlish
(informal) girlie
OPPOSITE masculine

fence NOUN
The garden was surrounded by a tall fence.
• railing, barrier, paling, stockade

fence VERB
a field fenced by hedgerows
• enclose, surround, bound, encircle

fend VERB

➤ **fend for yourself**
We were left to fend for ourselves.
• look after yourself, take care of yourself, care for yourself

➤ **fend off**
The small force managed to fend off the attack.
• repel, resist, ward off, fight off, hold off, repulse

ferment NOUN
All Europe was in a state of ferment.
• turmoil, unrest, upheaval, agitation, excitement, commotion, turbulence, confusion, disorder, tumult

ferocious ADJECTIVE
The gate was guarded by a ferocious dog.
• fierce, fiercesome, savage, vicious, violent, wild, brutal
OPPOSITES gentle, tame

fertile ADJECTIVE
The area has very fertile soil.
• fruitful, productive, rich, lush
OPPOSITES barren, sterile
a fertile imagination
• inventive, creative, rich, prolific, teeming

fertilize VERB
❶ a good compost to fertilize the soil
• manure, feed, enrich
❷ How do frogs fertilize their eggs?
• inseminate, pollinate

fervent ADJECTIVE
It was her fervent wish to return to Ireland.
• eager, keen, avid, ardent, intense, wholehearted, heartfelt, passionate
OPPOSITES indifferent, lukewarm

festival NOUN
❶ The town holds a music festival every summer.
• celebration, carnival, fiesta, fête, gala, fair, jubilee, jamboree
(informal) fest
❷ For religious festivals see religion.

festive ADJECTIVE
Chinese New Year is a festive occasion.
• cheerful, happy, merry, jolly, cheery, joyful, joyous, jovial, light-hearted, celebratory
OPPOSITES gloomy, sombre

fetch VERB
❶ I went to fetch a torch.
• get, bring, collect, pick up, retrieve, obtain, carry, convey, transport
❷ We had better fetch the doctor.
• send for, call for, summon, go for, get, bring
❸ How much will the painting fetch?
• sell for, go for, make, raise, bring in, earn

feud NOUN
a feud between two families
• quarrel, dispute, conflict, hostility, enmity, rivalry, strife, antagonism
– A feud that lasts a long time is a vendetta.

fever NOUN
❶ a fever of 39 degrees Celsius
• temperature, delirium
❷ We were all in a fever of impatience.
• frenzy, ferment, excitement, agitation, mania, passion

feverish ADJECTIVE
❶ I stayed in bed all day, feeling feverish.
• hot, burning, flushed, delirious
❷ There was feverish activity in the kitchen.
• frenzied, frantic, excited, agitated, hectic, frenetic, busy, hurried, restless

few ADJECTIVE
on a few occasions
• not many, hardly any, a small number of, a handful of, one or two
OPPOSITE many

fiasco NOUN
the fiasco of the cancelled concert
• failure, disaster, catastrophe, mess, farce, debacle
(informal) shambles
OPPOSITE success

fibre NOUN
❶ Nylon is a synthetic fibre.
• thread, strand, hair, filament
❷ She is on a diet low in fibre.
• roughage

fickle ADJECTIVE
the fickle support of the public
• changeable, erratic, unreliable, unsteady, unpredictable, inconstant
OPPOSITES constant, steady

fiction NOUN
❶ 'The Lord of the Rings' is a work of fiction.
• creative writing, storytelling
OPPOSITE non-fiction

❷ *Most of the newspaper story was pure fiction.*
• fantasy, invention, fabrication, lies
IDIOMS pack of lies, flight of fancy
OPPOSITE fact

fictional ADJECTIVE
Middle-earth is a fictional realm.
• imaginary, made-up, invented, fanciful
OPPOSITES factual, real

fictitious ADJECTIVE
She was travelling under a fictitious name.
• false, fake, fabricated, fraudulent, bogus, assumed, spurious, unreal
OPPOSITES genuine, real
The words fictional and fictitious do not mean the same thing. A *fictional* character exists only in fiction, whereas a *fictitious* identity is created to deceive others.

fiddle VERB
❶ *He was fiddling with the DVD player.*
• tinker, meddle, tamper, twiddle, play about, mess about
❷ *(informal) They had been fiddling the accounts for years.*
• falsify, alter, rig, doctor
IDIOM *(informal)* cook the books

fiddly *(informal)* ADJECTIVE
Wiring a plug can be a fiddly job.
• intricate, complicated, awkward, involved
OPPOSITE simple

fidget VERB
Luke was fidgeting in his chair.
• be restless, move about, wriggle, squirm

fidgety ADJECTIVE
After waiting an hour, we began to get fidgety.
• restless, unsettled, impatient, agitated, jumpy, nervy, twitchy, jittery, on edge

field NOUN
❶ *Cattle were grazing in the field.*
• meadow, pasture, paddock

❷ *a football field*
• ground, pitch, playing field
❸ *advances in the field of medicine*
• area, sphere, speciality, discipline, domain, province

fiend NOUN
❶ *like a fiend from Hell*
• demon, devil, evil spirit
❷ *(informal) a fresh-air fiend*
• enthusiast, fanatic, devotee
(informal) freak, nut

fierce ADJECTIVE
❶ *a fierce attack by armed robbers*
• vicious, ferocious, savage, brutal, violent, wild, cruel, merciless, ruthless, pitiless
❷ *Competition between the two companies was fierce.*
• strong, intense, keen, eager, aggressive, relentless, cut-throat
❸ *the fierce heat of the desert sun*
• intense, severe, blazing, raging

fiery ADJECTIVE
❶ *the fiery heat of the midday sun*
• burning, blazing, flaming, red-hot
OPPOSITES cool, mild
❷ *the fiery taste of chilli pepper*
• hot, spicy, peppery
OPPOSITE mild
❸ *a fiery temper*
• passionate, excitable, volatile, violent, raging, explosive
OPPOSITES calm, mild

fight NOUN
❶ *the fight to capture the island*
• battle, conflict, action, engagement, hostilities
❷ *a fight in the street*
• brawl, scuffle, skirmish, tussle, fracas, set-to
(informal) scrap, punch-up
– A fight arranged between two people is a **duel**.
❸ *a heavyweight fight*
• boxing match, contest, bout
❹ *a fight with your girlfriend*
• argument, quarrel, squabble, row, dispute

⑤ *the fight to save the rainforest*
• campaign, crusade, struggle, battle, effort

fight VERB
① *They were caught fighting in the playground.*
• brawl, exchange blows, come to blows, scuffle, grapple, wrestle (*informal*) scrap, have a punch-up
② *The boys were fighting over who should go first.*
• argue, quarrel, squabble, row, bicker, wrangle
③ *The two countries fought each other in the war.*
• do battle with, wage war with, attack
④ *Local people are fighting the decision to close the library.*
• protest against, oppose, resist, challenge, contest, make a stand against, campaign against

fighter NOUN
a guerrilla fighter
• soldier, warrior, combatant

fighting NOUN
soldiers killed during the fighting
• combat, hostilities, war, battle, conflict

figurative ADJECTIVE
the poet's use of figurative language
• metaphorical, symbolic
OPPOSITE literal

figure NOUN
① *I'd better check these figures again.*
• number, numeral, digit, integer
② *Can you put a figure on it?*
• price, value, amount, sum, cost
③ *See the figure on page 22.*
• diagram, graph, illustration, drawing
④ *Rose has a good figure.*
• body, build, frame, shape, physique
⑤ *an important figure in Irish history*
• person, character, individual
⑥ *a clay figure of a bison*
• statue, carving, sculpture

figure VERB
Wolves often figure in fairy tales.
• appear, feature, be mentioned, be referred to, take part

➤ **figure out**
I'm trying to figure out what it all means.
• work out, make out, understand, comprehend, make sense of, see, grasp, fathom
IDIOM get to the bottom of

file NOUN
① *I keep my notes in a file.*
• folder, binder, portfolio, wallet
② *The agency kept a secret file on her.*
• dossier, report, record, archive
③ *We followed her in single file.*
• line, row, column, queue, string, chain, procession

file VERB
① *The cards are filed alphabetically.*
• organize, arrange, categorize, classify, catalogue, store
② *We all filed out of the hall.*
• walk in a line, march, troop, parade
③ *She sat there filing her nails.*
• smooth, grind down, rub down, rasp, hone

fill VERB
① *Dad filled the trolley with shopping.*
• load, pack, stuff, cram, top up
– To fill something with air is to **inflate** it.
OPPOSITE empty
② *What can I use to fill this hole?*
• close up, plug, seal, block up, stop up
③ *The scent of roses filled the room.*
• spread through, permeate, pervade, suffuse
④ *Hundreds of protesters filled the streets.*
• crowd, throng, cram, pack
⑤ *That job has already been filled.*
• take up, occupy

filling NOUN
a sandwich filling
• stuffing, insides, innards, contents, padding, wadding

filling ADJECTIVE
That meal was very filling!
• substantial, hearty, ample, heavy

film NOUN
① *the latest James Bond film*
• movie, picture, video, DVD

❷ *a career in film*
• cinema, movies
IDIOMS the big screen, the silver screen
❸ *a film of grease on the wall*
• coat, coating, layer, covering, sheet, skin

WORD WEB

Types of film:

- action picture
- animation
- (*informal*) biopic
- (*informal*) buddy movie
- (*informal*) chick flick
- costume drama
- disaster movie
- documentary
- epic
- feature film
- film noir
- horror film
- road movie
- (*informal*) romcom
- short
- silent film
- thriller
- (*informal*) weepie
- western

People involved in films:

- actor
- animator
- camera crew
- cast
- cinematographer
- co-star
- director
- editor
- extras
- film crew
- film star
- film studio
- producer
- projectionist
- screenwriter
- sound engineer
- stunt artist
- voice coach

Other terms relating to film:

- 3-D
- adaptation
- CGI
- cinematography
- clip
- costumes
- credits
- cut
- dubbing
- editing
- fade-out
- film score
- flashback
- footage
- Hollywood
- IMAX
- leading role
- lighting
- montage
- nomination
- off-set
- on-set
- Oscar
- premiere
- release date
- remake
- rushes
- screenplay
- screen test
- script
- scene
- sequence
- slow motion (*informal* slo-mo)
- sound effects
- soundtrack
- special effects
- storyboard
- subtitles
- supporting role
- titles
- trailer
- voice-over
- wide-screen

filter *VERB*
❶ *The water must be filtered before drinking.*
• strain, sieve, sift, purify, refine
❷ *Rain began to filter through the roof.*
• pass, trickle, leak, seep, ooze, percolate

filth *NOUN*
The beach was covered in filth.
• dirt, grime, muck, mess, mud, sludge, scum, sewage, refuse

filthy *ADJECTIVE*
❶ *Those trainers are filthy!*
• dirty, mucky, messy, grimy, grubby, muddy, soiled, stained, unwashed
OPPOSITE clean
❷ *Don't drink the filthy water from the well.*
• impure, polluted, contaminated, foul
OPPOSITE pure
❸ *They were telling filthy jokes.*
• obscene, rude, dirty, vulgar, crude, bawdy, lewd

final *ADJECTIVE*
❶ *The final moments of the film were very tense.*
• last, closing, finishing, concluding, terminal
OPPOSITE opening
❷ *What was the final result?*
• eventual, ultimate
❸ *The judges' decision is final.*
• definite, conclusive, absolute, decisive

finally *ADVERB*
❶ *I've finally managed to finish my book.*
• eventually, at last, in the end
IDIOM at long last
❷ *Finally, I'd like to say a few words.*
• lastly, in conclusion

finance NOUN

❶ *He is an expert in finance.*
• financial affairs, money matters, economics, investment, commerce, banking, accounting

❷ *Our finances are in a good state.*
• money, bank account, funds, resources, assets, wealth

financial ADJECTIVE

She helps people with their financial affairs.
• monetary, money, economic, fiscal, commercial, banking

find VERB

❶ *Did you ever find your keys?*
• locate, spot, track down, trace, recover, retrieve, detect, identify
OPPOSITE lose

❷ *We found a perfect place for a picnic.*
• come across, discover, encounter, stumble on, unearth, uncover

❸ *You might find that you feel tired.*
• become aware, realize, learn, recognize, notice, observe
➤ **find out**
At last we will find out what happened.
• learn, discover, ascertain

findings PLURAL NOUN

the findings of the police investigation
• conclusions, judgement, verdict, decision

fine ADJECTIVE

❶ *a fine example of Dutch painting*
• excellent, first-class, superb, splendid, admirable, commendable, good
OPPOSITE bad

❷ *a day of fine weather*
• sunny, fair, dry, bright, clear, cloudless, pleasant
OPPOSITE dull

❸ *Spiders spin very fine thread for their webs.*
• delicate, fragile, thin, flimsy, slender, slim
OPPOSITE thick

❹ *a layer of fine sand*
• fine-grained, dusty, powdery
OPPOSITE coarse

❺ *I've had a cold but I'm feeling fine now.*
• well, healthy, all right, in good shape

❻ *That all sounds fine to me.*
• all right, acceptable, satisfactory
(*informal*) OK

fine NOUN

a fine for speeding
• penalty, charge, damages

finger NOUN

She wore a gold ring on her finger.
• digit

WORD WEB

The fingers on a hand (in order):

➤ thumb
➤ index finger
➤ middle finger
➤ ring finger
➤ little finger
(*Scottish & North American* pinkie)

finger VERB

The old man fingered his moustache nervously.
• touch, feel, handle, fondle, caress, play with, toy with

finicky ADJECTIVE

Cats can be finicky about their food.
• fussy, hard to please, particular
(*informal*) choosy, picky

finish VERB

❶ *Have you finished your homework?*
• complete, reach the end of, accomplish, round off
(*informal*) wrap up

❷ *I've already finished my bag of crisps.*
• consume, use up, get through, exhaust
(*informal*) polish off

❸ *The film should finish around nine o'clock.*
• end, stop, conclude, come to a stop, cease, terminate
(*informal*) wind up
OPPOSITES start, begin

finish NOUN

❶ *We watched the film until the finish.*
• end, close, conclusion, completion, result, termination
OPPOSITE start

❷ *furniture with a glossy finish*
• surface, polish, shine, gloss, glaze, sheen, lustre

fire NOUN

We warmed our hands in front of the fire.
• blaze, flames, burning, combustion
– A very big hot fire is an **inferno**.
– A great and destructive fire is a **conflagration**.
– An open fire out of doors is a **bonfire**.
➤ catch fire
The leaves caught fire quickly.
• catch light, ignite, kindle
IDIOMS burst into flames, go up in smoke
➤ on fire
The forest was soon on fire.
• burning, flaming, blazing, alight, in flames, aflame, ablaze
➤ set fire to
They tried to set fire to the school.
• set alight, set on fire, ignite, kindle
– The crime of deliberately setting fire to a building is **arson**.

fire VERB

❶ *The pots are fired to a red colour in the kiln.*
• bake, harden, heat
❷ *One of the guards fired a warning shot into the air.*
• shoot, discharge, let off, set off
– To fire a missile is to **launch** it.
❸ *(informal) He was fired for being late for work.*
• dismiss
(informal) sack
❹ *The story fired our imagination.*
• excite, stimulate, stir up, arouse

firm ADJECTIVE

❶ *The ground was firm underfoot.*
• hard, solid, dense, compact, rigid, inflexible, unyielding, set
OPPOSITE soft

❷ *She kept a firm grip on the reins.*
• secure, tight, strong, stable, fixed, rooted, sturdy, steady
❸ *He has a firm belief in ghosts.*
• definite, certain, sure, decided, determined, resolute, unshakeable, unwavering, unswerving
OPPOSITE unsure
❹ *The two girls became firm friends.*
• close, devoted, faithful, loyal, constant, steadfast, long-standing

firm NOUN

a family-run firm
• company, business, establishment, organization, enterprise, corporation

first ADJECTIVE

❶ *the first chapter of a book*
• earliest, opening, introductory, preliminary
– The first voyage of a ship is its **maiden** voyage.
❷ *The first thing to do in an emergency is to keep calm.*
• foremost, principal, key, main, fundamental, chief, primary
➤ at first
At first, no one spoke.
• at the beginning, to start with, initially, originally

first-class ADJECTIVE

He became a first-class detective.
• excellent, first-rate, outstanding, superb, exceptional, superior, superlative, top-notch
OPPOSITES second-rate, mediocre

fish NOUN

 WORD WEB

Some common fish:

➤ bream	➤ hake
➤ catfish	➤ halibut
➤ cod	➤ herring
➤ dogfish	➤ mackerel
➤ eel	➤ marlin
➤ flounder	➤ minnow
➤ haddock	➤ monkfish

> mullet
> pike
> pilchard
> roach
> salmon
> sardine
> shark
> sole
> sprat

> stickleback
> stingray
> sturgeon
> swordfish
> trout
> tuna
> turbot
> whiting

– Fish that live mainly in the sea are **marine fish** and fish that live mainly in rivers are **freshwater fish**. A tiny freshwater fish is a **minnow**.

Parts of a fish:

> backbone
> belly
> fins
> gills

> lateral line
> scales
> swim bladder
> tail

For shellfish see **crustacean**.

fish VERB

She fished in her pocket and pulled out a photo.
• rummage, search, delve, ferret

fishing NOUN

a fishing trip
• angling, trawling

fit ADJECTIVE

❶ *It was a meal fit for a king.*
• suitable, appropriate, fitting, right, good enough, worthy (of)
OPPOSITE unsuitable
❷ *Dad goes to the gym to keep fit.*
• healthy, well, strong, robust, in good shape, in trim
(*old use*) hale and hearty
OPPOSITES unfit, unhealthy
❸ *The horses were exhausted and fit to collapse.*
• ready, liable, likely, about

fit VERB

❶ *We need to fit a new lock on the door.*
• install, put in place, position, fix
❷ *It takes a long time to fit all the pieces together.*
• arrange, assemble, interlock, join

❸ *He fits the description in the paper.*
• match, correspond to, conform to, go together with, tally with
IDIOM fit the bill
❹ *I chose a dress to fit the occasion.*
• be suitable for, be appropriate to, suit

fit NOUN

❶ *The two of us had a fit of the giggles.*
• outburst, outbreak, bout, spell, attack
❷ *an epileptic fit*
• seizure, spasm, convulsion, attack

fitful ADJECTIVE

periods of fitful sleep
• sporadic, intermittent, irregular, spasmodic
OPPOSITES regular, steady

fitting ADJECTIVE

a fitting end to the evening
• suitable, appropriate, apt, proper
OPPOSITE inappropriate

fix VERB

❶ *She fixed the sign to the front gate.*
• fasten, attach, secure, connect, join, link
❷ *Let's fix a time to meet.*
• set, agree on, decide on, arrange, settle, determine
❸ (*informal*) *Can you fix my laptop?*
• repair, mend, sort, put right, restore

fix NOUN

(*informal*) *You've got yourself into a real fix.*
• difficulty, mess, predicament, plight, corner
(*informal*) jam, hole

fixed ADJECTIVE

The date is fixed for next Tuesday.
• set, arranged, decided, agreed, settled, confirmed, definite

fizz VERB

Shake the bottle to make it fizz.
• bubble, sparkle, effervesce, froth, foam, fizzle, hiss

fizzy ADJECTIVE

a bottle of fizzy water
• sparkling, bubbly, effervescent, gassy,

frothy, carbonated
OPPOSITE still

flabbergasted ADJECTIVE
She just stood there, flabbergasted.
• astonished, amazed, astounded, staggered, stunned, taken aback
(*British informal*) gobsmacked

flabby ADJECTIVE
A flabby white arm was flung up over his face.
• fat, fleshy, sagging, slack, loose, floppy, limp
OPPOSITE firm

flag NOUN
the Olympic flag
• banner, pennant, streamer
- The flag of a regiment is its **colours** or **standard**.
- Strips of small flags hung up for decoration are called **bunting**.

flag VERB
❶ *My enthusiasm was beginning to flag.*
• diminish, decrease, decline, lessen, fade, dwindle, wane
❷ *The runners were flagging towards the finish.*
• tire, weaken, wilt, droop
OPPOSITE revive

flair NOUN
❶ *a flair for drawing cartoons*
• talent, aptitude, skill, gift, knack
❷ *She dresses with great flair.*
• style, elegance, panache

flake NOUN
a flake of plaster from the ceiling
• sliver, shaving, wafer, fragment, chip

flamboyant ADJECTIVE
a flamboyant style of dress
• ostentatious, exuberant, showy, flashy, colourful
OPPOSITES restrained, modest

flammable ADJECTIVE
made of flammable material
• inflammable
OPPOSITES non-flammable, fireproof, fire-resistant, fire-retardant

The words flammable and inflammable mean the same thing. They are not opposites of each other.

flap VERB
❶ *The sail flapped in the wind.*
• flutter, sway, swing, wave about, thrash about
❷ *a bat flapping its wings*
• beat, flutter, thrash

flare VERB
A match flared suddenly in the darkness.
• blaze, burn, flash, flame
➤ **flare up**
❶ *The rash tends to flare up at night.*
• break out, erupt, burst out, blow up, reappear
❷ *Elizabeth flared up at his words.*
• lose your temper, fly into a rage, become angry

flash NOUN
❶ *the flash of lightning*
• blaze, flare, beam, burst, gleam, glint, flicker, glimmer, sparkle
SEE ALSO light
❷ *an occasional flash of genius*
• burst, outburst, show, display

flash VERB
❶ *Two searchlights flashed across the sky.*
• shine, blaze, flare, glare, gleam, beam, glint, flicker, glimmer, sparkle
❷ *The train flashed past us.*
• speed, fly, rush, hurtle

flashy ADJECTIVE
Fraser was wearing a flashy tie.
• showy, ostentatious, ornate, flamboyant, gaudy
(*informal*) snazzy, jazzy
OPPOSITE plain

flat ADJECTIVE
❶ *You need a flat surface to write on.*
• level, even, smooth, plane
OPPOSITE uneven
❷ *lying flat on the ground*
• horizontal, outstretched, spread out
- To lie flat, face downwards, is to be **prone**.

A
B
C
D
E
F
G
H
I
J
K
L
M
N
O
P
Q
R
S
T
U
V
W
X
Y
Z

– To lie flat, face upwards, is to be
supine.
OPPOSITE upright
❸ *a flat tyre*
• deflated, punctured, burst
OPPOSITE inflated
❹ *a flat refusal*
• outright, straight, direct, positive,
absolute, definite, point-blank
❺ *speaking in a flat tone*
• monotonous, droning, lifeless, dull,
tedious, boring
OPPOSITE lively

flat NOUN
a two-bedroom flat in the city
• apartment, rooms
– A luxurious flat at the top of a building
is a **penthouse**.
SEE ALSO building

flatten VERB
❶ *Flatten the dough with your hands.*
• smooth, press, roll out, iron out
❷ *The bombing flattened most of the
city.*
• demolish, destroy, knock down, pull
down, level, raze
❸ *a track where feet had flattened the
grass*
• squash, press down, compress, crush,
trample

flatter VERB
❶ *He was only trying to flatter you.*
• compliment, praise, fawn on, toady
(informal) butter up
❷ *I was flattered to be invited.*
• honour, gratify, please
(informal) tickle pink

flattery NOUN
Flattery never works on her.
• compliments, praise, fawning,
toadying
(informal) sweet talk

flaunt VERB
celebrities flaunting their wealth
• show off, display, parade, exhibit

flavour NOUN
❶ *a strong flavour of garlic*
• taste, tang, savour, smack

❷ *a city with an East European flavour*
• quality, style, character, feeling, feel,
atmosphere, air, mood, ambience

flavour VERB
*The sauce was flavoured with garlic and
herbs.*
• season, spice

flaw NOUN
❶ *His only real flaw is vanity.*
• weakness, fault, shortcoming, failing,
weak point, Achilles' heel
OPPOSITES strength, strong point
❷ *I can see a flaw in your argument.*
• error, inaccuracy, mistake, slip
❸ *There is a tiny flaw in the glass.*
• imperfection, defect, blemish, chip,
crack

flawless ADJECTIVE
It was a flawless performance.
• perfect, faultless, immaculate,
impeccable, spotless
OPPOSITES imperfect, flawed

fleck NOUN
*There were a few flecks of paint on the
carpet.*
• spot, speck, mark, dot, dab
SEE ALSO bit

flee VERB
The crowd fled in panic.
• run away, run off, bolt, fly, escape, get
away, take off, hurry off
(informal) clear off, scram, scarper
IDIOMS take to your heels, beat a hasty
retreat

fleet NOUN
a fleet of sixty ships
– A fleet of boats or small ships is a
flotilla.
– A fleet of warships is an **armada**.
– A military fleet belonging to a country
is its **navy**.

fleeting ADJECTIVE
a fleeting glimpse of a deer
• brief, momentary, quick, short, short-
lived, cursory, passing, transient
OPPOSITES lengthy, lasting

flesh NOUN
The knife slipped and cut into his flesh.
• skin, tissue, muscle

flew
past tense see fly

flex VERB
a weightlifter flexing his muscles
• bend, contract, tighten
OPPOSITE straighten

flex NOUN
a long flex for the computer
• cable, lead, wire, cord

flexible ADJECTIVE
❶ a pair of trainers with flexible soles
• bendable, supple, pliable, bendy, elastic, springy
OPPOSITES rigid, inflexible
❷ flexible working hours
• adjustable, adaptable, variable, open
OPPOSITES fixed, inflexible

flick NOUN
a quick flick of the wrist
• swish, twitch, jerk, snap, flip

flick VERB
❶ a horse flicking its tail
• swish, twitch, jerk, whip
❷ flicking a light switch
• press, flip, throw, activate
➤ flick through
flicking through a magazine
• leaf through, thumb through, browse through, skim, scan

flicker VERB
❶ candles flickering in the draught
• glimmer, sparkle, twinkle, shimmer, flutter, blink, wink, dance
SEE ALSO light
❷ I thought I saw her eyelids flicker.
• flutter, quiver, tremble, twitch

flight NOUN
❶ a book about the history of flight
• flying, aviation, aeronautics, air travel
❷ the refugees' flight to safety
• escape, getaway, retreat, exodus

flimsy ADJECTIVE
❶ a flimsy ladder made of rotting wood
• fragile, delicate, frail, brittle, weak, wobbly, shaky, rickety
OPPOSITES sturdy, robust
❷ She wore a flimsy white gown.
• thin, fine, light, lightweight
❸ He listened to their flimsy excuses.
• weak, insubstantial, feeble, unconvincing, implausible
OPPOSITES sound, substantial

flinch VERB
I flinched as a stone flew past my head.
• back off, draw back, recoil, shrink back, start, wince

fling VERB
I flung a stone into the pond.
• throw, cast, sling, toss, hurl, heave, pitch, lob
(informal) chuck

flip VERB
Flip the pancake to cook the other side.
• toss, turn, turn over, flick, spin

flippant ADJECTIVE
He made a flippant remark about the war.
• frivolous, facetious, disrespectful, irreverent, cheeky
OPPOSITE serious

float VERB
❶ The raft floated gently down the river.
• sail, drift, bob, glide, slip, slide, waft
❷ I was floating around inside the spaceship.
• drift, bob, glide, waft, hover

flock NOUN
❶ a flock of geese
see bird
❷ a flock of sheep
see animal

flock VERB
Fans flocked round the stage door.
• crowd, gather, collect, congregate, assemble, mass, throng, swarm, herd, cluster

b
c
d
e
f
g
h
i
j
k
l
m
n
o
p
q
r
s
t
u
v
w
x
y
z

flog VERB
Slaves used to be flogged for running away.
• whip, thrash, beat, lash, scourge, flay

flood NOUN
❶ *The flood swept away several cars.*
• deluge, inundation, torrent, spate
❷ *We received a flood of emails.*
• succession, barrage, storm, volley, rush, torrent, spate
OPPOSITE trickle

flood VERB
❶ *The river burst its banks and flooded the village.*
• inundate, swamp, drown, submerge, immerse, engulf, drench
❷ *Shops have been flooded with cheap imports.*
• saturate, swamp, overwhelm

floor NOUN
❶ *a rug on the floor*
• ground, flooring, base
❷ *the top floor of the building*
• storey, level, tier, deck, stage

flop VERB
❶ *Fiona came in and flopped onto the sofa.*
• collapse, drop, fall, slump, sink
❷ *His red hair flopped over his eyes.*
• dangle, droop, hang down, sag, wilt
❸ (*informal*) *The first film flopped, but the sequel was a big hit.*
• be unsuccessful, fail, founder, fall flat

floppy ADJECTIVE
a rabbit with long, floppy ears
• drooping, droopy, hanging, dangling, limp, saggy
OPPOSITES stiff, rigid

flounder VERB
❶ *The horses were floundering in the mud.*
• struggle, stumble, stagger, fumble, wallow

❷ *I was floundering to answer the question.*
• struggle, falter, hesitate, blunder
IDIOM be out of your depth

flourish VERB
❶ *Our strawberries are flourishing this year.*
• grow well, thrive, bloom, blossom, flower
OPPOSITE die
❷ *Art and music flourished in this period.*
• be successful, do well, prosper, thrive, boom, succeed, progress, develop, increase
OPPOSITE fail
❸ *A man appeared, flourishing an umbrella.*
• brandish, wield, wave, shake

flout VERB
Players were accused of flouting the rules.
• disobey, disregard, defy, ignore, breach, break, contravene, infringe, violate

flow VERB
❶ *A river flowed through the forest.*
• run, pour, stream, roll, course, circulate, sweep, swirl
– To flow slowly is to dribble, drip, ooze, seep or trickle.
– To flow fast is to cascade, gush or surge.
– To flow with sudden force is to spurt or squirt.
– When the tide flows out, it ebbs.
❷ *Traffic was flowing in both directions.*
• move, go, run, stream, rush

flow NOUN
❶ *a steady flow of water*
• stream, course, current, tide, drift, circulation, flood, gush, spate
❷ *the constant flow of traffic*
• movement, motion, stream, circulation, rush

flower NOUN
a bunch of wild flowers
• bloom, blossom, bud

– A bunch of cut flowers is also called a
bouquet or **posy**.

WORD WEB

Some common flowers:

➤ African violet	➤ iris
➤ anemone	➤ lilac
➤ aster	➤ lily
➤ bluebell	➤ lupin
➤ carnation	➤ marigold
➤ chrysanthemum	➤ narcissus
➤ cornflower	➤ orchid
➤ crocus	➤ pansy
➤ daffodil	➤ petunia
➤ dahlia	➤ phlox
➤ daisy	➤ poinsettia
➤ delphinium	➤ primrose
➤ forget-me-not	➤ rose
➤ foxglove	➤ snapdragon
➤ freesia	➤ snowdrop
➤ fuchsia	➤ sunflower
➤ geranium	➤ sweet pea
➤ gladiolus	➤ tulip
➤ hyacinth	➤ violet

- The scientific study of plants and
flowers is **botany**.

- A person who sells or arranges cut
flowers is a **florist**.

Parts of a flower:

➤ anthers	➤ pistil
➤ filaments	➤ sepals
➤ ovary	➤ stamen
➤ ovules	➤ stigma
➤ petals	➤ style

- The parts of the **stamen** are: **anthers**
(containing **pollen**) and **filaments**.

- The parts of the **pistil** are: **stigma**,
style and **ovary** (containing **ovules**).

SEE ALSO plant

flower VERB
*Our snowdrops started to flower in
January.*
• bloom, blossom, bud

flowery ADJECTIVE
a flowery passage from the novel
• ornate, elaborate, florid, fancy, purple

fluctuate VERB
Prices have fluctuated in the past year.
• vary, change, alter, shift, waver, rise
and fall

fluent ADJECTIVE
*She is a fluent speaker on almost any
topic.*
• articulate, eloquent, communicative
OPPOSITES inarticulate,
uncommunicative

fluffy ADJECTIVE
a fluffy scarf
• feathery, downy, furry, fuzzy, hairy,
shaggy

fluid NOUN
Fluid was leaking from the engine.
• liquid, solution, juice
OPPOSITE solid

fluid ADJECTIVE
❶ *Try to keep the mixture fluid.*
• liquid, free-flowing, runny, watery,
molten, melted, liquefied
OPPOSITE solid
❷ *In one fluid movement he drew out his
sword.*
• flowing, smooth, graceful
❸ *Our holiday plans are still fluid.*
• changeable, variable, flexible, open
OPPOSITES fixed, firm

fluke NOUN
*It was a fluke that the ball went into the
net.*
• chance, accident, piece of luck, stroke
of luck

flurry NOUN
❶ *a flurry of snow*
• swirl, whirl, gust
❷ *a flurry of activity*
• burst, outbreak, spurt, fit, bout, spell

flush VERB
❶ *Toby flushed with embarrassment.*
• blush, go red, colour, redden, glow,
burn

A B C D E F G H I J K L M N O P Q R S T U V W X Y Z

❷ *The rain flushed away all the dirt.*
• wash, rinse, sluice, swill

flustered ADJECTIVE
She arrived late, looking flustered.
• confused, upset, bothered, agitated, unsettled, unnerved, ruffled
(*informal*) rattled
OPPOSITE calm

flutter VERB
❶ *A robin fluttered its wings.*
• flap, beat, flicker, quiver, shake, tremble, vibrate
❷ *Flags fluttered in the breeze.*
• waver, flap, flit, ripple, ruffle, undulate

fly VERB
❶ *Two eagles flew high above our heads.*
• glide, soar, swoop, wheel, wing, flit, flutter, hover, float
❷ *Suddenly the hawk flew into the air.*
• rise, soar, ascend, take off
❸ *Everyone was flying past us in a hurry.*
• run, speed, rush, hurry, tear, zoom, hurtle
❹ *The morning just seemed to fly.*
• go quickly, pass quickly, rush by

fly NOUN
see insect

foam NOUN
a layer of white foam
• bubbles, froth, suds, lather
- Foam made by sea water is **surf** or **spume**.

foam VERB
Water foamed around the rocks.
• froth, bubble, seethe, boil, lather, fizz, ferment, effervesce

focus NOUN
❶ *How do you adjust the focus on this camera?*
• clarity, sharpness
❷ *The new lion cubs were the focus of everyone's attention.*
• centre, focal point, target, core, heart, nucleus, pivot, hub

focus VERB
➤ focus on
I'm trying to focus on my work.
• concentrate on, pay attention to, centre on, zero in on, spotlight, pinpoint

fog NOUN
Fog was rolling in from the sea.
- Thin fog is **mist** or **haze**.
- A thick mixture of fog and smoke is **smog**.

foggy ADJECTIVE
❶ *a cold and foggy morning*
• misty, hazy, murky, cloudy, smoggy
❷ *a foggy memory of events*
• blurred, fuzzy, dim, indistinct

foil VERB
The robbery was foiled by French police.
• thwart, frustrate, prevent, block, obstruct, stop, check
(*informal*) scupper

fold VERB
Fold the paper along the dotted line.
• bend, double over, crease, pleat

fold NOUN
❶ *a fold in the centre of the map*
• crease, pleat, furrow, tuck
❷ *a sheep fold*
• enclosure, pen

folder NOUN
I keep all my art work in a folder.
• file, binder, wallet, portfolio

follow VERB
❶ *I think that car is following us.*
• go after, chase, pursue, track, trail, tail, stalk, shadow
❷ *Why does thunder always follow lightning?*
• come after, succeed, replace
OPPOSITE precede
❸ *Follow the directions on the map.*
• carry out, comply with, heed, obey, observe, keep to, adhere to
❹ *I like to follow current events.*
• take an interest in, pay attention to, keep up with, support

❺ *We couldn't follow what she was saying.*
• understand, comprehend, grasp, take in, catch, fathom

❻ *If you're all here, then it follows that your house is empty.*
• mean, happen, result, ensue, arise, come about

follower NOUN
Sir John had a small band of followers.
• supporter, adherent, disciple, admirer

following ADJECTIVE
the following day
• next, succeeding, subsequent, ensuing

folly NOUN
an act of sheer folly
• foolishness, senselessness, stupidity, foolhardiness

fond ADJECTIVE
❶ *a fond farewell*
• loving, tender, affectionate, warm, caring
❷ *a fond hope*
• foolish, unrealistic, fanciful, vain, naive
➤ **be fond of**
I'm very fond of blueberry muffins.
• be keen on, be partial to, have a liking for, like, love
IDIOM have a soft spot for

fondle VERB
She stooped down to fondle the kitten.
• caress, stroke, nudge, pet, play with

food NOUN
The table was laid out with all kinds of delicious food.
• foodstuffs, refreshments, eatables, nourishment, nutrition, nutriment, sustenance, rations, provisions, victuals, fare
(*informal*) grub, nosh
- The food you normally eat or choose to eat is your **diet**.
- Food for farm animals is **feed** or **fodder**.
For ways to prepare food see **cook**.
For tips on describing taste see **taste**.

fool NOUN
❶ *Only a fool would believe that story.*
• idiot, ass, clown, halfwit, dunce, simpleton, blockhead, buffoon, dunderhead, imbecile, moron
(*informal*) chump, dope, dummy, dimwit, nitwit, nincompoop, ninny
(*British informal*) twit, clot, wally
❷ *a medieval fool with cap and bells*
• jester, clown

fool VERB
Don't be fooled by her friendly smile.
• deceive, trick, mislead, delude, dupe, hoodwink, hoax
(*informal*) con, kid, have on, take in
IDIOMS pull the wool over your eyes, take you for a ride
➤ **fool about** or **around**
Stop fooling around and listen!
• play about, mess about, misbehave

foolish ADJECTIVE
It was a foolish idea.
• stupid, silly, idiotic, senseless, ridiculous, nonsensical, unwise, ill-advised, half-witted, unintelligent, absurd, crazy, mad, hare-brained, foolhardy
(*informal*) dim-witted, dumb
(*British informal*) daft, barmy
OPPOSITE sensible

foot NOUN
❶ *to put one foot in front of the other*
❷ *the foot of the page*
• bottom, base
OPPOSITES top, head, summit

🟦	WORD WEB

Parts of a foot:	
➤ ankle	➤ instep
➤ arch	➤ sole
➤ ball	➤ toes
➤ heel	

Types of animal and bird feet:	
➤ claw	➤ hoof

a b c d e f g h i j k l m n o p q r s t u v w x y z

211

> ➤ pad ➤ talon
> ➤ paw ➤ trotter

football NOUN
a friendly game of football
• (North American & Australian) soccer

WORD WEB

Terms used in football:

> ➤ back of the net ➤ linesman
> ➤ booking ➤ midfield
> ➤ captain ➤ near post
> ➤ corner flag ➤ offside
> ➤ corner kick ➤ penalty kick
> ➤ crossbar ➤ penalty
> ➤ defender shoot-out
> ➤ deflection ➤ penalty spot
> ➤ dugout ➤ pitch
> ➤ far post ➤ possession
> ➤ forward ➤ red card
> ➤ foul ➤ referee
> ➤ free kick ➤ relegation
> ➤ fullback ➤ sending off
> ➤ goalkeeper ➤ set play
> ➤ goal kick ➤ sideline
> ➤ goal line ➤ stadium
> ➤ goalpost ➤ striker
> ➤ halftime ➤ substitution
> ➤ hat-trick ➤ suspension
> ➤ header ➤ tackle
> ➤ injury time ➤ throw-in
> ➤ kick-off ➤ yellow card

For tips on writing about sport see
sport.

footprint NOUN
We followed the footprints in the snow.
• track, print, footmark
- The tracks left by an animal are also
called a **spoor**.

footstep NOUN
the sound of footsteps
• step, tread, footfall

forbid VERB
I forbid you to see her again.
• prohibit, ban, bar, rule out,
proscribe, veto, debar
OPPOSITES permit, allow

forbidden ADJECTIVE
Taking photographs is strictly forbidden.
• prohibited, banned, barred, outlawed,
vetoed
OPPOSITES permitted, allowed

forbidding ADJECTIVE
The prison had a grim, forbidding look.
• threatening, menacing, sinister, grim,
ominous, uninviting, daunting
OPPOSITE inviting

force NOUN
❶ They had to use force to open the
door.
• strength, power, might, muscle, vigour,
effort, energy
❷ The force of the explosion broke all
the windows.
• impact, shock, intensity
❸ an international peace-keeping force
• group, unit, team, corps, body, squad

force VERB
❶ They were forced to work for low
wages.
• compel, make, coerce, drive, impel,
order, pressure into, bully into
❷ I had to force my way through the
crowd.
• push, shove, drive, propel, press, thrust
❸ Firefighters had to force the door.
• break open, burst open, break down,
kick in

forceful ADJECTIVE
❶ a forceful personality
• strong, powerful, dynamic, vigorous,
assertive, pushy
(informal) in-your-face
OPPOSITES weak, submissive
❷ a forceful argument
• convincing, compelling, strong,
powerful, persuasive
OPPOSITES weak, unconvincing

forecast VERB
Gales have been forecast for Tuesday.
• predict, foresee, foretell, prophesy

forecast NOUN
the weather forecast for tomorrow
• outlook, prediction, prognosis, prophecy

foreign ADJECTIVE
❶ Every summer the town is full of foreign tourists.
• overseas, international, non-native
OPPOSITES native, domestic
❷ I like travelling to foreign countries.
• overseas, distant, faraway, exotic, remote, far-flung
❸ The idea of cooking is foreign to him.
• unnatural, unfamiliar, strange, alien

foreigner NOUN
Many foreigners have come to live here.
• overseas visitor, stranger, outsider, newcomer, incomer
(formal) alien
– A foreigner who comes to live in a country is an **immigrant**.

foremost ADJECTIVE
He was one of the foremost artists of his day.
• leading, greatest, best, pre-eminent, principal, premier, supreme, chief, top

foresee VERB
She could foresee many problems ahead.
• anticipate, expect, predict, forecast, prophesy, foretell

forest NOUN
see tree

foretell VERB
The witches foretold that Macbeth would be king.
• predict, prophesy, forecast, foresee

forever ADVERB
❶ Will you love me forever?
• for all time, for ever and ever, for good, for eternity, until the end of time, evermore
❷ Cal is forever complaining about something.
• constantly, continually, always, perpetually, incessantly, repeatedly, regularly

forge VERB
❶ Modern horseshoes are forged from steel.
• fashion, cast, hammer out, beat out
❷ That signature has been forged.
• fake, copy, counterfeit
➤ **forge ahead**
The steamship was soon forging ahead.
• advance, make progress, make headway

forgery NOUN
One of these paintings is a forgery.
• fake, copy, counterfeit, fraud, imitation, replica
(informal) phoney

forget VERB
❶ Did you forget your phone?
• leave behind, leave out, overlook
❷ I forgot to switch off the computer.
• omit, neglect, fail
OPPOSITE remember

forgetful ADJECTIVE
He's getting forgetful in his old age.
• absent-minded, dreamy, inattentive, careless, oblivious

forgive VERB
❶ She never forgave him for what he did.
• pardon, excuse, let off, absolve, exonerate
❷ Please forgive my rudeness.
• excuse, pardon, overlook, disregard, indulge, make allowances for
IDIOM turn a blind eye to

fork VERB
The path ahead forks into two.
• split, branch, divide, separate, diverge

forlorn ADJECTIVE
She looked so forlorn.
• sad, unhappy, miserable, sorrowful, dejected, wretched, downcast, crestfallen
OPPOSITE cheerful

form NOUN
❶ The stones are arranged in the form of a cross.
• shape, structure, design, outline,

format, layout, formation, configuration, arrangement
❷ *She is good at drawing the human form.*
• body, figure, shape, frame, physique, anatomy
❸ *Haiku is a form of poetry.*
• kind, sort, type, variety, category, class, genre
❹ *Please fill in this form.*
• questionnaire, document, sheet, slip
❺ *Which form is your sister in?*
• class, year
(*North American*) grade

form VERB
❶ *The bat is formed from a single piece of wood.*
• shape, mould, model, fashion, build, fabricate, construct
❷ *We decided to form a book club.*
• set up, establish, found, create, start, institute, launch
❸ *Icicles had formed on the roof of the cave.*
• appear, develop, grow, emerge, materialize, take shape

formal ADJECTIVE
❶ *Dinner was to be a formal occasion.*
• ceremonious, ceremonial, official, grand, solemn
OPPOSITES informal, casual, unofficial
❷ *Her manner was always very formal.*
• correct, proper, dignified, reserved, stiff, cold, aloof
(*informal*) stand-offish
OPPOSITES informal, friendly, warm

formation NOUN
❶ *an unusual rock formation*
• structure, construction, configuration, arrangement, grouping, pattern
❷ *the formation of a new team*
• creation, establishment, setting up, foundation, institution

former ADJECTIVE
❶ *the former head of the FBI*
• previous, preceding, past, ex-, one-time
(*formal*) erstwhile

❷ *a photograph of the house in former times*
• earlier, past, previous, prior, bygone, olden, of old

formerly ADVERB
Machines were used to do the work formerly done by hand.
• previously, earlier, before, in the past, once, at one time, until now

formidable ADJECTIVE
We face a formidable challenge.
• daunting, intimidating, forbidding, difficult, tough, stiff

formula NOUN
a formula for making invisible ink
• recipe, prescription, procedure

fort NOUN
the remains of a Roman fort
• fortress, fortification, stronghold, castle, citadel, tower
SEE ALSO castle

forthcoming ADJECTIVE
a list of forthcoming events
• upcoming, future, approaching, impending, imminent

fortify VERB
❶ *The wall was built to fortify the old city.*
• defend, protect, secure, strengthen, reinforce
❷ *I felt fortified after breakfast.*
• invigorate, energize, enliven, strengthen, bolster, boost
OPPOSITE weaken

fortress NOUN
see fort

fortunate ADJECTIVE
We were fortunate to have good weather.
• lucky, in luck, favoured
OPPOSITES unfortunate, unlucky

fortunately ADVERB
Fortunately, no one was injured.
• luckily, happily, thankfully, mercifully,

by good fortune
IDIOM as luck would have it

fortune NOUN
❶ She was hoping for a change in fortune.
• luck, fate, destiny
❷ By good fortune, I stumbled across a secret doorway.
• chance, luck, accident, providence
❸ The family had built up a vast fortune.
• wealth, riches, assets, possessions, property, estate
(informal) millions

fortune-teller NOUN
A fortune-teller offered to read my palm.
• soothsayer, clairvoyant, psychic, seer

forward ADJECTIVE
❶ a forward dive from a springboard
• front-facing, front, frontal, onward
OPPOSITES backward, rear
❷ We need to do some forward planning for the camping trip.
• advance, early, future
OPPOSITE retrospective
❸ Would it be too forward to ask him out?
• bold, cheeky, brash, familiar, impudent, presumptuous
OPPOSITE shy

forwards or **forward** ADVERB
❶ The queue moved forwards very slowly.
• on, onwards, along, ahead
❷ Can I have a seat facing forwards?
• to the front, towards the front, ahead
OPPOSITES backwards, back

foster VERB
❶ My aunt has fostered several children.
• bring up, rear, raise, care for, look after, take care of
– To **adopt** a child is to make them legally a full member of your family.
❷ Reading to young children can foster a long-lasting love of books.
• encourage, promote, nurture, stimulate, cultivate, develop

fought
past tense see fight

foul ADJECTIVE
❶ the foul smell of rotting food
• disgusting, revolting, repulsive, repugnant, offensive, loathsome, nasty, horrible, vile, stinking, sickening, nauseating
(informal) gross
OPPOSITE pleasant
❷ the foul state of the kitchen
• dirty, unclean, filthy, mucky, messy
OPPOSITES clean, pure
❸ The referee sent him off for using foul language.
• rude, offensive, improper, indecent, coarse, crude, vulgar, obscene
❹ That was a foul shot.
• illegal, prohibited, unfair
OPPOSITE fair

found VERB
The society was founded a hundred years ago.
• establish, set up, start, begin, create, initiate, institute
OPPOSITE dissolve

foundation NOUN
❶ There is no foundation for that rumour.
• basis, grounds, evidence, justification
❷ It's a hundred years since the foundation of the museum.
• founding, beginning, establishment, setting up, creation, institution

founder NOUN
James Hutton was the founder of modern geology.
• originator, creator, inventor, father, architect

founder VERB
❶ The ship had foundered on the rocks.
• go under, sink, submerge
❷ The project foundered because of lack of money.
• fail, fall through, collapse, come to nothing
(informal) fold, flop, bomb

fountain NOUN

a fountain of water
• jet, spout, spray, spring, cascade

fox NOUN

the rare sight of an Arctic fox
– A female fox is a **vixen**.
– A young fox is a **cub**.
– The burrow of a fox is an **earth**.
For tips on describing animals see animal.

fox VERB

The last question foxed everyone.
• puzzle, baffle, bewilder, mystify,
perplex, stump
(*informal*) flummox, floor

fraction NOUN

I only paid a fraction of the full price.
• tiny part, fragment, scrap, snippet
SEE ALSO bit

fracture VERB

*Jo fell off her bike and fractured her
wrist.*
• break, crack, split, splinter, snap

fracture NOUN

The X-ray showed a bone fracture.
• break, breakage, crack, split, fissure

fragile ADJECTIVE

Reptile eggs are very fragile.
• breakable, delicate, frail, brittle, flimsy,
weak
OPPOSITES sturdy, robust

fragment NOUN

❶ *a fragment of broken pottery*
• bit, piece, chip, sliver, shard, splinter
❷ *She overheard fragments of a
conversation.*
• part, portion, scrap, snippet, snatch

fragrance NOUN

the heady fragrance of jasmine
• scent, smell, aroma, perfume, bouquet
For tips on describing smells see smell.

fragrant ADJECTIVE

The air was fragrant with spices.
• sweet-smelling, perfumed, scented,
aromatic
OPPOSITES foul-smelling, smelly

frail ADJECTIVE

❶ *My grandad is still feeling frail after
his illness.*
• weak, infirm, feeble
❷ *That footbridge looks a bit frail.*
• flimsy, fragile, delicate, rickety,
unsound
OPPOSITES strong, robust

frame NOUN

❶ *a picture frame*
• mount, mounting, surround, border,
setting, edging
❷ *the frame of an old bicycle*
• framework, structure, shell, skeleton,
casing
– The framework under a car is the
chassis.

framework NOUN

❶ *the wooden framework of the roof*
• frame, structure, shell, skeleton,
scaffolding, support
❷ *a new framework for teaching*
• plan, system, scheme, strategy,
programme, blueprint

frank ADJECTIVE

May I be frank with you?
• direct, candid, plain, straight,
straightforward, open, honest, sincere,
genuine, forthright, blunt, matter-of-
fact
(*informal*) upfront
OPPOSITES insincere, evasive

frantic ADJECTIVE

❶ *His parents were going frantic with
worry.*
• beside yourself, fraught, desperate,
distraught, overwrought, hysterical,
worked up, berserk
IDIOMS at your wits' end, in a state
❷ *It was a scene of frantic activity.*
• excited, hectic, frenzied, frenetic,
feverish, wild, mad
OPPOSITE calm

fraud NOUN

❶ *She was found guilty of fraud.*
• deceit, deception, dishonesty,
cheating, swindling, sharp practice

② *The phone-in competition was a fraud.*
• swindle, trick, hoax, pretence, sham
(*informal*) con, scam
③ *The author was later exposed as a fraud.*
• cheat, swindler, fraudster, trickster, charlatan
(*informal*) con man, con artist, phoney

frayed ADJECTIVE
a frayed woollen carpet
• tattered, ragged, worn, threadbare
(*informal*) tatty

freak NOUN
① *a freak of nature*
• oddity, aberration, abnormality, anomaly
② (*informal*) *a health-food freak*
• enthusiast, fan, fanatic, devotee
(*informal*) fiend, nut

free ADJECTIVE
① *You are free to do as you wish.*
• able, allowed, permitted, at liberty
OPPOSITE restricted
② *All the hostages are now free.*
• freed, liberated, released, emancipated, at large
IDIOM on the loose
OPPOSITES imprisoned, captive
③ *I got a free drink with my sandwich.*
• complimentary, free of charge, gratis
IDIOM on the house
④ *The bathroom is free now.*
• available, unoccupied, vacant, empty
OPPOSITES occupied, engaged
⑤ *Are you free this weekend?*
• available, unoccupied, not busy
OPPOSITES busy, occupied
⑥ *He is very free with his money.*
• generous, lavish, liberal
OPPOSITE mean
➤ **free from** or **free of**
food which is free of additives
• without, clear of, rid of, unaffected by

free VERB
① *The hostages were eventually freed.*
• release, liberate, set free, let go, set loose, untie
– To free slaves is to **emancipate** them.

– To free hostages by paying money to the captors is to **ransom** them.
OPPOSITES imprison, confine
② *Rescuers freed the driver from the wreckage.*
• extricate, undo, untangle, work loose

freedom NOUN
① *The prisoners were finally given their freedom.*
• liberty, liberation
② *the freedom to decide for yourself*
• right, power, entitlement, licence

freely ADVERB
① *Elephants roam freely in the national park.*
• unrestricted, unrestrained, free, at large
② *He freely admits to taking bribes.*
• readily, willingly, voluntarily, openly, frankly, candidly

freeze VERB
① *Pure water begins to freeze at 0° C.*
• become ice, ice over, harden, solidify
OPPOSITE thaw
② *Vince froze when he heard the scream.*
• stand still, remain stationary
IDIOM stop dead in your tracks
③ *Season-ticket prices have been frozen for another year.*
• fix, hold, keep as they are

freezing ADJECTIVE
① *a freezing winter's day*
• chilly, frosty, icy, wintry, raw, bitter, arctic
② *Your hands are freezing!*
• frozen, chilled, numb with cold
IDIOM chilled to the bone

frenzy NOUN
a frenzy of last-minute preparations
• excitement, fever, madness, mania, hysteria, panic, fury

frequent ADJECTIVE
① *We send frequent text messages to each other.*
• numerous, continual, constant, recurring, recurrent, repeated
OPPOSITE infrequent

a b c d e f g h i j k l m n o p q r s t u v w x y z

A
B
C
D
E
F
G
H
I
J
K
L
M
N
O
P
Q
R
S
T
U
V
W
X
Y
Z

❷ *She is a frequent visitor to our house.*
• regular, habitual, common, familiar, persistent
OPPOSITE rare

frequent *VERB*
We frequent the same coffee shops.
• visit, attend, spend time in, patronize, haunt

frequently *ADVERB*
These two words are frequently confused.
• often, continually, repeatedly, regularly, routinely, again and again

fresh *ADJECTIVE*
❶ *The shop bakes fresh bread every day.*
• new
OPPOSITES old, stale
❷ *We are looking for fresh ideas.*
• original, novel, new, different, innovative
OPPOSITES tired, stale
❸ *a bowl of fresh fruit*
• natural, raw, unprocessed
OPPOSITES preserved, processed, tinned
❹ *Use a fresh sheet of paper.*
• clean, unused
OPPOSITE used
❺ *She went outside to get some fresh air.*
• cool, crisp, refreshing, bracing
OPPOSITE stuffy
❻ *You'll feel fresh in the morning.*
• refreshed, revived, restored, invigorated
OPPOSITES tired, weary

fret *VERB*
She's always fretting about her school work.
• worry, be anxious, concern yourself, agonize, lose sleep, get worked up

friction *NOUN*
❶ *Engine oil reduces friction.*
• rubbing, chafing, abrasion, resistance, drag
❷ *There was friction between the two teams.*
• conflict, disagreement, discord, hostility, antagonism, animosity, acrimony, bad feeling

friend *NOUN*
Helen is an old friend of mine.
• companion, comrade, ally
(*informal*) pal, buddy, chum
(*British informal*) mate
– A friend you know only slightly is an **acquaintance**.
OPPOSITE enemy

friendly *ADJECTIVE*
❶ *Everyone in our street is very friendly.*
• amiable, amicable, neighbourly, genial, sociable, convivial, affable, likeable, good-natured, warm, kind-hearted, approachable, cordial, kindly
(*informal*) pally, chummy
❷ *a cafe with a friendly atmosphere*
• warm, welcoming, hospitable, cordial, informal
OPPOSITES unfriendly, hostile

friendship *NOUN*
Their friendship has lasted for many years.
• relationship, attachment, closeness, affection, fondness, familiarity, intimacy, bond, tie, fellowship, comradeship
OPPOSITE hostility

fright *NOUN*
❶ *The children were speechless with fright.*
• fear, terror, alarm, horror, panic, dread
❷ *The explosion gave us all a fright.*
• scare, shock, surprise, start, turn, jolt

frighten *VERB*
Sorry, I didn't mean to frighten you.
• scare, terrify, alarm, startle, shock, petrify, panic
IDIOM (*informal*) give you the creeps

frightened *ADJECTIVE*
Were you frightened when the lights went out?
• afraid, scared, terrified, alarmed, fearful, panicky, petrified

frightening *ADJECTIVE*
The climb was a frightening experience.
• terrifying, horrifying, alarming, nightmarish, hair-raising, fearsome (*informal*) scary

frill *NOUN*
❶ *The dress has a lace frill.*
• ruffle, ruff, flounce, fringe
❷ *Our hotel was basic with no frills.*
• extra, luxury

fringe *NOUN*
❶ *a scarf with a beaded fringe*
• border, edging, frill, trimming
❷ *a region on the fringe of the solar system*
• edge, border, margin, rim, perimeter, periphery, outskirts

frisky *ADJECTIVE*
Our new kittens are very frisky.
• playful, lively, high-spirited, sprightly

fritter *VERB*
➤ **fritter away**
He frittered away all the money he had won.
• waste, squander, use up, get through

frivolous *ADJECTIVE*
Don't waste my time asking frivolous questions.
• foolish, silly, ridiculous, trifling, trivial, shallow, superficial, petty
OPPOSITES serious, weighty

frock *NOUN*
see **clothes**

frog *NOUN*

WORD WEB

The life cycle of a frog:
➤ **frogspawn**   ➤ **tadpole**
– The process whereby a tadpole develops into a frog is **metamorphosis**.
SEE ALSO **amphibian**

frolic *VERB*
Lambs frolicked in the fields.
• jump about, leap about, bound, caper, prance, gambol, romp, skip, play

front *NOUN*
❶ *We stood at the front of the queue.*
• head, start, beginning, lead, top
❷ *The front of the house was painted white.*
• face, facing, frontage, facade
– The front of a ship is the **bow** or **prow**.
– The front of a picture is the **foreground**.
OPPOSITES back, rear
❸ *She managed to put on a brave front.*
• appearance, act, show, exterior, face, facade
➤ **in front**
the team in front at the half-way stage
• ahead, in the lead, leading

front *ADJECTIVE*
the front page of the newspaper
• first, leading, lead, foremost
– The front legs of an animal are its **forelegs** (opposite **hind legs**).
OPPOSITES back, rear

frontier *NOUN*
the frontier between France and Belgium
• border, boundary, borderline, dividing line

frosty *ADJECTIVE*
❶ *a clear and frosty morning*
• cold, crisp, icy, freezing, wintry
❷ *The assistant gave us a frosty stare.*
• unfriendly, unwelcoming, cold, cool, stony
OPPOSITES warm, friendly

froth *NOUN*
Would you like froth on your hot chocolate?
• foam, bubbles, head
– The froth on top of soapy water is **lather** or **suds**.
– Dirty froth is **scum**.

A B C D E F G H I J K L M N O P Q R S T U V W X Y Z

frown VERB
She frowned as she stared at the screen.
• scowl, grimace, glower, glare
IDIOMS knit your brow, look daggers

frown NOUN
Benny had a frown on his face.
• scowl, grimace, glower, glare, black look

frozen ADJECTIVE
My feet are frozen!
• freezing, chilled, numb with cold
IDIOMS chilled to the bone, frozen solid

frugal ADJECTIVE
❶ *A frugal supper was laid out.*
• meagre, paltry, plain, simple
OPPOSITE lavish
❷ *People had to be frugal during the war.*
• thrifty, sparing, economical, prudent
OPPOSITES wasteful, spendthrift

fruit NOUN

WORD WEB

Some varieties of fruit:

➤ apple	➤ melon
➤ apricot	➤ nectarine
➤ avocado	➤ orange
➤ banana	➤ papaya
➤ blackberry or bramble	➤ peach
➤ blackcurrant	➤ pear
➤ blueberry	➤ persimmon
➤ cherry	➤ pineapple
➤ clementine	➤ plantain
➤ cranberry	➤ plum
➤ grape	➤ pomegranate
➤ grapefruit	➤ quince
➤ guava	➤ raspberry
➤ kiwi fruit	➤ redcurrant
➤ kumquat	➤ rosehip
➤ lemon	➤ satsuma
➤ lime	➤ sloe
➤ lychee	➤ strawberry
➤ mandarin	➤ tangerine
➤ mango	➤ tomato

- Lemons, limes, oranges and grapefruit are citrus fruits.

Dried fruits:

➤ currant	➤ raisin
➤ date	➤ sultana
➤ prune	

fruitful ADJECTIVE
Did you have a fruitful trip?
• successful, productive, useful, worthwhile, profitable, rewarding
OPPOSITE fruitless

fruitless ADJECTIVE
a fruitless search for clues
• unsuccessful, unprofitable, unproductive, futile, pointless, useless, vain
OPPOSITES fruitful, successful

frustrate VERB
❶ *People were frustrated by the long wait.*
• exasperate, discourage, dishearten, dispirit, irritate, infuriate
❷ *Our plans were frustrated by the weather.*
• block, foil, thwart, defeat, hinder, prevent

frustration NOUN
He banged the table in frustration.
• exasperation, annoyance, irritation, vexation, dissatisfaction

fry VERB
see cook

fuel NOUN

WORD WEB

Some types of fuel:

➤ biofuel	➤ hydrogen
➤ charcoal	➤ kerosene
➤ coal	➤ natural gas
➤ coke	➤ methane
➤ diesel	➤ petrol (*North American* gasoline)
➤ electricity	
➤ ethanol	

> ➤ petroleum or   ➤ uranium
>   crude oil   ➤ wood
> ➤ propane

- Coal, natural gas and petroleum are called **fossil fuels**.

fuel *VERB*
❶ *The rocket was fuelled by liquid hydrogen and oxygen.*
• power, drive, fire, run
❷ *The cinema fuelled his imagination.*
• feed, stimulate, incite, provoke, intensify, fire, stoke, fan

fugitive *NOUN*
Police are still searching for the fugitives.
• runaway, escapee, outlaw, deserter
– Someone who is a fugitive from war or persecution is a **refugee**.

fulfil *VERB*
❶ *She fulfilled her ambition to fly an aircraft.*
• achieve, realize, accomplish, attain, carry out, complete, succeed in
❷ *All contestants must fulfil these conditions.*
• meet, satisfy, conform to, comply with

full *ADJECTIVE*
❶ *My glass is already full.*
• filled, loaded, packed, topped up, brimming
OPPOSITE empty
❷ *The cinema is usually full on Saturdays.*
• busy, crowded, jammed, packed, crammed, congested
(*informal*) jam-packed
OPPOSITE empty
❸ *I can't eat any more—I'm full.*
• replete, full up, sated, satiated
(*informal*) stuffed
OPPOSITE hungry
❹ *You need to write a full account of what happened.*
• complete, detailed, comprehensive, thorough, exhaustive, in-depth, unabridged
OPPOSITES incomplete, partial, selective

❺ *They are working at full speed.*
• top, maximum, greatest, highest
OPPOSITE minimum
❻ *The dress has a very full skirt.*
• wide, broad, loose-fitting, voluminous
OPPOSITE tight

fully *ADVERB*
They were fully aware of the risks.
• completely, totally, entirely, wholly, perfectly, quite

fun *NOUN*
We had great fun playing in the attic.
• amusement, enjoyment, pleasure, entertainment, recreation, diversion, merriment, sport, play, a good time
➤ **make fun of**
Why do you always make fun of him?
• jeer at, laugh at, mock, ridicule, taunt, tease

function *NOUN*
❶ *Modern zoos have several functions.*
• purpose, role, use, task, job, duty, responsibility
❷ *The room is being used for a private function.*
• event, occasion, party, reception

function *VERB*
His heart isn't functioning properly.
• work, go, operate, run, perform

fund *NOUN*
a special emergency fund
• collection, reserve, savings, pool, kitty
➤ **funds**
The nature centre is running short of funds.
• money, cash, savings, capital, reserves

fund *VERB*
The website is funded entirely by donations.
• finance, pay for, sponsor, subsidize, back

fundamental *ADJECTIVE*
There are still some fundamental questions you haven't answered.
• basic, elementary, essential, important, main, necessary, principal

a b c d e f g h i j k l m n o p q r s t u v w x y z

funeral NOUN

The service was followed by a private funeral.

• burial, interment, entombment, cremation

funny ADJECTIVE

OVERUSED WORD

❶ A funny joke, situation:

➤ amusing	➤ farcical
➤ humorous	➤ witty
➤ comic	➤ entertaining
➤ comical	➤ diverting
➤ hilarious	➤ droll

(informal) hysterical, priceless, side-splitting, rib-tickling

The best part of the film is the hilarious car chase.

OPPOSITES serious, unfunny

❷ A funny feeling, look:

➤ strange	➤ puzzling
➤ odd	➤ perplexing
➤ peculiar	➤ weird
➤ unusual	➤ bizarre
➤ curious	

Being alone in the graveyard gave me a peculiar feeling.

❸ A funny taste, smell:

➤ strange	➤ puzzling
➤ odd	➤ perplexing
➤ peculiar	➤ weird
➤ unusual	➤ bizarre
➤ curious	

The rattlesnake stew had a curious flavour.

fur NOUN

the fur of an arctic fox

• hair, coat, hide, pelt

furious ADJECTIVE

❶ Tony was furious when he heard the news.

• angry, irate, enraged, infuriated, incensed, fuming, raging, seething, livid

(informal) mad

❷ We worked at a furious rate.

• frantic, hectic, frenzied, extreme, intense

OPPOSITE calm

furniture NOUN

WORD WEB

Some items of furniture:

➤ armchair	➤ dresser
➤ bed	➤ dressing table
➤ bookcase	➤ filing cabinet
➤ bureau	➤ settee
➤ chair	➤ sideboard
➤ chest of drawers	➤ sofa
➤ coffee table	➤ sofa bed
➤ couch	➤ stool
➤ cupboard	➤ table
➤ desk	➤ wardrobe

- The soft covering on a chair or sofa is upholstery.

- Old and valuable pieces of furniture are antiques.

furrow NOUN

The tractor wheels had made deep furrows in the mud.

• groove, rut, ditch, channel, trench

furry ADJECTIVE

a small, furry creature

• hairy, woolly, fleecy, fuzzy, fluffy, downy

further ADJECTIVE

See our website for further information.

• more, extra, additional, supplementary

furtive ADJECTIVE

She cast a furtive glance backwards.

• secretive, stealthy, surreptitious, conspiratorial, sneaky, sly, underhand

IDIOM cloak-and-dagger

OPPOSITE open

fury NOUN

❶ His eyes blazed with fury.

• anger, rage, wrath, indignation

Sidebar letters: A B C D E F G H I J K L M N O P Q R S T U V W X Y Z

❷ *There was no shelter from the fury of the storm.*
• ferocity, fierceness, intensity, severity, violence, turbulence, savagery

fuse VERB
Two or more cells can be fused together.
• merge, unite, join, combine, blend, melt
– To fuse metals together when making or mending something is to **solder** or **weld** them.

fuss NOUN
You're making a fuss about nothing.
• bother, commotion, excitement, trouble, hullabaloo, stir
(*informal*) to-do
IDIOM song and dance

fuss VERB
I wish you'd stop fussing.
• worry, fret, bother, get worked up
IDIOMS (*informal*) get in a flap, get in a tizzy

fussy ADJECTIVE
❶ *Our cat is fussy about her food.*
• finicky, hard to please, particular

(*informal*) choosy, picky, pernickety
❷ *a carpet with a fussy design*
• fancy, elaborate, busy, ornate, florid

futile ADJECTIVE
He made a futile attempt to escape.
• fruitless, pointless, unsuccessful, useless, ineffectual, vain, wasted
OPPOSITES successful, fruitful

future NOUN
He has a bright future as an actor.
• outlook, prospects
OPPOSITE past

future ADJECTIVE
at a future date
• later, following, ensuing, to come
OPPOSITES past, previous, earlier

fuzzy ADJECTIVE
❶ *A fuzzy image appeared on the screen.*
• blurred, bleary, unfocused, unclear, indistinct, hazy, cloudy
OPPOSITE clear
❷ *a fuzzy ball of wool*
• fluffy, frizzy, furry, woolly, fleecy

Gg

gadget NOUN
a handy kitchen gadget
• tool, instrument, implement, device, contraption
(*informal*) gizmo

gain VERB
❶ *Samira gained a place at art college.*
• get, acquire, obtain, achieve, attain, earn, win
(*informal*) land
OPPOSITE lose
❷ *The car began to gain speed.*
• increase, gather, pick up, build up

game NOUN
❶ *an old-fashioned party game*
• amusement, pastime, sport, activity, recreation
❷ *Are you going to the game this Saturday?*
• match, contest, competition, tournament, fixture, tie

gang NOUN
❶ *a gang of bullies*
• group, band, crowd, pack, set, mob
❷ *a gang of builders*
• team, unit, crew, squad, detachment, shift

gaol NOUN
see jail

gap NOUN
❶ *We can go through that gap in the fence.*
• opening, space, hole, aperture, break, breach, rift, crack
❷ *She is back in the team after a gap of two years.*
• break, interval, interruption, pause, lull
❸ *The gap between rich and poor is widening.*
• difference, disparity, separation, contrast, gulf, chasm

gape VERB
Anne could only gape in surprise.
• stare, be open-mouthed, gaze
(*informal*) gawp

gaping ADJECTIVE
a gaping hole in the ground
• wide, broad, yawning, vast, cavernous

garden NOUN
a vegetable garden
• plot, patch
– A rented garden for growing vegetables is an **allotment**.
– A garden planted with trees is an **orchard**.
– A formal word for gardening is **horticulture** and a word meaning 'to do with gardens or gardening' is **horticultural**.

garment NOUN
see clothes

gas NOUN
The air we breathe is a mixture of gases.
• vapour, fumes

gash NOUN
a deep gash on my knee
• cut, slash, slit, wound

gasp VERB
At the end of the race we lay down, gasping for breath.
• gulp, pant, puff, wheeze

gate NOUN
Please enter by the main gate.
• gateway, doorway, entrance, portal

gather VERB
❶ *A crowd gathered to watch the fireworks.*
• assemble, collect, come together, congregate, converge, rally
OPPOSITE disperse
❷ *He gathered up all his papers.*
• collect, assemble, bring together, round up, marshal
❸ *We've been gathering sticks of wood.*
• pick, pluck, collect, harvest

④ *I gather that you've been ill.*
• understand, hear, learn, believe

gathering NOUN
an annual family gathering
• assembly, meeting, get-together, party, convention, crowd

gaudy ADJECTIVE
The man on the TV was wearing a gaudy tie.
• flashy, showy, loud, glaring, garish, lurid
OPPOSITE subdued

gauge VERB
① *This instrument can gauge the temperature of the water.*
• measure, calculate, work out, compute, determine, ascertain
② *It was difficult to gauge the mood of the audience.*
• judge, estimate, assess, reckon

gaunt ADJECTIVE
an old woman with gaunt features
• haggard, drawn, thin, skinny, scraggy, scrawny, wasted, skeletal

gave
past tense see give

gaze VERB
He continued to gaze blankly out of the window.
• stare, look, gape

gear NOUN
(informal) *We put our camping gear in the back of the car.*
• equipment, apparatus, materials, paraphernalia, tackle, kit

gem NOUN
a silver casket studded with gems
• jewel, gemstone, precious stone

⊛ **WORD WEB**

Some common gemstones:
➤ agate   ➤ amber

➤ amethyst   ➤ moonstone
➤ aquamarine   ➤ onyx
➤ carnelian   ➤ opal
➤ diamond   ➤ pearl
➤ emerald   ➤ rose quartz
➤ garnet   ➤ ruby
➤ jade   ➤ sapphire
➤ jasper   ➤ tiger's eye
➤ jet   ➤ topaz
➤ lapis lazuli   ➤ tourmaline
➤ malachite   ➤ turquoise

general ADJECTIVE
① *There was a general feeling of relief.*
• widespread, extensive, broad, sweeping, overall, prevalent
IDIOM across the board
② *I've got a general idea of where we are.*
• rough, approximate, vague, broad, loose, indefinite, imprecise
OPPOSITES specific, detailed

generally ADVERB
① *I generally travel by bus.*
• usually, normally, as a rule, chiefly, mostly, mainly, predominantly, on the whole
② *He is generally considered to be the greatest player ever.*
• widely, commonly, popularly, universally

generate VERB
The website has generated a lot of interest.
• create, produce, bring about, give rise to, prompt, stimulate, trigger, spark

generous ADJECTIVE
① *He is always generous to his friends.*
• unselfish, charitable, kind-hearted, magnanimous, giving
OPPOSITES selfish, mean
② *We each got a generous portion of chips.*
• ample, large, lavish, plentiful, abundant, copious
OPPOSITE meagre

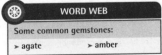

genial ADJECTIVE

He had a very pleasant, genial manner.
• friendly, kind, warm, warm-hearted, kindly, good-natured, pleasant, agreeable, cordial, amiable, affable
OPPOSITES unfriendly, cold

genius NOUN

Luke is a genius at maths.
• expert, master, mastermind, wizard, ace, virtuoso, maestro

gentle ADJECTIVE

❶ *She was shy and gentle by nature.*
• kind, tender, good-tempered, humane, mild, placid
OPPOSITES rough, harsh
❷ *Grasses swayed in the gentle breeze.*
• light, slight, mild, soft, faint
OPPOSITES strong, severe
❸ *There is a gentle slope down the hill.*
• gradual, slight, easy
OPPOSITE steep

genuine ADJECTIVE

❶ *a genuine diamond*
• real, actual, true, authentic
OPPOSITES fake, imitation
❷ *She seems like a very genuine person.*
• honest, sincere, frank, earnest, natural, candid
OPPOSITES false, insincere

gesture NOUN

The man raised his hands in a gesture of surrender.
• sign, signal, motion, movement, indication

gesture VERB

She gestured to us to keep quiet.
• signal, indicate, motion, give a sign

get VERB

❶ *Where did you get those trainers?*
• acquire, obtain, come by, get hold of, buy, purchase
❷ *She got an award for gymnastics.*
• receive, be given, gain, earn, win, achieve
❸ *It's starting to get dark outside.*
• become, grow, turn, go

❹ *What time did you get home?*
• reach, arrive at, come to
OPPOSITE leave
❺ *Could you get me a fork, please?*
• bring, fetch, collect, pick up, retrieve
❻ *You'll never get her to agree.*
• persuade, urge, influence, coax
❼ *We all got a stomach bug on holiday.*
• catch, develop, contract, pick up (*informal*) go down with, come down with
❽ (*informal*) *I don't get your point.*
• understand, comprehend, follow, grasp, see

➤ **get on or along**
❶ *How are you getting on with playing the guitar?*
• manage, fare, cope, prosper, succeed
❷ *We didn't get along at first.*
• harmonize, gel, connect
IDIOMS hit it off, see eye to eye

➤ **get out of**
I can't get out of going to the party.
• avoid, evade, escape, dodge, shirk (*informal*) wriggle out of

➤ **get over**
He never got over his disappointment.
• recover from, get better from, shake off, survive

➤ **have got to**
You've got to tell her the truth.
• must, need to, should, ought to, be obliged to

ghastly ADJECTIVE

The story is about a ghastly murder.
• appalling, awful, dreadful, frightful, grim, grisly, horrible, horrifying, shocking, monstrous, terrible

ghost NOUN

They say the house is haunted by ghosts.
• spirit, spectre, phantom, ghoul, apparition, shade, wraith (*informal*) spook
– A ghost or spirit that throws things about noisily is a **poltergeist**.
For tips on writing horror fiction see **horror**.

ghostly ADJECTIVE
the icy touch of a ghostly hand
• spectral, phantom, ghoulish, unearthly, eerie, sinister, uncanny
(*informal*) creepy, spooky

giant NOUN
Argus was a giant with a hundred eyes.
see fantasy

giant ADJECTIVE
the trunk of a giant redwood tree
• gigantic, huge, enormous, massive, immense, mammoth, colossal, mighty
(OPPOSITES) tiny, miniature
(SEE ALSO) big

giddy ADJECTIVE
I felt giddy when I looked down.
• dizzy, light-headed, faint, unsteady
(*informal*) woozy

gift NOUN
❶ *a birthday gift*
• present, offering
❷ *You have a real gift for drawing.*
• talent, ability, flair, knack, genius, aptitude, bent

gifted ADJECTIVE
He is a gifted pianist.
• talented, skilled, accomplished, capable, able, proficient, expert

gigantic ADJECTIVE
A gigantic wall surrounded the city.
• huge, giant, enormous, massive, colossal, immense, vast, mammoth, monumental, mountainous, gargantuan
(*informal*) whopping, humongous
(OPPOSITES) tiny, minuscule
(SEE ALSO) big

giggle VERB
I saw them whispering and giggling together.
• snigger, titter, chuckle, chortle, laugh

girl NOUN
a girl of thirteen or fourteen
• young woman, young lady, miss, lass
(*old use*) damsel, maid, maiden

give VERB
❶ *I gave her a brooch for her birthday.*
• present with, offer, supply with, issue with, hand over to, deliver to
❷ *We gave some money to the charity appeal.*
• contribute, donate, grant
❸ *He gave a loud yawn.*
• utter, emit, let out, produce, make
❹ *The band will be giving a free performance.*
• present, put on, lay on, organize, arrange, host, throw
❺ *The branch gave under their weight.*
• collapse, give way, bend, break, buckle
➤ **give in**
I'm not going to give in now!
• surrender, yield, submit, concede defeat
➤ **give up**
We gave up waiting for the bus.
• abandon, stop, cease, discontinue
(*informal*) quit

glad ADJECTIVE
I'm glad that you like your present.
• pleased, happy, delighted, thrilled
(OPPOSITES) sad, sorry
➤ **be glad of**
We'd be glad of your help.
• appreciate, be grateful for, value

glamorous ADJECTIVE
the glamorous life of a film star
• attractive, elegant, stylish, fashionable, chic, exotic, glittering
(*informal*) glitzy

glance VERB
❶ *Ravi glanced quickly at his watch.*
• look, peek, peep, glimpse
❷ *I glanced briefly through the papers.*
• browse, skim, scan, flick, leaf, thumb

glance NOUN
She gave a quick glance behind her.
• look, peek, peep, glimpse

glare VERB
❶ *She glared at him without speaking.*
• stare, frown, scowl, glower
(IDIOM) look daggers

a
b
c
d
e
f
g
h
i
j
k
l
m
n
o
p
q
r
s
t
u
v
w
x
y
z

② *A bright light glared in my face.*
• dazzle, blaze, shine, flash

glare NOUN
① *the glare of the headlights*
• dazzle, blaze, brightness, brilliance
② *The manager gave us an angry glare.*
• stare, scowl, glower, frown, black look

glaring ADJECTIVE
There were a few glaring errors.
• obvious, conspicuous, noticeable, unmistakable, unmissable, striking, blatant

glasses PLURAL NOUN
She put on her glasses to read the letter.
• spectacles
(*informal*) specs

gleam NOUN
a gleam of moonlight
• glimmer, glint, flash, ray, shaft

gleam VERB
Lights gleamed on the water.
• glimmer, glint, glisten, shimmer, shine

glide VERB
The balloon glided gently over the treetops.
• slide, slip, drift, float, coast

glimmer VERB
The city lights glimmered in the distance.
• gleam, glint, glow, glisten, shimmer, flicker, blink

glimpse NOUN
We caught a glimpse of a dolphin's tail.
• peek, peep, glance, sighting, view

glimpse VERB
I glimpsed a deer running through the forest.
• catch sight of, spot, spy, sight

glint VERB
Sunlight glinted off the windows.
• flash, glitter, sparkle, twinkle

glisten VERB
The pavement glistened with frost.
• gleam, shine, glint, shimmer, glimmer

glitter VERB
The jewels glittered under the lights.
• sparkle, twinkle, shimmer, glimmer, glint, glisten, flash, shine

gloat VERB
They were still gloating about the score.
• boast, brag, crow, show off

global ADJECTIVE
The Internet is a global network of computers.
• worldwide, international, universal
OPPOSITE local

globe NOUN
① *She has travelled all over the globe.*
• world, planet, earth
② *The fortune teller stared into a crystal globe.*
• ball, sphere, orb

gloom NOUN
① *We could hardly see in the gloom of the cave.*
• darkness, dimness, shade, shadow, murk
– The dim light of the evening is **dusk** or **twilight**.
② *A feeling of gloom descended on me.*
• depression, sadness, unhappiness, melancholy, misery, despair, dejection, woe

gloomy ADJECTIVE
① *It was cold and gloomy in the cellar.*
• dark, dingy, dim, shadowy, murky, dismal, dreary, sombre, cheerless
OPPOSITE bright
② *I stayed in bed feeling gloomy.*
• depressed, sad, unhappy, glum, miserable, melancholy, low, down, downcast, dejected, despondent, crestfallen
(*informal*) fed up
IDIOMS (*informal*) down in the dumps, down in the mouth
OPPOSITE cheerful

glorious ADJECTIVE
the sight of a glorious sunset
• magnificent, splendid, stunning,

spectacular, superb, magnificent,
wonderful, marvellous

glossy ADJECTIVE
a cat with a glossy coat
• shiny, shining, gleaming, lustrous,
sleek, silky, polished
OPPOSITE dull

glove NOUN
a pair of sheepskin gloves
– Gloves without separate parts for the
fingers are **mittens**.
– A glove with a wide cuff covering the
wrist is a **gauntlet**.
SEE ALSO clothes

glow NOUN
*The soft glow of candlelight lit the
room.*
• shine, gleam, radiance, glimmer

glow VERB
A flying saucer glowed in the night sky.
• shine, gleam, glimmer, beam, burn,
flare
– Something that glows in the dark is
luminous or **phosphorescent**.

glower VERB
The two men glowered at each other.
• glare, scowl, frown, stare angrily
IDIOM look daggers

glue NOUN
a tube of glue
• adhesive, paste, gum

glue VERB
Glue the edges together.
• stick, paste, bond, seal

glum ADJECTIVE
Why are you looking so glum?
• depressed, sad, unhappy, gloomy,
miserable, melancholy, low, down,
downcast, dejected, despondent,
crestfallen
(informal) fed up
IDIOM (informal) down in the dumps
OPPOSITE cheerful

gnarled ADJECTIVE
a gnarled tree trunk
• bent, twisted, crooked, distorted,
knobbly, knotty

gnaw VERB
A dog was gnawing at a bone.
• chew, bite, nibble, munch

go VERB
❶ *Our bus went slowly up the hill.*
• move, progress, proceed, advance,
make your way
SEE ALSO move
❷ *Are you going into town today?*
• travel, journey
❸ *Some of the guests had already
gone.*
• leave, depart, set off, withdraw
❹ *A path goes all the way to the
summit.*
• extend, lead, reach, stretch, run
❺ *My fingers went blue with cold.*
• become, turn, grow
❻ *The cups go on the top shelf.*
• belong, be kept, be placed
(informal) live
❼ *By morning, all the snow had gone.*
• disappear, vanish
❽ *All the money has gone.*
• be used up, be spent
❾ *Is that old clock still going?*
• function, operate, work, run
❿ *The morning went quickly.*
• pass, go by, elapse
➤ **go back**
Let's go back to the house.
• return, retreat, retrace your steps
➤ **go in for**
Are you going in for the race this year?
• enter, take part in, participate in
➤ **go off**
❶ *A firework went off by mistake.*
• explode, blow up, detonate
❷ *This milk has gone off.*
• go bad, turn sour, spoil, rot
➤ **go on**
❶ *What's going on over there?*
• happen, occur, take place
❷ *Please go on with your story.*
• carry on, continue, keep going,
proceed

➤ go through

The family were going through a hard time.

• experience, undergo, face, suffer, endure

➤ go with

Do these shoes go with my dress?

• match, suit, blend with

go NOUN

Can I have a go on your tablet?

• turn, try, chance, opportunity, spell, stint

(*informal*) shot, bash, stab

goal NOUN

The goal of the society is to protect wildlife.

• aim, objective, purpose, object, end, target, ambition, intention

god, goddess NOUN

the gods of ancient Greece

• deity, divine being, immortal

– A word meaning 'to do with a god or goddess' is **divine**.

golden ADJECTIVE

❶ *a golden helmet*

• gold

– Something that is covered with a thin layer of gold is **gilded** or **gilt**.

❷ *golden hair*

• fair, blonde, yellow

good ADJECTIVE

That's a really good idea!

• excellent, fine, lovely, nice, wonderful

(*informal*) fantastic, great, super, cool

OPPOSITES bad, poor, awful

▨ OVERUSED WORD

❶ **A good person, good deed:**

➤ honest	➤ noble
➤ worthy	➤ kind
➤ honourable	➤ humane
➤ moral	➤ charitable
➤ decent	➤ merciful
➤ virtuous	

Sir Lancelot is portrayed as an

honourable knight.

OPPOSITES wicked, evil

❷ **Good behaviour:**

➤ well-behaved	➤ exemplary
➤ obedient	➤ angelic

The kittens are well-behaved.

OPPOSITES naughty, disobedient

❸ **A good friend:**

➤ true	➤ reliable
➤ loyal	➤ trusty
➤ loving	➤ trustworthy

You have always been a true friend to me.

❹ **A good experience, good news:**

➤ pleasant	➤ agreeable
➤ enjoyable	➤ pleasing
➤ delightful	

I found the book more enjoyable than the film.

OPPOSITES unpleasant, disagreeable

❺ **Good food, a good meal:**

➤ delicious	➤ appetizing
➤ healthy	➤ well-cooked
➤ nourishing	➤ wholesome
➤ nutritious	➤ substantial
➤ tasty	➤ hearty

The crew ate a hearty breakfast.

❻ **Good weather:**

➤ fine	➤ favourable
➤ fair	

We are hoping for fine weather tomorrow.

OPPOSITES harsh, adverse

❼ **A good feeling, good mood:**

➤ happy	➤ contented
➤ cheerful	➤ good-humoured
➤ light-hearted	➤ buoyant
➤ positive	

(*informal*) chirpy

Ali began the day in a buoyant mood.

❽ A good performer, good work:

- capable
- skilled
- talented
- able
- competent
- commendable
- sound

My grandmother was a talented painter.

OPPOSITES poor, awful

❾ Good grammar, good spelling:

- accurate
- correct
- exact
- proper

Can you translate this into correct French?

OPPOSITES poor, awful

❿ Good timing, a good moment:

- convenient
- suitable
- fortunate
- appropriate
- opportune

Is this a convenient time for a chat?

OPPOSITES inconvenient, unsuitable

⓫ A good excuse, good reason:

- acceptable
- valid
- satisfactory
- proper
- legitimate
- strong
- convincing

That is not a valid excuse for being late.

OPPOSITES poor, unacceptable

⓬ A good look, good clean:

- thorough
- comprehensive
- rigorous
- careful
- complete
- full

My locker needs a thorough clean-out!

OPPOSITES rough, superficial

⓭ Something that is good for you:

- beneficial
- advantageous
- helpful
- valuable
- rewarding
- health-giving

Eating garlic is beneficial for your heart.

OPPOSITES harmful, detrimental

---

goodbye NOUN
It was time to say goodbye.
• farewell
(*informal*) cheerio, bye, bye bye, so long, see you

good-looking ADJECTIVE
I think your cousin is quite good-looking.
• attractive, handsome, pretty
OPPOSITE ugly

goods PLURAL NOUN
The smugglers hid the stolen goods in a cave.
• property, merchandise, wares, articles, produce, cargo

gorgeous ADJECTIVE
a gorgeous sunset
• beautiful, glorious, dazzling, stunning, splendid, superb, attractive, glamorous, handsome
SEE ALSO beautiful

gossip VERB
Those two are always gossiping.
• chatter, tell tales
(*informal*) natter

gossip NOUN
❶ *I want to hear all the gossip.*
• chatter, rumour, hearsay, scandal
(*informal*) tittle-tattle
❷ *She is a dreadful gossip.*
• busybody, chatterbox, telltale, scandalmonger

gouge VERB
Glaciers gouged out valleys from the hills.
• dig, hollow out, scoop out, excavate

govern VERB
The ancient Romans governed a vast empire.
• rule, run, administer, direct, command, manage, oversee, be in charge of

gown NOUN
a silk evening gown
• dress, frock, robe

grab VERB
She reached out and grabbed my hand.
• seize, grasp, catch, clutch, grip, get hold of, snatch

graceful ADJECTIVE
the graceful stride of a gazelle
• elegant, flowing, stylish, smooth, agile, nimble, fluid
OPPOSITES clumsy, graceless

gracious ADJECTIVE
Thank you for being such a gracious host.
• polite, courteous, good-natured, pleasant, agreeable, civil

grade NOUN
A black belt is the highest grade in judo.
• class, standard, level, stage, rank, degree

grade VERB
Eggs are graded according to size.
• classify, class, categorize, arrange, group, sort, rank

gradual ADJECTIVE
There's been a gradual change in the weather.
• steady, slow, gentle, moderate, unhurried, regular, even
OPPOSITES sudden, abrupt

gradually ADVERB
Add the water gradually to the mixture.
• steadily, slowly, gently, bit by bit, little by little
OPPOSITES suddenly, all at once

grain NOUN
❶ *a field of grain*
• cereal, corn
❷ *a few grains of sand*
• bit, particle, speck, granule

grand ADJECTIVE
❶ *Their wedding was a grand occasion.*
• magnificent, splendid, stately, impressive, big, great, important, imposing

❷ (*informal*) *Keep going—you're doing a grand job!*
• excellent, fine, good, splendid, first-class

grant VERB
❶ *We have decided to grant your request.*
• give, allow, permit, award
❷ *I grant that I'm no expert.*
• admit, accept, acknowledge, confess, recognize

graphic ADJECTIVE
a graphic description of war
• detailed, explicit, vivid, striking, colourful, realistic

grapple VERB
The guards grappled the man to the ground.
• wrestle, struggle, tussle, scuffle
➤ **grapple with**
I have lots of homework to grapple with.
• tackle, deal with, confront, face
IDIOM get to grips with

grasp VERB
❶ *He managed to grasp the end of the rope.*
• clutch, grab, grip, seize, catch, snatch, take hold of, hang on to
❷ *The idea of infinity is difficult to grasp.*
• understand, comprehend, follow, take in
IDIOM take on board

grasp NOUN
❶ *You will need a good grasp of German.*
• understanding, comprehension, knowledge, mastery, command
❷ *She broke free from the creature's grasp.*
• hold, grip, clutch

grass NOUN
Please keep off the grass.
• lawn, turf, green

grate VERB
❶ *I grated some cheese onto the pizza.*
• shred, grind, mince

❷ *The keel of the boat grated on the sand.*
• scrape, scratch, rasp
➤ **grate on**
His voice grates on my nerves.
• annoy, irritate, jar on

grateful ADJECTIVE
I was grateful for their help.
• thankful, appreciative, obliged, indebted
OPPOSITE ungrateful

gratitude NOUN
We sent some flowers to show our gratitude.
• thanks, appreciation

grave ADJECTIVE
❶ *She told him he was in grave danger.*
• serious, important, profound, weighty, significant, terrible, dire
OPPOSITE trivial
❷ *He turned to me with a grave expression.*
• solemn, serious, grim, sombre, dour, heavy-hearted
OPPOSITE cheerful

grave NOUN
see tomb

graveyard NOUN
Some famous people are buried in the graveyard.
• burial ground, cemetery, churchyard

graze VERB
I grazed my knee when I fell off my bike.
• scrape, scratch, skin, scuff, chafe, cut

greasy ADJECTIVE
a plate of greasy food
• fatty, oily

great ADJECTIVE
❶ *Theirs is a story of great courage.*
• considerable, exceptional, outstanding, extraordinary, prodigious, tremendous, extreme
OPPOSITE little
❷ *Mozart was a great composer.*
• famous, notable, celebrated, eminent, distinguished, important, outstanding,

major, leading, prominent
OPPOSITE insignificant, minor
❸ *A great canyon stretched before us.*
• large, huge, big, enormous, immense, gigantic, colossal, mighty, vast, extensive
OPPOSITE small
❹ (*informal*) *The food was great!*
• excellent, marvellous, outstanding, superb, tremendous, wonderful, enjoyable
(*informal*) brilliant, fantastic, super, smashing, terrific, fabulous
OPPOSITES bad, awful

greed NOUN
Midas was driven by his greed for gold.
• avarice, covetousness, acquisitiveness, hunger, craving, gluttony

greedy ADJECTIVE
❶ *Don't be greedy—leave some food for me!*
• gluttonous
(*informal*) piggish
❷ *a story about a greedy landowner*
• grasping, covetous, avaricious
(*informal*) money-grubbing

green ADJECTIVE
an awareness of green issues
• environmental, ecological, conservation, eco-
SEE ALSO environment

green ADJECTIVE & NOUN

✸ **WORD WEB**

Some shades of green:

➤ emerald	➤ mint
➤ jade	➤ olive
➤ khaki	➤ pea-green
➤ lime	➤ sea-green

For tips on describing colours see colour.

---

greet VERB
She greeted us with a friendly wave.
• welcome, hail, receive, salute

grew
past tense see **grow**

grey ADJECTIVE
❶ *His grey beard had grown very long.*
• silver, silvery, grizzly, hoary, whitish
❷ *Her face was grey with worry.*
• pale, pallid, pasty, ashen, wan
❸ *The day began cold and grey.*
• dull, cloudy, overcast, murky

grief NOUN
Juliet is overcome with grief at Romeo's death.
• sorrow, mourning, sadness, unhappiness, distress, anguish, heartache, heartbreak, woe
OPPOSITE joy

grieve VERB
❶ *The family is still grieving over their loss.*
• mourn, lament, sorrow, weep
OPPOSITE rejoice
❷ *It grieves me to tell you this.*
• sadden, upset, distress, hurt, pain, wound
OPPOSITE please

grim ADJECTIVE
❶ *The judge wore a grim expression on his face.*
• stern, severe, harsh, bad-tempered, sullen
OPPOSITE cheerful
❷ *the grim details of the murder*
• unpleasant, horrible, dreadful, terrible, hideous, shocking, gruesome, grisly
OPPOSITE pleasant

grime NOUN
The floor was covered with grime.
• dirt, filth, muck, mire, mess

grimy ADJECTIVE
a grimy pair of overalls
• dirty, filthy, grubby, mucky, soiled
OPPOSITE clean

grin NOUN & VERB
Everyone is grinning in the photograph.
• smile, beam, smirk

– A large grin is a **broad**, **wide** or **cheesy** grin.

grind VERB
❶ *Grind the spices into a fine powder.*
• crush, pound, powder, pulverize, mill
❷ *This tool is for grinding knives.*
• sharpen, file, hone, whet

grip VERB
❶ *Grip the handle tightly.*
• grasp, seize, clutch, clasp, hold
❷ *I was gripped by the last chapter.*
• fascinate, engross, enthral, absorb, captivate, rivet

grip NOUN
❶ *She kept a tight grip on my hand.*
• hold, grasp, clasp, clutch
❷ *People on the streets were in the grip of panic.*
• power, control, influence, clutches

grisly ADJECTIVE
the grisly discovery of a human skull
• gruesome, gory, ghastly, hideous, nasty, revolting, sickening

grit NOUN
❶ *I've got a piece of grit in my shoe.*
• gravel, dust, sand
❷ *The contestants showed grit and stamina.*
• bravery, courage, toughness, spirit, pluck
(informal) guts

groan VERB
The wounded soldier was groaning with pain.
• cry, moan, sigh, wail

groove NOUN
The skates cut grooves in the ice.
• channel, furrow, trench, rut, scratch

grope VERB
I groped in the dark for the light switch.
• fumble, feel about, flounder, scrabble

gross ADJECTIVE
❶ *That is a gross exaggeration!*
• extreme, glaring, obvious, sheer, blatant, outright

❷ *I was shocked by their gross behaviour.*
• offensive, rude, coarse, vulgar
❸ *(informal) Sweaty feet smell gross!*
• disgusting, repulsive, revolting, foul, obnoxious, sickening

ground NOUN
❶ *We planted some seeds in the ground.*
• earth, soil, land
❷ *a football ground*
• field, pitch, park, stadium, arena
❸ *Both books cover the same ground.*
• subject, topic, material, matter

grounds PLURAL NOUN
❶ *a country house with extensive grounds*
• gardens, estate, park, land
❷ *There are grounds for suspicion.*
• reason, basis, justification, cause, argument, excuse

group NOUN
❶ *Japan consists of a group of islands.*
• collection, set, batch, cluster, clump
❷ *A group of fans was waiting outside.*
• crowd, gathering, band, body, gang
(informal) bunch
❸ *The book group meets once a month.*
• club, society, association, circle
❹ *We sorted the fossils into different groups.*
• category, class, type, kind, sort
❺ For collective nouns see collective.

group VERB
Entries are grouped according to age.
• categorize, classify, class, organize, arrange, sort, range

grow VERB
❶ *I've grown an inch taller since last summer.*
• get bigger, put on growth, spring up, shoot up, sprout
❷ *Our website has grown over the past year.*
• increase, develop, enlarge, expand, build up, swell, flourish
OPPOSITE decrease

❸ *The local farm grows organic vegetables.*
• cultivate, produce, raise, farm, propagate
❹ *It is growing dark outside.*
• become, get, turn, begin to be

grown-up ADJECTIVE
a leopard with two grown-up cubs
• adult, mature, fully grown
OPPOSITES young, under age

growth NOUN
❶ *There's been a growth of interest in cycling.*
• increase, rise, spread, expansion, development, enlargement, build-up
❷ *an unusual growth on the skin*
• lump, swelling, tumour

grub NOUN
Moles feed on grubs and earthworms.
• larva, maggot, caterpillar

grubby ADJECTIVE
a set of grubby fingers
• dirty, filthy, grimy, messy, mucky, soiled
OPPOSITE clean

grudge NOUN
She isn't the sort of person who bears a grudge.
• grievance, bitterness, resentment, hard feelings, ill-will, spite

gruelling ADJECTIVE
It was a gruelling uphill climb.
• hard, tough, demanding, exhausting, challenging, difficult, laborious, strenuous, taxing, back-breaking, punishing
OPPOSITE easy

gruesome ADJECTIVE
The book is quite gruesome in places.
• grisly, gory, ghastly, hideous, horrific, monstrous, revolting, sickening, appalling, dreadful, shocking, horrifying, frightful

gruff ADJECTIVE
He spoke in a gruff voice.
• harsh, rough, hoarse, husky, throaty

grumble VERB
What are you grumbling about now?
• complain, protest, whine, grouse, carp, make a fuss
(*informal*) gripe, moan, whinge

grumpy ADJECTIVE
My brother is always grumpy in the morning.
• bad-tempered, cross, irritable, testy, tetchy, grouchy, cantankerous, crotchety
(*informal*) ratty
OPPOSITES good-humoured, cheerful

guarantee VERB
I guarantee that you will like this book.
• promise, assure, pledge, vow, give your word

guard VERB
The gate was guarded by men with spears.
• protect, defend, stand guard over, patrol, safeguard, shield, watch over

guard NOUN
a team of security guards
• sentry, sentinel, warder, lookout, watchman

guardian NOUN
The guardian of the treasure was a fierce dragon.
• defender, protector, keeper, minder, custodian

guess NOUN
My guess is that they have got lost.
• theory, conjecture, opinion, belief, feeling, suspicion, speculation, estimate, hunch

guess VERB
❶ *Can you guess how many sweets are in this jar?*
• estimate, judge, work out, gauge, reckon, predict, conjecture
❷ (*informal*) *I guess you must be feeling hungry.*
• suppose, imagine, expect, assume,

think, suspect
(*informal*) reckon
IDIOMS I take it, I dare say

guest NOUN
We are expecting guests this weekend.
• visitor, caller, company

guide NOUN
❶ *Our guide met us outside the hotel.*
• courier, escort, leader, chaperone
❷ *We bought a pocket guide to the town.*
• guidebook, handbook, manual, companion

guide VERB
We sailed east, guided by the stars.
• direct, lead, conduct, steer, pilot, escort, usher, shepherd, show the way

guilt NOUN
❶ *She tearfully admitted her guilt.*
• responsibility, liability, blame, wrongdoing
OPPOSITE innocence
❷ *You could see the look of guilt on her face.*
• shame, remorse, regret, contrition, shamefacedness, sheepishness

guilty ADJECTIVE
❶ *The two men were found guilty of kidnapping.*
• responsible, to blame, at fault, in the wrong, liable
OPPOSITE innocent
❷ *I felt guilty about not inviting her.*
• ashamed, guilt-ridden, remorseful, sorry, repentant, conscience-stricken, contrite, shamefaced, sheepish
OPPOSITE unrepentant

gulp VERB
He gulped down the sandwich in one go.
• swallow, bolt, gobble, guzzle, devour, down, wolf
SEE ALSO eat

gulp NOUN
She drank the milk in long gulps.
• swallow, mouthful
(*informal*) swig

gun *NOUN*
see weapon

gurgle *VERB*
The mountain stream gurgled over the rocks.
• burble, babble, trickle

gush *VERB*
Water gushed from the broken pipe.
• rush, stream, flow, pour, flood, spout, spurt, squirt

gush *NOUN*
There was a gush of water from the pipe.
• rush, stream, torrent, cascade, flood, jet, spout, spurt

gust *NOUN*
a sudden gust of wind
• blast, rush, puff, squall, flurry

guzzle *VERB*
The seagulls guzzled all the bread.
• gobble, gulp, bolt, devour, wolf
SEE ALSO eat

Hh

habit NOUN

❶ *It's good to develop a habit of regular exercise.*
• custom, practice, routine, rule

❷ *My sister has an odd habit of talking to herself.*
• mannerism, way, tendency, inclination, quirk

hack VERB
We hacked our way through the dense undergrowth.
• chop, cut, hew, slash, lop

had
past tense see have

haggard ADJECTIVE
The survivors looked tired and haggard.
• drawn, gaunt, thin, pinched, wasted, shrunken, wan

haggle VERB
They haggled over the price for several minutes.
• bargain, negotiate, argue, rangle

hair NOUN

❶ *a girl with wavy auburn hair*
• locks, tresses, curls
(*informal*) mop
– A mass of hair is a **head of hair** or **shock of hair**.
– A single thread of hair is a **strand**.

❷ *a poodle with short hair*
• fur, coat, wool, fleece, mane

 WRITING TIPS

DESCRIBING HAIR
Adjectives:

- bushy
- close-cropped
- curly
- dishevelled
- fine
- frizzy

- glossy
- greasy
- lank
- luxuriant
- shaggy
- shaven
- shock-headed
- silken
- silky
- sleek
- spiky
- straggly
- straight
- stringy
- stubbly
- tangled
- thick
- thinning
- tousled
- unkempt
- wavy
- windswept
- wispy

Colour:

- auburn
- blond (male) or blonde (female)
- brown
- brunette
- dark
- dyed
- fair
- flaxen
- ginger
- grizzled
- hoary
- mousy
- platinum blonde
- raven
- red
- silver
- strawberry blonde
- streaked
- white

Hairstyles:

- Afro
- beehive
- bob
- braid
- bun
- bunches
- chignon
- cornrows
- crew cut
- curls
- dreadlocks
- French braid
- fringe (*North American* bangs)
- highlights
- Mohican
- parting
- perm
- pigtail
- plait
- ponytail
- quiff
- ringlets
- skinhead
- spikes
- topknot

Facial hair:

- beard
- bristle
- goatee beard
- moustache
- sideburns
- stubble
- whiskers

– Someone with a lot of hair is **hairy** or (*formal*) **hirsute**.

Artificial hair:
➤ false beard or   ➤ toupee
  moustache   ➤ wig
➤ hairpiece
SEE ALSO colour, texture

hairy *ADJECTIVE*
❶ *Mammoths were like elephants with thick hairy coats.*
• shaggy, bushy, woolly, fleecy, furry, fuzzy, long-haired
❷ *a man with a hairy chin*
• bristly, stubbled, stubbly, bearded, unshaven
(*formal*) hirsute

half-hearted *ADJECTIVE*
She made a half-hearted attempt to smile.
• unenthusiastic, feeble, weak, indifferent, apathetic, lukewarm
OPPOSITE enthusiastic

halfway *ADJECTIVE*
the halfway point in the race
• midway, middle, mid, intermediate, centre

hall *NOUN*
❶ *Leave your umbrella in the hall.*
• entrance hall, hallway, lobby, foyer, vestibule
❷ *The hall was full for the concert.*
• assembly room, auditorium, concert hall, theatre

halt *VERB*
❶ *The bus halted at the red light.*
• stop, come to a halt, come to a standstill, draw up, pull up
OPPOSITES start, go
❷ *A sudden noise halted us in our tracks.*
• stop, check, stall, block, arrest, curb, stem
❸ *Work halted when the whistle went.*
• end, cease, terminate, break off

hammer *VERB*
I hammered on the door, but no one came.
• strike, beat, knock, batter, thump, pummel, pound

hamper *VERB*
Bad weather hampered the rescuers.
• hinder, obstruct, impede, restrict, handicap, frustrate, hold up, slow down, delay
OPPOSITE help

hand *NOUN*
❶ *a cold and clammy hand*
• (*informal*) paw, mitt
– When you clench your hand you make a **fist**.
– The flat part of the inside of your hand is the **palm**.
– Work that you do with your hands is **manual** work.
– Someone who is able to use their left and right hands equally well is **ambidextrous**.
❷ *a farm hand*
• labourer, worker, employee

hand *VERB*
The postman handed me several letters.
• give, pass, present, let someone have, offer
➤ **hand something down**
This ring has been handed down from generation to generation.
• pass down, pass on, bequeath

handicap *NOUN*
❶ *Lack of experience may be a handicap.*
• disadvantage, drawback, hindrance, obstacle, problem, difficulty, barrier, limitation
IDIOM stumbling block
OPPOSITE advantage
❷ *He was born with a visual handicap.*
• disability, impairment

handicap *VERB*
The search was handicapped by bad weather.
• hamper, hinder, impede, hold up, slow down, restrict
OPPOSITE help

handle NOUN

He slowly turned the door handle.
• grip, handgrip, knob, shaft
– The handle of a sword is the **hilt**.

handle VERB

❶ *Please don't handle the exhibits.*
• touch, feel, hold, stroke, fondle, finger, pick up, grasp
❷ *I thought you handled the situation well.*
• manage, tackle, deal with, cope with, control, see to

handsome ADJECTIVE

❶ *a handsome young man*
• attractive, good-looking, gorgeous, beautiful, striking
(*informal*) dishy
OPPOSITES ugly, unattractive
❷ *We should make a handsome profit.*
• big, large, substantial, sizeable, considerable, ample
OPPOSITE slight

handy ADJECTIVE

❶ *a handy kitchen tool*
• useful, helpful, convenient, practical, easy to use
OPPOSITES awkward, useless
❷ *Always keep an umbrella handy.*
• ready, available, accessible, close at hand, nearby, within reach, at the ready
OPPOSITE inaccessible
❸ *I'm not very handy with chopsticks.*
• skilled, adept, proficient, dexterous, deft
OPPOSITES clumsy, inept

hang VERB

❶ *A chandelier was hanging from the ceiling.*
• be suspended, dangle, swing, sway
❷ *Her long hair was hanging down her back.*
• droop, drape, flop, trail, cascade
❸ *I hung the picture on the wall.*
• fix, attach, fasten, stick, peg
❹ *The tree was hung with lights.*
• decorate, adorn, festoon, string, drape
❺ *Our breath hung in the icy air.*
• float, hover, drift, linger, cling

➤ **hang about** or **around**
We had to hang about in the cold for hours.
• wait around, linger, loiter, dawdle
➤ **hang on**
(*informal*) *Could you hang on for a second?*
• wait, stay, remain
➤ **hang on to something**
❶ *I hung on to the side of the boat.*
• hold, grip, grasp, clutch, clasp
❷ *Hang on to your entrance ticket.*
• keep, retain, save, keep a hold of

haphazard ADJECTIVE

The books were shelved in a haphazard way.
• random, unplanned, arbitrary, disorderly, chaotic, higgledy-piggledy
OPPOSITE orderly

happen VERB

What happened on the night of the murder?
• take place, occur, arise, come about, crop up, emerge, result

happening NOUN

There have been strange happenings in the village lately.
• event, occurrence, incident, episode, affair

happiness NOUN

His little face glowed with happiness.
• joy, joyfulness, pleasure, delight, jubilation, contentment, gladness, cheerfulness, merriment, ecstasy, bliss
OPPOSITE sorrow

happy ADJECTIVE

 OVERUSED WORD

❶ *A* **happy mood,** **happy person:**

➤ cheerful	➤ gleeful
➤ joyful	➤ light-hearted
➤ jolly	➤ contented
➤ merry	➤ carefree
➤ jovial	➤ upbeat

The girls look really cheerful in the photograph.
OPPOSITES unhappy, sad

❷ A very happy feeling:

➤ thrilled   ➤ elated
➤ ecstatic   ➤ overjoyed

(*informal*) over the moon, thrilled to bits, tickled pink

Fran was ecstatic when she heard the news.

❸ A happy time, happy experience:

➤ enjoyable   ➤ glorious
➤ pleasant   ➤ blissful
➤ delightful   ➤ heavenly
➤ joyous   ➤ idyllic

They spent a glorious summer on the island.

❹ Being happy to do something:

➤ glad   ➤ willing
➤ pleased   ➤ keen
➤ delighted

Would you be willing to sign our petition?

OPPOSITE unwilling

❺ A happy coincidence:

➤ lucky   ➤ favourable
➤ fortunate   ➤ timely

By a lucky coincidence, we took the same train.

OPPOSITE unfortunate

harass VERB
He claims he has been harassed by the police.
• pester, trouble, bother, annoy, disturb, plague, torment, badger, hound
(*informal*) hassle, bug

harbour NOUN
an old fishing harbour
• port, dock, mooring, quay, pier, wharf
– A harbour for yachts is a **marina**.

harbour VERB
❶ *I think she still harbours a grudge against them.*
• bear, hold, feel, nurse
❷ *He was arrested for harbouring a criminal.*
• shelter, protect, shield, hide, conceal

hard ADJECTIVE

🚫 **OVERUSED WORD**

❶ Hard ground, a hard surface:

➤ solid   ➤ compact
➤ firm   ➤ rigid
➤ dense   ➤ stiff

The core of the Moon is solid rock.

OPPOSITE soft

❷ A hard blow, hard thrust:

➤ strong   ➤ powerful
➤ forceful   ➤ violent
➤ heavy   ➤ mighty
➤ hefty

The injury was caused by a heavy blow to the head.

OPPOSITE light

❸ A hard task, hard work:

➤ strenuous   ➤ tiring
➤ arduous   ➤ exhausting
➤ tough   ➤ laborious
➤ difficult   ➤ back-breaking
➤ gruelling

Digging the tunnel was strenuous work.

OPPOSITES easy, light

❹ A hard worker:

➤ industrious   ➤ keen
➤ diligent   ➤ energetic

At first, he was a diligent student.

OPPOSITE lazy

❺ A hard person, hard treatment:

➤ harsh   ➤ severe
➤ stern   ➤ cruel
➤ strict   ➤ hard-hearted

➤ heartless   ➤ unkind
➤ unfeeling   ➤ unsympathetic

In the film, he plays a hard-hearted gangster.

OPPOSITE mild

❻ A hard problem, hard question:

➤ difficult   ➤ puzzling
➤ complicated   ➤ baffling
➤ complex   ➤ knotty
➤ intricate   ➤ thorny
➤ perplexing

No one has deciphered the intricate code.

OPPOSITE simple

hard *ADVERB*
❶ *I've been working hard all morning.*
• diligently, industriously, energetically, keenly, intently
(*informal*) like mad
❷ *It's been raining hard all afternoon.*
• heavily, steadily
(*informal*) cats and dogs
❸ *I stared hard at the screen.*
• intently, closely, carefully, searchingly

harden *VERB*
Leave the mixture to harden overnight.
• set, solidify, stiffen, thicken
OPPOSITE soften

hardly *ADVERB*
I could hardly see in the fog.
• barely, scarcely, only just, with difficulty
OPPOSITE easily

hardship *NOUN*
His childhood was full of hardship.
• suffering, trouble, distress, misery, misfortune, adversity, need, want, poverty
OPPOSITES prosperity, comfort

hardy *ADJECTIVE*
Highland cattle are hardy animals.
• tough, strong, robust, sturdy, hearty, rugged
OPPOSITES delicate, tender

harm *VERB*
❶ *No animals were harmed in making this film.*
• hurt, injure, ill-treat, mistreat, wound
IDIOM lay a finger on
❷ *Some of these chemicals can harm the environment.*
• damage, spoil, ruin, impair, do harm to

harm *NOUN*
You've done enough harm already.
• damage, injury, hurt, pain
OPPOSITES good, benefit

harmful *ADJECTIVE*
Ultraviolet rays are harmful to your skin.
• damaging, detrimental, dangerous, hazardous, destructive, injurious, unhealthy
OPPOSITES harmless, beneficial

harmless *ADJECTIVE*
❶ *The bite of a grass snake is harmless.*
• safe, innocuous, non-poisonous, non-toxic
OPPOSITES harmful, dangerous, poisonous
❷ *It was just a bit of harmless fun.*
• innocent, inoffensive

harsh *ADJECTIVE*
❶ *a harsh cry of a seagull*
• rough, rasping, grating, jarring, discordant, shrill, strident, raucous
OPPOSITES soft, gentle
❷ *the harsh light of a bare bulb*
• bright, brilliant, dazzling, glaring
OPPOSITES soft, subdued
❸ *The rescue was carried out in harsh weather conditions.*
• severe, adverse, tough, bleak, inhospitable
OPPOSITE mild
❹ *The prisoners suffered harsh treatment.*
• cruel, inhumane, brutal, ruthless, heartless
❺ *They exchanged harsh words.*
• sharp, stern, unkind, unfriendly, critical, scathing
OPPOSITE kind

harvest NOUN
There was a good harvest of rice this year.
• crop, yield, return, produce
– A plentiful harvest is a **bumper harvest**.

haste NOUN
In her haste, she forgot to lock the door.
• hurry, rush, speed, urgency

hasty ADJECTIVE
❶ *Don't make any hasty decisions.*
• hurried, rash, reckless, impulsive, impetuous, precipitate
IDIOM spur-of-the-moment
OPPOSITES careful, considered
❷ *We made a hasty exit.*
• fast, hurried, quick, sudden, swift, rapid, speedy
OPPOSITE slow

hat NOUN

WORD WEB

Some types of hat:
➤ balaclava	➤ kufi
➤ baseball cap	➤ mitre
➤ beanie	➤ mortarboard
➤ bearskin	➤ panama hat
➤ beret	➤ skullcap
➤ bobble hat	➤ sombrero
➤ bonnet	➤ sou'wester
➤ bowler	➤ stetson
➤ cap	➤ sun hat
➤ cloche	➤ tam-o'shanter
➤ deerstalker	➤ top hat
➤ fedora	➤ trilby
➤ fez	➤ turban
➤ hard hat	➤ woolly hat
➤ helmet	

hatch VERB
Together they began to hatch a plan.
• plan, develop, conceive, think up, devise
(*informal*) cook up, dream up

hate VERB
❶ *The two families hated each other.*
• dislike, detest, despise, loathe, be unable to bear, be unable to stand
(*formal*) abhor
OPPOSITES like, love
❷ *I hate to disturb you.*
• be sorry, be reluctant, be loath, regret

hate NOUN
❶ *His eyes were full of hate.*
see **hatred**
❷ *Name one of your pet hates.*
• dislike, bugbear

hatred NOUN
Her heart was filled with hatred and rage.
• hate, loathing, dislike, hostility, enmity, contempt, detestation, abhorrence
OPPOSITE love

haughty ADJECTIVE
The butler responded with a haughty look.
• proud, arrogant, conceited, lofty, superior, pompous, disdainful
(*informal*) stuck-up
OPPOSITE modest

haul VERB
He hauled his bike out of the shed.
• drag, pull, tow, heave, lug

haunt VERB
Her words came back to haunt her.
• torment, trouble, disturb, plague, prey on

have VERB
❶ *Do you have your own computer?*
• own, possess
❷ *Our house has two bedrooms.*
• contain, include, incorporate, comprise, consist of
❸ *We're having a barbecue at the weekend.*
• hold, organize, provide, host, throw
❹ *I'm having some trouble with my computer.*
• experience, go through, meet with, run into, face, suffer

a
b
c
d
e
f
g
h
i
j
k
l
m
n
o
p
q
r
s
t
u
v
w
x
y
z

⑤ *We had a great time at the party.*
• experience, enjoy
⑥ *We've had lots of messages of support.*
• receive, get, be given, be sent
⑦ *Who had the last piece of cake?*
• take, eat, consume
⑧ *One of the giraffes has had a baby.*
• give birth to, bear, produce
⑨ *I have to be home by nine o'clock.*
• must, need to, ought to, should

haven NOUN
The lake is a haven for wild birds.
• refuge, shelter, retreat, sanctuary

havoc NOUN
The floods caused havoc throughout the country.
• chaos, mayhem, disorder, disruption

hazard NOUN
Their journey was fraught with hazards.
• danger, risk, threat, peril, trap, pitfall, snag

hazardous ADJECTIVE
They made the hazardous journey to the South Pole.
• dangerous, risky, unsafe, perilous, precarious, high-risk
OPPOSITE safe

haze NOUN
I could hardly see through the haze.
• mist, cloud, fog, steam, vapour

hazy ADJECTIVE
① *The city looked hazy in the distance.*
• blurred, misty, unclear, dim, faint
OPPOSITES clear, sharp
② *I only have a hazy memory of that day.*
• uncertain, vague

head NOUN
① *He hit his head on a low beam.*
• skull, crown
(*informal*) nut
② *All the details are in my head.*
• brain, mind, intellect, intelligence

③ *Mrs Owen is the head of the music department.*
• chief, leader, manager, director, controller
(*informal*) boss
④ *Our friends were at the head of the queue.*
• front, start, lead, top
OPPOSITES back, rear

head VERB
Professor Rees headed the inquiry.
• lead, direct, command, manage, oversee, be in charge of
➤ **head for**
As night fell, we headed for home.
• go towards, make for, aim for

heading NOUN
Each chapter has a different heading.
• title, caption, headline, rubric

headlong ADJECTIVE
We made a headlong dash for shelter.
• quick, hurried, hasty, breakneck

heal VERB
It took a month for the wound to heal.
• get better, recover, mend, be cured

health NOUN
① *My gran is in excellent health.*
• condition, constitution, shape
② *I am slowly returning to health.*
• well-being, fitness, strength, vigour, good shape

healthy ADJECTIVE
① *She was always healthy as a child.*
• well, fit, strong, sturdy, vigorous, robust
(*informal*) in good shape
OPPOSITE ill
② *Porridge makes a healthy breakfast.*
• health-giving, wholesome, invigorating, nourishing, nutritious, good for you
OPPOSITE unhealthy

heap NOUN
There was an untidy heap of clothes on the floor.
• pile, stack, mound, mountain, collection, mass

heap VERB
We heaped up all the rubbish in the corner.
• pile, stack, collect, bank, mass

hear VERB
❶ Did you hear what she said?
• catch, listen to, make out, pick up, overhear, pay attention to
– A sound that you can hear is **audible**.
– A sound that you cannot hear is **inaudible**.
❷ Have you heard the news?
• be told, discover, find out, learn, gather

heart NOUN
❶ Have you no heart?
• compassion, feeling, sympathy, tenderness, affection, humanity, kindness, love
❷ We wandered deep into the heart of the forest.
• centre, middle, core, nucleus, hub
❸ Let's try to get to the heart of problem.
• core, essence, crux, root

heartless ADJECTIVE
How could she be so heartless?
• hard-hearted, callous, cruel, inhuman, unfeeling, unkind, pitiless, ruthless
OPPOSITES kind, compassionate

hearty ADJECTIVE
❶ He gave a hearty laugh.
• strong, forceful, vigorous, loud, spirited
OPPOSITE feeble
❷ They gave us a hearty welcome.
• enthusiastic, wholehearted, sincere, genuine, warm, heartfelt
OPPOSITES unenthusiastic, half-hearted
❸ She always ate a hearty breakfast.
• large, substantial, ample, satisfying, filling
OPPOSITE light

heat NOUN
❶ Last summer, the heat made me feel ill.
• hot weather, warmth, high temperature
– A long period of hot weather is a **heatwave**.
OPPOSITE cold
❷ The fire gives out a lot of heat.
• warmth, hotness, glow
❸ Voices were raised in the heat of the debate.
• passion, intensity, fervour, vehemence

heat VERB
The fire will gradually heat the room.
• warm, heat up
OPPOSITES cool, cool down

heave VERB
The men heaved the piano into position.
• haul, drag, pull, draw, tow, tug, hoist, lug

heavy ADJECTIVE
❶ The box was too heavy to lift.
• weighty, massive, bulky, hefty
OPPOSITE light
❷ A heavy mist hung over the valley.
• dense, thick, solid
OPPOSITE thin
❸ The rain has caused heavy flooding.
• severe, extreme, torrential
❹ Both sides suffered heavy losses in the battle.
• large, substantial, considerable
❺ Digging the garden is heavy work.
• hard, tough, gruelling, back-breaking, strenuous, arduous
❻ This book makes heavy reading.
• serious, intense, demanding
❼ I was feeling sleepy after such a heavy meal.
• filling, stodgy, rich

hectic ADJECTIVE
It's been a hectic day, getting the hall ready for the show.
• frantic, feverish, frenzied, frenetic, chaotic, busy
(informal) manic
OPPOSITES quiet, leisurely

heed *VERB*
They refused to heed our advice.
• listen to, pay attention to, take notice of, attend to, regard, obey, follow, mark, mind, note
OPPOSITE ignore

hefty *ADJECTIVE*
❶ *He was a hefty man with ginger hair.*
• strong, sturdy, muscular, powerful, brawny, burly, beefy, hulking, strapping
OPPOSITE slight
❷ *She lifted a hefty volume down from the shelf.*
• weighty, large, massive, bulky

height *NOUN*
❶ *We need to know the height of the tower.*
• tallness, elevation, altitude
– The natural height of your body is your **stature**.
❷ *the dizzying heights of the Himalayas*
• summit, peak, crest, crown, cap, pinnacle
❸ *They were at the height of their fame.*
• peak, high point, pinnacle, zenith, climax

held
past tense see **hold**

help *VERB*
❶ *Could you please help me with my luggage?*
• aid, assist, give assistance to
IDIOMS give a hand to, lend a hand to
❷ *The money will help victims of the earthquake.*
• be helpful to, benefit, support, serve, be of service to
❸ *This medicine will help your cough.*
• make better, cure, ease, relieve, soothe, improve
OPPOSITES aggravate, worsen
❹ *I couldn't help smiling.*
• avoid, resist, refrain from, keep from, stop

help *NOUN*
❶ *Thank you for your help.*
• aid, assistance, support, guidance, cooperation, advice
OPPOSITE hindrance
❷ *Would a torch be of any help to you?*
• use, benefit

helpful *ADJECTIVE*
❶ *The staff were friendly and helpful.*
• obliging, accommodating, considerate, thoughtful, sympathetic, kind, cooperative
OPPOSITE unhelpful
❷ *The website offers some helpful advice.*
• useful, valuable, worthwhile, beneficial, profitable
OPPOSITE worthless

helping *NOUN*
Would you like a second helping of trifle?
• serving, portion, plateful, amount, share, ration

helpless *ADJECTIVE*
The cubs are born blind and helpless.
• powerless, weak, feeble, dependent, defenceless, vulnerable
OPPOSITES independent, strong

hem *VERB*
➤ **hem someone in**
The bus was hemmed in by the traffic.
• shut in, box in, encircle, enclose, surround

herb *NOUN*

WORD WEB

Some common herbs:

➤ basil	➤ fennel
➤ camomile	➤ fenugreek
➤ caraway	➤ hyssop
➤ chervil	➤ lemon balm
➤ chicory	➤ lovage
➤ chive	➤ marjoram
➤ coriander	➤ mint
➤ cumin	➤ oregano
➤ dill	➤ parsley

> peppermint   > tarragon
> rosemary   > thyme
> sage

herd NOUN
For groups of animals see **collective noun.**

heritage NOUN
She has been exploring her African heritage.
• ancestry, background, descent, history, roots, tradition, culture

hero or **heroine** NOUN
❶ She is one of my sporting heroines.
• idol, role model, star, celebrity, legend
❷ The film has no real hero.
• protagonist, main character, lead

heroic ADJECTIVE
The firefighters made heroic efforts to put out the blaze.
• bold, brave, courageous, daring, fearless, intrepid, valiant
(informal) gutsy
OPPOSITE cowardly

hesitant ADJECTIVE
She took a hesitant step through the entrance.
• uncertain, unsure, doubtful, cautious, tentative, wary, undecided
OPPOSITE confident

hesitate VERB
I hesitated before picking up the phone.
• pause, delay, wait, hold back, falter, stall, dither, waver
(informal) dilly-dally
IDIOM think twice

hidden ADJECTIVE
❶ a hidden camera
• concealed, secret, unseen, out of sight, invisible, camouflaged
OPPOSITE visible
❷ The poem has a hidden meaning.
• obscure, mysterious, secret, coded, cryptic
OPPOSITE obvious

hide VERB
❶ We hid in the bushes until they had gone.
• go into hiding, take cover, take refuge, keep out of sight
IDIOMS lie low, go to ground
❷ She hid the letters in a secret drawer.
• conceal, secrete, bury, stow, put out of sight
(informal) stash
OPPOSITE expose
❸ The mist hid our view of the hills.
• cover, obscure, screen, mask, shroud, veil, blot out
OPPOSITE uncover
❹ I tried to hide my true feelings.
• disguise, conceal, keep secret, suppress, camouflage, cloak
IDIOM keep a lid on
OPPOSITES show, reveal

hideous ADJECTIVE
The legend tells of a hideous beast.
• ugly, grotesque, monstrous, revolting, repulsive, ghastly, gruesome, horrible, appalling, dreadful, frightful
OPPOSITE beautiful

high ADJECTIVE
❶ The castle was surrounded by a high wall.
• tall, towering, elevated, lofty
OPPOSITE low
❷ an officer of high rank
• senior, top, leading, important, prominent, powerful
OPPOSITES low, junior
❸ the high cost of living
• expensive, dear, costly, excessive, exorbitant
(informal) steep
OPPOSITE low
❹ a warning of high winds
• strong, powerful, forceful, extreme
OPPOSITES light, gentle
❺ She spoke in a high voice.
• high-pitched, squeaky, shrill, piercing
– A high singing voice is **soprano** or **treble.**
OPPOSITES deep, low

A
B
C
D
E
F
G
H
I
J
K
L
M
N
O
P
Q
R
S
T
U
V
W
X
Y
Z

highlight NOUN
What was the highlight of your trip?
• high point, high spot, best moment, climax
OPPOSITES low point, nadir

highly ADVERB
He is a highly experienced doctor.
• very, extremely, exceptionally, considerably, decidedly

hike VERB
We often go hiking across the moors.
• walk, trek, ramble, tramp, backpack

hilarious ADJECTIVE
a hilarious joke
• funny, amusing, comical, uproarious (*informal*) hysterical, priceless
SEE ALSO funny

hill NOUN
❶ *a valley between two hills*
• mount, peak, ridge, fell
– A small hill is a **hillock**, **knoll** or **mound**.
❷ *Their house is at the top of the hill.*
• slope, rise, incline, ascent, gradient

hinder VERB
Bad weather is hindering the rescue attempt.
• hamper, obstruct, impede, handicap, restrict, hold up, slow down, get in the way of, interfere with
OPPOSITE help

hindrance NOUN
Parked cars can be a hindrance to cyclists.
• obstacle, obstruction, inconvenience, handicap, disadvantage, drawback
OPPOSITE help

hint NOUN
❶ *Can you give me a hint?*
• clue, indication, sign, suggestion, inkling, intimation
❷ *The website offers some handy hints on taking good photos.*
• tip, pointer, suggestion, guideline
hint VERB
He hinted that he might be retiring soon.
• give a hint, suggest, imply, intimate

hire VERB
❶ *We hired a boat for the afternoon.*
• rent, lease, charter
❷ *They will be hiring extra staff for Christmas.*
• employ, engage, recruit, take on
OPPOSITE dismiss

historic ADJECTIVE
The Moon landing was a historic event.
• famous, important, notable, celebrated, renowned, momentous, significant, major, ground-breaking
OPPOSITES unimportant, minor
The words **historic** and **historical** do not mean the same thing. A historical event took place in the past, but a historic event is famous or important in history.

historical ADJECTIVE
❶ *The old library is full of useful historical documents.*
• past, former, old, ancient, bygone, olden
OPPOSITES contemporary, recent
❷ *Was King Arthur a historical figure?*
• real, real-life, true, actual, authentic, documented
OPPOSITES fictitious, legendary

W   **WRITING TIPS**

WRITING HISTORICAL FICTION
Clothes:

➤ bodice	➤ gauntlet
➤ bonnet	➤ gown
➤ breeches	➤ hose
➤ bustle	➤ petticoat
➤ cape	➤ raiment
➤ cloak	➤ robe
➤ corset	➤ ruff
➤ cravat	➤ shawl
➤ crinoline	➤ toga
➤ doublet	➤ top hat
➤ drawers	➤ tricorn hat
➤ farthingale	➤ tunic
➤ frock coat	

Occupations:

- apothecary
- barrow boy
- blacksmith
- chimney sweep
- clerk
- cobbler
- costermonger
- draper
- dressmaker
- executioner
- governess
- housemaid
- innkeeper
- kitchen maid
- laundress
- merchant
- pedlar
- seamstress
- spinner
- tanner
- weaver
- wheelwright
- wigmaker

Setting:

- battlefield
- frontier
- imperial court
- industrial town
- inn
- market
- monastery
- orphanage
- outpost
- tavern
- workhouse

Transport:

- airship
- chariot
- galleon
- hansom cab
- horse-drawn carriage
- penny-farthing
- sedan chair
- stagecoach
- steamboat
- steam train

Weapons:

- ballista
- blunderbuss
- bow and arrow
- broadsword
- cannon
- catapult
- claymore
- cutlass
- dagger
- gunpowder
- lance
- longbow
- mace
- musket
- sabre
- samurai sword
- siege tower
- shield
- spear
- sword
- trebuchet

Other details:

- candlelight
- farthing
- flagon
- gallows
- gaslight
- goblet
- groat
- guinea
- lantern
- oil lamp

- parasol
- parchment
- plague
- powdered wig
- quill pen
- shilling
- telegraph

For words in old and poetic use see old.

history NOUN

❶ *Dr Sachs is an expert on American history.*
• heritage, past, antiquity, past times, olden days

❷ *He is writing a history of the First World War.*
• account, chronicle, record

– The history of a person's life is their **biography**.

– The history of your own life is your **autobiography** or **memoirs**.

hit VERB

> ### ⬛ OVERUSED WORD

❶ Hit **a person, animal:**

- strike
- beat
- thump
- punch
- slap
- smack
- swipe
- slog
- cuff

(*informal*) whack, thump, wallop, clout, clobber, sock, belt, biff

– To hit someone with a stick is to **club** them.

In judo, you are not allowed to strike your opponent.

❷ Hit **an object, surface:**

- knock
- bang
- bump
- bash
- strike
- thump
- rap
- crack
- slam

(*informal*) whack

– To hit your toe on something is to **stub** it.

Mind you don't bump your head on the ceiling.

❸ Hit something in an accident:

> crash into   > run into
> smash into   > plough into
> collide with   > meet head on

A lorry had **ploughed into** the side of their house.

❹ Hit gently, lightly:

> tap   > patter
> pat   > rap

Pat the dough with your hands on a floured surface.

❺ Hit repeatedly:

> batter   > pummel
> buffet   > drum
> pound

She **drummed** her fingers impatiently on the desk.

❻ Hit a note, target:

> reach   > attain

Can you **reach** the high notes in this song?

OPPOSITES miss, fall short of

❼ Hit a problem, difficulty:

> run into   > face
> come across   > confront
> encounter

I **encountered** a snag while installing the program.

hit NOUN
❶ He got a nasty hit on the head.
• bump, blow, bang, strike, knock, whack, punch, slap, smack, swipe
❷ The book was an instant hit.
• success, triumph
(informal) winner
OPPOSITES failure, flop

hitch NOUN
The evening went without a hitch.
• problem, difficulty, snag, complication, obstacle, setback
(informal) hiccup, glitch

hitch VERB
She hitched up her skirt and waded into the river.
• pull, lift, raise, hoist, draw

hoard NOUN
The tomb contained a hoard of gold.
• cache, store, stock, supply, pile, stockpile
(informal) stash
– A hoard of treasure is a **treasure trove**.

hoard VERB
Squirrels hoard nuts for the winter.
• store, collect, gather, save, pile up, stockpile, put aside, put by
(informal) stash away

hoarse ADJECTIVE
Her voice was hoarse from shouting.
• rough, harsh, husky, croaky, throaty, gruff, rasping, gravelly

hoax NOUN
The email was just a hoax.
• joke, practical joke, prank, trick, spoof, fraud
(informal) con, scam

hobby NOUN
My favourite hobby is photography.
• pastime, pursuit, interest, activity, recreation, amusement

hoist VERB
The women hoisted the bundles onto their heads.
• lift, raise, heave, pull up, haul up, winch up

hold VERB
❶ Hold the reins loosely in your left hand.
• clasp, grasp, grip, cling to, hang on to, clutch, seize, squeeze
❷ Can I hold the baby?
• embrace, hug, cradle
❸ The tank should hold ten litres.
• contain, take, have space for, accommodate
❹ Will the ladder hold my weight?
• bear, support, carry, take

❺ *If our luck holds, we could reach the final.*
• continue, last, carry on, persist, stay
❻ *She has always held strong opinions.*
• believe in, maintain, stick to
❼ *We will be holding a public meeting.*
• host, put on, organize, arrange, convene, call
❽ *Three suspects are being held in prison.*
• confine, detain, keep

➤ **hold out**
❶ *The stranger held out his hand in greeting.*
• extend, reach out, stick out, stretch out
❷ *Our supplies won't hold out much longer.*
• keep going, last, carry on, continue, endure

➤ **hold up**
❶ *Hold up your hand if you know the answer.*
• lift, put up, raise, elevate, hoist
❷ *Roadworks were holding up the traffic.*
• delay, hinder, impede, slow down

hold NOUN
❶ *Keep a firm hold on the leash.*
• grip, grasp, clutch, clasp
❷ *The myth had a strange hold on my imagination.*
• influence, power, dominance, pull, sway

hole NOUN
❶ *The men were digging a large hole in the ground.*
• pit, hollow, crater, dent, depression, cavity, chasm, abyss
❷ *The rabbits escaped through a hole in the fence.*
• gap, opening, breach, break, cut, slit, gash, split, tear, rift, vent
❸ *a rabbit hole*
• burrow, lair, den, earth

holiday NOUN
We spent our summer holiday in France.
• vacation, break, leave, time off

hollow ADJECTIVE
❶ *a hollow tube*
• empty, unfilled
OPPOSITE solid
❷ *hollow cheeks*
• sunken, wasted, deep-set, concave
OPPOSITES plump, chubby
❸ *a hollow promise*
• insincere, empty, meaningless
OPPOSITE sincere

hollow NOUN
The ball rolled into a hollow in the ground.
• hole, pit, crater, cavity, depression, dent, dip

hollow VERB
We hollowed out a pumpkin to make a Halloween lantern.
• dig, excavate, gouge, scoop

holy ADJECTIVE
❶ *a pilgrimage to a holy shrine*
• sacred, blessed, revered, venerated, sanctified
❷ *The pilgrims were holy people.*
• religious, spiritual, devout, pious, godly, saintly

home NOUN
The cottage was their home for ten years.
• residence, house, dwelling, abode, lodging
– A home for the sick is a **convalescent home** or **nursing home**.
– A place where a bird or animal lives is its **habitat**.

homely ADJECTIVE
The hotel was small with a homely atmosphere.
• friendly, informal, cosy, familiar, relaxed, easy-going, comfortable, snug

honest ADJECTIVE
❶ *He's an honest boy, so he gave the money back.*
• good, honourable, upright, virtuous, moral, decent, law-abiding, scrupulous, trustworthy
OPPOSITE dishonest

a b c d e f g h i j k l m n o p q r s t u v w x y z

A
B
C
D
E
F
G
H
I
J
K
L
M
N
O
P
Q
R
S
T
U
V
W
X
Y
Z

❷ *Please give me your honest opinion.*
• sincere, genuine, truthful, direct, frank, candid, plain, straightforward, unbiased

OPPOSITE insincere

honour NOUN
❶ *Her success brought honour to the school.*
• reputation, good name, credit, repute, standing
❷ *I believe he is a man of honour.*
• integrity, honesty, fairness, morality, decency, principles
❸ *She knew that playing for her country was an honour.*
• privilege, distinction, glory, prestige, kudos

honour VERB
There will be a memorial service to honour the dead.
• pay tribute to, salute, recognize, celebrate, praise, acclaim

honourable ADJECTIVE
❶ *an honourable man*
• honest, virtuous, good, upright, moral, principled, decent, fair, noble, worthy, righteous
❷ *It was an honourable thing to do.*
• noble, admirable, praiseworthy, decent

OPPOSITE unworthy

hook NOUN
She hung her coat on one of the hooks.
• peg, nail

hook VERB
❶ *Dad hooked the trailer to the car.*
• attach, fasten, hitch, connect, couple
❷ *I managed to hook a small fish.*
• catch, land, take

hop VERB
The goblins were hopping about in excitement.
• jump, leap, skip, spring, bound, caper, prance, dance

hope NOUN
❶ *Her dearest hope was to see her family again.*
• ambition, wish, dream, desire,

aspiration
❷ *There was little hope of escape.*
• prospect, expectation, likelihood

hope VERB
I hope to see you again soon.
• wish, trust, expect, look forward

hopeful ADJECTIVE
❶ *I am feeling hopeful about tomorrow's match.*
• optimistic, confident, positive, buoyant, expectant

OPPOSITE pessimistic
❷ *Our chances are looking more hopeful.*
• promising, encouraging, favourable, reassuring

OPPOSITE discouraging

hopeless ADJECTIVE
❶ *The plight of the crew was hopeless.*
• desperate, wretched, impossible, futile, beyond hope

OPPOSITE hopeful
❷ *I'm hopeless at ice-skating.*
• bad, poor, incompetent, awful, (*informal*) useless, rubbish, lousy, pathetic

OPPOSITES good, competent

horde NOUN
Hordes of people thronged the streets.
• crowd, mob, throng, mass, swarm, gang, pack

horizontal ADJECTIVE
Draw a horizontal line.
• flat, level

OPPOSITES vertical, upright

horrible ADJECTIVE
What a horrible smell!
• awful, terrible, dreadful, appalling, unpleasant, disagreeable, offensive, objectionable, disgusting, repulsive, revolting, horrendous, horrid, nasty, hateful, odious, loathsome, ghastly

OPPOSITE pleasant

horrific ADJECTIVE
The film starts with a horrific battle scene.
• horrifying, terrifying, shocking,

gruesome, dreadful, appalling, ghastly, hideous, atrocious, grisly, sickening

horrify VERB
She was horrified when she discovered the truth.
• appal, shock, outrage, scandalize, disgust, sicken

horror NOUN
❶ *His eyes filled with horror.*
• terror, fear, fright, alarm, panic, dread
❷ *The film depicts the full horror of war.*
• awfulness, hideousness, gruesomeness, ghastliness, grimness

 **WRITING TIPS**

WRITING HORROR FICTION
Characters:

➤ ghost	➤ spectre
➤ ghoul	➤ spirit
➤ mummy	➤ vampire
➤ necromancer	➤ werewolf
➤ phantom	➤ wraith
➤ poltergeist	➤ zombie

Setting:

➤ catacombs	➤ haunted mansion
➤ cemetery	
➤ crypt	➤ mausoleum
➤ dungeon	➤ necropolis
➤ graveyard	➤ tomb

Useful words and phrases:

➤ accursed	➤ haunting
➤ afterlife	➤ hex
➤ apparition	➤ living dead
➤ beyond the grave	➤ lycanthropy
➤ coffin	➤ macabre
➤ corpse	➤ malediction
➤ curse	➤ mortal remains
➤ dark side	➤ necromancy
➤ eerie	➤ nightmare
➤ exorcism	➤ occult
➤ ghostly	➤ other-worldly
➤ ghoulish	➤ paranormal
➤ gore	➤ possession
➤ Halloween	➤ reanimation
	➤ sarcophagus

➤ seance	➤ uncanny
➤ shroud	➤ undead
➤ soul	➤ unearthly
➤ spectral	➤ vampirism
➤ supernatural	➤ voodoo
➤ trance	

horse NOUN
a horse pulling a carriage
• mount, nag
(*poetic*) steed

 WORD WEB

Some types of horse:

➤ bronco	➤ racehorse
➤ carthorse	➤ Shetland pony
➤ Clydesdale	➤ shire horse
➤ mustang	➤ warhorse
➤ pony	

- A male horse is a **stallion** and a female is a **mare**.
- A young horse is a **foal**, **colt** (male) or **filly** (female).
- A cross between a donkey and a horse is a **mule**.

Parts of a horse's body:

➤ coat	➤ hoof
➤ fetlock	➤ mane
➤ flank	➤ withers

Colours of a horse's coat:

➤ bay	➤ palomino
➤ chestnut	➤ piebald
➤ dappled	➤ pinto
➤ dun	➤ roan
➤ grey	

Noises made by a horse:

➤ neigh	➤ snort
➤ snicker	➤ whinny

Ways a horse can move:

➤ canter	➤ trot
➤ gallop	➤ walk

- Equine means 'to do with horses' and ➤

a b c d e f g h i j k l m n o p q r s t u v w x y z

equestrian means 'to do with horse-riding'.
- A person who rides a horse in a race is a **jockey**.
- Soldiers who fight on horseback are **cavalry**.

hospital NOUN
a small community hospital
• clinic, infirmary, sanatorium
SEE ALSO medicine

hostile ADJECTIVE
❶ The men glared at us in a hostile manner.
• aggressive, antagonistic, confrontational, unfriendly, unwelcoming, warlike, belligerent
OPPOSITE friendly
❷ The North Pole has a hostile climate.
• harsh, adverse, unfavourable, inhospitable
OPPOSITE favourable

hostility NOUN
The hostility between the two players was obvious.
• dislike, enmity, unfriendliness, aggression, antagonism, hate, hatred, bad feeling, ill-will, malice
OPPOSITE friendship

hot ADJECTIVE
❶ a hot summer's day
• warm, balmy, blazing, scorching, blistering, roasting, baking, sweltering, stifling
OPPOSITES cold, cool
❷ a bowl of hot soup
• burning, boiling, scalding, searing, sizzling, steaming, red-hot, piping hot
OPPOSITES cold, cool
❸ a hot curry sauce
• spicy, peppery, fiery
OPPOSITE mild
❹ a hot temper
• fierce, fiery, violent, passionate, raging, intense
OPPOSITES calm, mild

house NOUN
❶ She still lives in the family house.
• residence, home, dwelling, abode, lodging
SEE ALSO accommodation
❷ He was related to the House of Stuart.
• family, dynasty, clan, line

house VERB
The cabins are able to house twenty people.
• accommodate, lodge, shelter, take in, quarter, board

hover VERB
❶ A helicopter hovered overhead.
• hang, float, drift, be suspended, be poised
❷ I hovered just outside the door.
• linger, pause, wait about, dally, loiter, (informal) hang about

however ADVERB
❶ I can't remember, however hard I try.
• no matter how
❷ Spiders' silk is thin; however, it is also strong.
• nevertheless, nonetheless, yet, still, even so, for all that

howl VERB
❶ A baby was howling in its pram.
• cry, wail, bawl, scream, yell, shriek, (informal) holler
❷ They heard wolves howling in the night.
• bay, yowl, yelp

huddle VERB
❶ We huddled around the fire to get warm.
• crowd, gather, congregate, flock, cluster, pack, squeeze
❷ I huddled under the blankets and tried to sleep.
• curl up, nestle, cuddle, snuggle

hue NOUN
The leaves were various hues of red and gold.
• colour, shade, tint, tone, tinge

hug VERB
The two friends laughed and hugged each other.
• embrace, clasp, cuddle, squeeze, cling to, hold tight

hug NOUN
Izzie gave her dad a huge hug.
• embrace, clasp, cuddle, squeeze

huge ADJECTIVE
Woolly mammoths were huge creatures.
• enormous, gigantic, massive, colossal, giant, immense, vast, mighty, mammoth, monumental, hulking, great, big, large (*informal*) whopping, humongous (*literary*) gargantuan
OPPOSITES small, tiny

hum VERB
Insects were humming in the sunshine.
• drone, buzz, murmur, purr, whirr

hum NOUN
the hum of an engine
• drone, whirr, throb, murmur, purr

humane ADJECTIVE
A humane society should treat animals well.
• kind, compassionate, sympathetic, civilized, benevolent, kind-hearted, charitable, loving, merciful
OPPOSITE cruel

humans PLURAL NOUN
Humans have smaller brains than whales.
• human beings, the human race, people, humanity, humankind, mankind, Homo sapiens

humble ADJECTIVE
❶ *The book is about a humble watchmaker.*
• modest, meek, unassuming, self-effacing, unassertive, submissive
OPPOSITE proud
❷ *a painting of a humble domestic scene*
• simple, modest, plain, ordinary, commonplace, lowly
OPPOSITE grand

humid ADJECTIVE
It was a hot and humid day.
• muggy, clammy, close, sultry, sticky, moist, steamy
OPPOSITE fresh

humiliate VERB
He humiliated her in front of her friends.
• embarrass, disgrace, shame, make ashamed, humble, crush, degrade, demean, mortify
(*informal*) put someone in their place, take someone down a peg

humiliating ADJECTIVE
The team suffered a humiliating defeat.
• embarrassing, crushing, degrading, demeaning, humbling, undignified, ignominious, mortifying
OPPOSITE glorious

humorous ADJECTIVE
a humorous anecdote
• amusing, funny, comic, comical, witty, entertaining, droll
OPPOSITE serious

humour NOUN
❶ *I liked the humour in the film.*
• comedy, wit, hilarity, satire, irony, jokes, witticisms
OPPOSITE seriousness
❷ *She is in a good humour today.*
• mood, temper, disposition, frame of mind, spirits

hump NOUN
Camels have humps on their backs.
• bump, lump, bulge, swelling

hunch NOUN
I have a hunch that she won't come.
• feeling, intuition, inkling, guess, impression, suspicion, idea, notion
IDIOM gut feeling

hung
past tense see **hang**

hunger NOUN
I was feeling faint with hunger.
• lack of food, starvation, undernourishment

– A severe shortage of food in an area is **famine**.
– Bad health caused by not having enough food is **malnutrition**.

hungry ADJECTIVE
❶ *I was hungry again by 3 o'clock.*
• starving, starved, famished, ravenous
(*informal*) peckish
❷ *He was hungry for power.*
• eager, keen, longing, yearning, craving, greedy
(*informal*) itching

hunt VERB
❶ *Some Native American tribes used to hunt buffalo.*
• chase, pursue, track, trail, hound, stalk
– An animal which hunts other animals for food is a **predator**.
❷ *I hunted in the attic for our old photo albums.*
• search, seek, look, rummage, ferret, root around, scour around
IDIOM look high and low

hunt NOUN
Police have begun the hunt for clues.
• search, quest, chase, pursuit (of), forage

hurdle NOUN
❶ *The runners cleared the first hurdle.*
• fence, barrier, jump, barricade, obstacle
❷ *Our biggest hurdle was our lack of experience.*
• difficulty, problem, handicap, obstacle, hindrance, impediment, snag
IDIOM stumbling block

hurl VERB
I hurled the ball as far as I could.
• throw, fling, pitch, toss, cast, sling, launch
(*informal*) chuck

hurried ADJECTIVE
He gave the clock a hurried glance.
• quick, hasty, speedy, swift, rapid, rushed, brisk, cursory

hurry VERB
❶ *We'd better hurry or we'll miss the bus.*
• be quick, hasten, make speed
(*informal*) get a move on, step on it
IDIOM (*informal*) get your skates on
OPPOSITE dawdle
❷ *An ambulance crew hurried to the scene.*
• rush, dash, race, fly, speed, sprint, hurtle, scurry
OPPOSITES amble, stroll
❸ *I don't mean to hurry you.*
• hasten, hustle, speed up, urge on
OPPOSITE slow down

hurry NOUN
In my hurry, I forgot the tickets.
• rush, haste, speed, urgency

hurt VERB
❶ *I hurt my wrist playing hockey.*
• injure, wound, damage, harm, maim, bruise, cut
❷ *My feet hurt.*
• be sore, be painful, ache, throb, sting, smart
❸ *Your letter hurt me deeply.*
• upset, distress, offend, grieve, sadden, pain, wound, sting

hurtful ADJECTIVE
That was a very hurtful remark.
• upsetting, distressing, unkind, cruel, mean, spiteful, wounding, nasty, malicious

hurtle VERB
The train hurtled along at top speed.
• rush, speed, race, dash, fly, charge, tear, shoot, zoom

husband NOUN
She lives with her husband and two sons.
• spouse, partner
IDIOM other half

hush VERB
The speaker tried to hush the crowd.
• silence, quieten, settle, still, calm
(*informal*) shut up
➤ **hush something up**
They tried to hush up the scandal.
• cover up, hide, conceal, keep quiet,

keep secret, suppress
IDIOM sweep under the carpet

hush NOUN
There was a sudden hush in the room.
• silence, quiet, stillness, calm,
tranquillity

husky ADJECTIVE
a husky voice
• hoarse, throaty, gruff, rasping,
gravelly, rough, croaky

hut NOUN
*They came across a little hut in the
woods.*
• shed, shack, cabin, den, shelter, shanty,
hovel

hygienic ADJECTIVE
*Always use a hygienic surface for
preparing food.*
• sanitary, clean, disinfected, sterilized,
sterile, germ-free
OPPOSITES unhygienic, insanitary

hysterical ADJECTIVE
❶ *The fans became hysterical when the
band finally appeared.*
• crazy, frenzied, mad, delirious, raving,
wild, uncontrollable
❷ (*informal*) *Some of the scenes in the
film are hysterical.*
• hilarious, funny, amusing, comical,
uproarious
(*informal*) priceless, side-splitting

Ii

ice NOUN

🌐 **WORD WEB**

Various forms of ice:

- ➤ black ice
- ➤ floe
- ➤ frost
- ➤ glacier
- ➤ iceberg
- ➤ ice cap
- ➤ ice field
- ➤ icicle
- ➤ pack ice
- ➤ sheet ice

– A permanently frozen layer of soil is permafrost.

icy ADJECTIVE

❶ *There was an icy wind.*
• cold, freezing, frosty, wintry, arctic, bitter, biting, raw
❷ *Icy roads can be dangerous.*
• frozen, slippery, glacial, glassy

idea NOUN

❶ *I've got a great idea!*
• plan, scheme, proposal, suggestion, proposition, inspiration
❷ *He has some odd ideas about life.*
• belief, opinion, view, theory, notion, concept, conception, hypothesis
❸ *What's the central idea of the poem?*
• point, meaning, intention, thought
❹ *Have you any idea what will happen?*
• clue, hint, inkling, impression, sense, suspicion, hunch

ideal ADJECTIVE

These are ideal conditions for sailing.
• perfect, excellent, suitable, faultless, the best

identical ADJECTIVE

All the houses looked identical.
• matching, alike, indistinguishable, interchangeable, the same
OPPOSITE different

identify VERB

❶ *The suspect was identified by three witnesses.*
• recognize, name, distinguish, pick out, single out
❷ *The doctors couldn't identify what was wrong.*
• diagnose, discover, spot
(*informal*) put a name to
➤ **identify with**
Can you identify with the hero of the film?
• sympathize with, empathize with, feel for, relate to, understand
(*informal*) put yourself in someone's shoes

idiot NOUN

I felt like such an idiot.
• fool, ass, clown, halfwit, dunce, blockhead, buffoon, dunderhead, imbecile, moron
(*informal*) chump, dope, dummy, dimwit, nitwit, nincompoop

idiotic ADJECTIVE

That was an idiotic thing to say.
• stupid, foolish, senseless, silly, ridiculous, nonsensical, unintelligent, absurd, crazy, mad, hare-brained, foolhardy
(*informal*) dim-witted, dumb, daft, barmy
OPPOSITE sensible

idle ADJECTIVE

❶ *He's such an idle fellow.*
• lazy, indolent, slothful, work-shy
OPPOSITES hard-working, industrious
❷ *The machines lay idle all week.*
• inactive, unused, inoperative
OPPOSITES active, in use
❸ *She never makes idle threats.*
• pointless, aimless, meaningless, empty, trivial, frivolous
OPPOSITE serious

idol NOUN

❶ *He was a pop idol of the 1980s.*
• star, superstar, celebrity, icon
(*informal*) pin-up

❷ *an ancient clay idol*
• god, deity, effigy, statue, figurine

idolize VERB
He idolizes his big brother.
• adore, love, worship, be devoted to, look up to

ignite VERB
❶ *These sparks then ignite the gunpowder.*
• light, set fire to, set alight
❷ *The bonfire would not ignite.*
• catch fire, light, burn, kindle, spark

ignorant ADJECTIVE
What an ignorant lot you are!
• uneducated, uninformed, illiterate, stupid
➤ **ignorant of**
I'm ignorant of the facts in the case.
• unaware of, unfamiliar with, unacquainted with
OPPOSITE aware of

ignore VERB
❶ *Why are you ignoring me?*
• take no notice of, pay no attention to, neglect, spurn, snub
IDIOM give you the cold shoulder
❷ *I'll ignore that remark.*
• disregard, overlook, brush aside
IDIOM turn a blind eye to

ill ADJECTIVE
❶ *She was ill with flu for three weeks.*
• unwell, sick, poorly, sickly, ailing, infirm, unfit, indisposed
IDIOM under the weather
– Someone who feels ill may be **nauseous** or **queasy**.
– Someone who looks ill may be **peaky** or **off colour**.
OPPOSITES healthy, well
SEE ALSO **illness**
❷ *He suffered no ill effects from the fall.*
• bad, harmful, adverse, damaging, detrimental
OPPOSITES good, beneficial

illegal ADJECTIVE
Under-age drinking is illegal.
• unlawful, illicit, criminal, banned,

prohibited, forbidden, outlawed, against the law
OPPOSITE legal

illegible ADJECTIVE
The signature was illegible.
• unreadable, indecipherable, unintelligible, unclear, indistinct
OPPOSITES legible, readable

illness NOUN
She is suffering from a mysterious illness.
• sickness, ailment, disease, disorder, complaint, condition, affliction, malady, infirmity, infection, virus
(*informal*) bug
– A sudden illness is an **attack** or **fit**.
– A period of illness is a **bout**.
– A general outbreak of illness in a particular area is an **epidemic**.

WORD WEB

Some common illnesses:

➤ allergy	➤ hay fever
➤ anaemia	➤ headache
➤ appendicitis	➤ indigestion
➤ asthma	➤ influenza
➤ bronchitis	➤ jaundice
➤ chickenpox	➤ laryngitis
➤ chill	➤ measles
➤ cold	➤ migraine
➤ cough	➤ mumps
➤ diarrhoea	➤ pneumonia
➤ eczema	➤ stomach ache
➤ fever	➤ tonsillitis
➤ flu	➤ ulcer
➤ glandular fever	➤ whooping cough

illusion NOUN
❶ *The trick was a clever illusion created by mirrors.*
• deception, apparition, mirage, fantasy, hallucination
IDIOM figment of your imagination
❷ *He had no illusions about the danger he was in.*
• delusion, misapprehension, misconception

illustrate VERB
❶ These drawings illustrate scenes from 'The Hobbit'.
• depict, picture, portray
❷ To illustrate my point, let me tell you a little story.
• show, demonstrate, explain, make clear, get across
IDIOM bring home

illustration NOUN
❶ The book has beautiful colour illustrations.
• picture, photograph, print, plate, figure, drawing, sketch, diagram
❷ Let me give you an illustration of what I mean.
• example, instance, demonstration, specimen, case

image NOUN
❶ The film contains graphic images of war.
• picture, portrayal, depiction, representation
❷ Amy frowned at her image in the mirror.
• reflection, likeness
❸ Kabir is the image of his father.
• double, twin
❹ The company is trying to improve its image.
• reputation, profile, impression, perception

imaginary ADJECTIVE
The story is set in an imaginary world.
• imagined, non-existent, unreal, made-up, invented, fanciful, fictitious, fictional, make-believe, pretend
OPPOSITE real

imagination NOUN
❶ It's all in your imagination.
• mind, fancy, dreams
❷ The writing shows plenty of imagination.
• creativity, inventiveness, ingenuity, inspiration, originality, vision

imaginative ADJECTIVE
Roald Dahl wrote highly imaginative stories.
• creative, inventive, inspired, original, innovative, fanciful
OPPOSITES unimaginative, dull

imagine VERB
❶ Can you imagine life without computers?
• picture, visualize, envisage, conceive of
IDIOM see in your mind's eye
❷ I imagine you'd like something to eat.
• suppose, assume, presume, expect, guess, take it

imitate VERB
❶ At first, he imitated the style of other authors.
• copy, reproduce, echo, ape, simulate, follow, mirror, match
❷ He is good at imitating famous people.
• mimic, impersonate, do an impression of
(informal) send up, take off

imitation ADJECTIVE
The rug is made from imitation fur.
• artificial, synthetic, fake, sham, mock, man-made
OPPOSITES real, genuine

imitation NOUN
This is an imitation of a Roman coin.
• copy, replica, reproduction, duplicate
– An imitation made to deceive someone is a **fake** or **forgery**.

immature ADJECTIVE
He is quite immature for his age.
• childish, babyish, infantile, juvenile
OPPOSITE mature

immediate ADJECTIVE
❶ They sent an immediate response.
• instant, instantaneous, prompt, speedy, swift, urgent, quick, direct
(informal) snappy
OPPOSITE slow
❷ Are you friends with your immediate neighbours?
• closest, nearest, adjacent, next
OPPOSITE distant

immediately ADVERB
❶ *Call an ambulance immediately!*
• at once, now, straight away, right away, without delay, instantly, promptly
❷ *I was sitting immediately behind you.*
• right, exactly, directly, just

immense ADJECTIVE
At the top of the cliff was an immense boulder.
• huge, enormous, gigantic, massive, colossal, giant, vast, mighty, mammoth, monumental, great
(*informal*) whopping
OPPOSITE tiny
SEE ALSO big

imminent ADJECTIVE
By now, war was imminent.
• near, close, approaching, impending, forthcoming, looming

immobile ADJECTIVE
A figure stood immobile at the window.
• unmoving, motionless, stationary, still
OPPOSITE mobile

immoral ADJECTIVE
She believes that animal testing is immoral.
• wrong, unethical, bad, wicked, sinful, dishonest, corrupt, unprincipled
OPPOSITES moral, right

immortal ADJECTIVE
❶ *the immortal gods of Mount Olympus*
• undying, deathless, ageless, eternal
OPPOSITE mortal
❷ *the immortal words of Shakespeare*
• everlasting, enduring, timeless, perennial

immune ADJECTIVE
➤ **immune from**
No one is immune from the law.
• exempt from, not subject to, not liable to
OPPOSITE liable to
➤ **immune to**
Make your computer immune to viruses.
• resistant to, protected from, safe from, secure against
OPPOSITE susceptible to

impact NOUN
❶ *The crater was caused by the impact of a meteor.*
• crash, collision, smash, bump, blow, knock, bang, jolt
❷ *The Internet has had a huge impact on our lives.*
• effect, influence

impair VERB
Very loud noise can impair your hearing.
• damage, harm, injure, weaken, diminish

impartial ADJECTIVE
Referees must be impartial.
• unbiased, neutral, unprejudiced, disinterested, detached, objective, independent, non-partisan, even-handed
OPPOSITES biased, partisan

impatient ADJECTIVE
❶ *As time went on, I grew more and more impatient.*
• restless, agitated, anxious, edgy, fidgety, irritable, snappy, tetchy, testy
OPPOSITE patient
❷ *We were impatient for the show to begin.*
• anxious, eager, keen, in a hurry
(*informal*) itching
OPPOSITE reluctant

imperfect ADJECTIVE
The items on this shelf are imperfect.
• damaged, faulty, defective, flawed, substandard, incomplete
OPPOSITE perfect

impertinent ADJECTIVE
I've had enough of your impertinent questions.
• rude, cheeky, impolite, impudent, insolent, disrespectful
OPPOSITES respectful, polite

implement NOUN
The shed was full of garden implements.
• tool, appliance, device, utensil, gadget, instrument, contraption

a b c d e f g h i j k l m n o p q r s t u v w x y z

implore VERB
I implore you to reconsider.
• beg, entreat, plead with, appeal to, urge

imply VERB
Are you implying that I am a liar?
• suggest, hint, indicate, insinuate, make out
The words imply and infer are not synonyms.

impolite ADJECTIVE
It would be impolite to refuse the invitation.
• rude, bad-mannered, discourteous, disrespectful, insulting
OPPOSITE polite

import VERB
The UK imports tea and coffee.
• bring in, ship in
OPPOSITE export

important ADJECTIVE
❶ *It is an important moment for our country.*
• major, significant, momentous, big, central, historic
❷ *I have some important business to attend to.*
• serious, urgent, pressing, weighty, vital, essential, crucial
❸ *Abraham Lincoln is an important figure in American history.*
• prominent, influential, powerful, high-ranking, notable, eminent, distinguished
OPPOSITES unimportant, minor

impose VERB
A new tax was imposed on fuel.
• introduce, enforce, fix, inflict, prescribe, set
➤ **impose on**
Are you sure I'm not imposing on you?
• inconvenience, intrude on, take advantage of, put out

imposing ADJECTIVE
The castle is an imposing building.
• grand, great, impressive, stately, magnificent, splendid, majestic, dignified, striking
OPPOSITE insignificant

impossible ADJECTIVE
It's impossible to get there and back in a day.
• impractical, unrealistic, unworkable, unthinkable, unachievable, unattainable, not viable, out of the question
OPPOSITES possible, realistic

impress VERB
She tried hard to impress the judges.
• make an impression on, influence, leave your mark on, stick in the mind of

impression NOUN
❶ *The book made a big impression on me.*
• impact, influence, effect, mark
❷ *I had the impression that something was wrong.*
• feeling, sense, idea, notion, suspicion, hunch
❸ *My sister does a good impression of the Queen.*
• imitation, impersonation
(*informal*) send-up, take-off

impressive ADJECTIVE
The film includes some impressive special effects.
• striking, effective, powerful, spectacular, stunning, breathtaking, awesome, grand, imposing, prodigious
OPPOSITES unimpressive, uninspiring

imprison VERB
Galileo was arrested and imprisoned for his ideas.
• send to prison, jail, lock up, incarcerate, confine, detain
(*informal*) put away, send down
IDIOM put under lock and key
OPPOSITE release

improve VERB
❶ *My playing has improved this year.*
• get better, advance, progress, develop, move on
OPPOSITE deteriorate
❷ *How can I improve this story?*
• make better, refine, enhance, amend, revise, correct, upgrade

❸ *Her health is slowly improving.*
• get better, recover, recuperate, pick up, rally, revive
IDIOM be on the mend
OPPOSITE get worse

improvement NOUN
❶ *Your handwriting is showing signs of improvement.*
• getting better, advance, progress, development, recovery, upturn
❷ *We have made some improvements to the website.*
• amendment, correction, revision, modification, enhancement

impudent ADJECTIVE
The boy had an impudent grin on his face.
• cheeky, insolent, rude, impolite, impertinent, disrespectful
OPPOSITES respectful, polite

impulse NOUN
I had a sudden impulse to laugh out loud.
• desire, instinct, urge, compulsion, whim

impulsive ADJECTIVE
She regretted her impulsive decision to dye her hair.
• hasty, rash, reckless, sudden, spontaneous, unplanned, unpremeditated, thoughtless, unthinking, impetuous, impromptu, spur-of-the-moment
OPPOSITES deliberate, premeditated

inaccessible ADJECTIVE
The caves are in an inaccessible part of the island.
• unreachable, isolated, remote, out-of-the-way, hard to find
OPPOSITE accessible

inaccurate ADJECTIVE
The information you gave is inaccurate.
• wrong, incorrect, inexact, imprecise, mistaken, false, erroneous, untrue
OPPOSITES accurate, correct

inadequate ADJECTIVE
They had an inadequate supply of water.
• insufficient, deficient, not enough, poor, limited, scarce, scanty, meagre, paltry
OPPOSITE adequate

inappropriate ADJECTIVE
Some scenes are inappropriate for very young children.
• unsuitable, unfitting, out of place, ill-suited, improper, unseemly
OPPOSITE appropriate

inaudible ADJECTIVE
From that distance the voices were inaudible.
• indistinct, muffled, muted, faint
OPPOSITE audible

incapable ADJECTIVE
➤ incapable of
They seem incapable of making a decision.
• unable to, incompetent at, unfit to, unsuited to, ineffective at
(*informal*) not up to
OPPOSITE capable of

incident NOUN
There was an amusing incident at school today.
• event, happening, occurrence, episode, affair

incidental ADJECTIVE
Some of these details are incidental to the plot.
• unimportant, inessential, secondary, minor, subordinate, subsidiary, peripheral
OPPOSITES essential, key

incite VERB
They were accused of inciting rebellion.
• provoke, instigate, arouse, stir up, whip up, kindle, inflame

inclination NOUN
❶ *The child shows a strong inclination towards music.*
• tendency, leaning, propensity, predisposition, bent

(*formal*) penchant
❷ *That night, I felt no inclination for sleep.*
• desire, taste, liking, preference, urge

incline NOUN
The house was at the top of a steep incline.
• slope, hill, rise, gradient, ascent, ramp

inclined ADJECTIVE
➤ **be inclined to**
❶ *I'm inclined to agree with her.*
• be disposed to, be of a mind to
❷ *My brother is inclined to say the wrong thing.*
• tend to, be in the habit of, be liable to, be prone to, be given to, be apt to

include VERB
The cost includes postage and packing.
• contain, incorporate, cover, comprise, encompass, involve, take in, allow for, take into account
OPPOSITE exclude

income NOUN
Her income has gone up in the last year.
• earnings, pay, salary, wages, takings, revenue
OPPOSITE expenditure

incompetent ADJECTIVE
He is an incompetent buffoon!
• inept, unskilful, inexpert, amateurish, bungling
(*informal*) useless
OPPOSITE competent

incomplete ADJECTIVE
The new stadium is still incomplete.
• unfinished, uncompleted, not ready
OPPOSITE complete

incomprehensible ADJECTIVE
He left an incomprehensible message.
• unintelligible, unclear, indecipherable, unfathomable
OPPOSITES comprehensible, intelligible

inconsiderate ADJECTIVE
Some drivers are inconsiderate to cyclists.
• selfish, unthinking, thoughtless, insensitive, uncaring, tactless
OPPOSITE considerate

inconsistent ADJECTIVE
❶ *Their performance has been inconsistent this season.*
• changeable, variable, unreliable, unpredictable, erratic, fickle
❷ *The stories of the two witnesses are inconsistent.*
• contradictory, conflicting, irreconcilable, at odds, at variance
OPPOSITE consistent

inconspicuous ADJECTIVE
He stood in the corner, trying to remain inconspicuous.
• unnoticed, unobtrusive, camouflaged, out of sight
OPPOSITE conspicuous

inconvenient ADJECTIVE
I'm sorry if I've arrived at an inconvenient moment.
• awkward, difficult, bad, unsuitable, unfortunate, untimely, inopportune
OPPOSITE convenient

incorporate VERB
The show incorporates some well-known tunes.
• include, contain, embrace, take in
OPPOSITE exclude

incorrect ADJECTIVE
The next three answers were incorrect.
• wrong, mistaken, inaccurate, false, untrue
OPPOSITE correct

increase VERB
❶ *They have increased the size of the page.*
• make bigger, enlarge, expand, widen, broaden
❷ *We are increasing our efforts to reduce waste.*
• intensify, strengthen, develop, enhance, add to, step up

❸ *The train company will be increasing ticket prices soon.*
• put up, raise

❹ *How do you increase the volume on the TV?*
• turn up, amplify, boost

❺ *The population continues to increase.*
• grow, mount, go up, build up, rise, soar, escalate, multiply

❻ For opposites see **decrease**.

increase NOUN
There has been an increase in demand.
• rise, growth, expansion, enlargement, leap, surge
(*informal*) hike
OPPOSITE decrease

incredible ADJECTIVE
❶ *I find her story incredible.*
• unbelievable, unlikely, improbable, implausible, unconvincing, far-fetched
OPPOSITE credible

❷ *The new bridge is an incredible feat of engineering.*
• extraordinary, marvellous, amazing, astounding, phenomenal, spectacular, magnificent, breathtaking, prodigious

independence NOUN
The islanders value their independence.
• freedom, liberty, autonomy, self-rule
OPPOSITE dependence

independent ADJECTIVE
❶ *My granny is a very independent person.*
• self-sufficient, self-reliant
OPPOSITE dependent

❷ *Luxembourg is an independent country.*
• autonomous, self-governing

❸ *We need an independent opinion.*
• impartial, unbiased, neutral, objective, disinterested
OPPOSITE biased

indicate VERB
❶ *Please indicate your preference.*
• specify, point out, show, reveal, make known

❷ *A red light indicates danger.*
• mean, stand for, denote, express, signal, signify, communicate, convey

indication NOUN
He gave no indication of his feelings.
• sign, signal, hint, clue, inkling, evidence, token, warning, symptom, pointer

indifferent ADJECTIVE
❶ *Her voice showed how indifferent she was.*
• uninterested, unconcerned, detached, impassive, uncaring, unmoved, unenthusiastic
OPPOSITE enthusiastic

❷ *The food in the restaurant was indifferent.*
• mediocre, ordinary, average, unexciting, uninspired, middle-of-the-road
OPPOSITE excellent

indignant ADJECTIVE
The voice at the end of the phone was indignant.
• annoyed, displeased, angry, resentful, affronted, offended, outraged, aggrieved, piqued
(*informal*) peeved

indirect ADJECTIVE
The bus took an indirect route into town.
• roundabout, circuitous, winding, meandering, tortuous, zigzag
OPPOSITE direct

indistinct ADJECTIVE
❶ *In the photocopies, some of the numbers were indistinct.*
• unclear, blurred, blurry, fuzzy, indefinite, vague, obscure, hazy
OPPOSITE clear

❷ *I could hear indistinct sounds of people talking.*
• muffled, mumbled, muted, faint, weak, inaudible, unintelligible, incoherent
OPPOSITES distinct, clear

individual ADJECTIVE
❶ *Count each individual word.*
• single, separate, discrete

❷ *Her singing has an individual style.*
• characteristic, distinct, distinctive, special, unique, personal, singular

individual NOUN
He is a rather odd individual.
• person, character, man, woman (*informal*) sort, type

induce VERB
❶ *Nothing would induce me to live there.*
• persuade, convince, prompt, coax, tempt, prevail upon
❷ *Some headaches are induced by stress.*
• cause, produce, generate, provoke, bring on, lead to, give rise to

indulge VERB
❶ *She could not be accused of indulging her children.*
• spoil, pamper, pander to, mollycoddle, cosset
❷ *Her husband indulged her every wish.*
• satisfy, gratify, fulfil, meet, yield to, give in to
➤ **indulge in**
On the journey we indulged in jokes and bad puns.
• enjoy, treat yourself to, revel in

indulgent ADJECTIVE
They are very indulgent towards their grandchildren.
• tolerant, patient, permissive, lenient, easy-going, generous, liberal
OPPOSITE strict

industry NOUN
❶ *Many people in the area work in the car industry.*
• business, trade, commerce, manufacturing, production
❷ *The workshop was a hive of industry.*
• hard work, effort, energy, endeavour, industriousness, diligence, application
OPPOSITE laziness

ineffective ADJECTIVE
❶ *Her protests were ineffective.*
• unsuccessful, ineffectual, unproductive
OPPOSITES effective, successful

❷ *He was an ineffective captain of the team.*
• incompetent, inept, incapable, unfit, inadequate
(*informal*) useless

inefficient ADJECTIVE
❶ *It is an inefficient way of doing things.*
• ineffective, unproductive, unsystematic, disorganized, inept, slow, sloppy
❷ *The car is inefficient in its use of fuel.*
• wasteful, uneconomical, extravagant
OPPOSITE efficient

inequality NOUN
Is there still inequality between men and women?
• imbalance, inequity, disparity, discrepancy, unfairness, bias
OPPOSITE equality

inevitable ADJECTIVE
It was inevitable that they would meet one day.
• unavoidable, inescapable, certain, sure, definite

inexpensive ADJECTIVE
You can buy inexpensive clothes in the market.
• cheap, low-priced, low-cost, cut-price, affordable, economical, bargain, budget
OPPOSITE expensive

infamous ADJECTIVE
Jesse James was an infamous outlaw.
• notorious, villainous, disreputable, scandalous

infant NOUN
On the wall there's a picture of me as an infant.
• baby, newborn, small child, tot, toddler

infect VERB
A virus had infected the water supply.
• contaminate, pollute, poison

infection NOUN
The infection spread rapidly.
• disease, virus, contagion, contamination

infectious *ADJECTIVE*
Chickenpox is highly infectious.
• contagious, communicable
(*informal*) catching
OPPOSITE non-infectious

infer *VERB*
What can we infer from this letter?
• conclude, deduce, gather,
work out
SEE ALSO imply

inferior *ADJECTIVE*
❶ *The goods were of inferior quality.*
• poor, bad, second-rate, low-grade,
substandard, cheap, shoddy
❷ *Officers can give orders to those of
inferior rank.*
• lesser, lower, junior,
subordinate
OPPOSITE superior

infested *ADJECTIVE*
The cellar was infested with mice.
• swarming, teeming, crawling, overrun,
plagued

infinite *ADJECTIVE*
*You need infinite patience to train a
puppy.*
• unlimited, endless, limitless,
boundless, never-ending, unending,
inexhaustible, immeasurable
OPPOSITES finite, limited

infirm *ADJECTIVE*
*Most of the patients are elderly and
infirm.*
• frail, weak, feeble, poorly, ill,
unwell
– People who have to stay in bed are
bedridden.
OPPOSITE healthy

inflammable *ADJECTIVE*
see flammable

inflammation *NOUN*
*This ointment will soothe the
inflammation.*
• swelling, redness, soreness,
infection

inflate *VERB*
*We have ten minutes to inflate fifty
balloons.*
• blow up, pump up
OPPOSITE deflate

inflict *VERB*
*They inflicted a heavy defeat on us last
season.*
• administer, deal out, mete out, exact,
impose, force

influence *NOUN*
❶ *Jazz had a major influence on his
music.*
• effect, impact, hold, pull, sway
❷ *Europe had no influence in the region.*
• power, authority, dominance, control,
leverage, weight
(*informal*) clout

influence *VERB*
Did anything influence your decision?
• affect, have an impact on, guide,
shape, direct, control, govern, determine

influential *ADJECTIVE*
She knows some very influential people.
• important, leading, powerful,
significant
OPPOSITE unimportant

inform *VERB*
Please inform us if you move house.
• tell, let someone know, notify, advise,
send word to

informal *ADJECTIVE*
❶ *The dinner will be very informal.*
• casual, relaxed, easy-going, friendly,
homely
(*informal*) laid-back
❷ *Emails are usually written in an
informal style.*
• colloquial, vernacular, familiar,
everyday, popular, chatty
OPPOSITE formal

information *NOUN*
*There is more information on our
website.*
• details, particulars, facts, data,

a
b
c
d
e
f
g
h
i
j
k
l
m
n
o
p
q
r
s
t
u
v
w
x
y
z

advice, guidance, knowledge
(*informal*) info

informative ADJECTIVE
It's a very informative website.
• helpful, useful, instructive,
illuminating, revealing
OPPOSITE unhelpful

infuriate VERB
My answer just infuriated her.
• anger, enrage, incense, madden,
exasperate

ingenious ADJECTIVE
It seemed like an ingenious plan.
• clever, brilliant, inspired, inventive,
imaginative, original, crafty, cunning,
shrewd

inhabit VERB
People once inhabited these caves.
• live in, occupy, dwell in, reside in,
populate, settle in

inhabitant NOUN
The island has fewer than a hundred
inhabitants.
• resident, dweller, native, occupier,
occupant
– An inhabitant of a particular city or
country is a **citizen**.
– The inhabitants of a place are its
population.

inhabited ADJECTIVE
Is the island inhabited?
• occupied, lived-in
OPPOSITE uninhabited

inherit VERB
She inherited the farm from her uncle.
• succeed to, be left, come into

inherited ADJECTIVE
Eye colour is an inherited characteristic.
• hereditary, passed down, genetic

inhuman ADJECTIVE
It was an act of inhuman cruelty.
• barbaric, inhumane, savage, cruel,
merciless, heartless
OPPOSITE humane

initial ADJECTIVE
❶ My initial reaction was to run away.
• first, earliest, immediate
OPPOSITES final, eventual
❷ The initial part of the poem is about
the sea.
• opening, preliminary, introductory,
preparatory
OPPOSITES final, closing

initially ADVERB
Initially, I thought the book was boring.
• at first, in the beginning, to begin
with, to start with, at the outset

initiative NOUN
They had to use their initiative to survive.
• resourcefulness, inventiveness,
originality, ingenuity, enterprise

injection NOUN
The nurse gave me an injection.
• inoculation, vaccination, immunization
(*informal*) jab, shot

injure VERB
Some passengers were seriously injured.
• hurt, wound, harm
– To injure someone causing permanent
damage is to **maim** them.

injury NOUN
We all escaped without any serious
injury.
• wound, harm, hurt

WORD WEB

Some types of injury:

➤ bite	➤ graze
➤ bruise	➤ scald
➤ burn	➤ scratch
➤ cut	➤ sprain
➤ fracture	➤ sting
➤ gash	➤ strain

inner ADJECTIVE
❶ A passageway leads to the inner
chamber.
• central, inside, interior, internal,
inward, middle

❷ *She kept her inner feelings to herself.*
• innermost, personal, private, intimate, secret, hidden, concealed
OPPOSITE outer

innocent ADJECTIVE
❶ *He was found innocent of murder.*
• guiltless, blameless, faultless, free from blame
OPPOSITE guilty
❷ *She looks so sweet and innocent.*
• angelic, virtuous, pure, inexperienced, naive
OPPOSITES wicked, cunning
❸ *It was just a bit of innocent fun.*
• harmless, innocuous, inoffensive

innumerable ADJECTIVE
The sun is just one of innumerable stars.
• countless, numberless, uncountable, untold

inquire VERB
➤ **inquire into**
The police are inquiring into the case.
• look into, investigate, examine, explore

inquiry NOUN
There will be an official inquiry into the accident.
• investigation, inspection, examination

inquisitive ADJECTIVE
Chimpanzees are naturally inquisitive.
• curious, questioning, inquiring, probing
– An uncomplimentary word is **nosy**.

insane ADJECTIVE
❶ *It was rumoured that the king had gone insane.*
• mentally ill, mad, crazy, deranged, demented, unhinged
(*informal*) nuts, bonkers
IDIOMS off your head, stark raving mad
IDIOMS (*informal*) off your rocker, off your trolley
OPPOSITE sane
❷ *The whole idea seems insane now.*
• crazy, mad, senseless, stupid, foolish, idiotic, foolhardy, absurd, ludicrous, preposterous, hare-brained

(*informal*) nutty, daft, barmy
OPPOSITES sensible, wise

inscription NOUN
I tried to read the inscription on the tomb.
• engraving, carving, writing, lettering

insect NOUN
night-flying insects
• bug
(*informal*) creepy-crawly, minibeast

✸ WORD WEB

Some types of insect:

➤ ant	➤ gnat
➤ aphid	➤ grasshopper
➤ bee	➤ greenfly
➤ beetle	➤ hornet
➤ bluebottle	➤ horsefly
➤ bumblebee	➤ lacewing
➤ butterfly	➤ ladybird
➤ cicada	➤ locust
➤ cockroach	➤ louse
➤ crane fly	➤ mantis
(*informal*	➤ mayfly
daddy-long-	➤ midge
legs)	➤ mosquito
➤ cricket	➤ moth
➤ dragonfly	➤ stick insect
➤ earwig	➤ termite
➤ firefly	➤ tsetse fly
➤ flea	➤ wasp
➤ fly	➤ weevil
➤ glow-worm	

Life stages of insects:

➤ caterpillar	➤ larva
➤ chrysalis	➤ maggot
➤ grub	➤ pupa

Parts of an insect's body:

➤ head	➤ legs
➤ thorax	➤ mandibles
➤ abdomen;	➤ wings
antennae	

– The scientific study of insects is entomology.

insecure ADJECTIVE
I used to feel insecure around people.
• unconfident, uncertain, self-conscious, diffident, hesitant, anxious, nervous, apprehensive, uneasy
OPPOSITES secure, self-confident

insensitive ADJECTIVE
I'm sorry if my comments were insensitive.
• thoughtless, tactless, unfeeling, uncaring, unsympathetic, callous
OPPOSITE sensitive

insert VERB
Please insert a coin in the slot.
• put in, place, push in, slide in, slot in, install, implant, load
(*informal*) pop in, stick in

inside NOUN
❶ *The inside of the nest was lined with feathers.*
• interior, inner surface, centre, core, heart, middle
OPPOSITE outside
❷ (*informal*) *I felt a pain in my insides.*
• stomach, belly, gut, bowels, intestines
(*informal*) innards

inside ADJECTIVE
The inside walls of the house were damp.
• interior, inner, internal, innermost, indoor
OPPOSITES outside, outer

insignificant ADJECTIVE
These changes may seem insignificant to you.
• unimportant, minor, trivial, trifling, negligible, slight, insubstantial, paltry, petty
OPPOSITES significant, major

insincere ADJECTIVE
The waiter welcomed us with an insincere smile.
• false, pretended, feigned, hollow, hypocritical, disingenuous
(*informal*) two-faced, phoney, put-on
OPPOSITE sincere

insist VERB
He insisted that no one else was to blame.
• declare, state, assert, maintain, protest, stress, emphasize, swear, vow, claim
➤ **insist on**
I insist on seeing the manager.
• demand, require

insistent ADJECTIVE
There was an insistent tapping on the window.
• persistent, unrelenting, unremitting, dogged, tenacious

insolent ADJECTIVE
The boy gave him an insolent stare.
• rude, impudent, disrespectful, impolite, impertinent, arrogant, brazen
(*informal*) cheeky
OPPOSITES polite, respectful

inspect VERB
We inspected the damage done by the storm.
• examine, investigate, check, look over, study, survey, scrutinize, monitor, vet
(*informal*) check out
IDIOM (*informal*) give the once-over

inspection NOUN
There will be a safety inspection this afternoon.
• check, check-up, examination, review, survey, scrutiny, investigation

inspiration NOUN
❶ *I had a sudden inspiration.*
• idea, bright idea, thought, revelation
(*informal*) brainwave
❷ *What was the inspiration behind your story?*
• impulse, motivation, stimulus, influence, spur

inspire VERB
❶ *I felt inspired to write a poem.*
• motivate, stimulate, prompt, encourage, stir, rouse, spur on

❷ He's a manager who inspires loyalty in
his players.
• arouse, induce, awaken, kindle, trigger,
bring out

install VERB
We are having a new cooker installed.
• put in, set up, fix, place, position,
establish
OPPOSITE remove

instalment NOUN
I missed the first instalment of the new
series.
• episode, part, programme, issue,
section

instance NOUN
Give me an instance of what you mean.
• example, illustration, case, sample

instant ADJECTIVE
The show was an instant success.
• immediate, instantaneous, quick,
rapid, fast, prompt, snappy, speedy,
swift, direct
instant NOUN
I only saw the figure for an instant.
• moment, second, flash
(informal) tick, jiffy
IDIOMS split second, twinkling of an eye

instinct NOUN
Good detectives should always follow
their instincts.
• impulse, inclination, intuition, hunch,
feeling, urge

instinctive ADJECTIVE
Many people have an instinctive fear of
snakes.
• intuitive, natural, innate, inherent,
automatic, involuntary, reflex,
spontaneous, impulsive, unconscious,
unthinking
OPPOSITES deliberate, conscious

instruct VERB
❶ All the staff are instructed in first aid.
• teach, train, coach, tutor, educate,
school
❷ The guide instructed us to wait.
• tell, order, direct, command

instructions PLURAL NOUN
Please follow the instructions carefully.
• directions, guidelines, orders,
commands

instructor NOUN
She is a qualified skiing instructor.
• teacher, trainer, tutor, coach

instrument NOUN
They use a special instrument for
measuring wind speed.
• tool, implement, utensil, appliance,
device, gadget, contraption
(informal) gizmo
For musical instruments see music.

insufficient ADJECTIVE
The plants had an insufficient amount
of water.
• inadequate, deficient, not enough, too
little, scant, scanty
OPPOSITES enough, excessive

insult VERB
I apologize if I have insulted you.
• offend, outrage, be rude to, hurt,
injure, slight, snub
insult NOUN
Would it be an insult to refuse her offer?
• affront, slight, slur, snub
(informal) put-down

insulting ADJECTIVE
She made an insulting comment about
my hair.
• offensive, rude, impolite, derogatory,
disparaging, scornful, uncomplimentary
OPPOSITE complimentary

intact ADJECTIVE
The skeleton was largely intact.
• unbroken, whole, undamaged,
unharmed, complete, perfect
(informal) in one piece

integrate VERB
They decided to integrate the two
classes.
• combine, join, merge, unite, unify,
amalgamate, bring together
OPPOSITE separate

a
b
c
d
e
f
g
h
i
j
k
l
m
n
o
p
q
r
s
t
u
v
w
x
y
z

integrity NOUN
Is there any reason to doubt his integrity?
• honesty, honour, loyalty, trustworthiness, reliability, sincerity, fidelity, virtue
OPPOSITE dishonesty

intelligence NOUN
❶ *The robot shows signs of intelligence.*
• cleverness, understanding, comprehension, reason, sense, wisdom, insight, intellect, brainpower, wits (*informal*) brains
❷ *He was sent on a spying mission to gather secret intelligence.*
• information, knowledge, data, facts, reports

intelligent ADJECTIVE
He was an intelligent boy for his age.
• clever, bright, smart, quick-witted, sharp, perceptive, shrewd, able, brilliant, rational, thinking (*informal*) brainy
OPPOSITES unintelligent, stupid

intelligible ADJECTIVE
The message was barely intelligible.
• understandable, comprehensible, clear, plain, unambiguous, coherent, lucid
OPPOSITE incomprehensible

intend VERB
What do you intend to do?
• plan, aim, mean, have in mind, plot, propose
➤ **be intended for**
The class is intended for beginners.
• be aimed at, be designed for, be meant for, be set up for

intense ADJECTIVE
❶ *I felt a sudden, intense pain in my chest.*
• extreme, acute, severe, sharp, great, strong, violent
OPPOSITES slight, mild
❷ *The debate aroused intense feelings.*
• deep, passionate, powerful, strong, profound
OPPOSITE mild

intensive ADJECTIVE
Police carried out an intensive search of the area.
• detailed, thorough, rigorous, exhaustive, concentrated, in-depth, methodical, painstaking
OPPOSITE superficial

intent ADJECTIVE
He read the letter with an intent look of concentration.
• attentive, focused, absorbed, engrossed, preoccupied, rapt
➤ **intent on**
Why are you intent on leaving?
• determined to, resolved to, committed to, set on, fixed on, bent on

intention NOUN
Our only intention is to win.
• aim, objective, target, goal, ambition, plan, intent

intentional ADJECTIVE
It was clearly an intentional foul.
• deliberate, conscious, calculated, planned, intended, meant, wilful, done on purpose
OPPOSITE accidental

intercept VERB
A defender intercepted the pass.
• check, stop, block, catch, cut off, head off, deflect

interest NOUN
❶ *He listened with increasing interest.*
• curiosity, attention, involvement, attentiveness, regard, notice
❷ *The information is of no interest to anyone.*
• importance, significance, concern, consequence, relevance, note, value
❸ *My interests include painting and photography.*
• hobby, pastime, pursuit, activity, diversion, amusement

interest VERB
Astronomy has always interested me.
• appeal to, be of interest to, attract, excite, fascinate, absorb, capture your imagination
OPPOSITE bore
➤ **be interested in**
Are you interested in fashion?
• be keen on, care about, follow

interesting ADJECTIVE
She is full of interesting ideas.
• fascinating, stimulating, intriguing, absorbing, captivating, engrossing, entertaining, diverting
OPPOSITES boring, dull

interfere VERB
➤ **interfere in**
Please stop interfering in my affairs!
• intervene in, intrude in, meddle in, pry into, encroach on, butt in on
IDIOM (*informal*) poke your nose into
➤ **interfere with**
The weather interfered with our plans.
• hamper, hinder, get in the way of, obstruct

interior ADJECTIVE & NOUN
see **inside**

intermediate ADJECTIVE
Should I join the intermediate or the advanced class?
• middle, midway, halfway, in-between, transitional

internal ADJECTIVE
This is a diagram of the internal parts of the engine.
• inner, inside, interior
OPPOSITE external

international ADJECTIVE
An international rescue team was put together.
• global, worldwide, multinational, intercontinental

interpret VERB
Can you interpret this old writing?
• explain, make sense of, clarify, translate, decipher, decode

interrogate VERB
The police interrogated the two suspects for several hours.
• question, interview, examine, cross-examine, quiz
(*informal*) grill

interrupt VERB
❶ *Please don't interrupt while I am speaking.*
• intervene, interject, break in, butt in, cut in
❷ *Heavy rain interrupted the match.*
• stop, suspend, disrupt, break off, cut short

interruption NOUN
I worked for an hour without any interruption.
• break, pause, stop, gap, halt, disruption, suspension

interval NOUN
❶ *There will be a short interval after the first act.*
• intermission, interlude, recess, break, pause, time-out
(*informal*) breather
❷ *There are signs at regular intervals along the road.*
• space, gap, distance

intervene VERB
A man intervened to stop the fight.
• intercede, step in, interfere, interrupt, butt in

interview VERB
The actress was being interviewed about her new film.
• question, talk to, interrogate, examine, quiz, sound out
(*informal*) grill

intimate ADJECTIVE
❶ *They have been intimate friends for years.*
• close, cherished, dear, bosom
OPPOSITE distant
❷ *The restaurant has an intimate atmosphere.*
• friendly, warm, welcoming, informal, cosy

a
b
c
d
e
f
g
h
i
j
k
l
m
n
o
p
q
r
s
t
u
v
w
x
y
z

❸ *They printed intimate details about her life.*
• personal, private, confidential, secret
❹ *He has an intimate knowledge of this area.*
• detailed, thorough, deep, profound, exhaustive, in-depth

intimidate VERB
He was accused of trying to intimidate a witness.
• bully, threaten, frighten, menace, scare, terrify, terrorize, persecute

intrepid ADJECTIVE
The intrepid explorers finally reached the North Pole.
• daring, bold, fearless, courageous, brave, valiant, heroic, plucky

intricate ADJECTIVE
The clock has an intricate mechanism.
• complex, complicated, elaborate, sophisticated, involved, convoluted
OPPOSITE simple

intriguing ADJECTIVE
The results of the experiment are intriguing.
• interesting, fascinating, absorbing, captivating, beguiling

introduce VERB
❶ *When was printing introduced in Europe?*
• establish, institute, bring in, set up, create, start, begin, initiate, launch, inaugurate
❷ *Let me introduce you to my friend.*
• present, make known, acquaint (with)
❸ *The director stood up to introduce the film.*
• announce, give an introduction to, lead into

introduction NOUN
The plot is outlined in the introduction.
• preface, foreword, preamble, prelude (*informal*) intro
– An introduction to a play is a **prologue**.
– An introduction to an opera or a ballet is an **overture**.

intrude VERB
I hope I'm not intruding.
• interrupt, intervene, break in, butt in
➤ **intrude on**
I don't mean to intrude on your privacy.
• encroach on, infringe on, trespass on, violate, invade

intruder NOUN
Some intruders broke into the building.
• trespasser, interloper, prowler, burglar

invade VERB
The Vikings invaded many parts of Europe.
• attack, raid, occupy, overrun, conquer, capture, seize

invalid ADJECTIVE
❶ *Your ticket is invalid because it is out of date.*
• unacceptable, illegitimate, void
❷ *That is an invalid argument.*
• false, unsound, unjustifiable, spurious, fallacious
OPPOSITE valid

invaluable ADJECTIVE
She is an invaluable member of the team.
• indispensable, irreplaceable, crucial, essential, vital, all-important
OPPOSITES dispensable, worthless

invasion NOUN
the Viking invasion of Ireland
• attack, raid, occupation, capture, seizure, conquest

invent VERB
❶ *Who invented the telescope?*
• create, design, devise, originate, think up, conceive
❷ *He had to invent an excuse quickly.*
• make up, fabricate, concoct, dream up

invention NOUN
❶ *The recipe is my own invention.*
• creation, design, discovery, innovation (*informal*) brainchild
❷ *The newspaper article was mostly invention.*
• fantasy, fiction, fabrication, lies, deceit, falsehood

inventive ADJECTIVE
She has an inventive mind.
• creative, original, imaginative, ingenious, inspired, innovative

inventor NOUN
James Watt was the inventor of the steam engine.
• creator, designer, originator, discoverer, author, architect

investigate VERB
Police are investigating the cause of the accident.
• examine, explore, inquire into, look into, study, scrutinize, consider, follow up, probe, research
(informal) go into

investigation NOUN
There will be an investigation into the accident.
• examination, inquiry, inspection, study, review, survey

invigorating ADJECTIVE
We had an invigorating walk before breakfast.
• refreshing, stimulating, reviving, bracing

invisible ADJECTIVE
These creatures are so tiny that they are invisible to the human eye.
• out of sight, unseen, undetectable, unnoticeable, unnoticed, unobserved, inconspicuous, hidden, concealed, covered, obscured
OPPOSITE visible

invitation NOUN
I received an invitation to attend the ceremony.
• request, call, summons
(informal) invite

invite VERB
❶ Who are you inviting to your party?
• ask, summon, have someone round
(formal) request someone's company
❷ That sort of thing just invites trouble.
• ask for, lead to, bring about, encourage, induce, provoke

inviting ADJECTIVE
An inviting smell came from the kitchen.
• attractive, appealing, pleasant, welcoming, agreeable, appetizing, tempting, enticing
OPPOSITE repulsive

involve VERB
❶ Her job involves a lot of travel.
• include, comprise, require, demand, necessitate, mean
❷ These are decisions that involve everybody.
• affect, concern, interest, touch

involved ADJECTIVE
The plot is too involved to summarize.
• complex, complicated, elaborate, intricate, convoluted
OPPOSITE simple
➤ **be involved in**
Are you involved in the theatre?
• associated with, connected with, concerned with, caught up in, mixed up in

irrational ADJECTIVE
I have an irrational fear of spiders.
• unreasonable, illogical, senseless, groundless, unfounded, nonsensical, absurd
OPPOSITE rational

irregular ADJECTIVE
❶ The bricks were arranged in an irregular pattern.
• varying, variable, erratic, unpredictable, uneven, random, haphazard, fitful, patchy
OPPOSITES regular, orderly
❷ The suggestion is highly irregular!
• abnormal, unusual, exceptional, unconventional, improper
OPPOSITES normal, usual

irrelevant ADJECTIVE
Don't waste time on irrelevant details.
• inappropriate, unnecessary, inessential, pointless, immaterial, unrelated, unconnected, extraneous
IDIOM beside the point
OPPOSITE relevant

A
B
C
D
E
F
G
H
I
J
K
L
M
N
O
P
Q
R
S
T
U
V
W
X
Y
Z

irresistible ADJECTIVE
I had an irresistible urge to giggle.
• overwhelming, overpowering, uncontrollable, unavoidable, powerful, compelling

irresponsible ADJECTIVE
It's irresponsible to drive too fast.
• reckless, rash, thoughtless, inconsiderate, uncaring, unthinking, negligent
OPPOSITE responsible

irritable ADJECTIVE
He arrived in an irritable mood.
• bad-tempered, grumpy, short-tempered, cross, impatient, irascible, snappy, touchy, testy, grouchy, prickly, peevish, quarrelsome
OPPOSITES good-humoured, cheerful

irritate VERB
❶ *The noise began to irritate me.*
• annoy, bother, exasperate, anger, provoke, madden, vex
(*informal*) bug, rile, get to
IDIOM get on your nerves
❷ *Soap may irritate sensitive skin.*
• inflame, itch, burn

island NOUN
Fiji is an island in the South Pacific.
• (*literary*) isle
– A small island is an **islet**.
– A coral island is an **atoll**.
– A group of islands is an **archipelago**.
– An uninhabited island is a **desert island**.

isolated ADJECTIVE
❶ *They found their way to an isolated village in the mountains.*
• remote, secluded, out-of-the-way, outlying, inaccessible, cut off
OPPOSITE accessible

❷ *There was an isolated sighting of a UFO.*
• single, solitary, lone, unique, uncommon, unusual, exceptional
(*informal*) one-off
OPPOSITE common

issue VERB
❶ *They issued blankets to the refugees.*
• give out, distribute, supply, furnish, equip
❷ *The ambassador issued a strongly-worded statement.*
• put out, send out, bring out, produce, publish, release, circulate, print, broadcast
❸ *Black smoke issued from the chimneys.*
• come out, emerge, appear, flow out, gush, erupt

issue NOUN
❶ *The paper mainly covers local issues.*
• matter, subject, topic, affair, concern, question, problem, situation
❷ *There will be a special issue of the magazine next month.*
• edition, number, instalment, copy

itch NOUN
❶ *I had an annoying itch on my foot.*
• tickle, tingling, prickle
❷ *You've always had an itch to travel.*
• desire, longing, yearning, craving, hankering, urge, wish, ache, thirst, hunger

item NOUN
❶ *I bought a few items in the sale.*
• thing, object, article
❷ *There was an item about our school in the paper.*
• article, piece, report, feature, write-up

jab *VERB*
A passer-by jabbed me in the ribs.
• poke, prod, elbow, nudge, stab, dig

jagged *ADJECTIVE*
Holly leaves have jagged edges.
• spiky, toothed, serrated, prickly, thorny, barbed, ragged
OPPOSITE smooth

jail *NOUN*
see prison

jam *NOUN*
❶ *We got stuck in a jam on the motorway.*
• traffic jam, hold-up, tailback, blockage, congestion, bottleneck
❷ (*informal*) *I'm in a bit of a jam.*
• difficulty, mess, predicament, plight (*informal*) fix
IDIOM tight corner

jam *VERB*
❶ *Someone had jammed the door open.*
• prop, wedge, stick
❷ *The paper has jammed in the printer.*
• become stuck, stick, catch
❸ *I jammed my things into a backpack.*
• cram, pack, stuff, squeeze, squash, crush, ram, crowd
❹ *The roads are jammed at rush hour.*
• block, clog, obstruct, congest (*informal*) bung up

jangle *NOUN & VERB*
His keys jangled in his pocket.
• jingle, tinkle, ring, chink, clink

jar *NOUN*
an earthenware jar
• pot, container, vase, crock

jar *VERB*
❶ *I jarred my wrist when I fell.*
• jolt, jerk, shake, vibrate
❷ *Those colours jar with each other.*
• clash, conflict, be incompatible, be at odds
OPPOSITES harmonize, go together

jealous *ADJECTIVE*
❶ *Some people were jealous of her popularity.*
• envious, resentful, grudging
IDIOM green with envy (at)
❷ *In the story she is locked away by her jealous lover.*
• suspicious, distrustful, possessive

jealousy *NOUN*
❶ *I couldn't help feeling a twinge of jealousy at his good fortune.*
• envy, resentment, bitterness
❷ *She could no longer stand her lover's jealousy.*
• suspicion, distrust, possessiveness

jeer *VERB*
Some of the audience whistled and jeered.
• boo, hiss, sneer, taunt, mock, scoff, ridicule
OPPOSITE cheer

jerk *VERB*
❶ *The train suddenly jerked to a halt.*
• jolt, lurch, judder, shudder, bump, bounce
❷ *I just managed to jerk my arm free.*
• pull, tug, yank, pluck, wrench

jerky *ADJECTIVE*
The stagecoach drew to a jerky halt.
• jolting, jumpy, shaky, bouncy, bumpy, twitchy, uneven
OPPOSITES steady, smooth

jet *NOUN*
A jet of water shot high in the air.
• spout, spurt, spray, squirt, gush, stream, fountain

jewel *NOUN*
see gem

A
B
C
D
E
F
G
H
I
J
K
L
M
N
O
P
Q
R
S
T
U
V
W
X
Y
Z

jewellery NOUN

WORD WEB

Some items of jewellery:

- ➤ anklet
- ➤ bangle
- ➤ beads
- ➤ bindi
- ➤ body jewel
- ➤ bracelet
- ➤ brooch
- ➤ cameo
- ➤ chain
- ➤ charm
- ➤ choker
- ➤ clasp
- ➤ crown
- ➤ cufflinks
- ➤ diadem

- ➤ earring
- ➤ engagement ring
- ➤ lapel pin
- ➤ locket
- ➤ necklace
- ➤ necklet
- ➤ pendant
- ➤ pin
- ➤ ring
- ➤ tiara
- ➤ tiepin
- ➤ toe ring
- ➤ wedding ring

- A person who sells or makes jewellery is a **jeweller**.

- A person who makes gold or silver jewellery is a **goldsmith** or **silversmith**.

SEE ALSO **gem**

jingle NOUN & VERB
We heard the sound of sleigh bells jingling.
• tinkle, jangle, ring, chink, clink

job NOUN
❶ *My sister has a job as a teaching assistant.*
• post, position, profession, occupation, employment, trade, work, career, vocation, calling
For types of job see **occupation**.
❷ *Whose job is it to do the washing-up?*
• duty, task, assignment, chore, errand

jog VERB
❶ *He jogs round the park every morning.*
• run, trot
❷ *I jogged his elbow by accident.*
• nudge, prod, jolt, jostle, jar, knock, bump
❸ *The photograph may jog your memory.*
• prompt, stir, arouse, stimulate, spark, set off

join VERB
❶ *The two roads join here.*
• come together, meet, converge, merge, unite, combine, amalgamate
OPPOSITES divide, separate
❷ *Join the two pieces of rope together.*
• put together, connect, fasten, attach, fix, link, couple, bond
OPPOSITES detach, separate
❸ *I joined the crowd going into the cinema.*
• follow, go with, accompany
(*informal*) tag along with
❹ *We have joined a local sports club.*
• become a member of, enrol in, sign up for
– To join the army is to **enlist**.
OPPOSITES leave, resign from

join NOUN
If you look hard, you can still see the join.
• joint, connection, link, mend, seam

joint ADJECTIVE
Putting on the show was a joint effort.
• combined, shared, common, communal, cooperative, united, collective, mutual, concerted
OPPOSITE individual

joke NOUN
Do you know any good jokes?
• jest, quip, witticism, wisecrack
(*informal*) gag, crack

joke VERB
Those two are always laughing and joking.
• jest, clown, have a laugh, make jokes, tease

jolly ADJECTIVE
He was in his usual, jolly mood.
• cheerful, good-humoured, happy, merry, joyful, cheery, bright, sunny, chirpy
(*informal*) upbeat
OPPOSITE gloomy

jolt VERB
The car jolted over the bumps in the road.
• jerk, lurch, judder, shudder, bump, bounce

jostle VERB
People jostled to get a better view.
• push, shove, elbow, barge, press, scramble, jockey

jot VERB
➤ **jot down**
I quickly jotted down a few ideas.
• make a note of, write down, take down, note, scribble

journal NOUN
❶ *She has had a few articles published in academic journals.*
• magazine, periodical, newspaper, review, bulletin, gazette
❷ *He kept a journal of the voyage.*
• diary, log, logbook, record, account, chronicle

journalist NOUN
She works as a journalist on the local paper.
• reporter, correspondent, columnist, writer

journey NOUN
The journey takes you through three countries.
• voyage, trip, expedition, passage, tour, route, travels

jovial ADJECTIVE
A jovial old man greeted them.
• cheerful, happy, jolly, merry, good-humoured, cheery
OPPOSITE sad

joy NOUN
My heart leaped with joy.
• happiness, joyfulness, delight, cheerfulness, gladness, glee, jubilation, rejoicing, bliss, ecstasy, elation, exultation, euphoria, rapture
OPPOSITE sorrow

joyful ADJECTIVE
The wedding was a joyful occasion.
• happy, cheerful, merry, joyous, jolly, good-humoured
OPPOSITE sad

judge NOUN
The judges could not agree on a winner.
• adjudicator, assessor, referee, umpire

judge VERB
❶ *The umpire judged that the ball was out.*
• rule, decide, decree, pronounce, adjudicate
❷ *Entries will be judged by a panel of experts.*
• assess, evaluate, appraise, rate, examine
❸ *She judged the helmet to be about a thousand years old.*
• gauge, estimate, reckon, deduce, guess

judgement NOUN
❶ *What is the judgement of the court?*
• decision, verdict, finding, ruling, pronouncement, decree
❷ *In my judgement, you're making a big mistake.*
• opinion, view, belief, assessment, appraisal, estimate
❸ *His comments show a lack of judgement.*
• wisdom, sense, common sense, understanding, perception, discrimination, discernment

juice NOUN
Add the juice of a lemon.
• liquid, fluid, sap, extract

jumble VERB
Please don't jumble the pages.
• muddle, mix up, mess up, disorganize, disorder, shuffle, tangle
OPPOSITES arrange, order

jumble NOUN
His clothes were in a jumble on the floor.
• mess, muddle, clutter, chaos, confusion, disarray, disorder
(informal) hotchpotch

jump VERB
❶ *Suddenly a deer jumped in front of us.*
• leap, spring, bound, hop, skip, prance, pounce
❷ *All the horses jumped the first hurdle.*
• leap over, vault, clear
❸ *The loud bang made everyone jump.*
• start, flinch, jolt

jump NOUN
❶ *With a jump she reached the other side.*
• leap, spring, bound, vault, hop, skip
❷ *I awoke with a jump.*
• start, jolt, jerk, spasm, judder
❸ *There has been a sharp jump in prices.*
• increase, rise, leap, surge
(*informal*) hike

junction NOUN
Turn left at the junction.
• intersection, crossroads, interchange

junior ADJECTIVE
❶ *I play for the junior hockey team.*
• younger
❷ *He's a junior officer in the army.*
• low-ranking, minor, lesser, subordinate
OPPOSITE senior

junk NOUN
The garage is full of old junk.
• rubbish, clutter, jumble, trash, garbage, waste, refuse, scrap, odds and ends

just ADJECTIVE
❶ *It was a just decision.*
• fair, impartial, unbiased, even-handed, honourable, upright, principled
OPPOSITES unjust, unfair

❷ *I think it was a just punishment for the crime.*
• deserved, fair, fitting, merited, appropriate, due, rightful, reasonable, proper
OPPOSITE undeserved

just ADVERB
❶ *The colour is just right.*
• exactly, precisely, absolutely
❷ *She was just a child then.*
• only, simply, merely
❸ *It's just after nine o'clock.*
• slightly, barely, scarcely

justice NOUN
❶ *We demand to be treated with justice.*
• fairness, justness, right, honesty, impartiality, even-handedness, equity, fair play
OPPOSITE injustice
❷ *They were tried in a court of justice.*
• law

justify VERB
How can you justify the cost?
• defend, excuse, account for, explain, vindicate

jut VERB
➤ jut out
A large nail jutted out from the wall.
• stick out, project, protrude, extend, overhang

juvenile ADJECTIVE
❶ *The bookshop sells a range of juvenile fiction.*
• children's, young people's
OPPOSITE adult
❷ *His jokes are really juvenile.*
• childish, babyish, immature
OPPOSITE mature

keen *ADJECTIVE*
❶ *Layla is a keen photographer.*
• enthusiastic, eager, fervent, avid, devoted, committed, motivated
OPPOSITE unenthusiastic
❷ *A carving knife should have a keen edge.*
• sharp, razor-sharp, honed
OPPOSITE blunt
❸ *Owls have keen eyesight.*
• sharp, acute, piercing
OPPOSITE poor
❹ *A keen wind was blowing from the east.*
• bitter, cold, icy, biting, penetrating
OPPOSITE mild
➤ **be keen on**
I'm not very keen on flying.
• be fond of, like, enjoy, be partial to (*informal*) be mad on, be into
IDIOM have a soft spot for

keep *VERB*
❶ *I've kept all of her letters.*
• save, conserve, preserve, retain, hang on to, hold on to, guard, store
❷ *It costs money to keep a pet.*
• support, maintain, provide for, pay for
❸ *She tried to keep calm.*
• stay, remain
❹ *I won't keep you long.*
• delay, detain, hold up, keep waiting
❺ *Why do you keep asking me questions?*
• persist in, go on, carry on, continue, insist on
❻ *The milk will keep until tomorrow.*
• last, be usable, stay good
❼ *Where do you keep the knives and forks?*
• store, house, put, stow
➤ **keep off**
❶ *Let's hope the rain keeps off.*
• stay away
❷ *Please keep off the grass.*
• avoid, stay away from, steer clear of
➤ **keep to**

❶ *Keep to the cycle path.*
• stay on, stay within
❷ *You must keep to your promise.*
• abide by, adhere to, hold to, carry out, make good, honour
➤ **keep something up**
Keep up the good work!
• carry on, continue, maintain

keeper *NOUN*
For years he was the keeper of the lighthouse.
• guardian, curator, custodian, caretaker, steward

key *NOUN*
At last I found the key to the riddle.
• answer, solution, explanation, clue

keyboard *NOUN*
For musical instruments see music.

kick *VERB*
❶ *He kicked the ball over the wall.*
• strike, boot, drive, send, propel, punt
❷ *The beetle was kicking its legs in the air.*
• wave, flail, swing, shake

kick *NOUN*
❶ *She gave the door a kick.*
• strike, boot, hit, blow, punt, flick
❷ (*informal*) *I still get a kick out of watching this film.*
• thrill, excitement, tingle (*informal*) buzz

kidnap *VERB*
This is a story about a boy who is kidnapped by bandits.
• abduct, capture, seize, carry off, snatch, take hostage

kill *VERB*
The victim was killed by an unknown poison.
• (*informal*) bump off, do away with (*old use*) slay
– To kill someone deliberately is to **murder** them.
– To kill someone brutally is to **butcher** them.
– To kill large numbers of people is to

massacre or slaughter them.
– To kill someone as a punishment is to
execute them or put them to death.
– To kill someone for political reasons is
to assassinate them.

kind NOUN
What kind of music do you like?
• sort, type, variety, style, category,
class, genre

kind ADJECTIVE
It was very kind of you to help me.
• kind-hearted, caring, good-natured,
kindly, affectionate, warm, genial,
loving, sweet, gentle, amiable, friendly,
generous, sympathetic, thoughtful,
obliging, considerate, understanding,
compassionate, unselfish, giving,
gracious, merciful, benevolent,
charitable, humane, neighbourly
OPPOSITES unkind, cruel

kindness NOUN
*The family treated me with great
kindness.*
• kind-heartedness, benevolence,
compassion, generosity, warmth,
affection, sympathy, good nature
OPPOSITE cruelty

king NOUN
Neptune is the King of the Sea.
• monarch, sovereign, ruler

kingdom NOUN
*One day the prince will rule over a vast
kingdom.*
• realm, monarchy, empire, dominion,
domain

kiss NOUN
She gave him a kiss on the cheek.
• (informal) peck

kit NOUN
❶ *The box contains an emergency repair
kit.*
• equipment, apparatus, materials,
paraphernalia, tools, tackle
❷ *I've forgotten my football kit.*
• clothing, clothes, outfit, strip
(informal) gear, get-up

kitchen NOUN
He worked in the kitchen of a large hotel.
– A small kitchen is a kitchenette.
– The kitchen on a ship or aircraft is the
galley.

knack NOUN
*You have a knack for taking unusual
photographs.*
• skill, talent, gift, flair, instinct

knead VERB
Knead the dough until it is smooth.
• work, press, squeeze, pummel

knew
past tense see know

knife NOUN
a sharp kitchen knife
• blade, cutter
– A large heavy knife used by a butcher
is a cleaver.
– A sharp thin knife used by a surgeon is
a scalpel.
SEE ALSO weapon

knight NOUN
a medieval knight
– A boy training to be a knight was first a
page and then a squire.
For tips on writing historical fiction see
historical.

knit VERB
❶ *The broken bones will eventually knit
together.*
• join, fuse, bond, unite, combine
❷ *Mrs Oliphant knitted her brows.*
• furrow, wrinkle, gather

knob NOUN
❶ *a old wooden door knob*
• handle
❷ *Melt a small knob of butter in a pan.*
• piece, bit, pat, lump, chunk

knobbly ADJECTIVE
I picked up a knobbly piece of wood.
• lumpy, bumpy, gnarled

knock *VERB*
❶ *Someone is knocking at the door.*
• rap, tap, pound, pummel, hammer, bang, thump
❷ *Don't knock your head on the way out.*
• bump, bang, bash, hit, strike, crack (*informal*) whack
SEE ALSO hit

knock *NOUN*
❶ *We heard a knock at the door.*
• rap, tap, pounding, pummelling, hammering, banging
❷ *The bike has had a few knocks over the years.*
• bump, bang, bash, hit, strike, blow, crash, collision

knot *NOUN*
❶ *I was combing the knots out of my hair.*
• tangle, snarl, lump, mass
❷ *We were surrounded by a knot of people.*
• cluster, group, huddle, circle, ring, band, bunch

knot *VERB*
Knot the two threads together.
• tie, bind, fasten, join, lash, entwine
OPPOSITE untie

know *VERB*
❶ *None of us knew how to speak Russian.*
• understand, comprehend, have knowledge of, be versed in
OPPOSITE be ignorant of

❷ *Do you know where we are?*
• recognize, realize, appreciate, be aware of
OPPOSITE be unaware of
❸ *I know her sister quite well.*
• be acquainted with, be familiar with, be a friend of
OPPOSITE be unfamiliar with

knowledge *NOUN*
❶ *She has a good knowledge of Italian.*
• understanding, grasp, command, mastery, familiarity (with), grounding (in)
– a slight knowledge of a subject is a **smattering** of it
❷ *There is much ancient knowledge contained in this book.*
• learning, wisdom, scholarship, erudition
(*informal*) know-how

knowledgeable *ADJECTIVE*
We were shown around by a knowledgeable guide.
• well-informed, learned, erudite, scholarly, educated, cultured
OPPOSITE ignorant
➤ **be knowledgeable about**
My dad is surprisingly knowledgeable about rap music.
• be well informed about, know a lot about, be familiar with
(*informal*) be up on

a
b
c
d
e
f
g
h
i
j
k
l
m
n
o
p
q
r
s
t
u
v
w
x
y
z

Ll

label *NOUN*
an address label
• tag, ticket, sticker, tab

label *VERB*
❶ *I've labelled all the boxes.*
• tag, mark, name, identify
❷ *He was soon labelled as a troublemaker.*
• categorize, classify, mark out, stamp, brand, dub

laborious *ADJECTIVE*
It was a laborious climb to the top of the hill.
• strenuous, arduous, hard, tough, difficult, stiff, tiring, exhausting, gruelling, punishing, back-breaking
OPPOSITES easy, effortless

labour *NOUN*
❶ *It took hours of painstaking labour to restore the painting.*
• work, effort, industry, exertion, toil, drudgery
(*informal*) slog
❷ *The factory had to take on extra labour.*
• workers, employees

labour *VERB*
Rescuers laboured through the night to reach survivors.
• work hard, exert yourself, toil
(*informal*) slave away

lack *NOUN*
I was suffering from lack of sleep.
• absence, shortage, scarcity, want, dearth, deficiency, shortfall
– A general lack of food is a **famine**.
– A general lack of water is a **drought**.
OPPOSITE abundance

lack *VERB*
The match lacked excitement.
• be without, be short of, be deficient in, be low on, miss
OPPOSITE possess

lady *NOUN*
see woman

lag *VERB*
One runner lagged behind the others.
• straggle, trail, fall behind, drop behind, dawdle

laid
past tense see lay

lair *NOUN*
The hunters tracked the beast back to its lair.
• den, refuge, shelter, hideout, hiding place

lake *NOUN*
We rowed across the lake.
• pond, pool
– A lake in Scotland is a **loch**.
– A salt-water lake is a **lagoon**.
– A lake used to supply water is a **reservoir**.

lame *ADJECTIVE*
❶ *a lame horse*
• disabled, crippled, limping, hobbling
❷ *What a lame excuse!*
• feeble, flimsy, poor, unconvincing, inadequate, weak, tame

lamp *NOUN*
see light

land *NOUN*
❶ *It's a large house, surrounded by several acres of land.*
• grounds, estate, property
❷ *The land here is good for growing strawberries.*
• ground, soil, earth
❸ *China is a land with an ancient history.*
• country, nation, state, region, territory, province, realm

land *VERB*
❶ *The plane landed exactly on time.*
• touch down, arrive
OPPOSITE take off
❷ *The ship will land at Dover.*
• dock, berth, come ashore, put in

❸ *How did these papers land on my desk?*
• arrive, turn up, end up, wind up, settle

landmark NOUN
❶ *The tower is a landmark that can be seen for miles around.*
• feature, sight, monument
❷ *This was a landmark in the history of science.*
• milestone, turning point, watershed

landscape NOUN
The best way to see the landscape is on foot or by bike.
• countryside, scenery, terrain, view, scene, outlook, prospect, panorama

---

W WRITING TIPS

DESCRIBING LANDSCAPE
Areas of landscape:

➤ bush	➤ prairie
➤ desert	➤ rainforest
➤ grassland	➤ savannah
➤ island	➤ steppe
➤ marsh	➤ swamp
➤ moor	➤ tundra
➤ peninsula	➤ wasteland
➤ plain	➤ wetland
➤ plateau	

Landscape features:

➤ beach	➤ gully
➤ bog	➤ hill
➤ brae	➤ hillock
➤ cave	➤ hillside
➤ cavern	➤ hummock
➤ copse	➤ knoll
➤ crag	➤ ledge
➤ crevasse	➤ meadow (*poetic* lea)
➤ crevice	
➤ dell	➤ mountain
➤ dune	➤ pass
➤ escarpment	➤ peak
➤ fell	➤ precipice
➤ fen	➤ range
➤ forest	➤ ridge
➤ glen	➤ rise
➤ gorge	➤ riverbank
➤ slope	➤ valley
➤ wood	

Areas of water:

➤ bay	➤ lake
➤ bayou	➤ loch
➤ billabong	➤ oasis
➤ cove	➤ pond
➤ creek	➤ pool
➤ estuary (*Scottish* firth)	➤ ravine
	➤ river
➤ fjord	➤ rivulet
➤ geyser	➤ sound
➤ glacier	➤ spring
➤ ice floe	➤ stream
➤ inlet	➤ waterhole
➤ lagoon	

Man-made features:

➤ bridge	➤ field
➤ canal	➤ furrow
➤ dam	➤ path
➤ dyke	➤ track

Adjectives:

➤ arid	➤ jagged
➤ bare	➤ lunar
➤ barren	➤ lush
➤ bleak	➤ mountainous
➤ craggy	➤ open
➤ enclosed	➤ patchwork
➤ exposed	➤ pitted
➤ fallow	➤ ploughed
➤ farmed	➤ rocky
➤ fenced	➤ rugged
➤ fertile	➤ shady
➤ furrowed	➤ sheltered
➤ hilly	➤ steep
➤ inhospitable	➤ sun-drenched
➤ irrigated	➤ wooded

---

lane NOUN
a narrow country lane
• track, path, trail, walk, passageway, alley

language NOUN
❶ *The scroll was written in an ancient language.*
• tongue, speech, dialect
(*informal*) lingo

A B C D E F G H I J K L M N O P Q R S T U V W X Y Z

❷ *In this piece of writing, the author uses very poetic language.*
• wording, phrasing, vocabulary, expression, style, turn of phrase, terminology

lap NOUN
❶ *Rachael was happy to have the baby on her lap for the evening.*
• knees, thighs
❷ *The runners were on the last lap of the race.*
• circuit, round, leg

lapse NOUN
❶ *I made a mistake because of a short lapse in concentration.*
• failure, error, fault, slip, flaw, weakness, shortcoming
❷ *After a lapse of six months work began again.*
• interval, gap, break, interlude, lull, pause

lapse VERB
❶ *Your membership has lapsed.*
• expire, become void, run out
❷ *He lapsed into unconsciousness.*
• drift, slip, slide, sink

large ADJECTIVE
❶ *Elephants have large skulls.*
• big, huge, enormous, gigantic, great, immense, giant, colossal, massive, mammoth, bulky, hefty, weighty, mighty (*informal*) whopping
❷ *I had a large helping of pudding.*
• ample, generous, plentiful, abundant, lavish
❸ *The living room is the largest room in the house.*
• spacious, extensive, sizeable, roomy
❹ *We were flying over a large area of desert.*
• wide, broad, extensive, widespread, vast
❺ *The programme received a large number of complaints.*
• considerable, substantial, high
OPPOSITES small, tiny
SEE ALSO **big**

largely ADVERB
The abbey was largely destroyed by fire.
• mainly, chiefly, mostly, principally, to a large extent

lash VERB
❶ *Rain was lashing against the window.*
• beat, pound, pelt, batter
❷ *The crocodile started lashing its tail.*
• swish, flick, whip
❸ *During the storm they lashed the boxes to the mast.*
• tie, fasten, bind, tether, knot, hitch

last ADJECTIVE
❶ *I have just started the last chapter.*
• final, closing, concluding, terminating, ultimate
OPPOSITE first
❷ *Did you see her last film?*
• latest, most recent
OPPOSITE next

last NOUN
➤ **at last**
At last someone was listening to me.
• finally, eventually, in the end

last VERB
❶ *Let's hope our luck will last.*
• carry on, continue, keep on, stay, remain, persist, endure, hold
OPPOSITES end, wear out
❷ *The plants won't last long without water.*
• hold out, keep going, live, survive

lasting ADJECTIVE
The Australian landscape left a lasting impression on me.
• enduring, abiding, long-lasting, long-lived, undying, everlasting, permanent, durable

late ADJECTIVE
❶ *My bus was late again.*
• delayed, overdue
OPPOSITES early, punctual, on time
❷ *There was a portrait of his late wife on the wall.*
• dead, deceased, departed, former

lately ADVERB
It has been a lot warmer lately.
• recently, latterly, of late

later ADJECTIVE
The mystery is revealed in a later chapter.
• subsequent, future, following,
succeeding, upcoming, ensuing, to come

later ADVERB
❶ *The letter arrived a week later.*
• afterwards, after that, subsequently
❷ *I'll phone you later.*
• in a while, at a later date, in the
future, in due course

latter ADJECTIVE
*We played better in the latter part of the
year.*
• later, more recent, second, last, final

laugh VERB
That story always makes me laugh.
• chuckle, chortle, guffaw, giggle, titter,
burst out laughing, roar with laughter,
fall about laughing
(*informal*) crack up,
IDIOMS be in stitches, have hysterics, be
rolling in the aisles
➤ **laugh at**
Many people laughed at Newton's ideas.
• make fun of, mock, ridicule, scoff at,
jeer at, deride, poke fun at
IDIOM (*informal*) take the mickey out of

laughter NOUN
*We heard laughter coming from the next
room.*
• laughing, amusement, humour,
hilarity, mirth, merriment

launch VERB
❶ *The space rocket will be launched next
month.*
• send off, set off, blast off
❷ *She sprinted up and launched a javelin
into the air.*
• throw, propel, hurl, pitch, fling, let fly,
fire, shoot
❸ *Their website was launched last year.*
• begin, start, set up, open, establish,
found, initiate, inaugurate, introduce

lavatory NOUN
a public lavatory
• toilet, bathroom, WC, convenience,
cloakroom, washroom
(*informal*) loo

lavish ADJECTIVE
❶ *The wedding was followed by a lavish
feast.*
• sumptuous, luxurious, extravagant,
opulent, rich, grand, splendid
OPPOSITES meagre, paltry
❷ *He had been spending lavish amounts
of money.*
• abundant, copious, generous, plentiful,
extravagant

law NOUN
a law against child labour
• regulation, statute, rule, ruling, decree,
edict, order, commandment, directive
– A law passed by parliament is an **act**.
– A proposed law to be discussed by
parliament is a **bill**.

lay VERB
❶ *She laid the book down carefully on
her desk.*
• put down, set down, place, position,
deposit, rest, leave
❷ *I was laying the table for dinner.*
• set out, set, arrange
❸ *He laid the blame on his sister.*
• assign, attach, attribute, ascribe, fix
❹ *We began to lay our plans for the
future.*
• devise, prepare, plan, conceive,
concoct, formulate, work out, hatch
➤ **lay something on**
Our hosts had laid on entertainment.
• provide, supply, furnish, prepare,
organize, line up

layer NOUN
❶ *The walls needed two layers of paint.*
• coat, coating, covering, film, skin,
blanket, sheet
❷ *You can see various layers of rock in
the cliff.*
• seam, stratum, tier, thickness

a
b
c
d
e
f
g
h
i
j
k
l
m
n
o
p
q
r
s
t
u
v
w
x
y
z

laze VERB

We spent all day lazing in the garden.
• be lazy, idle, loaf, lounge, relax, take it easy, lie about

lazy ADJECTIVE

He was too lazy to walk to the shops.
• idle, indolent, slothful, inactive, lethargic, sluggish

lead VERB

❶ *Our guide led us through the underground caves.*
• guide, conduct, escort, usher, steer, pilot, shepherd
OPPOSITE follow
❷ *She led from the start of the race.*
• be in front, be in the lead, head the field
❸ *He was chosen to lead the expedition.*
• be in charge of, direct, command, head, manage, supervise, preside over
(*informal*) head up
❹ *This path leads to the beach.*
• go, run, make its way
❺ *I prefer to lead a quiet life.*
• live, pass, spend, experience, enjoy
➤ **lead to**
Their carelessness led to the accident.
• result in, cause, bring about, give rise to, occasion, generate, spark

lead NOUN

❶ *Our team were in the lead.*
• first place, front position
❷ *Detectives are following up a new lead.*
• clue, pointer, tip-off
❸ *The older students provide a lead for the younger ones.*
• example, model, pattern, guidance, leadership, direction
❹ *My sister is playing the lead in the school play.*
• principal part, starring role, title role
❺ *Keep your dog on a lead.*
• leash, strap, chain, tether, rein
❻ *The toaster needs a new lead.*
• cable, flex, wire

leader NOUN

The leader of the gang was called Redbeard.
• head, chief, commander, captain, director, principal, ruler
(*informal*) boss
– The leader of a group of wrongdoers is the **ringleader**.
OPPOSITE follower

leaf NOUN

❶ *the leaf of a maple tree*
– A mass of leaves is **foliage** or **greenery**.
❷ *A single leaf had been torn from the book.*
• page, sheet

leak NOUN

❶ *The plumber came to mend a leak in one of the pipes.*
• crack, hole, opening, split, rupture, perforation
– A leak in a tyre is a **puncture**.
❷ *We had a gas leak.*
• escape, discharge, leakage, drip

leak VERB

❶ *Gallons of oil leaked from the tanker.*
• escape, seep, ooze, drain, drip, dribble, trickle
❷ *Details of the plan were leaked to the press.*
• reveal, disclose, divulge, pass on, let out, make known, make public

lean VERB

❶ *Two boys were leaning against the front wall.*
• recline, rest, prop yourself, support yourself
❷ *The Tower of Pisa leans to one side.*
• slope, tilt, tip, incline, slant, list, bank

lean ADJECTIVE

a dancer with a strong, lean figure
• slim, slender, thin, trim, wiry
OPPOSITES fat, plump
For tips on describing bodies see **body**.

leap VERB

❶ *The dog leapt in the air to catch the ball.*
• jump, spring, bound, vault
❷ *The price of fuel has leapt in the last*

few months.
• rise sharply, jump, soar, rocket, shoot up

leap NOUN
With one leap he cleared the stream.
• jump, spring, bound, vault

learn VERB
❶ We have started to learn French.
• acquire, master, pick up, absorb (informal) get the hang of
❷ I need to learn the words of this song.
• learn by heart, memorize, master
❸ I later learned that we had met before.
• discover, find out, hear, gather, grasp

learner NOUN
The swimming class is for learners only.
• beginner, starter, novice
– Someone learning things at school or college is a **pupil** or **student**.
– Someone learning a trade is an **apprentice** or **trainee**.
OPPOSITE expert

learning NOUN
The city became a centre of learning.
• study, education, knowledge, erudition, scholarship

least ADJECTIVE
❶ Who got the least number of points?
• fewest, lowest
❷ I found the house without the least difficulty.
• slightest, smallest, tiniest

leave VERB
❶ We'll be leaving tomorrow morning.
• go, go away, depart, withdraw, take your leave, go out, set off, say goodbye (informal) take off, disappear
OPPOSITE arrive
❷ She left the room suddenly.
• exit, go out of, depart from, quit, vacate
OPPOSITE enter
❸ Don't leave me here on my own!
• abandon, desert, forsake
❹ You can leave your coat in here.
• place, position, put down, set down, deposit

❺ My sister has left her job at the bank.
• give up, quit, resign from, step down from
❻ I'll leave all the arrangements to you.
• pass on, hand over, refer, entrust
❼ She left all her money to charity.
• bequeath, hand down, will, endow
➤ leave someone or something out
You've left out the best part of the story.
• miss out, omit, exclude, overlook, pass over, skip, drop

leave NOUN
❶ The doctor is away on leave for two weeks.
• holiday, vacation, time off
❷ Will you give me leave to speak?
• permission, authorization, consent, approval

lecture NOUN
❶ There is a lecture on dinosaurs at the museum today.
• talk, speech, address, lesson, presentation
❷ He got a stern lecture about being late.
• reprimand, warning, scolding (informal) telling-off, talking-to, dressing-down

led
past tense see lead

ledge NOUN
She was standing on a narrow ledge of rock.
• shelf, projection
– A ledge under a window is a **windowsill**.

left ADJECTIVE
on the left side of the road
• left-hand
– The left side of a ship when you face forwards is the **port** side.
OPPOSITE right

leg NOUN
❶ Callum fell and bruised his leg.
see body

a
b
c
d
e
f
g
h
i
j
k
l
m
n
o
p
q
r
s
t
u
v
w
x
y
z

❷ We were on the final leg of the journey.
• part, stage, section, phase, stretch

legal ADJECTIVE
Is it legal to download this file?
• lawful, legitimate, within the law, permissible, permitted, allowed
OPPOSITE illegal

legend NOUN
the legend of the Loch Ness Monster
• myth, story, folk tale, fairy tale, fable, saga, tradition
For tips on writing fantasy fiction see fantasy.

legendary ADJECTIVE
❶ the legendary city of Camelot
• mythical, mythological, fabulous, fabled, fairy-tale
OPPOSITE real
❷ Her cooking is legendary.
• famous, well-known, celebrated, renowned, acclaimed

legible ADJECTIVE
The inscription is now barely legible.
• readable, clear, distinct, neat
OPPOSITE illegible

legitimate ADJECTIVE
Many people believed he had a legitimate claim to the throne.
• legal, proper, rightful, authorized, permitted

leisure NOUN
His busy life leaves little time for leisure.
• free time, spare time, relaxation, recreation, rest

leisurely ADJECTIVE
We went for a leisurely stroll in the park.
• unhurried, relaxed, relaxing, gentle, easy, restful, slow
OPPOSITE fast

lend VERB
❶ Could you lend me some money?
• loan, advance, let someone have
OPPOSITE borrow

❷ Moonlight lent an air of mystery to the scene.
• give, add, impart, bestow, confer, contribute

length NOUN
❶ My heart sank when I saw the length of the queue.
• extent, size, distance, expanse, range, span
❷ We only had to wait a short length of time.
• period, duration, space, stretch

lengthen VERB
❶ Maya deliberately lengthened her stride.
• extend, make longer, elongate, stretch
OPPOSITE shorten
❷ The afternoon shadows began to lengthen.
• draw out, get longer, stretch out

lengthy ADJECTIVE
There was a lengthy argument over who was to blame.
• long, drawn-out, extended, prolonged, protracted, time-consuming, long-running
OPPOSITES short, brief

lenient ADJECTIVE
I think the referee was too lenient.
• easy-going, soft-hearted, tolerant, forgiving, indulgent, charitable, merciful
OPPOSITE strict

lessen VERB
❶ He was given medicine to lessen the pain.
• minimize, reduce, relieve
❷ Her fear gradually lessened.
• diminish, decrease, dwindle, subside, weaken, ease off, tail off, die down, ebb, wane, recede
OPPOSITE increase

lesson NOUN
I have a piano lesson every week.
• class, period, session, tutorial, instruction

let *VERB*

❶ *My parents would not let me go on the trip.*
• allow, permit, give permission to, consent to, agree to, authorize
OPPOSITE forbid

❷ *A microscope lets you see tiny objects.*
• enable, allow, equip

❸ *Our neighbours are letting their house for the summer.*
• lease, rent out, hire out

➤ **let someone off**
We were let off classes for the day.
• excuse from, exempt from, spare from

➤ **let something out**
Suddenly Molly let out a scream.
• utter, emit, give, produce, express

➤ **let up**
The rain didn't let up.
• ease, subside, abate, slacken, diminish

lethal *ADJECTIVE*

He had been given a lethal dose of poison.
• deadly, fatal, mortal, life-threatening, poisonous, toxic

letter *NOUN*

❶ *The sign was written in large letters.*
• character, symbol, sign, figure
– The letters a, e, i, o, u and sometimes y are **vowels**.
– The other letters are **consonants**.

❷ *Did you remember to sign your letter?*
• note, message, communication
– Letters people send each other are **correspondence**.

level *ADJECTIVE*

❶ *Put the tent up on a level piece of ground.*
• even, flat, horizontal, plane, smooth, flush
OPPOSITE uneven

❷ *At half-time the scores were level.*
• equal, even, the same, matching, tied, drawn
IDIOMS all square, neck and neck

level *NOUN*

❶ *The water rose to a dangerous level.*
• height, position

❷ *The lift takes you up to the sixth level.*
• floor, storey, tier

❸ *She has reached a high level of skill.*
• grade, standard, stage, rank, degree

lever *VERB*

Slowly, they levered open the coffin.
• prise, wrench, force

liable *ADJECTIVE*

❶ *You're liable to make mistakes when you're tired.*
• likely, inclined, disposed, prone, apt, given
OPPOSITE unlikely

❷ *We are not liable for any loss or damage.*
• responsible, answerable, accountable

liberal *ADJECTIVE*

❶ *Apply a liberal amount of hair gel.*
• generous, abundant, copious, ample, plentiful, lavish, unstinting
OPPOSITES meagre, miserly

❷ *She has a liberal attitude towards such things.*
• broad-minded, open-minded, tolerant, permissive, enlightened, lenient, easy-going
OPPOSITE strict

liberate *VERB*

The prisoners were liberated at the end of the war.
• free, set free, release, emancipate, discharge, let go, set loose
OPPOSITE imprison

liberty *NOUN*

❶ *The king granted the prisoners their liberty.*
• liberation, release, emancipation
OPPOSITES imprisonment, slavery

❷ *You have the liberty to come and go as you please.*
• freedom, independence
OPPOSITE constraint

licence *NOUN*

He has a licence to practise as a vet.
• permit, certificate, authorization, warrant, pass

A
B
C
D
E
F
G
H
I
J
K
L
M
N
O
P
Q
R
S
T
U
V
W
X
Y
Z

license *VERB*
Are you licensed to drive this vehicle?
• permit, allow, authorize, entitle, certify

lid *NOUN*
Can you help me get the lid off this jar?
• cover, covering, cap, top

lie *NOUN*
She can't help telling lies.
• untruth, falsehood, fib, fabrication, deception
(*informal*) whopper
OPPOSITE truth

lie *VERB*
❶ *Why would he lie about his past?*
• tell a lie, fib, bluff
OPPOSITE tell the truth
❷ *He was lying on the grass.*
• recline, stretch out, sprawl, lounge, rest, repose
– To lie face downwards is to **be prone** or **be prostrate**.
– To lie face upwards is to **be supine**.
❸ *The village lies ten miles from the coast.*
• be sited, be situated, be located, be placed, be found

life *NOUN*
❶ *I owe you my life.*
• existence, being, survival
❷ *Our dog leads a very easy life.*
• way of life, lifestyle
❸ *You seem to be full of life today!*
• energy, liveliness, vigour, vitality, vivacity, spirit, sprightliness, animation, exuberance, dynamism
❹ *I'm reading a life of Charles Dickens.*
• life story, biography, autobiography
❺ *The battery has a life of two years.*
• duration, lifetime, lifespan

lift *VERB*
❶ *The box is too heavy to lift.*
• raise, pick up, pull up, elevate, hoist
❷ *One by one, the balloons lifted off the ground.*
• rise, ascend, soar
❸ *The ban has finally been lifted.*
• remove, withdraw, cancel, revoke

light *NOUN*

WORD WEB

Some kinds of natural light:

➤ daylight	➤ sunlight
➤ moonlight	➤ twilight
➤ starlight	

Sources of artificial light:

➤ bulb	➤ lantern
➤ candle	➤ laser
➤ chandelier	➤ LED or
➤ flambeau	light-emitting
➤ floodlight	diode
➤ fluorescent	➤ neon light
lamp	➤ searchlight
➤ headlamp or	➤ spotlight
headlight	➤ street light
➤ lamp	➤ torch

WRITING TIPS

DESCRIBING LIGHT
Effects of light:

➤ beam	➤ glitter
➤ blaze	➤ glow
➤ burn	➤ lustre
➤ dazzle	➤ radiance
➤ flame	➤ ray
➤ flare	➤ reflection
➤ flash	➤ shaft
➤ flicker	➤ shimmer
➤ glare	➤ shine
➤ gleam	➤ sparkle
➤ glimmer	➤ twinkle
➤ glint	➤ wink
➤ glisten	

Adjectives:

➤ bright	➤ diffused
➤ brilliant	➤ dim
➤ dappled	➤ harsh

➤ luminous   ➤ soft
➤ lustrous   ➤ sparkling
➤ muted   ➤ strong
➤ pale   ➤ warm
➤ radiant   ➤ weak
➤ scintillating

light *ADJECTIVE*
❶ *Artists like to work in light and airy studios.*
• bright, well-lit, illuminated, sunny
OPPOSITES dim, gloomy
❷ *My new scarf is a light shade of grey.*
• pale, faint, delicate, subtle
OPPOSITES dark, deep
❸ *The cart was only carrying a light load.*
• lightweight, portable, weightless, slight
OPPOSITES heavy, weighty
❹ *A light breeze rippled the water.*
• gentle, faint, slight, soft
OPPOSITES strong, forceful
❺ *We ate a light breakfast before setting out.*
• small, modest, simple, insubstantial
OPPOSITES heavy, substantial
❻ *Are you well enough to do some light housework?*
• easy, undemanding, effortless
OPPOSITES heavy, demanding
❼ *I bought a magazine for some light reading.*
• undemanding, entertaining, lightweight, superficial
OPPOSITE serious

light *VERB*
❶ *Let's light the candles on your cake.*
• ignite, set alight, set fire to, kindle, switch on
OPPOSITE extinguish
❷ *The stage was lit by a bright spotlight.*
• light up, illuminate, brighten, shine on, shed light on
OPPOSITE darken

like *VERB*

OVERUSED WORD

❶ To **like** a person, animal or possession:

➤ admire   ➤ cherish
➤ adore   ➤ esteem
➤ love   ➤ hold dear
➤ be attached to   ➤ be attracted to
➤ be fond of   ➤ be interested in
➤ care for

(informal) fancy

IDIOM have a soft spot for

He is very attached to his new puppy.

❷ To **like** a taste, book, film, etc.:

➤ be partial to   ➤ be keen on
➤ have a taste for   ➤ enjoy
➤ have a liking for ➤ appreciate
➤ have a prefer-   ➤ prefer
  ence for

(informal) be mad on

My mum is partial to chocolate cake.

I used to enjoy fantasy, but now I prefer science fiction.

OPPOSITE dislike

❸ To **like** doing something:

➤ delight in   ➤ relish
➤ take pleasure in   ➤ savour
➤ enjoy   ➤ revel in

My brother delights in telling rude jokes.

like *PREPOSITION*
He made a noise like a strangled cat.
• similar to, the same as, resembling, identical to, akin to, in the manner of
OPPOSITE unlike

likeable *ADJECTIVE*
The main character is a likeable lad called Seth.
• pleasant, appealing, attractive, agreeable, amiable, engaging, charming

a b c d e f g h i j k l m n o p q r s t u v w x y z

293

likely ADJECTIVE

❶ *Heavy rain and high winds are likely this afternoon.*
• probable, expected, anticipated, predictable, foreseeable
OPPOSITE unlikely

❷ *I can think of a more likely reason for their defeat.*
• plausible, credible, reasonable, feasible, believable
OPPOSITE implausible

likeness NOUN

❶ *There is a strong likeness between the two sisters.*
• resemblance, similarity, correspondence
OPPOSITE difference

❷ *This photo is a good likeness of my grandfather.*
• image, representation, picture, portrait, depiction, portrayal

liking NOUN

She has a liking for large earrings and flowery hats.
• fondness, taste, love, passion, affection, preference, partiality, penchant
OPPOSITES dislike, distaste

limb NOUN
see **body**

limit NOUN

❶ *This stone marks the limit of the old city.*
• border, boundary, edge, perimeter, frontier

❷ *The course has a limit of twenty places.*
• maximum, restriction, threshold, ceiling, cut-off point
– A limit on time is a **deadline** or **time limit**.

limit VERB

I had to limit the invitations to my party.
• put a limit on, restrict, ration, curb, cap

limited ADJECTIVE

❶ *We only had a limited supply of water.*
• restricted, short, inadequate, insufficient, rationed, finite, fixed
OPPOSITE limitless

❷ *It was hard to move about in the limited space.*
• small, cramped, restricted, narrow, tight, confined

limp VERB

She limped off the pitch with a twisted ankle.
• hobble, hop, falter, stumble

limp ADJECTIVE

The child's hand was quite limp and cold.
• floppy, drooping, droopy, sagging, wilting, soft, flabby, slack
OPPOSITES rigid, firm

line NOUN

❶ *I drew a pencil line across the page.*
• stroke, rule, dash, underline, stripe, strip, streak, band, bar, belt
– A line cut into a surface is a **groove**, **score** or **scratch**.
– A line on a person's skin is a **wrinkle**.
– A deep groove or wrinkle is a **furrow**.
– A line on fabric is a **crease**.

❷ *There was a long line of people at the bus stop.*
• queue, row, file, column, rank, procession, chain
– A line of schoolchildren walking in pairs is a **crocodile**.

❸ *Clothes were drying on a washing line.*
• cord, rope, string, thread, wire, cable, flex, lead

linger VERB

❶ *The smell of burning lingered in the air.*
• continue, remain, stay, last, persist, endure
OPPOSITE disappear

❷ *We mustn't linger any longer.*
• hang about, wait about, loiter, dawdle, dally, delay
(*old use*) tarry
OPPOSITE hurry

link NOUN
The two schools have close links with each other.
• relationship, association, connection, bond, tie

link VERB
❶ *The two trains were linked together.*
• connect, attach, fasten, join, couple, hook up
OPPOSITE separate
❷ *Police are linking this death with a series of other murders.*
• connect, associate, relate, bracket

lion NOUN
Lions usually stalk their prey.
– A female lion is a **lioness**.
– A young lion is a **cub**.
– A group of lions is a **pride**.
– The fur collar on a male lion is its **mane**.
SEE ALSO cat
For tips on describing animals see **animal**.

liquid NOUN
Stir the liquid until it thickens.
• fluid, solution, juice, liquor
– The liquid inside a plant is **sap**.
OPPOSITE solid

liquid ADJECTIVE
Pour the liquid jelly into a mould.
• runny, watery, fluid, flowing, running, sloppy
– To make food into a liquid or pulp is to **liquidize** it.
– To make something liquid by heating it is to **melt** it.
– Liquid metal or rock is **molten**.
OPPOSITE solid

list NOUN
I'll add your name to the list.
• register, roll, rota, catalogue, directory, inventory, checklist
– A list of topics mentioned in a book is an **index**.
– A list of things to choose from is a **menu**.

list VERB
❶ *She spent an hour listing the books in in alphabetical order.*
• record, register, write down, catalogue,

index, itemize
❷ *The ship was listing dangerously to one side.*
• lean, tilt, tip, pitch, incline, slant, slope

listen VERB
Do you think anyone is listening?
• pay attention, attend
IDIOMS keep your ears open, be all ears
– To listen secretly to a private conversation is to **eavesdrop**.
➤ **listen to someone**
Nobody ever listens to me.
• pay attention to, take notice of, attend to, heed

literature NOUN
The publisher specializes in children's literature.
• writing, books
For types of literature see **drama, fiction, poetry**.

litter NOUN
The street was covered with litter.
• rubbish, refuse, waste, garbage, junk, clutter, mess

litter VERB
The desk was littered with scraps of paper.
• scatter, strew, clutter

little ADJECTIVE

OVERUSED WORD

❶ **Little in size, scale:**

➤ small	➤ mini
➤ tiny	➤ miniature
➤ minute	➤ minuscule
➤ petite	➤ midget
➤ compact	➤ diminutive

(*informal*) teeny, titchy
(*Scottish*) wee

Microbes are so minute they can only be seen through a microscope.

OPPOSITES big, large

Side alphabet tabs: a b c d e f g h i j k l m n o p q r s t u v w x y z

② Little in age:

> young   > small

(*Scottish*) wee

My granny lived in India when she was young.

OPPOSITES old, big

③ A little time, a little while:

> brief   > passing
> short   > cursory
> fleeting

It was a short while before our friends arrived.

OPPOSITES lengthy, long

④ A little problem:

> slight   > insignificant
> minor   > trivial
> unimportant   > trifling

I have a slight problem with my bike.

OPPOSITE major

⑤ Little left of something:

> hardly any   > paltry
> insufficient   > scarcely any
> meagre

There was scarcely any food left by the time we arrived.

OPPOSITES ample, plenty

⑥ A little amount of something:

> some   > a touch of
> a bit of   > a dash of
> a drop of   > a pinch of
> a spot of

Would you like a drop of milk in your tea?

OPPOSITES plenty of, lots of

⑦ A little:

> a bit   > somewhat
> slightly   > to some degree
> rather

I'm feeling slightly tired now.

live VERB

① *Giant tortoises can live for over a hundred years.*
• stay alive, survive, exist
OPPOSITE die
② *She has lived a happy life.*
• lead, experience, go through, spend, pass
③ *Where do you live?*
• reside, dwell
> live in
We used to live in a basement flat.
• inhabit, occupy, dwell in, reside in
> live on
Some whales live entirely on plankton.
• eat, feed on, subsist on

live ADJECTIVE

The fishermen caught a live octopus in their nets.
• alive, living, breathing
OPPOSITE dead

lively ADJECTIVE

① *The toddlers were in a lively mood.*
• active, energetic, vigorous, dynamic, animated, spirited, vibrant, vivacious, buoyant, exuberant, sprightly, frisky, chirpy, perky
IDIOM full of beans
OPPOSITE inactive
② *The city centre is always lively at night.*
• busy, bustling, crowded, exciting, buzzing, vibrant
OPPOSITES quiet, dead

livid ADJECTIVE

He was livid when he saw the damage to his bike.
• angry, furious, fuming, incensed, enraged, seething, raging

living ADJECTIVE

① *Miss Cooper had no living relatives.*
• alive, surviving
OPPOSITES dead, deceased
② *Basque is a living language.*
• current, existing, in use
OPPOSITES dead, extinct

living NOUN

① *He makes a living from painting.*
• income, livelihood, subsistence

❷ *What does she do for a living?*
• job, occupation, profession, trade, career

load NOUN
❶ *Camels can carry heavy loads.*
• burden, weight
❷ *The lorry was picking up a load for delivery.*
• cargo, consignment, goods, freight
➤ **loads of**
(*informal*) *We had loads of time to spare.*
• plenty of, lots of
(*informal*) tons of, masses of

load VERB
❶ *We loaded the suitcases into the car.*
• pack, stack, pile, heap, stow
❷ *The men were loading a van with furniture.*
• fill up, pack, stock
❸ *She arrived loaded with shopping bags.*
• weigh down, burden, saddle, encumber

loan NOUN
They needed a loan from the bank.
• advance
– A system which allows you to pay for something later is **credit**.
– A loan to buy a house is a **mortgage**.

loath ADJECTIVE
I'm loath to ask for their help again.
• reluctant, unwilling, disinclined
OPPOSITES willing, keen

loathe VERB
My brother loathes the colour pink.
• hate, detest, despise, can't bear, can't stand
(*formal*) abhor
OPPOSITES love, adore

local ADJECTIVE
There are story-telling sessions at our local library.
• neighbourhood, community, nearby, neighbouring

locate VERB
❶ *I can't locate the book you asked for.*
• find, discover, track down, detect,

pinpoint, unearth
IDIOM lay your hands on
OPPOSITE lose
❷ *The gallery is located in the city centre.*
• place, position, site, situate, set up, establish, station, base

location NOUN
What is the exact location of the submarine?
• position, situation, place, site, spot, setting, whereabouts, locality, locale

lock NOUN
❶ *There was a heavy lock on the door.*
• fastening, clasp, catch, padlock, bolt, latch
❷ *The princess gave him a lock of her hair.*
• tress, curl, tuft, wisp, coil, ringlet

lock VERB
Remember to lock the door.
• fasten, secure, bolt, latch, padlock, chain, seal

lodge VERB
❶ *Where are you lodging at present?*
• reside, stay, board, live, dwell
(*North American*) room
❷ *The animals are lodged indoors in the winter.*
• house, accommodate, board, put up
❸ *The bullet had lodged in his chest.*
• get caught, become stuck, jam, wedge, fix, embed

log NOUN
Keep a log of your computer time.
• record, register, account, tally, diary, journal, logbook

logical ADJECTIVE
❶ *Holmes used logical methods of deduction.*
• rational, analytical, methodical, systematic, sound, valid
OPPOSITE illogical
❷ *That would be the logical thing to do.*
• sensible, reasonable, natural, understandable

lone ADJECTIVE
A lone figure appeared on the horizon.
• single, solitary, unaccompanied, isolated, solo

lonely ADJECTIVE
❶ *I felt lonely in the house by myself.*
• alone, friendless, lonesome, abandoned, neglected, forlorn, forsaken
❷ *She took me to a lonely place by the river.*
• deserted, isolated, remote, secluded, out-of-the-way

long ADJECTIVE
There was a long and awkward silence.
• lengthy, prolonged, extended, extensive, long-lasting, drawn-out, interminable
OPPOSITES short, brief

long VERB
➤ **long for something**
We were all longing for a rest.
• yearn for, crave, wish for, desire, hunger for, pine for, hanker after, itch for, be desperate for
(*informal*) be dying for

look VERB
❶ *A woman was looking in our direction.*
• gaze, peer, glance, watch, stare
❷ *You look a bit sad.*
• appear, seem, come across as
➤ **look after someone or something**
Would you look after my cat while I'm away?
• care for, take care of, tend, mind, watch over, guard, protect
IDIOM keep an eye on
– To look after sick people is to **nurse** them.
➤ **look for something**
I spent ages looking for my keys.
• search for, hunt for, seek
➤ **look into something**
We've been looking into our family history.
• investigate, inquire into, find out about, examine, explore
➤ **look out for something**
Look out for sharp bends in the road.
• beware of, watch out for, be careful of,

pay attention to
IDIOM keep an eye open for
➤ **look something up**
If you don't know what a word means, look it up in the dictionary.
• find, search for, track down, research, locate

OVERUSED WORD

❶ To look at something:

> watch
> observe
> view
> regard

> contemplate
> inspect
> take in
> eye

He inspected himself in the mirror.

❷ To look quickly:

> glance
> glimpse
> peek

> peep
> sneak a look

I thought I glimpsed the fin of a shark.

❸ To look carefully, look intently:

> stare
> peer
> squint
> study
> scrutinize

> examine
> inspect
> take a good
>   look at

She knelt down and peered at the footprints.

❹ To look angrily:

> glare
> glower
> grimace

> frown
> scowl

Mr Davies merely glowered at us in silence.

❺ To look in amazement:

> gape
> stare wide-eyed

> stare open-
>   mouthed
> goggle

(*informal*) gawk, gawp
IDIOM have your eyes on stalks
I found myself gaping in genuine surprise.

look NOUN
① *Take a look at this website.*
• glance, gaze, glimpse, peek, peep, sight, view, squint
(*informal*) eyeful
② *I don't like the look of this place.*
• appearance, air, aspect, bearing, manner
③ *The girl turned to us with a look of horror.*
• expression, face, countenance

lookout NOUN
Lookouts were posted along the wall.
• sentry, guard, sentinel, watchman

loom VERB
① *A figure loomed out of the mist.*
• appear, emerge, arise, take shape
② *A sheer cliff face loomed before us.*
• rise, tower, stand out, hang over

loop NOUN
Make a loop in the string.
• coil, ring, hoop, circle, noose, bend, curl, twist, kink

loop VERB
Loop the thread around your finger.
• coil, wind, twist, curl, bend, turn, snake

loose ADJECTIVE
① *Some of the roof tiles are loose.*
• insecure, unfixed, movable, unsteady, shaky, wobbly
OPPOSITES firm, secure
② *She likes to wear her hair loose.*
• untied, free, down
OPPOSITE tied
③ *These jeans are loose around the waist.*
• slack, baggy, roomy, loose-fitting
OPPOSITE tight
④ *The chickens wander loose about the farm.*
• free, at large, at liberty, on the loose, unconfined, unrestricted
OPPOSITE confined
⑤ *Here is a loose translation of the poem.*
• rough, general, vague, inexact
OPPOSITES exact, literal

loosen VERB
① *Can you loosen this knot?*
• undo, unfasten, untie, free, loose, slacken
OPPOSITE tighten
② *I loosened my grip on the rope.*
• relax, slacken, ease, release, let go
OPPOSITE tighten

loot NOUN
Under the floorboards was a bag full of stolen loot.
• spoils, plunder, stolen goods, booty, haul

loot VERB
Rioters looted the shops.
• raid, ransack, rob, steal from, pillage, plunder

lorry NOUN
see vehicle

lose VERB
① *I've lost one of my gloves.*
• mislay, misplace
OPPOSITE find
② *By now, we had lost a lot of time.*
• waste, squander, let pass
③ *Our team lost 3-0.*
• be defeated, get beaten, suffer a defeat
OPPOSITE win

loss NOUN
① *She is suffering from a loss of memory.*
• failure, disappearance, deprivation, depletion
② *I want to report the loss of my phone.*
• disappearance, misplacement, theft
③ *They were devastated by the loss of their dear friend.*
• death, decease, passing

lost ADJECTIVE
① *I eventually found my lost keys.*
• missing, mislaid, misplaced
OPPOSITE found
② *He appeared to be lost in thought.*
• absorbed, engrossed, preoccupied, deep, immersed, rapt

a
b
c
d
e
f
g
h
i
j
k
l
m
n
o
p
q
r
s
t
u
v
w
x
y
z

lot NOUN

We are having another lot of visitors this weekend.
• group, batch, set, crowd, collection

➤ **a lot of**

These patients need a lot of care.
• a large amount of, a good deal of, a great deal of, plenty of

➤ **lots of**

I got lots of cards on my birthday.
• a great number of, many, numerous, plenty, plenty of, a wealth of, an abundance of, galore
(*informal*) loads of, tons of, masses of, stacks of, oodles of, hundreds of, umpteen

The word galore comes after a noun: a film that offers action and stunts galore.

loud ADJECTIVE

❶ *That music is too loud!*
• noisy, blaring, booming, deafening, resounding, thunderous, penetrating, piercing, ear-splitting
– A noise which is loud enough to hear is **audible**.
OPPOSITES quiet, soft

❷ *He was wearing a very loud shirt.*
• bright, gaudy, garish, showy
(*informal*) flashy
OPPOSITES muted, subdued

lounge VERB

She lounged on the sofa all morning.
• laze, idle, loaf, relax, take it easy, sprawl, slouch, lie around, loll

lovable ADJECTIVE

Our neighbours have a lovable new cat.
• adorable, dear, sweet, charming, likeable, lovely, appealing, attractive, cuddly, enchanting, endearing
OPPOSITE hateful

love NOUN

❶ *the love between Romeo and Juliet*
• adoration, infatuation, affection, fondness, attachment, tenderness, passion, warmth, intimacy

❷ *She had a love of the outdoors.*
• liking, fondness, taste, passion, enthusiasm, keenness

❸ *Emma was his true love.*
• sweetheart, beloved, loved one, darling, dearest

love VERB

❶ *It's obvious that those two love each other.*
• be in love with, adore, care for, cherish, hold dear, treasure, worship, idolize, be infatuated with, be besotted with, be smitten with
(*informal*) be crazy about
– A relationship between two people who love each other is a **romance**.

❷ *My brother loves anything to do with football.*
• like, be fond of, be partial to, have a weakness for, have a passion for, delight in, enjoy
IDIOMS have a soft spot for, (*informal*) have a thing about
OPPOSITE hate

lovely ADJECTIVE

 OVERUSED WORD

❶ **A lovely person:**

➤ charming
➤ delightful
➤ lovable
➤ likeable
➤ dear
➤ sweet
➤ enchanting
➤ endearing
➤ adorable

She is a charming girl.

❷ **A lovely day, lovely weather:**

➤ fine
➤ glorious
➤ bright
➤ fair
➤ sunny

It was glorious weather for a bike ride.

❸ **A lovely view:**

➤ scenic
➤ picturesque
➤ pleasing
➤ glorious
➤ splendid

You get a splendid view from the cable car.

4 A lovely experience, a lovely time:

➤ pleasant   ➤ delightful
➤ pleasing   ➤ marvellous
➤ enjoyable   ➤ wonderful

(*informal*) fantastic, terrific, brilliant, smashing

I had an enjoyable time doing absolutely nothing!

5 Looking lovely:

➤ appealing   ➤ pretty
➤ attractive   ➤ glamorous
➤ good-looking   ➤ alluring
➤ beautiful   ➤ ravishing

(*informal*) cute

(*Scottish*) bonny

You look particularly attractive in that hat.

lover NOUN
➊ *Some lovers send each other Valentine cards.*
• boyfriend, girlfriend, sweetheart, beloved
➋ *He is a great lover of musicals.*
• admirer, fan, devotee, enthusiast

loving ADJECTIVE
She grew up in a loving family.
• affectionate, kind, friendly, warm, tender, fond, devoted, passionate
OPPOSITE unfriendly

low ADJECTIVE
➊ *The garden is surrounded by a low wall.*
• short, shallow, sunken, squat
OPPOSITES high, tall
➋ *You can tell from his uniform that he was a soldier of low rank.*
• junior, inferior, lowly, modest, humble
OPPOSITES high, senior
➌ *This work is of low quality.*
• poor, inferior, substandard, unsatisfactory
OPPOSITES high, superior
➍ *The tuba plays low notes.*
• bass, deep, sonorous
OPPOSITE high

➎ *We spoke in low whispers.*
• quiet, soft, muted, subdued, muffled, hushed
OPPOSITE loud

lower VERB
➊ *Some shops have lowered their prices.*
• reduce, cut, drop, decrease, lessen, bring down
(*informal*) slash
➋ *Please lower your voices.*
• quieten, soften, turn down, tone down, muffle, hush
➌ *At the end of the ceremony, soldiers lower the flag.*
• take down, let down, dip, let fall
OPPOSITE raise

loyal ADJECTIVE
He has always been a loyal supporter of the club.
• faithful, devoted, true, steadfast, constant, staunch, reliable, dependable, trusty
OPPOSITE disloyal

luck NOUN
➊ *I found the hidden entrance by pure luck.*
• chance, accident, fortune, fate, fluke
➋ *She had a bit of luck today.*
• good fortune, good luck, success

lucky ADJECTIVE
➊ *It was just a lucky guess.*
• accidental, chance, fortuitous, providential
➋ *Are you feeling lucky today?*
• fortunate, favoured, charmed, blessed, in luck
OPPOSITE unlucky

ludicrous ADJECTIVE
The film has a ludicrous plot.
• ridiculous, absurd, laughable, idiotic, nonsensical, foolish, preposterous, crazy
(*informal*) daft

luggage NOUN
Put your luggage on the trolley.
• baggage, cases, suitcases, bags

a
b
c
d
e
f
g
h
i
j
k
l
m
n
o
p
q
r
s
t
u
v
w
x
y
z

lull *VERB*
She lulled the baby to sleep by rocking it gently.
• soothe, calm, hush, quieten, pacify, subdue

lull *NOUN*
There was a brief lull in the conversation.
• pause, break, gap, interval, respite, calm
(*informal*) let-up

lumber *VERB*
❶ *A rhinoceros lumbered past our jeep.*
• trundle, shamble, trudge, tramp, blunder, clump
❷ (*informal*) *Why am I lumbered with all the washing-up?*
• burden, encumber, saddle, land

lump *NOUN*
❶ *Lumps of sticky clay stuck to his boots.*
• chunk, piece, cluster, clump, wad, mass, hunk, wedge, block
– A lump of gold is a **nugget**.
– A lump of earth is a **clod**.
– A lump of blood is a **clot**.
❷ *I could feel a lump where I'd banged my head.*
• bump, swelling, bulge, protrusion

lump *VERB*
➤ **lump things together**
The newspaper reports lumped together two different incidents.
• put together, combine, merge, bunch up

lunge *VERB*
The creature lunged forward and grabbed my leg.
• thrust, charge, rush, dive, spring, pounce, throw yourself, launch yourself

lurch *VERB*
❶ *It looked like a zombie lurching towards us.*

• stagger, stumble, totter, sway, reel, roll, rock
❷ *The bus suddenly lurched to one side.*
• veer, swerve, swing, lean, list

lure *VERB*
It was a trick to lure him into the forest.
• attract, entice, tempt, coax, draw, invite, persuade, seduce
– Something used to lure an animal into a trap is **bait**.
OPPOSITES deter, put off

lurk *VERB*
I had the feeling that someone was lurking in the shadows.
• skulk, loiter, prowl, crouch, hide, lie in wait, lie low

lush *ADJECTIVE*
Rainforests have lush vegetation.
• rich, dense, thick, profuse, abundant, rampant, luxuriant

luxurious *ADJECTIVE*
He was shown into a room with luxurious furnishings.
• rich, expensive, costly, lavish, lush, sumptuous, opulent, de luxe, magnificent, splendid, extravagant
(*informal*) plush, swanky
The words *luxurious* and *luxuriant* do not mean the same thing. A *luxurious hair salon* is expensive and comfortable, but *luxuriant hair* is thick and abundant.
OPPOSITES simple, austere

luxury *NOUN*
❶ *Dining out is a luxury these days.*
• indulgence, extravagance, treat, frill
OPPOSITE necessity
❷ *Only the nobility lived in luxury.*
• affluence, wealth, richness, splendour, opulence, sumptuousness
OPPOSITE poverty

machine NOUN
Do you know how this machine works?
• appliance, device, apparatus, engine, contraption, mechanism

mad ADJECTIVE
❶ *Have you gone completely mad?*
• insane, crazy, deranged, demented, unbalanced
(*informal*) nuts, bonkers, loopy, crackers, potty
IDIOMS (*informal*) off your head, round the bend, round the twist
OPPOSITE sane
❷ *It is a mad idea but it might just work.*
• foolish, idiotic, senseless, crazy, stupid, silly, absurd, hare-brained
(*informal*) crackpot, cockeyed, daft
❸ (*informal*) *Shami is mad about football.*
• fanatical, enthusiastic, passionate, fervent, wild
(*informal*) crazy, nuts
❹ (*informal*) *Please don't get mad when you hear this.*
• angry, furious, infuriated, annoyed, cross, beside yourself, frenzied, hysterical

made
past tense see **make**

magazine NOUN
I bought a magazine to read on the train.
• journal, periodical, supplement, comic
(*informal*) mag

magic NOUN
❶ *The wizard used magic to make himself invisible.*
• sorcery, witchcraft, wizardry, enchantment, black magic, the black arts, white magic, the supernatural, the occult
For tips on writing fantasy fiction see **fantasy**.

❷ *She is good at performing magic with a pack of cards.*
• conjuring, illusion, sleight of hand
❸ *The place has lost none of its magic.*
• charm, allure, fascination, mystery, enchantment, wonder

magic ADJECTIVE
❶ *The castle was surrounded by a magic spell.*
• magical, supernatural, mystical, occult
❷ *My uncle taught me some magic tricks.*
• conjuring

magical ADJECTIVE
❶ *The ring had magical powers.*
• supernatural, magic, mystical, occult
❷ *It was a magical evening.*
• enchanting, entrancing, captivating, spellbinding, bewitching, charming, alluring, enthralling, delightful

magician NOUN
❶ *The magician performed card tricks at our table.*
• conjuror, illusionist
❷ *Merlin, the legendary magician.*
• sorcerer, sorceress, witch, wizard, warlock, enchanter, enchantress

magnificent ADJECTIVE
❶ *The mountain scenery was magnificent.*
• splendid, spectacular, glorious, superb, impressive, striking, dazzling, breathtaking, awe-inspiring
OPPOSITES uninspiring, ordinary
❷ *They lived in a magnificent mansion.*
• grand, imposing, stately, majestic, palatial, luxurious
❸ *What a magnificent goal!*
• excellent, first-class, outstanding, wonderful, marvellous, superb
(*informal*) fabulous, fantastic, terrific, brilliant

magnify VERB
This image has been magnified many times.
• enlarge, make larger, amplify, boost
(*informal*) blow up
OPPOSITES reduce, minimize

mail NOUN
  Have we had a delivery of mail yet?
  • post, letters, correspondence

mail VERB
  Can you mail this letter for me?
  • post, send, dispatch, ship

maim VERB
  Many people were killed or maimed in
  the attack.
  • injure, wound, mutilate, disfigure

main ADJECTIVE
  What is the main theme of the play?
  • principal, chief, major, central,
  leading, dominant, key, basic,
  essential, fundamental, primary, prime,
  predominant, pre-eminent, foremost
  OPPOSITES minor, secondary

mainly ADVERB
  Vitamin C is found mainly in fruits and
  vegetables.
  • mostly, chiefly, principally, primarily,
  predominantly, largely, on the whole, for
  the most part

maintain VERB
  ❶ The referee tried to maintain order.
  • keep, preserve, sustain, retain,
  perpetuate
  ❷ A team of gardeners maintain the
  grounds.
  • look after, take care of, keep in order
  ❸ He still maintains that he's innocent.
  • claim, insist, assert, declare, state,
  affirm, contend, profess

majestic ADJECTIVE
  These are the ruins of what was once a
  majestic city.
  • grand, magnificent, splendid,
  impressive, imposing, stately, noble

major ADJECTIVE
  ❶ Winning the Oscar was a major
  achievement.
  • big, great, considerable, significant,
  important, serious, weighty
  OPPOSITES minor, trivial

❷ There are delays on all the major
roads into the city.
• chief, principal, primary, leading,
foremost
OPPOSITES minor, lesser

majority NOUN
➤ the majority of
The majority of Americans live in cities.
• the greater number of, the bulk of,
most
IDIOM the lion's share of
OPPOSITE minority

make VERB
❶ We were making a model aeroplane.
• build, construct, assemble, put
together, manufacture, fashion
❷ Try not to make a noise.
• cause, produce, create, generate
❸ The company made a huge profit last
year.
• gain, get, obtain, acquire, earn, win
❹ They made me do it.
• force to, compel to, drive to, order to,
press into
❺ We should make the coast before
nightfall.
• reach, arrive at, get to, get as far as
❻ I think she'll make a good actress.
• become, grow into, turn into, change
into
❼ What time do you make it?
• calculate, estimate, reckon
❽ 5 and 8 make 13.
• add up to, come to, total
❾ He stood up and made a little bow.
• perform, execute, carry out, give, do
❿ I'm just making my bed.
• arrange, tidy
⓫ I'll make you an offer.
• propose, suggest
➤ make for
We made for the nearest exit.
• go towards, head for
IDIOM make a beeline for
➤ make off
The gang made off in a stolen car.
• leave, escape, get away, run away,
disappear
(informal) clear off, scarper
➤ make something out

❶ *Can you make out a figure in the background?*
• see, detect, discern, distinguish, recognize, spot
❷ *I can't make out what you're saying.*
• understand, follow, grasp, work out, comprehend, fathom, make sense of
❸ *My brother always makes out that he's some kind of genius.*
• claim, allege, suggest, imply, insinuate, pretend
➤ make something up
She was good at making up stories.
• create, invent, think up, concoct, fabricate
➤ make up for something
The acting makes up for the far-fetched plot.
• compensate for, cancel out, offset

make NOUN
What make of phone do you have?
• brand, model, label

male ADJECTIVE
a male model
• masculine
– Something that is suitable for a man is **manly**.
OPPOSITE female
SEE ALSO man

malicious ADJECTIVE
Someone has been spreading malicious rumours.
• malevolent, hostile, malign, spiteful, vindictive, vicious, hurtful

mammal NOUN

WORD WEB

Some animals which are mammals:
➤ aardvark	➤ beaver
➤ anteater	➤ bison
➤ antelope	➤ camel
➤ armadillo	➤ cat
➤ baboon	➤ chimpanzee
➤ badger	➤ chipmunk
➤ bat	➤ cow
➤ bear	➤ deer

➤ dog	➤ narwhal
➤ dolphin	➤ orang-utan
➤ dormouse	➤ otter
➤ echidna	➤ panda
➤ elephant	➤ pig
➤ elk	➤ polar bear
➤ ferret	➤ porcupine
➤ fox	➤ porpoise
➤ gazelle	➤ rabbit
➤ gibbon	➤ raccoon
➤ giraffe	➤ rat
➤ goat	➤ reindeer
➤ gorilla	➤ rhinoceros
➤ hare	➤ seal
➤ hedgehog	➤ sea lion
➤ hippopotamus	➤ sheep
➤ horse	➤ shrew
➤ hyena	➤ skunk
➤ lemming	➤ sloth
➤ lemur	➤ squirrel
➤ leopard	➤ tapir
➤ lion	➤ tiger
➤ lynx	➤ vole
➤ manatee	➤ walrus
➤ meerkat	➤ weasel
➤ mole	➤ whale
➤ mongoose	➤ wildebeest
➤ monkey	➤ wolf
➤ moose	➤ yak
➤ mouse	➤ zebra

– A related adjective is **mammalian**.

– When a female mammal produces milk she is **lactating**.

SEE ALSO cat, dog, horse, rodent

For tips on describing animals see **animal**.

man NOUN
❶ *The man at the ticket desk was very helpful.*
• gentleman, male, fellow
(*informal*) guy, gent, bloke, chap
– An unmarried man is a **bachelor**.
– A man whose wife has died is a **widower**.
❷ *Early man lived by hunting.*
• mankind, humankind, the human race, humanity, Homo sapiens

manage VERB

❶ *His son manages the business now.*
• be in charge of, run, direct, lead, control, govern, rule, supervise, oversee, preside over

❷ *I can't manage any more work just now.*
• cope with, deal with, take on, carry out

❸ *I don't know how we'll manage without you.*
• cope, make do, get along, get by, survive, fare
(*informal*) muddle through

manager NOUN

She is the manager of a bookshop.
• director, head, chief, proprietor
(*informal*) boss

mania NOUN

A mania for this new hobby swept the country.
• craze, enthusiasm, passion, obsession (with), fixation (with), fad, rage

manipulate VERB

❶ *She began to manipulate the controls and levers.*
• work, handle, pull, push, turn, twist
(*informal*) twiddle

❷ *He uses his charm to manipulate people.*
• take advantage of, use, exploit, impose on

man-made ADJECTIVE

a man-made fibre
• synthetic, artificial, imitation, mock, fake
OPPOSITES natural, real

manner NOUN

❶ *They dealt with the problem in a very efficient manner.*
• way, style, fashion, method, mode, means, system, technique

❷ *I was put off by her frosty manner.*
• behaviour, conduct, attitude, air, aspect, demeanour, bearing

➤ **manners**

Some people have no manners at all!
• politeness, courtesy, civility, etiquette, social graces

manoeuvre NOUN

Parking a bus is a difficult manoeuvre.
• move, operation

manoeuvre VERB

She manoeuvred the boat through the gap in the rocks.
• guide, move, pilot, steer, navigate

manufacture VERB

The factory manufactures tyres.
• make, build, construct, assemble, put together, turn out

many DETERMINER

I've been on a boat many times.
• numerous, a lot of, plenty of, countless, innumerable, untold
(*informal*) umpteen, lots of, masses of
OPPOSITE few

map NOUN

She had a map of France on the wall.
• chart, diagram, plan
– A book of maps is an **atlas**.
– A person who draws maps is a **cartographer**.

mar VERB

The film is marred by a terrible soundtrack.
• spoil, ruin, wreck, damage, impair, tarnish
OPPOSITE enhance

march VERB

A brass band was marching down the street.
• parade, troop, stride, strut, pace, tread, file

margin NOUN

❶ *Leave a wide margin around the text.*
• border, edge, rim, verge, fringe

❷ *We won by a narrow margin.*
• gap, amount, distance

marginal ADJECTIVE
I can see a marginal improvement.
• slight, small, minimal, minor, unimportant, negligible, borderline
OPPOSITES great, marked

mark NOUN
❶ *The dog left muddy paw marks on the floor.*
• spot, stain, blemish, blotch, blot, smear, smudge, streak, speck
(*informal*) splodge
❷ *What mark did you get in the test?*
• score, grade
❸ *They stood in silence as a mark of respect.*
• sign, token, indication, symbol, emblem

mark VERB
❶ *Please try not to mark the pages.*
• stain, dirty, blot, smudge, smear, streak
❷ *He had exam papers to mark that evening.*
• correct, grade, assess
❸ *She'll be back, you mark my words!*
• mind, heed, attend to, listen to, note, take note of

marked ADJECTIVE
You can see a marked improvement in his health.
• noticeable, considerable, pronounced, clear, obvious, distinct, decided, striking
OPPOSITES slight, marginal

marriage NOUN
❶ *My grandparents are celebrating forty years of marriage.*
• matrimony, wedlock
❷ *Today is the anniversary of their marriage.*
• wedding, union
(*formal*) nuptials

marry VERB
In what year did your grandparents marry?
• get married, wed
IDIOMS (*informal*) tie the knot, get hitched
– A couple who have promised to marry

are **engaged** to each other.
– A man who is engaged to be married is a **fiancé** and a woman who is engaged to be married is a **fiancée**.

marsh NOUN
Wading birds are found in coastal marshes.
• swamp, bog, wetland, marshland, fen

marvel NOUN
the marvels of modern science
• wonder, miracle, phenomenon, sensation

marvel VERB
➤ marvel at
Audiences marvelled at the acrobats' skill.
• admire, wonder at, be amazed by, be astonished by

marvellous ADJECTIVE
What a marvellous achievement!
• excellent, superb, splendid, magnificent, glorious, sublime, wonderful, tremendous, amazing, remarkable, extraordinary, incredible, phenomenal
(*informal*) brilliant, fantastic, terrific, super, smashing
OPPOSITES terrible, awful

masculine ADJECTIVE
The singer had a deep, masculine voice.
• male, manly, macho, virile
OPPOSITE feminine

mash VERB
Mash the potatoes with a little butter.
• crush, pound, pulp, smash, squash
– To make something into powder is to **grind** or **pulverize** it.

mask VERB
The entrance was masked by a curtain.
• conceal, hide, cover, obscure, screen, veil, shroud, camouflage

mass NOUN
She sifted through the mass of papers on her desk.
• heap, pile, mound, stack, collection,

a b c d e f g h i j k l m n o p q r s t u v w x y z

A B C D E F G H I J K L M N O P Q R S T U V W X Y Z

quantity, accumulation
(*informal*) load

massacre VERB
see kill

massive ADJECTIVE
Near the entrance stood a massive
bronze statue.
• enormous, huge, gigantic, colossal,
giant, immense, vast, mighty, mammoth,
monumental, great, big, large
(*informal*) whopping
(*literary*) gargantuan
OPPOSITES small, tiny
SEE ALSO big

master NOUN
❶ a computer game called Masters of
the Universe
• lord, ruler, sovereign, governor
❷ Sherlock Holmes was a master of
disguise.
• expert, genius, ace, wizard, virtuoso,
maestro
(*informal*) whizz

master VERB
❶ Have you mastered the guitar yet?
• grasp, learn, understand, become
proficient in, pick up
(*informal*) get the hang of, get to grips
with
❷ She succeeded in mastering her fear
of heights.
• overcome, conquer, defeat, triumph
over, get the better of, control, curb,
subdue, tame
OPPOSITES succumb to, give in to

match NOUN
❶ We lost the first match of the season.
• game, contest, competition, fixture,
tournament, tie
❷ Those colours are a good match.
• combination, pairing
OPPOSITE contrast

match VERB
Does this tie match my shirt?
• go with, suit, fit with, blend with, tone
in with
OPPOSITES contrast with, clash with

matching ADJECTIVE
She wore a red hat with a matching
scarf.
• coordinating, corresponding,
complementary, equivalent, twin, paired
OPPOSITES contrasting, clashing

mate NOUN
❶ (*informal*) Jermaine is one of my best
mates.
• friend
(*informal*) pal, chum, buddy
❷ I could hear a bird calling for its mate.
• partner
❸ He got a job as a plumber's mate.
• assistant, helper, apprentice

material NOUN
❶ I'm collecting material for the school
magazine.
• information, facts, data, ideas, notes,
details
❷ We have a range of art materials in
the cupboard.
• supplies, stuff, substances, things
❸ The curtains are made of heavy
material.
• cloth, fabric, textile
SEE ALSO fabric

mathematics NOUN
a professor of mathematics
• (*informal*) maths
(*North American*) math

🌐 WORD WEB

Branches of mathematics:

➤ algebra	➤ set theory
➤ arithmetic	➤ statistics
➤ calculus	➤ trigonometry
➤ geometry	

Terms used in mathematics:

➤ acute angle	➤ cosine
➤ addition	➤ decimal
➤ calculation	➤ diameter
➤ calculator	➤ digit
➤ cardinal number	➤ division
➤ constant	➤ equation

> exponent
> factor
> formula
> fraction
> hypotenuse
> index
> integer
> locus
> long division
> matrix
> median
> multiplication
> obtuse angle
> ordinal number
> pi

> power
> prime number
> product
> quotient
> reciprocal
> remainder
> sector
> sine
> square root
> subtraction
> symbol
> symmetry
> tangent
> vector
> whole number

matted ADJECTIVE
The dog's coat was dirty and matted.
• tangled, knotted, uncombed

matter NOUN
❶ This is a matter of great importance.
• affair, concern, issue, business,
situation, incident, subject, topic, thing
❷ What's the matter with the car?
• problem, difficulty, trouble, worry
❸ Peat consists mainly of plant matter.
• material, stuff, substance

matter VERB
Will it matter if I'm late?
• be important, count, make a
difference

mature ADJECTIVE
❶ The zoo has two mature gorillas.
• adult, fully grown, well developed
OPPOSITE young
❷ He is very mature for his age.
• grown-up, responsible, sensible
OPPOSITES immature, childish

maximum NOUN
The heat is at its maximum at midday.
• highest point, peak, top, upper limit,
ceiling

maximum ADJECTIVE
The ship has a maximum speed of
40 knots.
• greatest, top, highest, biggest, largest,
fullest, utmost
OPPOSITE minimum

maybe ADVERB
Maybe they've got lost.
• perhaps, possibly
OPPOSITE definitely

maze NOUN
We were lost in a maze of underground
tunnels.
• labyrinth, network, web, tangle,
warren

meadow NOUN
Cows were grazing in the meadow.
• field, pasture

meagre ADJECTIVE
The prisoners were given meagre rations
of rice and water.
• scant, sparse, poor, scanty, inadequate,
insufficient, skimpy, paltry
(informal) measly, stingy
OPPOSITES generous, ample

meal NOUN
a simple meal of bread and cheese
• (informal) bite
(formal) repast

✺ WORD WEB

Some types of meal:

> afternoon tea
> barbecue
> breakfast
> banquet
> brunch
> buffet
> dinner
> (informal)
  elevenses
> feast

> high tea
> lunch
> (formal)
  luncheon
> picnic
> snack
> supper
> takeaway
> tea
> tea break

SEE ALSO food

mean VERB
❶ Do you know what this symbol
means?
• indicate, signify, denote, symbolize,
represent, stand for, express, convey,
communicate, suggest, imply

a
b
c
d
e
f
g
h
i
j
k
l
m
n
o
p
q
r
s
t
u
v
w
x
y
z

A
B
C
D
E
F
G
H
I
J
K
L
M
N
O
P
Q
R
S
T
U
V
W
X
Y
Z

❷ *I didn't mean to cause any harm.*
• intend, aim, plan, set out, propose, want, have in mind

mean *ADJECTIVE*
❶ *Scrooge was too mean to buy any presents.*
• selfish, miserly, uncharitable, penny-pinching
(*informal*) stingy, tight, tight-fisted
OPPOSITE generous
❷ *That was a mean thing to say.*
• unkind, unpleasant, spiteful, vicious, cruel, malicious, horrible, nasty
(*informal*) rotten
OPPOSITE kind

meaning *NOUN*
What is the meaning of this word?
• sense, explanation, interpretation, definition, significance, import, gist

meaningful *ADJECTIVE*
The two friends exchanged a meaningful look.
• pointed, significant, expressive, suggestive, revealing
OPPOSITES insignificant, inconsequential

meaningless *ADJECTIVE*
It was a meaningless promise.
• empty, hollow, insincere, pointless, worthless, ineffectual
OPPOSITES serious, worthwhile

means *PLURAL NOUN*
❶ *Camels are used as a means of transport.*
• method, mode, medium, channel, course, way
❷ *They don't have the means to buy a house.*
• money, resources, assets, funds, finance, capital, wherewithal

measure *VERB*
Now measure the height of the wall.
• calculate, gauge, determine, quantify, assess

measure *NOUN*
❶ *You can't use money alone as a measure of success.*
• gauge, standard, scale, indicator, yardstick, barometer
❷ *At least we know the measure of the problem.*
• size, extent, magnitude
❸ *They are taking measures to improve the park.*
• step, action, course, procedure, initiative

WORD WEB

Metric weights and measures:

➤ centimetre	➤ litre
➤ gram	➤ metre
➤ hectare	➤ milligram
➤ kilo or kilogram	➤ millilitre
➤ kilolitre	➤ millimetre
➤ kilometre	➤ tonne

Imperial weights and measures:

➤ acre	➤ pint
➤ foot	➤ pound
➤ gallon	➤ quart
➤ inch	➤ stone
➤ mile	➤ ton
➤ ounce	➤ yard

- The depth of the sea is measured in **fathoms**.
- The speed of a boat or ship is measured in **knots**.
- The distance of an object in space is measured in **light years**.

For measurements used in cooking see **cook**.

measurement *NOUN*
What are the measurements of the room?
• dimensions, size, extent, proportions

meat *NOUN*
Dad was carving the meat from the turkey.
• flesh

WORD WEB

Some kinds of meat:

- bacon
- beef
- chicken
- duck
- game
- gammon
- goose
- ham
- lamb
- mutton
- offal
- pork
- turkey
- veal
- venison

medal NOUN

We won the bronze medal in the relay race.
• award, prize, trophy
– A person who wins a medal is a **medallist**.

meddle VERB

❶ *He's always meddling in other people's affairs.*
• interfere, intrude, intervene, pry
IDIOMS (*informal*) poke your nose in, stick your oar in
❷ *Someone has been meddling with my phone.*
• fiddle about, tinker, tamper

medicine NOUN

❶ *Have you taken your cough medicine?*
• drug, medication, treatment, remedy, cure
– An amount of medicine taken at one time is a **dose**.
– Medicine which a doctor gives you is a **prescription**.
❷ *The plant is used in herbal medicine.*
• therapy, treatment, healing

WORD WEB

Some types of medicine:

- anaesthetic
- antibiotic
- antidote
- antiseptic
- expectorant
- painkiller
- sedative
- stimulant
- tonic
- tranquillizer

Methods of taking medicine:

- capsule
- eardrops
- eyedrops
- gargle
- inhaler
- injection
- lotion
- lozenge
- ointment
- pill
- tablet

Medical instruments:

- forceps
- scalpel
- stethoscope
- syringe
- thermometer
- tweezers

Some forms of alternative therapy:

- acupuncture
- aromatherapy
- herbal medicine or herbalism
- homeopathy
- reflexology

People involved in health and medicine:

- anaesthetist
- cardiologist
- chiropodist
- dentist
- dermatologist
- doctor
- GP
- gynaecologist
- herbalist
- homeopath
- midwife
- neurologist
- nurse
- obstetrician
- oncologist
- ophthalmologist
- optician
- orthodontist
- osteopath
- paediatrician
- paramedic
- pharmacist
- physician
- physiotherapist
- podiatrist
- psychiatrist
- psychologist
- radiographer
- speech therapist
- surgeon

mediocre ADJECTIVE

I thought the film was rather mediocre.
• ordinary, average, commonplace, indifferent, second-rate, run-of-the-mill, undistinguished, uninspiring, forgettable, lacklustre, pedestrian (*informal*) so-so
OPPOSITES outstanding, exceptional

medium ADJECTIVE

She is of medium height.
• average, middle, middle-sized, middling, standard, moderate, normal

medium NOUN

The Internet is a powerful medium of communication.
• means, mode, method, way, channel, vehicle

meek ADJECTIVE

That cat looks meek but she has sharp claws.
• gentle, mild, docile, tame, obedient, submissive
OPPOSITE aggressive

meet VERB

❶ *We're meeting outside the cinema.*
• assemble, gather, get together, congregate, convene
❷ *I met an old friend from university at the party.*
• encounter, run into, come across, stumble across, chance on, happen on
(informal) bump into
❸ *When did you two first meet?*
• become acquainted (with), be introduced (to), get to know
❹ *The two roads meet here at the crossroads.*
• come together, converge, connect, touch, join, cross, intersect, link up
❺ *My parents met me at the arrivals hall at the airport.*
• greet, pick up, welcome
❻ *She meets all the requirements for the job.*
• fulfil, satisfy, match, answer, comply with

meeting NOUN

❶ *We held a meeting to discuss our plans.*
• gathering, assembly, council, forum, congress, conference
– A large outdoor public meeting is a **rally**.
– A formal meeting with an important person is an **audience**.
❷ *It is a story about the meeting of two cultures.*
• coming together, convergence, intersection, confluence, union

melancholy ADJECTIVE

She was playing a melancholy tune.
• sad, sorrowful, mournful, doleful, unhappy, gloomy, wistful, sombre
OPPOSITE cheerful
SEE ALSO sad

melody NOUN

The song has a simple melody.
• tune, air, theme

melt VERB

❶ *The snow has already begun to melt.*
• thaw, defrost, soften, liquefy
– To melt ore to extract its metal is to **smelt** it.
– Rock or metal that has melted through great heat is **molten**.
OPPOSITE freeze
❷ *Soon the crowd began to melt away.*
• disperse, break up, drift away, disappear, vanish, fade

member NOUN

➤ be a member of something
Are you a member of the sports club?
• belong to, subscribe to

memorable ADJECTIVE

It was a memorable holiday.
• unforgettable, notable, remarkable, noteworthy, significant, outstanding
OPPOSITE ordinary

memorize VERB

He is good at memorizing long numbers.
• learn, learn by heart, commit to memory, remember
OPPOSITE forget

memory NOUN

My earliest memory is of watching the sea.
• recollection, remembrance, reminiscence, reminder, impression

menace NOUN

❶ *Sharks can be a menace to divers.*
• danger, threat, risk, hazard, peril
❷ *That cat is an absolute menace!*
• nuisance, annoyance, irritation, inconvenience
(informal) pest

mend VERB

Workmen were mending a hole in the road.
• repair, fix, put right, restore, renovate, patch

mention VERB

❶ *Please don't mention this to anyone.*
• refer to, speak about, touch on, hint at, allude to
❷ *She mentioned that she had been ill.*
• say, remark, reveal, disclose, divulge
(*informal*) let out
❸ *The programme mentioned all the cast.*
• name, acknowledge, list

mercy NOUN

The queen showed no mercy to her enemies.
• compassion, humanity, sympathy, pity, leniency, kindness, charity, clemency
OPPOSITE cruelty

merge VERB

❶ *They plan to merge the two schools.*
• join together, combine, integrate, unite, amalgamate, conflate, consolidate
❷ *Two smaller rivers merge to form the Danube.*
• come together, converge, join, meet
OPPOSITE separate

merit NOUN

❶ *She's a writer of great merit.*
• excellence, quality, calibre, distinction, worth, talent
❷ *I can see the merits of this argument.*
• benefit, advantage, virtue, asset, value, good point

merit VERB

This suggestion definitely merits further discussion.
• deserve, justify, warrant, be worthy of, be entitled to, earn, rate

merry ADJECTIVE

A boy sat on a wall, whistling a merry tune.
• cheerful, happy, light-hearted, joyful, jolly, bright, sunny, cheery, lively, chirpy
OPPOSITES sad, gloomy

mess NOUN

❶ *Please clear up this mess.*
• untidiness, clutter, jumble, muddle, chaos, disorder, disarray, litter
(*informal*) shambles, tip
❷ *I've made a real mess of things, haven't I?*
• disaster, botch
(*informal*) hash
❸ *How can we get out of this mess?*
• difficulty, problem, predicament, plight, trouble
(*informal*) fix, jam
IDIOMS tight spot, tight corner

mess VERB

➤ mess about or around
I spent the day messing about at home.
• potter about, lounge about, play about, fool around
(*informal*) muck about
➤ mess something up
❶ *I don't want to mess up my hair.*
• make a mess of, mix up, muddle, jumble, tangle, dishevel
❷ *I think I messed up my audition.*
• make a mess of, bungle
(*informal*) botch, make a hash of

message NOUN

❶ *Did you get my message?*
• note, letter, communication, memo, dispatch
(*formal*) missive
❷ *What is the main message of the poem?*
• meaning, sense, import, idea, point, moral, gist, thrust

messy ADJECTIVE

This kitchen is really messy!
• untidy, disorderly, chaotic, muddled, dirty, filthy, grubby, mucky
(*informal*) higgledy-piggledy
OPPOSITES neat, tidy, clean

met

past tense see meet

metal NOUN

WORD WEB

Some common metals:

- aluminium   ➤ mercury
- brass   ➤ nickel
- bronze   ➤ pewter
- copper   ➤ platinum
- gold   ➤ silver
- iron   ➤ steel
- lead   ➤ tin
- magnesium   ➤ zinc

- A metal formed by mixing two or more metals is an **alloy**.
- Rock which contains a particular metal is **ore**.
  ➤ iron ore
- Something that looks or sounds like metal is **metallic**.

method NOUN
They practised new methods of farming.
• technique, way, procedure, process, system, approach, routine

methodical ADJECTIVE
She has a methodical way of working.
• orderly, systematic, structured, organized, well-ordered, disciplined, deliberate, efficient, businesslike
OPPOSITES disorderly, haphazard

middle NOUN
❶ *There is an island in the middle of the lake.*
• centre, midpoint, core, heart, hub
❷ *Tie the rope around your middle.*
• waist, midriff, stomach, belly
(*informal*) tummy

middle ADJECTIVE
❶ *I keep my paints in the middle drawer.*
• central, midway, mid, inner
❷ *a middle size of egg*
• medium, average, moderate

might NOUN
I banged at the door with all my might.
• strength, power, force, energy, vigour

mighty ADJECTIVE
The creature let out a mighty roar.
• powerful, forceful, vigorous, ferocious, violent, hefty, great
OPPOSITES weak, feeble

mild ADJECTIVE
❶ *Her horse has a mild temper.*
• easy-going, gentle, docile, placid, good-tempered, kind, soft-hearted
❷ *There is a mild flavour of garlic.*
• slight, faint, subtle, light
OPPOSITES strong, pronounced
❸ *It was a mild form of the disease.*
• light, gentle, slight, soft
OPPOSITES severe, harsh
❹ *The weather should turn mild this week.*
• pleasant, warm, balmy, temperate, clement
OPPOSITES harsh, inclement

milky ADJECTIVE
Rubber trees produce a milky sap.
• whitish, cloudy, misty, chalky, opaque
OPPOSITE clear

mimic VERB
My brother is good at mimicking other people.
• do impressions of, imitate, impersonate, pretend to be, caricature, parody
(*informal*) take off

mind NOUN
❶ *Her mind was as sharp as ever.*
• brain, intelligence, intellect, head, sense, understanding, wits, judgement, mental powers, reasoning
❷ *Are you sure you won't change your mind?*
• wishes, intention, fancy, inclination, thoughts, opinion, point of view

mind VERB
❶ *Would you mind my bag for a minute?*
• guard, look after, watch, care for
IDIOM keep an eye on
❷ *Mind the step.*
• look out for, watch out for, beware of, pay attention to, heed, note

❸ *They won't mind if I'm late.*
• bother, care, worry, be upset, take offence, object, disapprove

mine NOUN
The village was next to an abandoned coal mine.
• pit, colliery
– A place where coal is removed from the surface is an **opencast mine**.
– A place where stone or slate is removed is a **quarry**.

mingle VERB
I tried to mingle with the other guests.
• mix in, circulate, blend, combine, merge, fuse

miniature ADJECTIVE
His glasses were fitted with a miniature camera.
• tiny, minute, diminutive, small-scale, baby, mini
SEE ALSO small

minimum ADJECTIVE
Set the oven to the minimum temperature.
• least, smallest, lowest, bottom
OPPOSITE maximum

minor ADJECTIVE
I only had a minor part in the play.
• small, unimportant, insignificant, inferior, lesser, subordinate, trivial, trifling, petty
OPPOSITE major

minute ADJECTIVE
❶ *You can hardly see the minute crack.*
• tiny, minuscule, microscopic, negligible
OPPOSITE large
❷ *Each flower is drawn in minute detail.*
• exhaustive, thorough, meticulous, painstaking
OPPOSITE rough

miraculous ADJECTIVE
The patient made a miraculous recovery.
• amazing, astonishing, astounding, extraordinary, incredible, inexplicable, phenomenal

misbehave VERB
The puppies have been misbehaving again!
• behave badly, be naughty, be disobedient, get up to mischief
OPPOSITE behave

miscellaneous ADJECTIVE
The box contained miscellaneous musical instruments.
• assorted, various, varied, different, mixed, sundry, diverse

mischief NOUN
The twins are always getting up to mischief.
• naughtiness, bad behaviour, misbehaviour, disobedience, playfulness

miser NOUN
The old miser kept his money hidden under the floorboards.
• penny-pincher, Scrooge
(*informal*) skinflint

miserable ADJECTIVE
❶ *You look miserable. What's the matter?*
• sad, unhappy, sorrowful, gloomy, glum, downhearted, despondent, dejected, depressed, melancholy, mournful, tearful
IDIOMS (*informal*) down in the mouth, down in the dumps
OPPOSITES cheerful, happy
❷ *The animals lived in miserable conditions.*
• distressing, uncomfortable, wretched, pitiful, pathetic, squalid
OPPOSITE comfortable
❸ *The weather was cold and miserable.*
• dismal, dreary, bleak, depressing, cheerless, drab
OPPOSITES fine, mild

miserly ADJECTIVE
He was too miserly to donate any money.
• mean, selfish, penny-pinching
(*informal*) stingy, tight, tight-fisted
OPPOSITE generous

a
b
c
d
e
f
g
h
i
j
k
l
m
n
o
p
q
r
s
t
u
v
w
x
y
z

misery NOUN
They thought they were doomed to a life of misery.
• unhappiness, wretchedness, sorrow, sadness, gloom, grief, distress, despair, anguish, suffering, torment, heartache, depression
OPPOSITE happiness

misfortune NOUN
I heard about her family's misfortune.
• bad luck, trouble, hardship, adversity, affliction, setback, mishap
OPPOSITE good luck

mishap NOUN
I had a slight mishap with my computer.
• accident, problem, difficulty, setback

mislay VERB
I seem to have mislaid my watch.
• lose, misplace
OPPOSITE find

misleading ADJECTIVE
The directions they gave us were misleading.
• confusing, unreliable, deceptive, ambiguous, unclear

miss VERB
❶ I don't want to miss the start of the film.
• be too late for
❷ The bullet missed him by inches.
• fall short of, go wide of, overshoot
❸ If we leave now, we should miss the traffic.
• avoid, evade, bypass, beat
❹ I missed my friends over the holidays.
• long for, yearn for, pine for
➤ miss something out
Don't miss out the gory details!
• leave out, omit, exclude, cut out, pass over, ignore, skip

missile NOUN
see weapon

missing ADJECTIVE
❶ She found the missing keys in a drawer.
• lost, mislaid, misplaced, absent, astray
❷ What is missing from this photograph?
• absent, lacking, wanting, left out, omitted

mission NOUN
❶ The mission of the society is to protect wildlife.
• aim, purpose, objective, task, job, vocation, calling
❷ The astronauts are on a mission to Mars.
• expedition, journey, voyage, exploration, quest

mist NOUN
❶ The hills were enveloped in mist.
• fog, haze, cloud, drizzle
❷ I wiped the mist from the window.
• condensation, steam, vapour

mistake NOUN
This article is full of mistakes.
• error, fault, inaccuracy, miscalculation, blunder, lapse, slip, slip-up
(informal) howler
– A spelling mistake is a **misspelling**.
– A mistake made during printing is a **misprint**.
– A mistake where something is left out is an **omission** or **oversight**.
➤ make a mistake
You've made a mistake in the formula.
• err, miscalculate, blunder, slip up

mistake VERB
At first, I mistook the meaning of her letter.
• misunderstand, misinterpret, misconstrue, misread, get wrong
➤ mistake someone for someone
People often mistake him for his brother.
• confuse someone with, take someone for, mix someone up with

mistrust VERB
Do you have any reason to mistrust him?
• distrust, have doubts about, suspect, be wary of, have misgivings about, have reservations about
OPPOSITE trust

316

misty ADJECTIVE

❶ *It was a cold and misty morning.*
• foggy, hazy
❷ *I couldn't see through the misty windows.*
• steamy, cloudy, smoky, opaque
❸ *I have misty memories of that day.*
• indistinct, vague, faint, dim, hazy, fuzzy, blurred
OPPOSITE clear

misunderstand VERB

I think you misunderstood what I said.
• mistake, misinterpret, misconstrue, misread, get wrong, miss the point of
IDIOM get the wrong end of the stick
OPPOSITE understand

mix VERB

Mix the ingredients in a bowl.
• combine, blend, mingle, amalgamate, fuse
➤ **mix something up**
Please don't mix up my DVDs.
• muddle, jumble, shuffle, confuse
➤ **mix with**
She's been mixing with the wrong sort of people.
• associate with, socialize with, keep company with, consort with
IDIOM rub shoulders with

mix NOUN

The style is a strange mix of ancient and modern.
• mixture, blend, combination, compound, mingling, amalgamation, fusion, union

mixed ADJECTIVE

Add a teaspoon of mixed herbs.
• assorted, varied, various, different, miscellaneous, sundry, diverse
OPPOSITE separate

mixture NOUN

❶ *I felt a mixture of fear and excitement.*
• mix, blend, combination, compound, mingling
– A mixture of metals is an **alloy**.
– A mixture of two different species of plant or animal is a **hybrid**.

❷ *The book contains an odd mixture of stories.*
• assortment, collection, variety, miscellany, medley, jumble, ragbag
– A confused mixture is a **mishmash**.

mix-up NOUN

There was a mix-up with our tickets.
• confusion, misunderstanding, mistake, error, blunder, muddle

moan VERB

❶ *He lay on the ground, moaning in pain.*
• cry, groan, sigh, wail, howl, whimper
❷ (*informal*) *My sister is always moaning about something.*
• complain, grumble, grouse, carp, bleat, whine
(*informal*) gripe, whinge

mob NOUN

There was an angry mob of protesters outside the gate.
• crowd, horde, throng, mass, multitude, rabble, gang, pack, herd

mob VERB

The singer was mobbed by fans as he left the hotel.
• surround, crowd round, besiege, hem in, jostle

mobile ADJECTIVE

❶ *A mobile library visits once a fortnight.*
• movable, transportable, portable, travelling
OPPOSITES stationary, fixed
❷ *You should be mobile again in a day or two.*
• moving about, active
(*informal*) up and about
OPPOSITE immobile

mock VERB

It was mean of them to mock his singing.
• ridicule, laugh at, make fun of, jeer at, scoff at, sneer at, scorn, deride
IDIOM (*informal*) take the mickey out of

a b c d e f g h i j k l m n o p q r s t u v w x y z

mock ADJECTIVE
He held up his hands in mock surprise.
• imitation, pretend, simulated, fake, artificial, sham
OPPOSITES real, genuine

mode NOUN
The normal mode of transport on the island is horse and cart.
• way, manner, method, system, means, style, approach

model NOUN
❶ *I'm building a model of the Eiffel Tower.*
• replica, copy, reproduction, miniature, toy, dummy
❷ *Her dad always has the latest model of car.*
• design, type, version
❸ *He is a model of good behaviour.*
• example, ideal

model ADJECTIVE
❶ *We went to an exhibition of model railways.*
• miniature, replica, toy, dummy
❷ *She is a model student.*
• ideal, perfect, exemplary, faultless

model VERB
We learnt how to model figures in clay.
• make, mould, shape, construct, fashion

moderate ADJECTIVE
Her first book was a moderate success.
• average, fair, modest, medium, reasonable, passable, tolerable
OPPOSITES exceptional, great

moderately ADVERB
I'm moderately happy with my score.
• fairly, reasonably, relatively, quite, rather, somewhat
(*informal*) pretty

modern ADJECTIVE
❶ *The speed of modern computers is amazing.*
• present-day, current, contemporary, the latest, recent, advanced
OPPOSITE past

❷ *She has a very modern hairstyle.*
• fashionable, up to date, stylish, modish, trendsetting
(*informal*) trendy, hip
OPPOSITES old-fashioned, out of date, retro

modest ADJECTIVE
❶ *He's very modest about his work.*
• humble, unassuming, self-effacing, diffident, reserved, shy, bashful, coy
OPPOSITES conceited, boastful
❷ *There has been a modest increase in sales.*
• moderate, reasonable, average, medium, limited
OPPOSITE considerable
❸ *She always dressed in a modest style.*
• demure, decent, decorous, proper, seemly
OPPOSITES immodest, indecent

modify VERB
We've had to modify our travel plans.
• adapt, alter, change, adjust, refine, revise, vary
(*informal*) tweak

moist ADJECTIVE
❶ *a current of warm, moist air*
• damp, dank, wet, humid, muggy, clammy, steamy
❷ *a rich and moist fruitcake*
• juicy, soft, tender, succulent
OPPOSITE dry

moisture NOUN
There was a patch of moisture on the wall.
• wetness, dampness, damp, wet, condensation, humidity, dew

moment NOUN
❶ *I'll be ready in a moment.*
• short while, minute, second, instant, flash
(*informal*) jiffy, tick
❷ *It was a great moment in the history of science.*
• time, occasion, point

momentary ADJECTIVE
There was a momentary pause.
• brief, short, short-lived, temporary, fleeting, passing
OPPOSITES lengthy, long-lived

momentous ADJECTIVE
We have reached a momentous decision.
• very important, significant, historic, major, far-reaching, pivotal (*informal*) earth-shattering
OPPOSITES insignificant, trivial

monarch NOUN
see ruler

money NOUN
❶ *How much money do you have with you?*
• cash, currency, change, coins, notes (*informal*) dough, dosh
❷ *The family lost all their money when the business collapsed.*
• funds, finance, capital, wealth, riches, fortune, means, wherewithal

monster NOUN
A sea monster reared its head above the waves.
• beast, giant, ogre, brute, fiend, demon (*literary*) leviathan

monstrous ADJECTIVE
❶ *The volcano triggered a monstrous tidal wave.*
• huge, gigantic, enormous, massive, immense, colossal, great, mighty, towering, vast
❷ *The whole country was shocked by this monstrous crime.*
• horrifying, shocking, wicked, evil, hideous, vile, atrocious, abominable, dreadful, horrible, gruesome, grisly, outrageous, scandalous

mood NOUN
He arrived in a foul mood.
• temper, humour, state of mind, frame of mind, disposition

moody ADJECTIVE
She slumped on the chair, looking moody.
• sulky, sullen, grumpy, bad-tempered, temperamental, touchy, miserable, gloomy, glum, morose
OPPOSITE cheerful

moon NOUN
Saturn has a large number of moons.
• satellite

WORD WEB

Phases of the moon:
➤ new moon   ➤ gibbous moon
➤ crescent moon   ➤ full moon
➤ half moon

- The Moon **waxes** when it appears gradually bigger before a full moon.
- The Moon **wanes** when it appears gradually smaller after a full moon.
- A landscape on the Moon is a **moonscape**.
- A word meaning 'to do with the Moon' is **lunar**.
  ➤ *a lunar eclipse*
  SEE ALSO **planet, space**

moor NOUN
The tower stands on a windswept moor.
• moorland, heath, fell

moor VERB
Several yachts were moored in the harbour.
• tie up, secure, fasten, anchor, berth, dock

moral ADJECTIVE
She tried her best to lead a moral life.
• good, virtuous, upright, honourable, principled, honest, just, truthful, decent, ethical, righteous
OPPOSITE immoral

moral NOUN
The moral of this story is to be careful what you wish for.
• lesson, message, meaning, teaching

morale NOUN
A win would improve the team's morale.
• confidence, self-esteem, spirit, mood, attitude, motivation, state of mind

319

more DETERMINER
We need more light in this room.
• extra, further, added, additional, supplementary
OPPOSITES less, fewer

morning NOUN
We set off in the early morning.
• daybreak, dawn, first light, sunrise

morsel NOUN
You haven't eaten a morsel of food.
• bite, crumb, mouthful, taste, nibble, piece, scrap, fragment

mortal ADJECTIVE
❶ *All of us are mortal.*
OPPOSITE immortal
❷ *I believe you are in mortal danger.*
• deadly, lethal, fatal
❸ *The brothers became mortal enemies.*
• bitter, deadly, irreconcilable

mostly ADVERB
❶ *The account is written mostly from memory.*
• mainly, largely, chiefly, primarily, principally, predominantly, in the main, for the most part
❷ *Floods mostly occur during monsoon season.*
• generally, usually, normally, typically, ordinarily, as a rule

mother NOUN
My mother uses her maiden name.
• (*informal*) mum, mummy, ma
(*North American informal*) mom, mommy
– A word meaning 'to do with a mother' is **maternal**.
For other members of a family see **family**.

motion NOUN
He silenced the audience with a motion of his hand.
• gesture, movement, gesticulation

motivate VERB
What motivated you to write a book?
• prompt, drive, stimulate, influence, inspire, urge, induce, impel, provoke, spur

motive NOUN
The police can find no motive for the crime.
• cause, motivation, reason, rationale, purpose, grounds

motor NOUN
see **engine**

motto NOUN
Her motto has always been 'Keep it simple'.
• slogan, proverb, saying, maxim, adage, axiom, golden rule

mould VERB
The little figures on the cake are moulded out of marzipan.
• shape, form, fashion, model, sculpt, work, cast

mouldy ADJECTIVE
At the back of the fridge was a lump of mouldy cheese.
• rotten, rotting, decaying, musty

mound NOUN
❶ *The letter was buried under a mound of paper.*
• heap, pile, stack, mountain, mass
❷ *There used to be a castle on top of that mound.*
• hill, hillock, rise, hump
– An ancient mound of earth over a grave is a **barrow**.

mount VERB
❶ *She slowly mounted the stairs.*
• go up, climb, ascend, scale
OPPOSITE descend
❷ *He mounted his bicycle and rode off.*
• get on, climb onto, jump onto, hop onto
OPPOSITE dismount
❸ *Tension began to mount in the audience.*
• grow, increase, rise, escalate, intensify, build up
OPPOSITES fall, lessen
❹ *The library is mounting a new exhibition.*
• put on, set up, display, install, stage, present

mountain NOUN

❶ *They had to make their way through the mountains.*
- mount, peak, summit
- A line of mountains is a **range**.
- A long narrow hilltop or mountain range is a **ridge**.
- An area of land with many mountains is said to be **mountainous**.

❷ *I have a mountain of work to get through.*
- heap, pile, mound, stack, mass

mourn VERB

He was still mourning the loss of his dear friend.
- grieve for, lament for

mouth NOUN

❶ *He was staring into the mouth of a crocodile.*
- jaws, muzzle, maw
(*informal*) chops, trap
- A word meaning 'to do with your mouth' is **oral**.

❷ *They lived in a village at the mouth of the river.*
- outlet, estuary, delta
(*Scottish*) firth

❸ *The mouth of the cave was hidden by trees.*
- entrance, opening

move VERB

❶ *The robot can move in any direction.*
- go, walk, step, proceed, travel, change position, budge, stir, shift

❷ *We need to move the piano to the front of the stage.*
- shift, lift, carry, push, slide, transport, remove, transfer

❸ *I heard you were moving to Cardiff.*
- move house, move away, relocate, transfer, decamp
- To move abroad permanently is to **emigrate**.

❹ *Her sad story moved me deeply.*
- affect, touch, stir, shake, impress, inspire

OVERUSED WORD

❶ **To move forwards, move towards a place:**

➤ advance	➤ press on
➤ approach	➤ make headway
➤ proceed	➤ gain ground
➤ progress	

*They saw a pirate ship **approaching**.*

❷ **To move back, move away:**

➤ retreat	➤ back away
➤ withdraw	➤ fall back
➤ reverse	➤ give way
➤ retire	

*The werewolves **fell back** as dawn began to break.*

❸ **To move upwards:**

➤ rise	➤ mount
➤ ascend	➤ soar
➤ climb	

*I looked out of the window as we **climbed** above the clouds.*

❹ **To move downwards:**

➤ drop	➤ plunge
➤ descend	➤ sink
➤ fall	➤ swoop
➤ dive	➤ nosedive

*The film captures a falcon **swooping** down on its prey.*

❺ **To move from side to side:**

➤ sway	➤ swish
➤ swing	➤ flourish
➤ wave	➤ brandish
➤ rock	➤ undulate
➤ wag	

*The knight stepped forward, **swinging** his sword.*

❻ **To move quickly:**

➤ hurry	➤ run
➤ dash	➤ rush
➤ race	➤ hasten

---

a
b
c
d
e
f
g
h
i
j
k
l
m
n
o
p
q
r
s
t
u
v
w
x
y
z

> hurtle   > sweep
> career   > shoot
> fly   > zoom
> speed

A boy went careering past on a skateboard.

❼ To move slowly, aimlessly:

> amble   > crawl
> stroll   > drift
> saunter   > wander
> dawdle   > meander

(*informal*) mosey

The cat yawned and strolled over to her basket.

❽ To move clumsily:

> stumble   > flounder
> stagger   > reel
> shuffle   > totter
> lurch   > trundle
> lumber   > trip

He stumbled up the narrow steps.

❾ To move gracefully:

> flow   > flit
> glide   > float
> dance   > slide
> drift   > slip

Swans glided gently across the pond.

❿ To move restlessly:

> toss   > fidget
> turn   > twitch
> stir   > jerk
> twist   > flap
> shake

The children kept fidgeting in their seats.

⓫ To move stealthily:

> creep   > slink
> crawl   > slither
> edge   > tiptoe
> inch

Agent 007 edged carefully along the window ledge.

move NOUN
❶ *Someone was watching our every move.*
• movement, motion, action, gesture, step, deed, manoeuvre
❷ *It's your move next.*
• turn, go

movement NOUN
❶ *The robot made a sudden, jerky movement.*
• motion, move, action, gesture
❷ *Has there been any movement in their attitude?*
• progress, advance, development, change, shift
❸ *Her mother was involved in the peace movement.*
• organization, group, party, faction, campaign

movie NOUN
see film

moving ADJECTIVE
The story was so moving that I started to cry.
• emotional, affecting, touching, poignant, heart-rending, stirring, inspiring
(*informal*) tear-jerking

much DETERMINER
There is still much work to be done.
• a lot of, a great deal of, plenty of, ample
OPPOSITE little

much ADVERB
I find messaging much quicker than email.
• a great deal, a lot, considerably, substantially, markedly, greatly, far

muck NOUN
❶ *We had to clear the muck out of the stable.*
• dung, manure, droppings
❷ (*informal*) *I'll just scrape the muck off the windscreen.*
• dirt, filth, grime, mud, sludge, mess
(*informal*) gunge, gunk

mucky ADJECTIVE
She took off her mucky football boots.
• dirty, messy, muddy, grimy, grubby, filthy, foul, soiled
OPPOSITE clean

mud NOUN
He slipped and fell in the mud.
• dirt, muck, mire, sludge, clay, soil, silt

muddle NOUN
❶ *There was a muddle over the invitations.*
• confusion, misunderstanding (*informal*) mix-up
❷ *These files are all in a muddle.*
• jumble, mess, tangle, disorder, disarray

muddle VERB
❶ *The words to the song are all muddled.*
• mix up, mess up, disorder, jumble up, shuffle, tangle
OPPOSITE tidy
❷ *I got muddled trying to follow the instructions.*
• confuse, bewilder, puzzle, perplex, baffle, mystify

muddy ADJECTIVE
❶ *Take off your muddy trainers before you come in.*
• dirty, messy, mucky, filthy, grimy, caked, soiled
OPPOSITE clean
❷ *The ground was very muddy.*
• boggy, marshy, swampy, waterlogged, wet, sodden, squelchy
OPPOSITES dry, firm

muffle VERB
❶ *We muffled ourselves up to play in the snow.*
• wrap up, cover up, swathe, cloak, enfold
❷ *I closed the door to muffle the noise.*
• deaden, dampen, dull, stifle, smother, soften, mask

muffled ADJECTIVE
We heard muffled voices from the next room.
• faint, indistinct, unclear, muted,

deadened, stifled
OPPOSITE clear

muggy ADJECTIVE
The weather is often muggy before a storm.
• humid, close, clammy, sticky, moist, damp, oppressive
OPPOSITE fresh

multiply VERB
❶ *Multiply the remaining number by ten.*
– To multiply a number by two is to **double** it; to multiply it by three is to **triple** it; and to multiply it by four is to **quadruple** it.
OPPOSITE divide
❷ *The problems seemed to be multiplying.*
• increase, grow, spread, proliferate, mount up, accumulate, mushroom, snowball
OPPOSITE decrease

mumble VERB
He mumbled an apology.
• mutter, murmur
IDIOM talk under your breath

munch VERB
We munched popcorn all through the film.
• chew, chomp, crunch

murder VERB
The woman is accused of murdering her husband.
• kill, assassinate
(*informal*) bump off, do away with

murder NOUN
Detectives are treating the case as murder.
• homicide, killing, assassination

murky ADJECTIVE
❶ *The sky was murky and drizzle was falling.*
• dark, dull, clouded, overcast, foggy, misty, grey, leaden, dismal, dreary, dingy
OPPOSITES fine, bright

a b c d e f g h i j k l m n o p q r s t u v w x y z

murmur

2 The water in the well was green and murky.
• muddy, cloudy, dirty
OPPOSITE clear

murmur VERB
The crowd murmured their approval.
• mutter, mumble, whisper

muscular ADJECTIVE
He's tall and muscular.
• brawny, beefy, burly, well built, athletic, sinewy, strapping, strong
OPPOSITES puny, weak

music NOUN

WORD WEB

Musical styles and genres:

- bebop
- bhangra
- blues
- bluegrass
- classical music
- country music
- dance music
- disco music
- early music
- flamenco
- folk music
- funk
- gospel
- heavy metal
- hip-hop
- jazz
- pop music
- punk
- ragtime
- rap
- reggae
- rock
- ska
- soul
- swing

Musical forms and compositions:

- anthem
- ballad
- carol
- concerto
- folk song
- fugue
- hymn
- lullaby
- march
- mass
- musical
- opera
- operetta
- oratorio
- prelude
- raga
- requiem
- sonata
- song
- suit
- symphony
- tune

Families of musical instruments:

- brass
- keyboard
- percussion
- strings

- woodwind

Stringed instruments:

- acoustic guitar
- balalaika
- banjo
- bass guitar
- bouzouki
- cello
- double bass
- dulcimer
- electric guitar
- harp
- hurdy gurdy
- lute
- lyre
- mandolin
- pedal steel guitar
- sitar
- ukulele
- viol or viola da gamba
- viola
- violin (*informal* fiddle)
- zither

Wind and brass instruments:

- bagpipes
- bassoon
- bugle
- clarinet
- cor anglais
- cornet
- euphonium
- flugelhorn
- flute
- French horn
- harmonica
- oboe
- panpipes
- piccolo
- recorder
- saxophone
- tin whistle
- trombone
- trumpet
- tuba
- uilleann pipes

Keyboard instruments:

- accordion
- clavichord
- harmonium
- harpsichord
- keyboard
- organ
- piano
- spinet
- synthesizer

Percussion instruments:

- bass drum
- bongo drum
- castanets
- cymbals
- drum
- gamelan
- glockenspiel
- gong
- maracas
- marimba
- mbira or thumb piano
- rattle
- snare drum
- steel drum or steelpan
- tabla
- tambourine
- timpani or kettledrums
- triangle
- tubular bells
- vibraphone
- xylophone

Other terms used in music:

- chord
- clef
- counterpoint
- crotchet (*North American quarter note*)
- discord
- flat
- harmony
- key signature
- melody
- metronome
- minim
- natural
- note
- octave
- pitch
- quaver (*North American eighth note*)
- rhythm
- scale
- semibreve (*North American whole note*)
- semiquaver (*North American sixteenth note*)
- semitone
- sharp
- stave
- tempo
- theme
- time signature
- tone

musical *ADJECTIVE*
My mum has a very musical voice.
• tuneful, melodic, melodious, harmonious, sweet-sounding
OPPOSITE discordant

musician *NOUN*
a musician in an orchestra
• performer, instrumentalist

WORD WEB

Some types of musician:

- bassist or bass player
- bugler
- cellist
- chorister
- clarinettist
- composer
- conductor
- drummer
- fiddler
- flautist
- guitarist
- harpist or harper
- lutenist
- oboist
- organist
- percussionist
- pianist
- piper
- singer
- timpanist
- trombonist
- trumpeter
- violinist (*informal* fiddler)
- vocalist

- A musician who plays music or sings alone is a **soloist**.

- A musician who plays music to support a singer or another musician is an **accompanist**.

Groups of musicians:

- band
- choir or chorus
- duet or duo
- ensemble
- group
- orchestra
- quartet
- quintet
- trio

musty *ADJECTIVE*
There is a musty smell in the cellar.
• damp, dank, mouldy, stale, stuffy, airless
OPPOSITE fresh

mute *ADJECTIVE*
She could only stare, mute with terror.
• silent, speechless, unspeaking, dumb, tongue-tied

mutilate *VERB*
His right hand was mutilated by a firework.
• maim, disfigure, injure, wound, mangle

mutiny *NOUN*
The ship's crew were plotting a mutiny.
• rebellion, revolt, uprising

mutter *VERB*
She sat muttering to herself in the corner.
• mumble, murmur, whisper
IDIOM talk under your breath

mutual *ADJECTIVE*
It is in our mutual interest to work together.
• joint, common, shared, reciprocal

mysterious *ADJECTIVE*
The letter contained a mysterious message.
• puzzling, strange, baffling, perplexing, mystifying, bizarre, curious, weird, obscure, unexplained, incomprehensible, inexplicable

a b c d e f g h i j k l m n o p q r s t u v w x y z

mystery *NOUN*
What really happened remains a mystery.
• puzzle, riddle, secret, enigma,
conundrum

mystify *VERB*
I was completely mystified by the plot.
• puzzle, baffle, bewilder, perplex

myth *NOUN*
*My story is based on the ancient myth of
the Minotaur.*
• legend, fable, saga, folklore

mythical *ADJECTIVE*
The unicorn is a mythical beast.
• fabulous, fanciful, imaginary, invented,
fictional, legendary, mythological
OPPOSITE real

nag VERB
He was always nagging her to work harder.
• badger, pester, hound, harass, keep on at

naive ADJECTIVE
She was still hopelessly naive about life.
• innocent, inexperienced, unsophisticated, immature, unworldly, artless, gullible, green
IDIOM wet behind the ears

naked ADJECTIVE
He walked naked into the bathroom.
• bare, nude, unclothed, undressed, stripped, with nothing on
IDIOMS (*humorous*) without a stitch on, in the buff, in your birthday suit
OPPOSITE clothed

name NOUN
What's your name?
– The official names you have are your **first names** or **forenames** and **surname**.
– Names a Christian is given at baptism are **Christian names**.
– A false name is an **alias**.
– A name people use instead of your real name is a **nickname**.
– A false name an author uses is a **pen name** or **pseudonym**.
– The name of a book or film is its **title**.

name VERB
❶ *They named the puppy Ricky.*
• call, label, dub, term, title
– To name someone at the ceremony of baptism is to **baptize** or **christen** them.
❷ *The victim has not been named.*
• identify, specify

nap NOUN
She was on the sofa, taking a nap.
• rest, sleep, doze, lie-down
(*informal*) snooze
IDIOM forty winks

narrate VERB
The story is narrated by the main character.
• tell, recount, relate, report
– The person who narrates a story is the **narrator**.

narrative NOUN
We were spellbound by his narrative of the voyage.
• account, history, story, tale, chronicle
(*informal*) yarn

narrow ADJECTIVE
❶ *We had to crawl through a narrow tunnel.*
• thin, slender, slight, slim, tight, constricted, confined
OPPOSITES wide, broad
❷ *He has a narrow outlook on life.*
• limited, restricted, close-minded, inadequate, deficient
OPPOSITES broad, open-minded

nasty ADJECTIVE
❶ *This medicine has a nasty taste.*
• unpleasant, offensive, disgusting, revolting, repulsive, repellent, obnoxious, horrible, horrid, foul, vile, rotten, sickening
(*informal*) yucky
OPPOSITES pleasant, agreeable
❷ *That was a nasty thing to say.*
• unkind, unpleasant, unfriendly, disagreeable, malicious, cruel, spiteful, vicious, mean
OPPOSITES likeable, agreeable
❸ *She's had a nasty accident.*
• serious, dreadful, awful, terrible, severe, painful
OPPOSITE slight

nation NOUN
People from many nations compete in the Olympic Games.
• country, state, land, realm, race, people

a b c d e f g h i j k l m n o p q r s t u v w x y z

national ADJECTIVE
The interview will be broadcast on national television.
• nationwide, countrywide, state
OPPOSITE local

native ADJECTIVE
❶ *the native population of Hawaii*
• indigenous, original, local
OPPOSITES immigrant, imported
❷ *Is Urdu your native language?*
• mother, first, home

natural ADJECTIVE
❶ *Is that your natural hair colour?*
• real, original, normal
OPPOSITES unnatural, fake
❷ *Our smoothies are made with natural ingredients.*
• unprocessed, unrefined, pure
OPPOSITES artificial, processed
❸ *It's only natural to be nervous before a race.*
• normal, common, understandable, reasonable, predictable
OPPOSITES abnormal, unnatural
❹ *She has a natural gift for music.*
• born, inborn, instinctive, intuitive, native

nature NOUN
❶ *I like TV programmes about nature.*
• the natural world, wildlife, the environment, natural history
❷ *Labradors are known for their mild nature.*
• character, disposition, temperament, personality, manner, make-up
❸ *I collect coins, medals and things of that nature.*
• kind, sort, type, order, description, variety, category

naughty ADJECTIVE
He had been the naughtiest kid in his class.
• badly behaved, disobedient, bad, troublesome, mischievous, uncontrollable, unmanageable, wayward, unruly
OPPOSITE well behaved

navigate VERB
She managed to navigate her boat through the rocks.
• steer, pilot, guide, direct, manoeuvre

navy NOUN
see fleet

near ADJECTIVE
❶ *We get on well with our near neighbours.*
• nearby, next-door, close, adjacent, accessible
OPPOSITES far, remote
❷ *The message warned us that danger was near.*
• imminent, approaching, coming, looming, impending, on its way (old use) nigh
IDIOMS round the corner, in the offing
OPPOSITE far off
❸ *We sent cards to all our near relatives.*
• close, dear, familiar, intimate
OPPOSITE distant

nearby ADVERB
A photographer happened to be standing nearby.
• close by, not far off, close at hand, within reach
IDIOMS a stone's throw away, within spitting distance
OPPOSITES far away, far off

nearly ADVERB
You're nearly as tall as I am.
• almost, practically, virtually, just about

neat ADJECTIVE
❶ *Please leave the room as neat as possible.*
• clean, tidy, orderly, uncluttered, immaculate, trim, in good order
IDIOM spick and span
OPPOSITES untidy, messy
❷ *He always looks very neat in his school uniform.*
• smart, elegant, spruce, trim, dapper, well turned out
OPPOSITE scruffy

❸ *That is the neatest handwriting I've ever seen.*
• clear, precise, well formed, elegant
❹ *She produced a neat pass into the penalty area.*
• skilful, deft, clever, adroit, adept, well executed
OPPOSITE clumsy

necessary ADJECTIVE
Are all these forms strictly necessary?
• essential, required, needed, requisite, compulsory, obligatory, mandatory, unavoidable, imperative
OPPOSITE unnecessary

need VERB
❶ *I need a pound coin for the locker.*
• require, want, be short of, lack
❷ *It's a charity which needs our support.*
• depend on, rely on
➤ **need to**
We need to leave by 6 o'clock.
• have to, must, be required to, be supposed to, be expected to

need NOUN
There's definitely a need for more shops in our area.
• call, demand, requirement, necessity, want

needless ADJECTIVE
They went to a lot of needless expense.
• unnecessary, unwanted, uncalled for, excessive, superfluous, redundant, gratuitous

needlework NOUN
see textiles

needy ADJECTIVE
They set up a fund to help needy children.
• poor, deprived, underprivileged, disadvantaged, poverty-stricken, penniless, destitute, in need
OPPOSITES wealthy, privileged

negative ADJECTIVE
❶ *Why are you being so negative?*
• pessimistic, defeatist, fatalistic, unenthusiastic, gloomy, cynical,

downbeat
OPPOSITES positive, optimistic, upbeat
❷ *Stress can have a negative effect on your health.*
• bad, adverse, unfavourable, detrimental, harmful, damaging
OPPOSITES positive, beneficial

neglect VERB
❶ *She's been neglecting her work recently.*
• ignore, overlook, disregard, pay no attention to, shirk, abandon
❷ *You neglected to mention a few things.*
• fail, omit, forget

negligible ADJECTIVE
There is a negligible difference in price.
• slight, insignificant, unimportant, minor, trivial, trifling, minimal
OPPOSITES considerable, significant

negotiate VERB
❶ *They refused to negotiate with the kidnappers.*
• bargain, haggle, deal, confer, discuss terms
❷ *They finally negotiated a treaty.*
• work out, agree on, broker
(*informal*) thrash out
❸ *We first had to negotiate a five-metre wall.*
• get past, get round, get over, manoeuvre round

neighbourhood NOUN
They lived in a run-down neighbourhood.
• area, district, community, locality, locale, quarter, vicinity

neighbouring ADJECTIVE
We went on a tour of the neighbouring villages.
• nearby, bordering, adjacent, adjoining, surrounding, nearest, next-door

neighbourly ADJECTIVE
It was neighbourly of her to offer to feed the cat.
• friendly, helpful, obliging, kind, sociable
OPPOSITE unfriendly

a
b
c
d
e
f
g
h
i
j
k
l
m
n
o
p
q
r
s
t
u
v
w
x
y
z

nerve NOUN

❶ *It takes nerve to be a trapeze artist.*
• bravery, courage, daring, fearlessness, pluck, grit
(*informal*) guts, bottle
❷ *He had the nerve to ask me to leave!*
• cheek, impudence, audacity, effrontery, impertinence, presumption

nervous ADJECTIVE

Do you get nervous before you go on stage?
• anxious, worried, apprehensive, concerned, uneasy, fearful, edgy, fraught, tense, worked up, keyed up (*informal*) uptight, jittery, twitchy
IDIOMS (*informal*) in a flap, in a state
OPPOSITES calm, confident

nestle VERB

She nestled her head on his shoulder.
• snuggle, nuzzle, cuddle, huddle, curl up

neutral ADJECTIVE

❶ *A referee has to be neutral.*
• impartial, detached, uninvolved, disinterested, objective, unbiased, even-handed
OPPOSITE biased
❷ *The room was decorated in neutral colours.*
• dull, drab, cool, muted, colourless, indefinite, nondescript
OPPOSITES colourful, vibrant

new ADJECTIVE

❶ *Start on a new sheet of paper.*
• fresh, unused, pristine, brand new – Something new and unused is in mint condition.
OPPOSITES old, used
❷ *Have you read the new issue of the magazine?*
• latest, current, recent, up-to-date
❸ *I've added a new paragraph to my story.*
• additional, extra, further, supplementary
❹ *He introduced a whole new style of acting.*
• fresh, original, novel, innovative,

cutting-edge, state-of-the-art, contemporary
❺ *Flying was a new experience for me.*
• unfamiliar, unknown, different, alternative, strange
OPPOSITE familiar

news NOUN

Have you heard the news?
• information, word, report, bulletin (*old use*) tidings

next ADJECTIVE

❶ *What time is the next train?*
• following, subsequent, succeeding, upcoming
OPPOSITE previous
❷ *I could hear people laughing in the next room.*
• adjacent, closest, nearest, next door
OPPOSITE distant

nice ADJECTIVE

❶ *That's not a very nice thing to say!*
• pleasant, agreeable
OPPOSITES unpleasant, nasty
❷ *There's a nice distinction between telling a lie and not telling the whole truth.*
• fine, subtle, delicate, precise

S   **OVERUSED WORD**

❶ A nice person:

➤ good	➤ personable
➤ kind	➤ charming
➤ pleasant	➤ engaging
➤ friendly	➤ sympathetic
➤ agreeable	➤ polite
➤ likeable	➤ civil
➤ amiable	➤ courteous
➤ genial	

The film features a cast of likeable characters.

❷ A nice experience, nice feeling:

➤ enjoyable	➤ satisfying
➤ pleasant	➤ agreeable
➤ good	➤ entertaining
➤ delightful	➤ amusing

> ➤ wonderful ➤ splendid
> ➤ marvellous

Did you have an **enjoyable** *time on holiday?*

❸ Looking nice:

> ➤ beautiful ➤ fine
> ➤ attractive ➤ handsome
> ➤ pleasing ➤ striking
> ➤ lovely

There is an **attractive** *view from the upstairs window.*

❹ A nice smell:

> ➤ fragrant ➤ perfumed
> ➤ pleasant ➤ aromatic
> ➤ sweet

The **fragrant** *scent of lavender filled the garden.*

OPPOSITE smelly

❺ A nice taste, nice food:

> ➤ appetizing ➤ delicious
> ➤ tasty ➤ delectable
> ➤ flavoursome ➤ mouth-watering

(informal) yummy, scrumptious

Slow cooking will make the dish more **flavoursome.**

❻ Nice weather, a nice day:

> ➤ fine ➤ mild
> ➤ sunny ➤ balmy
> ➤ warm ➤ dry

The weather has been **fine** *all week.*

SEE ALSO **good, lovely**

night NOUN

Badgers usually come out at night.
• night-time, dark, the hours of darkness
– The time immediately after sunset when the sky is still light is **twilight**.
– The time when the evening twilight ends is **dusk** or **nightfall**.
– A **nightly** event happens every night.
– Animals which are active at night are **nocturnal**.

OPPOSITES day, daytime

nil NOUN

The score was nil all at half-time.
• zero, nought, nothing, none
– A score of nil in cricket is a **duck**.
– A score of nil in tennis is **love**.

nimble ADJECTIVE

You need nimble fingers for that job.
• agile, skilful, quick, deft, dexterous, adroit

OPPOSITE clumsy

nip VERB

❶ *Frost had begun to nip at our toes.*
• bite, nibble, peck, pinch, tweak, catch
❷ *(informal) I'm just nipping out to the shops.*
• dash, run, rush
(informal) pop

noble ADJECTIVE

❶ *The count came from an ancient noble family.*
• aristocratic, high-born, upper-class, titled

OPPOSITES low-born, humble, base
❷ *Their noble sacrifice will be remembered.*
• brave, heroic, courageous, valiant, honourable, worthy, virtuous, gallant

OPPOSITES cowardly, unworthy
❸ *The oak is a noble tree.*
• grand, stately, magnificent, impressive, imposing, dignified, proud, majestic

noble NOUN

A group of nobles were loyal to the king.
• aristocrat, nobleman, noblewoman, lord, lady, peer

OPPOSITE commoner

nod VERB

The others nodded their heads in agreement.
• bob, bow, dip, lower, incline
➤ **nod off**
She sometimes nods off in front of the fire.
• fall asleep, doze off, drop off, have a nap

noise NOUN

My computer is making a peculiar noise.
• sound, racket, din, row, uproar, commotion, clamour, hullabaloo
For tips on describing sounds see **sound**.

noisy ADJECTIVE

❶ *It was noisy in the classroom.*
• rowdy, raucous, clamorous, uproarious
OPPOSITES quiet, silent

❷ *The plane completed its noisy take-off.*
• loud, blaring, booming, deafening, ear-splitting, thunderous
OPPOSITES quiet, soft

nominate VERB

His latest novel has been nominated for several prizes.
• propose, put forward, recommend, select, choose, name, elect

nonsense NOUN

Stop talking such nonsense!
• rubbish, drivel, gibberish, claptrap, garbage
(*informal*) gobbledegook, baloney, rot, tripe, twaddle, piffle
(*old use*) balderdash, poppycock
OPPOSITES sense, reason

nonsensical ADJECTIVE

It was a nonsensical suggestion.
• absurd, ridiculous, ludicrous, senseless, irrational, illogical, preposterous, crazy, laughable, silly, stupid, foolish, idiotic
(*British informal*) daft
OPPOSITES sensible, reasonable

non-stop ADJECTIVE

❶ *All he could hear was the sound of non-stop traffic.*
• constant, continual, continuous, endless, ceaseless, incessant, never-ending, unending, perpetual, round-the-clock

❷ *We took a non-stop train from Paris to Nice.*
• direct, express

normal ADJECTIVE

❶ *It began as just a normal day.*
• ordinary, average, typical, usual, common, standard, regular, routine, familiar, habitual, customary, conventional
IDIOM run-of-the-mill
OPPOSITE abnormal

❷ *It can't be normal to feel this way.*
• healthy, natural, rational, reasonable, sane
OPPOSITES unhealthy, unnatural

north NOUN, ADJECTIVE & ADVERB

The Sahara is in the north of Africa.
– The parts of a country or continent in the north are the **northern** parts.
– To travel towards the north is to travel **northward** or **northwards**.
– A wind from the north is a **northerly** wind.
– A person who lives in the north of a country is a **northerner**.

nose NOUN

❶ *Someone punched me on the nose.*
– The openings in your nose are your **nostrils**.
– An animal's nose is its **muzzle** or **snout**.
– A long flexible snout is a **trunk** or **proboscis**.
– A word meaning 'to do with your nose' is **nasal**.

❷ *I was sitting in the nose of the boat.*
• front, bow, prow

nosy (*informal*) ADJECTIVE

A nosy reporter was asking a lot of questions.
• inquisitive, curious, prying, snooping, intrusive

notable ADJECTIVE

❶ *It was a notable date in American history.*
• memorable, noteworthy, significant, major, important, well known, famous, celebrated, renowned, noted, prominent
OPPOSITES insignificant, minor

❷ *He was showing a notable lack of enthusiasm.*
• distinct, definite, obvious, conspicuous, marked, pronounced, striking, remarkable

notch NOUN
She cut a small notch in the tree trunk.
• cut, nick, groove, score, scratch, incision

note NOUN
❶ *Someone had written a note in the margin.*
• comment, annotation, jotting, entry, record, memo
❷ *I sent her a brief thank-you note.*
• message, letter, line, communication
❸ *There was a note of warning in his voice.*
• tone, feeling, quality, sense, hint, suggestion

note VERB
❶ *I noted the address on a scrap of paper.*
• jot down, make a note of, write down, take down, scribble, record, list, enter, pencil in
❷ *Did you note what she was wearing?*
• notice, take note of, pay attention to, heed, mark, register, observe

nothing NOUN
❶ *There's nothing more we can do.*
• not a thing
(*informal*) zilch
IDIOM (*humorous*) not a sausage
❷ *They scored nothing in the first round.*
• nought, zero, nil
SEE ALSO nil

notice NOUN
❶ *There was a notice pinned to the wall.*
• sign, advertisement, poster, placard
❷ *Some islands received no notice of the tsunami.*
• warning, notification, announcement
➤ **take notice of something**
They took no notice of the warning.
• pay attention to, heed, mark

notice VERB
❶ *Did you notice the tattoo on his arm?*
• note, take note of, heed, mark, register, observe, spot
❷ *I noticed a funny smell in the room.*
• become aware of, detect, discern

noticeable ADJECTIVE
❶ *There has been a noticeable improvement in the weather.*
• notable, distinct, definite, measurable, perceptible, appreciable, significant, marked, pronounced, salient, unmistakable, striking
❷ *She spoke with a noticeable foreign accent.*
• obvious, conspicuous, visible, detectable, discernible, evident, apparent
OPPOSITE imperceptible

notion NOUN
He has some old-fashioned notions about women.
• belief, idea, view, thought, opinion, theory, concept

notorious ADJECTIVE
They were the most notorious criminal gang in the country.
• infamous, disreputable, disgraceful

nought NOUN
see nil

nourish VERB
Plants are nourished by water drawn up through their roots.
• feed, sustain, support, nurture

nourishing ADJECTIVE
She used to make us bowls of hot, nourishing soup.
• nutritious, wholesome, healthy, health-giving

novel ADJECTIVE
They came up with a novel method of filming underwater.
• original, new, innovative, fresh, different, imaginative, creative, unusual, unconventional, unorthodox
OPPOSITES traditional, familiar

now ADVERB
❶ *My sister is now living in Melbourne.*
• at present, at the moment, at this time, currently, nowadays
❷ *I'll send them an email now.*
• immediately, at once, straight away,

right away, without delay, instantly, directly, this instant

nude *ADJECTIVE*
On the wall was a painting of a nude figure.
• naked, bare, unclothed, undressed
OPPOSITE clothed

nudge *VERB*
❶ *She nudged me with her elbow.*
• poke, prod, dig, elbow, jab, jolt, bump
❷ *We nudged the piano into position.*
• ease, inch, manoeuvre

nuisance *NOUN*
Mosquitoes can be a nuisance in the summer.
• annoyance, irritation, inconvenience, bother, menace, pest, drawback
(*informal*) bind, hassle, pain, headache, drag

numb *ADJECTIVE*
My toes were numb with cold.
• unfeeling, deadened, frozen, insensitive, paralysed
OPPOSITE sensitive

number *NOUN*
❶ *The paper had a line of numbers written on it.*
• figure, numeral
– Any of the numbers from 0 to 9 is a **digit**.
– A negative or positive whole number is an **integer**.
– An amount used in measuring or counting is a **unit**.
❷ *We received a large number of emails.*

• amount, quantity, collection, quota, total, tally
❸ *I've ordered the latest number of the magazine.*
• edition, issue
❹ *The musical features some well-known numbers.*
• song, piece, tune

numerous *ADJECTIVE*
The book contains numerous errors.
• many, a lot of, plenty of, abundant, copious, countless, innumerable, untold, myriad
(*informal*) umpteen, lots of, masses of
OPPOSITE few

nurse *NOUN*
see medicine

nurse *VERB*
She nursed her sick mother for years.
• look after, care for, take care of, tend, treat

nut *NOUN*

WORD WEB

Some edible nuts:

➤ almond	➤ macadamia
➤ Brazil	➤ peanut
➤ cashew	➤ pecan
➤ chestnut	➤ pine nut
➤ coconut	➤ pistachio
➤ hazelnut	➤ walnut

– The part inside the shell of a nut is the **kernel**.

oath NOUN

❶ *The knights swore an oath of allegiance.*
• pledge, promise, vow, word of honour
❷ *He banged his head, letting out a stream of oaths.*
• swear word, curse, expletive, profanity

obedient ADJECTIVE

Your dog seems very obedient.
• well-behaved, disciplined, manageable, dutiful, docile, compliant
OPPOSITE disobedient

obey VERB

❶ *The robot will obey any command.*
• follow, carry out, execute, implement, observe, heed, comply with, adhere to, submit to
❷ *Do you always obey without question?*
• do what you are told, take orders, be obedient, conform
OPPOSITE disobey

object NOUN

❶ *There were reports of a strange object in the sky.*
• article, item, thing
❷ *What is the object of this experiment?*
• point, purpose, aim, goal, intention, objective
❸ *He has become an object of pity.*
• target, focus

object VERB

➤ object to something
Only one person objected to the plan.
• oppose, be opposed to, disapprove of, take exception to, take issue with, protest against, complain about
OPPOSITES accept, agree to

objection NOUN

Has anybody got any objections?
• protest, complaint, opposition, disapproval, disagreement, dissent

objectionable ADJECTIVE

He can be thoroughly objectionable when he wants to be.
• unpleasant, disagreeable, disgusting, foul, offensive, repellent, revolting, obnoxious, nasty
OPPOSITE acceptable

objective NOUN

My main objective is to tell a good story.
• aim, goal, intention, target, ambition, object, purpose, plan

objective ADJECTIVE

She tried to give an objective account of what happened.
• impartial, neutral, unbiased, unprejudiced, even-handed, disinterested, dispassionate, detached
OPPOSITE subjective

obligatory ADJECTIVE

The wearing of seat belts is obligatory.
• compulsory, mandatory, required, prescribed, necessary
OPPOSITE optional

oblige VERB

Would you oblige me by delivering this letter?
• do someone a favour, help, assist, indulge

obliged ADJECTIVE

❶ *I felt obliged to accept the invitation.*
• bound, compelled, expected, required, constrained
❷ *I'm much obliged to you for your help.*
• thankful, grateful, appreciative, indebted

oblong NOUN

The garden was simply an oblong of grass.
• rectangle
SEE ALSO shape

obscene ADJECTIVE

The film contains some obscene language.
• indecent, offensive, explicit, rude, vulgar, coarse, lewd
OPPOSITES clean, decent

a b c d e f g h i j k l m n o p q r s t u v w x y z

obscure *ADJECTIVE*

❶ *The origins of the stone circle remain obscure.*
• uncertain, unclear, mysterious, vague, hazy, shadowy, murky, dim
OPPOSITE clear

❷ *The poem is full of obscure references.*
• oblique, enigmatic, cryptic, puzzling, perplexing
OPPOSITE obvious

❸ *He is an obscure Russian poet.*
• unknown, unheard of, little known, minor, unrecognized, forgotten
OPPOSITES famous, well known

obscure *VERB*

A tall hedge obscured the view.
• block out, cover, hide, conceal, mask, screen, veil, shroud
OPPOSITE reveal

observant *ADJECTIVE*

If you're observant, you might see a badger tonight.
• alert, attentive, sharp-eyed, vigilant, watchful
OPPOSITE inattentive

observation *NOUN*

❶ *You will need a telescope for observation of the Moon.*
• study, watching, scrutiny, surveillance, monitoring

❷ *The author makes some interesting observations.*
• comment, remark, statement, reflection

observe *VERB*

❶ *He has spent his life observing elephants in the wild.*
• watch, look at, view, study, survey, monitor, scrutinize, regard
IDIOMS keep an eye on, keep tabs on

❷ *I observed her putting the letter into her bag.*
• notice, note, see, detect, spot, discern, perceive, witness

❸ *You must observe the rules of the game.*
• comply with, abide by, keep to, adhere to, obey, honour, respect, follow, heed

❹ *'This is a most curious case,' observed Holmes.*
• remark, comment, mention, say, state, declare
SEE ALSO say

obsessed *ADJECTIVE*

Raheem is completely obsessed with cars.
• infatuated, fixated, preoccupied, besotted, smitten
IDIOM (*informal*) have a thing about

obsession *NOUN*

She seems to have an obsession with aliens.
• passion, fixation, infatuation, preoccupation, mania, compulsion
IDIOMS a bee in your bonnet, (*informal*) a thing about

obsolete *ADJECTIVE*

That piece of software is now obsolete.
• out of date, outdated, outmoded, passé, antiquated, dated, archaic, defunct, extinct
IDIOM past its sell-by date
OPPOSITES current, modern

obstacle *NOUN*

❶ *I cycled around the obstacles in the road.*
• obstruction, barrier, barricade, block

❷ *Your age should not be an obstacle.*
• problem, difficulty, hindrance, hurdle, snag, catch, disadvantage, drawback, stumbling block, impediment
IDIOMS a fly in the ointment, a spanner in the works
OPPOSITES aid, advantage

obstinate *ADJECTIVE*

He's too obstinate to admit that he's wrong.
• stubborn, uncooperative, wilful, self-willed, headstrong, pig-headed, inflexible, unyielding
OPPOSITES cooperative, compliant

obstruct *VERB*

The path was obstructed by a fallen tree.
• block, jam, clog, choke,

make impassable
(*informal*) bung up

obstruction NOUN
A fallen tree was causing an obstruction.
• blockage, barrier, obstacle, hindrance,
impediment, stoppage, hold-up, check

obtain VERB
You must obtain a permit to park here.
• get, get hold of, acquire, pick up,
procure, come by
IDIOM lay your hands on

obvious ADJECTIVE
❶ *There were no obvious marks on the
body.*
• noticeable, conspicuous, visible,
prominent, pronounced, distinct, glaring
OPPOSITES inconspicuous, imperceptible
❷ *It was obvious that the woman was
lying.*
• clear, evident, apparent, plain,
manifest, patent, undeniable,
unmistakable
OPPOSITE unclear

obviously ADVERB
There has obviously been some mistake.
• clearly, plainly, evidently, apparently,
patently, of course, needless to say
OPPOSITES perhaps, arguably

occasion NOUN
❶ *We met on a number of occasions.*
• time, moment, instance
❷ *Is the dress for a special occasion?*
• event, affair, function, happening,
incident, occurrence

occasional ADJECTIVE
The forecast is for occasional showers.
• intermittent, infrequent, irregular,
periodic, sporadic, odd, scattered
OPPOSITES frequent, regular

occasionally ADVERB
*He nodded occasionally to show he was
listening.*
• sometimes, every so often, once in
a while, now and again, from time to
time, on occasion, periodically
OPPOSITES frequently, often

occupant NOUN
*The only occupants of the castle were a
family of bats.*
• resident, inhabitant, occupier, tenant

occupation NOUN
❶ *The birth certificate lists his father's
occupation.*
• job, employment, profession, post,
position, trade, work, line of work,
calling
❷ *My favourite occupation is reading.*
• activity, pastime, hobby, pursuit,
recreation
❸ *the Roman occupation of Gaul*
• capture, seizure, conquest, invasion,
takeover, colonization

✺ WORD WEB

Some occupations:

➤ accountant	➤ florist
➤ actor or actress	➤ footballer
➤ architect	➤ gardener
➤ artist	➤ hairdresser
➤ astronaut	➤ imam
➤ banker	➤ janitor
➤ barber	➤ joiner
➤ bookseller	➤ journalist
➤ builder	➤ lawyer
➤ bus driver	➤ lecturer
➤ care worker	➤ lexicographer
➤ chef	➤ librarian
➤ cleaner	➤ mechanic
➤ coach	➤ midwife
➤ cook	➤ miner
➤ curator	➤ minister
➤ dancer	➤ model
➤ dentist	➤ musician
➤ detective	➤ nurse
➤ diver	➤ office worker
➤ doctor	➤ optician
➤ editor	➤ painter
➤ electrician	➤ paramedic
➤ engineer	➤ pharmacist
➤ farmer	➤ photographer
➤ film-maker	➤ pilot
➤ firefighter	➤ plumber
➤ fisherman	➤ police officer
➤ flight attendant	➤ politician

a
b
c
d
e
f
g
h
i
j
k
l
m
n
o
p
q
r
s
t
u
v
w
x
y
z

> postal worker
> priest
> professor
> programmer
> psychiatrist
> psychologist
> rabbi
> receptionist
> reporter
> sailor
> scientist
> secretary
> security guard
> shepherd
> shopkeeper
> singer
> soldier

> solicitor
> stockbroker
> surgeon
> tailor
> teacher
> traffic warden
> train driver
> TV presenter
> undertaker
> vet
> vicar
> waiter or waitress
> web designer
> writer
> zookeeper

For occupations in the past see historical.

For medical occupations see medicine.

occupied ADJECTIVE
❶ *This game will keep you occupied for hours.*
• busy, engaged, absorbed, engrossed, involved, active, tied up
OPPOSITE idle
❷ *Is this seat occupied?*
• in use, taken, engaged, full
OPPOSITES free, vacant

occupy VERB
❶ *A young couple occupy the flat upstairs.*
• live in, reside in, dwell in, inhabit
❷ *The piano occupies most of the room.*
• fill, take up, use up
❸ *This game should occupy them for a few hours.*
• keep you busy, engage your attention, divert, amuse, absorb, engross
❹ *The Romans occupied Britain for nearly 400 years.*
• capture, seize, take over, conquer, colonize

occur VERB
❶ *She told them what had occurred.*
• happen, take place, come about, arise

❷ *It is a disease which occurs mainly in childhood.*
• appear, develop, be found, crop up, turn up
> occur to
Just then an idea occurred to me.
• cross your mind, enter your head

occurrence NOUN
Highway robbery was once a common occurrence.
• event, happening, incident, phenomenon

ocean NOUN

⊕ **WORD WEB**

The oceans of the world:
> Antarctic
> Arctic
> Atlantic
> Indian
> Pacific
SEE ALSO sea

odd ADJECTIVE
❶ *Her behaviour seems rather odd.*
• strange, unusual, abnormal, peculiar, curious, puzzling, extraordinary, funny, weird, bizarre, eccentric, quirky, outlandish
IDIOM (informal) off the wall
OPPOSITES normal, ordinary
❷ *I could only find one odd sock.*
• unmatched, unpaired, single, lone, leftover, spare
❸ *He does odd jobs around the house.*
• occasional, casual, irregular, various, sundry

odour NOUN
There's a strange odour coming from the kitchen.
• smell, aroma, scent, perfume, fragrance, bouquet
(informal) whiff
– An unpleasant odour is a **reek**, **stench** or **stink**.
For tips on describing smells see smell.

offence NOUN
 1 They were only charged with minor offences.
• crime, wrongdoing, misdeed, misdemeanour, felony, sin
– In sports, an offence is a **foul** or an **infringement**.
 2 I didn't mean to cause any offence.
• annoyance, anger, displeasure, resentment, hard feelings, animosity

offend VERB
 1 I hope my email didn't offend you.
• upset, hurt your feelings, annoy, anger, displease, insult, affront
 2 Some criminals are likely to offend again.
• break the law, commit a crime, do wrong

offensive ADJECTIVE
 1 He apologized for his offensive remarks.
• insulting, rude, impolite, disrespectful, abusive, upsetting, hurtful
OPPOSITE complimentary
 2 The gas produces an offensive smell.
• unpleasant, disagreeable, distasteful, objectionable, off-putting, repellent, repulsive, disgusting, obnoxious, revolting, nasty
OPPOSITES pleasant, agreeable

offer VERB
 1 May I offer a suggestion?
• propose, put forward, suggest, submit, present, proffer
OPPOSITES withdraw, retract
 2 A few people offered to help us clear up.
• volunteer, come forward
OPPOSITE refuse

offer NOUN
Thank you for your offer of help.
• proposal, suggestion, proposition

office NOUN
 1 Over the summer he is working in a newspaper office.
• workplace, bureau, department

 2 She took up the office of vice president immediately.
• post, position, appointment, job, role, function

officer NOUN
a customs officer
• official, office-holder, executive

official ADJECTIVE
The official opening of the museum is next month.
• formal, authorized, legitimate, approved, recognized, proper, valid
OPPOSITES unofficial, unauthorized

official NOUN
We spoke to a high-ranking official in the ministry.
• officer, office-holder, executive, representative, agent

often ADVERB
It often rains in April.
• frequently, regularly, commonly, constantly, repeatedly, again and again, time after time, many times

oil VERB
She was oiling her bicycle chain.
• lubricate, grease

oily ADJECTIVE
I'm cutting down on oily foods.
• greasy, fatty

ointment NOUN
Here's some ointment for your rash.
• cream, lotion, salve, liniment, balm

OK or **okay** (informal) ADJECTIVE
see **all right**

old ADJECTIVE

> **S**   **OVERUSED WORD**
>
> **1** An **old** person:
> ➤ elderly   ➤ senior
> ➤ aged
> Bus tickets are free for **elderly** people.
> OPPOSITE young

❷ An old building, old document:

> historical
> early
> ancient

> archaic
> antiquarian

The church stands on the site of an ancient Celtic monastery.

OPPOSITE modern

❸ An old machine, old vehicle:

> old-fashioned
> out of date
> antiquated
> antique

> vintage
> veteran
> early
> obsolete

My uncle collects and restores vintage motorcycles.

OPPOSITES up to date, current

❹ Old clothes, old furnishings:

> worn
> scruffy
> shabby

> frayed
> threadbare
> (informal) tatty

IDIOM falling to pieces

I was wearing a pair of scruffy jeans and a t-shirt.

OPPOSITE new

❺ The old days, old times:

> past
> former
> earlier

> previous
> bygone
> olden

– Times before written records were kept were **prehistoric** times.

We did a project on how children lived in former times.

OPPOSITES modern, recent

old-fashioned ADJECTIVE

The illustrations look old-fashioned now.

• out of date, dated, outdated, outmoded, unfashionable, antiquated, passé
(informal) old hat
IDIOM behind the times
OPPOSITES modern, up to date

omit VERB

❶ *These scenes were omitted from the final film.*
• exclude, leave out, cut, drop, eliminate, miss out, skip
OPPOSITE include
❷ *You omitted to mention the author's name.*
• forget, fail, neglect
OPPOSITE remember

once ADVERB

❶ *California was once part of Mexico.*
• formerly, at one time, previously, in the past
❷ *We spoke only once on the phone.*
• one time, on one occasion

once CONJUNCTION

The show will begin once everyone is seated.
• as soon as, when, after

one-sided ADJECTIVE

❶ *The game has been one-sided so far.*
• uneven, unequal, unbalanced
❷ *This book gives a one-sided account of the conflict.*
• biased, prejudiced, partisan, partial, slanted, distorted

only ADVERB

❶ *There is only room for one passenger.*
• just, no more than, at most, at best
❷ *This email is for your eyes only.*
• solely, purely, exclusively

ooze VERB

The jam was oozing from my doughnut.
• seep, leak, escape, dribble, drip

opaque ADJECTIVE

The window was fitted with opaque glass.
• cloudy, dull, obscure
OPPOSITES transparent, translucent

open ADJECTIVE

❶ *Just leave the door open.*
• unlocked, unfastened, ajar, gaping
OPPOSITES closed, shut

❷ *There was an open packet of crisps on the table.*
• opened, unsealed, uncovered, unwrapped
OPPOSITES closed, sealed

❸ *Several maps were open on the desk.*
• unfolded, spread out, unrolled, unfurled

❹ *Through the window was a view of open countryside.*
• clear, unrestricted, unenclosed, extensive, rolling, sweeping
OPPOSITE enclosed

❺ *He was open about his mistakes.*
• frank, honest, candid, direct, forthcoming, unreserved, outspoken (*informal*) upfront
OPPOSITES secretive, evasive

❻ *The idea was met with open hostility.*
• plain, undisguised, unconcealed, overt, manifest, blatant, public
OPPOSITES hidden, suppressed

➤ **be open to**
❶ *I am always open to suggestions.*
• receptive to, willing to listen to, responsive to

❷ *Computers are open to online attacks.*
• vulnerable to, susceptible to, exposed to, liable to, subject to

open VERB
❶ *Let me open a window.*
• unfasten, unlock, unbolt

❷ *I can't wait to open my presents.*
• undo, unwrap, untie, unseal, unfold, unroll
– To open an umbrella is to **unfurl** it.
– To open a wine bottle is to **uncork** it.

❸ *The exhibition opens next Friday.*
• begin, start, commence, get under way (*informal*) kick off
OPPOSITE close

opening NOUN
❶ *The sheep got through an opening in the fence.*
• gap, hole, breach, break, split

❷ *The film has a very dramatic opening.*
• beginning, start, commencement (*informal*) kick-off

❸ *We are invited to the opening of the new sports centre.*
• launch, inauguration

– The opening of a new play or film is the **first night** or **premiere**.

❹ *The job offers a good opening for a keen young person.*
• chance, opportunity

opening ADJECTIVE
Can you remember the opening lines of the song?
• first, initial, introductory, preliminary
OPPOSITES final, closing

operate VERB
❶ *Do you know how to operate this camera?*
• use, work, run, drive, handle, control, manage

❷ *This watch operates even underwater.*
• work, function, go, run, perform

❸ *They had to operate to save his life.*
• carry out an operation, perform surgery

operation NOUN
❶ *This lever controls the operation of the robot.*
• performance, working, functioning, running, action

❷ *Defusing a bomb is a dangerous operation.*
• task, activity, action, exercise, manoeuvre, process, procedure

❸ *I had an operation to remove my appendix.*
• surgery

opinion NOUN
What was your honest opinion of the film?
• view, judgement, impression, assessment, estimation, point of view, thought, belief, feeling, attitude, idea, notion

opponent NOUN
He was one of the main opponents of slavery.
• critic, objector, challenger, rival, adversary, enemy, foe
– Your opponents in a game are the **opposition**.
OPPOSITES supporter, ally

a b c d e f g h i j k l m n o p q r s t u v w x y z

opportunity *NOUN*
There weren't many opportunities to relax.
• chance, possibility, occasion, moment, time

oppose *VERB*
Many people opposed the plans for a new runway.
• object to, be against, disapprove of, disagree with, argue against, be hostile towards, fight against, resist, challenge
OPPOSITES support, defend

opposite *ADJECTIVE*
❶ *My friend lives on the opposite side of the street.*
• facing
❷ *They hold opposite opinions on the subject.*
• contrasting, conflicting, contradictory, opposed, opposing, different, contrary
OPPOSITES the same, similar

opposite *NOUN*
She always says one thing and does the opposite.
• reverse, converse, contrary, antithesis

opposition *NOUN*
❶ *There was fierce opposition to the new road.*
• resistance, objection, disapproval, hostility, antagonism, dissent
OPPOSITE support
❷ *Our team easily beat the opposition.*
• opponents, rivals

optimistic *ADJECTIVE*
I'm feeling optimistic about the future.
• positive, confident, cheerful, buoyant, hopeful, expectant, (*informal*) upbeat
OPPOSITE pessimistic

option *NOUN*
We had the option to walk or take the bus.
• choice, alternative, selection, possibility

optional *ADJECTIVE*
Art is an optional subject at the school.
• voluntary, non-compulsory, discretionary
OPPOSITE compulsory

oral *ADJECTIVE*
Students take an oral exam in each language.
• spoken, verbal, unwritten
OPPOSITE written

orange *ADJECTIVE*
a bright orange colour
For tips on describing colours see **colour**.

orbit *VERB*
The earth orbits the sun in about 365 days.
• circle, travel round, go round

ordeal *NOUN*
One of the survivors gave an account of their ordeal.
• suffering, hardship, trial, trauma, torment, anguish, torture, nightmare

order *NOUN*
❶ *The captain gave the order to abandon ship.*
• command, instruction, direction, decree, edict
❷ *You can put in an advance order for the DVD.*
• request, demand, reservation, booking
❸ *The films are listed in alphabetical order.*
• arrangement, sequence, series, succession
❹ *She keeps her bike in good order.*
• condition, state, shape, repair
❺ *The police eventually restored order to the streets.*
• peace, calm, control, quiet, harmony, law and order
OPPOSITE chaos

order *VERB*
❶ *The crew were ordered to return.*
• command, instruct, direct, tell, require, charge
❷ *I ordered the tickets over the Internet.*
• request, reserve, apply for, book

❸ *He needed a few minutes to order his thoughts.*
• arrange, organize, sort, put in order

orderly ADJECTIVE
❶ *Plants are named according to an orderly system.*
• organized, well ordered, systematic, methodical, neat, tidy
OPPOSITES untidy, haphazard
❷ *Please form an orderly queue.*
• well behaved, controlled, disciplined
OPPOSITE disorderly

ordinary ADJECTIVE
❶ *It began as just an ordinary day.*
• normal, typical, usual, customary, habitual, regular, routine
❷ *The picture was taken with an ordinary camera.*
• standard, average, common, conventional, run-of-the-mill, everyday
IDIOM common or garden
OPPOSITES special, unusual

organization NOUN
❶ *The UN is an international organization.*
• institution, operation, enterprise, company
(*informal*) outfit, set-up
❷ *She is responsible for the organization of this year's parade.*
• coordination, planning, arrangement, running

organize VERB
❶ *Can you help me to organize the party?*
• coordinate, plan, see to, set up, put together, run
❷ *I'm trying to organize all my notebooks.*
• arrange, put in order, sort out, tidy up, classify, collate

origin NOUN
❶ *We know very little about the origin of life on Earth.*
• beginning, start, creation, birth, dawn, emergence, source, cause, root
OPPOSITE end

❷ *He was proud of his humble origins.*
• background, ancestry, descent, parentage, pedigree, lineage, roots, stock, birth, family, extraction

original ADJECTIVE
❶ *The settlers drove out the original inhabitants.*
• earliest, first, initial, native, indigenous
❷ *It's certainly an original idea for a story.*
• inventive, innovative, new, novel, fresh, creative, imaginative, unusual, unconventional, unorthodox
❸ *Is that an original painting or a copy?*
• genuine, real, authentic, true

originate VERB
❶ *Rock music originated in the 1950s.*
• begin, start, arise, emerge, emanate, spring up, crop up
❷ *He originated his own style of playing the guitar.*
• invent, create, design, conceive, dream up, devise, formulate, develop, pioneer

ornament NOUN
The shelf was covered with ornaments.
• decoration, bauble, trinket, knick-knack

ornamental ADJECTIVE
There was an ornamental fountain in the garden.
• decorative, fancy, ornate, decorated

ornate ADJECTIVE
The frame around the mirror was very ornate.
• elaborate, decorative, fancy, showy, fussy
OPPOSITE plain

orthodox ADJECTIVE
She wasn't taught to play the piano in the orthodox way.
• conventional, accepted, customary, usual, standard, traditional, regular, established, approved, recognized, official
OPPOSITES unorthodox, unconventional

other ADJECTIVE
❶ *It is more expensive than other brands.*
• alternative, different, separate, distinct
❷ *I have some other questions.*
• more, further, additional, supplementary, extra

outbreak NOUN
❶ *People in the town fear an outbreak of violence.*
• outburst, eruption, flare-up, upsurge (in), spate, wave, rash
– An outbreak of disease that spreads quickly is an **epidemic**.
❷ *They left the country a year after the outbreak of the war.*
• beginning, start, onset, commencement

outburst NOUN
There was an outburst of laughter from the next room.
• explosion, eruption, outbreak, fit, storm, surge

outcome NOUN
What was the outcome of your experiment?
• result, consequence, effect, upshot, end result

outcry NOUN
There was a massive outcry over the closure of the hospital.
• protest, protestation, complaints, objections, uproar, fuss, furore, dissent

outdoor ADJECTIVE
The hotel has an outdoor swimming pool.
• open-air, out of doors, outside, al fresco
OPPOSITE indoor

outer ADJECTIVE
They finally broke through the outer walls of the city.
• external, exterior, outside, outermost, outward
OPPOSITE inner

outfit NOUN
❶ *She was wearing her new outfit.*
• clothes, costume, suit, ensemble (*informal*) get-up
❷ *Do you have a puncture repair outfit?*
• equipment, apparatus, kit (*informal*) set-up, gear

outing NOUN
We went on a family outing to the coast.
• trip, excursion, expedition, jaunt, day out

outlaw NOUN
A band of outlaws held up the train.
• bandit, fugitive, wanted criminal, highwayman, brigand

outlet NOUN
❶ *The basin has an outlet for excess water.*
• opening, way out, exit, vent, channel, conduit, duct
OPPOSITE inlet
❷ *The company has outlets throughout Europe.*
• shop, store, branch, market

outline NOUN
❶ *He first drew the outline of a face.*
• profile, silhouette, shape, form, contour
❷ *Write a brief outline of the plot.*
• summary, sketch, synopsis, precis, résumé, rough idea, rundown, gist
IDIOM bare bones

outline VERB
She quickly outlined her plan.
• summarize, sketch out, rough out

outlook NOUN
❶ *The cottage has a beautiful outlook over the lake.*
• view, vista, prospect, panorama
❷ *She has a gloomy outlook on life.*
• point of view, view, attitude, frame of mind, standpoint, stance
❸ *The outlook for tomorrow is bright and sunny.*
• forecast, prediction, prospect, prognosis

out of date ADJECTIVE
　❶ The information in the article is already out of date.
　• outdated, dated, old-fashioned, obsolete, obsolescent
　IDIOMS behind the times, past its sell-by date
　OPPOSITES modern, up to date
　❷ Your library card is out of date.
　• expired, invalid, void, lapsed
　OPPOSITES valid, current

outrage NOUN
　❶ There was public outrage at the government's decision.
　• anger, fury, indignation, rage, disgust, horror
　❷ Such a waste of public money is an outrage.
　• disgrace, scandal, crime, atrocity

outrage VERB
　He was outraged at the way he had been treated.
　• shock, anger, enrage, infuriate, affront

outrageous ADJECTIVE
　❶ It was an outrageous way to behave.
　• disgraceful, scandalous, shocking, atrocious, appalling, monstrous, shameful
　OPPOSITES acceptable, reasonable
　❷ They charge outrageous prices at that shop.
　• excessive, exorbitant, extortionate, inflated, unreasonable, preposterous

outset NOUN
　The plan was doomed from the outset.
　• start, beginning, starting point
　IDIOM the word go

outside NOUN
　Insects have their skeletons on the outside of their bodies.
　• exterior, shell, surface, case, skin, facade
　OPPOSITE inside

outside ADJECTIVE
　We have an outside light above the front door.
　• exterior, external, outer
　OPPOSITE inside

outsider NOUN
　She's lived in the village for years, but still feels like an outsider.
　• newcomer, stranger, alien, foreigner, immigrant, incomer

outskirts PLURAL NOUN
　We live on the outskirts of town.
　• edges, fringes, periphery, outer areas
　– The outskirts of a large town or city are the suburbs.
　OPPOSITE centre

outspoken ADJECTIVE
　He's always been outspoken in his views.
　• frank, open, forthright, direct, candid, plain-spoken, blunt, straightforward

outstanding ADJECTIVE
　❶ She is an outstanding athlete.
　• excellent, exceptional, first-rate, first-class, tremendous, marvellous, wonderful, superb, great, fine, superior, superlative, top-notch
　(informal) brilliant, fantastic, terrific, fabulous, sensational, super
　OPPOSITES ordinary, second-rate, unexceptional
　❷ There are still some outstanding bills to pay.
　• unpaid, unsettled, overdue, owing

outward ADJECTIVE
　His outward manner was bright and cheerful.
　• external, exterior, outside, outer, surface, superficial
　OPPOSITE inward

outwit VERB
　Somehow she always manages to outwit her opponents.
　• outsmart, outfox, get the better of, beat, defeat

oval ADJECTIVE
　Our garden has an oval lawn.
　• egg-shaped, elliptical

oven NOUN
　The meat was roasting in the oven.
　• cooker, stove, range

– A special oven for firing pottery is a **kiln**.

overcast ADJECTIVE
The sky has been overcast all day.
• cloudy, dull, grey, sunless, dark, leaden
For tips on describing the weather see **weather**.

overcome VERB
❶ *He managed to overcome his fear of flying.*
• conquer, defeat, master, get the better of, prevail over
❷ *Rescuers were overcome by the fumes.*
• overpower, overwhelm

overflow VERB
I left the tap on and the bath overflowed.
• spill over, pour over, brim over, run over, flood

overgrown ADJECTIVE
The back garden was completely overgrown.
• unkempt, untidy, tangled, weedy, wild

overhaul VERB
The engine has been completely overhauled.
• service, check over, inspect, repair, restore, refit, refurbish

overhead ADVERB
A flock of geese flew overhead.
• above, high up, in the sky, above your head

overlook VERB
❶ *You have overlooked one important fact.*
• miss, fail to see, fail to notice
❷ *I am willing to overlook the error.*
• disregard, ignore, pay no attention to, forget about, pass over
IDIOM turn a blind eye to
❸ *The villa overlooks an olive grove.*
• have a view of, look on to, look out on, face

overpowering ADJECTIVE
❶ *The stench was overpowering.*
• overwhelming, strong, intense,

pungent, oppressive, suffocating, unbearable
❷ *I felt an overpowering urge to giggle.*
• overwhelming, powerful, compelling, irresistible, uncontrollable

overrun VERB
The barn was overrun with rats and mice.
• invade, take over, spread over, swarm over, inundate, overwhelm

overtake VERB
We overtook the car in front.
• pass, go past, pull ahead of, leave behind

overthrow VERB
The rebels planned to overthrow the president.
• depose, bring down, topple, defeat, remove, oust, drive out, unseat

overturn VERB
❶ *Our canoe overturned.*
• capsize, turn over, keel over, turn turtle
❷ *I accidentally overturned a milk jug.*
• knock over, tip over, topple, upset, upend
❸ *The court overturned the judge's decision.*
• cancel, reverse, repeal, rescind, revoke, overrule

overwhelm VERB
❶ *We have been overwhelmed by the response.*
• affect deeply, move deeply, overcome
IDIOMS bowl you over, leave you speechless
❷ *The attackers overwhelmed us with sheer numbers.*
• defeat, overcome, overpower, crush, trounce
❸ *A huge tidal wave overwhelmed the village.*
• engulf, flood, inundate, submerge, swallow up, bury

overwhelming ADJECTIVE
❶ *It was another overwhelming defeat.*
• decisive, devastating, crushing, massive, monumental

A
B
C
D
E
F
G
H
I
J
K
L
M
N
O
P
Q
R
S
T
U
V
W
X
Y
Z

– An overwhelming victory at an election
is a **landslide**.

② *I had an overwhelming desire to see
him again.*
• strong, powerful, overpowering,
irresistible, compelling

owe *VERB*
How much do you owe her?
• be in debt (to), be in arrears (to)

owing *ADJECTIVE*
➤ **owing to**
It was a difficult journey owing to the
heavy snow and ice.
• because of, on account of, as a result
of, thanks to, due to

own *VERB*
It was the first bike she had owned.
• be the owner of, have, possess
➤ **own up to**
*No one owned up to breaking the
window.*
• confess to, admit to, tell the truth
about
IDIOM come clean about

Pp

pace NOUN
❶ Take a pace backwards.
• step, stride
❷ The runners set off at a fast pace.
• speed, rate, velocity, tempo

pace VERB
She was pacing anxiously around the room.
• walk, step, stride, march, pound
SEE ALSO walk

pacify VERB
It was too late to pacify her now and she stormed off.
• calm, quieten, soothe, humour, appease
OPPOSITES anger, annoy

pack NOUN
❶ He took out a pack of chewing gum.
• packet, box, carton, package, bundle
❷ The hikers picked up their packs and trudged off.
• bag, rucksack, backpack, haversack, knapsack
❸ Wolves hunt in packs.
• group, herd, troop, band

pack VERB
❶ She was packing a suitcase.
• fill, load up
❷ I packed everything away in the cupboards.
• stow, store, put away
❸ Over a hundred people packed into the hall.
• cram, crowd, squeeze, stuff, jam, wedge

package NOUN
The postman delivered a huge package.
• parcel, packet, bundle

pad NOUN
❶ She put a pad of cotton wool over the wound.
• wad, dressing, cushion, pillow
❷ There's a pad for messages next to the phone.
• notebook, notepad, jotter

pad VERB
❶ The seats are padded with foam rubber.
• stuff, fill, pack, wad
– To put covers and padding on furniture is to **upholster** it.
❷ He padded along to the bathroom.
see walk

padding NOUN
The padding is coming out of this cushion.
• stuffing, filling, wadding
– The covers and padding on furniture is **upholstery**.

paddle VERB
The children were paddling in rock pools.
• splash about, dabble
– To walk through deep water is to **wade**.

page NOUN
❶ The last page had been torn from the book.
• sheet, leaf, folio
❷ I wrote two whole pages of notes.
• side

paid
past tense see **pay**

pain NOUN
❶ I felt a sharp pain in my ankle.
• soreness, ache, pang, stab, throbbing, twinge
– A slight pain is **discomfort**.
❷ She had suffered the pain of losing her husband.
• anguish, agony, suffering, torment, torture

painful ADJECTIVE
❶ Is your knee still painful?
• sore, aching, tender, hurting, smarting, stinging, throbbing
OPPOSITES painless, pain-free
❷ We looked at the photographs and it

brought back painful memories.
• unpleasant, upsetting, distressing, disagreeable, traumatic, agonizing, harrowing
OPPOSITE pleasant

painless ADJECTIVE
❶ *The treatment is quite painless.*
• comfortable, pain-free
OPPOSITE painful
❷ *This is a quick and painless way to make a cake.*
• easy, simple, effortless, trouble-free, undemanding

painstaking ADJECTIVE
He showed a painstaking attention to detail.
• meticulous, thorough, careful, conscientious, rigorous, scrupulous

paint VERB
❶ *Each wall was painted a different colour.*
• colour, decorate, dye, stain, tint
❷ *Cézanne often painted apples.*
• depict, portray, represent

painting NOUN
Most of his paintings are landscapes.
• picture, artwork, canvas, oil painting, watercolour
– *A painting of a person or an animal is a* **portrait**.
– *A picture painted on a wall is a* **mural** *or* **fresco**.
– *A painting by a famous artist of the past is an* **old master**.
SEE ALSO picture

pair NOUN
Next to the bowl were a pair of chopsticks.
• couple, brace, set
– *Two people who sing or play music together are a* **duet** *or* **duo**.
– *Two people who work or play together are* **partners** *or a* **partnership**.

palace NOUN
The palace once belonged to the royal family.
• mansion, stately home, castle, chateau

pale ADJECTIVE
❶ *His face suddenly turned pale.*
• white, pallid, pasty, wan, ashen, sallow, anaemic, colourless
– *To go pale with fear is to* **blanch**.
OPPOSITES rosy-cheeked, flushed
❷ *Her jacket was a pale shade of blue.*
• light, pastel, faint, subtle, faded, muted, bleached
OPPOSITES bright, dark
❸ *It was difficult to see much in the pale moonlight.*
• dim, faint, low, weak, feeble
OPPOSITES bright, strong

pamper VERB
The twins' grandparents liked to pamper them.
• spoil, indulge, cosset, mollycoddle, humour

pamphlet NOUN
She had several pamphlets on bee-keeping.
• leaflet, booklet, brochure, circular

pan NOUN
Heat some milk in a pan.
• pot, saucepan, frying pan

panel NOUN
❶ *He stared at the control panel, looking for the right switch.*
• board, unit, console, array
❷ *The contest was judged by a panel of experts.*
• group, team, body, board, committee

panic NOUN
People fled the streets in panic.
• alarm, fear, fright, terror, frenzy, hysteria
OPPOSITE calm

panic VERB
If the alarm goes off, don't panic.
• be alarmed, take fright, become hysterical, be panic-stricken (*informal*) freak out
IDIOM lose your head

pant VERB
He stood panting at the top of the hill.
• gasp, wheeze, puff, breathe heavily
IDIOM huff and puff

pants PLURAL NOUN
see clothes

paper NOUN
❶ We are out of printing paper.
– A single piece of paper is a **leaf** or **sheet**.
– Paper and other writing materials are **stationery**.
❷ The story made the front page of the local paper.
• newspaper, journal, gazette, bulletin
❸ Excuse me, there are some papers I need to sign.
• document, deed, certificate, paperwork

⊛ WORD WEB

Some types of paper:
- ➤ blotting paper
- ➤ card
- ➤ cardboard
- ➤ cartridge paper
- ➤ crêpe paper
- ➤ graph paper
- ➤ greaseproof paper
- ➤ papyrus
- ➤ parchment
- ➤ recycled paper
- ➤ rice paper
- ➤ tissue paper
- ➤ toilet paper
- ➤ tracing paper
- ➤ wallpaper
- ➤ wrapping paper
- ➤ vellum

---

parade NOUN
The circus parade passed along the street.
• procession, march, spectacle, show, display
– A parade of people in costume is a **pageant**.
– A parade of vehicles or people on horseback is a **cavalcade**.

parade VERB
❶ A brass band paraded past our window.
• march, troop, file

❷ My sister paraded round the room in her new dress.
• strut, stride, swagger

parallel ADJECTIVE
The two main characters have led parallel lives.
• similar, corresponding, comparable, analogous, matching, twin
OPPOSITES divergent, contrasting

paralyse VERB
❶ Scorpions paralyse their prey with venom.
• disable, immobilize, incapacitate, deaden, numb
❷ I stood and stared, paralysed with fear.
• immobilize, freeze, petrify

parcel NOUN
I received a parcel in the post this morning.
• package, packet

parched ADJECTIVE
❶ Nothing was growing in the parched fields.
• dry, arid, baked, scorched, barren, sterile, waterless
❷ (informal) I need a drink of water – I'm parched!
• thirsty, dry

pardon VERB
❶ Pardon me for asking.
• excuse, forgive
❷ One of the conspirators was later pardoned.
• exonerate, reprieve, let off, spare, forgive

parent NOUN
see family

park NOUN
❶ In the afternoon we went for a walk in the park.
• recreation ground, public garden
❷ The house and surrounding park are open to visitors.
• parkland, gardens, grounds, estate

park *VERB*
You may park your car outside.
• leave, position, station

parliament *NOUN*
The Isle of Man has its own parliament.
• assembly, legislature, congress, senate, chamber, house

part *NOUN*
❶ *All the parts of the engine are now working properly.*
• component, constituent, bit, element, module
❷ *I missed the first part of the film.*
• section, piece, portion, bit, division, instalment
❸ *Our friends are moving to another part of town.*
• area, district, region, neighbourhood, sector, quarter
❹ *She has the lead part in the school play.*
• character, role

part *VERB*
❶ *The clouds parted to reveal a full moon.*
• separate, divide, move apart, split
OPPOSITE join
❷ *We parted on friendly terms.*
• part company, say goodbye, take your leave, go your separate ways
OPPOSITE meet
➤ **part with**
I couldn't bear to part with any of my books.
• discard, get rid of, give away, dispense with, throw out, hand over, surrender

partial *ADJECTIVE*
The show was only a partial success.
• limited, imperfect, incomplete, qualified
OPPOSITES complete, total
➤ **be partial to**
My sister has always been partial to chocolate.
• like, love, enjoy, be fond of, be keen on
IDIOMS have a soft spot for, have a taste for, have a weakness for

participate *VERB*
Twenty-two choirs will be participating in the event.
• take part, join in, be involved, contribute, play a part
IDIOM have a hand in

particle *NOUN*
There were particles of dust on the camera lens.
• speck, grain, fragment, bit, piece, scrap, shred, sliver
SEE ALSO bit

particular *ADJECTIVE*
❶ *Do you have a particular date in mind?*
• specific, certain, distinct, definite, exact, precise
❷ *Please take particular care with this package.*
• special, exceptional, unusual, extreme, marked, notable
❸ *My cat's very particular about her food.*
• fussy, finicky, fastidious, faddy, hard to please
(*informal*) choosy, picky

particularly *ADVERB*
❶ *The view is particularly good from here.*
• especially, exceptionally, remarkably, outstandingly, unusually, uncommonly, uniquely
❷ *I particularly asked for front-row seats.*
• specifically, explicitly, expressly, specially, in particular

particulars *PLURAL NOUN*
A police officer took down all the particulars.
• details, facts, information, circumstances

partition *NOUN*
A partition separates the two classrooms.
• room divider, screen, barrier, panel

partly ADVERB
The accident was partly my own fault.
• in part, to some extent, up to a point
OPPOSITE entirely

partner NOUN
❶ *The two women had been business partners for years.*
• colleague, associate, collaborator, ally
❷ *Staff were encouraged to bring their partners to the party.*
• spouse, husband, wife, boyfriend, girlfriend, lover
– An animal's partner is its **mate**.

party NOUN
❶ *We're all going to a New Year party.*
• celebration, festivity, function, gathering, reception
(*informal*) get-together, bash, do
❷ *A party of tourists was going round the museum.*
• group, band, crowd, company
(*informal*) bunch, gang
❸ *They have formed a new political party.*
• alliance, association, faction, league

pass VERB
❶ *A crowd watched as the parade passed.*
• go by, move past
❷ *The soldiers passed over the bridge.*
• go, advance, proceed, progress, travel, make your way
❸ *We tried to pass the car in front.*
• overtake, go past, go ahead of
❹ *Three years passed before we met again.*
• go by, elapse, roll by
❺ *Could you pass me the sugar, please?*
• hand, give, deliver, offer, present
❻ *Did you pass your audition?*
• be successful in, get through, succeed in
– To pass something easily is to **sail through** and to pass it barely is to **scrape through**.
OPPOSITE fail

❼ *They passed the time playing cards.*
• spend, occupy, fill, use, employ, while away
❽ *The pain will soon pass.*
• go away, come to an end, disappear, fade
IDIOMS run its course, blow over
➤ **pass out**
One of the runners passed out in the heat.
• faint, lose consciousness, black out

pass NOUN
❶ *You'll need a pass to go backstage.*
• permit, licence, ticket
❷ *We went through a narrow mountain pass.*
• gap, gorge, ravine, canyon, valley

passage NOUN
❶ *A secret passage leads to the inner chamber.*
• passageway, corridor, hallway, tunnel
❷ *The ship managed to force a passage through the ice.*
• path, route, way
❸ *They finally reached land after a long sea passage.*
• journey, voyage, crossing
❹ *We all had to read out a passage from the book.*
• excerpt, extract, quotation, piece, section
❺ *He hadn't changed at all, despite the passage of time.*
• passing, progress, advance

passenger NOUN
The bus has seats for 30 passengers.
• traveller
– Passengers who travel regularly to work are **commuters**.

passion NOUN
❶ *It is a story about youthful passion.*
• love, emotion, desire
❷ *She has a passion for sports.*
• enthusiasm, eagerness, appetite, craving, urge, zest, thirst, mania, obsession

passionate ADJECTIVE
❶ *He gave a passionate speech before the battle.*
• emotional, intense, impassioned, heartfelt, vehement, fervent
OPPOSITE unemotional
❷ *She is a passionate collector of art.*
• eager, keen, avid, enthusiastic, fanatical
OPPOSITE apathetic

passive ADJECTIVE
Owls are normally passive during the daytime.
• inactive, docile, submissive
OPPOSITE active

past ADJECTIVE
❶ *Things were very different in past centuries.*
• earlier, former, previous, old, olden, bygone, of old, gone by
OPPOSITE future
❷ *The road has been closed for the past month.*
• last, preceding, recent
OPPOSITE next

past NOUN
❶ *The story is set in the distant past.*
• past times, old days, olden days, days gone by
OPPOSITE future
❷ *I knew nothing about her colourful past.*
• history, background, past life
OPPOSITE future

paste NOUN
❶ *Mix the powder with water to make a paste.*
• pulp, mash, purée
❷ *We were both covered in wallpaper paste.*
• glue, gum, adhesive

pastime NOUN
Ice skating is a popular winter pastime.
• activity, hobby, recreation, pursuit, amusement, interest, diversion, entertainment, relaxation, game, sport

pasture NOUN
Sheep were grazing on the hill pastures.
• grassland, field, meadow

pat VERB
I reached down and patted the horse's neck.
• tap, touch, stroke, pet
– To touch something quickly and lightly is to **dab** it.
– To stroke someone with an open hand is to **caress** them.

pat NOUN
He gave me a reassuring pat on the shoulder.
• tap, touch, stroke

patch NOUN
❶ *There is a damp patch on the carpet.*
• mark, area, spot, blotch, stain, blemish
❷ *Harry had a small vegetable patch.*
• plot, area, piece, strip, parcel, bed, allotment

patch VERB
I need some material to patch a hole in my jeans.
• mend, repair, stitch up, darn

patchy ADJECTIVE
There will be patchy outbreaks of rain overnight.
• irregular, uneven, varying, inconsistent, unpredictable

path NOUN
❶ *A path winds through the forest.*
• pathway, track, trail, footpath, walk, walkway, lane
– A path for horse-riding is a **bridleway**.
– A path along a canal is a **towpath**.
❷ *The tornado destroyed everything in its path.*
• way, route, course
❸ *He is now surely on the path to success.*
• course of action, approach, method, line, tack

a b c d e f g h i j k l m n o p q r s t u v w x y z

pathetic ADJECTIVE
❶ *The girl came in, a pathetic little creature in rags.*
• pitiful, wretched, sorry, heartbreaking, moving, touching, plaintive
❷ (*informal*) *What a pathetic excuse!*
• hopeless, useless, weak, feeble, inadequate, incompetent

patience NOUN
Bird-watching requires great patience.
• perseverance, persistence, endurance, tenacity, staying power, forbearance, tolerance, restraint
OPPOSITE impatience

patient ADJECTIVE
❶ *Please be patient while we connect you.*
• calm, composed, uncomplaining, forbearing, tolerant, understanding, long-suffering
❷ *It took hours of patient work to restore the painting.*
• persevering, persistent, unhurried, untiring, dogged, determined, tenacious
OPPOSITE impatient

patrol VERB
A security guard patrols the grounds at night.
• guard, keep watch over, stand guard over, do the rounds of, inspect

patrol NOUN
An armed military patrol was guarding the gates.
• guard, force, party, squad, detail

patter NOUN & VERB
For tips on describing sounds see **sound**.

pattern NOUN
❶ *Do you like the pattern on this wallpaper?*
• design, decoration, motif
❷ *His films follow a set pattern.*
• example, model, standard, norm
❸ *How do you explain this strange pattern of behaviour?*
• system, structure, scheme, plan, arrangement

WORD WEB

Some types of pattern:
- checked
- criss-cross
- dotted
- floral or flowery
- geometric
- herringbone
- mosaic
- paisley
- pinstriped
- polka dot
- spiral
- spotted or spotty
- striped or stripy
- swirling
- symmetrical
- tartan
- wavy
- zigzag

pause NOUN
There was a long pause before she answered.
• break, gap, halt, rest, lull, stop, wait, interruption, stoppage
(*informal*) **let-up**
– A pause in the middle of a performance is an **interlude** or **interval**.
– A pause in the middle of a cinema film is an **intermission**.
– A pause for rest is a **breathing space** or (*informal*) **breather**.

pause VERB
❶ *I paused at the door before knocking.*
• hesitate, wait, delay, hang back
❷ *The speaker paused to sip some water.*
• halt, stop, break off, rest, take a break
(*informal*) take a breather

paw NOUN
She stroked the cat's paw.
• foot, pad
– A horse's foot is a **hoof**.
– A pig's feet are its **trotters**.
– A bird's feet are its **claws**.

pay VERB
❶ *How much did you pay for your new phone?*
• spend, give out, hand over
(*informal*) fork out, shell out, cough up
❷ *Who's going to pay the bill?*
• pay off, repay, settle, clear
❸ *Sometimes it pays to complain.*
• be worthwhile, be beneficial, be to your advantage, be profitable

❹ *I'll make you pay for this!*
• suffer

pay *NOUN*
You should get an increase in pay next year.
• wages, salary, income, earnings, revenue, remuneration
– A payment for doing a single job is a **fee**.

payment *NOUN*
❶ *She never received any payment for her work.*
• earnings, pay, income, fee, revenue, remuneration, reimbursement
– A voluntary payment to a charity is a **contribution** or **donation**.
– Money that is paid back to you is a **refund**.
❷ *We require prompt payment of all bills.*
• settlement, clearance, remittance

peace *NOUN*
❶ *After the war there was a period of peace.*
• agreement, harmony, friendliness, truce, ceasefire
OPPOSITES war, conflict
❷ *She enjoys the peace of the countryside.*
• calm, peacefulness, quiet, tranquillity, stillness, serenity, silence, hush
OPPOSITES noise, bustle

peaceful *ADJECTIVE*
We found a peaceful spot by the water's edge.
• calm, quiet, relaxing, tranquil, restful, serene, undisturbed, untroubled, gentle, placid, soothing, still
OPPOSITES noisy, busy

peak *NOUN*
❶ *There was a stunning view of snow-capped mountain peaks.*
• summit, cap, crest, crown, pinnacle, top, tip, point
❷ *She is at the peak of her career as a gymnast.*
• top, height, high point, climax, pinnacle, culmination, zenith

peculiar *ADJECTIVE*
❶ *What's that peculiar smell?*
• strange, unusual, odd, curious, puzzling, extraordinary, abnormal, funny, weird, bizarre
OPPOSITES normal, ordinary
❷ *Her way of writing is peculiar to her.*
• characteristic, distinctive, individual, particular, personal, special, unique, identifiable

pedigree *NOUN*
This horse has an impressive pedigree.
• ancestry, lineage, descent, bloodline, parentage, background

peek *VERB*
see look

peel *NOUN*
a strip of lemon peel
• rind, skin, zest

peel *VERB*
❶ *I peeled a banana.*
• pare, skin
❷ *You can see the paintwork starting to peel.*
• fall off, flake off, be shed

peep *VERB*
❶ *I found her peeping through the keyhole.*
• peek, glance, squint
❷ *The sun was just peeping out from the clouds.*
• emerge, appear, issue, come into view

peer *VERB*
see look

peg *NOUN*
I hung my coat and scarf on the peg.
• hook, knob, pin, nail

pelt *VERB*
❶ *We pelted each other with snowballs.*
• attack, bombard, shower
❷ *It's still pelting down outside.*
• rain hard, pour, teem
(*informal*) bucket
❸ *Two lads came pelting down the street.*
see run

pen NOUN
❶ *My pen has run out of ink.*
see **writing**
❷ *The dog drove the sheep into the pen.*
• enclosure, fold

penalize VERB
You will be penalized if you handle the ball.
• punish, discipline

penalty NOUN
The penalty for murder is life imprisonment.
• punishment, sanction, sentence, fine
OPPOSITE reward

penetrate VERB
❶ *The bullet had penetrated the man's chest.*
• pierce, puncture, perforate, bore through, enter
❷ *Your mission is to penetrate deep into enemy territory.*
• get through, enter, infiltrate

penetrating ADJECTIVE
❶ *She gave him a penetrating look.*
• piercing, searching, probing, intent, keen, sharp
❷ *The students asked some penetrating questions.*
• perceptive, insightful, sharp, acute, astute

penniless ADJECTIVE
The family was left penniless and homeless.
• poor, impoverished, poverty-stricken, destitute
OPPOSITE rich

people PLURAL NOUN
❶ *How many people are you inviting?*
• persons, individuals
(*informal*) folk
– People as opposed to animals are **humans, human beings** or **mankind**.
❷ *the people of the United States*
• population, citizens, populace, public, inhabitants, society, nation, race

perceive VERB
❶ *I perceived a change in her voice.*
• notice, become aware of, recognize, detect, discern, make out
❷ *I began to perceive what she meant.*
• realize, understand, comprehend, grasp

perceptive ADJECTIVE
❶ *It was very perceptive of you to spot my mistake.*
• observant, sharp, quick, alert
IDIOM (*informal*) on the ball
OPPOSITE unobservant
❷ *She asked some perceptive questions.*
• insightful, penetrating, discerning, shrewd, astute, intelligent
OPPOSITE obtuse

perch VERB
A robin was perching on the fence.
• sit, settle, rest, balance

percussion NOUN
see **music**

perfect ADJECTIVE
❶ *The guitar is in perfect condition.*
• faultless, flawless, intact, undamaged, complete, whole, mint, pristine, immaculate
(*informal*) tip-top
OPPOSITES imperfect, flawed
❷ *He produced a perfect copy of my signature.*
• exact, faithful, accurate, precise, correct
❸ *That dress is perfect on you.*
• ideal, just right
(*informal*) spot on, just the job
❹ *Today I received a letter from a perfect stranger.*
• complete, absolute, total, utter

perfect VERB
She spent months perfecting some new magic tricks.
• make perfect, improve, refine, polish, hone, fine-tune

perfectly ADVERB
❶ *Please stand perfectly still.*
• completely, absolutely, totally, utterly,

entirely, wholly, altogether
❷ *The TV works perfectly now.*
• superbly, faultlessly, flawlessly, immaculately, to perfection

perform *VERB*
❶ *Do you enjoy performing on stage?*
• act, appear, play, dance, sing
❷ *We performed the play in the school hall.*
• present, stage, produce, put on
❸ *The robot is programmed to perform simple tasks.*
• do, carry out, execute, fulfil, accomplish

performance *NOUN*
❶ *This evening's performance is already sold out.*
• show, production, presentation, showing, screening, staging, concert, recital
❷ *It was the team's best performance of the season.*
• effort, work, endeavour, exertion, behaviour, conduct

performer *NOUN*
We stopped to watch a group of street performers.
• actor, actress, musician, singer, dancer, artist, entertainer, player
  SEE ALSO drama, music

perfume *NOUN*
The perfume of roses filled the room.
• smell, scent, fragrance, aroma, bouquet

perhaps *ADVERB*
Perhaps no one will notice.
• maybe, possibly, conceivably, for all you know
  OPPOSITE definitely

peril *NOUN*
The crew faced many perils on their voyage.
• danger, hazard, risk, menace, threat
  OPPOSITE safety

perimeter *NOUN*
The dotted line marks the perimeter of the old city.
• edge, border, boundary, limits, bounds
– The distance round the edge of something round is the **circumference**.

period *NOUN*
❶ *After a period of silence he spoke again.*
• time, span, interval, spell, stretch, phase
❷ *These rocks date from the Jurassic Period.*
• age, era, epoch

perish *VERB*
❶ *Without sunlight, the plants will perish.*
• die, be killed, pass away
❷ *The rubber ring has started to perish.*
• rot, decay, disintegrate, decompose, crumble away

permanent *ADJECTIVE*
❶ *Sugar can do permanent damage to your teeth.*
• lasting, long-lasting, long-term, irreparable, irreversible, everlasting, enduring
❷ *Pollution is a permanent problem in the city.*
• never-ending, perpetual, persistent, chronic, perennial
❸ *She has been offered a permanent job in the firm.*
• fixed, long-term, stable, secure
  OPPOSITE temporary

permission *NOUN*
Do you have permission to leave early?
• authorization, consent, agreement, approval, leave, licence
(*informal*) go-ahead, say-so

permit *VERB*
The gallery doesn't permit photographs.
• allow, consent to, give permission for, authorize, license, grant

permit *NOUN*
You need a permit to fish in the river.
• licence, pass, ticket

a b c d e f g h i j k l m n o p q r s t u v w x y z

A
B
C
D
E
F
G
H
I
J
K
L
M
N
O
P
Q
R
S
T
U
V
W
X
Y
Z

perpetual ADJECTIVE
The machine produces a perpetual hum.
• constant, continual, continuous, never-ending, non-stop, endless, ceaseless, incessant, persistent, unceasing, unending
OPPOSITES intermittent, short-lived

perplexing ADJECTIVE
It is one of the most perplexing problems in science.
• puzzling, confusing, bewildering, baffling, mystifying

persecute VERB
❶ *Galileo and his followers were persecuted for their beliefs.*
• oppress, discriminate against, victimize
❷ *She claimed she was being persecuted by the media.*
• harass, hound, intimidate, bully, pick on, pester, torment

persevere VERB
The rescuers persevered despite the conditions.
• continue, carry on, keep going, persist
(*informal*) keep at it, stick at it
OPPOSITE give up

persist VERB
If the pain persists, you should see a doctor.
• continue, carry on, last, linger, remain, endure
OPPOSITES stop, cease
➤ **persist in**
Why do you persist in arguing with me?
• keep on, insist on
OPPOSITE give up

persistent ADJECTIVE
❶ *There was a persistent drip from the tap.*
• constant, continual, incessant, never-ending, steady, non-stop
OPPOSITE intermittent
❷ *The interviewer was very persistent.*
• determined, persevering, insistent, tenacious, obstinate, stubborn, dogged, resolute, unrelenting, tireless

person NOUN
Not a single person has replied to my email.
• individual, human being, man, woman, character, soul

personal ADJECTIVE
❶ *The book is based on her personal experience.*
• own, individual, particular, special, unique
❷ *The contents of the letter are personal.*
• confidential, private, secret, intimate

personality NOUN
❶ *She has a warm and cheerful personality.*
• character, nature, disposition, temperament, make-up
❷ *He is a well-known TV personality.*
• celebrity, star
(*informal*) celeb

persuade VERB
I persuaded my friends to sign the petition.
• convince, coax, induce, talk into, prevail on, win over, bring round
OPPOSITE dissuade

persuasive ADJECTIVE
She used some very persuasive arguments.
• convincing, compelling, effective, telling, strong, powerful, forceful, valid, sound
OPPOSITE unconvincing

pessimistic ADJECTIVE
I'm pessimistic about our chances of winning.
• negative, gloomy, downbeat, despairing, unhopeful, resigned, cynical
OPPOSITES optimistic, hopeful

pest NOUN
❶ *Here are some tips to help you get rid of garden pests.*
– Pests in general are **vermin**.
– An informal word for insect pests is **bugs**.
– A pest which lives on or in another creature is a **parasite**.

❷ (informal) My cousin can be a pest at times.
• nuisance, bother, annoyance
IDIOM (informal) pain in the neck

pester VERB
Please stop pestering me with questions!
• annoy, bother, trouble, harass, badger, hound, nag, plague
(informal) bug, hassle

pet ADJECTIVE
❶ My brother keeps a pet snake in his bedroom.
• tame, domesticated
❷ Have I told you my pet theory about UFOs?
• favourite, favoured, cherished, personal

petrified ADJECTIVE
I stood for a moment petrified, then turned and fled.
• terrified, horrified, terror-struck, paralysed, frozen
IDIOM rooted to the spot

petty ADJECTIVE
❶ There was a long list of petty rules and regulations.
• minor, trivial, trifling, unimportant, insignificant, inconsequential, footling
OPPOSITE important
❷ It was a petty act of revenge.
• small-minded, mean, mean-spirited, spiteful, ungracious

phase NOUN
This was the start of a new phase in my life.
• period, time, stage, step, spell, episode, chapter

phenomenal ADJECTIVE
She was blessed with a phenomenal memory.
• exceptional, remarkable, extraordinary, outstanding, incredible, miraculous, amazing, astonishing, astounding, staggering, awesome
OPPOSITE ordinary

phenomenon NOUN
❶ A solar eclipse is an extraordinary natural phenomenon.
• happening, occurrence, event, fact
❷ The band soon became a worldwide phenomenon.
• sensation, wonder, marvel, prodigy

phobia NOUN

WORD WEB

Some types of phobia:

➤ acrophobia
(fear of heights)
➤ agoraphobia
(fear of open or crowded spaces)
➤ arachnophobia
(fear of spiders)
➤ claustrophobia
(fear of enclosed spaces)
➤ xenophobia
(fear or dislike of foreigners)

phone VERB
I'll phone you later this evening.
• telephone, call, ring, give someone a call
(informal) give someone a ring, give someone a bell

photograph NOUN
I have an old photograph of my great grandmother.
• photo, picture, snap, snapshot, shot, print, still

photograph VERB
He loves photographing the night sky.
• take a picture of, shoot, snap

phrase NOUN
She liked the sound of the phrase 'the bee's knees'.
• expression, saying, construction, idiom

phrase VERB
I tried to phrase my email carefully.
• express, put into words, formulate, couch, frame

a b c d e f g h i j k l m n o **p** q r s t u v w x y z

A
B
C
D
E
F
G
H
I
J
K
L
M
N
O
P
Q
R
S
T
U
V
W
X
Y
Z

physical ADJECTIVE

❶ *Rugby is a game with a lot of physical contact.*
• bodily, corporeal, corporal
OPPOSITES mental, spiritual

❷ *There was no physical evidence of the crime.*
• material, concrete, solid, substantial, tangible

pick VERB

❶ *We picked some flowers from the garden.*
• pluck, gather, collect, cut, harvest

❷ *Pick a number from one to twenty.*
• choose, select, decide on, settle on, opt for, single out, nominate, elect

❸ *She was picking the polish off her fingernails.*
• pull off, scrape, remove, extract

➤ **pick on**
Why are they always picking on me?
• victimize, bully, persecute, torment, single out

➤ **pick up**
Sales have started to pick up.
• improve, recover, rally, bounce back, perk up

➤ **pick something up**
❶ *It took two men to pick up the wardrobe.*
• lift, raise, hoist

❷ *I'll pick up some milk on the way home.*
• get, collect, fetch, call for

❸ *You'll pick up the language in no time.*
• acquire, learn

❹ *We have picked up a distress signal from a ship.*
• receive, detect, hear

picture NOUN

❶ *There's a picture of a volcano on the cover.*
• illustration, image, painting, drawing, sketch, print
– A picture which represents a particular person is a **portrait**.

– A picture which represents the artist himself or herself is a **self-portrait**.
– A picture which represents a group of objects is a **still life**.
– A picture which represents a country scene is a **landscape**.
– Pictures on a computer are **graphics**.
SEE ALSO painting

❷ *I took a lot of pictures on holiday.*
• photograph, photo, snapshot, snap

picture VERB

❶ *She is pictured here with her two brothers.*
• depict, illustrate, represent, show, portray, paint, photograph

❷ *He pictured himself holding up the trophy.*
• imagine, visualize
IDIOM see in your mind's eye

picturesque ADJECTIVE

❶ *We stayed in a picturesque thatched cottage.*
• attractive, pretty, charming, quaint, scenic
OPPOSITE ugly

❷ *She wrote a picturesque account of her travels.*
• colourful, descriptive, imaginative, expressive, lively, poetic, vivid

piece NOUN

❶ *They collected pieces of wood to build a raft.*
• bar, block, length, stick, chunk, lump, hunk, bit, chip, fragment, particle, scrap, shred

❷ *Who wants the last piece of chocolate?*
• bit, portion, part, section, segment, share, slice

❸ *There wasn't a single piece of furniture in the room.*
• item, article

❹ *I've lost one of the pieces of this jigsaw.*
• part, element, unit, component, constituent

❺ *There's a piece about our school in the local paper.*
• article, item, report, feature

pier NOUN
Fishing boats were tied up at the pier.
• quay, wharf, jetty, landing stage

pierce VERB
The arrow pierced his armour.
• penetrate, perforate, puncture, enter, make a hole in, go through, bore through
– To pierce someone with a spear or spike is to **impale** them.

piercing ADJECTIVE
❶ *From the wood came a piercing screech.*
• high-pitched, shrill, strident, penetrating, ear-splitting, deafening
❷ *The girl had piercing blue eyes.*
• penetrating, intense, sharp, keen, searching, probing

pig NOUN
The farm rears free-range pigs.
– An old word for pigs is **swine**.
– A wild pig is a **wild boar**.
– A male pig is a **boar** or **hog**.
– A female pig is a **sow**.
– A young pig is a **piglet**.
– A family of piglets is a **litter**.
– The smallest piglet in a litter is the **runt**.

pile NOUN
❶ *In the corner was a pile of old newspapers.*
• heap, stack, mound, mass, collection, accumulation, stockpile, hoard
❷ (*informal*) *I still have piles of work to do.*
• plenty, a lot, a great deal
(*informal*) lots, masses, loads, heaps, a stack, a ton

pile VERB
Just pile the dirty dishes in the sink.
• heap, stack
➤ **pile up**
The bills are beginning to pile up.
• build up, mount up, accumulate, multiply, grow

pill NOUN
Take one pill every four hours.
• tablet, capsule, pellet, lozenge

pillar NOUN
The dome was supported by marble pillars.
• column, post, support, upright, pier, prop

pillow NOUN
She rested her head on a pillow.
• cushion, pad
– A long kind of pillow is a **bolster**.

pilot NOUN
see aircraft

pilot VERB
He piloted the little plane to the island.
• navigate, steer, guide, control, manoeuvre, captain, fly

pimple NOUN
I had a pimple on the end of my nose.
• spot, boil, swelling
(*informal*) zit

pin NOUN
She wore a shawl fastened with a pin.
• brooch, fastener, tack, staple, nail

pin VERB
❶ *I pinned the list on the noticeboard.*
• attach, fasten, secure, tack, nail
❷ *He was pinned under the wreckage for hours.*
• hold down, press, pinion

pinch VERB
❶ *Pinch the dough between your fingers.*
• nip, squeeze, press, tweak, grip
❷ (*informal*) *Who pinched my calculator?*
• steal, take, snatch, pilfer
(*informal*) swipe, lift, nick, make off with

pine VERB
The dog pined when its master died.
• mope, languish, sicken, waste away
➤ **pine for**
She was pining for the sight of the sea again.
• long for, yearn for, miss, crave, hanker after

pink ADJECTIVE & NOUN

⊛ **WORD WEB**

Some shades of pink:

➤ coral   ➤ puce
➤ fuchsia   ➤ rose
➤ peach   ➤ salmon

For tips on describing colours see colour.

pip NOUN
Remove the pips from the grapes.
• seed
– To remove pips from fruit is to **deseed** it.

pipe NOUN
The water flows away along this pipe.
• tube, duct, conduit, channel
– A pipe used for watering the garden is a **hose**.
– A pipe in the street which supplies water for fighting fires is a **hydrant**.
– A pipe for carrying oil or gas over long distances is a **pipeline**.
– The system of water pipes in a house is the **plumbing**.

pipe VERB
Water is piped from the reservoir to the town.
• carry, convey, run, channel, funnel, siphon

pirate NOUN
Pirates attacked the ship.
• buccaneer, marauder, freebooter

pit NOUN
❶ We first dug a deep pit.
• hole, crater, cavity, hollow, depression, pothole, chasm, abyss
❷ The town is next to a disused coal pit.
• mine, colliery, quarry

pitch NOUN
❶ The football pitch was covered in snow.
• ground, field, playing field, park

❷ Dogs can hear at a higher pitch than humans.
• tone, frequency
❸ a roof with a steep pitch
• slope, slant, gradient, incline, angle, tilt

pitch VERB
❶ Boys were pitching pebbles into the pond.
• throw, toss, fling, hurl, sling, cast, lob (informal) chuck
❷ This is a perfect place to pitch a tent.
• erect, put up, set up
❸ She tripped and pitched headlong into the water.
• plunge, dive, drop, topple, plummet
❹ The little boat pitched about in the storm.
• lurch, toss, rock, roll, reel

pitfall NOUN
Being famous has some serious pitfalls.
• difficulty, problem, hazard, danger, snag, catch, trap

pitiful ADJECTIVE
❶ We could hear pitiful cries for help.
• sad, sorrowful, mournful, pathetic, plaintive, piteous, heart-rending, moving, touching
❷ What a pitiful excuse!
• feeble, weak, pathetic, hopeless, useless, inadequate, incompetent

pity NOUN
They showed no pity towards their captives.
• mercy, compassion, sympathy, humanity, kindness, concern, feeling
OPPOSITE cruelty
➤ **a pity**
It's a pity you have to leave so soon.
• a shame, unfortunate, bad luck, too bad

pity VERB
I pity anyone who has to live there.
• feel sorry for, feel for, sympathize with, take pity on, commiserate with

pivot NOUN
The wheel on the barrow acts as a pivot.
– The point on which a lever turns is

A B C D E F G H I J K L M N O P Q R S T U V W X Y Z

called the **fulcrum**.
– The point on which a spinning object turns is its **axis**.
– The point on which a wheel turns is the **axle** or **hub**.

place NOUN

❶ *This is a good place to park.*
• site, spot, location, position, situation, venue
❷ *They are looking for a quiet place to live.*
• area, district, locality, neighbourhood, region, vicinity, locale
❸ *Save me a place on the bus.*
• seat, space
❹ *She was offered a place as a trainee.*
• job, position, post, appointment
❺ *Let's go back to my place.*
• home, house, flat, apartment, quarters
(*informal*) pad
➤ **in place of**
You can use honey in place of sugar.
• instead of, rather than, in exchange for, in lieu of

place VERB

❶ *Our table was placed next to the window.*
• locate, situate, position, station
❷ *You can place your coats on the bed.*
• put down, set down, lay, deposit, stand, leave

placid ADJECTIVE

❶ *Her pony has a very placid nature.*
• calm, composed, unexcitable, even-tempered
OPPOSITE excitable
❷ *The sea was placid at that time of the day.*
• calm, quiet, tranquil, peaceful, undisturbed, unruffled
OPPOSITE stormy

plague NOUN

❶ *Millions of people died of the plague.*
• pestilence, epidemic, pandemic, contagion, outbreak
❷ *There was a plague of wasps this summer.*
• invasion, infestation, swarm

plague VERB

❶ *Stop plaguing me with questions!*
• pester, bother, annoy, badger, harass, hound
(*informal*) nag, hassle, bug
❷ *I've been plagued by bad luck recently.*
• afflict, beset, trouble, torment, dog, curse

plain ADJECTIVE

❶ *The furniture in the room was very plain.*
• simple, modest, basic, unelaborate
OPPOSITES elaborate, ornate
❷ *Jodie was rather plain compared with her sister.*
• unattractive, ordinary
OPPOSITE attractive
❸ *It is plain to me that you are not interested.*
• clear, evident, obvious, apparent, unmistakable
OPPOSITE unclear
❹ *Let me tell you what I think in plain terms.*
• direct, frank, candid, blunt, honest, sincere, straightforward, forthright, outspoken
OPPOSITE obscure

plain NOUN

He missed the wide open plains of Wyoming.
• grassland, prairie, pampas, savannah, steppe, veld

plan NOUN

❶ *We'd better come up with a plan quickly!*
• scheme, strategy, proposal, idea, suggestion, proposition, stratagem
– A plan to do something bad is a **plot**.
❷ *On the wall were the plans for the new sports centre.*
• design, diagram, chart, map, drawing, blueprint

plan VERB

❶ *Some of us are planning a surprise party.*
• organize, arrange, devise, design, scheme, plot, work out, map out, formulate

❷ *What do you plan to do next?*
• aim, intend, propose, mean

plane NOUN
see aircraft

planet NOUN
Could there be life on planets beyond our solar system?
• world

🌀 **WORD WEB**

The planets of our solar system (in order from the sun):

➤ Mercury   ➤ Jupiter
➤ Venus   ➤ Saturn
➤ Earth   ➤ Uranus
➤ Mars   ➤ Neptune

- The path followed by a planet is its **orbit**.
- Pluto is classified as a **dwarf planet**.
- Minor planets orbiting the Sun are **asteroids** or **planetoids**.
- Something which orbits a planet is a **satellite**.
- The Earth's large satellite is the **Moon**.

SEE ALSO **space**

---

plant NOUN
Most of these plants are native to Australia.
• vegetation, greenery, plantlife
- The plants of a particular place or time are its **flora**.

🌀 **WORD WEB**

Some types of plant:

➤ algae   ➤ herb
➤ bush   ➤ house plant
➤ cactus   ➤ lichen
➤ cereal   ➤ moss
➤ evergreen   ➤ pot plant
➤ fern   ➤ shrub
➤ flower   ➤ tree
➤ grass   ➤ vegetable

➤ vine   ➤ wild flower
➤ weed

SEE ALSO **flower, fruit, herb, tree, vegetable**

Parts of a plant:

➤ bloom   ➤ pod
➤ blossom   ➤ root
➤ branch   ➤ seed
➤ bud   ➤ shoot
➤ bulb   ➤ stalk
➤ flower   ➤ stem
➤ fruit   ➤ trunk
➤ leaf   ➤ twig
➤ petal

- A young plant is a **seedling**.
- A piece cut off a plant to form a new plant is a **cutting**.
- The scientific study of plants and flowers is **botany**.
- A word meaning 'to do with plants' is **botanical**.
➤ *an exhibition of botanical art*

---

plant VERB
❶ *Plant the seeds in September.*
• sow, put in the ground
- To move a growing plant to a new position is to **transplant** it.
❷ *He planted his feet on the ground and took hold of the rope.*
• place, set, position

plaster NOUN
You should put a plaster on your finger.
• dressing, sticking plaster, bandage

plate NOUN
❶ *They piled their plates with food.*
• dish, platter, salver
❷ *The design is first etched on a metal plate.*
• panel, sheet
❸ *The book includes thirty two full-page colour plates.*
• illustration, picture, photograph, print

platform NOUN
People gathered round as he made a speech from the platform.
• dais, podium, stage, stand, rostrum

play VERB
❶ *Children were playing in the street.*
• amuse yourself, have fun, romp about
❷ *Do you like playing basketball?*
• take part in, participate in, compete in
❸ *We are playing the defending champions.*
• compete against, oppose, challenge, take on
❹ *I am learning to play the piano.*
• perform on
❺ *Who is going to play the lead role?*
• act, perform, take the part of, portray, represent

play NOUN
❶ *We both had parts in the school play.*
• drama, theatrical work, piece, performance, production
SEE ALSO drama
❷ *The weekend was a mixture of work and play.*
• recreation, amusement, leisure, fun, games, sport

player NOUN
❶ *You need four players for this game.*
• contestant, participant, competitor, contender
❷ *We have some experienced players in the band.*
• performer, musician, artist, instrumentalist
– Someone who plays music on their own is a **soloist**.

playful ADJECTIVE
❶ *The kittens are in a playful mood.*
• lively, spirited, frisky, frolicsome, mischievous, roguish, impish
❷ *He made a few playful remarks.*
• light-hearted, joking, teasing, frivolous, flippant
OPPOSITE serious

plea NOUN
The emperor ignored his plea for mercy.
• appeal, request, call, entreaty, petition

plead VERB
➤ **plead with**
They pleaded with us to listen to them.
• beg, entreat, implore, appeal to, ask, petition

pleasant ADJECTIVE
❶ *We spent a pleasant afternoon in the park.*
• enjoyable, agreeable, pleasing, pleasurable, delightful, lovely, entertaining
OPPOSITES unpleasant, disagreeable
❷ *The staff there are always pleasant.*
• kind, friendly, likeable, charming, amiable, amicable, cheerful, genial, good-natured, good-humoured, approachable, hospitable, welcoming
❸ *The forecast is for a spell of pleasant weather.*
• fine, mild, sunny, warm

please VERB
❶ *I wish I knew how to please her.*
• make happy, satisfy, gratify, delight, amuse, entertain, charm
❷ *Everyone just does as they please.*
• like, want, wish, choose, prefer, see fit

pleased ADJECTIVE
I'm very pleased to meet you.
• happy, glad, delighted, content, contented, satisfied, gratified, thankful, grateful, elated, thrilled
OPPOSITES unhappy, dissatisfied, discontented

pleasure NOUN
❶ *My aunt gets a lot of pleasure from her garden.*
• enjoyment, happiness, delight, satisfaction, gratification, comfort, contentment, gladness, joy, fun
– Very great pleasure is **bliss** or **ecstasy**.
❷ *He talked of the pleasures of living in the country.*
• joy, comfort, delight

pleat NOUN
It takes ages to iron the pleats in this skirt.
• crease, fold, tuck

pledge NOUN
The knights swore a pledge of allegiance to the king.
• oath, vow, promise, word, commitment, guarantee

plentiful ADJECTIVE
There is a plentiful supply of berries in the forest.
• abundant, ample, copious, profuse, generous, lavish, bountiful, prolific
OPPOSITE scarce

plenty NOUN
There should be plenty for everyone.
• an ample supply, a sufficiency, quite enough, more than enough
OPPOSITE a shortage
➤ **plenty of**
We've still got plenty of time.
• a lot of, lots of, a great deal of, many, ample, abundant
(*informal*) loads of, masses of, stacks of, tons of

plight NOUN
He was concerned about the plight of the homeless.
• predicament, trouble, difficulty, problem, dilemma
IDIOM dire straits

plod VERB
❶ *We plodded back through the snow.*
• tramp, trudge, lumber
❷ *I'm still plodding through all the paperwork.*
• slog, plough, wade, toil, labour

plot NOUN
❶ *They were part of a plot against the government.*
• conspiracy, scheme, secret plan, intrigue
❷ *It was hard to follow the plot of the film.*
• story, storyline, narrative, thread
❸ *He bought a small plot of land.*
• area, piece, lot, patch
– A plot of ground for growing flowers or vegetables is an **allotment**.
– A large plot of land is a **tract** of land.

plot VERB
❶ *The men were plotting a daring escape from prison.*
• plan, devise, concoct, hatch
(*informal*) cook up
❷ *They were accused of plotting against the queen.*
• conspire, intrigue, scheme
❸ *The captain plotted the course of the ship.*
• chart, map, mark

plough VERB
❶ *A tractor was ploughing the field.*
• cultivate, till, turn over
❷ *Are you still ploughing through that book?*
• wade, labour, toil, slog, plod

ploy NOUN
It was a clever ploy to attract publicity.
• scheme, plan, ruse, trick, tactic, stratagem, manoeuvre

pluck VERB
❶ *We started plucking berries off the bush.*
• pick, pull off, remove, gather, collect, harvest
❷ *A seagull plucked the sandwich out of her hand.*
• grab, seize, snatch, jerk, pull, tug, yank
❸ *The guitarist plucked the strings very gently.*
– To run your finger or plectrum across the strings of a guitar is to **strum**.

plug NOUN
She took the plug out of the side of the barrel.
• stopper, cork, bung

plug VERB
❶ *We managed to plug the leak in the pipe.*
• stop up, block, close, fill, seal, bung up
❷ (*informal*) *The author was there to plug her new book.*
• advertise, publicize, promote, market, push

plump *ADJECTIVE*
He was a plump little man with a bald head.
• chubby, dumpy, fat, tubby, podgy, round, stout, portly
OPPOSITE skinny

plunder *VERB*
Viking raiders plundered the villages near the coast.
• loot, pillage, raid, ransack, rob, steal from

plunge *VERB*
❶ *One by one, the girls plunged into the pool.*
• dive, jump, leap, throw yourself
❷ *Temperatures have plunged overnight.*
• drop, fall, tumble, plummet, nosedive
❸ *I plunged my hand in the cold water.*
• dip, lower, dunk, sink, immerse, submerge
❹ *You must plunge a stake into the vampire's heart.*
• thrust, stab, stick, push, shove, sink, force, drive, ram

poem *NOUN*
I was reading a poem about winter.
• rhyme, verse, lyric
SEE ALSO **poetry**

poetic *ADJECTIVE*
The book is written in a poetic style.
• expressive, imaginative, lyrical, poetical
– An uncomplimentary synonym is **flowery**.

poetry *NOUN*
This is a book of First World War poetry.
• poems, verse, rhyme, lyrics

⚙ **WORD WEB**

Some forms of poetry:
➤ acrostic	➤ concrete poetry
➤ ballad	➤ elegy
➤ blank verse	➤ epic
➤ cinquain	➤ free verse
➤ clerihew	➤ haiku

➤ limerick	➤ ode
➤ lyric	➤ rap
➤ narrative poetry	➤ sonnet
➤ nonsense verse	➤ tanka
➤ nursery rhyme	

– A group of lines forming a section of a poem is a **stanza**.
– A pair of rhyming lines within a poem is a **couplet**.
– The rhythm of a poem is its **metre**.

point *NOUN*
❶ *That knife has a very sharp point.*
• tip, end, nib, spike, prong, barb
❷ *The stars looked like points of light in the sky.*
• dot, spot, speck, fleck
❸ *We headed for the point where the two rivers meet.*
• location, place, position, site, spot
❹ *Just at that point, the doorbell rang.*
• moment, instant, second, time, stage
❺ *His sense of humour is one of his good points.*
• characteristic, feature, attribute, trait, quality, side, aspect
❻ *I agree with your last point.*
• idea, argument, thought
❼ *I didn't get the point of that film at all.*
• meaning, essence, core, gist, nub, crux
❽ *There is no point in phoning at this hour.*
• purpose, reason, aim, object, use, usefulness, sense, advantage

point *VERB*
❶ *An arrow points the way to the exit.*
• indicate, show, signal
❷ *Can you point me in the right direction?*
• direct, aim, guide, lead, steer
➤ **point out**
I'd like to point out that this was your idea.
• make known, mention, indicate, specify, detail, draw someone's attention to

pointed *ADJECTIVE*
❶ *I used the pointed end of the stick.*
• sharp, spiked, spiky, barbed

a b c d e f g h i j k l m n o p q r s t u v w x y z

A
B
C
D
E
F
G
H
I
J
K
L
M
N
O
P
Q
R
S
T
U
V
W
X
Y
Z

(*informal*) pointy
OPPOSITES rounded, blunt
❷ *It was a rather pointed remark.*
• deliberate, clear, unmistakable, obvious, conspicuous
OPPOSITES oblique, obscure

pointless *ADJECTIVE*
It would be pointless to continue the experiment.
• useless, senseless, futile, idle, vain
OPPOSITE worthwhile

poise *NOUN*
She shows great poise for her age.
• calmness, composure, calm, assurance, self-confidence, dignity, aplomb

poised *ADJECTIVE*
He raised his arm, poised to strike.
• ready, prepared, waiting, all set, set

poison *NOUN*
He had been given a lethal dose of poison.
• toxin, venom
– A poison to kill plants is **herbicide** or **weedkiller**.
– A poison to kill insects is **insecticide** or **pesticide**.
– A substance which counteracts the effects of a poison is an **antidote**.

poisonous *ADJECTIVE*
This particular mushroom is poisonous.
• toxic, deadly, lethal, fatal
– Snakes and other animals which produce a toxic venom are said to be **venomous**.

poke *VERB*
Someone poked me in the back with an umbrella.
• prod, dig, jab, stab, nudge
➤ **poke out**
Bits of straw were poking out of the mattress.
• stick out, jut out, project, protrude

poke *NOUN*
She gave me a poke in the back.
• prod, dig, jab, stab, nudge

polar *ADJECTIVE*
Sea ice is melting in the polar regions.
• Arctic or Antarctic
SEE ALSO ice

pole *NOUN*
The huts are supported on wooden poles.
• post, pillar, stick, rod, shaft, stake, staff, prop
– A strong pole to support sails on a ship is a **mast** or **spar**.

police *NOUN*
I think you'd better call the police.
• police force, constabulary
(*informal*) the law, the cops, the fuzz

police officer *NOUN*
Two police officers arrived in a patrol car.
• policeman or policewoman, officer, constable
(*informal*) cop, copper
– Police officers of higher rank are **sergeant**, **inspector** and **superintendent**.
– The head of a police force is the **chief constable**.
– Someone training for the police force is a **cadet**.
– A person who investigates crimes is a **detective**.

policy *NOUN*
What is the school's policy on bullying?
• approach, strategy, plan of action, guidelines, code, line, position, stance

polish *VERB*
❶ *I need to polish my shoes.*
• rub down, shine, buff, burnish, wax
❷ *She sat down to polish the final draft of the script.*
• refine, improve, perfect, hone, revise, edit, touch up
➤ **polish something off**
We polished off a whole plate of sandwiches.
• finish, get through, eat up

polish *NOUN*
Marble can be given a high polish.
• shine, sheen, gloss, lustre, sparkle, brightness, glaze, finish

polished *ADJECTIVE*
❶ *She could see her face in the polished surface.*
• shining, shiny, bright, gleaming, glossy, lustrous
(OPPOSITES) dull, tarnished
❷ *The cast gave a polished performance.*
• accomplished, skilful, masterly, expert, adept

polite *ADJECTIVE*
They were too polite to complain.
• courteous, well mannered, respectful, civil, well behaved, gracious, gentlemanly or ladylike, chivalrous, gallant
(OPPOSITES) rude, impolite

politics *NOUN*

WORD WEB

Some terms used in uk politics:

➤ alliance	➤ manifesto
➤ AM (Assembly Member)	➤ Member of Parliament or MP
➤ assembly	➤ minister
➤ ballot	➤ ministry
➤ bill	➤ minority
➤ cabinet	➤ MLA (Member of the Legisla-
➤ campaign	tive Assembly)
➤ coalition	➤ MSP (Member of the Scottish
➤ conservative	Parliament)
➤ constituency	➤ opinion poll
➤ constitution	➤ parliament
➤ devolution	➤ party
➤ election	➤ policy
➤ electorate	➤ politician
➤ executive	➤ Prime Minister
➤ First Minister	➤ proportional
➤ general election	representation
➤ government	➤ radical
➤ House of Commons	➤ referendum
➤ House of Lords	➤ right-wing
➤ liberal	➤ socialist
➤ left-wing	➤ speaker
➤ lobby	➤ upper house
➤ local election	➤ vote
➤ lower house	
➤ majority	

Some terms used in other political systems:

➤ congress	➤ president
➤ congressman or congresswoman	➤ senate
➤ House of Representatives	➤ senator
	➤ vice-president

poll *NOUN*
The results of a nationwide poll have been published.
• election, vote, ballot
– A vote on a particular question by all the people in a country is a **referendum**.
– An official survey to find out about the population is a **census**.

pollute *VERB*
Industrial waste has polluted the lake.
• contaminate, poison, infect, dirty, foul
(OPPOSITE) purify

pompous *ADJECTIVE*
He sounded so pompous I couldn't help smiling.
• arrogant, self-important, haughty, conceited, pretentious, puffed up
(OPPOSITE) modest

pond *NOUN*
see **pool**

pool *NOUN*
❶ *The surface of the pool was covered with frogspawn.*
• pond
– A larger area of water is a **lake** or (in Scotland) a **loch**.
– A salt-water lake is a **lagoon**.
– A pool of water in the desert is an **oasis**.
– A pool among rocks on a seashore is a **rock pool**.
❷ *On the floor was a pool of spilled milk.*
• puddle, patch
❸ *The sports centre has an indoor and an outdoor pool.*
• swimming pool, swimming bath

a b c d e f g h i j k l m n o p q r s t u v w x y z

poor *ADJECTIVE*
❶ *He was the son of a poor farm labourer.*
• impoverished, poverty-stricken, penniless, impecunious, needy, destitute, badly off
(*informal*) hard up
OPPOSITES rich, affluent
❷ *Her handwriting is very poor.*
• bad, inferior, inadequate, unsatisfactory, substandard, deficient, imperfect, incompetent, shoddy
OPPOSITES good, superior
❸ *The poor man had to wait for ages in the rain.*
• unlucky, unfortunate, pitiful, wretched
OPPOSITE lucky

poorly *ADJECTIVE*
I've been feeling poorly for weeks.
• ill, unwell, unfit, ailing
IDIOMS off colour, under the weather
OPPOSITE well

pop *NOUN & VERB*
For tips on describing sounds see sound.

popular *ADJECTIVE*
❶ *She is a popular children's author.*
• well liked, well loved, celebrated, favourite
OPPOSITES unpopular, little known
❷ *These hats have suddenly become popular.*
• fashionable, widespread, current, in demand, in vogue
(*informal*) trendy, hot, big
IDIOM all the rage
OPPOSITES unpopular, out of fashion

population *NOUN*
China has the largest population of any country in the world.
• inhabitants, residents, occupants, citizens, people, populace, community

pore *VERB*
➤ **pore over**
I've pored over the letter a hundred times.
• examine, study, inspect, look closely at, scrutinize, peruse

port *NOUN*
Rotterdam is a major European port.
• harbour, docks, seaport
– A harbour for yachts and pleasure boats is a **marina**.

portable *ADJECTIVE*
They took a portable TV on holiday.
• transportable, mobile, compact, lightweight

portion *NOUN*
❶ *He ordered a large portion of chips.*
• helping, serving, ration, share, quantity, measure, serving, plateful, slice
❷ *The central portion of the bridge collapsed.*
• part, piece, section, division, segment

portrait *NOUN*
This is a portrait of the artist's mother.
• picture, image, likeness, representation, painting, drawing, photograph
– A portrait which shows a side view of someone is a **profile**.
– A portrait which shows someone in outline is a **silhouette**.
– A portrait which exaggerates some aspect of a person is a **caricature**.

portray *VERB*
❶ *The book portrays life in rural Australia.*
• depict, represent, show, describe, illustrate
❷ *In the film, he portrays a notorious gangster.*
• play, act the part of, appear as

pose *VERB*
❶ *She loves posing in front of the camera.*
• model, posture
❷ *Flooding poses a serious threat at this time of year.*
• present, put forward, offer, constitute
➤ **pose as someone**
He posed as a newspaper reporter.
• impersonate, pretend to be, pass yourself off as, masquerade as

posh (*informal*) ADJECTIVE
❶ *We went to a posh restaurant.*
• smart, stylish, high-class, upmarket, fancy, elegant, fashionable, chic, exclusive, luxury, de luxe
(*informal*) classy, swanky, swish, snazzy
❷ *She has a very posh accent.*
• upper-class, aristocratic

position NOUN
❶ *Mark the position on the map.*
• location, place, point, spot, site, situation, whereabouts, locality
❷ *My arms were aching so I shifted my position slightly.*
• pose, posture, stance
❸ *What would you do in my position?*
• situation, state, condition, circumstances, predicament
❹ *He made his position on nuclear energy very clear.*
• opinion, attitude, outlook, view, viewpoint, thinking, stand
❺ *She now has a senior position in the government.*
• job, post, appointment, situation, rank, status, standing

positive ADJECTIVE
❶ *Are you positive this is the man you saw?*
• certain, sure, convinced, assured, confident, satisfied
OPPOSITES uncertain, doubtful
❷ *We received a positive reply.*
• favourable, affirmative
OPPOSITE negative
❸ *Don't you have anything positive to say?*
• constructive, supportive, encouraging, helpful, useful, productive
OPPOSITE negative

possess VERB
❶ *The gallery possesses a number of his early paintings.*
• own, have
❷ *My brother does not really possess a sense of humour.*
• have, be blessed with, be endowed with, enjoy, boast

❸ *What possessed you to take up snorkelling?*
• make you think of, come over you

possession NOUN
The photograph is no longer in my possession.
• ownership, keeping, care, custody, charge, hands
➤ **possessions**
The refugees had lost all of their possessions.
• belongings, property, things, worldly goods, personal effects

possibility NOUN
There's a possibility of snow tomorrow.
• chance, likelihood, hope, danger, risk

possible ADJECTIVE
❶ *Is it possible that life exists on other planets?*
• likely, probable, conceivable, credible, plausible, imaginable
OPPOSITES impossible, unlikely
❷ *It's not possible to get there before nightfall.*
• feasible, practicable, viable, attainable, workable
(*informal*) doable
OPPOSITES impossible, out of the question

possibly ADVERB
❶ *This is possibly the best film ever made.*
• maybe, perhaps, arguably
OPPOSITES definitely, without a doubt
❷ *I couldn't possibly accept the money.*
• in any way, under any circumstances, conceivably, at all, ever

post NOUN
❶ *The fence is supported by wooden posts.*
• pole, pillar, shaft, stake, support, prop, strut
❷ *I am expecting a package in the post.*
• mail, letters, delivery

A
B
C
D
E
F
G
H
I
J
K
L
M
N
O
P
Q
R
S
T
U
V
W
X
Y
Z

❸ Are you thinking of applying for the post?
• job, position, situation, appointment, vacancy, opening

post VERB
❶ The timetable will be posted on the noticeboard.
• display, put up, pin up, announce, advertise
❷ Did you post those letters?
• mail, send, dispatch
❸ Guards were posted along the wall.
• station, position, place, mount

poster NOUN
He collects old film posters.
• advertisement, notice, bill, sign, placard

postpone VERB
The match has been postponed because of bad weather.
• put off, defer, delay, put back, hold over
– To stop a game or meeting that you intend to start again later is to **adjourn** or **suspend** it.
OPPOSITE bring forward

posture NOUN
He tried to raise himself into a sitting posture.
• pose, position, stance, attitude

pot NOUN
On the table were little pots of jam and honey.
• jar, dish, bowl, pan, vessel

potent ADJECTIVE
❶ The local wine is potent.
• strong, powerful, pungent, heady, intoxicating
❷ She persuaded us with her potent arguments.
• effective, forceful, strong, compelling, persuasive, convincing
OPPOSITE weak

potential ADJECTIVE
❶ He is a potential Wimbledon champion.
• prospective, budding, future, likely, possible, probable, promising
❷ These floods are a potential disaster.
• looming, threatening

potential NOUN
She is a young actress with great potential.
• prospects, promise, capability, future

potion NOUN
The witch gave him a magic potion to drink.
• concoction, brew, compound, medicine, drug, draught

pottery NOUN

✺ WORD WEB

Some types of pottery:

➤ bone china   ➤ raku
➤ china   ➤ slipware
➤ earthenware   ➤ stoneware
➤ porcelain   ➤ terracotta

– Pottery used to serve food and drink is **crockery**.
– A formal word for pottery is **ceramics**.
– A person who creates pottery is a **potter** or **ceramic artist**.

pouch NOUN
He kept his coins in a leather pouch.
• bag, purse, sack

poultry NOUN
see **bird**

pounce VERB
A tiger will stalk its prey before pouncing.
• jump, leap, spring, swoop down, lunge, attack, ambush

pound VERB
❶ Huge waves pounded against the sea wall.
• batter, buffet, beat, hit, smash, dash

❷ *I heard heavy footsteps pounding up the stairs.*
• stamp, stomp, tramp, thud, thump, clump, clomp
❸ *She felt her heart pounding faster.*
• beat, thump, hammer, pulse, race

pour VERB
❶ *Sunlight poured through the front window.*
• flow, stream, run, gush, spill, flood
❷ *I poured some milk into a saucer.*
• tip, splash, spill
(*informal*) slosh
– To pour wine or other liquid from one container to another is to **decant** it.
❸ *It's absolutely pouring outside!*
• rain heavily, teem, lash down, tip down, pelt down
(*informal*) bucket down
❹ *Crowds poured through the gate.*
• surge, stream, crowd, swarm, throng

poverty NOUN
Bad harvests have caused widespread poverty and famine.
• pennilessness, hardship, need, want, destitution
– Extreme poverty is known as **abject poverty.**
OPPOSITES wealth, affluence

powder NOUN
Ginger root is dried and then ground to powder.
• dust, particles, grains

powdery ADJECTIVE
The ground was covered with powdery snow.
• powder-like, fine, light, loose, dusty, grainy, sandy, chalky

power NOUN
❶ *The film shows the immense power of a tsunami.*
• strength, force, might, energy, vigour
❷ *As a storyteller he has the power to move an audience to tears.*
• skill, talent, ability, capacity, capability

❸ *Roman slave-owners had absolute power over their slaves.*
• authority, command, control, dominance, domination, sway

powerful ADJECTIVE
❶ *He has one of the most powerful serves in tennis.*
• strong, forceful, hard, mighty, vigorous, formidable, potent
OPPOSITES weak, ineffective
❷ *Persia was once a powerful empire.*
• influential, leading, commanding, dominant, high-powered, formidable
OPPOSITES powerless, weak
❸ *She used some powerful arguments.*
• strong, convincing, compelling, effective, persuasive, impressive

powerless ADJECTIVE
❶ *A normal bullet is powerless against a werewolf.*
• ineffective, impotent, useless, weak, feeble
❷ *The citizens were powerless to defend themselves.*
• helpless, defenceless, vulnerable

practical ADJECTIVE
❶ *We need a practical person to lead the team.*
• down-to-earth, matter-of-fact, sensible, level-headed, commonsensical, no-nonsense
OPPOSITE impractical
❷ *The idea was not practical from the start.*
• workable, realistic, sensible, feasible, viable, achievable
(*informal*) doable
OPPOSITE impractical
❸ *Do you have any practical experience of sailing?*
• real, actual, hands-on
OPPOSITE theoretical

practically ADVERB
The place was practically deserted.
• almost, just about, nearly, virtually, as good as

a
b
c
d
e
f
g
h
i
j
k
l
m
n
o
p
q
r
s
t
u
v
w
x
y
z

practice NOUN
❶ *We have extra football practice this week.*
• training, exercises, drill, preparation, rehearsal, run-through
❷ *His usual practice was to work until midnight.*
• custom, habit, convention, routine, procedure
➤ **in practice**
What will the plan involve in practice?
• in effect, in reality, actually, really

practise VERB
❶ *I've spent weeks practising for my music exam.*
• do exercises, rehearse, train, drill, prepare
IDIOM go through your paces
– To practise just before the start of a performance is to **warm up.**
❷ *Let's practise that scene again.*
• rehearse, go over, go through, run through, work at
❸ *She was accused of practising witchcraft.*
• do, perform, carry out, observe, follow, pursue

praise VERB
The judge praised her for her bravery.
• commend, applaud, pay tribute to, compliment, congratulate, speak highly of
(*informal*) rave about
IDIOM sing the praises of
OPPOSITES criticize, condemn

praise NOUN
His performance has received a lot of praise.
• approval, acclaim, admiration, commendation, compliments, congratulations, plaudits
IDIOM a pat on the back

prance VERB
The lead guitarist was prancing about on stage.
• leap, skip, romp, cavort, caper, frolic

precarious ADJECTIVE
❶ *She was in a precarious position on the ledge.*
• dangerous, perilous, risky, hazardous
OPPOSITE safe
❷ *That chimney looks a bit precarious.*
• unsafe, unstable, unsteady, insecure, shaky, wobbly, rickety
OPPOSITE secure

precaution NOUN
Always wear a helmet as a precaution.
• safeguard, safety measure, preventative measure

precede VERB
A firework display preceded the concert.
• come before, go before, lead into, lead up to
IDIOM pave the way for
OPPOSITES follow, succeed

precious ADJECTIVE
❶ *Trading ships arrived carrying precious silks and spices.*
• valuable, costly, expensive, priceless
OPPOSITE worthless
For precious stones see **gem**.
❷ *Her most precious possession was a faded letter.*
• treasured, cherished, valued, prized, dearest, beloved

precise ADJECTIVE
❶ *Can you tell me the precise time?*
• exact, accurate, correct, true, right
OPPOSITE rough
❷ *We were given precise instructions.*
• careful, detailed, specific, particular, definite, explicit
OPPOSITES vague, imprecise

predict VERB
Scientists try to predict when earthquakes will happen.
• forecast, foresee, foretell, prophesy

predictable ADJECTIVE
The outcome of the match was predictable.
• foreseeable, to be expected, likely, unsurprising, inevitable
OPPOSITE unpredictable

A B C D E F G H I J K L M N O P Q R S T U V W X Y Z

prediction NOUN
What is your prediction for next year?
• forecast, prophecy, prognosis

preface NOUN
The title of the book is explained in the preface.
• introduction, prologue

prefer VERB
Would you prefer rice or pasta?
• rather have, sooner have, go for, opt for, plump for, choose, fancy

preferable ADJECTIVE
➤ preferable to
She finds country life preferable to living in the city.
• better than, superior to, more suitable than, more desirable than
OPPOSITE inferior to

preference NOUN
I have a slight preference for the red one.
• liking, fondness, taste, fancy, partiality, inclination, penchant

pregnant ADJECTIVE
She was six months pregnant at the time.
• expectant, carrying a baby
(*informal*) expecting
– A pregnant woman is an **expectant mother.**

prehistoric ADJECTIVE

WORD WEB

Prehistoric remains:
➤ barrow or tumulus
➤ cromlech or stone circle
➤ dolmen
➤ hill fort
➤ menhir or standing stone
– A person who studies prehistory by examining remains is an **archaeologist.**

Prehistoric periods:
➤ Stone Age
➤ Bronze Age
➤ Iron Age
➤ Ice Age
– Formal names for the Old, Middle and New Stone Ages are **Palaeolithic, Mesolithic** and **Neolithic** periods.
– A prehistoric species of humans who lived during the Stone Age were the **Neanderthals.**

Some prehistoric animals:
➤ cave bear
➤ dinosaur
➤ glyptodon
➤ ground sloth
➤ macrauchenia
➤ sabre-toothed cat or smilodon
➤ sabre-toothed squirrel
➤ woolly mammoth
➤ woolly rhino
– A person who studies fossils of prehistoric life is a **palaeontologist.**

prejudice NOUN
The school has a policy against any form of racial prejudice.
• discrimination, intolerance, bigotry, narrow-mindedness, bias, partiality
– Prejudice against other races is **racism.**
– Prejudice against other nations is **xenophobia.**
– Prejudice against the other sex is **sexism.**
– Prejudice against older or younger people is **ageism.**
OPPOSITES impartiality, tolerance

preliminary ADJECTIVE
Our team was knocked out in the preliminary round.
• first, initial, introductory, early, opening, preparatory

prelude NOUN
The award was a prelude to a glittering career.
• introduction, precursor, preamble, lead-in, opening
OPPOSITE swansong

premises PLURAL NOUN
No one is allowed on the premises after dark.
• property, grounds, site, buildings

preoccupied ADJECTIVE
➤ **preoccupied with something**
She was so preoccupied with her work that she forgot the time.
• absorbed in, engrossed in, wrapped up in, concerned with, involved with, obsessed with

preparation NOUN
An event like this requires months of preparation.
• planning, organization, arrangement, setting-up, development, groundwork

prepare VERB
❶ *The city is preparing to host the Olympics.*
• get ready, plan, make preparations, make arrangements, make provisions
– To prepare for a play is to **rehearse**.
– To prepare to take part in a sport is to **train**.
❷ *We are preparing a surprise party for her.*
• arrange, organize, make arrangements for, plan, set up
❸ *He was in the kitchen preparing lunch.*
• make, produce, put together, make ready, get ready, assemble

prepared ADJECTIVE
❶ *I don't feel prepared for this exam at all.*
• ready, all set
❷ *Are you prepared to take the risk?*
• willing, disposed, inclined, of a mind

presence NOUN
Your presence is required upstairs.
• attendance, appearance, existence

present ADJECTIVE
❶ *Is everyone present?*
• here, in attendance, at hand
❷ *He is the present world record holder.*
• current, existing
OPPOSITES past, former

present NOUN
❶ *The opening chapter takes place in the present.*
• now, today, the here and now, the present time, nowadays
OPPOSITES past, future
❷ *I have a birthday present for you.*
• gift, offering, donation

present VERB
❶ *A local celebrity was asked to present the prizes.*
• hand over, award, bestow
❷ *I'd like to present my latest invention.*
• introduce, put forward, show, display, exhibit, make known
❸ *Our drama group is presenting a series of one-act plays.*
• put on, perform, stage, mount
❹ *Translating a poem presents a number of problems.*
• offer, provide, set out, open up

preserve VERB
❶ *Salt was used to preserve meat and fish.*
• keep, save, store
❷ *We are campaigning to preserve the rainforest.*
• look after, protect, conserve, defend, safeguard, maintain
OPPOSITE destroy

press VERB
❶ *The olives are then pressed to extract their oil.*
• push, squeeze, squash, crush, cram, compress, hold down, force down
❷ *She pressed her blouse for the party.*
• iron, flatten, smooth
❸ *I must press you for an answer.*
• urge, push, force, implore
(*informal*) lean on

press NOUN
❶ *The story has been reported in the press.*
• newspapers, magazines
❷ *All the press came to the opening night of the show.*
• journalists, reporters, the media

pressure NOUN
❶ *Apply steady pressure to the wound.*
• force, compression, squeezing, weight, load
❷ *I've been under a lot of pressure lately.*
• stress, strain, tension
❸ *The newspapers are putting pressure on her to resign.*
• influence, persuasion, intimidation, coercion, duress

prestige NOUN
There's a lot of prestige in winning an Oscar.
• glory, honour, credit, renown, distinction, status, kudos

prestigious ADJECTIVE
Her books have won several prestigious awards.
• distinguished, respected, renowned, highly regarded

presume VERB
❶ *I presume you know how to use a camera.*
• assume, suppose, imagine, expect
IDIOM take it
❷ *I wouldn't presume to doubt your word.*
• dare, venture, be so bold as, go so far as

pretend VERB
❶ *Let's pretend we're snakes.*
• act like, make as if, make believe, play at
❷ *Is he really crying or just pretending?*
• bluff, sham, pose, fake it
(informal) kid on, put it on

pretend ADJECTIVE (informal)
That's just a pretend spider, not a real one.
• fake, false, artificial, made-up, imaginary

pretty ADJECTIVE
That's a pretty brooch you're wearing.
• attractive, beautiful, lovely, nice, appealing, pleasing, charming, dainty, picturesque

(informal) cute
OPPOSITE ugly

prevent VERB
❶ *The driver could do nothing to prevent the accident.*
• avert, avoid, stop, forestall, head off
IDIOM nip in the bud
❷ *Her illness prevented her from travelling.*
• stop, bar, block, obstruct, impede, inhibit, thwart
❸ *Some people say that garlic prevents colds.*
• stave off, ward off, fend off
IDIOM keep at bay

previous ADJECTIVE
❶ *The couple had met on a previous occasion.*
• earlier, former, prior, past
❷ *There had been a storm the previous night.*
• preceding, former, last, most recent
OPPOSITE subsequent

prey NOUN
The eagle swooped down on its prey.
• quarry, kill, victim
OPPOSITE predator

prey VERB
➤ prey on
Owls prey on small animals.
• hunt, kill, feed on

price NOUN
❶ *What's the price of a return ticket to Sydney?*
• cost, charge, fee, fare, rate, expense, amount, figure, sum
– The price you pay to send a letter is the **postage**.
– The price you pay to use a private road, bridge or tunnel is a **toll**.
❷ *He was paying the price of failure.*
• consequence, result, penalty, cost, downside

priceless ADJECTIVE
❶ *The museum contains many priceless works of art.*
• precious, rare, invaluable,

irreplaceable, expensive, costly
OPPOSITE worthless
❷ (*informal*) The joke she told at the end
was *priceless*.
• funny, amusing, comic, hilarious, witty

prick VERB
Prick the pastry all over with a fork.
• pierce, puncture, stab, jab, perforate,
spike

prickle NOUN
A hedgehog uses its *prickles* for defence.
• spike, spine, needle, barb, thorn
– The prickles on a hedgehog or
porcupine are also called **quills**.

prickly ADJECTIVE
❶ Holly leaves are very *prickly*.
• spiky, spiked, thorny, spiny, bristly
❷ He's quite a *prickly* character.
• bad-tempered, irritable, grumpy,
tetchy, testy

pride NOUN
❶ She takes great *pride* in her work.
• satisfaction, pleasure, delight, joy,
fulfilment, gratification
❷ My heart swelled with *pride*.
• self-esteem, self-respect, dignity,
honour
OPPOSITE shame
❸ Finally, the hero is forced to swallow
his *pride*.
• arrogance, conceitedness, vanity, self-
importance, big-headedness, egotism,
snobbery
OPPOSITE humility

priest NOUN
see religion

prim ADJECTIVE
She was a rather *prim* and proper young
lady.
• prudish, strait-laced, formal, demure

primarily ADVERB
The website is aimed *primarily* at
teenagers.
• chiefly, especially, mainly, mostly,
largely, predominantly, principally,
above all, first and foremost

primary ADJECTIVE
The *primary* aim of a website is to
communicate.
• main, chief, principal, foremost, most
important, key, central
OPPOSITE secondary

prime ADJECTIVE
❶ The bad weather was the *prime* cause
of the accident.
• main, chief, top, principal, foremost,
leading
(*informal*) number-one
❷ The dish is made from *prime* cuts of
meat.
• best, superior, first-class, choice,
select, top-quality, finest

primitive ADJECTIVE
❶ *Primitive* humans were hunters rather
than farmers.
• ancient, early, prehistoric, primeval
OPPOSITES civilized, advanced
❷ It was a *primitive* type of computer.
• crude, basic, simple, rudimentary,
undeveloped
OPPOSITES advanced, sophisticated

principal ADJECTIVE
What is the *principal* aim of the
experiment?
• main, chief, primary, foremost, most
important, key, central, predominant,
pre-eminent, leading, supreme,
major, top
OPPOSITES secondary, minor

principle NOUN
❶ He follows the *principles* of Buddhism.
• rule, standard, code, ethic, precept,
doctrine, creed
❷ She taught me the *principles* of good
design.
• basics, fundamentals, essentials

print NOUN
❶ The tiny *print* was difficult to read.
• type, printing, lettering, letters,
characters
❷ Detectives searched the building for
prints.
• mark, impression, footprint,

fingerprint
❸ *On the wall was a full-size print of the Mona Lisa.*
• copy, reproduction, duplicate, photograph

priority NOUN
❶ *Traffic on the main road has priority.*
• precedence, right of way
❷ *Emergency cases are given priority in hospital.*
• preference, precedence, favour, first place

prise VERB
Slowly, we began to prise the lid off the chest.
• lever, force, wrench

prison NOUN
He was sentenced to six months in prison.
• jail, imprisonment, confinement, custody

prisoner NOUN
Two escaped prisoners are on the run.
• convict, inmate, captive
(*informal*) jailbird, con
– A person who is held prisoner until some demand is met is a **hostage**.
– A person who is captured by the opposite side during a war is a **prisoner-of-war**.

private ADJECTIVE
❶ *Always keep your password private.*
• secret, confidential, personal, intimate
– Secret official documents are **classified** documents.
OPPOSITES public, known
❷ *Can we go somewhere a little more private?*
• quiet, secluded, hidden, concealed
OPPOSITES public, open

privilege NOUN
Club members enjoy special privileges.
• advantage, benefit, concession, right, entitlement

privileged ADJECTIVE
❶ *She comes from a privileged family background.*
• affluent, wealthy, prosperous, rich, well off, well-to-do
OPPOSITES disadvantaged, poor
❷ *I feel privileged to be here.*
• honoured, fortunate, lucky, favoured

prize NOUN
Our team won first prize in the relay race.
• award, reward, trophy
– Money that you win as a prize is your **winnings**.
– Prize money that keeps increasing until someone wins it is a **jackpot**.

prize VERB
They prize their freedom above all else.
• treasure, value, cherish, hold dear, esteem, revere
IDIOM set great store by
OPPOSITE disdain

probable ADJECTIVE
A burst pipe was the most probable cause of the flood.
• likely, feasible, possible, expected, predictable
OPPOSITE improbable

probe VERB
❶ *The inquiry will probe the circumstances surrounding the accident.*
• investigate, inquire into, examine, study, scrutinize, look into, go into
❷ *This small spacecraft will probe the outer solar system.*
• explore, penetrate, see into, plumb

problem NOUN
❶ *I'm having problems with my computer.*
• difficulty, trouble, complication, snag, hitch, hiccup, setback
(*informal*) headache
❷ *I was struggling with a complicated maths problem.*
• puzzle, question, riddle, conundrum
(*informal*) brain-teaser, poser

a
b
c
d
e
f
g
h
i
j
k
l
m
n
o
p
q
r
s
t
u
v
w
x
y
z

procedure NOUN

What is the procedure for making a complaint?
• method, process, system, mechanism, practice, routine, technique, way

proceed VERB

❶ *The sheep proceeded slowly along the lane.*
• go forward, move forward, make your way, advance, progress
❷ *NASA has decided to proceed with the launch.*
• go ahead, carry on, continue, get on, press on, push on
❸ *The stranger proceeded to tell me his life story.*
• go on to, move on to, begin to, start to

proceedings PLURAL NOUN

A thunderstorm interrupted the day's proceedings.
• events, happenings, activities, affairs (*informal*) goings-on

proceeds PLURAL NOUN

All proceeds from the auction will go to charity.
• income, takings, money, earnings, profit, revenue, returns

process NOUN

This is a new process for storing solar energy.
• method, procedure, operation, system, technique, way, means

process VERB

We are still processing your application.
• deal with, attend to, see to, handle, treat, prepare

procession NOUN

The procession made its way slowly down the hill.
• parade, march, column, line
– A procession of mourners at a funeral is a **cortège**.

proclaim VERB

Two teams were proclaimed joint winners of the title.
• declare, announce, pronounce, state

prod VERB

He prodded the worm to see if it was alive.
• poke, dig, jab, nudge, push

produce VERB

❶ *Some lorries produce a lot of fumes.*
• create, generate, emit, give out, yield
❷ *The company produces computer games.*
• make, manufacture, construct, fabricate, put together, assemble, turn out
❸ *The writers have produced an award-winning comedy.*
• create, compose, invent, think up, come up with
❹ *His speech produced boos and whistles from the crowd.*
• provoke, arouse, stimulate, prompt, give rise to, result in, trigger
❺ *Brandon produced a letter from his pocket.*
• bring out, pull out, fish out, extract, present, show, reveal

produce NOUN

She works in a shop which sells organic produce.
• food, foodstuffs, crops, fruit and vegetables

product NOUN

❶ *The company launched a new range of beauty products.*
• article, commodity, merchandise, goods
❷ *The famine is the product of years of drought.*
• result, consequence, outcome, upshot

production NOUN

❶ *The firm is famous for the production of luxury cars.*
• manufacture, making, construction, creation, assembly, building, fabrication
❷ *Production at the factory has increased thus year.*
• output, yield
❸ *We went to see a production of 'Oliver'.*
• performance, show, staging, presentation

productive ADJECTIVE
❶ She had a long and productive literary career.
• prolific, creative, fruitful, fertile
❷ It wasn't a very productive meeting.
• useful, valuable, worthwhile, constructive, profitable
OPPOSITE unproductive

profession NOUN
Why did you chose acting as a profession?
• career, job, occupation, vocation, business, trade, line of work

professional ADJECTIVE
❶ His ambition is to be a professional footballer.
• paid, full-time
OPPOSITES amateur, non-professional
❷ The plans were drawn by a professional architect.
• qualified, chartered, skilled, trained, experienced
❸ This is a very professional piece of work.
• skilled, expert, proficient, accomplished, competent, polished
OPPOSITE incompetent

proficient ADJECTIVE
It takes years to become proficient in judo.
• skilful, skilled, accomplished, capable, expert, able
OPPOSITE incompetent

profile NOUN
❶ He was a handsome man with a strong profile.
• silhouette, side view, outline, shape
❷ Write a short profile of a famous person.
• biography, portrait, sketch, study, account

profit NOUN
The business made a small profit last year.
• gain, surplus, excess
– The extra money you get on your savings is **interest**.
OPPOSITE loss

programme NOUN
❶ There was a really good programme on TV last night.
• broadcast, show, production, transmission
❷ We worked out a varied programme of events.
• plan, schedule, timetable, calendar, line-up
– A list of things to be done at a meeting is an **agenda**.
– A list of places to visit on a journey is an **itinerary**.

progress NOUN
❶ Scientists monitored the progress of the hurricane.
• journey, route, movement, travels
❷ I'm not making much progress with the trumpet.
• advance, development, improvement, growth, headway, step forward
– An important piece of progress is a **breakthrough**.

progress VERB
❶ You can now progress to the next level of the game.
• go forward, move forward, proceed, advance
❷ The chicks are progressing at a steady rate.
• develop, grow, improve
(informal) come along

prohibit VERB
Taking photographs is prohibited here.
• ban, forbid, disallow, outlaw, rule out, veto
OPPOSITES permit, allow

project NOUN
❶ We did a history project on the Victorians.
• assignment, task, activity, piece of research
❷ There is a project to create a bird sanctuary in the area.
• plan, scheme, undertaking, enterprise, venture, proposal, bid

a b c d e f g h i j k l m n o p q r s t u v w x y z

project VERB
- ❶ *A narrow ledge projects from the cliff.*
- • extend, protrude, stick out, jut out, overhang
- ❷ *The laser projects a narrow beam of light.*
- • emit, throw out, cast, shine
- ❸ *He likes to project an image of absent-minded brilliance.*
- • give out, send out, convey, communicate

prolong VERB
There is no point in prolonging the argument.
- • extend, lengthen, protract, stretch out, draw out, drag out, spin out
- OPPOSITES shorten, curtail

prominent ADJECTIVE
- ❶ *She had a long nose and prominent teeth.*
- • noticeable, conspicuous, striking, eye-catching, protruding
- OPPOSITE inconspicuous
- ❷ *He became a prominent member of the government.*
- • well-known, famous, celebrated, major, leading, notable, distinguished, eminent
- OPPOSITES unknown, obscure

promise NOUN
- ❶ *We had promises of help from many people.*
- • assurance, pledge, guarantee, commitment, vow, oath, word of honour
- ❷ *This group of young actors show great promise.*
- • potential, talent, ability, aptitude

promise VERB
- ❶ *Do you promise not to tell anyone?*
- • give your word, guarantee, swear, take an oath, vow, pledge
- ❷ *I promise you I'll be there.*
- • assure, swear to, give your word to

promising ADJECTIVE
- ❶ *The weather looks promising for tomorrow.*
- • encouraging, hopeful, favourable, auspicious
- ❷ *She is a promising young singer.*
- • talented, gifted, budding, aspiring (*informal*) up-and-coming

promote VERB
- ❶ *Rory has been promoted to captain.*
- • move up, advance, upgrade, elevate
- ❷ *The band are here to promote their new album.*
- • advertise, publicize, market, push (*informal*) plug, hype
- ❸ *The school launched a campaign to promote healthy eating.*
- • encourage, foster, advocate, back, support, boost

prompt ADJECTIVE
I received a prompt reply to my email.
- • quick, speedy, swift, rapid, punctual, immediate, instant, direct
- OPPOSITES late, belated

prompt VERB
What prompted you to start writing a diary?
- • induce, lead, cause, motivate, persuade, inspire, stimulate, encourage, provoke, spur

prone ADJECTIVE
- ❶ *My sister is prone to exaggerate things.*
- • inclined, apt, liable, likely, given
- ❷ *The victim was lying prone on the floor.*
- • face down, on the front

pronounce VERB
- ❶ *Try to pronounce the words clearly.*
- • say, speak, utter, articulate, enunciate, sound
- ❷ *The man was pronounced dead on arrival.*
- • declare, announce, proclaim, judge

pronounced ADJECTIVE
She spoke with a pronounced Australian accent.
- • marked, strong, clear, distinct, definite, noticeable, obvious, striking, unmistakable, prominent
- OPPOSITE imperceptible

proof NOUN
Do you have any proof of your identity?
• evidence, confirmation, verification, authentication

prop NOUN
The tunnel roof is supported by metal props.
• support, strut, pole, post, upright
– A stick used to support an injured leg is a **crutch**.
– Part of a building which props up a wall is a **buttress**.

prop VERB
I propped my bike against the railing.
• lean, rest, stand, balance
➤ **prop something up**
The old tree was propped up with posts.
• support, hold up, reinforce, shore up

propel VERB
The steamboat was propelled by a huge paddle wheel.
• drive, push, power, move forward

proper ADJECTIVE
❶ *This is the proper way to hold a tennis racket.*
• correct, right, accepted, established, conventional, appropriate, suitable
OPPOSITES wrong, incorrect
❷ *He looks just like a proper movie star.*
• real, actual, genuine, true
OPPOSITE fake
❸ *I could do with a proper meal.*
• good, decent, adequate, substantial
OPPOSITE inadequate
❹ *Her whole family is very proper and polite.*
• formal, correct, respectable, conventional, polite
OPPOSITES informal, unconventional
❺ (informal) *I must have looked a proper idiot!*
• complete, total, utter, absolute, thorough, downright
(informal) right

property NOUN
❶ *This box contains lost property.*
• belongings, possessions, goods, personal effects

❷ *The newspaper has lists of property for sale.*
• buildings, houses, land, premises
❸ *Many herbs have healing properties.*
• quality, characteristic, feature, attribute, trait

prophecy NOUN
The witch's prophecy came true.
• prediction, forecast

prophesy VERB
Many people have been prophesying disaster.
• predict, forecast, foresee, foretell

proportion NOUN
❶ *A large proportion of the earth's surface is covered by sea.*
• part, section, portion, segment, share, fraction, percentage
❷ *What is the proportion of girls to boys in the class?*
• ratio, balance, distribution, relationship
➤ **proportions**
The dining hall was a room of large proportions.
• size, dimensions, measurements, area, expanse

proposal NOUN
There is a proposal to build a new skate park.
• plan, project, scheme, suggestion, proposition, recommendation

propose VERB
❶ *We are proposing a change in the rules.*
• suggest, ask for, put forward, submit, recommend
❷ *How do you propose to pay for this?*
• intend, mean, plan, aim

proprietor NOUN
Who is the proprietor of the bicycle shop?
• manager, owner, landlord or landlady
(informal) boss

a
b
c
d
e
f
g
h
i
j
k
l
m
n
o
p
q
r
s
t
u
v
w
x
y
z

prosecute VERB
Anyone caught shoplifting will be prosecuted.
• charge, take to court, bring to trial, indict
– To take someone to court to try to get money from them is to **sue** them.

prospect NOUN
❶ *There is little prospect of success.*
• chance, hope, promise, expectation, likelihood, possibility, probability
❷ *The terrace outside has a prospect over the sea.*
• outlook, view, vista, panorama

prosper VERB
Over time, the settlement prospered.
• do well, be successful, flourish, thrive, grow, progress, boom
OPPOSITES fail, flounder

prosperity NOUN
Tourism has brought prosperity to the region.
• wealth, affluence, growth, success

prosperous ADJECTIVE
She was the daughter of a prosperous farmer.
• wealthy, rich, well-off, well-to-do, affluent, successful, thriving, booming
OPPOSITE poor

protect VERB
❶ *The magpie was protecting its nest.*
• guard, defend, keep safe, safeguard, secure, keep from harm
OPPOSITE neglect
❷ *Sunscreen will protect your skin from harmful rays.*
• shield, shade, shelter, screen, insulate
OPPOSITE expose

protection NOUN
The trees gave some protection from the rain.
• shelter, cover, defence, insulation, security, refuge, sanctuary

protest NOUN
❶ *There were protests at the plan to close the cinema.*
• complaint, objection
– A general protest is an **outcry**.
❷ *Supporters staged a protest outside parliament.*
• demonstration, march, rally, sit-in (informal) demo

protest VERB
We wrote a letter protesting about the programme.
• complain, make a protest, object (to), take exception (to), take issue (with), express disapproval (of)

protrude VERB
His tongue protruded from his lips.
• stick out, poke out, bulge, swell, project, stand out, jut out

proud ADJECTIVE
❶ *You should be proud of your work this year.*
• delighted (with), pleased (with), satisfied, gratified
OPPOSITE ashamed (of)
❷ *He's too proud to admit his mistakes.*
• conceited, arrogant, vain, haughty, superior, self-important, pompous (informal) stuck-up, big-headed
OPPOSITE humble

prove VERB
❶ *Can you prove you were at home on the night of the murder?*
• demonstrate, provide proof, provide evidence, establish, confirm, verify
OPPOSITE disprove
❷ *The idea proved unpopular with the public.*
• turn out to be, be found to be

proverb NOUN
see saying

provide VERB
❶ *We'll provide the tea and coffee.*
• supply, contribute, arrange for, lay on, come up with
– To provide food and drink for people is to **cater** for them.

❷ *Our website should provide you with
all the information you need.*
• equip, supply, furnish, issue

provisions PLURAL NOUN
We have enough provisions for a week.
• supplies, food and drink, rations,
stores

provoke VERB
❶ *Rattlesnakes are dangerous if
provoked.*
• annoy, irritate, anger, enrage, incense,
infuriate, exasperate, madden, nettle,
rile, taunt, goad
(*informal*) wind up
OPPOSITE pacify
❷ *The decision provoked anger from the
crowd.*
• arouse, produce, prompt, cause,
generate, instigate, induce, stimulate,
trigger, kindle, spark off, stir up

prowl VERB
Dogs prowled about at night.
• creep, sneak, slink, steal, skulk, roam

prudent ADJECTIVE
❶ *It would be prudent to get some
advice first.*
• wise, sensible, shrewd
OPPOSITES unwise, rash
❷ *She has always been prudent with her
money.*
• careful, cautious, thoughtful, thrifty
OPPOSITES wasteful, reckless

prune VERB
Roses should be pruned every spring.
• cut back, trim, clip, shear

pry VERB
*I don't mean to pry, but I overheard your
conversation.*
• be curious, be inquisitive, interfere
(*informal*) be nosy, nose around, snoop
➤ **pry into something**
*She was always prying into other
people's affairs.*
• interfere in, meddle in, spy on
IDIOM (*informal*) poke your nose into

psychological ADJECTIVE
*The doctor thinks her illness is
psychological.*
• mental, emotional
OPPOSITE physical

public ADJECTIVE
❶ *The public entrance is at the front.*
• common, communal, general, open,
shared, collective
OPPOSITE private
❷ *The name of the author is now public
knowledge.*
• known, acknowledged, published,
available, open, general, universal
OPPOSITE secret

public NOUN
➤ **the public**
*This part of the house is not open to the
public.*
• people, everyone, the community,
society, the nation

publication NOUN
❶ *She is celebrating the publication of
her first novel.*
• issuing, printing, production,
appearance
❷ *Here is a list of our latest publications.*
• book, newspaper, magazine, periodical,
title, work

publicity NOUN
❶ *The band got some free publicity for
their latest album.*
• advertising, advertisements,
promotion
(*informal*) hype, build-up
❷ *He is an actor who shies away from
publicity.*
• attention, exposure, the limelight
IDIOM the public eye

publish VERB
❶ *The magazine is published twice a
month.*
• issue, print, produce, bring out,
release, circulate
❷ *When will they publish the results?*
• announce, declare, disclose, make
known, make public, report, reveal

385

a b c d e f g h i j k l m n o p q r s t u v w x y z

– To publish information on radio or TV is to **broadcast** it.

pudding NOUN
There is strawberry ice cream for pudding.
• dessert, sweet
(informal) afters

puff NOUN
❶ A puff of wind caught his hat.
• gust, draught, breath, flurry
❷ A puff of smoke rose from the chimney.
• cloud, whiff, waft, wisp

puff VERB
❶ High chimneys puffed clouds of black smoke.
• blow out, send out, emit, belch
❷ A red-faced man stood puffing in the doorway.
• breathe heavily, pant, gasp, wheeze
❸ The sails puffed out as the wind rose.
• become inflated, billow, swell

pull VERB
❶ Can you pull your chair a bit closer?
• drag, draw, haul, lug, trail, tow
OPPOSITE push
❷ Be careful, you nearly pulled my arm off!
• tug, rip, wrench, jerk, pluck
(informal) yank
➤ **pull off**
They've pulled off an amazing stunt.
• achieve, accomplish, manage, fulfil, bring off
➤ **pull out**
❶ The dentist pulled out one of my teeth.
• extract, take out, remove
❷ One team had to pull out of the race.
• back out, withdraw, retire, step down, bow out
(informal) quit
➤ **pull through**
It was a bad accident, but the doctors expect him to pull through.
• get better, recover, revive, rally, survive
➤ **pull up**
A taxi pulled up at the door.
• draw up, stop, halt

pulse NOUN
❶ See if you can feel your own pulse.
• heartbeat, heart rate
❷ I love the pulse of Brazilian samba music.
• beat, rhythm, throb, drumming

pump VERB
The crew had to pump water out of the boat.
• drain, draw off, empty
– To move liquid between containers through a tube is to **siphon** it.
➤ **pump up**
You need to pump up the tyre.
• inflate, blow up
OPPOSITES deflate, let down

punch VERB
❶ She punched him on the nose.
• strike, hit, jab, poke, prod, thump, smash
(informal) biff, slug, sock
SEE ALSO hit
❷ I need to punch a hole through the card.
• bore, pierce, puncture

punch NOUN
He received a punch on the nose.
• blow, hit, box, jab, poke, thump, smash
(informal) biff, slug, sock

punctual ADJECTIVE
Please be punctual so we can start early.
• prompt, on time, on schedule, in good time
OPPOSITE late

punctuation NOUN

WORD WEB

Punctuation marks:
➤ apostrophe
➤ brackets
➤ colon
➤ comma
➤ dash
➤ exclamation mark
➤ full stop
➤ hyphen
➤ question mark
➤ inverted commas or speech marks
➤ semicolon
➤ square brackets

Other marks used in writing:

➤ accent   ➤ capital letters
➤ asterisk   ➤ emoticon
➤ at sign   ➤ forward slash
➤ bullet point

For tips on using punctuation see the
Young Writer's Toolkit.

puncture NOUN
  ❶ *I found the puncture in my tyre.*
  • hole, perforation, rupture, leak
  ❷ *I had a puncture on the way home.*
  • burst tyre, flat tyre

puncture VERB
  A nail must have punctured the tyre.
  • perforate, pierce, rupture

punish VERB
  *Anyone who breaks the rules will be
  punished.*
  • penalize, discipline, chastise

punishment NOUN
  *The punishment for dropping litter is a
  fine.*
  • penalty, sentence
  – Punishing someone by taking their life
  is **capital punishment** or **execution**.

puny ADJECTIVE
  He was rather a puny child.
  • delicate, weak, feeble, frail, slight,
  undersized
  (*informal*) weedy
  OPPOSITES strong, sturdy

pupil NOUN
  How many pupils are in the class?
  • schoolchild, student, learner, scholar
  – Someone who follows a great teacher
  is a **disciple**.

purchase VERB
  *The library has purchased new
  computers.*
  • buy, pay for, get, obtain, acquire,
  procure

purchase NOUN
  ❶ *Keep the receipt as proof of your
  purchase.*
  • acquisition, buying, shopping

  ❷ *I couldn't get any purchase on the
  slippery rock.*
  • grasp, grip, hold, leverage, traction

pure ADJECTIVE
  ❶ *The coin is made of pure gold.*
  • solid, genuine, unadulterated,
  undiluted
  OPPOSITES impure, adulterated
  ❷ *All our dishes are made from pure
  ingredients.*
  • natural, unprocessed, unrefined,
  wholesome
  OPPOSITE processed
  ❸ *She loved the pure mountain air.*
  • clean, clear, fresh, unpolluted,
  uncontaminated
  OPPOSITES polluted, stale
  ❹ *This book is pure nonsense.*
  • complete, absolute, utter, sheer, total,
  out-and-out

purify VERB
  A filter is used to purify the rainwater.
  • clean, make pure, decontaminate
  – You destroy germs by **disinfecting** or
  sterilizing things.
  – You take solid particles out of liquids by
  filtering them.
  – To purify water by boiling it and
  condensing the vapour is to **distil** it.
  – To purify crude oil is to **refine** it.

purple ADJECTIVE & NOUN

WORD WEB

Some shades of purple:

➤ lavender   ➤ mauve
➤ lilac   ➤ plum
➤ magenta   ➤ violet

For tips on describing colours see
colour.

purpose NOUN
  ❶ *What was your purpose in coming
  here?*
  • intention, motive, aim, objective, goal,
  end, target

❷ *She began to feel that her life had no purpose.*
• point, use, usefulness, value
➤ **on purpose**
Did you trip me up on purpose?
• deliberately, intentionally, purposely, knowingly, consciously

purposeful ADJECTIVE
She set off with a purposeful look on her face.
• determined, decisive, resolute, positive, committed
OPPOSITE aimless

purse NOUN
I always keep some change in my purse.
• money bag, pouch, wallet

pursue VERB
❶ *The thief ran off, pursued by two police officers.*
• chase, follow, run after, tail, track, hunt, trail, shadow
❷ *She plans to pursue a career as a musician.*
• follow, undertake, practise, conduct, take up, carry on, continue, maintain

pursuit NOUN
❶ *The film is about one man's pursuit of happiness.*
• hunt (for), search (for), striving (for), chase, quest
❷ *Guests can enjoy a range of outdoor pursuits.*
• activity, pastime, hobby, recreation, amusement, interest

push VERB
❶ *Push the red button.*
• press, depress, hold down
❷ *She pushed a chair against the door.*
• shove, thrust, drive, propel, send
OPPOSITE pull
❸ *Push the mixture down with the back of a spoon.*
• pack, press, cram, crush, compress, ram, squash, squeeze
❹ *We pushed our way through the*

large crowd.
• force, barge, shove, thrust, elbow, jostle
❺ *I think she pushes herself too hard.*
• pressurize, press, drive, urge, compel, bully
(*informal*) lean on
❻ *They are really pushing the new TV series.*
• promote, publicize, advertise
(*informal*) plug, hype

put VERB
❶ *Just put the parcels by the door.*
• place, set down, leave, deposit, stand
(*informal*) dump, stick, park, plonk
❷ *Maria put her head on my shoulder.*
• lay, lean, rest
❸ *I was putting a picture on the wall.*
• attach, fasten, fix, hang
❹ *Where are you planning to put the piano?*
• locate, situate
❺ *They always put a lifeguard on duty.*
• position, post, station
❻ *I'm not sure of the best way to put this.*
• express, word, phrase, say, state
➤ **put someone off**
The stench put me off eating.
• deter, discourage, dissuade
➤ **put something off**
We can't put off the decision any longer.
• delay, postpone, defer, shelve
➤ **put something out**
It took three hours to put out the blaze.
• extinguish, quench, smother, douse, snuff out
➤ **put something up**
❶ *We put up the tent in the garden.*
• set up, construct, erect, raise
❷ *They have put up their prices.*
• increase, raise, inflate
➤ **put up with something**
How do you put up with that racket?
• bear, stand, tolerate, endure, stomach, abide

puzzle NOUN
Has anyone managed to solve the puzzle?
• mystery, riddle, conundrum, problem,

A B C D E F G H I J K L M N O P Q R S T U V W X Y Z

enigma
(*informal*) brain-teaser, poser

puzzle VERB
❶ *Your response puzzled me.*
• confuse, baffle, bewilder, bemuse,
mystify, perplex
(*informal*) fox
❷ *We spent all night puzzling over the
problem.*
• ponder, think, meditate, worry, brood

puzzled ADJECTIVE
Why are you looking so puzzled?
• confused, baffled, bewildered,
mystified, perplexed

puzzling ADJECTIVE
*There was something puzzling about the
photograph.*
• confusing, baffling, bewildering,
mystifying, perplexing, mysterious,
inexplicable
OPPOSITES clear, straightforward

Qq

quaint ADJECTIVE

We stayed in a quaint thatched cottage.
• charming, picturesque, sweet, old-fashioned, old-world

quake VERB

The whole building quaked with the blast.
• shake, shudder, tremble, quiver, rock, sway, wobble

qualification NOUN

❶ She has a qualification in healthcare.
• diploma, certificate, degree, licence, training, skill
❷ I'd like to add a qualification to what I said.
• condition, reservation, limitation, proviso

qualified ADJECTIVE

❶ This job needs a qualified electrician.
• certified, chartered, licensed, experienced, skilled, trained, professional
OPPOSITE amateur
❷ The plan has been given qualified approval.
• conditional, limited, partial, guarded, cautious, half-hearted

qualify VERB

❶ The course will qualify you to administer first aid.
• authorize, certify, license, permit, allow, entitle
❷ The first three runners will qualify for the final.
• be eligible, be entitled, get through, pass
❸ I'd like to qualify that statement.
• limit, modify, restrict, moderate

quality NOUN

❶ We only use ingredients of the highest quality.
• grade, class, standard, calibre, merit

❷ It has all the qualities of a good detective story.
• characteristic, feature, property, attribute, trait

quantity NOUN

❶ Add a very small quantity of baking powder.
• amount, mass, volume, bulk, weight (informal) load
❷ We received a large quantity of emails.
• number, sum, total

quarrel NOUN

My brother and I have quarrels all the time.
• argument, disagreement, dispute, difference of opinion, row, tiff, fight, squabble, wrangle, clash
– Continuous quarrelling is **strife**.
– A long-lasting quarrel is a **feud** or **vendetta**.
– A quarrel in which people become violent is a **brawl**.

quarrel VERB

What are you two quarrelling about?
• argue, disagree, fight, row, squabble, bicker, clash, fall out
IDIOM cross swords
➤ quarrel with something
I won't quarrel with your decision.
• disagree with, object to, oppose, take exception to, take issue with, criticize, fault

quarrelsome ADJECTIVE

They were a quarrelsome family.
• argumentative, belligerent, confrontational, aggressive, bad-tempered, irritable
OPPOSITES placid, peaceable

quarry NOUN

He filmed a leopard stalking its quarry.
• prey, victim, kill

quarters PLURAL NOUN

The attic was originally the servants' quarters.
• accommodation, lodging, rooms, housing

quaver VERB
I was so nervous my voice began to quaver.
• shake, tremble, waver, quake, quiver, falter

quay NOUN
Boats were moored alongside the quay.
• dock, harbour, pier, wharf, jetty, landing stage, marina

queasy ADJECTIVE
Long bus journeys make me feel queasy.
• sick, nauseous, ill, unwell, groggy

queen NOUN
The infant Mary was crowned Queen of Scots.
• monarch, sovereign, ruler

queer ADJECTIVE
There's a queer smell in here.
• odd, peculiar, strange, unusual, abnormal, curious, funny, weird, bizarre, mysterious, puzzling
OPPOSITES normal, ordinary

quench VERB
❶ They gave us water to quench our thirst.
• satisfy, ease, relieve, cool
IDIOM take the edge off
OPPOSITE intensify
❷ Firefighters are struggling to quench a forest fire.
• extinguish, put out, smother, snuff out
OPPOSITE kindle

query NOUN
Please email your queries to this address.
• question, enquiry, problem

query VERB
No one queried the referee's decision.
• question, challenge, dispute, argue over, quarrel with, object to
OPPOSITE accept

quest NOUN
He set off on a quest for adventure.
• search, hunt, expedition, mission

question NOUN
❶ Does anyone have any questions?
• enquiry, query
– A question which someone sets as a puzzle is a **brain-teaser**, **conundrum** or **riddle**.
– A series of questions asked as a game is a **quiz**.
– A set of questions which someone asks to get information is a **questionnaire** or **survey**.
❷ There's some question over his fitness to play.
• uncertainty, doubt, argument, debate, dispute
❸ There is also the question of cost.
• matter, issue, topic, subject, concern, problem

question VERB
❶ Detectives have been questioning the suspect.
• interrogate, cross-examine, interview, quiz
(informal) grill, pump for information
❷ She never questioned his right to be there.
• query, challenge, dispute, argue over, quarrel with, object to
OPPOSITE accept

queue NOUN
There was a queue of people waiting for tickets.
• line, file, column, string, procession, train
– A long queue of traffic on a road is a **tailback**.

queue VERB
Please queue at the door.
• line up, form a queue

quick ADJECTIVE
❶ You need to be quick when applying the paint.
• fast, swift, rapid, speedy, snappy, brisk
(informal) nippy
OPPOSITES slow, unhurried
❷ Do you mind if I make a quick phone call?
• short, brief, momentary, hurried, hasty, cursory
OPPOSITES long, lengthy

A
B
C
D
E
F
G
H
I
J
K
L
M
N
O
P
Q
R
S
T
U
V
W
X
Y
Z

❸ *I would appreciate a quick reply.*
• prompt, immediate, instant, direct
OPPOSITE delayed
❹ *She's very quick at mental arithmetic.*
• bright, sharp, clever, acute, alert, perceptive
IDIOM (informal) on the ball
OPPOSITES slow, dull

quicken VERB
The pace quickens as the story unfolds.
• accelerate, speed up, step up, pick up speed

quickly ADVERB
❶ *She began to walk more quickly.*
• fast, hurriedly, swiftly, rapidly, speedily, briskly, at speed
IDIOMS at the double, at full tilt
OPPOSITES slowly, unhurriedly
❷ *I had to come up with a plan quickly.*
• immediately, at once, soon, straight away, right away, directly, instantly
(informal) pronto, asap
IDIOM in a heartbeat

quiet ADJECTIVE
❶ *Suddenly the whole room went quiet.*
• silent, still, noiseless, soundless, mute
OPPOSITE noisy
❷ *He spoke in a quiet voice.*
• hushed, low, soft, faint, muted, muffled, whispered
– Something that is too quiet to hear clearly is **inaudible**.
OPPOSITE loud
❸ *She has always been a quiet child.*
• shy, reserved, subdued, placid, uncommunicative, retiring, withdrawn
OPPOSITE talkative
❹ *I found a quiet place to sit and read.*
• peaceful, tranquil, secluded, restful, calm, serene
OPPOSITE busy

quieten VERB
➤ **quieten down**
Eventually the audience quietened down.
• fall silent, calm down, settle

quietly ADVERB
❶ *I crept quietly along the corridor.*
• silently, noiselessly, without a sound, inaudibly
OPPOSITE noisily
❷ *A voice whispered quietly into my ear.*
• softly, faintly, in a whisper, under your breath
OPPOSITE loudly

quit VERB
❶ *He decided to quit his job and go abroad.*
• leave, give up, resign from
(informal) pack in
❷ (informal) *Quit asking me all these questions!*
• stop, cease
(informal) leave off

quite ADVERB
❶ *His sisters have quite different personalities.*
• completely, totally, utterly, entirely, wholly, absolutely, altogether
OPPOSITE slightly
❷ *It's still quite dark outside.*
• fairly, reasonably, moderately, comparatively, rather, somewhat
(informal) pretty

quiver VERB
The dog was wet through and quivering with cold.
• shiver, shake, shudder, tremble, quake, quaver, wobble

quiz NOUN
We took part in a general knowledge quiz.
• test, competition

quiz VERB
Detectives quizzed him about his missing wife.
• question, interrogate, cross-examine, interview
(informal) grill

quota *NOUN*
 We are given a quota of work to get through each week.
 • allocation, allowance, ration, share, portion

quotation *NOUN*
 The title is a quotation from Shakespeare.
 • extract, excerpt, passage, piece, quote

– A piece taken from a newspaper is a **cutting**.
– A piece taken from a film or TV programme is a **clip**.

quote *VERB*
 He ended by quoting a few lines from a poem.
 • recite, repeat

Rr

race NOUN
❶ *We had a race across the field.*
• competition, contest, chase
– A race to decide who will take part in the final is a **heat**.
❷ *People of many different races lived together in the city.*
• ethnic group, people, nation

race VERB
❶ *I'll race you to the corner.*
• have a race with, run against, compete with
❷ *I raced home to tell them the exciting news.*
• run, rush, hurry, dash, sprint, fly, tear, whizz, zoom

rack NOUN
Cooking pots hung from a rack on the wall.
• frame, framework, support, holder, stand, shelf

racket NOUN
The chickens are making a terrible racket!
• noise, din, row, commotion, clamour, uproar, rumpus, hubbub

radiant ADJECTIVE
She gave him a radiant smile.
• bright, dazzling, happy, cheerful, joyful, warm

radiate VERB
❶ *All stars radiate light.*
• give off, send out, emit
❷ *She is a woman who radiates confidence.*
• show, exhibit, exude, ooze
❸ *The city's streets radiate from the central square.*
• spread out, fan out, branch out

radical ADJECTIVE
❶ *We had to make radical changes to the script.*
• fundamental, drastic, thorough, comprehensive, extensive, sweeping, wide-ranging, far-reaching
OPPOSITE superficial
❷ *She has radical views on education.*
• extreme, revolutionary, militant
OPPOSITE moderate

rage NOUN
He let out a cry of rage.
• anger, fury, wrath, temper, outrage, indignation, pique

rage VERB
❶ *She just sat there, raging inwardly.*
• be angry, be enraged, fume, seethe, rant, rave
❷ *The storm was still raging outside.*
• blow, storm, rampage

ragged ADJECTIVE
❶ *A man came to the door wearing ragged clothes.*
• tattered, torn, frayed, threadbare, ripped, patched, shabby, worn out (*informal*) tatty
❷ *A ragged line of people waited in the rain.*
• irregular, uneven, rough

raid NOUN
The bombing raids continued for weeks.
• attack, assault, strike, onslaught, invasion, foray, blitz

raid VERB
❶ *The monastery was raided by Vikings in 795.*
• attack, invade, ransack, plunder, loot, pillage
❷ *Police raided the house at dawn.*
• descend on, break into, rush, storm, swoop on

rail NOUN
The track is made of steel rails.
• bar, rod, spar
– A fence made of rails is also called **railings**.

railway NOUN
see **transport**

rain NOUN
We were caught in a shower of rain.
• rainfall, raindrops, drizzle
(*formal*) precipitation
– The rainy season in south and south-east Asia is the **monsoon**.
– A long period without rain is a **drought**.
– A fall of rain is a **shower** or **downpour**.
– A heavy fall of rain is a **deluge**.
For tips on describing weather see **weather**.

rain VERB
Is it still raining outside?
• pour, teem, bucket, pelt, spit, drizzle

rainy ADJECTIVE
It was a cold and rainy day.
• wet, showery, drizzly, damp
OPPOSITES dry, fine
For tips on describing weather see **weather**.

raise VERB
❶ *Raise your hand if you need help.*
• put up, hold up, lift
❷ *The box was too heavy for him to raise.*
• lift, pick up, elevate, hoist
❸ *The company was forced to raise its prices.*
• increase, put up, push up, inflate
(*informal*) bump up
❹ *They raised thousands of pounds for charity.*
• collect, gather, take in, make
❺ *She raised three children on her own.*
• bring up, care for, look after, nurture, rear
❻ *Several objections have been raised.*
• put forward, bring up, mention, present, air
❼ *I don't want to raise your hopes.*
• encourage, build up, arouse
❽ *The accident raises questions about rail safety.*
• produce, create, give rise to, prompt

rally NOUN
Demonstrators held a rally in the town square.
• demonstration, meeting, march, protest
(*informal*) demo

rally VERB
They tried to rally support for the campaign.
• gather, collect, amass, raise

ram VERB
❶ *He quickly rammed the wallet into his pocket.*
• thrust, force, push, jam, stuff, plunge, stick
❷ *The car skidded and rammed into a lamp post.*
• hit, strike, bump, crash into, collide with, smash into

ramble VERB
❶ *We both enjoy rambling in the countryside.*
• walk, hike, trek, backpack, roam, rove, range
❷ *The speaker rambled on for hours.*
• chatter, babble, prattle
(*informal*) rabbit, witter

rambling ADJECTIVE
It was a long rambling speech.
• confused, disorganized, unfocused, roundabout, meandering
OPPOSITE focused

rampage VERB
An angry mob rampaged through the streets.
• run riot, run amok, go berserk, storm, charge

ran
past tense see **run**

random ADJECTIVE
Make the longest word you can out of a random selection of letters.
• arbitrary, unplanned, haphazard, chance, casual, indiscriminate
OPPOSITE deliberate

rang
past tense see **ring**

range NOUN
❶ *Supermarkets sell a wide range of goods.*
• variety, assortment, mixture, collection, selection, choice
❷ *The competition is open to children in the age range 8 to 12.*
• span, scope, spectrum, compass
❸ *There is a range of mountains in the south.*
• chain, line, row, series, string

range VERB
❶ *Prices range from fifteen to twenty pounds.*
• vary, differ, extend, run, fluctuate
❷ *Jars of preserves were ranged on the shelf.*
• arrange, order, lay out, set out, line up
❸ *Wild deer range over the hills.*
• wander, ramble, roam, rove, stray

rank NOUN
❶ *Ranks of marching soldiers approached the town.*
• row, line, file, column
❷ *He holds the rank of sergeant.*
• grade, level, position, status
– To raise someone to a higher rank is to **promote** them.
– To reduce someone to a lower rank is to **demote** them.

ransack VERB
❶ *She ransacked the wardrobe for something to wear.*
• search, scour, rummage through, comb
(*informal*) turn upside down
❷ *Thieves had ransacked the building.*
• loot, pillage, plunder, rob, wreck

rap VERB
❶ *Someone rapped urgently on the door.*
• knock, tap
❷ *She rapped her knuckles on the desk.*
• strike, hit, drum

rapid ADJECTIVE
They set off at a rapid pace.
• fast, quick, speedy, swift, brisk
OPPOSITE slow

rare ADJECTIVE
❶ *This is a rare species of orchid.*
• uncommon, unusual, infrequent, scarce, sparse
OPPOSITE common
❷ *She has a rare talent for storytelling.*
• exceptional, remarkable, outstanding, special

rarely ADVERB
He is rarely seen in public.
• seldom, infrequently, hardly ever
OPPOSITE often

rash ADJECTIVE
Don't make any rash promises.
• reckless, foolhardy, hasty, hurried, impulsive, impetuous, unthinking
OPPOSITES prudent, considered

rash NOUN
❶ *I had an itchy red rash on my leg.*
• spots
❷ *There has been a rash of break-ins lately.*
• series, succession, wave, flurry, outbreak, flood, spate

rate NOUN
❶ *The boys were pedalling at a furious rate.*
• speed, pace, velocity, tempo
❷ *What's the usual rate for washing a car?*
• charge, cost, fee, payment, price, figure, amount

rate VERB
How do you rate your chances of winning?
• assess, judge, estimate, evaluate, gauge, weigh up

rather ADVERB
❶ *It's rather chilly today.*
• slightly, fairly, moderately, somewhat, quite, a bit, a little
❷ *I'd rather not discuss it on the phone.*
• preferably, sooner

➤ **rather than**
We decided to walk rather than wait for the bus.
• as opposed to, instead of

ratio NOUN
Mix oil and vinegar in the ratio of three to one.
• proportion, balance
– You can express a ratio as a **percentage**.

ration NOUN
Each of us was allowed a daily ration of water.
• allowance, allocation, quota, share, portion, helping, measure
➤ **rations**
We took plenty of rations for our camping trip.
• provisions, food, supplies, stores

ration VERB
Food had to be rationed during the war.
• limit, restrict, share out, allocate, allot

rational ADJECTIVE
There was no rational explanation for what had happened.
• logical, reasonable, sensible, sane, common-sense
OPPOSITE irrational

rattle VERB
Something rattled inside the parcel.
• clatter, clink, clunk
For tips on describing sounds see **sound**.

rave VERB
❶ *Liz started raving at me down the phone.*
• rage, rant, storm, fume, shout, yell
❷ *Everyone is raving about the new book.*
• enthuse, be excited, talk wildly

ravenous ADJECTIVE
By evening we were all ravenous.
• hungry, famished, starving, starved

raw ADJECTIVE
❶ *He was eating a piece of raw carrot.*
• uncooked
OPPOSITE cooked

❷ *The factory imports most of its raw materials from abroad.*
• unprocessed, crude, natural, untreated
OPPOSITES manufactured, processed
❸ *She started as a raw trainee reporter.*
• inexperienced, untrained, new, green
OPPOSITE experienced
❹ *The fall had left a patch of raw skin on my knee.*
• red, rough, sore, tender, inflamed
❺ *There was a raw north-east wind blowing.*
• bitter, cold, chilly, biting, freezing, piercing

ray NOUN
A ray of sunlight shone through the branches.
• beam, shaft, stream

reach VERB
❶ *After a while we reached a small village.*
• arrive at, go as far as, get to, make, end up at
❷ *The appeal fund has reached its target.*
• achieve, attain, hit
OPPOSITES miss, fall short of
❸ *I can't reach the top shelf.*
• get hold of, grasp, touch
❹ *You can reach me on my mobile.*
• contact, get in touch with, get through to, speak to, get hold of
➤ **reach out**
Reach out your hands.
• extend, hold out, stretch out, thrust out, stick out

reach NOUN
❶ *The lower branches were just out of my reach.*
• grasp, range, stretch
❷ *The island is within easy reach of the mainland.*
• distance, range

react VERB
The woman reacted oddly when I gave my name.
• respond, behave, answer, reply

a b c d e f g h i j k l m n o p q r s t u v w x y z

A
B
C
D
E
F
G
H
I
J
K
L
M
N
O
P
Q
R
S
T
U
V
W
X
Y
Z

reaction NOUN
What was your immediate reaction to the news?
• response, answer, reply

read VERB
❶ *Can you read this signature?*
• make out, understand, decipher
❷ *I read through my notes again quickly.*
• look over, study, scan, leaf through, peruse
IDIOM cast your eye over
– To read through something very quickly is to **skim through** it.
– To read here and there in a book is to **dip into** it.
– To read something intently is to **pore over** it.

readily ADVERB
❶ *My friends readily agreed to help.*
• willingly, gladly, happily, eagerly
OPPOSITES reluctantly, grudgingly
❷ *All the ingredients are readily available.*
• easily, conveniently, without any difficulty

ready ADJECTIVE
❶ *When will tea be ready?*
• prepared, all set, done, organized, arranged, available, in place
OPPOSITE not ready
❷ *He's always ready to help a friend.*
• willing, glad, pleased, happy, keen, eager
OPPOSITES reluctant, unwilling
❸ *She has a ready answer for everything.*
• prompt, swift, immediate
OPPOSITE slow

real ADJECTIVE
❶ *The play is based on a real story.*
• actual, true, factual, verifiable
OPPOSITES fictitious, imaginary
❷ *Is that a real diamond?*
• genuine, authentic, natural
OPPOSITES artificial, imitation

❸ *She doesn't often show her real feelings.*
• sincere, honest, genuine, true, heartfelt
OPPOSITES insincere, put on

realistic ADJECTIVE
❶ *It's a very realistic portrait.*
• lifelike, true to life, faithful, authentic, convincing, natural
❷ *It's not realistic to expect a puppy to be quiet.*
• feasible, practical, sensible, possible, workable
(*informal*) doable
OPPOSITES unrealistic, impractical

reality NOUN
You need to stop daydreaming and face reality.
• the facts, the real world, real life, the truth
OPPOSITE fantasy

realize VERB
❶ *Don't you realize what this means?*
• understand, appreciate, comprehend, perceive, recognize, grasp, see
(*informal*) catch on to, tumble to, twig
❷ *She realized her ambition to become a racing driver.*
• fulfil, achieve, accomplish, attain

really ADVERB
❶ *Can there really be life on other planets?*
• actually, definitely, genuinely, honestly, certainly, truly, in fact, in truth, in reality
❷ *I thought that was a really good film.*
• very, extremely, exceptionally

realm NOUN
❶ *Hobbits live in the mythical realm of Middle-earth.*
• country, kingdom, domain, empire
❷ *Perhaps the answer lies beyond the realm of science.*
• sphere, domain, field, area

rear NOUN
The buffet car is at the rear of the train.
• back, end, tail end

– The rear of a ship is the **stern**.
OPPOSITES front, head

rear ADJECTIVE
Our seats were in the rear coach of the train.
• back, end, last
– The rear legs of an animal are its **hind** legs.
OPPOSITES front, leading

rear VERB
❶ The couple have reared three children.
• bring up, raise, nurture
❷ The cobra reared its head.
• hold up, lift, raise
❸ Ahead of us reared the Himalayas.
• rise up, tower, loom, soar

rearrange VERB
❶ Someone has rearranged the furniture.
• reorganize, reorder, reposition
(informal) rejig
❷ Let's rearrange our meeting.
• reschedule

reason NOUN
❶ What was the reason for the delay?
• cause, grounds, explanation, motive, justification, basis, excuse
❷ He never listens to reason.
• sense, common sense, logic, rationality
❸ It was clear that the poor woman had lost her reason.
• sanity, mind, senses, wits
(informal) marbles

reason VERB
➤ reason with someone
It's no use reasoning with him.
• argue with, persuade, talk round

reasonable ADJECTIVE
❶ That seems like a reasonable plan.
• sensible, intelligent, realistic, rational, logical, sane, sound, valid
OPPOSITES irrational, illogical
❷ It's a reasonable price for a camera.
• fair, moderate, affordable, respectable, acceptable
OPPOSITES excessive, exorbitant
❸ The bike is in reasonable condition.
• satisfactory, acceptable, adequate, average, tolerable, passable, not bad,

fairly good
(informal) OK

reassure VERB
She tried hard to reassure us.
• calm, comfort, encourage, hearten, give confidence to
IDIOM put your mind at rest
OPPOSITE alarm

rebel VERB
The people of the south rebelled.
• revolt, rise up
– To rebel against the captain of a ship is to **mutiny**.
OPPOSITE obey

rebellion NOUN
❶ The protest soon became a widespread rebellion.
• revolt, revolution, uprising, insurgence, insurrection
– A rebellion on a ship is a **mutiny**.
❷ She was showing signs of teenage rebellion.
• resistance, defiance, disobedience, insubordination

rebellious ADJECTIVE
My sister is going through a rebellious phase.
• defiant, disobedient, insubordinate, mutinous, unruly, obstreperous

rebound VERB
The ball rebounded off the keeper's chest.
• bounce back, spring back, ricochet

recall VERB
Can you recall any of their names?
• remember, recollect, think back to
OPPOSITE forget

recede VERB
❶ The flood water slowly receded.
• go back, retreat, withdraw, subside, ebb
OPPOSITE advance
❷ His fear began to recede.
• lessen, diminish, decline, subside, ebb, fade, dwindle
OPPOSITES grow, intensify

receive VERB
❶ *I went up to the stage to receive the trophy.*
• be given, be presented with, be awarded, take, accept, collect
OPPOSITES give, present
❷ *Some passengers received minor injuries.*
• experience, suffer, undergo, sustain
OPPOSITE inflict
❸ *He received the news in complete silence.*
• react to, respond to
❹ *We went to the front door to receive our visitors.*
• greet, meet, welcome

recent ADJECTIVE
She tries to keep up with recent fashion trends.
• current, contemporary, new, fresh, modern, the latest, up to date, up to the minute
OPPOSITE old

recently ADVERB
I've not heard from her recently.
• lately, of late, latterly

reception NOUN
❶ *The landlady gave us a frosty reception.*
• greeting, welcome, treatment
❷ *The wedding reception will be held at a nearby hotel.*
• party, function, gathering, get-together, celebration
(*informal*) do

recipe NOUN
Here is a simple recipe for carrot cake.
• directions, instructions
– The items you use for a recipe are the **ingredients**.

recital NOUN
❶ *There will be a short piano recital at noon.*
• concert, performance
❷ *He stood up to give a recital of one of his poems.*
• recitation, reading

recite VERB
She recited the whole poem from memory.
• say aloud, read out, narrate, deliver, declaim

reckless ADJECTIVE
A man has been charged with reckless driving.
• careless, thoughtless, rash, irresponsible, heedless, foolhardy, negligent
OPPOSITE careful

reckon VERB
❶ (*informal*) *I reckon it's going to rain.*
• think, believe, guess, imagine, feel
❷ *I tried to reckon how much she owed me.*
• calculate, work out, add up, assess, estimate
(*informal*) tot up
➤ **reckon on**
They hadn't reckoned on it being so expensive.
• be prepared for, plan for, anticipate, foresee, expect, consider, bargain on

recline VERB
She reclined lazily on the sofa.
• lean back, lie back, lounge, rest, stretch out, sprawl, loll

recognize VERB
❶ *I didn't recognize the voice at first.*
• identify, know, distinguish, recall, recollect, put a name to, place
❷ *They refuse to recognize that there is a problem.*
• acknowledge, admit, accept, grant, concede, confess, realize

recoil VERB
She recoiled at the sight of blood.
• draw back, shrink back, flinch, quail, wince

recollect VERB
Do you recollect what happened?
• remember, recall, have a memory of
OPPOSITE forget

recommend VERB
❶ *I recommend that you book in advance.*
• advise, counsel, propose, suggest, advocate, prescribe, urge
OPPOSITE advise against
❷ *I recommend the strawberry ice cream.*
• endorse, praise, commend, vouch for, speak favourably of
IDIOM put in a good word for

reconsider VERB
Would you like to reconsider your answer?
• rethink, review, reassess, re-evaluate
IDIOM have second thoughts about

record NOUN
I keep a record of my dreams.
• account, report, register, diary, journal, log, chronicle
– The records of what happened at a meeting are the **minutes**.
– Records consisting of historical documents are **archives**.

record VERB
❶ *He recorded everything he heard in a notebook.*
• write down, note, document, set down, put down, enter, register, log
❷ *The concert is being recorded live.*
• tape, film, video

recover VERB
❶ *She is still recovering from her illness.*
• get better, recuperate, convalesce, heal, mend, improve, pick up, revive, bounce back
OPPOSITE deteriorate
❷ *The police have recovered the stolen painting.*
• get back, retrieve, regain, reclaim, recoup, repossess, find, trace
OPPOSITE lose

recovery NOUN
We all wish you a speedy recovery.
• recuperation, improvement, convalescence, healing, revival

recreation NOUN
❶ *What do you do for recreation around here?*
• leisure, fun, relaxation, enjoyment, amusement, entertainment, pleasure, diversion, play
❷ *Curling is a popular recreation in Canada.*
• pastime, hobby, leisure activity

recruit NOUN
The centre is where new recruits are trained in fire fighting.
• trainee, apprentice, learner, novice
– A recruit training to be in the armed services is a **cadet**.

recruit VERB
We have recruited two new members for our book club.
• bring in, take on, enrol, sign up, hire
– To be recruited into the armed services is to **enlist**.

rectangle NOUN
You will need a rectangle of fabric.
– A rectangle with adjacent sides of unequal length is also called an **oblong**.

recur VERB
Go to the doctor if the symptoms recur.
• reappear, be repeated, come back, happen again, return

recycle VERB
We recycle all our plastic and glass.
• reuse, reprocess, salvage, reclaim

red ADJECTIVE
❶ *He wore a bright red T-shirt.*
see **red** adjective
❷ *She had flaming red hair.*
• ginger, auburn, chestnut, coppery (informal) carroty
For tips on describing hair see **hair**.
❸ *My eyes were red from lack of sleep.*
• bloodshot, inflamed, red-rimmed
❹ *Xiang went red with embarrassment.*
• flushed, blushing, rosy, ruddy

red ADJECTIVE & NOUN

> ### WORD WEB
>
> Some shades of red:
>
> | | |
> |---|---|
> | ➤ brick red | ➤ pink |
> | ➤ burgundy | ➤ rose |
> | ➤ cherry | ➤ ruby |
> | ➤ crimson | ➤ scarlet |
> | ➤ maroon | ➤ vermilion |
> | ➤ pillar-box red | ➤ wine |
>
> For tips on describing colours see colour.

reduce VERB

I have reduced the amount of sugar in my diet.

• decrease, lessen, lower, diminish, minimize, cut, cut back, slash

– To reduce something by half is to **halve** it.

– To reduce the width of something is to **narrow** it.

– To reduce the length of something is to **shorten** or **trim** it.

– To reduce speed is to **decelerate**.

– To reduce the strength of a liquid is to **dilute** it.

OPPOSITE increase

➤ **reduce to**

The audience were reduced to tears.

• drive to, bring to

reel NOUN

I bought a reel of black cotton thread.

• spool

reel VERB

❶ *He reeled as if he was going to faint.*

• stagger, lurch, sway, rock, totter, stumble, wobble

❷ *All these questions are making my head reel.*

• spin, whirl, swirl, swim, feel dizzy

➤ **reel off**

The chef reeled off a long list of ingredients.

• recite, rattle off, fire off

refer VERB

Your doctor may refer you to a specialist.

• hand over, pass on, direct, send

➤ **refer to**

❶ *Which book are you referring to?*

• allude to, make reference to, mention, comment on, touch on, call attention to, bring up

❷ *Refer to our website for more information.*

• look up, consult, go to, turn to, call up

➤ **refer to as**

Junk email is often referred to as 'spam'.

• call, term, style, dub, describe as

referee NOUN

The referee blew his whistle.

• umpire, adjudicator, judge (*informal*) ref

refill VERB

Can I refill your glass?

• top up

– To refill a fuel tank is to **refuel**.

refine VERB

❶ *This chapter explains the process of refining sugar.*

• purify, filter, process, distil

❷ *I'm trying to refine my juggling skills.*

• improve, perfect, polish, hone, fine-tune

reflect VERB

❶ *Mirrored surfaces reflect sunlight.*

• send back, throw back, shine back

❷ *Her love of adventure is reflected in her writing.*

• show, indicate, demonstrate, exhibit, reveal

➤ **reflect on**

I have been reflecting on the events of the past week.

• think about, contemplate, consider, ponder, mull over

reflection NOUN

❶ *I could see my reflection in the pond.*

• image, likeness

❷ *His art is a reflection of his passion for life.*

• indication, demonstration, evidence, expression, manifestation, result

❸ *We need more time for reflection.*

• thinking, contemplation,

consideration, deliberation, meditation, musing

reform VERB
❶ *We need to reform the way we live on this planet.*
• improve, better, rectify, revise, refine, revamp, modify, adapt
❷ *He promised to reform in the future.*
• change for the better, mend your ways
IDIOM turn over a new leaf
Note that re-form, spelled with a hyphen, is a different word meaning 'get back together': *The band are re-forming after twenty years.*

reform NOUN
They are making reforms to the school curriculum.
• improvement, amendment, refinement, revision, modification

refrain VERB
➤ refrain from
I found it hard to refrain from smiling.
• stop yourself, avoid, hold back from, abstain from

refresh VERB
❶ *Maybe a walk will refresh me.*
• revive, revitalize, reinvigorate, restore, freshen, wake up, perk up
OPPOSITE weary
❷ *Let me refresh your memory.*
• jog, prompt, prod

refreshing ADJECTIVE
We went for a refreshing dip in the pool.
• reviving, invigorating, restorative, bracing, stimulating, fortifying

refuge NOUN
❶ *A cave provided refuge from the blizzard.*
• shelter, cover, protection, safety
❷ *The outlaws hid in their secret mountain refuge.*
• hideaway, hideout, retreat, haven, sanctuary

refund VERB
She asked them to refund her money.
• repay, pay back, give back, return

refusal NOUN
❶ *I sent them a polite refusal.*
• non-acceptance, rejection
OPPOSITE acceptance
❷ *I can't understand her refusal to cooperate.*
• unwillingness, reluctance, disinclination
OPPOSITE willingness

refuse VERB
❶ *He refused all offers of help.*
• decline, reject, turn down, say no to, rebuff, spurn
(*informal*) pass up
OPPOSITE accept
❷ *We were refused permission to take photos inside.*
• deny, deprive of
OPPOSITES grant, allow

refuse NOUN
We recycle most of our household refuse.
• rubbish, waste, litter, junk
(*North American*) trash, garbage

regain VERB
Mike slowly began to regain consciousness.
• get back, get back to, return to

regard VERB
❶ *I still regard it as a great film.*
• think of, consider, judge, value, estimate, rate, look on
❷ *The boy regarded us suspiciously.*
• look at, gaze at, stare at, eye, view, observe, scrutinize, watch, contemplate

regard NOUN
➤ regards
Give my regards to your family.
• best wishes, greetings, compliments, respects

regarding PREPOSITION
For more information regarding our products, visit our website.
• about, concerning, on the subject of, with reference to, with regard to, with respect to, in connection with

a b c d e f g h i j k l m n o p q r s t u v w x y z

regardless ADJECTIVE
➤ **regardless of**
I kept on reading, regardless of the time.
• indifferent to, not caring about,
unconcerned about, irrespective of,
without regard to, disregarding

region NOUN
*They lived in a remote region of northern
Australia.*
• area, district, territory, province,
sector, quarter, zone, neighbourhood

register VERB
❶ *You need to register your username.*
• record, enter, submit, lodge
❷ *This dial registers the oven
temperature.*
• indicate, display, read, show
❸ *His face registered deep suspicion.*
• show, express, display, exhibit, reveal

regret VERB
Do you now regret your decision?
• be sorry about, feel remorse for,
repent, rue

regular ADJECTIVE
❶ *Try to eat regular meals.*
• evenly spaced, fixed
OPPOSITES irregular, haphazard
❷ *The drummer kept up a regular
rhythm.*
• steady, even, uniform, unvarying,
constant, consistent
OPPOSITES irregular, erratic, uneven
❸ *Is this your regular route to school?*
• normal, usual, customary, habitual,
ordinary, routine, standard
OPPOSITE unusual
❹ *She is one of our regular customers.*
• frequent, familiar, habitual, persistent
OPPOSITES rare, occasional

regulate VERB
❶ *Turn the dial to regulate the
temperature.*
• control, set, adjust, alter, moderate
❷ *The broadcasting industry is strictly
regulated.*
• manage, direct, control, govern,
monitor, supervise, police

regulation NOUN
*There are new regulations on school
uniform.*
• rule, order, law, directive, decree,
statute

rehearsal NOUN
*This morning we have a rehearsal for the
school concert.*
• practice, run-through, dry run, drill
– A rehearsal in which the cast wear
costumes is a **dress rehearsal**.

rehearse VERB
*We need to rehearse the final scene
again.*
• go over, practise, run over, read
through

reign VERB
How long did Queen Victoria reign?
• be king or queen, sit on the throne,
govern, rule

reject VERB
❶ *Why did you reject their offer?*
• decline, refuse, turn down, say no to,
spurn, rebuff
OPPOSITE accept
❷ *Faulty parts are rejected at the
factory.*
• discard, get rid of, throw out, scrap
OPPOSITE keep

rejoice VERB
*Everyone rejoiced when the fighting
ceased.*
• be happy, celebrate, delight, exult
OPPOSITE grieve

relate VERB
*They have many stories to relate about
their adventures abroad.*
• tell, narrate, recount, report, describe
➤ **relate to**
❶ *The rest of the letter relates to her
family.*
• be about, refer to, have to do with,
concern
❷ *How does this scene relate to the rest
of the play?*
• fit in with, connect to, be linked to

❸ *I find it hard to relate to any of the characters.*
• empathize with, identify with, feel for, get on with

related ADJECTIVE
Do you think the murders are related?
• connected, linked, interconnected, allied
OPPOSITES unrelated, unconnected

relation NOUN
❶ *The stolen car has no relation to the robbery.*
• connection, relationship, association, link, bond
❷ *Are you a relation of hers?*
• relative, member of the family
(*old use*) kinsman or kinswoman
SEE ALSO family

relationship NOUN
❶ *There is a relationship between your diet and your health.*
• connection, relation, association, link, bond
– The relationship between two numbers is a **ratio**.
❷ *She has a good relationship with her stepmother.*
• friendship, attachment (to), understanding (of), rapport (with)

relative NOUN
see relation

relax VERB
❶ *I like to relax by listening to music.*
• unwind, rest, take it easy
(*informal*) chill out
IDIOM put your feet up
❷ *A warm bath always relaxes me.*
• calm down, soothe
❸ *Try to relax your grip on the racket.*
• slacken, loosen, unclench, ease, soften
OPPOSITES tighten, tense

relaxed ADJECTIVE
The cafe had a relaxed atmosphere.
• informal, casual, carefree, leisurely, easy-going, peaceful, restful, unhurried, calm

(*informal*) laid-back, chilled-out
OPPOSITES tense, stressful

release VERB
❶ *All the hostages have been released.*
• free, let go, discharge, liberate, set free
OPPOSITES capture, imprison
❷ *What if they release the guard dogs?*
• let loose, set loose, unfasten, unleash, untie
❸ *Her new album will be released in April.*
• issue, publish, put out

relent VERB
In the end Mum and Dad relented and let me go to the party.
• give in, give way, yield, soften, weaken

relentless ADJECTIVE
He faced relentless criticism.
• constant, continuous, never-ending, incessant, perpetual, persistent, unrelenting, unremitting

relevant ADJECTIVE
Make sure your answer is relevant to the question.
• applicable, pertinent, to the point, appropriate, suitable, related
OPPOSITE irrelevant

reliable ADJECTIVE
❶ *This website is a reliable source of information.*
• dependable, valid, trustworthy, safe, sound, steady, sure
OPPOSITES unreliable, untrustworthy
❷ *He's a reliable boy and won't let you down.*
• faithful, dependable, trustworthy, loyal, constant, devoted, staunch, true

relief NOUN
❶ *The pills gave some relief from the pain.*
• comfort, easing, soothing, alleviation
❷ *I watched TV for some light relief.*
• relaxation, rest, respite, diversion
❸ *The charity is involved in famine relief.*
• aid, assistance, help

a
b
c
d
e
f
g
h
i
j
k
l
m
n
o
p
q
r
s
t
u
v
w
x
y
z

relieve VERB
❶ *The doctor said the pills would relieve the pain.*
• alleviate, ease, soothe, lessen, diminish, dull
OPPOSITE intensify
❷ *We played cards to relieve the boredom.*
• reduce, lighten, dispel, counteract

religion NOUN
Prayers are used in many religions.
• faith, belief, creed, denomination, sect

✦ WORD WEB

Major world religions:

➤ Buddhism	➤ Shintoism
➤ Christianity	➤ Sikhism
➤ Hinduism	➤ Taoism
➤ Islam	➤ Zen
➤ Judaism	

- The study of religion is **divinity** or **theology**.

Major religious festivals:

➤ (*Buddhist*) Buddha Day, Nirvana Day
➤ (*Christian*) Lent, Easter, Christmas
➤ (*Hindu*) Holi, Diwali
➤ (*Muslim*) Ramadan, Eid
➤ (*Jewish*) Passover, Rosh Hashana, Yom Kippur, Hanukkah
➤ (*Sikh*) Baisakhi, Birth of Guru Nanak

Religious leaders:

➤ cleric, clergyman or clergywoman
➤ (*Buddhist*) lama
➤ (*Christian*) priest, minister, vicar, bishop, cardinal, pope, chaplain
➤ (*Hindu or Sikh*) guru
➤ (*Muslim*) imam
➤ (*Jewish*) rabbi

Places of religious worship:

➤ temple
➤ shrine
➤ (*Christian*) church, chapel, cathedral
➤ (*Muslim*) mosque
➤ (*Jewish*) synagogue

religious ADJECTIVE
❶ *The choir sang a selection of religious music.*
• sacred, spiritual, holy, divine
OPPOSITE secular
❷ *My grandparents were very religious.*
• devout, pious, reverent, god-fearing, churchgoing

relish VERB
Many people would relish the chance to be on TV.
• enjoy, delight in, appreciate, savour, revel in

reluctant ADJECTIVE
I was reluctant to admit defeat.
• unwilling, disinclined, loath, resistant, hesitant, grudging
OPPOSITES eager, willing

rely VERB
➤ rely on
Can I rely on you to keep a secret?
• depend on, count on, have confidence in, trust in, be sure of
(*informal*) bank on

remain VERB
❶ *A few people remained in their seats.*
• stay, wait, linger, stay put
(*informal*) hang about
❷ *The heatwave is forecast to remain all week.*
• continue, persist, last, keep on, carry on
❸ *Little remained of the house after the fire.*
• be left, survive, endure, abide

remainder NOUN
We watched a film for the remainder of the afternoon.
• rest, what is left, surplus, residue

remains PLURAL NOUN
They cleared away the remains of the picnic.
• leftovers, remnants, residue, fragments, traces, scraps, debris
- The remains at the bottom of a cup are **dregs**.

– Remains still standing after a building
has collapsed are **ruins**.
– Historic remains are **relics**.

remark NOUN
*We exchanged a few remarks about the
weather.*
• comment, observation, word,
statement, reflection, mention

remark VERB
*He remarked that it was very quiet in the
room.*
• say, state, comment, note, declare,
mention, observe
SEE ALSO say

remarkable ADJECTIVE
❶ *This was a remarkable stroke of good
luck.*
• extraordinary, astonishing, amazing,
incredible, wonderful
❷ *She has a remarkable ear for music.*
• exceptional, outstanding, striking,
notable, noteworthy, impressive,
phenomenal
OPPOSITE ordinary

remedy NOUN
❶ *This is a traditional remedy for sore
throats.*
• cure, treatment, medicine, medication,
therapy
– A remedy for the effects of poison is an
antidote.
❷ *I may have found the remedy to all
your problems.*
• solution, answer, relief

remember VERB
❶ *Can you remember what she looked
like?*
• recall, recollect, recognize, place
OPPOSITE forget
❷ *I'll never remember all this
information.*
• memorize, retain, learn, keep in your
head
❸ *My granny likes to remember the old
days.*
• reminisce about, think back to, look
back on

remind VERB
Remind me to buy a newspaper.
• prompt, jog someone's memory
➤ **remind you of**
What does this tune remind you of?
• make you think of, be reminiscent of,
take you back to

reminder NOUN
❶ *The photos are a reminder of our
holiday.*
• souvenir, memento
❷ *I sent round a reminder about the
party.*
• prompt, cue, hint, nudge

reminiscent ADJECTIVE
➤ **be reminiscent of something**
*The tune is reminiscent of an old folk
song.*
• remind you of, make you think of, call
to mind, evoke, conjure up

remnants PLURAL NOUN
Remnants of the meal lay on the floor.
• remains, remainder, residue, traces,
scraps, debris, dregs

remorse NOUN
*He showed no remorse for causing the
accident.*
• regret, repentance, guilt, contrition,
sorrow, shame

remote ADJECTIVE
❶ *They went on an expedition to a
remote part of Brazil.*
• isolated, faraway, distant, inaccessible,
cut off, secluded, out of the way,
unfrequented
IDIOM off the beaten track
OPPOSITE accessible
❷ *There is only a remote chance of us
winning.*
• unlikely, improbable, slight, slim, faint,
doubtful
OPPOSITES likely, strong

remove VERB
❶ *Please remove your rubbish.*
• clear away, take away
❷ *The dentist removed my bad tooth.*
• extract, take out, pull out, withdraw

❸ *Some protesters were removed from the building.*
• throw out, turn out, eject, expel, evict (*informal*) kick out
– To remove someone from power is to **depose** them.
❹ *I decided to remove the last paragraph.*
• get rid of, delete, cut, cut out, erase, do away with, eliminate, abolish
❺ *The divers removed their wetsuits.*
• take off, peel off, strip off, shed, cast off

render VERB
❶ *The shock rendered her speechless.*
• make, leave, cause to be
❷ *We are asking the public to render their support.*
• give, provide, offer, furnish, supply

renew VERB
❶ *The paintwork has been completely renewed.*
• repair, renovate, restore, replace, rebuild, reconstruct, revamp, refurbish, overhaul
(*informal*) do up
❷ *We stopped for a snack to renew our energy.*
• refresh, revive, restore, replenish, revitalize, reinvigorate
❸ *I need to renew my bus pass.*
• bring up to date, update

renowned ADJECTIVE
Venice is renowned for its canals.
• famous, celebrated, well known, famed, noted, notable, acclaimed
OPPOSITE unknown

rent VERB
We rented bikes to tour the island.
• hire, charter, lease

repair VERB
Will you be able to repair the damage?
• mend, fix, put right, patch up

repair NOUN
❶ *The ceiling is badly in need of repair.*
• restoration, renovation, mending, fixing
❷ *Keep your bike in good repair.*
• condition, working order, state, shape

repay VERB
❶ *You can repay me later.*
• pay back, refund, reimburse
❷ *How can I ever repay their kindness?*
• return, reciprocate

repeat VERB
❶ *Could you please repeat your name?*
• say again, restate, reiterate, go through again, echo
❷ *We will have to repeat the experiment.*
• do again, redo, replicate

repeatedly ADVERB
I knocked repeatedly, but there was no answer.
• again and again, over and over, time after time, frequently, regularly, often, many times

repel VERB
❶ *They fought bravely and repelled the attackers.*
• drive back, beat back, fight off, fend off, hold off, resist
❷ *You can use this spray to repel insects.*
• keep away, ward off, deter, scare off
OPPOSITE attract
❸ *I was repelled by the awful smell.*
• disgust, revolt, sicken, nauseate, offend
(*informal*) turn off
OPPOSITE tempt

repellent ADJECTIVE
The villain is portrayed as truly repellent.
• repulsive, revolting, hideous, horrible, loathsome, vile, objectionable, offensive, foul, disgusting
OPPOSITE attractive

replace VERB
❶ *Please replace books on the correct shelf.*
• put back, return, restore, reinstate

❷ *Who will replace the coach next season?*
• follow, succeed, take over from, take the place of
IDIOM step into someone's shoes
❸ *I need to replace one of the tyres on my bike.*
• change, renew, swap, exchange

replacement NOUN
They needed to find a replacement for the injured player.
• substitute, standby, stand-in, reserve
– Someone who can take the place of an actor is an **understudy**.

replica NOUN
He built a replica of the Statue of Liberty.
• copy, reproduction, model, duplicate, imitation
– An exact copy of a document is a **facsimile**.

reply NOUN
I got an immediate reply to my email.
• response, answer, reaction, acknowledgement
– An angry reply is a **retort**.

reply VERB
➤ reply to
I'd better reply to her text.
• answer, respond to, send a reply to, react to, acknowledge

report VERB
❶ *We had to report our findings to the rest of the group.*
• communicate, give an account of, describe, announce, publish, broadcast, disclose
❷ *He threatened to report us to the police.*
• complain about, inform on, denounce
(*informal*) tell on, rat on, shop
❸ *Please report to reception when you arrive.*
• present yourself, make yourself known, check in

report NOUN
❶ *There is a full report of the incident in the paper.*
• account, description, story, record,

article, piece, bulletin
❷ *We heard the loud report of a rifle.*
• bang, crack, noise, explosion

reporter NOUN
She is a reporter for the local newspaper.
• journalist, correspondent

represent VERB
❶ *The dove usually represents peace.*
• stand for, symbolize, personify, epitomize, embody
❷ *The statue represents the god Zeus.*
• depict, portray, illustrate, picture, show
❸ *He appointed a lawyer to represent him.*
• speak for, appear for, speak on someone's behalf, stand in for

reprimand VERB
They were reprimanded for their bad behaviour.
• reproach, rebuke, scold
(*informal*) tell off, tick off
OPPOSITE praise

reproduce VERB
❶ *The robot can reproduce a human voice.*
• copy, duplicate, replicate, imitate, simulate, mimic
❷ *Rats and mice reproduce quickly.*
• breed, procreate, produce offspring, multiply
– Fish reproduce by **spawning**.
– To reproduce plants is to **propagate** them.

reproduction NOUN
❶ *Is that an original painting or a reproduction?*
• copy, replica, imitation, duplicate, likeness
– An exact reproduction of a document is a **facsimile**.
– A reproduction which is intended to deceive people is a **fake** or **forgery**.
❷ *The programme is all about the cycle of animal reproduction.*
• breeding, procreation, propagation

reptile NOUN

WORD WEB

Some animals which are reptiles:

- ➤ alligator
- ➤ chameleon
- ➤ crocodile
- ➤ gecko
- ➤ iguana
- ➤ Komodo dragon
- ➤ lizard
- ➤ salamander
- ➤ skink
- ➤ slow-worm
- ➤ snake
- ➤ terrapin
- ➤ tortoise
- ➤ turtle

– A **basilisk** is a reptile found in myths and legends.

repulsive ADJECTIVE

We were put off eating by the repulsive smell.

• disgusting, revolting, offensive, repellent, disagreeable, foul, repugnant, obnoxious, sickening, nauseating, loathsome, objectionable, nasty, vile

OPPOSITE attractive

reputation NOUN

She is a singer with an international reputation.

• fame, celebrity, name, renown, eminence, standing, stature

request VERB

❶ *Several players are requesting a transfer.*

• ask for, appeal for, call for, seek, apply for, beg for, demand

❷ *They requested us to stop.*

• ask, call on, invite, entreat, implore, beg, beseech

request NOUN

❶ *They have ignored our request for help.*

• appeal, plea, entreaty, call, cry, demand

– A request for a job or membership is an **application**.

– A request signed by a lot of people is a **petition**.

❷ *It was her last request before she died.*

• wish, desire, requirement

require VERB

❶ *These patients require immediate treatment.*

• need, must have, demand, depend on

❷ *Visitors are required to sign the register.*

• instruct, oblige, request, direct, order, command

❸ *Is there anything in particular that you require?*

• want, desire, be short of, lack

rescue VERB

❶ *A helicopter was sent to rescue the climbers.*

• free, liberate, release, save, set free

❷ *The divers rescued some items from the sunken ship.*

• retrieve, recover, salvage

resemblance NOUN

He bears a remarkable resemblance to my brother.

• likeness, similarity, closeness, correspondence, comparability

OPPOSITES difference, dissimilarity

resemble VERB

She closely resembles my sister.

• look like, be similar to, remind you of, mirror, echo

(*informal*) take after

OPPOSITE differ from

resent VERB

She resents having to work such long hours.

• feel bitter about, feel aggrieved about, take exception to, be resentful of, object to, begrudge, grudge

reservation NOUN

❶ *We have a reservation for bed and breakfast.*

• booking

❷ *I still have reservations about the idea.*

• doubt, misgiving, hesitation, qualm, scruple

– If you have reservations about something, you are **sceptical** about it.

reserve VERB
❶ *The astronauts had to reserve fuel for the return voyage.*
• set aside, put aside, save, keep, preserve, retain, hold back
❷ *Have you reserved your seats on the train?*
• book, order, secure

reserve NOUN
❶ *The climbers had a week's reserve of food.*
• stock, store, supply, hoard, stockpile, pool, fund
❷ *He was named as a reserve for the semi-final.*
• substitute, standby, stand-in, replacement
– Someone who can take the place of an actor is an **understudy**.
❸ *We visited a wild bird reserve.*
• reservation, park, preserve, sanctuary
❹ *She has a natural air of reserve.*
• shyness, timidity, reticence, inhibition, modesty, diffidence

reserved ADJECTIVE
❶ *These seats are reserved.*
• booked, set aside, ordered, taken, spoken for
❷ *He was unusually reserved that evening.*
• shy, timid, taciturn, quiet, uncommunicative, withdrawn, reticent, inhibited, diffident
OPPOSITE outgoing

residence NOUN
The palace is the official residence of the queen.
• home, house, address, dwelling
(old use) abode

resident NOUN
The residents of the town love their new sports centre.
• inhabitant, citizen, native, occupant, householder
– A temporary resident in a hotel is a **guest**.
– A resident in rented accommodation is a **boarder**, **lodger** or **tenant**.

resign VERB
The team manager has been forced to resign.
• leave, stand down, step down, give in your notice, quit, bow out
– When a monarch resigns from the throne, he or she **abdicates**.

resist VERB
❶ *They were too weak to resist the sorcerer's magic.*
• stand up to, withstand, defend yourself against, fend off, combat, oppose, defy
OPPOSITES succumb to, give in to
❷ *Some residents are resisting the plan.*
• oppose, object to, fight against, defy
OPPOSITES agree to, welcome
❸ *I couldn't resist taking a peek.*
• refrain from, hold back from, restrain yourself from
OPPOSITE allow yourself to

resolve VERB
❶ *We resolved to press on until nightfall.*
• decide, determine, make up your mind
❷ *They held a meeting to try to resolve the dispute.*
• settle, sort out, straighten out, end, overcome

resort VERB
➤ resort to
In the end, they resorted to violence.
• turn to, fall back on, stoop to

resort NOUN
As a last resort, we could always walk.
• option, alternative, choice, course of action

resound VERB
Frantic screams resounded through the crowd.
• echo, reverberate, resonate, ring, boom

resources PLURAL NOUN
❶ *It is a country rich in natural resources.*
• materials, raw materials, reserves

❷ *The business had to survive on limited resources.*
• funds, money, capital, assets, means, wealth

respect NOUN
❶ *Her colleagues have the deepest respect for her.*
• admiration, esteem, regard, reverence, honour
❷ *Have some respect for other people's feelings.*
• consideration, politeness, courtesy, thought
❸ *In some respects, he's a better player than I am.*
• aspect, way, sense, regard, detail, feature, point, particular

respect VERB
❶ *He was highly respected as a songwriter.*
• admire, esteem, think highly of, look up to, honour, revere
OPPOSITES scorn, despise
❷ *You must respect other people's privacy.*
• show consideration for, be mindful of, have regard for
OPPOSITE disregard
❸ *She tried to respect the wishes of her dead husband.*
• obey, follow, observe, adhere to, comply with
OPPOSITES ignore, defy

respectable ADJECTIVE
❶ *He came from a very respectable family.*
• decent, honest, upright, honourable, reputable, worthy
❷ *What would be a respectable score?*
• reasonable, satisfactory, acceptable, passable, adequate, fair, tolerable

respective ADJECTIVE
The pets were returned to their respective owners.
• own, personal, individual, separate, particular, specific

respond VERB
➤ **respond to**
He responded to each question with a shrug.
• reply to, answer, react to, acknowledge

response NOUN
Did you get a response to your letter?
• reply, answer, reaction, acknowledgement
– An angry response is a **retort**.

responsible ADJECTIVE
❶ *Miss Kumar is responsible for the school's website.*
• in charge (of), in control (of)
❷ *You seem to be a responsible sort of person.*
• reliable, sensible, trustworthy, dependable, conscientious, dutiful
OPPOSITE irresponsible
❸ *Looking after people's money is a responsible job.*
• important, serious
❹ *I hope they find whoever is responsible.*
• to blame, guilty (of), at fault, culpable

rest NOUN
❶ *The actors had a short rest in the middle of the rehearsal.*
• break, pause, respite, breathing space, nap, lie-down
(*informal*) breather
❷ *Try to get as much rest as you can.*
• relaxation, inactivity, leisure, ease, quiet, time off
➤ **the rest**
I spent the rest of the money on clothes.
• the remainder, the surplus, the remains, the others

rest VERB
❶ *Let's stop and rest for a while.*
• have a rest, take a break, relax, have a nap, take it easy, lie down
(*informal*) have a breather
IDIOM put your feet up
❷ *Rest the ladder against the wall.*
• lean, prop, stand, place, support

restaurant NOUN

WORD WEB

Some types of restaurant:

- bistro
- brasserie
- buffet
- cafe
- cafeteria
- canteen
- carvery
- chip shop
- coffee shop
- diner
- grill room
- ice cream parlour
- pizzeria
- snack bar
- steakhouse
- takeaway
- tea room
- wine bar

restful ADJECTIVE

What I needed was a restful night's sleep.
• peaceful, undisturbed, quiet, relaxing, leisurely, calm, tranquil
OPPOSITES stressful, disturbed

restless ADJECTIVE

❶ I'd been feeling strangely restless all morning.
• agitated, nervous, anxious, uneasy, edgy, jumpy, jittery, tense
(informal) uptight, nervy
OPPOSITE relaxed
❷ She spent a restless night worrying.
• sleepless, wakeful, troubled, disturbed, unsettled
OPPOSITES restful, peaceful

restore VERB

❶ Please restore the book to its proper place on the shelf.
• put back, return, replace
❷ They are restoring the Sunday bus service.
• bring back, reinstate
❸ My uncle loves restoring old motorcycles.
• renew, repair, renovate, recondition, fix, mend, rebuild
(informal) do up

restrain VERB

❶ Dogs must be restrained on a lead in the park.
• hold back, keep back, keep under control, restrict
❷ She tried to restrain her anger.
• control, check, curb, suppress, contain, hold in
IDIOM keep the lid on

restrict VERB

❶ The new law restricts the sale of fireworks.
• control, limit, regulate, moderate, keep within bounds
❷ Dancers wear clothes that don't restrict their movement.
• hinder, impede, obstruct, block

result NOUN

❶ The forest fires were the result of a long drought.
• consequence, effect, outcome, upshot, sequel (to)
OPPOSITE cause
❷ What was the result of the match?
• score, tally

result VERB

The bruising on his leg resulted from a bad fall.
• come about, develop, emerge, happen, occur, follow, ensue
➤ result in
The flooding resulted in chaos on the roads.
• cause, bring about, give rise to, lead to, develop into

resume VERB

The class will resume after lunch.
• restart, start again, recommence, proceed, continue, carry on
OPPOSITES discontinue, cease

retain VERB

❶ Please retain your ticket for inspection.
• hold on to, keep, preserve, reserve, save
(informal) hang on to
OPPOSITE surrender

❷ *This type of soil is good at retaining water.*
• hold in, keep in, hold back
OPPOSITE release

retire VERB
❶ *He retired two years ago after a long career in teaching.*
• give up work, stop working, bow out
– To leave your job voluntarily is to **resign**.
❷ *She retired to her room with a headache.*
• withdraw, retreat, adjourn

retort NOUN
see **reply**

retreat VERB
❶ *We retreated to a safe distance from the bonfire.*
• move back, draw back, fall back, withdraw, retire
OPPOSITE advance
❷ *The snail retreated into its shell.*
• shrink back, recoil

retrieve VERB
I had to climb over the fence to retrieve the ball.
• get back, bring back, recover, rescue, salvage

return VERB
❶ *I hope to return to New Zealand some day.*
• go back, revisit
❷ *I'll see you when I return.*
• get back, come back, come home
❸ *Take these pills if the symptoms return.*
• reappear, come back, recur
❹ *I returned the cat to its rightful owner.*
• give back, send back, restore
❺ *Faulty goods may be returned to the shop.*
• send back, take back

return NOUN
❶ *She was looking forward to her*

friends' return.
• homecoming, reappearance
❷ *The museum is hoping for the safe return of the stolen painting.*
• retrieval, recovery
❸ *We are all waiting for the return of spring.*
• reappearance, recurrence
❹ *He gets a good return on his savings.*
• profit, interest, gain

reveal VERB
❶ *The bookcase swung out to reveal a secret room.*
• uncover, unveil, expose
OPPOSITES hide, conceal
❷ *She never revealed her real identity.*
• disclose, make known, divulge, confess, admit, make public, give away, let slip

revel VERB
➤ **revel in**
My sister revelled in all the attention.
• enjoy, delight in, love, adore, relish, savour, lap up

revenge NOUN
The story is about a man who seeks revenge for his brother's murder.
• vengeance, reprisal, retribution, retaliation
➤ **take revenge on someone**
He swore to take revenge on them all.
• get even with, make someone pay (*informal*) get your own back on

revere VERB
The painter was greatly revered by his fellow artists.
• admire, respect, esteem, think highly of, look up to, venerate
OPPOSITE despise

reverse NOUN
❶ *This is the reverse of what I expected.*
• opposite, contrary, converse, antithesis
❷ *The letter had a handwritten note on the reverse.*
• other side, back

reverse VERB
❶ *You can use tracing paper to reverse a drawing.*
• turn round, swap round, turn back to front, transpose, invert, flip
❷ *The driver was reversing into a parking space.*
• back, move backwards, go backwards
❸ *The referee refused to reverse his decision.*
• go back on, overturn, overrule, cancel, revoke

review NOUN
❶ *After the accident they carried out a review of safety procedures.*
• study, survey, examination, inspection, enquiry, probe
❷ *The reviews of her latest film aren't good.*
• report, commentary, appraisal, assessment
(*informal*) crit

review VERB
❶ *The judge began to review the evidence.*
• examine, go over, study, survey, consider, assess, evaluate, appraise, weigh up, size up
❷ *On Friday they always review the latest films.*
• write a review of, comment on, criticize

revise VERB
❶ *We revised the work we did last term.*
• go over, review, reread, study, cram
❷ *The last chapter has been revised by the author.*
• correct, amend, edit, rewrite, update
❸ *I have revised my opinion about that.*
• change, modify, alter, reconsider, re-examine

revive VERB
❶ *He fainted but soon revived.*
• come round, come to, recover, regain consciousness
❷ *A cup of tea should revive you.*
• refresh, restore, reinvigorate, revitalize, bring back to life

revolt VERB
❶ *The stench in the dungeon revolted him.*
• disgust, repel, sicken, nauseate, offend, appal, put off
(*informal*) turn off
IDIOM turn your stomach
❷ *The people revolted against their Roman masters.*
• rebel, riot, rise up
– To revolt on a ship is to **mutiny**.

revolt NOUN
Boudicca led a revolt against the Romans.
• rebellion, riot, uprising, revolution
– A revolt on a ship is a **mutiny**.

revolting ADJECTIVE
What is that revolting smell?
• disgusting, foul, horrible, nasty, loathsome, offensive, obnoxious, repulsive, repugnant, sickening, nauseating, vile, unpleasant
OPPOSITES pleasant, attractive

revolution NOUN
❶ *The Russian Revolution took place in 1917.*
• rebellion, revolt, uprising
❷ *Computers brought about a revolution in the way people work.*
• change, transformation, shift
(*informal*) shake-up
❸ *One revolution of the Earth takes 24 hours.*
• rotation, turn, circuit, cycle, orbit, lap

revolutionary ADJECTIVE
He invented a revolutionary type of battery.
• new, novel, innovative, unconventional, unorthodox, radical

revolve VERB
❶ *The Earth revolves once every 24 hours.*
• rotate, turn, spin
❷ *The Moon revolves around the Earth.*
• circle, go around, orbit

a b c d e f g h i j k l m n o p q r s t u v w x y z

reward NOUN

❶ *You deserve a reward for all your hard work.*
- award, bonus, treat
(*informal*) pay-off
OPPOSITE punishment

❷ *The dog's owners have offered a reward for its safe return.*
- payment, bounty

reward VERB

It is good to reward your pet for good behaviour.
- recompense, give a treat to, give a bonus to, repay
OPPOSITE punish

rewarding ADJECTIVE

Being a vet must be a rewarding job.
- satisfying, gratifying, fulfilling, pleasing, worthwhile
OPPOSITE thankless

rhyme NOUN

I have a book of nonsense rhymes.
- poem, verse
SEE ALSO poem

rhythm NOUN

Everyone clapped to the rhythm of the music.
- beat, pulse, tempo
– The rhythm of a poem is its **metre**.

rich ADJECTIVE

❶ *He came from a rich family.*
- wealthy, affluent, prosperous, well-off, well-to-do
(*informal*) flush, loaded, well-heeled
OPPOSITES poor, impoverished

❷ *The room was decorated with rich fabrics.*
- luxurious, lavish, sumptuous, opulent, ornate, splendid, expensive, costly

❸ *She has hair of a rich chestnut colour.*
- deep, strong, vivid, intense

❹ *I'm cutting down on rich foods.*
- fatty, creamy, heavy

❺ *Plant the bulbs in moist rich soil.*
- fertile, fruitful, productive
➤ **be rich in**
The islands are rich in animal and

plant species.
- be full of, abound in, teem with, overflow with, be well supplied with, be well stocked with

riches PLURAL NOUN

They acquired riches beyond their wildest dreams.
- wealth, money, affluence, prosperity, fortune, treasure

rickety ADJECTIVE

She pulled out a rickety old step ladder.
- shaky, unsteady, unstable, wobbly, flimsy
OPPOSITES solid, firm

rid VERB

He rid the town of rats.
- clear, free, empty, strip, purge
➤ **get rid of**
She decided to get rid of her old guitar.
- dispose of, throw away, throw out, discard, scrap, dump, jettison
(*informal*) ditch, chuck out

riddle NOUN

They had to solve the riddle to find the treasure.
- puzzle, question, conundrum, problem, mystery
(*informal*) brain-teaser, poser

ride VERB

❶ *My little brother is learning to ride a bike.*
- control, handle, manage, steer

❷ *She used to ride around on a scooter.*
- travel, drive, cycle, pedal

ride NOUN

We took a ride on a snowmobile.
- drive, run, journey, trip
(*informal*) spin

ridicule VERB

People have often ridiculed great inventors at first.
- laugh at, make fun of, mock, scoff at, jeer at, sneer at, taunt, tease, deride
OPPOSITE respect

ridiculous ADJECTIVE
❶ *You look ridiculous in those trousers.*
• silly, stupid, foolish, absurd, laughable, farcical
OPPOSITE sensible
❷ *That is a ridiculous price for a pair of shoes.*
• ludicrous, senseless, nonsensical, preposterous, outrageous, absurd, unreasonable
OPPOSITE reasonable

right ADJECTIVE
❶ *The entrance is on the right side of the building.*
• right-hand
– The right side of a ship when you face forwards is the **starboard** side.
OPPOSITE left
❷ *That is the right answer.*
• correct, accurate, true, exact
OPPOSITE wrong
❸ *She was waiting for the right moment to tell him.*
• proper, appropriate, fitting, suitable, ideal, perfect
OPPOSITE wrong
❹ *It's not right to cheat.*
• fair, honest, moral, just, honourable, decent, upright, virtuous, ethical
OPPOSITE wrong

right ADVERB
❶ *Turn right at the corner.*
OPPOSITE left
❷ *Go right ahead.*
• directly, straight
❸ *We had walked right round in a circle.*
• all the way, completely
❹ *There is a dot right in the centre of the screen.*
• exactly, precisely, squarely, dead (*informal*) bang
❺ *Did I do that right?*
• correctly, properly, accurately, perfectly
❻ (*informal*) *I'll be right back.*
• immediately, promptly, soon

right NOUN
❶ *Take the turning on the right.*
OPPOSITE left

❷ *We both know the difference between right and wrong.*
• goodness, fairness, virtue, morality, truth, justice
OPPOSITE wrong
❸ *People over 18 have the right to vote in elections.*
• entitlement, privilege, prerogative, freedom, liberty, licence, power

rigid ADJECTIVE
❶ *The tent was supported by a rigid framework.*
• stiff, firm, hard, inflexible, unbending
OPPOSITES flexible, pliable
❷ *The referee was rigid in applying the rules.*
• strict, inflexible, uncompromising
OPPOSITES flexible, lenient

rigorous ADJECTIVE
Detectives carried out a rigorous investigation.
• thorough, careful, meticulous, painstaking, conscientious, scrupulous

rim NOUN
She peered at us over the rim of her glasses.
• brim, edge, lip, brink

ring NOUN
❶ *Mushrooms were growing in a ring.*
• circle, round, loop, circuit
❷ *Each bird is tagged with a metal ring.*
• band, hoop
❸ *Four gladiators entered the ring.*
• arena, circus, enclosure

ring VERB
❶ *The whole area was ringed by barbed wire.*
• surround, encircle, enclose, circle
❷ *Church bells rang all morning.*
• chime, peal, toll, clang
❸ *The doorbell rang unexpectedly.*
• sound, buzz, jangle, tinkle
❹ *Ring me later this evening.*
• phone, call, telephone, give someone a call
(*informal*) give someone a ring, give someone a bell

a
b
c
d
e
f
g
h
i
j
k
l
m
n
o
p
q
r
s
t
u
v
w
x
y
z

rinse VERB
Rinse the wound carefully with clean water.
• wash, clean, cleanse, bathe, swill, flush out

riot NOUN
The incident sparked a riot in the capital.
• disturbance, commotion, turmoil, disorder, uproar, uprising

riot VERB
Students rioted in the streets of the capital.
• run riot, run wild, run amok, rampage, revolt, rise up, rebel

rip VERB
❶ *She read the note and ripped it into little pieces.*
• tear
❷ *He ripped the letter out of my hands.*
• pull, tug, wrench, snatch, tear

ripe ADJECTIVE
❶ *You need ripe berries for making jam.*
• mature, ready to eat
– To become ripe is to **ripen**.
❷ *I feel that the time is ripe for change.*
• ready, right, suitable, favourable

ripple VERB
A light breeze rippled the tree tops.
• ruffle, stir, disturb, make waves on

rise VERB
❶ *A plume of smoke rose high into the air.*
• climb, mount, ascend, soar, fly up, take off, lift off
OPPOSITE descend
❷ *The castle walls rose above us.*
• tower, loom, soar, reach up
❸ *Prices are set to rise again.*
• go up, increase, escalate, jump, leap
OPPOSITE fall
❹ *I rose to greet our visitor.*
• stand up, get up, leap up, get to your feet
OPPOSITE sit down
❺ *They rose early winter and summer.*
• awake, get up, stir
OPPOSITES go to bed, retire

rise NOUN
❶ *There will be a rise in temperature over the next few days.*
• increase, jump, leap, hike
OPPOSITE fall
❷ *The hill fort sits at the top of a rise.*
• hill, slope, ascent, incline

risk NOUN
❶ *She was aware of the risks involved in mountaineering.*
• danger, hazard, peril
❷ *There is a risk of further delays.*
• chance, likelihood, possibility, prospect

risk VERB
❶ *I decided to risk taking a look outside.*
• chance, dare, gamble, venture
❷ *She risked her life to save others.*
• endanger, put at risk, jeopardize, imperil

risky ADJECTIVE
Bungee jumping is a risky activity.
• dangerous, hazardous, perilous, unsafe, precarious
(*informal*) dicey
IDIOM touch and go
OPPOSITE safe

ritual NOUN
The temple was used for ancient religious rituals.
• ceremony, rite

rival NOUN
The two players became friendly rivals.
• opponent, adversary, challenger, competitor, contender

rival VERB
This scenery can rival any in the world.
• compete with, contend with, vie with, compare with, match, equal

rivalry NOUN
There was intense rivalry between the two local teams.
• competition, competitiveness, opposition
OPPOSITE cooperation

river NOUN
We took a ferry across the river.
– A small river is a **stream**, **brook**, **rivulet** or (*Scottish*) **burn**.
– A small river which flows into a larger river is a **tributary**.
– The place where a river begins is its **source**.
– The place where a river goes into the sea is its **mouth**.
– A wide river mouth is an **estuary** or (*Scottish*) **firth**.
– The place where the mouth of a river splits before going into the sea is a **delta**.

road NOUN
We have to cross a busy road.
• street, lane, alley, avenue, boulevard, highway, motorway, bypass
– A road which is closed at one end is a **dead end**.
– A private road up to a house is a **drive**.

roam VERB
❶ *We roamed about town aimlessly.*
• wander, drift, stroll, amble, traipse
❷ *Herds of buffalo used to roam the plains.*
• range, rove

roar NOUN
❶ *It sounded like the roar of a wild animal.*
• bellow, howl, cry
❷ *Outside the stadium we heard the roars of the crowd.*
• shout, cry, yell, clamour

roar VERB
The monster lifted its head and roared.
• bellow, cry, howl, thunder, bawl, yell

rob VERB
Masked highwaymen used to rob stagecoaches.
• steal from, break into, burgle, hold up, raid, loot, ransack, rifle
➤ **be robbed of something**
We were robbed of victory in the last minute of the match.
• be deprived of, be denied, be cheated out of

robber NOUN
The money was stolen by a gang of armed robbers.
• thief, burglar, housebreaker, looter

robbery NOUN
He planned a daring robbery on a jewellery store.
• theft, stealing, burglary, housebreaking, looting

robe NOUN
He wore the ceremonial robes of a chief.
• gown, vestments

robot NOUN
In the future, housework will be done by robots.
• automaton, android
– A robot which is part-human is a **cyborg**.

robust ADJECTIVE
❶ *He is in a robust state of health.*
• strong, vigorous, fit, hardy, healthy, rugged
OPPOSITE weak
❷ *Bring a robust pair of boots.*
• sturdy, tough, durable, hard-wearing
OPPOSITE flimsy

rock NOUN
We clambered over the rocks on the seashore.
• stone, boulder, pebble

WORD WEB

Some rocks and minerals:

➤ basalt	➤ marble
➤ chalk	➤ pumice
➤ flint	➤ quartz
➤ granite	➤ sandstone
➤ gypsum	➤ shale
➤ limestone	➤ slate

– Rock from which metal or valuable minerals can be extracted is **ore**.
– A layer of rock is a **stratum**.

a b c d e f g h i j k l m n o p q r s t u v w x y z

- The scientific study of rocks and rock formations is **geology**.
- The scientific study of minerals is **mineralogy**.

rock VERB
❶ *At each turn, the bus rocked from side to side.*
• roll, toss, lurch, pitch, tilt, reel
❷ *I rocked the baby's cradle to and fro.*
• sway, swing

rocky ADJECTIVE
❶ *Nothing was growing in the rocky ground.*
• stony, pebbly, rough, craggy, shingly
❷ *I wish this chair wasn't so rocky.*
• unsteady, unstable, rickety, shaky, wobbly, tottery

rod NOUN
He was putting up a metal curtain rod.
• bar, rail, pole, strut, shaft, stick, spoke, staff

rode
past tense see ride

rodent NOUN

WORD WEB

Some animals which are rodents:

➤ beaver	➤ marmot
➤ chinchilla	➤ mouse
➤ chipmunk	➤ muskrat
➤ coypu	➤ porcupine
➤ gerbil	➤ prairie dog
➤ gopher	➤ rat
➤ groundhog	➤ squirrel
➤ guinea pig	➤ vole
➤ hamster	➤ water vole or
➤ jerboa	water rat
➤ lemming	

rogue NOUN
What a rogue he turned out to be!
• rascal, scoundrel, villain, cheat, fraud, swindler

role NOUN
❶ *Who played the lead role in the film?*
• part, character
❷ *Each player has an important role in the team.*
• job, task, function, position, responsibility, duty

roll VERB
❶ *Slowly the wheels began to roll.*
• move round, turn, revolve, rotate, spin, whirl
❷ *Roll the ribbon around your finger.*
• curl, wind, wrap, twist, coil, twirl
– To roll up a sail is to **furl** it.
❸ *Roll out the pastry into a large circle.*
• flatten, level out, smooth
❹ *A tiny boat was rolling about in the storm.*
• rock, sway, pitch, toss, lurch

romantic ADJECTIVE
❶ *Do you think they had a romantic relationship?*
• amorous, loving, passionate, affectionate, tender
❷ *The film had a very romantic ending.*
• sentimental, emotional
(*informal*) soppy, mushy
❸ *She has a romantic view of life in the countryside.*
• idealistic, unrealistic, fanciful, fairy-tale

roof NOUN
The shed has a sloping roof.
– The sloping beams in the framework of a roof are **rafters**.
– The overhanging edges of a roof are the **eaves**.
– The triangular section of wall under a sloping roof is the **gable**.

room NOUN
❶ *There is a small room at the top of the stairs.*
• (*old use*) chamber
❷ *Do you have room for another passenger?*
• space, capacity

❸ *There is still room for improvement.*
• scope, opportunity

WORD WEB

Some types of room:

➤ anteroom	➤ lavatory or toilet
➤ bathroom	➤ library
➤ bedroom	➤ living room
➤ box room	➤ lounge
➤ classroom	➤ music room
➤ cloakroom	➤ nursery
➤ conservatory	➤ pantry
➤ dining room	➤ parlour
➤ dormitory	➤ playroom
➤ drawing room	➤ scullery
➤ dressing room	➤ sitting room
➤ games room	➤ spare room
➤ guest room	➤ staffroom
➤ hall	➤ storeroom
➤ kitchen	➤ study
➤ kitchenette	➤ utility room
➤ landing	

– A sleeping room on a ship is a **cabin**.
– A small room in a monastery or prison is a **cell**.
– An underground room is a **basement** or **cellar**. In a church it is a **vault**.
– The space in the roof of a house is the **attic** or **loft**.
– A room where an artist works is a **studio**.
– A room where you wait to see a doctor or dentist is a **waiting room**.

roomy *ADJECTIVE*
The flat is surprisingly roomy inside.
• spacious, extensive, big, sizeable

root *NOUN*
We need to get to the root of the problem.
• source, cause, basis, origin, starting point

rope *NOUN*
He lowered down a length of rope.
• cable, cord, line

– The ropes which support a ship's mast and sails are the **rigging**.
– The ropes which hold down a tent are the **guy ropes**.
– A rope with a loop at one end used for catching cattle is a **lasso**.

rose
past tense see **rise**

rot *VERB*
The floorboards had begun to rot.
• decay, decompose, become rotten, disintegrate, crumble
– If metal rots it is said to **corrode**.
– If rubber rots it is said to **perish**.
– If food rots it is said to **go bad** or **putrefy**.

rotate *VERB*
A day is the time it takes the Earth to rotate once on its axis.
• revolve, turn, spin, pivot, gyrate, wheel, swivel, twirl, whirl

rotten *ADJECTIVE*
❶ *The window frame is rotten.*
• decayed, decaying, decomposed, crumbling, disintegrating
OPPOSITE sound
❷ *The fridge smelled of rotten eggs.*
• bad, mouldy, putrid, rancid, gone off
OPPOSITE fresh
❸ *(informal) I've had a rotten week!*
• bad, unpleasant, disagreeable, awful, dreadful, terrible, abysmal *(informal)* lousy
OPPOSITE good

rough *ADJECTIVE*
❶ *A rough track led to the farm.*
• uneven, irregular, rugged, bumpy, rocky, stony
OPPOSITES even, level
❷ *Feel the rough texture of this handmade paper.*
• coarse, harsh, scratchy, bristly
OPPOSITES smooth, soft
❸ *She pushed him away with a rough shove.*
• hard, forceful, violent, severe,

a b c d e f g h i j k l m n o p q r s t u v w x y z

tough, brutal

OPPOSITES gentle, mild

❹ The sea was rough that day.
• stormy, choppy, turbulent, heaving

OPPOSITES calm, smooth

❺ He's been having a rough time.
• hard, difficult, troublesome, bad, disagreeable, unpleasant

OPPOSITES good, easy

❻ I had only a rough idea of where we were.
• approximate, vague, inexact, imprecise

OPPOSITES exact, precise

❼ I've written a rough draft of the first chapter.
• preliminary, basic, rudimentary, unfinished, unpolished, sketchy

OPPOSITES finished, final

roughly ADVERB

The cinema seats roughly a hundred people.
• approximately, about, around, close to, nearly

round ADJECTIVE

❶ The room had a little round window.
• circular, disc-shaped

❷ Holly bushes have small round berries.
• spherical, ball-shaped, globular

round NOUN

❶ We got through to the second round of the competition.
• stage, level, heat, game, bout, contest

❷ My brother does a morning paper round.
• route, circuit, tour

– The regular round of a police officer is their **beat**.

round VERB

A large van slowly rounded the corner.
• go round, travel round, turn

➤ round something off

We rounded off the meal with coffee and cake.
• finish off, conclude, complete, end, crown, cap

➤ round someone up

The teacher was rounding up the children.
• gather together, assemble, collect, muster, rally

roundabout ADJECTIVE

That is a very roundabout way of answering the question.
• indirect, circuitous, winding, meandering

OPPOSITE direct

rouse VERB

❶ The doorbell roused her from her daydream.
• awaken, wake up, arouse

❷ My curiosity was roused by a flashing light in the sky.
• excite, arouse, stir up, stimulate, activate, galvanize, provoke, agitate

route NOUN

We took the quickest route home.
• way, course, path, road, direction

routine NOUN

❶ A morning run is part of her daily routine.
• procedure, practice, regime, drill, pattern, custom, habit, programme, schedule

❷ I've been practising a new dance routine.
• act, programme, performance, number

row (rhymes with go) NOUN

Across the road was a neat row of houses.
• line, column, file, series, sequence, string, chain

– A row of people waiting for something is a **queue**.

row (rhymes with cow) NOUN

❶ The people next door were making a terrible row.
• noise, din, racket, commotion, clamour, uproar, rumpus, hubbub

❷ Some of the players were having a row with the referee.
• argument, fight, disagreement, dispute, quarrel, squabble, tiff

rowdy ADJECTIVE

A rowdy group of men got on the train.
• noisy, unruly, wild, disorderly,

boisterous, riotous
OPPOSITE quiet

royal ADJECTIVE
These pyramids were built as royal tombs.
• regal, kingly, queenly, princely

royalty NOUN

WORD WEB

Some members of a royal family:

➤ king
➤ monarch
➤ prince
➤ princess
➤ queen
➤ queen mother
➤ sovereign

- The way to address a king or queen is **Your Majesty.**
- The way to address a prince or princess is **Your Highness.**
- The husband or wife of a royal person is a **consort.**
- A person who rules while a monarch is too young or unable to rule is a **regent.**

rub VERB
❶ *Try not to rub your eyes.*
• stroke, knead, massage, pat
❷ *Rub some suncream on your arms.*
• spread, smear, apply (to), smooth
❸ *I rubbed the window to see outside.*
• wipe, polish, shine, buff
❹ *These boots are rubbing against my ankles.*
• graze, scrape, chafe
➤ **rub something out**
I just need to rub out the pencil marks.
• erase, wipe out, delete, remove

rubbish NOUN
❶ *Dad took the rubbish out to the bin.*
• refuse, waste, junk, litter, scrap
(North American) trash, garbage
❷ *Don't talk rubbish!*
• nonsense, drivel, gibberish, claptrap,
(North American) garbage
(informal) gobbledegook, baloney, rot,
tripe, twaddle, piffle, codswallop

(old use) balderdash, poppycock
OPPOSITE sense

rude ADJECTIVE
❶ *It was rude of me to interrupt.*
• impolite, discourteous, bad-mannered,
impertinent, impudent, insolent,
offensive, insulting, abusive
OPPOSITE polite
❷ *He's always telling rude jokes.*
• indecent, coarse, crude, dirty, smutty,
vulgar, lewd, obscene
OPPOSITE clean

ruffle VERB
❶ *A light breeze ruffled the waters of the lake.*
• stir, disturb, ripple
❷ *Lukasz's dad leaned over and ruffled his hair.*
• tousle, mess up, rumple, dishevel

ruin NOUN
❶ *The city was in a state of ruin.*
• destruction, disintegration, decay,
collapse
❷ *They now face financial ruin.*
• failure, loss, bankruptcy, insolvency,
destitution
➤ **ruins**
Archaeologists discovered the ruins of an ancient Mayan city.
• remains, remnants, fragments

ruin VERB
❶ *A sudden rainstorm could ruin the entire harvest.*
• destroy, wreck, devastate, demolish,
ravage, lay waste, wipe out
❷ *The ending ruined the whole film for me.*
• spoil, mar, blight, mess up
(informal) scupper

ruined ADJECTIVE
Bats flew in and out of the ruined abbey.
• wrecked, crumbling, derelict,
dilapidated, tumbledown, ramshackle

rule NOUN
❶ *Players must stick to the rules of the game.*
• regulation, law, principle, statute

a b c d e f g h i j k l m n o p q r s t u v w x y z

❷ The country was formerly under
French rule.
• control, authority, command, power,
government, jurisdiction
❸ The usual rule is to leave a tip.
• custom, convention, practice, habit,
norm

rule VERB
❶ The Romans ruled a vast empire.
• govern, control, command, direct, lead,
manage, run, administer
❷ Queen Elizabeth I ruled for over 40
years.
• reign, be ruler
❸ The umpire ruled that the ball was
out.
• judge, decree, pronounce, decide,
determine, find
➤ **rule something out**
We can't rule out the possibility
of sabotage.
• eliminate, exclude, disregard, disallow

ruler NOUN

WORD WEB

Some titles of ruler:

➤ emir
➤ emperor
➤ empress
➤ governor
➤ head of state
➤ king
➤ monarch
➤ potentate
➤ premier
➤ president
➤ prince
➤ princess
➤ queen
➤ sovereign
➤ viceroy

– A person who rules while a monarch
is too young or unable to rule is a
regent.
– A single ruler with unlimited power is
an autocrat or a dictator.

Historical rulers:

➤ caesar
➤ caliph
➤ kaiser
➤ maharaja
➤ maharani
➤ pharaoh
➤ raja
➤ rani
➤ shah
➤ sultan
➤ tsar
➤ tsarina

rummage VERB
She started rummaging in her bag for
her keys.
• search, hunt, root about

rumour NOUN
All kinds of rumours were flying round
the school.
• gossip, hearsay, talk, speculation,
story
(informal) tittle-tattle

run VERB
❶ We ran at full speed down the hill.
• race, sprint, dash, speed, rush, hurry,
tear, bolt, fly, streak, whizz, zoom, zip,
pelt, hurtle, scurry, scamper, career
(informal) scoot
– To run at a gentle pace is to jog.
❷ Beads of sweat ran down his face.
• stream, flow, pour, gush, flood,
cascade, spill, trickle, dribble
❸ My old laptop still runs well.
• function, operate, work, go, perform
❹ Her dream is to run her own
restaurant.
• manage, be in charge of, direct,
control, supervise, oversee, govern, rule
❺ The river Amazon runs through seven
countries.
• go, extend, pass, stretch, reach
❻ Could you please run me to the
station?
• give someone a lift, drive, take,
transport, convey
➤ **run away or off**
The boys ran off when they saw me.
• flee, take flight, take off, escape, fly,
bolt
(informal) make off, clear off, scarper
IDIOM take to your heels
➤ **run into**
❶ Guess who I ran into at the weekend?
• meet, come across, encounter
(informal) bump into
❷ Two lorries nearly ran into each
other.
• hit, collide with

run NOUN
❶ She likes to go for a morning run
along the beach.
• jog, trot, sprint, race, dash

❷ *We went for a run in the car.*
• drive, journey, ride, trip, outing, excursion
(*informal*) spin
❸ *They've had a run of good luck recently.*
• sequence, stretch, series
❹ *The farmer had to build a new chicken run.*
• enclosure, pen, coop

runaway NOUN
We watched a film about three teenage runaways.
• missing person
– A person who has run away from the army is a **deserter**.
– A person who is running away from the law is a **fugitive** or an **outlaw**.

runner NOUN
Over a thousand runners will take part in the marathon.
• athlete, competitor, racer
– Someone who runs fast over short distances is a **sprinter**.
– Someone who runs to keep fit is a **jogger**.

runny ADJECTIVE
This sauce is too runny.
• watery, thin, liquid, fluid
OPPOSITE thick

rural ADJECTIVE
They live in a remote rural area.
• country, rustic, agricultural, pastoral
OPPOSITE urban

rush VERB
❶ *I rushed home with the good news.*
• hurry, hasten, race, run, dash, fly, bolt, charge, speed, sprint, tear, hurtle, scurry
❷ *Don't rush me – I'm thinking.*
• push, hurry, press, hustle

rush NOUN
❶ *What's the rush?*
• hurry, haste, urgency
❷ *There was a sudden rush of water.*
• flood, gush, spurt, stream, spate
❸ *I was surprised by the rush for tickets.*
• demand, call, clamour, run (on)

rustic ADJECTIVE
On the wall was a painting of a rustic scene.
• country, rural, pastoral

rustle VERB
The trees rustled in the breeze.
• crackle, swish, whisper

rut NOUN
There were deep ruts made by a tractor.
• furrow, groove, channel, trough

ruthless ADJECTIVE
He was a ruthless dictator who terrorized his people.
• merciless, pitiless, heartless, hard-hearted, cold-blooded, callous, cruel, vicious, brutal
OPPOSITE merciful

a
b
c
d
e
f
g
h
i
j
k
l
m
n
o
p
q
r
s
t
u
v
w
x
y
z

Ss

sack NOUN
In the corner was a large sack of potatoes.
• bag, pack, pouch
➤ the sack
(*informal*) If the boss finds out, he'll get the sack.
• dismissal, discharge, redundancy
(*informal*) the boot, the axe

sack VERB
They threatened to sack the whole workforce.
• dismiss, discharge, let go
(*informal*) fire, give someone the sack

sacred ADJECTIVE
The Koran is the sacred book of Muslims.
• holy, religious, hallowed, divine, heavenly
OPPOSITE secular

sacrifice VERB
❶ She sacrificed her career to bring up the children.
• give up, surrender, forfeit, go without
❷ Animals were sacrificed on this altar.
• offer up, slaughter, kill

sad ADJECTIVE

OVERUSED WORD

❶ A sad mood, sad feeling:

➤ unhappy	➤ blue
➤ sorrowful	➤ low
➤ miserable	➤ down
➤ depressed	➤ dejected
➤ downcast	➤ forlorn
➤ downhearted	➤ morose
➤ despondent	➤ desolate
➤ crestfallen	➤ doleful
➤ dismal	➤ wretched
➤ gloomy	➤ woeful
➤ glum	➤ woebegone

➤ tearful	➤ broken-hearted
➤ heartbroken	

(*informal*) down in the dumps, down in the mouth
He has been miserable since his dog died.
OPPOSITES happy, cheerful

❷ A sad situation, sad news:

➤ unfortunate	➤ deplorable
➤ upsetting	➤ grim
➤ distressing	➤ serious
➤ painful	➤ grave
➤ disheartening	➤ desperate
➤ discouraging	➤ tragic
➤ regrettable	➤ grievous
➤ lamentable	

I'm afraid I have some upsetting news.
OPPOSITES fortunate, good

❸ A sad story, sad tune:

➤ depressing	➤ heart-rending
➤ melancholy	➤ pitiful
➤ mournful	➤ pathetic
➤ moving	➤ plaintive
➤ touching	➤ wistful
➤ heartbreaking	

She stayed in her room, listening to mournful music.
OPPOSITES cheering, uplifting

sadden VERB
I was saddened by how much the town had changed.
• depress, upset, dispirit, dishearten, discourage, grieve
IDIOM break your heart
OPPOSITE cheer up

sadness NOUN
There was sadness and despair in her eyes.
• unhappiness, sorrow, grief, misery, depression, dejection, melancholy, gloom
OPPOSITES happiness, joy

safe ADJECTIVE

❶ *The missing hillwalkers were found safe and well.*
• unharmed, unhurt, uninjured, undamaged, unscathed, sound, intact (*informal*) in one piece
OPPOSITES hurt, damaged
❷ *He felt safe up in the tree.*
• protected, defended, secure, out of danger, out of harm's way
OPPOSITES vulnerable, insecure
❸ *She knew she was leaving her dog in safe hands.*
• reliable, trustworthy, dependable, sound
OPPOSITES dangerous, risky
❹ *Is the tap water safe to drink?*
• harmless, uncontaminated, innocuous, non-poisonous
OPPOSITE harmful

safety NOUN

These rules are for your own safety.
• protection, security, well-being
OPPOSITE danger

sag VERB

❶ *The tent began to sag under the weight of the rain.*
• sink, slump, bulge, dip
❷ *His shoulders sagged.*
• hang down, droop, flop

said

past tense see **say**

sail VERB

❶ *Tall ships used to sail right into the harbour.*
• travel, voyage, cruise
– To begin a sea voyage is to **put to sea** or **set sail**.
❷ *They learned how to sail a yacht.*
• pilot, steer, navigate
❸ *The ball sailed over the fence.*
• glide, drift, float, flow, sweep

sailor NOUN

We have a crew of experienced sailors.
• seaman, seafarer, mariner, hand
– A person who sails a yacht is a **yachtsman** or **yachtswoman**.

sake NOUN

➤ **for the sake of**
He was told to lose weight for the sake of his health.
• for the good of, in the interests of, to benefit, to help

salary NOUN

The job has an annual salary of £30,000.
• income, pay, earnings, wages

sale NOUN

They made a lot of money from the sale of the painting.
• selling, dealing, trading, marketing, vending
OPPOSITE purchase

salvage VERB

The crew tried to salvage some supplies from the wreck.
• save, rescue, recover, retrieve, reclaim

same ADJECTIVE

➤ **the same**
❶ *My sister and I like the same kinds of music.*
• similar, alike, equivalent, comparable, matching, identical
– Words which mean the same are **synonymous**.
OPPOSITES different, contrasting
❷ *Our recipe has remained the same for years.*
• unaltered, unchanged, constant
OPPOSITES different, new

sample NOUN

The detective asked for a sample of her handwriting.
• specimen, example, illustration, snippet, taster

sample VERB

Would you like to sample the new flavour?
• try out, test, taste

sands PLURAL NOUN

The children played on the sands for hours.
• beach, shore
– Hills of sand along the coast are **dunes**.

a b c d e f g h i j k l m n o p q r s t u v w x y z

sane ADJECTIVE
He was the only sane member of an eccentric family.
• sensible, rational, reasonable, balanced, level-headed
OPPOSITE insane

sang
past tense see **sing**

sank
past tense see **sink**

sarcastic ADJECTIVE
It's hard to tell if the author is being sarcastic.
• mocking, satirical, ironic, sneering, cutting

sat
past tense see **sit**

satisfaction NOUN
He looked at his work with a sense of satisfaction.
• pleasure, contentment, enjoyment, gratification, fulfilment, sense of achievement, pride
OPPOSITE dissatisfaction

satisfactory ADJECTIVE
That is not a satisfactory explanation.
• acceptable, adequate, passable, tolerable, sufficient, competent, good enough
IDIOMS up to scratch, up to the mark
OPPOSITE unsatisfactory

satisfied ADJECTIVE
❶ *Are you satisfied with your score?*
• pleased, contented, happy
OPPOSITES dissatisfied, discontented
❷ *The police are satisfied that the death was accidental.*
• certain, sure, convinced

satisfy VERB
❶ *Some days, nothing seemed to satisfy him.*
• please, content, gratify, make you happy

– To satisfy your thirst is to **quench** or **slake** it.
OPPOSITES dissatisfy, frustrate
❷ *I think this should satisfy your requirements.*
• meet, fulfil, answer

saturate VERB
❶ *Several days of rain have saturated the soil.*
• soak, drench, waterlog
❷ *The Internet is saturated with cat photos.*
• flood, inundate, overwhelm, overload

saunter VERB
We sauntered slowly along the footpath.
• amble, stroll, wander, ramble

savage ADJECTIVE
❶ *It was a savage attack on a defenceless young man.*
• vicious, cruel, barbaric, brutal, bloodthirsty, pitiless, ruthless, merciless, inhuman
OPPOSITE humane
❷ *A pack of savage dogs roamed the streets.*
• wild, feral, untamed, ferocious, fierce
OPPOSITE domesticated

save VERB
❶ *Firefighters managed to save most of the building.*
• preserve, protect, safeguard, rescue, recover, retrieve, reclaim, salvage
❷ *You saved me from making a big mistake!*
• stop, prevent, spare, deter
❸ *I saved you a piece of cake.*
• keep, reserve, set aside, retain, hold on to, store, hoard
❹ *Here are some ways to save household energy.*
• conserve, be sparing with, use wisely

savings *PLURAL NOUN*
The couple have lost all of their savings.
• reserves, funds, capital, resources, investments
IDIOM nest egg

savour *VERB*
He was savouring every mouthful.
• relish, enjoy, appreciate, delight in, revel in

saw
past tense see **see**

say *VERB*
❶ *He found it hard to say what he meant.*
• express, communicate, articulate, put into words, convey
❷ *I'd like to say a few words before we start.*
• utter, speak, voice, recite, read

◢ OVERUSED WORD

❶ To say something loudly:

➤ call	➤ bawl
➤ cry	➤ shout
➤ exclaim	➤ yell
➤ bellow	➤ roar

'Not much farther to go!' he yelled above the roar of the engine.

❷ To say something quietly:

➤ whisper	➤ mutter
➤ mumble	

'Now would be a good time to leave,' I whispered.

❸ To say something casually:

➤ remark	➤ note
➤ comment	➤ mention
➤ observe	➤ blurt out

'Lovely morning,' a passer-by remarked.

❹ To say something strongly:

➤ state	➤ declare
➤ announce	➤ pronounce
➤ assert	➤ insist

➤ maintain	➤ command
➤ profess	➤ demand
➤ order	

His wife maintains that he is innocent.

❺ To say something angrily:

➤ snap	➤ bark
➤ snarl	➤ rasp
➤ growl	➤ rant
➤ thunder	➤ rave

'I don't have time to talk to you!' barked the voice on the phone.

❻ To say something unclearly:

➤ babble	➤ stammer
➤ burble	➤ stutter
➤ gabble	

The stranger kept babbling about an ancient prophecy.

❼ To say something again:

➤ repeat	➤ echo
➤ reiterate	

Could you please repeat your email address?

❽ To say something in reply:

➤ answer	➤ respond
➤ reply	➤ retort

'Certainly not!' retorted the judge.

saying *NOUN*
There is an old saying, 'look before you leap'.
• proverb, motto, maxim, aphorism, phrase, expression
– An overused saying is a **cliché**.

scamper *VERB*
The rabbits scampered away to safety.
• scurry, scuttle, hurry, dash, dart, run, rush, hasten

scan *VERB*
❶ *The lookout scanned the horizon, hoping to see land.*
• search, study, survey, examine, inspect, scrutinize, scour, stare at, eye

② *I scanned through some magazines in the waiting room.*
• skim, glance at, flick through, browse through
IDIOM cast your eye over

scandal NOUN
① *He discovered a scandal in his family's past.*
• disgrace, shame, embarrassment
IDIOMS skeleton in the cupboard, (North American) skeleton in the closet
② *The amount of money wasted was a scandal.*
• outrage, disgrace
③ *The papers were full of the latest scandal.*
• gossip, rumours, muckraking
(informal) dirt

scanty ADJECTIVE
Details of his life are scanty.
• meagre, paltry, inadequate, insufficient, sparse, scarce
(informal) measly
OPPOSITES abundant, plentiful

scar NOUN
He had a scar on his left cheek.
• mark, blemish, disfigurement

scar VERB
The victim may be scarred for life.
• mark, disfigure

scarce ADJECTIVE
Food was becoming scarce.
• hard to find, in short supply, sparse, scanty, uncommon, rare
(informal) thin on the ground, few and far between
OPPOSITES plentiful, abundant

scarcely ADVERB
She was so tired that she could scarcely speak.
• barely, hardly, only just

scare VERB
You scared me creeping up like that!
• frighten, terrify, petrify, alarm, startle, panic, unnerve

scare NOUN
You gave me quite a scare!
• fright, shock, start, turn

scared ADJECTIVE
Were you scared of the dark when you were little?
• frightened, afraid, terrified, petrified, alarmed, fearful, panicky

scary (informal) ADJECTIVE
It's quite a scary film.
• frightening, terrifying, chilling, hair-raising, spine-tingling, spine-chilling, blood-curdling, eerie, sinister, nightmarish
(informal) creepy, spooky

scatter VERB
① *She scattered breadcrumbs on the ground.*
• spread, strew, distribute, sprinkle, shower, sow
OPPOSITE collect
② *The crowd scattered in all directions.*
• break up, separate, disperse, disband
OPPOSITE gather

scene NOUN
① *Police were called to the scene of the accident.*
• location, position, site, place, situation, spot
② *We were rehearsing a scene from the play.*
• episode, part, section, sequence, extract
③ *On the wall was a painting of a winter scene.*
• landscape, view, outlook, prospect, vista, sight, spectacle, setting, scenery, backdrop
④ *He didn't want to create a scene in the restaurant.*
• fuss, commotion, disturbance, quarrel, row
(informal) to-do, carry-on

scenery NOUN
We stopped to admire the scenery.
• landscape, outlook, prospect, scene, view, vista, panorama

scent NOUN
There was an overpowering scent of vanilla.
• smell, fragrance, perfume, aroma, odour
SEE ALSO smell

sceptical ADJECTIVE
At first, I was sceptical about these results.
• disbelieving, doubtful, doubting, dubious, incredulous, unconvinced, suspicious
OPPOSITES certain, convinced

schedule NOUN
We have a busy training schedule.
• programme, timetable, plan, calendar, diary
– A schedule for a meeting is an **agenda**.
– A schedule of places to visit is an **itinerary**.

scheme NOUN
They worked out a scheme to raise more money.
• plan, proposal, project, strategy, tactic, method, procedure, system

scheme VERB
She felt they were all scheming against her.
• plot, conspire, intrigue

school NOUN
He goes to a school for international students.
• academy, college, institute

science NOUN
He is an expert in the science of genetics.
• discipline, subject, field of study, branch of knowledge

WORD WEB

Some branches of science:

- aeronautics
- anatomy
- astronomy
- biochemistry
- biology
- botany
- chemistry
- computer science
- earth science
- ecology
- electronics
- engineering
- environmental science
- food science
- forensic science
- genetics
- geography
- geology
- information technology
- mathematics
- mechanical engineering
- medical science
- meteorology
- nuclear science
- oceanography
- pathology
- physics
- psychology
- robotics
- space technology
- veterinary science
- zoology

science fiction NOUN

WRITING TIPS

WRITING SCIENCE FICTION
Characters:

- alien life-form
- android
- artificial life-form
- astronaut
- cyborg
- robot
- space traveller
- time traveller

Setting:

- alien planet
- deep space
- mother ship
- outer space
- parallel universe
- space colony
- spacecraft
- spaceship
- space shuttle
- space station
- starship
- time machine

Useful words and phrases:

- bionic
- black hole
- extraterrestrial
- force field
- futuristic
- galactic
- home planet
- humanoid
- hyperspace
- intelligent life
- inter-galactic
- inter-planetary
- inter-stellar
- light year
- orbit
- portal
- post-apocalyptic
- spacesuit
- space-time continuum
- space walk
- suspended animation
- telepathic

> ➤ teleport   ➤ UFO
> ➤ time warp   ➤ wormhole
> SEE ALSO **moon, planet, space**

scoff VERB
➤ scoff at
Everyone scoffed at her ideas.
• mock, ridicule, sneer at, deride, make fun of, poke fun at

scold VERB
She scolded us for being late.
• reprimand, reproach
(*informal*) tell off, tick off

scoop VERB
❶ *Scoop out the middle of the pineapple.*
• dig, gouge, scrape, excavate, hollow
❷ *She scooped the kitten up in her arms.*
• lift, pick, gather, take, snatch

scope NOUN
❶ *There is plenty of scope for new ideas.*
• opportunity, space, room, capacity, freedom, leeway
❷ *Those questions are outside the scope of this essay.*
• range, extent, limit, reach, span

scorch VERB
The sand was so hot, it scorched our feet.
• burn, singe, sear, blacken, char

score NOUN
What was your final score?
• mark, points, total, tally, count, result

score VERB
❶ *How many goals did you score?*
• win, get, gain, earn, make, notch up, chalk up
❷ *Someone had scored their initials on the tree.*
• cut, gouge, notch, scratch, scrape

scorn NOUN
She dismissed my suggestion with scorn.
• contempt, derision, disrespect, mockery, ridicule, sneers
OPPOSITES admiration, respect

scour VERB
❶ *He was at the sink, scouring pots and pans.*
• scrub, rub, clean, polish, burnish, buff
❷ *They scoured the room for clues.*
• search, hunt through, ransack, comb, turn upside-down

scowl VERB
❶ *She scowled and folded her arms across her chest.*
• frown, glower
IDIOM knit your brows
❷ For facial expressions see face.

scramble VERB
❶ *The quickest route is to scramble over the rocks.*
• clamber, climb, crawl, scrabble
❷ *Everyone scrambled to get the best seats.*
• push, jostle, struggle, fight, scuffle

scrap NOUN
❶ *He wrote his number on a scrap of paper.*
• bit, piece, fragment, snippet, oddment
– Scraps of cloth are **rags** or **shreds**.
❷ *They fed scraps of food to the birds.*
• remnant, leftovers, morsel, crumb, speck
❸ *The lorry was loaded with scrap.*
• rubbish, waste, junk, refuse, litter
❹ *There was a scrap between rival fans.*
• fight, brawl, scuffle, tussle, squabble

scrap VERB
❶ *I decided to scrap the last paragraph.*
• discard, throw away, throw out, abandon, cancel, delete, drop
(*informal*) dump, ditch
❷ *The cubs enjoy scrapping with each other.*
• fight, brawl, tussle, scuffle

scrape VERB
❶ *How did you manage to scrape your knee?*
• graze, scratch, scuff
❷ *He was outside the door, scraping mud off his trainers.*
• rub, scour, scrub, clean

scrape NOUN
My little brother is always getting into scrapes.
• trouble, mischief
(*informal*) jam, pickle

scratch VERB
❶ *Try not to scratch the paintwork.*
• mark, score, scrape, gouge, graze
❷ *The dog was scratching at the door.*
• claw

scratch NOUN
There was a tiny scratch on the surface.
• score, line, mark, gash, groove, scrape, graze

scrawl VERB
He scrawled his name on a piece of paper.
• jot down, scribble, write

scream NOUN
He let out a scream of pain.
• shriek, screech, shout, yell, cry, bawl, howl, wail, squeal, yelp

scream VERB
People screamed and ran in all directions.
• shriek, screech, shout, yell, cry, bawl, howl, wail, squeal, yelp

screen NOUN
❶ *The room was divided into two by a screen.*
• partition, divider, curtain
❷ *Look at the image on the screen.*
• monitor, display

screen VERB
❶ *She used her hand to screen her eyes from the sun.*
• shield, protect, shelter, shade, cover, hide, mask, veil
❷ *All employees are screened before being appointed.*
• examine, investigate, check, test, vet
❸ *The match will be screened live on Saturday.*
• show, broadcast, transmit, air, put out

screw VERB
❶ *Screw the lid on tightly.*
• twist, wind, turn, tighten

❷ *Nail or screw the panel to the wall.*
• fasten, secure, fix, attach

scribble VERB
She was always scribbling ideas on scraps of paper.
• scrawl, write, jot down, note, dash off
– To scribble a rough drawing is to **doodle**.

script NOUN
She rewrote the original script for the film version.
– The script for a film is a **screenplay**.
– A handwritten or typed script is a **manuscript**.

scrub VERB
She was scrubbing the kitchen floor.
• scour, rub, brush, clean, wash

scruffy ADJECTIVE
He was wearing an old T-shirt and scruffy jeans.
• untidy, messy, ragged, tatty, tattered, worn-out, shabby
OPPOSITE smart

scrutinize VERB
They scrutinized her passport for a few minutes.
• examine, inspect, look at, study, peruse, investigate, explore

scuffle NOUN
A scuffle broke out between rival fans.
• fight, brawl, tussle, scrap, squabble

sculpture NOUN
The temple was full of marble sculptures.
• carving, figure, statue, effigy, model
– A sculpture of a person's head, shoulders and chest is a **bust**.
– A small sculpture of a person is a **figurine** or **statuette**.

sea NOUN
❶ *70 per cent of the Earth's surface is covered by sea.*
• ocean, waves
(*literary*) the deep

A
B
C
D
E
F
G
H
I
J
K
L
M
N
O
P
Q
R
S
T
U
V
W
X
Y
Z

② *She looked out at a sea of adoring fans.*
• expanse, stretch, mass, host, swathe, carpet

🌀 WORD WEB

- An area of sea partly enclosed by land is a **bay** or **gulf**.
- A wide inlet of the sea is a **sound**.
- A wide inlet where a river joins the sea is an **estuary** or in Scotland a **firth**.
- A narrow stretch of water linking two seas is a **strait**.
- The bottom of the sea is the **seabed**.
- The land near the sea is the **coast** or the **seashore**.
- Creatures that live in the sea are **marine** creatures.
- People who work or travel on the sea are **seafaring** people.

Creatures that live in the sea:

➤ coral	➤ sea cucumber
➤ dogfish	➤ seahorse
➤ dolphin	➤ seal
➤ eel	➤ sea lion
➤ fish	➤ sea otter
➤ jellyfish	➤ sea turtle
➤ killer whale	➤ sea urchin
➤ manta ray	➤ shark
➤ octopus	➤ squid
➤ plankton	➤ starfish
➤ porpoise	➤ stingray
➤ sea anemone	➤ whale

seal *VERB*
The entrance to the burial chamber had been sealed.
• close, fasten, shut, secure, lock
– To seal a leak is to **plug** it or **stop** it.

seam *NOUN*
① *The seam on his trousers split.*
• join, stitching
② *Geologists discovered a rich seam of coal.*
• layer, stratum, vein

search *VERB*
① *He was searching for the book he had lost.*
• hunt, look, seek
IDIOM look high and low
– To search for gold or other minerals is to **prospect**.
② *Police searched the house for clues.*
• explore, scour, ransack, rummage through, go through, comb
IDIOM turn upside down
③ *Security staff searched all the passengers.*
• check, inspect, examine, scrutinize (*informal*) frisk

search *NOUN*
After a long search, she found her keys.
• hunt, look, exploration, check
– A long journey in search of something is a **quest**.

seashore *NOUN*
We explored the seashore, looking for fossils.
• seaside, beach, shore, coast, sands

seaside *NOUN*
On Saturday we had a trip to the seaside.
• beach, sands, seashore, coast

season *NOUN*
Autumn is traditionally the season for harvest.
• period, time, time of year, term

seat *NOUN*
There were two empty seats in the front row.
• chair, place
– A long seat for more than one person is a **bench**.
– A long wooden seat in a church is a **pew**.
– A seat on a bicycle or horse is a **saddle**.

seat *VERB*
① *Please seat yourselves in a circle.*
• place, position, sit down, settle
② *The theatre can seat two hundred people.*
• accommodate, have room for, hold, take

secluded ADJECTIVE
The path leads down to a secluded beach.
• quiet, isolated, private, lonely, remote, cut off, sheltered, hidden
OPPOSITES crowded, busy

second ADJECTIVE
Would anyone like a second helping?
• another, additional, extra, further

second NOUN
I'll be with you in a second.
• moment, little while, instant, flash
(informal) jiffy, tick

second VERB
Will anyone second the proposal?
• support, back, approve, endorse

secondary ADJECTIVE
She loves to run and winning is of secondary importance to her.
• lesser, lower, minor, subordinate, subsidiary
OPPOSITES primary, main

second-hand ADJECTIVE
The shop sells second-hand computers.
• used, pre-owned, handed-down, cast-off
OPPOSITE new

secret ADJECTIVE
❶ It's important to keep your password secret.
• private, confidential, personal, undisclosed, classified, restricted
IDIOM under wraps
OPPOSITE public
❷ The detectives are part of a secret operation.
• undercover, covert, clandestine
(informal) hush-hush
IDIOM cloak-and-dagger
❸ We were shown a secret entrance to an underground cave.
• hidden, concealed, disguised
OPPOSITE open
❹ For secret agents see spy.

➤ in secret
Talks were held in secret.
• in private, privately, on the quiet
IDIOM behind closed doors

secretive ADJECTIVE
He was very secretive about his past.
• uncommunicative, reticent, reserved, tight-lipped, mysterious, quiet
(informal) cagey
OPPOSITES communicative, open

section NOUN
The website has a section on wind energy.
• part, division, bit, sector, segment, portion, compartment, module, chapter
– A section from a piece of classical music is a **movement**.

sector NOUN
❶ This is the residential sector of the city.
• area, part, district, region, section, zone
❷ People from all sectors of the music industry attend the awards ceremony.
• branch, part, division, department, area, arm

secure ADJECTIVE
❶ They bolted all the doors and windows to make the house secure.
• safe, protected, defended, guarded
OPPOSITES insecure, vulnerable
❷ Tie the ropes together with a secure knot.
• steady, firm, solid, fixed, fast, immovable
OPPOSITE loose
❸ She is trying to find a secure job.
• permanent, regular, steady, reliable, dependable, settled

secure VERB
❶ The door wasn't properly secured.
• fasten, lock, seal, bolt
❷ They secured their place in the semi-final.
• make certain of, gain, acquire, obtain
(informal) land

security NOUN

❶ *You must wear a seat belt for your own security.*
• safety, protection
❷ *There was increased security at the airport.*
• safety measures, surveillance, policing

see VERB

❶ *If you look closely, you might see a dragonfly.*
• catch sight of, spot, sight, notice, observe, make out, distinguish, note, perceive, spy, glimpse, witness (*informal*) clap eyes on
SEE ALSO look
❷ *Did you see the news last night?*
• watch, look at, view, catch
❸ *You should see a doctor about that cough.*
• consult, call on, visit, report to
❹ *I see what you mean.*
• understand, appreciate, comprehend, follow, grasp, realize, take in (*informal*) get
❺ *Can you see yourself as a teacher?*
• imagine, picture, visualize, view
❻ *I'll see what I can do.*
• think about, consider, ponder, reflect on, weigh up
❼ *Please see that the lights are switched off.*
• make sure, make certain, ensure, check, verify, confirm
❽ *She went to see what all the fuss was about.*
• find out, discover, learn, establish, ascertain
❾ *I'll see you to the door.*
• escort, conduct, accompany, guide, lead, take

➤ see to something
Will you see to the invitations?
• deal with, attend to, take care of, sort out

seed NOUN

The fruit was full of seeds.
– The seeds in an orange, lemon, etc. are the **pips**.
– The seed in a date, plum, etc. is the **stone**.

seek VERB

❶ *For many years he sought his long-lost brother.*
• search for, hunt for, look for, try to find
❷ *We always seek to please our customers.*
• try, attempt, strive, want, wish, desire

seem VERB

Everything seems to be in working order.
• appear, look, give the impression of being, strike you as

seep VERB

Water began to slowly seep through the roof.
• leak, ooze, escape, drip, dribble, trickle, flow, soak

seethe VERB

❶ *The mixture in the cauldron began to seethe.*
• boil, bubble, foam, froth up
❷ *Inwardly he was seething with indignation.*
• be angry, be furious, rage, storm

segment NOUN

Divide the orange into segments.
• section, portion, piece, part, bit, wedge, slice

seize VERB

❶ *He stretched out to seize the rope.*
• grab, catch, snatch, take hold of, grasp, grip, clutch
❷ *The town was seized by rebels last year.*
• capture, take over, conquer, occupy, overrun
❸ *Customs officers seized the smuggled goods.*
• take possession of, confiscate, impound, commandeer

➤ seize up
Without oil, the engine will seize up.
• become jammed, become clogged, become stuck

seldom ADVERB

He seldom spoke.
• rarely, infrequently, hardly ever, scarcely
IDIOM once in a blue moon
OPPOSITE often

select VERB

We have to select a new team captain.
• choose, pick, decide on, opt for, settle on, appoint, elect

select ADJECTIVE

Only a select few were invited to the party.
• chosen, special, hand-picked, privileged

selection NOUN

❶ *Have you made your selection?*
• choice, option, pick, preference
❷ *They stock a wide selection of games.*
• range, variety, assortment, array

selfish ADJECTIVE

It was selfish of him to keep all the chocolate for himself.
• self-centred, thoughtless, inconsiderate, uncharitable, mean, miserly
OPPOSITES unselfish, generous

sell VERB

The corner shop sells newspapers and sweets.
• deal in, trade in, stock, market
– Uncomplimentary synonyms are peddle and hawk.
OPPOSITE buy

send VERB

❶ *I'll send you a text message.*
• dispatch, post, mail, transmit, forward
OPPOSITE receive
❷ *They are sending a satellite into orbit.*
• launch, propel, direct, fire, shoot
❸ *This computer is sending me crazy!*
• drive, make, turn
➤ **send for someone**
I think we should send for a doctor.
• call, summon, fetch

➤ **send something out**
The device was sending out weird noises.
• emit, discharge, give off, issue, release

senior ADJECTIVE

❶ *She is one of the senior players in the squad.*
• older, long-standing
OPPOSITES younger, junior
❷ *He is a senior officer in the navy.*
• high-ranking, superior
OPPOSITES junior, subordinate

sensation NOUN

❶ *She had a tingling sensation in her fingers.*
• feeling, sense, perception
❷ *The unexpected news caused a sensation.*
• stir, thrill, commotion, fuss, furore, to-do

sensational ADJECTIVE

❶ *The newspaper printed a sensational account of the murder.*
• shocking, horrifying, scandalous, lurid (*informal*) juicy
❷ (*informal*) *Wow, that was a sensational goal!*
• amazing, extraordinary, stunning, spectacular, stupendous, tremendous, wonderful, fantastic, fabulous, terrific

sense NOUN

❶ *A baby learns about the world through its senses.*
– The five human senses are **hearing, sight, smell, taste** and **touch**.
❷ *He has a good sense of rhythm.*
• appreciation, awareness, consciousness, feeling (for)
❸ *At least she had the sense to keep quiet.*
• common sense, wisdom, wit, intelligence, brains
❹ *The sense of the word is not clear.*
• meaning, significance, import, definition
➤ **make sense of something**
No one could make sense of the code.
• understand, make out, interpret, decipher

a b c d e f g h i j k l m n o p q r s t u v w x y z

sense VERB

❶ *We sensed that we were not welcome.*
• be aware, realize, perceive, feel, notice, observe
❷ *This device can sense any change in temperature.*
• detect, respond to, pick up, recognize

senseless ADJECTIVE

❶ *It was a senseless act of violence.*
• pointless, mindless, futile, foolish, stupid, irrational, illogical, mad, crazy
OPPOSITE sensible
❷ *His attackers left him senseless on the ground.*
• unconscious, knocked out
OPPOSITE conscious

sensible ADJECTIVE

❶ *She gave me some sensible advice.*
• wise, shrewd, reasonable, rational, logical, sane, sound, prudent, level-headed
OPPOSITES foolish, unwise
❷ *Bring a pair of sensible shoes.*
• comfortable, practical
OPPOSITE impractical

sensitive ADJECTIVE

❶ *This cream is for sensitive skin.*
• delicate, tender, fine, soft
❷ *Don't be so sensitive!*
• touchy, defensive, thin-skinned
OPPOSITES insensitive, thick-skinned
❸ *This is still a sensitive subject.*
• difficult, delicate, tricky, awkward
❹ *She's very sensitive towards other people.*
• tactful, considerate, thoughtful, sympathetic, understanding
OPPOSITES insensitive, thoughtless

sentence NOUN

The judge will decide on a sentence next week.
• judgement, verdict, decision, ruling

sentence VERB

Both men were sentenced to five years in prison.
• condemn, convict

sentimental ADJECTIVE

❶ *The song has sentimental value to me.*
• emotional, nostalgic
❷ *The film is spoiled by a sentimental ending.*
• romantic, saccharine, mawkish
(*informal*) soppy, mushy

sentry NOUN

A sentry was on duty at the gate.
• guard, lookout, sentinel, watchman

separate ADJECTIVE

❶ *Raw food and cooked food should be kept separate.*
• apart, separated, detached, isolated, segregated
OPPOSITE together
❷ *Contestants have to cook three separate dishes.*
• different, distinct, discrete, independent, unrelated
OPPOSITES related, shared

separate VERB

❶ *The two sides of the city are separated by a river.*
• divide, split, beak up, part
– To separate something which is connected to something else is to **detach** or **disconnect** it.
OPPOSITES combine, mix
❷ *Separate the yolks of the eggs from the whites.*
• keep apart, set apart, isolate, cut off, remove
❸ *The trail separates from here onwards.*
• branch, fork, split, divide, diverge
OPPOSITE merge
❹ *Her friend's parents have separated.*
• split up, break up, part company
– To end a marriage legally is to **divorce**.

sequence NOUN

We tried to piece together the sequence of events.
• order, progression, series, succession, course, flow, chain, train

serene ADJECTIVE

A serene smile spread across her face.
• calm, contented, untroubled, peaceful,

quiet, placid, tranquil
OPPOSITE agitated

series NOUN
I had to answer a series of questions.
• succession, sequence, string, set,
round, chain, train

serious ADJECTIVE
❶ *She wore a serious expression.*
• solemn, sombre, sober, earnest, grave,
grim, unsmiling, humourless
OPPOSITES light-hearted, cheerful
❷ *We need a serious talk.*
• important, significant, momentous,
weighty, major
OPPOSITES unimportant, insignificant
❸ *He was writing a serious book about
global warming.*
• learned, intellectual, scholarly, heavy,
in-depth
OPPOSITES light, casual
❹ *Are you serious about wanting to
help?*
• sincere, genuine, in earnest,
committed, wholehearted
❺ *She was recovering from a serious
illness.*
• severe, grave, bad, major, acute,
critical, dangerous
OPPOSITES minor, trivial

seriously ADVERB
❶ *Erin nodded seriously.*
• solemnly, soberly, earnestly, gravely,
grimly
OPPOSITE cheerfully
❷ *Are you seriously interested?*
• genuinely, truly, honestly, sincerely
❸ *No one was seriously injured.*
• severely, badly, gravely, acutely,
critically
OPPOSITES slightly, mildly
❹ (informal) *a seriously bad film*
• extremely, exceptionally,
extraordinarily

seriousness NOUN
❶ *I saw the seriousness in her eyes.*
• solemnity, gravity, sobriety,
humourlessness
OPPOSITES cheerfulness, levity

❷ *You must understand the seriousness
of the situation.*
• gravity, severity, importance, weight

servant NOUN
A servant entered with a tray of food.
• attendant, domestic, maid, retainer,
minion

serve VERB
❶ *Is anyone waiting to be served?*
• help, assist, attend to, deal with
❷ *Serve the rice in separate bowls.*
• give out, dish up, present, pass round,
distribute
❸ *He served the school for 40 years until
his retirement.*
• work for, contribute to
❹ *An old crate served as a table.*
• be used, act, function

service NOUN
❶ *Let me know if I can be of any service.*
• help, assistance, aid, use, usefulness,
benefit
❷ *The funeral service was held in the
local church.*
• ceremony, ritual, rite
❸ *Treat your bike to an annual service.*
• check-up, overhaul, maintenance,
servicing

service VERB
A local garage services their car.
• maintain, check, go over, overhaul

session NOUN
❶ *We have a training session on
Saturday mornings.*
• period, time
❷ *The Queen will open the next session
of Parliament.*
• meeting, sitting, assembly

set VERB
❶ *He set the microphone on its stand.*
• place, put, stand, position, lay
❷ *Have they set a date for the wedding?*
• appoint, specify, name, decide,
determine, choose, fix, establish, settle
❸ *She set the alarm for five the next
morning.*
• adjust, regulate, correct

❹ *Leave the jelly to set in the fridge.*
• become firm, solidify, harden, stiffen
❺ *The sun was just beginning to set.*
• go down, sink
➤ **set about something**
We set about clearing the table immediately.
• begin, start, commence
➤ **set off**
❶ *They set off early for the airport.*
• depart, get going, leave, set out, start out
❷ *I set off the smoke alarm by mistake.*
• activate, start, trigger
➤ **set something out**
The information is clearly set out on the page.
• lay out, arrange, display, present
➤ **set something up**
❶ *Can you set up the table-tennis table?*
• put up, erect, construct, build
❷ *A few of us are setting up a film club.*
• create, establish, institute, start, found

set NOUN
❶ *There is a set of measuring spoons in the drawer.*
• collection, batch, kit, series
❷ *There is a quick change of set after Act One.*
• scenery, backdrop, setting

set ADJECTIVE
❶ *The evening meal is served at a set time.*
• fixed, established, definite
OPPOSITE variable
❷ *Everything is set for the big finale.*
• ready, prepared, organized, primed

setback NOUN
We ran into a setback before we even started.
• difficulty, problem, complication, snag, hitch, hiccup, glitch

setting NOUN
The abbey stands in a rural setting.
• surroundings, location, situation, position, place, site, environment, background

settle VERB
❶ *It's time to settle our differences.*
• resolve, sort out, work out, clear up, iron out, end
❷ *I had just settled down on the sofa when the doorbell rang.*
• sit, get comfortable
❸ *A crow settled on a nearby branch.*
• land, alight, perch, come to rest
❹ *The family settled in Canada after the war.*
• emigrate (to), move (to), set up home (in)
IDIOM put down roots
❺ *Wait until the mud settles.*
• sink to the bottom, clear, subside
❻ *We can settle the bill in the morning.*
• pay, clear, square
➤ **settle on**
Have you settled on a name for the puppy?
• agree on, decide on, choose, pick, determine, establish, fix

settlement NOUN
This was the site of an old Viking settlement.
• community, colony, encampment, outpost, village

settler NOUN
a book about early European settlers in America
• colonist, immigrant, pioneer, incomer

sever VERB
❶ *The builders accidentally severed a water pipe.*
• cut through, shear through
– To sever a limb is to **amputate** it.
❷ *He threatened to sever all ties with his family.*
• break off, end, terminate

several ADJECTIVE
I made several attempts to contact them.
• a number of, many, some, a few, various

severe ADJECTIVE
❶ *Mum gave me one of her severe looks.*
• harsh, strict, stern, hard, disapproving,

withering

OPPOSITES gentle, lenient

❷ He suffered a severe neck injury in the accident.
• bad, serious, acute, grave

OPPOSITE mild

❸ Siberia has a severe climate.
• extreme, tough, harsh, hostile, sharp, intense

OPPOSITE mild

sew VERB
She sewed a name tag on to my coat.
• stitch, tack, embroider
– To sew a picture or design is to **embroider** it.

sex NOUN
❶ What sex is the hamster?
• gender
❷ education about sex and relationships
• sexual intercourse, lovemaking

sexual ADJECTIVE
❶ the sexual parts of a flower
• reproductive, procreative
❷ The film contains scenes of a sexual nature.
• erotic, carnal, sensual

shabby ADJECTIVE
❶ He was wearing a shabby pair of slippers.
• ragged, scruffy, tattered, frayed, worn out, threadbare
(informal) tatty

OPPOSITE smart

❷ They lived in a shabby boarding house.
• dilapidated, run down, seedy, dingy, squalid, sordid
❸ That was a shabby trick!
• mean, nasty, unfair, unkind, dishonest, shameful, low, cheap

shade NOUN
❶ They were sitting in the shade of a palm tree.
• shadow, cover
❷ The porch had a shade to keep out the sun.
• screen, blind, canopy, awning
– A type of umbrella used as a sun shade

is a **parasol**.
❸ The walls are a pale shade of blue.
• hue, tinge, tint, tone, colour

shade VERB
❶ She used her hand to shade her eyes from the sun.
• shield, screen, protect, hide, mask
❷ Use small pencil strokes to shade the edges.
• fill in, darken

shadow NOUN
❶ The candlelight cast weird shadows on the wall.
• silhouette, shape, figure, outline
❷ Her face was deep in shadow.
• shade, darkness, semi-darkness, gloom
❸ Not a shadow of doubt remained.
• trace, hint, flicker, suggestion, suspicion

shadow VERB
Police have been shadowing the suspect for weeks.
• follow, pursue, stalk, track, trail
(informal) tail

shady ADJECTIVE
❶ We found a shady spot under a tree.
• shaded, shadowy, sheltered, dark, sunless

OPPOSITE sunny

❷ He was involved in some shady business deals.
• dishonest, disreputable, suspicious, dubious, suspect, untrustworthy
(informal) fishy, dodgy

OPPOSITE honest

shaft NOUN
❶ The arrow has a wooden shaft.
• pole, rod, stick, staff, spine
❷ A shaft of moonlight shone through the window.
• beam, ray, gleam, streak
❸ He nearly fell into an old mine shaft.
• pit, tunnel, hole

shaggy ADJECTIVE
Highland cows have long shaggy coats.
• bushy, woolly, fleecy, hairy, thick

a b c d e f g h i j k l m n o p q r s t u v w x y z

shake *VERB*

❶ *The walls and floor shook with the blast.*
• quake, shudder, vibrate, rattle, rock, sway, totter, wobble, judder
❷ *The driver shook his fist as he overtook us.*
• wave, brandish, flourish, wield, wag, waggle, joggle
❸ *She was so upset that her voice was shaking.*
• tremble, quaver, quiver
❹ *They were shaken by the terrible news.*
• shock, distress, upset, disturb, unsettle, unnerve, startle, alarm, agitate, rattle, fluster

shaky *ADJECTIVE*

❶ *We sat at a shaky table.*
• unsteady, wobbly, unstable, insecure, rickety
OPPOSITES steady, stable
❷ *He was so nervous that his hands were shaky.*
• trembling, quavering, quivering, faltering
OPPOSITE steady

shallow *ADJECTIVE*

No diving in the shallow end of the pool.
OPPOSITE deep

sham *NOUN*

I later found out that her illness was a sham.
• pretence, deception, lie, act

shame *NOUN*

❶ *He hung his head in shame.*
• remorse, contrition, guilt
❷ *Their actions brought shame to our community.*
• disgrace, dishonour, ignominy, humiliation, embarrassment
➤ **a shame**
It's a shame you have to leave.
• a pity, unfortunate

shameful *ADJECTIVE*

It was a shameful incident involving eight players.
• disgraceful, deplorable, reprehensible,

discreditable, dishonourable, contemptible, despicable, outrageous, scandalous
OPPOSITES admirable, honourable

shape *NOUN*

❶ *He sent her a Valentine card in the shape of a heart.*
• form, figure, outline
– A dark outline seen against a light background is a **silhouette**.
❷ *For his age he was feeling in good shape.*
• condition, health, form, order, fettle, trim

WORD WEB

Two-dimensional geometric shapes:

➤ circle	➤ oval
➤ decagon (10 sides)	➤ parallelogram
➤ diamond	➤ pentagon (5 sides)
➤ ellipse	➤ polygon
➤ heptagon (7 sides)	➤ quadrilateral
➤ hexagon (6 sides)	➤ rectangle
➤ nonagon (9 sides)	➤ rhombus
➤ oblong	➤ ring
➤ octagon (8 sides)	➤ semicircle
	➤ square
	➤ trapezium
	➤ triangle

Three-dimensional geometric shapes:

➤ cone	➤ polyhedron
➤ cube	➤ prism
➤ cuboid	➤ pyramid
➤ cylinder	➤ sphere
➤ hemisphere	

---

shape *VERB*

Shape the dough into a ball.
• form, mould, fashion, make
– To shape metal or plaster in a mould is to **cast** it.

share *NOUN*

Everyone gets a fair share of computer time.
• portion, quota, allocation, allowance,

ration, helping
(*informal*) cut

share VERB
❶ *We shared the cost of a taxi between us.*
• divide, split
❷ *They finally got round to sharing out the prizes.*
• distribute, deal out, ration out, allocate, allot

sharp ADJECTIVE
❶ *Use a pair of sharp scissors.*
• keen, sharpened, razor-sharp
OPPOSITE blunt
❷ *Many species of cactus have sharp spines.*
• pointed, spiky, jagged
OPPOSITE rounded
❸ *I felt a sharp pain in my ankle.*
• acute, piercing, stabbing
OPPOSITE dull
❹ *I'm trying to make the image on the screen sharper.*
• clear, distinct, well defined, crisp
OPPOSITE blurred
❺ *She has a sharp eye for detail.*
• keen, observant, perceptive
OPPOSITE unobservant
❻ *He had a quick wit and a sharp mind.*
• clever, quick, shrewd, perceptive
OPPOSITES dull, slow
❼ *Just ahead there's a sharp bend in the road.*
• abrupt, sudden, steep
– A bend that doubles back on itself is a **hairpin** bend.
OPPOSITE gradual
❽ *There is likely to be a sharp overnight frost.*
• severe, extreme, intense, serious
OPPOSITE slight, mild
❾ *This salad dressing is a bit sharp.*
• sour, tart, bitter
OPPOSITES mild, sweet

sharpen VERB
You will need to sharpen the knife.
• make sharp, grind, whet, hone

shatter VERB
❶ *The mirror fell and shattered into tiny pieces.*
• smash, break, splinter, fracture, fragment, disintegrate
❷ *Her dreams of being a writer were shattered.*
• destroy, wreck, ruin, demolish, crush, dash
(*informal*) scupper

sheaf NOUN
He handed me a sheaf of handwritten pages.
• bunch, bundle

sheath NOUN
Keep the thermometer in its plastic sheath.
• casing, covering, sleeve
– A sheath for a sword or dagger is a **scabbard**.

shed NOUN
We have a shed full of garden tools.
• hut, shack, outhouse, cabin

shed VERB
All the trees had shed their leaves.
• drop, let fall, spill, scatter

sheen NOUN
He waxed the table to give it a sheen.
• shine, gloss, lustre, polish

sheep NOUN
We could see a flock of sheep on the hill.
– A female sheep is a **ewe**.
– A male sheep is a **ram**.
– A young sheep is a **lamb**.
– Meat from sheep is **mutton** or lamb.
– The woolly coat of a sheep is its **fleece**.

sheer ADJECTIVE
❶ *That story he told was sheer nonsense.*
• complete, total, utter, absolute, pure, downright, out-and-out
❷ *The path ran alongside a sheer cliff.*
• vertical, perpendicular, precipitous
– A sheer or steep cliff face is a **precipice**.
❸ *She wore a scarf of sheer silk.*
• fine, thin, transparent, see-through

sheet NOUN

❶ *Start on a fresh sheet of paper.*
• page, leaf, piece
❷ *We need to fit a new sheet of glass.*
• pane, panel, plate
❸ *The pond was covered with a thin sheet of ice.*
• layer, film, coating, covering, surface

shelf NOUN

Please put the books back on the shelf.
• ledge, rack
– A shelf above a fireplace is a **mantelpiece**.

shell NOUN

Tortoises have hard shells.
• covering, case, casing, outside, exterior

shellfish NOUN

WORD WEB

Some types of shellfish:

➤ barnacle
➤ clam
➤ cockle
➤ conch
➤ crab
➤ crayfish
➤ cuttlefish
➤ limpet
➤ lobster
➤ mussel
➤ oyster
➤ prawn
➤ razor shell
➤ scallop
➤ shrimp
➤ whelk
➤ winkle

- Shellfish with legs, such as crabs, lobsters and shrimps, are **crustaceans**.

- Shellfish such as clams and oysters, with soft bodies and often an external shell, are **molluscs**.

shelter NOUN

The tents provide shelter from the desert winds.
• cover, protection, safety, security, refuge

shelter VERB

❶ *An overhanging rock sheltered us from the rain.*
• protect, shield, screen, guard, defend, safeguard, cushion
❷ *They sheltered in a cave until morning.*
• take shelter, take refuge, take cover

shelve VERB

The news is that the film has been shelved.
• postpone, put off, put back, defer, suspend, put to one side
IDIOMS put on ice, put on the back burner

shield NOUN

The trees act as an effective wind shield.
• screen, barrier, defence, guard, protection, cover, shelter
– The part of a helmet that shields your face is the **visor**.

shield VERB

A hat will shield your eyes from the sun.
• protect, screen, cover, shelter, guard, safeguard, defend, keep safe

shift VERB

❶ *Do you need help to shift the furniture?*
• move, rearrange, reposition
❷ *These stains won't be easy to shift.*
• remove, get off, lift, get rid of
❸ *Attitudes have shifted in recent years.*
• change, alter, modify

shine VERB

❶ *A light shone from an upstairs window.*
• beam, gleam, glow, glare, blaze, radiate
For tips on describing light see **light**.
❷ *He shines his shoes every morning.*
• polish, brush, buff
❸ *She's good at all sports, but she shines at tennis.*
• excel, stand out, be outstanding

shiny ADJECTIVE
She polished the mirror until it was shiny.
• shining, gleaming, glistening, polished, glossy, burnished, lustrous
OPPOSITES matt, dull

ship NOUN
❶ *Another big wave hit the ship.*
• boat, craft, vessel
– A large passenger ship is a **liner.**
– Ships that travel long distances at sea are **ocean-going** or **seagoing** ships.
– A word that means 'to do with ships' is **nautical.**
❷ For types of boat or ship see **boat.**

ship VERB
Your parcel was shipped on Tuesday.
• dispatch, send, post, mail, deliver

shirk VERB
He promised not to shirk his fair share of the work.
• avoid, evade, get out of, dodge, duck

shiver VERB
A boy stood on the doorstep, shivering with cold.
• tremble, quiver, shake, shudder, quake

shock NOUN
❶ *News of his death came as a great shock.*
• blow, surprise, fright, upset
IDIOM bolt from the blue
❷ *The driver is still in a state of shock.*
• trauma, distress
❸ *The shock of the explosion was felt for miles.*
• impact, jolt, reverberation

shock VERB
The whole town was shocked by the news.
• horrify, appal, startle, stun, stagger, astonish, astound, shake, rock, scandalize, outrage

shocking ADJECTIVE
❶ *There were shocking scenes of violence on the news.*
• appalling, horrifying, horrific, dreadful, horrendous, atrocious, horrible, terrible, distressing, sickening

❷ *(informal) It is a shocking waste of money.*
• very bad, awful, terrible, deplorable, disgraceful, dreadful
(informal) abysmal

shoes PLURAL NOUN
The shop sells fancy shoes and bags.
• footwear

WORD WEB

Some types of shoe or boot:

➤ ankle boots	➤ plimsolls
➤ ballet shoes	➤ pumps
➤ baseball boots	➤ sandals
➤ brogues	➤ slippers
➤ clogs	➤ stilettos
➤ court shoes	➤ tap shoes
➤ espadrilles	➤ tennis shoes
➤ flip-flops	➤ trainers (North
➤ football boots	American
➤ gym shoes	sneakers)
➤ high heels	➤ wellingtons
➤ moccasins	(informal
➤ mules	wellies)
➤ platform shoes	

shone
past tense see **shine**

shook
past tense see **shake**

shoot VERB
❶ *She shot an arrow into the air.*
• fire, discharge, launch, aim, propel
❷ *It is now illegal to hunt and shoot tigers.*
• fire at, hit, open fire on, gun down
❸ *An ambulance shot past with its lights flashing.*
• race, speed, dash, rush, tear, streak, hurtle, fly, whizz, zoom
❹ *He shot the penalty into the corner of the net.*
• kick, strike, hit, drive, boot
❺ *Most of the film was shot in New Zealand.*
• film, photograph, record

A
B
C
D
E
F
G
H
I
J
K
L
M
N
O
P
Q
R
S
T
U
V
W
X
Y
Z

shop NOUN
The high street has a good range of shops.
• store, boutique
(*old use*) emporium

⚙ **WORD WEB**

Some types of shop and shopkeeper:

➤ antique shop
➤ bakery
➤ bookshop
➤ butcher
➤ cheesemonger
➤ chemist or
  pharmacy
  (*North American*
  drugstore)
➤ clothes shop
➤ confectioner
➤ corner shop
➤ delicatessen
➤ department
  store
➤ fishmonger
➤ florist
➤ garden centre
➤ greengrocer
➤ grocer
➤ haberdasher

➤ hardware shop
➤ health-food
  shop
➤ hypermarket
➤ ironmonger
➤ jeweller
➤ music shop
➤ newsagent
➤ off-licence
➤ pharmacy
➤ post office
➤ shoe shop
➤ shopping arcade
➤ shopping centre
  (*North American*
  shopping mall)
➤ stationer
➤ supermarket
➤ toyshop
➤ watchmaker

shopping NOUN
We put our shopping in the back of the car.
• goods, purchases

shore NOUN
see seashore

short ADJECTIVE
❶ *They live a short distance from the shops.*
• little, small
OPPOSITE long
❷ *We had to write a short summary of the story.*
• concise, brief, succinct, condensed, pithy
OPPOSITES long, lengthy

❸ *It was a very short visit.*
• brief, quick, fleeting, hasty, cursory
OPPOSITES long, lengthy
❹ *My brother is short for his age.*
• small, tiny, little, diminutive, petite
– Someone who is short and fat is **squat** or **dumpy**.
OPPOSITE tall
❺ *Our food supplies were running short.*
• low, meagre, scant, sparse, inadequate, insufficient
OPPOSITE plentiful
❻ *The receptionist was short with me.*
• abrupt, rude, sharp, curt, brusque, terse, blunt, snappy
OPPOSITES polite, courteous

shortage NOUN
There is a severe shortage of basic medicines.
• scarcity, deficiency, lack, want, dearth, shortfall
– A shortage of water is a **drought**.
– A shortage of food is a **famine**.

shortcoming NOUN
She was aware of her own shortcomings.
• fault, failing, imperfection, defect, flaw, weakness, limitation, weak point
OPPOSITES strength, strong point

shorten VERB
Most people shorten Janet's name to Jan.
• cut down, reduce, cut, trim, abbreviate, abridge, condense, compress, curtail
OPPOSITE lengthen

shortly ADVERB
The guests will be arriving shortly.
• soon, before long, in a little while, in no time, any minute, presently, by and by

shot NOUN
❶ *We heard a noise like the shot of a rifle.*
• crack, report, bang, blast
❷ *He had an easy shot at goal.*
• strike, kick, hit, stroke
❸ *This is an unusual shot which is taken*

from the air.
• photograph, photo, picture, snap, snapshot
❹ (*informal*) *We each had a shot at solving the puzzle.*
• try, go, attempt
(*informal*) bash, crack, stab

shout VERB
She had to shout to be heard above the din.
• call, cry out, yell, roar, bellow, bawl, raise your voice
(*informal*) holler
OPPOSITE whisper

shove VERB
❶ *I shoved my bag into the locker.*
• push, thrust, force, ram, cram
❷ *Stop shoving at the back!*
• barge, push, elbow, jostle

shovel VERB
We shovelled the snow into a huge heap.
• dig, scoop, shift, clear, move

show VERB
❶ *You promised to show me your photos.*
• present, display, exhibit, set out
❷ *The painting shows a hunting scene.*
• portray, picture, depict, illustrate, represent
❸ *Can you show me how to do it?*
• explain to, make clear to, instruct, teach, tell
❹ *The evidence shows that he was right.*
• reveal, make plain, demonstrate, prove, confirm, verify
❺ *We were shown into the waiting room.*
• guide, direct, conduct, escort, accompany, usher
❻ *The dots show where to put your fingers.*
• indicate, point out
❼ *Does my T-shirt show through the blouse?*
• be seen, be visible, appear
➤ **show off**
Ignore him: he's just showing off.
• boast, brag, swagger, posture
IDIOM blow your own trumpet

➤ **show up**
The lines don't show up on the screen.
• appear, be visible, be evident

show NOUN
❶ *We have tickets for tonight's show.*
• performance, production, entertainment
❷ *There is a show of students' artwork at the end of term.*
• display, exhibition, presentation

shower NOUN
There was a sudden shower of rain.
• fall, downpour, sprinkling, drizzle
For tips on describing weather see **weather**.

shower VERB
The eruption showered a wide area with volcanic ash.
• spray, spatter, sprinkle, splash

showy ADJECTIVE
Is this tie too showy?
• gaudy, flashy, bright, loud, garish, conspicuous
OPPOSITES plain, restrained

shred NOUN
There's not a shred of evidence against her.
• bit, piece, scrap, trace, jot
➤ **shreds**
The gale ripped the tent to shreds.
• tatters, ribbons, rags, strips

shrewd ADJECTIVE
That was a shrewd decision.
• clever, astute, sharp, quick-witted, intelligent, smart, canny, perceptive
OPPOSITE stupid

shriek NOUN & VERB
see **shriek**

shrill ADJECTIVE
I could hear the shrill sound of a whistle.
• high, high-pitched, piercing, sharp, screechy
OPPOSITES low, soft

shrink VERB
❶ *My jeans have shrunk in the wash.*
• become smaller, contract, narrow, reduce, decrease
OPPOSITE expand
❷ *The creature shrank back instinctively from the light.*
• recoil, flinch, shy away

shrivel VERB
Many plants shrivelled in the heat.
• wilt, wither, droop, dry up, wrinkle, shrink

shroud VERB
The summit was shrouded in clouds.
• cover, envelop, wrap, blanket, cloak, mask, hide, conceal, veil

shrub NOUN
This shrub grows in northern Chile.
• bush
– An area planted with shrubs is a **shrubbery**.

shudder VERB
He shuddered at the thought of being left alone.
• tremble, quake, quiver, shiver, shake, judder

shuffle VERB
❶ *The old man shuffled over to the fireplace.*
• shamble, hobble, scuffle, scrape, drag your feet
❷ *Did you remember to shuffle the cards?*
• mix, mix up, jumble, rearrange

shut VERB
Please shut the door behind you.
• close, fasten, seal, secure, lock, bolt, latch
– To shut a door with a bang is to **slam** it.
➤ **shut down**
The hotel shut down years ago.
• close down, go out of business
OPPOSITE open up
➤ **shut something down**
I'll show you the best way to shut down the computer.
• switch off, shut off, close down

OPPOSITE start up
➤ **shut up**
(informal) I wish those people behind us would shut up!
• be quiet, be silent, stop talking, hush up
IDIOM hold your tongue
➤ **shut someone up**
❶ *I hate to see animals shut up in cages.*
• imprison, confine, detain
❷ *(informal) This should shut them up for a while.*
• silence, quieten, quiet down, hush up

shy ADJECTIVE
At first, she was too shy to say anything.
• bashful, timid, coy, reserved, hesitant, self-conscious, inhibited, modest
OPPOSITES bold, confident

sick ADJECTIVE
❶ *She was sick with a chest infection all last week.*
• ill, unwell, poorly, sickly, ailing, infirm, indisposed
IDIOM under the weather
OPPOSITES healthy, well
❷ *The sea was rough and I felt sick.*
• nauseous, queasy
➤ **be sick**
He suddenly felt he was going to be sick.
• vomit, heave
(informal) throw up, puke
➤ **be sick of**
I'm sick of all this miserable weather.
• be fed up with, be tired of, be weary of, have had enough of

sicken VERB
Many people were sickened by the violence in the film.
• disgust, revolt, repel, nauseate, make you sick
IDIOM turn your stomach

sickly ADJECTIVE
❶ *He had always been a sickly child.*
• unhealthy, weak, delicate, frail
OPPOSITES healthy, strong

❷ *The air was thick with a sickly, sweet smell.*
• nauseating, sickening, cloying, stomach-turning

sickness *NOUN*
❶ *A deadly sickness swept across the continent.*
• illness, disease, ailment, malady, infection, virus
(*informal*) bug
❷ *A sudden wave of sickness came over her.*
• nausea, queasiness, vomiting

side *NOUN*
❶ *A cube has six sides.*
• face, surface
❷ *He had a scar on the right side of his face.*
• half, part
❸ *The path runs along the side of a large playing field.*
• edge, border, boundary, fringe, perimeter, verge, margin
❹ *I could see both sides of the argument.*
• point of view, viewpoint, standpoint, position, perspective, angle, slant
❺ *We have the best side in the league.*
• team, squad, line-up

side *VERB*
➤ **side with someone**
Why do you always side with her?
• support, favour, take the side of, back, agree with, stand by

siege *NOUN*
The city was under siege for a year.
• blockade

sift *VERB*
Sift the flour to get rid of any lumps.
• sieve, strain, filter
➤ **sift through something**
Police have been sifting through piles of evidence.
• look through, examine, inspect, pore over, analyse, scrutinize, review

sigh *VERB*
'Not again,' he sighed.
• moan, complain, lament, grumble

sight *NOUN*
❶ *Owls have sharp sight and excellent hearing.*
• eyesight, vision, eyes
– Words meaning 'to do with sight' are **optical** and **visual**.
❷ *Later that day they had their first sight of land.*
• view, glimpse, look (at)
❸ *Niagara Falls is a breathtaking sight.*
• spectacle, display, show, scene
❹ *We spent the week seeing the sights of New York.*
• attraction, landmark
➤ **be in sight**
❶ *Not a single person was in sight.*
• be visible, be in view, be in range
❷ *At last victory was in sight.*
• approach, loom, be imminent

sight *VERB*
After eight days at sea we sighted land.
• see, catch sight of, spot, spy, glimpse, make out, notice, observe, distinguish, recognize

sign *NOUN*
❶ *A sign pointed to the exit.*
• notice, placard, poster, signpost
– The sign belonging to a particular business or organization is a **logo**.
– The sign on a particular brand of goods is a **trademark**.
❷ *There are no signs yet of a change in the weather.*
• indication, hint, clue, suggestion, warning
❸ *I'll give you the sign when I'm ready.*
• signal, gesture, cue, reminder

sign *VERB*
❶ *Please sign your name here.*
• write, inscribe, autograph
❷ *The club signed two new players this month.*
• take on, engage, recruit, enrol

signal *NOUN*
Don't move until I give the signal.
• sign, gesture, cue, prompt, indication

signal *VERB*
The photographer signalled that she was ready.
• give a sign, indicate, gesture, motion

a
b
c
d
e
f
g
h
i
j
k
l
m
n
o
p
q
r
s
t
u
v
w
x
y
z

significance NOUN
❶ *The significance of these carvings is not clear.*
• meaning, message, import, importance, point, relevance
❷ *Their discovery was of major significance.*
• importance, consequence, seriousness, magnitude
OPPOSITE insignificance

significant ADJECTIVE
❶ *Here is a list of some significant events in French history.*
• important, major, noteworthy, notable, influential
OPPOSITES insignificant, minor
❷ *Climate change is having a significant effect on wildlife.*
• noticeable, considerable, substantial, perceptible, striking
OPPOSITE negligible

signify VERB
❶ *A red light signifies danger.*
• indicate, denote, mean, symbolize, represent, stand for
❷ *Everyone nodded to signify agreement.*
• show, express, indicate, communicate, convey

silence NOUN
An eerie silence filled the room.
• quiet, quietness, hush, stillness, calm, peace, tranquillity
OPPOSITE noise

silence VERB
She silenced him with a glare.
• quieten, quiet, hush, muffle
– To silence someone by putting something over their mouth is to **gag** them.

silent ADJECTIVE
❶ *Outside, the night was cold and silent.*
• quiet, noiseless, soundless, still, hushed
– A sound you cannot hear is **inaudible**.
OPPOSITE noisy
❷ *He was silent for a few minutes.*
• speechless, quiet, mute

(*informal*) mum
– To be too shy to speak is to be **tongue-tied**.
OPPOSITE talkative

silky ADJECTIVE
This breed of rabbit has long silky fur.
• smooth, soft, fine, sleek, velvety

silly ADJECTIVE
That was a really silly idea!
• foolish, stupid, idiotic, foolhardy, senseless, brainless, thoughtless, unwise, unintelligent, half-witted, hare-brained, scatterbrained
(*informal*) daft
OPPOSITE sensible

similar ADJECTIVE
The two species are similar in appearance.
• alike, nearly the same, comparable
OPPOSITES dissimilar, different
➤ similar to
Her views are similar to my own.
• like, close to, comparable to
OPPOSITES unlike, different from

similarity NOUN
Notice the similarity between the paintings.
• likeness, resemblance, correspondence, parallel
OPPOSITE difference

simple ADJECTIVE
❶ *Can you answer this simple question?*
• easy, elementary, straightforward
OPPOSITE difficult
❷ *The forms are written in simple language.*
• clear, plain, uncomplicated, understandable, intelligible
OPPOSITE complicated
❸ *She was wearing a simple cotton dress.*
• plain, undecorated
OPPOSITES elaborate, showy
❹ *He enjoys simple pleasures like walking and gardening.*
• ordinary, unsophisticated, humble,

modest, homely
OPPOSITE sophisticated

simply ADVERB
❶ *I'll try to put it simply.*
• clearly, plainly, straightforwardly, in simple terms
❷ *It is simply the best book I've ever read.*
• absolutely, wholly, completely, totally, utterly
❸ *She was silenced simply for telling the truth.*
• only, just, merely, purely, solely

sin NOUN
They believed that the plague was a punishment for their sins.
• wrong, evil, wickedness, wrongdoing, immorality, vice

sincere ADJECTIVE
Please accept our sincere apologies.
• genuine, honest, true, real, earnest, wholehearted, heartfelt
OPPOSITE insincere

sing VERB
❶ *They started singing an old folk song.*
• chant, croon, chorus
❷ *A small bird was singing outside the window.*
• chirp, trill, warble

singe VERB
The flames singed the inside of the roof.
• burn, scorch, sear, blacken, char

singer NOUN
The band comprises two guitarists and a singer.
• vocalist
– A singer who sings alone is a **soloist**.
– A group of singers is a **choir** or **chorus**.
– A member of a church choir is a **chorister**.

single ADJECTIVE
❶ *A single tree stood out against the sky.*
• solitary, isolated, sole, lone
– When only a single example of something exists, it is **unique**.

❷ *She listened to every single word.*
• individual, distinct, separate
❸ *He had remained single all his life.*
• unmarried, unattached
(*old use*) unwed
– An unmarried man is a **bachelor**.
– An old-fashioned word for an unmarried woman is a **spinster**.
OPPOSITE married

single VERB
➤ **single someone out**
A few of us were singled out for special training.
• pick out, select, choose, identify, earmark, target

sinister ADJECTIVE
There was something sinister about the housekeeper.
• menacing, threatening, malevolent, dark, evil, disturbing, unsettling, eerie
(*informal*) creepy

sink VERB
❶ *The ship sank off the coast of Florida.*
• submerge, go down, founder
– To sink a ship deliberately by letting in water is to **scuttle** it.
❷ *The sun began to sink below the horizon.*
• go down, fall, drop, dip, descend, subside, set
❸ *She sank back in her chair.*
• slump, flop, collapse

sister NOUN
She has a younger sister.
• (*informal*) sis
– A formal name for a sister or brother is a **sibling**.
For other members of a family see **family**.

sit VERB
❶ *She sat on the sofa reading a magazine.*
• be seated, take a seat, settle down, rest, perch
– To sit on your heels is to **squat**.
– To sit for a photograph or portrait is to **pose**.
❷ *The house sits on top of a hill.*
• stand, lie, rest, is situated, is set

a
b
c
d
e
f
g
h
i
j
k
l
m
n
o
p
q
r
s
t
u
v
w
x
y
z

❸ When are you sitting your music exam?
• take
(*informal*) go in for

site NOUN
This is the site of an ancient burial ground.
• location, place, position, situation, setting, whereabouts, venue

situated ADJECTIVE
➤ **be situated**
This small village is situated in a valley.
• be located, be positioned, sit in

situation NOUN
❶ I found myself in an awkward situation.
• position, circumstances, condition, state of affairs
– A bad situation is a **plight** or **predicament**.
❷ The house is in a pleasant situation.
• location, locality, place, position, setting, site, spot
❸ She applied for a situation in advertising.
• job, post, position, appointment

size NOUN
❶ What size is the garden?
• dimensions, proportions, measurements, area, extent
❷ They were amazed by the sheer size of the pyramids.
• scale, magnitude, immensity

sizeable ADJECTIVE
The bullet left a sizeable hole in the wall.
• large, considerable, substantial, fair-sized, appreciable, noticeable
OPPOSITES small, unnoticeable

sizzle VERB
Heat the oil until it begins to sizzle.
• crackle, sputter, spit, hiss

skeleton NOUN
The model shows the skeleton of the building.
• frame, framework, shell
IDIOM bare bones

sketch NOUN
❶ She drew a quick sketch of the scene.
• drawing, outline, plan, doodle
❷ They performed a short comic sketch.
• play, scene, skit, routine

sketch VERB
Sketch your design on a piece of paper first.
• draw, draft, outline, rough out

skid VERB
Several cars skidded on the icy road.
• slide, slip

skilful ADJECTIVE
He was a skilful writer of detective stories.
• expert, skilled, accomplished, able, capable, talented, brilliant, clever, masterly, deft, dexterous
OPPOSITE incompetent

skill NOUN
Balancing on a snowboard requires a lot of skill.
• expertise, ability, accomplishment, talent, competence, proficiency, mastery, deftness, dexterity, prowess

skilled ADJECTIVE
see skilful

skim VERB
❶ Dragonflies skimmed across the still water.
• glide, slide, slip, flit
❷ I only had time to skim the papers.
• scan, glance through, flick through, leaf through
IDIOM cast your eye over

skin NOUN
❶ Drinking water is good for your skin.
– The appearance of the skin of your face is your **complexion**.
❷ The drums were originally made from animal skins.
• hide, pelt, fur
❸ He nearly slipped on a banana skin.
• peel, rind
❹ When it cools the mixture will form a

thin skin on the top.
• film, coating, membrane, crust

skinny ADJECTIVE
A skinny girl in bare feet answered the door.
• thin, lean, bony, gaunt, lanky, scrawny, scraggy
OPPOSITE plump

skip VERB
❶ *The little boy was skipping along the pavement.*
• hop, jump, leap, bound, caper, dance, prance
❷ *I skipped most of the first chapter.*
• pass over, miss out, ignore, omit, leave out

skirt VERB
The path skirts the east side of the lake.
• go past, go round, border, edge

sky NOUN
Clouds drifted slowly across the sky.
• air, heavens, atmosphere
IDIOM (*literary*) blue yonder

slab NOUN
The words were inscribed on a slab of marble.
• block, piece, tablet, slice, chunk, hunk, lump

slack ADJECTIVE
❶ *Suddenly the rope went slack.*
• loose, limp
OPPOSITES tight, taut
❷ *This is usually a slack time of year.*
• slow, quiet, sluggish
OPPOSITES busy, hectic
❸ *Standards of hygiene in the restaurant are slack.*
• lax, careless, negligent, slapdash, sloppy
OPPOSITE strict

slacken VERB
❶ *He undid his collar and slackened his tie.*
• loosen, relax, release, ease off
OPPOSITE tighten

❷ *Her pace gradually slackened.*
• lessen, reduce, decrease, slow down
OPPOSITE increase

slam VERB
He stormed out and slammed the door.
• bang, shut loudly

slant VERB
❶ *Italic text usually slants to the right.*
• lean, slope, tilt, incline, be at an angle, be angled
❷ *They slanted the story to suit themselves.*
• skew, twist, distort, bias

slant NOUN
❶ *Here, the graph shows a steep slant upwards.*
• slope, angle, tilt, incline, gradient
– The slant of a roof is its **pitch**.
❷ *The film brings a new slant to an old story.*
• point of view, angle, viewpoint, perspective, bias

slap VERB
He slapped his forehead and groaned.
• smack, strike, hit, spank, clout, cuff (*informal*) whack

slap NOUN
The cold air hit me like a slap in the face.
• smack, blow, spank, clout, cuff (*informal*) whack

slash VERB
❶ *Several cars had their tyres slashed overnight.*
• cut, gash, slit, knife, nick
❷ *Shops are slashing prices even further.*
• reduce, lower, cut, drop, bring down

slaughter VERB
Waves of soldiers were slaughtered as they advanced.
• kill, butcher, massacre, cull

slaughter NOUN
The battle ended in terrible slaughter.
• bloodshed, killing, butchery, carnage, massacre, bloodbath

slave VERB

He's been slaving away in the kitchen.
- work hard, labour, toil, grind, sweat

slavery NOUN

The central character is kidnapped and sold into slavery.
- captivity, bondage, servitude
- OPPOSITE freedom

sledge NOUN

We pulled our sledges up the snowy slope.
- toboggan
- (North American) sled
– A large sledge pulled by horses is a **sleigh**.
– A sledge used in winter sports is a **bobsleigh**.

sleek ADJECTIVE

Seal pups are born with sleek coats.
- smooth, glossy, shiny, silky, silken
- OPPOSITES coarse, matted

sleep NOUN

He usually has a short sleep after lunch.
- nap, rest, doze, catnap, siesta
- (informal) snooze, kip
- (literary) slumber
- IDIOM (informal) forty winks
➤ **go to sleep**
That night I was too restless to go to sleep.
- fall asleep, doze, drop off, nod off

sleep VERB

The baby is sleeping in the next room.
- be asleep, doze, take a nap
- (informal) snooze
- (literary) slumber

sleepless ADJECTIVE

We spent a sleepless night waiting for news.
- restless, wakeful, troubled, disturbed
– The formal name for sleeplessness is **insomnia**.
- OPPOSITE restful

sleepy ADJECTIVE

I didn't feel sleepy, so I decided to walk round for a bit.
- drowsy, tired, lethargic, heavy-eyed
- (informal) dopey
– Something that makes you feel sleepy is **soporific**. the soporific warmth of the fire
- OPPOSITE wide awake

slender ADJECTIVE

❶ He was a slender youth with dark hair.
- slim, lean, slight, thin, trim, svelte, willowy
- OPPOSITE fat
❷ The spider dangled on a slender thread.
- thin, fine, fragile, delicate
- OPPOSITE thick
❸ We only have a slender chance of winning.
- poor, slight, slim, faint, negligible, remote
- OPPOSITES good, strong
❹ They won by a slender margin.
- narrow, small, slim
- OPPOSITE wide

slice NOUN

Would you like a slice of cheesecake?
- piece, bit, wedge, slab, portion
– A thin slice is a **sliver**.

slice VERB

Slice the vegetables into thick chunks.
- cut, carve, chop

slick ADJECTIVE

The team have a slick passing style.
- skilful, artful, clever, cunning, smooth, deft
- OPPOSITE clumsy

slide VERB

The spoon slid across the table.
- glide, slip, slither, skim, skate, skid

slight ADJECTIVE

❶ I have a slight problem with my computer.
- small, minor, modest, negligible, trivial, insignificant
- OPPOSITE large

❷ There was a slight pause before anyone spoke.
• short, brief, fleeting
OPPOSITE long

❸ There is a slight chance of rain tomorrow.
• slim, slender, faint, remote
OPPOSITE strong

❹ A slight figure emerged from the shadows.
• slender, slim, petite, delicate, fragile, frail
OPPOSITE stout

slightly ADVERB
He was slightly hurt in the accident.
• a little, a bit, somewhat, rather, moderately
OPPOSITES very, seriously

slim ADJECTIVE
❶ She is tall and slim.
• slender, thin, lean, spare, trim, svelte
OPPOSITES fat, plump

❷ Their chances of winning are slim at best.
• poor, faint, slight, slender, negligible, remote
OPPOSITES good, strong

❸ He won the election by a slim margin.
• narrow, small, slender
OPPOSITE wide

slimy ADJECTIVE
The floor of the tunnel was covered in slimy mud.
• slippery, slithery, sticky, oozy
(informal) gooey, icky

sling VERB
❶ He slung his rucksack over his shoulder.
• swing, hang, suspend
❷ (informal) She slung the letter away in disgust.
• throw, fling, hurl, cast, toss, pitch, lob
(informal) chuck

slink VERB
I tried to slink away from the party unnoticed.
• slip, sneak, steal, creep, edge, sidle

slip VERB
❶ I slipped on a patch of ice outside.
• skid, slide, slither, lose your balance
❷ One by one, the seals slipped into the water.
• glide, slide
❸ He slipped out while the others were talking.
• sneak, steal, slink, sidle, creep, tiptoe

slip NOUN
❶ The rehearsal went off without any slips.
• mistake, error, fault, blunder, gaffe, lapse
❷ A name was written on a slip of paper.
• piece, scrap
➤ give someone the slip
It won't be easy to give your friends the slip.
• escape from, get away from, run away from

slippery ADJECTIVE
The stone steps were worn and slippery.
• slithery, slick, smooth, glassy, slimy, greasy, oily
(informal) slippy

slit NOUN
Daylight shone through a slit in the tent.
• cut, split, tear, gash, rent, chink, gap, opening, slot

slit VERB
She used her nail to slit open the envelope.
• cut, split, slice, slash, gash

slither VERB
A snake slithered through the grass.
• slip, slide, glide, slink, snake

slogan NOUN
We need a catchy slogan for the poster.
• motto, catchphrase, jingle

slope VERB
The beach slopes gently down to the sea.
• tilt, slant, incline, fall, drop, rise, climb, bank, shelve

a
b
c
d
e
f
g
h
i
j
k
l
m
n
o
p
q
r
s
t
u
v
w
x
y
z

A B C D E F G H I J K L M N O P Q R S T U V W X Y Z

slope NOUN

❶ *It was hard work pushing my bike up the slope.*
• hill, rise, bank, ramp
– An upward slope is an **ascent** and a downward slope is a **descent**.

❷ *Rain runs down the roof because of the slope.*
• tilt, slant, pitch, gradient, incline

sloppy ADJECTIVE

❶ *The batter should have a sloppy texture.*
• runny, watery, liquid, slushy, mushy
(*informal*) gloopy
OPPOSITE stiff

❷ *That was a sloppy performance from the team.*
• careless, slapdash, slack, messy, untidy, slovenly, slipshod
OPPOSITE careful

slot NOUN

❶ *Insert a coin or token in the slot.*
• slit, opening, aperture, chink, gap

❷ *The show has been moved to a late-night slot.*
• time, spot, space, place

slouch VERB

She sat slouched over her laptop.
• hunch, stoop, slump, droop, flop

slow ADJECTIVE

❶ *They walked on at a slow pace.*
• unhurried, leisurely, steady, sedate, plodding, dawdling, sluggish

❷ *Erosion is usually a slow process.*
• lengthy, prolonged, protracted, gradual, drawn-out

❸ *She's often slow to reply to emails.*
• tardy, late, sluggish, hesitant, reluctant
OPPOSITE quick

slow VERB
➤ slow down

❶ *The boat slowed down as it approached the island.*
• go slower, reduce speed, brake, decelerate
OPPOSITES speed up, accelerate

❷ *The storm slowed us down.*
• make slower, delay, hold up, impede, set back

sludge NOUN

They cleared a lot of sludge out of the pond.
• muck, mud, ooze, slime
(*informal*) gunge, gunk

slump VERB

❶ *I slumped exhausted into an armchair.*
• flop, collapse, sink, sag, slouch

❷ *CD sales continue to slump.*
• fall, decline, drop, plummet, tumble, plunge

slump NOUN

There was a slump in trade after Christmas.
• collapse, drop, fall, decline, downturn, slide
– A general slump in trade is a **depression** or **recession**.
OPPOSITE boom

sly ADJECTIVE

❶ *Foxes are traditionally portrayed as sly creatures.*
• crafty, cunning, artful, clever, wily, tricky, sneaky, devious, furtive, secretive, stealthy, underhand
OPPOSITES straightforward, honest

❷ *He looked up with a sly grin on his face.*
• mischievous, playful, impish, roguish, knowing, arch

smack VERB

She groaned and smacked her forehead in dismay.
• slap, strike, hit, cuff, clip, spank
(*informal*) whack

small ADJECTIVE

 OVERUSED WORD

❶ Small **in size, scale:**

➤ little	➤ compact
➤ tiny	➤ miniature
➤ minute	➤ microscopic

> minuscule   > baby
> mini

(*informal*) teeny, titchy, dinky

(*Scottish*) wee

He spotted a minuscule speck of dirt on his collar.

OPPOSITES big, large

❷ A small person, creature:

> little   > dainty
> short   > diminutive
> squat   > miniature
> petite   > undersized

(*informal*) pint-sized

The fossil belonged to a diminutive species of dinosaur.

OPPOSITES giant, tall, well-built

❸ Small inside:

> cramped   > narrow
> confined   > poky
> restricted

The cabin was a bit cramped for three people plus luggage.

OPPOSITES spacious, roomy

❹ A small amount, small portion:

> meagre   > scanty
> inadequate   > skimpy
> insufficient   > mean
> paltry   > stingy

(*informal*) measly

For breakfast there was stale bread with a meagre scraping of butter.

OPPOSITES ample, substantial

❺ A small change, small problem:

> minor   > trivial
> slight   > trifling
> unimportant   > negligible
> insignificant

We made some minor changes to the script.

OPPOSITES major, significant

smart ADJECTIVE

❶ *He looked smart in his new suit.*
• well-dressed, elegant, stylish, fashionable, chic, spruce, neat, dapper, well-groomed
(*informal*) natty
– To make yourself smart is to **smarten up.**
OPPOSITE scruffy

❷ *They booked a table at a smart restaurant in the city centre.*
• fashionable, upmarket, high-class, exclusive, fancy
(*informal*) posh, swanky, swish

❸ *That was a very smart move!*
• clever, ingenious, intelligent, shrewd, astute, crafty
OPPOSITE stupid

❹ *They set off at a smart pace.*
• fast, quick, rapid, speedy, swift, brisk
(*informal*) cracking
OPPOSITES slow, gentle

smart VERB

Chopping onions makes my eyes smart.
• sting, prick, prickle, tingle, burn

smash VERB

❶ *Every window in the building had been smashed.*
• break, crush, shatter, splinter, crack

❷ *He smashed the ball past the keeper.*
• hit, strike, kick, shoot, drive, slam

> **smash into**
The truck left the road and smashed into a wall.
• crash into, collide with, bang into, bump into, hit

smear VERB

Smear butter over the inside of the dish.
• spread, rub, wipe, plaster, smother, coat, smudge, dab, daub

smear NOUN

There was a smear of blood on the carpet.
• streak, smudge, daub, patch, splodge, mark, blotch

smell VERB

❶ *I could smell something baking in*

a
b
c
d
e
f
g
h
i
j
k
l
m
n
o
p
q
r
s
t
u
v
w
x
y
z

the oven.
• scent, sniff
(*informal*) get a whiff of
❷ *My shoes were beginning to smell.*
• stink, reek
(*informal*) pong

smell NOUN
❶ *Don't you love the smell of fresh popcorn?*
• scent, aroma, perfume, fragrance, bouquet
❷ *What is that awful smell?*
• odour, stench, stink, reek, whiff
(*informal*) pong, niff

WRITING TIPS

DESCRIBING SMELLS
Pleasant:

➤ aromatic	➤ perfumed
➤ delicate	➤ scented
➤ fragrant	➤ sweet-smelling

Unpleasant:

➤ evil-smelling	➤ rank
➤ fetid	➤ reeking
➤ foul	➤ rotten
➤ foul-smelling	➤ sickly
➤ musty	➤ smelly
➤ nauseating	➤ stinking
➤ odorous	➤ (*informal*) stinky
➤ (*informal*)	➤ (*informal*)
pong	whiffy
➤ rancid	

Strong:

➤ choking	➤ pungent
➤ heady	➤ rich
➤ overpowering	➤ sharp

smile VERB & NOUN
The woman smiled and waved at us from the window.
• grin, beam
– To smile in a silly way is to **simper**.
– To smile in a self-satisfied way is to **smirk**.
– To smile in an insulting way is to **sneer**.

smoke NOUN
Thick smoke billowed from the roof.
• fumes
– The smoke given out by a vehicle is **exhaust**.
– A mixture of smoke and fog is **smog**.
smoke VERB
❶ *The bonfire was still smoking next morning.*
• smoulder
❷ *A man stood silently smoking a cigar.*
• puff at

smooth ADJECTIVE
❶ *Roll out the dough on a smooth surface.*
• flat, even, level
OPPOSITE uneven
❷ *In the early morning, the lake was perfectly smooth.*
• calm, still, unruffled, undisturbed, glassy
OPPOSITE rough
❸ *Otters have smooth and shiny coats.*
• silky, sleek, velvety
OPPOSITE coarse
❹ *Stir the mixture until it is smooth.*
• creamy, velvety, silky
OPPOSITE lumpy
❺ *The take-off was surprisingly smooth.*
• comfortable, steady
OPPOSITES bumpy, rocky
❻ *Installing the software was a smooth operation.*
• straightforward, easy, effortless, trouble-free
OPPOSITES difficult, troublesome
smooth VERB
She stood up and smoothed her dress.
• flatten, level, even out
– To smooth cloth you can **iron** or **press** it.
– To smooth wood you can **plane** or **sand** it.

smother VERB
❶ *Pythons smother their prey to death.*
• suffocate, choke, stifle
❷ *Rescuers tried to smother the flames.*
• extinguish, put out, snuff out, douse
❸ *The chips were smothered in ketchup.*
• cover, coat, spread, smear, daub

❹ *She managed to smother a yawn.*
• suppress, stifle, muffle, hold back, conceal

smoulder VERB
❶ *The fire was still smouldering a week later.*
• smoke, glow, burn slowly
❷ *She was smouldering with rage.*
• fume, seethe, burn, boil

smudge NOUN
There were smudges of ink all over the page.
• smear, blot, streak, stain, mark, splodge

smug ADJECTIVE
Why are you looking so smug all of a sudden?
• self-satisfied, pleased with yourself, complacent, superior

snack NOUN
They had a quick snack before leaving.
• refreshments, bite to eat
(*informal*) nibbles
– A mid-morning snack is sometimes called **elevenses**.

snag NOUN
Our holiday plans have hit a snag.
• problem, difficulty, obstacle, hitch, complication, setback, catch
(*informal*) hiccup, glitch

snake NOUN

WORD WEB

Some types of snake:
- adder
- anaconda
- asp
- boa constrictor
- cobra
- garter snake
- grass snake
- mamba
- puff adder
- python
- rattlesnake
- sand snake
- sea snake
- sidewinder
- viper

– A literary word for a snake is a serpent.

snap VERB
❶ *One of the ropes snapped under the strain.*
• break, split, crack, fracture
❷ *The dogs were snapping at them.*
• bite, nip
❸ *'Leave me alone!' the boy snapped.*
• snarl, bark, retort

snare NOUN
A rabbit was caught in a snare.
• trap, wire, net
(*old use*) gin
– To catch an animal in a snare is to **ensnare** or **snare** it.

snarl VERB
❶ *A guard dog snarled as we approached.*
• growl, bare its teeth
❷ *'What do you want?' snarled a voice.*
• snap, bark, growl, thunder

snatch VERB
She snatched the letter from my hand.
• grab, seize, grasp, pluck, wrench away, wrest away

sneak VERB
I managed to sneak in without anyone noticing.
• slip, steal, creep, slink, tiptoe, sidle, skulk

sneaky ADJECTIVE
That was a really sneaky trick.
• sly, underhand, cunning, crafty, devious, furtive, dishonest
OPPOSITE honest

sneer VERB
➤ sneer at
He sneered at my attempts to build a sandcastle.
• make fun of, mock, ridicule, scoff at, jeer at, deride

snigger VERB
Someone sniggered at the back of the room.
• giggle, titter, chuckle, laugh

snip VERB
She snipped off a lock of her hair.
• cut, clip, trim, chop

snippet NOUN
We could hear snippets of their conversation.
• piece, fragment, bit, scrap, morsel, snatch

snivel VERB
For goodness' sake, stop snivelling!
• cry, sob, weep, sniff, whimper, whine

snobbish ADJECTIVE
I didn't like the snobbish atmosphere in the club.
• arrogant, pompous, superior, haughty (*informal*) stuck-up, snooty, toffee-nosed
IDIOM high and mighty
OPPOSITE humble

snoop VERB
A man was seen snooping round the building at night.
• sneak, pry, poke, rummage, spy

snout NOUN
Aardvarks have long, narrow snouts.
• muzzle, nose

snub VERB
She felt snubbed by not being invited.
• insult, offend, slight, spurn, brush off

snug ADJECTIVE
❶ *These boots will keep your feet snug through the winter.*
• cosy, comfortable, warm, relaxed (*informal*) comfy
❷ *Choose a smaller size for a snug fit.*
• tight, close-fitting, figure-hugging
OPPOSITES loose, roomy

soak VERB
❶ *You'll get soaked without a raincoat!*
• wet through, drench, saturate
❷ *Leave the beans to soak in water overnight.*
• steep, immerse, submerge

> **soak something up**
The roots act like a sponge, soaking up rainwater.
• take in, absorb, suck up

soaking ADJECTIVE
They arrived at the campsite soaking and exhausted.
• wet through, drenched, dripping, wringing, saturated, sodden, sopping, soggy
– Ground that has been soaked by rain is **waterlogged**.

soar VERB
❶ *A seagull soared into the air.*
• climb, rise, ascend, fly up
❷ *The number of complaints has soared recently.*
• go up, rise, increase, escalate, shoot up
IDIOMS go through the roof, go sky-high
OPPOSITE plummet

sob VERB
She threw herself on the bed, sobbing uncontrollably.
• cry, weep, bawl, snivel, shed tears (*informal*) blubber

sober ADJECTIVE
❶ *He drank a little wine, but he stayed sober.*
• clear-headed
OPPOSITE drunk
❷ *The funeral was a sober occasion.*
• serious, solemn, sombre, grave, dignified, sedate, subdued
OPPOSITES light-hearted, frivolous

sociable ADJECTIVE
Our new neighbours seem very sociable.
• friendly, outgoing, gregarious, neighbourly, amiable
OPPOSITE unfriendly

social ADJECTIVE
❶ *Chimpanzees live in social groups.*
• communal, collective, community, group
OPPOSITES individual, solitary

❷ *Here is a list of this month's social events.*
• recreational, leisure
OPPOSITE work-related

society NOUN
❶ *We live in a multiracial society.*
• community, culture, civilization, people
❷ *She is a member of the local music society.*
• association, group, organization, club, league, union
❸ *He shunned the society of his fellow students.*
• company, companionship, fellowship, friendship

soft ADJECTIVE
❶ *My head sank into the soft pillow.*
• supple, pliable, springy, spongy, yielding, flexible, squashy
OPPOSITES firm, hard
❷ *The rabbit's fur felt very soft.*
• smooth, silky, velvety, fleecy, feathery, downy
OPPOSITES coarse, rough
❸ *We spoke in soft whispers.*
• quiet, muted, muffled, hushed, low, faint
OPPOSITE loud
❹ *A soft breeze stirred the leaves.*
• gentle, light, mild, delicate
OPPOSITES strong, forceful
❺ *Through the window came the soft light of early morning.*
• pale, muted, subdued, dim, low
OPPOSITES bright, dazzling
❻ *You're being too soft with that puppy.*
• lenient, easy-going, tolerant, indulgent
OPPOSITES strict, tough

soggy ADJECTIVE
The pitch was still soggy underfoot.
• wet, moist, soaked, saturated, sodden, drenched, waterlogged
OPPOSITE dry

soil NOUN
❶ *These plants grow best in well-drained soil.*
• earth, ground, land
– Good fertile soil is **loam**.
– The upper layer of soil is **topsoil**.
❷ *We were glad to be back on home soil.*
• territory, turf, ground, country

sold
past tense see **sell**

soldier NOUN
Two soldiers stood guard outside the gate.
• serviceman or servicewoman
– A soldier paid to fight for a foreign country is a **mercenary**.
– An old word for a soldier is **warrior**.
– Soldiers who use large guns are **artillery**.
– Soldiers who fight on horseback or in armoured vehicles are **cavalry**.
– Soldiers who fight on foot are **infantry**.

sole ADJECTIVE
She was the sole survivor of the shipwreck.
• only, single, one, solitary, lone, unique

solemn ADJECTIVE
❶ *Both men wore a solemn expression.*
• serious, grave, sober, sombre, unsmiling, grim, dour
OPPOSITE cheerful
❷ *The coronation was a solemn occasion.*
• formal, dignified, ceremonial, grand, stately, majestic
OPPOSITE frivolous

solid ADJECTIVE
❶ *These bars are made of solid steel.*
OPPOSITE hollow
❷ *Leave the plaster to turn solid.*
• hard, firm, dense, compact, rigid, unyielding
OPPOSITES soft, liquid
❸ *He slept for a solid nine hours.*
• continuous, uninterrupted, unbroken
❹ *The crown was made of solid gold.*
• pure, genuine

⑤ *The house is built on solid foundations.*
• firm, robust, sound, strong, stable, sturdy
OPPOSITES weak, flimsy

⑥ *She got solid support from her team mates.*
• firm, reliable, dependable, united, unanimous
OPPOSITES weak, divided

solidify VERB
The lava solidifies as it cools.
• harden, become solid, set, stiffen
OPPOSITES soften, liquefy

solitary ADJECTIVE
❶ *He leads a solitary existence.*
• unaccompanied, on your own, reclusive, withdrawn, isolated, friendless, unsociable
OPPOSITE sociable
❷ *There was a solitary light in the distance.*
• single, sole, lone, individual, one, only

solitude NOUN
She longed for peace and solitude.
• privacy, seclusion, isolation, loneliness

solve VERB
There's a mystery we've been trying to solve.
• interpret, explain, answer, work out, find the solution to, unravel, decipher (*informal*) crack

sombre ADJECTIVE
❶ *The hall was painted in sombre shades of grey.*
• dark, dull, dim, dismal, dingy, drab, cheerless
OPPOSITE bright
❷ *Everyone was in a sombre mood that night.*
• gloomy, serious, sober, grave, grim, sad, melancholy, mournful
OPPOSITE cheerful

song NOUN

WORD WEB

Some types of song:

➤ anthem	➤ lay
➤ aria	➤ love song
➤ ballad	➤ lullaby
➤ calypso	➤ madrigal
➤ carol	➤ nursery rhyme
➤ chant	➤ pop song
➤ ditty	➤ psalm
➤ folk song	➤ rap
➤ hymn	➤ round
➤ jingle	➤ shanty
➤ lament	➤ spiritual

- A play or film that includes many songs is a **musical**.

- A song from a musical is a **number**.

- The words for a song are the **lyrics**.

Types of singing voice:

➤ alto	➤ soprano
➤ baritone	➤ tenor
➤ bass	➤ treble
➤ contralto	

soon ADVERB
The others will be back soon.
• before long, in a minute, shortly, presently, quickly

soothe VERB
❶ *The soft music soothed her nerves.*
• calm, comfort, settle, quieten, pacify, relax
❷ *This cream should soothe the pain.*
• ease, alleviate, relieve, lessen, reduce

soothing ADJECTIVE
Soothing music played in the background.
• calming, relaxing, restful, peaceful, gentle

sophisticated ADJECTIVE

❶ *She looks quite sophisticated with her hair up.*
• grown-up, mature, cultivated, cultured, refined
OPPOSITE naive

❷ *He has a sophisticated digital camera.*
• advanced, high-level, complex, intricate, elaborate
OPPOSITES simple, basic

sore ADJECTIVE

My feet are still sore from the walk.
• painful, aching, hurting, smarting, throbbing, tender, sensitive, inflamed, raw

sore NOUN

The dog had a sore on its paw.
• wound, inflammation, swelling, ulcer

sorrow NOUN

❶ *The song expresses the sorrow of parting.*
• sadness, unhappiness, misery, woe, grief, anguish, heartache, heartbreak, melancholy, gloom, wretchedness, despair
– Sorrow because of someone's death is **mourning**.
– Sorrow at being away from home is **homesickness**.
OPPOSITES happiness, joy

❷ *She expressed her sorrow for what she had done.*
• regret, remorse, repentance, apologies

sorry ADJECTIVE

I'm sorry if I upset you in any way.
• apologetic, regretful, remorseful, contrite, ashamed (of), repentant
OPPOSITE unapologetic

➤ **feel sorry for someone**
I actually began to feel sorry for him.
• sympathize with, pity, feel compassion for

sort NOUN

What sort of music do you like?
• kind, type, variety, style, form, class, category, genre
– A sort of animal is a **breed** or **species**.

sort VERB

The books are sorted according to size.
• arrange, organize, class, group, categorize, classify
OPPOSITE mix

➤ **sort something out**
• resolve, settle, deal with, put right, fix, clear up, straighten out

sought

past tense see **seek**

sound NOUN

I heard the sound of approaching footsteps.
• noise, tone
– A loud, harsh sound is a **din** or **racket**.
– Words meaning 'to do with sound' are **acoustic** and **sonic**.
➤ **sonic** waves

WRITING TIPS

DESCRIBING SOUNDS
Types of sound:

➤ bang	➤ gurgle
➤ beep	➤ jangle
➤ blare	➤ jingle
➤ bleep	➤ hiss
➤ boom	➤ honk
➤ buzz	➤ hoot
➤ chime	➤ knock
➤ chug	➤ patter
➤ clang	➤ peal
➤ clank	➤ ping
➤ clap	➤ plop
➤ clash	➤ pop
➤ clatter	➤ putter
➤ click	➤ rap
➤ clink	➤ rasp
➤ clunk	➤ rattle
➤ crack	➤ ring
➤ crackle	➤ roar
➤ crash	➤ rumble
➤ creak	➤ rustle
➤ crunch	➤ scrape
➤ ding	➤ scrunch
➤ drone	➤ sizzle
➤ drum	➤ snap
➤ fizz	➤ sputter

- squeak
- squelch
- swish
- tap
- thud
- thunder
- tick
- tinkle
- toot
- trill
- twang
- whirr
- whistle
- whoosh

Sounds made by people:

- bawl
- bellow
- boo
- boom
- cackle
- chortle
- croak
- cry
- gasp
- groan
- hiccup
- hiss
- howl
- hum
- moan
- murmur
- puff
- scream
- shout
- shriek
- sigh
- sing
- sniff
- snort
- sob
- splutter
- squeal
- stammer
- stutter
- wail
- wheeze
- whimper
- whine
- whisper
- whoop
- yell
- yodel

Adjectives describing sounds:

- blaring
- brittle
- croaky
- deafening
- discordant
- droning
- dulcet
- ear-splitting
- grating
- gruff
- harmonious
- harsh
- high-pitched
- hoarse
- husky
- jarring
- lilting
- mellifluous
- melodious
- piercing
- piping
- rasping
- raucous
- shrill
- squeaky
- sweet
- thin
- throaty
- tinny

sound VERB

A siren sounds when a shark is spotted.
• make a noise, resound, go off, be heard

sound ADJECTIVE

❶ *Parts of the outer wall are still sound.*
• firm, solid, stable, safe, secure, intact, undamaged, in good condition
OPPOSITES unsound, unstable

❷ *The travellers returned safe and sound.*
• well, fit, healthy, in good shape
OPPOSITES unhealthy, unfit

❸ *She gave us a piece of sound advice.*
• good, sensible, wise, reasonable, reliable, trustworthy, valid
OPPOSITES unwise, unreliable

❹ *He fell into a sound sleep.*
• thorough, deep, undisturbed, peaceful
OPPOSITES broken, fitful

sour ADJECTIVE

❶ *These apples are a bit sour.*
• tart, bitter, sharp, acidic
OPPOSITE sweet

❷ *The milk has gone sour.*
• bad, off, rancid, curdled
OPPOSITE fresh

❸ *He gave me a sour look.*
• cross, bad-tempered, grumpy, resentful, bitter

source NOUN

They've found the source of the infection.
• origin, start, starting point, root, cause, head
– The source of a river or stream is usually a **spring**.

south NOUN, ADJECTIVE & ADVERB

Portugal is in the south of Europe.
– The parts of a country or continent in the south are the **southern** parts.
– To travel towards the south is to travel **southward** or **southwards**.
– A wind from the south is a **southerly** wind.
– A person who lives in the south of a country is a **southerner**.

sow VERB

Sow the seeds in parallel rows.
• plant, scatter, disperse, distribute
– To sow an area of ground with seeds is to **seed** it.

space NOUN
① *The spacecraft's mission was to explore deep space.*
• outer space, the cosmos, the universe
② *There wasn't much space to move about.*
• room, capacity, area, volume, expanse
③ *There is a space at the back of the cupboard.*
• gap, hole, cavity, opening, aperture
– A space without any air in it is a **vacuum**.
④ *We moved house twice in the space of a year.*
• period, span, interval, duration, stretch

WORD WEB

Natural objects found in space:

➤ asteroid or planetoid
➤ black hole
➤ comet
➤ constellation
➤ dwarf planet
➤ galaxy
➤ meteor (*informal* shooting star)
➤ meteor shower

➤ Milky Way
➤ moon
➤ nebula
➤ nova
➤ planet
➤ red dwarf
➤ red giant
➤ solar system
➤ star
➤ sun
➤ supernova

SEE ALSO **planet, moon**

– A word that means 'to do with space' is **cosmic**.
➤ cosmic rays

– The scientific study of natural objects in space is **astronomy**.

Terms used in space exploration:

➤ astronaut
➤ heat shield
➤ intergalactic
➤ interplanetary
➤ interstellar
➤ launch
➤ mission
➤ orbit
➤ orbiter

➤ probe
➤ re-entry
➤ rover
➤ satellite
➤ spacecraft
➤ space shuttle
➤ space station
➤ spacesuit
➤ spacewalk

spacious ADJECTIVE
The front room is bright and spacious.
• big, large, roomy, sizeable
OPPOSITES small, cramped

span NOUN
① *The bridge has a span of 200 metres.*
• breadth, length, width, extent, distance, reach
– The length between the wing tips of a bird or an aircraft is its **wingspan**.
② *His novels were published over a span of forty years.*
• period, time, space, interval, duration, stretch

span VERB
A rickety footbridge spanned the river.
• cross, extend across, pass over, stretch over, straddle, bridge, traverse

spare VERB
① *Can you spare any money for a good cause?*
• afford, part with, give, provide, do without, manage without
② *The duke agreed to spare their lives.*
• pardon, have mercy on, reprieve, let off, release, free

spare ADJECTIVE
① *The spare tyre is in the boot.*
• additional, extra, supplementary, reserve, standby, backup, relief, substitute
② *Have you any spare change?*
• surplus, leftover, unused, unwanted, excess, superfluous
③ *The figure in the doorway was tall and spare.*
• lean, thin, skinny, gaunt, spindly

spark NOUN
One firework exploded in a shower of sparks.
• flash, gleam, glint, flicker, twinkle, sparkle

sparkle VERB & NOUN
Her earrings sparkled in the lamplight.
• glitter, glisten, glint, flash, twinkle, shimmer
For tips on describing light see **light**.

a b c d e f g h i j k l m n o p q r s t u v w x y z

sparse ADJECTIVE
Vegetation is more sparse in the dry season.
• scarce, scanty, patchy, thinly scattered (*informal*) thin on the ground
OPPOSITES plentiful, abundant

spatter VERB
The bus spattered mud all over us.
• splash, spray, sprinkle, scatter, shower

speak VERB
❶ *Mitchell was too nervous to speak.*
• talk, communicate, say something, express yourself
❷ *Speak the words clearly into the microphone.*
• say, utter, voice, pronounce, articulate, enunciate

speaker NOUN
We have a line-up of guest speakers.
• lecturer
– A person who makes formal speeches is an **orator**.
– A person who speaks on behalf of an organization is a **spokesperson**.

spear NOUN
The gladiator was armed with a spear and shield.
– A spear used in whaling is a **harpoon**.
– A spear thrown as a sport is a **javelin**.
– A spear carried by a medieval knight on horseback is a **lance**.

special ADJECTIVE
❶ *Today we are celebrating a special occasion.*
• important, significant, memorable, noteworthy, momentous, historic, out-of-the-ordinary
OPPOSITES ordinary, everyday
❷ *Early autumn has its own special beauty.*
• unique, individual, characteristic, distinctive, peculiar
❸ *You need a special camera to film underwater.*
• specific, particular, specialized, tailor-made, purpose-built

speciality NOUN
As an actor, his speciality is playing villains.
• strength, strong point, expertise, forte

specific ADJECTIVE
Can you give us some specific examples?
• detailed, particular, definite, precise, exact, explicit, clear-cut
OPPOSITES general, vague

specify VERB
Please specify your shoe size.
• state, identify, name, detail, define

specimen NOUN
The police asked for a specimen of his handwriting.
• sample, example, illustration, instance, model

speck NOUN
She brushed a speck of dust from her shoes.
• bit, dot, spot, fleck, grain, particle, trace

speckled ADJECTIVE
A brown, speckled egg lay on the nest.
• flecked, speckly, spotted, spotty, mottled
– If you have a lot of brown spots on your skin you are **freckled** or **freckly**.
– Something with patches of colour is **dappled** or **patchy**.

spectacle NOUN
The Mardi Gras parade is a colourful spectacle.
• display, show, sight, performance, exhibition, extravaganza

spectacles PLURAL NOUN
see **glasses**

spectacular ADJECTIVE
❶ *The film opens with a spectacular action sequence.*
• dramatic, exciting, impressive, thrilling, breathtaking, sensational

❷ *The tulips are spectacular at this time of year.*
• eye-catching, showy, striking, stunning, glorious, magnificent

spectator NOUN
Spectators lined the streets.
• watcher, viewer, observer, onlooker
– The spectators at a show are the **audience**.
– The spectators at a sporting event are the **crowd**.
– A person who sees an accident or a crime is a **witness** or an **eyewitness**.

speech NOUN
❶ *His speech was slurred.*
• speaking, talking, articulation, pronunciation, enunciation, diction
❷ *She was invited to give a short speech.*
• talk, address, lecture, oration
– A talk given as part of a religious service is a **sermon**.
– The art of making speeches in public is **oratory**.
❸ *I had learned a speech from Shakespeare.*
– Speech between actors in a play is **dialogue**.
– A speech delivered by a single actor is a **monologue** or **soliloquy**.

speechless ADJECTIVE
She was speechless with surprise.
• dumbstruck, dumbfounded, tongue-tied

speed NOUN
❶ *Could a spaceship travel faster than the speed of light?*
• pace, rate, velocity
– The speed of a piece of music is its **tempo**.
– To increase speed is to **accelerate**.
– To reduce speed is to **decelerate**.
❷ *The rumour spread with astonishing speed.*
• quickness, rapidity, swiftness, alacrity
OPPOSITE slowness

speed VERB
The train sped by.
• race, rush, dash, dart, hurry, hurtle, career, fly, streak, tear, shoot, zoom, zip
➤ **speed up**
The car behind us started to speed up.
• go faster, hurry up, accelerate, pick up speed
OPPOSITE slow down

speedy ADJECTIVE
We wish you a speedy recovery.
• fast, quick, swift, rapid, prompt, brisk, hasty
OPPOSITE slow

spell NOUN
❶ *The spell was believed to ward off evil.*
• charm, incantation
❷ *We are hoping for a spell of dry weather.*
• period, interval, time, stretch, run
➤ **put a spell on someone**
An evil sorcerer had put a spell on her.
• enchant, bewitch

spend VERB
❶ *How much money did you spend today?*
• pay out, use up, expend, get through (*informal*) fork out, shell out
– To spend money unwisely is to **waste**, **squander** or **fritter** it.
OPPOSITE save
❷ *I spent the whole day working on the script.*
• pass, occupy, fill, while away

sphere NOUN
❶ *A glass sphere hung from the ceiling.*
• ball, globe, orb
❷ *She is an expert in the sphere of astronomy.*
• subject, area, field, arena, realm, domain

spherical ADJECTIVE
The earth is roughly spherical.
• round, ball-shaped, globe-shaped

spice NOUN

WORD WEB

Some spices used in cooking:

➤ allspice	➤ garam masala
➤ aniseed	➤ ginger
➤ bay leaf	➤ juniper
➤ black pepper	➤ mace
➤ caraway	➤ mustard
➤ cardamom	➤ nutmeg
➤ cayenne	➤ paprika
➤ chilli	➤ pimento
➤ cinnamon	➤ saffron
➤ cloves	➤ sesame
➤ coriander	➤ star anise
➤ cumin	➤ turmeric
➤ curry powder	➤ white pepper
➤ fennel seed	

spicy ADJECTIVE

He made a spicy vegetable curry for us.
• hot, peppery, fiery, piquant
OPPOSITE mild

spike NOUN

His shirt got caught on a metal spike.
• point, prong, spear, skewer, stake, barb, thorn

spill VERB

❶ He spilled his juice all over the table.
• overturn, upset, tip over
❷ Water spilled onto the floor.
• overflow, pour, splash, slop, slosh
❸ The coins came spilling out.
• pour, stream, flood, surge, swarm

spin VERB

A wheel spins on an axle.
• revolve, rotate, go round, turn, whirl, twirl

spine NOUN

❶ They took an X-ray of the patient's spine.
• backbone, spinal column
– The bones in your spine are your **vertebrae**.

❷ A porcupine has sharp spines.
• spike, prickle, barb, quill, needle, thorn, bristle

spiral NOUN

The staircase wound upwards in a long spiral.
• coil, twist, corkscrew, whorl, helix
– A tight spiral of swirling air or water is a **vortex**.

spirit NOUN

❶ They believe the house is haunted by an evil spirit.
• ghost, phantom, spectre, ghoul, demon
❷ The orchestra played the piece with great spirit.
• energy, liveliness, enthusiasm, vigour, zest, zeal, fire
❸ We come together today in a spirit of friendship and cooperation.
• feeling, mood, atmosphere

spiritual ADJECTIVE

The Pope is the spiritual leader of Catholics around the world.
• religious, holy, sacred
OPPOSITES secular, worldly

spite NOUN

Someone wrote the email out of spite.
• malice, malevolence, ill will, meanness, spitefulness, vindictiveness, nastiness, venom
➤ in spite of
In spite of its name, the dogfish is a type of shark.
• despite, notwithstanding, regardless of

spiteful ADJECTIVE

Any spiteful comments will be deleted.
• malicious, malevolent, vindictive, hateful, venomous, mean, nasty, unkind
OPPOSITE kind

splash VERB

❶ The bus splashed water over us.
• shower, spray, spatter, splatter, squirt, slop, spill
(informal) slosh

❷ *Children splashed about in the water.*
• wade, paddle, wallow
(*informal*) slosh

splendid ADJECTIVE
❶ *There was a splendid banquet in their honour.*
• magnificent, lavish, luxurious, grand, imposing, rich, sumptuous, gorgeous, glorious, resplendent, dazzling
❷ *That's a splendid idea!*
• excellent, first-class, admirable, superb, wonderful, marvellous
(*informal*) brilliant, fantastic, terrific

splendour NOUN
We all admired the splendour of the palace.
• magnificence, grandeur, richness, sumptuousness, glory, resplendence

splinter NOUN
There were splinters of broken glass all over the floor.
• fragment, sliver, shard, chip, flake

splinter VERB
The boat's hull began to splinter and crack.
• shatter, smash, fracture, crack, split

split VERB
❶ *The rock had split into several pieces.*
• break apart, crack open, fracture, rupture, splinter, snap
❷ *He split his trousers climbing over a fence.*
• rip open, tear
❸ *She split the class into two groups.*
• divide, separate, part
❹ *We split the money between us.*
• distribute, share out, divide up, parcel out
➤ split up
The band announced they were splitting up.
• break up, separate, part company, go your separate ways

split NOUN
❶ *There was a large split in the rock.*
• crack, break, breach, fracture, fissure, rupture

❷ *He had a split in the seat of his trousers.*
• tear, rip, slash, slit, cut, rent

spoil VERB
❶ *If I tell you, it'll spoil the surprise.*
• ruin, wreck, destroy, upset, mess up, scupper
❷ *Overcooking will spoil the flavour of the fish.*
• damage, impair, mar, blight
– To spoil the look of something is to **disfigure** or **deface** it.
❸ *Maybe he was spoilt as a child.*
• indulge, pamper, cosset, make a fuss of

spoke
past tense see **speak**

spoken ADJECTIVE
a long section of spoken dialogue
• oral, unwritten
OPPOSITE written

spongy ADJECTIVE
The mossy ground felt spongy to walk on.
• soft, springy, squashy, absorbent, porous

spontaneous ADJECTIVE
The audience broke into spontaneous applause.
• unplanned, impromptu, unpremeditated, unrehearsed, impulsive, instinctive
IDIOMS off-the-cuff, spur-of-the-moment
– An action done without any conscious thought is a **reflex** action.

sport NOUN

WORD WEB
Some team sports:
- ➤ American football
- ➤ baseball
- ➤ basketball
- ➤ bobsleigh
- ➤ bowls
- ➤ cricket
- ➤ curling

a b c d e f g h i j k l m n o p q r s t u v w x y z

A
B
C
D
E
F
G
H
I
J
K
L
M
N
O
P
Q
R
S
T
U
V
W
X
Y
Z

➤ football or soccer	➤ polo
➤ hockey	➤ rounders
➤ ice hockey	➤ rowing
➤ lacrosse	➤ rugby
➤ netball	➤ volleyball
	➤ water polo

Some individual sports:

➤ angling	➤ luge
➤ archery	➤ motor racing
➤ athletics	➤ mountaineering
➤ badminton	➤ orienteering
➤ billiards	➤ pool
➤ bowling	➤ rowing
➤ boxing	➤ sailing
➤ canoeing	➤ showjumping
➤ climbing	➤ skiing
➤ croquet	➤ snooker
➤ cross-country running	➤ snowboarding
➤ cycling	➤ speed skating
➤ darts	➤ squash
➤ diving	➤ surfing
➤ fencing	➤ swimming
➤ golf	➤ table tennis
➤ gymnastics	➤ tae kwon do
➤ horse racing	➤ tennis
➤ ice skating	➤ waterskiing
➤ jogging	➤ weightlifting
➤ judo	➤ windsurfing
➤ karate	➤ wrestling

- Someone who takes part in sport is a sportsman or sportswoman.

SEE ALSO athletics

WRITING TIPS

WRITING ABOUT SPORT
Useful words and phrases:

➤ amateur	➤ first half
➤ arena	➤ foul
➤ champion	➤ full time
➤ coach	➤ game plan
➤ commentator	➤ half time
➤ cup tie	➤ hat trick
➤ draw	➤ heats
➤ extra time	➤ highlights
➤ final whistle	➤ injury time

➤ in play	➤ qualifying round
➤ key player	➤ quarter-final
➤ kick-off	➤ referee
➤ man or woman of the match	➤ score sheet
➤ offside	➤ second half
➤ off target	➤ semi-final
➤ onside	➤ sending off
➤ on target	➤ squad
➤ opponents	➤ stadium
➤ out of bounds	➤ substitute
➤ penalty	➤ supporters
➤ player	➤ tactics
➤ possession	➤ team captain
➤ professional	➤ teammate
	➤ turning point

Verbs:

➤ arc	➤ save
➤ bowl	➤ scoop
➤ catch	➤ score
➤ chip	➤ shoot
➤ curl	➤ slam
➤ dive	➤ smash
➤ dribble	➤ spin
➤ drive	➤ strike
➤ field	➤ swerve
➤ flick	➤ swing
➤ head	➤ swipe
➤ hurl	➤ tap
➤ kick	➤ throw
➤ lob	➤ toss
➤ miss	➤ trickle
➤ pass	➤ volley
➤ pitch	➤ weave
➤ power	

SEE ALSO football

sporting ADJECTIVE
It was sporting of him to admit defeat.
• sportsmanlike, fair, generous, honourable
OPPOSITE unsporting

spot NOUN
❶ *There were a few spots of rust here and there.*
• mark, patch, fleck, speck, dot, blot, stain, blotch, splodge
- Small brown spots on your skin are **freckles**.

– A small dark spot on your skin is a
mole.
– Spots on a bird's egg or plumage are
speckles.
❷ *Her skin is prone to spots.*
• pimple, blackhead
– An area of spots on your skin is a **rash**.
❸ *Here's a good spot for a photograph.*
• place, position, location, site, situation,
setting, venue
❹ *The first spots of rain began to fall.*
• drop, blob, bead

spot VERB
❶ *Did you spot your friends in the
crowd?*
• see, sight, spy, catch sight of, notice,
observe, make out, recognize, detect
❷ *My best coat was all spotted with
mud.*
• mark, stain, blot, spatter, fleck, dot,
speckle, mottle

spotless ADJECTIVE
*The house was spotless from top to
bottom.*
• clean, unmarked, immaculate,
gleaming
(OPPOSITES) dirty, grubby

spout VERB
Molten lava spouted far into the air.
• gush, spew, pour, stream, spurt,
squirt, jet

sprawl VERB
❶ *We found him asleep, sprawling on
the sofa.*
• stretch out, spread out, lean back, loll,
lounge, slouch, slump
❷ *I could see the town sprawling across
the hillside.*
• spread, stretch, scatter

spray VERB
*A burst pipe was spraying water
everywhere.*
• shower, spatter, sprinkle, splash,
squirt, scatter

spray NOUN
❶ *Give the plants a daily spray of water.*
• shower, sprinkling, squirt, mist

❷ *She took out her perfume spray.*
• aerosol, sprinkler, atomizer, mister
❸ *I picked a spray of spring flowers from
the garden.*
• bunch, posy

spread VERB
❶ *Just spread the map on the table.*
• lay out, open out, fan out, unfold,
unfurl, unroll
❷ *Newspapers were spread all over
the floor.*
• scatter, strew
❸ *I spread some butter on my toast.*
• smear, plaster, daub
❹ *A big grin spread across the girl's face.*
• expand, extend, stretch, broaden,
enlarge, swell
❺ *Someone has been spreading
malicious rumours.*
• communicate, circulate, distribute,
transmit, disseminate, make known,
pass round

spread NOUN
❶ *Nothing could stop the spread of the
disease.*
• advance, expansion, diffusion,
circulation, distribution, transmission,
dissemination
❷ *The bird's wings have a spread of
nearly a metre.*
• span, width, extent, stretch,
reach

sprightly ADJECTIVE
She still looks sprightly for her age.
• lively, energetic, active, agile, nimble,
frisky, spry
(OPPOSITE) inactive

spring VERB
❶ *She sprang to her feet in alarm.*
• jump, leap, bound, hop, vault, pounce
❷ *Where did the idea for the character
spring from?*
• originate, arise, derive, stem, come
➤ **spring up**
*Weeds are springing up all over the
garden.*
• appear, develop, emerge, shoot up,
sprout

a
b
c
d
e
f
g
h
i
j
k
l
m
n
o
p
q
r
s
t
u
v
w
x
y
z

A
B
C
D
E
F
G
H
I
J
K
L
M
N
O
P
Q
R
S
T
U
V
W
X
Y
Z

springy ADJECTIVE
The bed felt soft and springy.
• bouncy, elastic, stretchy, flexible, pliable
OPPOSITE rigid

sprinkle VERB
❶ *She sprinkled a little perfume onto a handkerchief.*
• spray, shower, splash, drizzle
❷ *I like to sprinkle sugar over strawberries.*
• scatter, strew, dust

sprout VERB
❶ *Leave the seeds in a warm place to sprout.*
• grow, germinate, put out shoots
❷ *Sites like this are sprouting all over the Internet.*
• spring up, appear, develop, emerge

spruce ADJECTIVE
He looked spruce in his new uniform.
• smart, well-dressed, well-groomed, elegant, neat, trim
OPPOSITE scruffy

spun
past tense see spin

spur VERB
➤ spur someone on
We were spurred on by the thought of adventure.
• encourage, stimulate, motivate, inspire, prompt, galvanize, urge on, egg on

spurt VERB
Dirty water spurted from the pipe.
• gush, spout, shoot out, stream, squirt, jet

spy NOUN
He once worked as a spy.
• agent, secret agent, mole
– A spy who works for two rival countries or organizations is a **double agent**.

W WRITING TIPS

WRITING SPY FICTION
Characters:

➤ agent	➤ operative
➤ codebreaker	➤ secret agent
➤ controller	➤ sleeper
➤ cryptographer	➤ spy catcher
➤ double agent	➤ spymaster
➤ mole	

Useful words and phrases:

➤ behind enemy lines	➤ espionage
➤ briefing	➤ false identity
➤ CIA	➤ FBI
➤ cipher	➤ headquarters
➤ clandestine operation	➤ hidden camera
➤ code book	➤ infiltration
➤ code-breaking	➤ intelligence
➤ counter-espionage	➤ listening device (*informal* bug)
➤ counter-intelligence	➤ MI5
➤ covert	➤ MI6
➤ debriefing	➤ mission
➤ decode	➤ password
➤ decryption	➤ recruitment
➤ deep cover	➤ secret service
➤ defection	➤ special operations
➤ disinformation	➤ spying
➤ encode	➤ surveillance
➤ encryption	➤ transmitting device
	➤ under cover

spy VERB
I thought I spied a familiar face.
• see, sight, spot, catch sight of, notice, observe, make out, detect

squabble VERB
Those two are always squabbling!
• argue, fight, quarrel, bicker, wrangle

squalid ADJECTIVE
The prisoners were kept in a squalid little room.
• dirty, filthy, foul, dingy, degrading, nasty, unpleasant
OPPOSITE clean

squander VERB
He squandered his fortune in gambling.
• waste, throw away, fritter away, misuse
(*informal*) blow
OPPOSITE save

square ADJECTIVE
All the tiles have square corners.
• right-angled
– A pattern of squares is a **chequered** pattern.

squarely ADVERB
The ball hit him squarely in the face.
• directly, straight, head on
OPPOSITE obliquely

squash VERB
❶ The cake got a bit squashed in my bag.
• crush, flatten, press, compress, mangle, mash, pulp
(*informal*) squish
❷ Just squash everything into the suitcase.
• force, stuff, squeeze, cram, jam, pack, ram, wedge

squat VERB
We squatted by the fire, trying to keep warm.
• crouch, huddle, sit on your heels
squat ADJECTIVE
He was a squat little man with a reddish face.
• dumpy, stocky, plump, podgy, portly

squeak NOUN & VERB
❶ The door squeaked.
• creak, grate, rasp
❷ The bird squeaked in its cage.
• chirp, peep, cheep

squeal NOUN & VERB
She squealed with pain.
• cry, yell, yelp, screech, scream, shriek

squeeze VERB
❶ She squeezed my hand tightly.
• press, compress, crush, grip, clasp, pinch, nip
❷ Now squeeze the juice out of lemon.
• extract, press, express, force, wring

❸ Five of us squeezed into the back of the car.
• squash, cram, crowd, stuff, jam, push, ram, shove, wedge

squeeze NOUN
❶ She gave my hand a squeeze.
• press, grip, clasp, pinch, nip
❷ It was a tight squeeze in the back seat.
• squash, crush, jam

squirm VERB
A rabbit had squirmed through a hole in the fence.
• wriggle, writhe, twist

squirt VERB
Tap water squirted all over the floor.
• spurt, spray, shower, gush, spout, shoot, jet

stab VERB
❶ The victim had been stabbed in the chest.
• knife, spear, jab, pierce, impale, run through, skewer
❷ A man was shouting and stabbing a finger in the air.
• stick, thrust, push, jab

stab NOUN
I felt a sudden stab of pain in my chest.
• pang, twinge, prick, sting

stable ADJECTIVE
❶ The ladder doesn't look very stable.
• steady, secure, firm, balanced, solid, fixed
OPPOSITES unstable, wobbly
❷ He's been in a stable relationship for the last few years.
• steady, established, lasting, durable, strong
OPPOSITES casual, temporary

stack NOUN
On the table was a stack of unanswered letters.
• pile, heap, mound, mountain, tower
– A stack of hay is also called a **rick** of hay.

a
b
c
d
e
f
g
h
i
j
k
l
m
n
o
p
q
r
s
t
u
v
w
x
y
z

stack VERB
Just stack the dishes in the sink.
• heap up, pile up

staff NOUN
He knows all the staff at the local library.
• workers, employees, personnel, workforce, team
– The staff on a ship or an aircraft are the **crew**.

stage NOUN
❶ *They went up on the stage to collect their prizes.*
• platform, podium
❷ *This was the final stage of our journey.*
• part, leg, step, phase, portion, section, stretch
❸ *At this stage in her life, she wants to try something new.*
• point, time, juncture, period, phase

stagger VERB
❶ *Dad staggered in carrying a huge parcel.*
• reel, stumble, lurch, totter, teeter, sway, waver, wobble
❷ *I was staggered at the price of the tickets.*
• amaze, astonish, astound, surprise, stun, startle, dumbfound, flabbergast

stagnant ADJECTIVE
Mosquitoes swarmed around the pool of stagnant water.
• still, motionless, static
OPPOSITES flowing, fresh

stain NOUN
There were a few coffee stains on the tablecloth.
• mark, spot, blot, blotch, smear, smudge

stain VERB
❶ *Her trainers were stained with mud.*
• discolour, mark, smear, smudge, soil, dirty, blacken, tarnish
❷ *The wood can be stained a darker shade.*
• dye, colour, tint, tinge

stairs PLURAL NOUN
The stairs up to the front door were worn with age.
• steps
– A set of stairs from one floor to another is a **flight** of stairs or a **staircase** or **stairway**.
– A moving staircase is an **escalator**.
– A handrail at the side of a staircase is a **banister**.

stake NOUN
The fence was made with sharp wooden stakes.
• pole, post, stick, spike, stave, pile

stale ADJECTIVE
❶ *All he had to eat were some stale crusts of bread.*
• old, dry, hard, mouldy, musty, rancid
OPPOSITE fresh
❷ *He keeps coming out with the same old stale ideas.*
• overused, tired, hackneyed, banal, clichéd
OPPOSITES original, fresh

stalk NOUN
❶ *The boy was holding a sunflower stalk.*
• stem, shoot, twig
❷ For parts of a plant see **plant**.

stalk VERB
❶ *The panther began stalking its prey.*
• hunt, pursue, track, trail, follow, shadow, tail
❷ *She turned and stalked out of the room.*
• stride, strut, march, stomp

stall NOUN
We had a stall selling home-made jam.
• stand, table, counter, kiosk, booth

stall VERB
❶ *I could tell the assistant was stalling.*
• play for time, delay, procrastinate, hedge
❷ *See if you can stall them for a few days.*
• delay, detain, hold off

stamina NOUN
Do you have the stamina to run a marathon?
• endurance, staying power, toughness, grit

stammer VERB
He stammered over his opening lines.
• stutter, falter, stumble, splutter

stamp NOUN
I put a first-class stamp on the letter.
– A person who studies or collects stamps is a **philatelist**.

stamp VERB
❶ *Please don't stamp on the flowers.*
• step, tread, trample, crush, flatten
❷ *We stamped our feet to get warm.*
• tramp, stomp
❸ *The librarian stamped my books.*
• print, mark
– To stamp a postmark on a letter is to **frank** it.
– To stamp a mark on cattle with a hot iron is to **brand** them.

stampede NOUN
When the bell went, there was a stampede towards the door.
• charge, rush, dash, rout

stance NOUN
❶ *Try to keep a relaxed stance.*
• posture, position, pose
❷ *What is your stance on nuclear power?*
• opinion, attitude, standpoint, position, policy, line

stand VERB
❶ *Please stand when your name is called.*
• get up, get to your feet, rise
❷ *Stand the ladder against the wall.*
• put, place, set, prop, position, station, erect
❸ *My offer still stands.*
• be valid, remain in force, apply, continue, hold
❹ *How can you stand the noise?*
• bear, abide, endure, put up with, tolerate, withstand
➤ **stand for something**

❶ *What do these initials stand for?*
• mean, indicate, signify, represent
❷ *She won't stand for any arguments.*
• put up with, tolerate, accept, allow, permit
➤ **stand out**
The lettering really stands out.
• catch your eye, leap out, be noticeable, be prominent
➤ **stand up for someone**
He always stands up for his friends.
• support, defend, side with, speak up for
(*informal*) stick up for

stand NOUN
The trophy stood on a wooden stand.
• base, rest, pedestal, plinth
– A three-legged stand for a camera or telescope is a **tripod**.

standard NOUN
❶ *Their writing is of a very high standard.*
• grade, level, quality, calibre
❷ *The house was small by modern standards.*
• criterion, measure, model, guide, benchmark, yardstick
❸ *At dawn they raised the regimental standard for the last time.*
• colours, flag, banner

standard ADJECTIVE
❶ *This is the standard way to set out a letter.*
• normal, usual, common, conventional, typical, customary, established, accepted, orthodox, regular, traditional
OPPOSITES unusual, unorthodox
❷ *It is the standard guide to North American birds.*
• definitive, authoritative, classic, ultimate, best, approved

standstill NOUN
➤ **come to a standstill**
Traffic had come to a standstill.
• stop moving, draw up, pull up, halt, stop
IDIOM grind to a halt

a
b
c
d
e
f
g
h
i
j
k
l
m
n
o
p
q
r
s
t
u
v
w
x
y
z

staple *ADJECTIVE*
> *Rice is the staple food in many countries.*
> • chief, main, principal, standard, basic

star *NOUN*
> ❶ *The sky was full of stars.*
> • celestial body, heavenly body
> – The scientific study of stars is
> **astronomy**.
> – A word meaning 'to do with stars' is
> **stellar**.
> ❷ *Several Hollywood stars attended the
> premiere of the film.*
> • celebrity, idol, superstar

stare *VERB*
> *The eyes in the portrait were staring
> straight at me.*
> • gaze, gape, peer, look
> (*informal*) gawk, gawp
> – To stare angrily at someone is to **glare**
> at them.

start *VERB*
> ❶ *The new series will start in the
> autumn.*
> • begin, commence, get under way, get
> going
> (*informal*) kick off
> OPPOSITES finish, end
> ❷ *Modern ice hockey started in Canada.*
> • originate, arise, begin, be born, come
> into being
> OPPOSITE stop
> ❸ *We're planning to start a film club.*
> • establish, set up, create, found,
> institute, initiate, inaugurate, launch
> OPPOSITES close down, wind up
> ❹ *Press here to start the computer.*
> • switch on, activate, fire up, boot up
> OPPOSITES shut down, deactivate
> ❺ *A crash in the kitchen made me start.*
> • jump, flinch, jerk, twitch, wince

start *NOUN*
> ❶ *Try not to miss the start of the film.*
> • beginning, opening, introduction,
> commencement
> OPPOSITES end, close, finish
> ❷ *She has been with the theatre
> company right from the start.*
> • beginning, outset, creation, inception,
> origin, onset, birth, dawn

> ❸ *Her voice gave me a nasty start.*
> • jump, jolt, shock, surprise

startle *VERB*
> *A sudden noise startled the horses.*
> • alarm, panic, frighten, scare, surprise,
> take someone by surprise, make
> someone jump

starve *VERB*
> *People were left to starve in freezing
> conditions.*
> • die of starvation, go hungry
> – To choose to go without food is to **fast**.

starving (*informal*) *ADJECTIVE*
> *By teatime we were all starving.*
> • hungry, famished, ravenous

state *NOUN*
> ❶ *Much of the building is in a rundown
> state.*
> • condition, shape, order
> ❷ (*informal*) *He gets into a terrible state
> before an exam.*
> • panic, fluster
> (*informal*) flap
> ❸ *The Queen is the head of state.*
> • country, nation

state *VERB*
> *The sign states that photography is
> allowed.*
> • declare, announce, say, express, report,
> proclaim, pronounce, communicate

stately *ADJECTIVE*
> *The funeral service was a stately affair.*
> • dignified, grand, formal, ceremonious,
> imposing, majestic, noble

statement *NOUN*
> *The prime minister made a statement to
> the press.*
> • announcement, declaration,
> communication, report, testimony

station *NOUN*
> ❶ *Does the train stop at the next
> station?*
> – The station at the end of a line is
> the **terminus**.

❷ He was taken to the police station for questioning.
• depot, office, base, headquarters
❸ She usually listens to the local radio station.
• channel, wavelength

station VERB
Two guards were stationed at the entrance.
• post, position, situate, locate, base

stationary ADJECTIVE
The car was stationary when the van hit it.
• still, static, unmoving, immobile, motionless, standing, at rest
OPPOSITE moving

statue NOUN
There is a statue of Nelson Mandela in the park.
• figure, sculpture, carving
– A small statue is a **statuette**.

status NOUN
❶ What was the status of women in Victorian society?
• rank, level, position, grade, place
❷ They were a family of wealth and status.
• importance, prestige, stature, standing

staunch ADJECTIVE
He was a staunch ally of the President.
• firm, strong, faithful, loyal, true, reliable, dependable, steadfast, trusty
OPPOSITES disloyal, unreliable

stay VERB
❶ I'll stay here until you get back.
• wait, remain, hang on, linger
(informal) hang about
OPPOSITES leave, depart
❷ Please try to stay calm.
• keep, remain, carry on being
❸ Do you plan to stay in America long?
• live, reside, dwell, lodge, settle, stop, stop over

stay NOUN
Our friends are here for a short stay.
• visit, stopover, holiday, break

steady ADJECTIVE
❶ Keep a steady grip on the handle.
• stable, secure, fixed, firm, fast, solid, balanced
OPPOSITES unsteady, shaky
❷ We had a steady stream of visitors.
• continuous, uninterrupted, non-stop, constant, consistent, reliable
OPPOSITE intermittent
❸ The runners kept up a steady pace.
• regular, constant, even, smooth, settled, rhythmic, unvarying
OPPOSITE irregular

steady VERB
She steadied herself against the wall.
• balance, stabilize, hold steady

steal VERB
❶ The thieves stole several valuable paintings.
• take, snatch, pilfer
(informal) swipe, lift, nick, pinch, make off with
❷ We both stole quietly out of the room.
• creep, sneak, tiptoe, slip, slink, slope

stealing NOUN
He was found guilty of stealing from his employers.
• robbery, theft
– Stealing from a private house is **burglary** or **housebreaking**.
– Stealing small goods from a shop is **shoplifting**.
– Stealing things of little value is **pilfering**.

stealthy ADJECTIVE
She inched forward with slow, stealthy movements.
• furtive, secretive, surreptitious, sly, sneaky, underhand
OPPOSITES conspicuous, open

steam NOUN
The kitchen was full of steam.
• vapour, mist, haze
– Steam on a cold window is **condensation**.

a b c d e f g h i j k l m n o p q r s t u v w x y z

steamy ADJECTIVE
❶ *The atmosphere in the greenhouse was warm and steamy.*
• humid, muggy, close, damp, moist
❷ *The bathroom mirror was steamy.*
• misty, hazy, cloudy

steep ADJECTIVE
❶ *Steep cliffs overlook the sea.*
• abrupt, sharp, precipitous
– A cliff or drop which is straight up and down is **sheer** or **vertical**.
OPPOSITES gradual, gentle
❷ *(informal) They charge very steep prices.*
• high, overpriced, inflated, exorbitant, extortionate

steer VERB
It can be tricky steering a shopping trolley.
• guide, direct, manoeuvre, drive
– To steer a boat is to **navigate** or **pilot** it.

stem NOUN
It's a plant with a woody stem.
• stalk, shoot, twig

stem VERB
She could no longer stem the flow of tears.
• stop, check, hold back, curb, staunch
➤ **stem from**
His love of writing stems from childhood.
• come from, arise from, spring from, derive from, originate in, have its origins in

step NOUN
❶ *We each took a step closer to the door.*
• pace, stride
❷ *I heard the sound of heavy steps outside.*
• footstep, tread, footfall
❸ *Mind the step as you go in.*
• doorstep, stair, tread
– The steps of a ladder are the **rungs**.
❹ *The first step in making a cake is to weigh the ingredients.*
• stage, phase, action, operation, move

step VERB
Don't step on the broken glass.
• put your foot, tread, walk, stamp, trample, stride, pace
➤ **step down**
He's stepping down at the end of the season.
• resign, stand down, quit, bow out
➤ **step something up**
They have stepped up security at the airport.
• increase, intensify, strengthen, boost

sterile ADJECTIVE
❶ *Very little grows in the sterile soil of the desert.*
• barren, dry, arid, infertile, lifeless
OPPOSITE fertile
❷ *The nurse put a sterile bandage on my arm.*
• sterilized, disinfected, uncontaminated, clean, hygienic, germ-free, antiseptic
OPPOSITE contaminated

stern ADJECTIVE
He gave them a stern look.
• severe, strict, hard, harsh, grim, austere, forbidding, disapproving
OPPOSITES kindly, lenient

stew VERB
see **cook**

stick NOUN
❶ *They collected dry sticks to make a fire.*
• twig, branch, stalk
❷ *He walked with a stick.*
• cane, rod, staff, pole
– A stick used by a conductor is a **baton**.
– A stick carried by a police officer is a **truncheon**.
– A stick used as a weapon is a **club** or **cudgel**.

stick VERB
❶ *He stuck a few drawing pins into the wall.*
• poke, prod, stab, thrust, dig, jab
❷ *Stick the label on the front of the parcel.*
• attach, affix, fasten, join, fix, paste,

glue, tape
❸ The stamp won't stick to the envelope.
• adhere, cling, bond
❹ The rear wheels stuck fast in the mud.
• jam, wedge, catch, get trapped
❺ (informal) I can't stick it here any longer.
• endure, tolerate, stand, bear, abide, put up with
➤ stick out
The shelf sticks out too far.
• jut out, poke out, project, protrude
➤ stick up for
(informal) Thanks for sticking up for me.
• support, stand up for, side with, speak up for, defend

sticky ADJECTIVE
❶ There was a sticky blob of chewing gum on the seat.
• tacky, gummy, gluey
(informal) gooey, icky
❷ It was a hot sticky afternoon.
• humid, muggy, clammy, close, steamy, sultry
OPPOSITE dry
❸ (informal) The hero finds himself in a sticky situation.
• awkward, difficult, tricky, ticklish
(informal) hairy

stiff ADJECTIVE
❶ Use a stiff piece of cardboard as a base.
• rigid, inflexible, firm
OPPOSITES flexible, pliable
❷ Add flour to make a stiff dough.
• thick, solid, firm
OPPOSITES soft, loose
❸ My legs were stiff from crouching.
• aching, achy, painful, taut, tight
OPPOSITE supple
❹ They face stiff opposition in the final.
• strong, powerful, difficult, tough, determined
OPPOSITE weak
❺ There are stiff penalties for dropping litter.
• harsh, severe, tough, strict, stringent, heavy
OPPOSITES lenient, mild

❻ His stiff manner made him hard to talk to.
• formal, awkward, wooden, strained, stilted
OPPOSITES informal, casual, relaxed

stifle VERB
❶ We were nearly stifled by the midday heat.
• suffocate, smother, choke
❷ She tried to stifle a yawn.
• suppress, muffle, hold back, repress, restrain
OPPOSITE let out

still ADJECTIVE
❶ He stood still and held his breath.
• motionless, unmoving, immobile, stationary, static, inert
IDIOM rooted to the spot
❷ It was a crisp still morning.
• quiet, silent, peaceful, tranquil, calm, serene, noiseless, windless

still VERB
I tried to still the trembling in my hand.
• calm, quieten, soothe, settle, silence, hush, lull
OPPOSITES stir, disturb

stimulate VERB
❶ Her travels stimulated her to write a book.
• encourage, inspire, prompt, spur
OPPOSITE discourage
❷ What stimulated your interest in science?
• arouse, provoke, trigger, excite, kindle, stir up
OPPOSITE dampen

sting VERB
❶ I was stung by a wasp.
• bite, nip
❷ The smoke made our eyes sting.
• smart, burn, prick, prickle, tingle

stingy (informal) ADJECTIVE
They're a bit stingy with their portions.
• mean, miserly, penny-pinching
(informal) tight-fisted
OPPOSITE generous

stink NOUN
The stink hits you as soon as you open the door.
• reek, stench, odour, smell
(*informal*) pong

stink VERB
The room stank of smoke.
• reek, smell

stir VERB
❶ *Stir the mixture until it is smooth.*
• mix, beat, blend, whisk
❷ *Something stirred in the bushes behind us.*
• move slightly, shift, rustle
➤ **stir something up**
They are always stirring up trouble.
• arouse, encourage, provoke, set off, trigger, whip up

stir NOUN
The news caused quite a stir.
• fuss, commotion, excitement, to-do

stock NOUN
❶ *Stocks of food were running low.*
• supply, store, reserve, hoard, stockpile
❷ *The grocer was waiting for new stock to arrive.*
• goods, merchandise, wares
❸ *He is descended from Italian stock.*
• descent, ancestry, origin, lineage, family, pedigree, line

stock VERB
Many supermarkets now stock organic food.
• sell, carry, trade in, deal in, keep in stock

stocky ADJECTIVE
He was a short, stocky man.
• dumpy, squat, thickset, solid, sturdy
OPPOSITE thin

stodgy ADJECTIVE
❶ *The pudding was rich and stodgy.*
• heavy, solid, starchy, filling
OPPOSITE light
❷ *It's quite a stodgy book, isn't it?*
• dull, boring, uninteresting, slow, tedious
OPPOSITES lively, interesting

stole
past tense see **steal**

stomach NOUN
I was hungry and my stomach started to rumble.
• belly, abdomen, gut
(*informal*) tummy
– A large rounded stomach is a **paunch**.

stomach VERB
She found it hard to stomach the truth.
• stand, bear, take, accept, tolerate, put up with, endure

stone NOUN
❶ *A boy was throwing stones into the sea.*
• rock, pebble
– A large rounded stone is a **boulder**.
– A mixture of sand and small stones is **gravel**.
– Pebbles on the beach are **shingle**.
– Round stones used to pave a path are **cobbles**.
❷ *The ring had a bright red stone.*
• jewel, gem, gemstone, precious stone

stony ADJECTIVE
❶ *We walked along a stony footpath.*
• pebbly, rocky, shingly
OPPOSITES smooth, sandy
❷ *We were greeted with stony silence.*
• unfriendly, cold, hostile, frosty, icy
OPPOSITES warm, friendly

stood
past tense see **stand**

stoop VERB
We had to stoop to go through the tunnel.
• bend, duck, bow, crouch

stop VERB
❶ *There was no sign of the rain stopping.*
• come to an end, end, finish, cease, conclude, terminate
OPPOSITE start
❷ *How do you stop this machine?*
• switch off, turn off, shut down, halt, deactivate, immobilize

❸ *Please stop asking me questions.*
• give up, cease, discontinue, suspend, leave off, break off
(*informal*) knock off, pack in, quit
OPPOSITES continue, resume
❹ *The bus will stop at the front gates.*
• come to a stop, halt, pull up, draw up, come to rest
❺ *They put a fence up to stop the dog getting out.*
• prevent, obstruct, bar, block, hinder
❻ *She was busy stopping a gap in the window frame.*
• close, plug, seal, block up, bung up

stop NOUN
❶ *Everything suddenly came to a stop.*
• end, finish, conclusion, halt, standstill
❷ *We had a short stop for lunch on the way.*
• break, pause, rest, stay, stopover

store NOUN
❶ *He kept a large store of wine in the cellar.*
• hoard, supply, quantity, stock, stockpile, reserve
❷ *The library has an underground book store.*
• storeroom, storehouse, repository, vault
– A store for food is a **larder** or **pantry**.
– A store for weapons is an **armoury** or **arsenal**.
❸ *She's the manager of the local grocery store.*
For more types of store see **shop**.

store VERB
Squirrels need to store food for the winter.
• save, reserve, set aside, stow away, hoard, stockpile
(*informal*) stash

storey NOUN
There is a restaurant on the top storey.
• floor, level, tier

storm NOUN
❶ *Heavy storms are forecast throughout the country.*
• squall, blizzard, gale, thunderstorm, snowstorm, hurricane, typhoon

(*literary*) tempest
– When a storm begins to develop it is **brewing.**
For tips on describing the weather see **weather.**
❷ *Plans to close the library caused a storm of protest.*
• outburst, outcry, uproar, clamour, fuss, furore

storm VERB
❶ *She stormed out in a rage.*
• march, stride, stalk, stomp, flounce
❷ *Police stormed the building.*
• charge at, rush at, swoop on, attack

stormy ADJECTIVE
❶ *It was a wild and stormy night.*
• blustery, squally, windy, gusty, blowy, thundery, tempestuous
OPPOSITE calm
❷ *Fighting broke out at the end of a stormy meeting.*
• angry, heated, turbulent, violent, passionate

story NOUN
❶ *Do you know any good ghost stories?*
• tale, narrative, anecdote
(*informal*) yarn
❷ *The book tells the story of her childhood.*
• account, history, narrative, saga, plot
– The story of a person's life is their **biography.**
– The story which a person writes of their own life is their **autobiography.**
❸ *It was the front-page story in all the papers.*
• article, item, feature, report, piece
❹ (*informal*) *Have you been telling stories again?*
• lie, tale
(*informal*) fib

stout ADJECTIVE
❶ *Inside was a rather stout lady dressed in black.*
• fat, plump, dumpy, tubby, portly, podgy, rotund, overweight
OPPOSITE thin

❷ *You will need a pair of stout walking boots.*
• strong, sturdy, tough, robust, hardwearing, durable
OPPOSITE flimsy

❸ *The enemy put up a stout resistance.*
• brave, courageous, spirited, plucky, determined, resolute, firm
OPPOSITE weak

stow VERB
We stowed the boxes away in the attic.
• store, put away, pack, hoard

straight ADJECTIVE
❶ *They were driving along a straight stretch of road.*
• direct, unbending
OPPOSITE winding

❷ *Is this mirror straight?*
• level, even, aligned, horizontal, vertical, upright
OPPOSITE crooked

❸ *It took ages to get the room straight.*
• neat, orderly, tidy, in order, shipshape
OPPOSITE untidy

❹ *I just want a straight answer.*
• honest, plain, frank, direct, straightforward, candid
OPPOSITES indirect, evasive

straight ADVERB
❶ *She was looking straight at me.*
• right, directly
❷ *They left straight after breakfast.*
• immediately, promptly, right

straightaway or **straight away** ADVERB
She replied to my text straightaway.
• immediately, at once, right away, without delay, instantly, promptly

straightforward ADJECTIVE
❶ *The recipe is quite straightforward.*
• uncomplicated, simple, easy, clear
OPPOSITE complicated

❷ *I found him straightforward to deal with.*
• frank, honest, straight, direct, plain, candid
OPPOSITE evasive

strain VERB
❶ *The dog was straining at its lead.*
• pull, tug, stretch
❷ *I was straining to see what was happening.*
• struggle, strive, make an effort, endeavour, try, attempt
❸ *I think I've strained a muscle.*
• sprain, injure, pull, twist, wrench
❹ *Take it easy and don't strain yourself.*
• overtax, overreach, exhaust, wear out, tire out
❺ *Strain the liquid to get rid of any lumps.*
• sieve, sift, filter

strain NOUN
❶ *The ropes creaked under the strain.*
• tension, tightness, tautness, stretch
❷ *The strain was beginning to tell on us all.*
• stress, tension, worry, anxiety, pressure

strand NOUN
The strands of the wool began to unravel.
• thread, filament, fibre

stranded ADJECTIVE
❶ *A whale lay stranded on the beach.*
• run aground, beached, marooned
❷ *She found herself stranded without any money.*
• abandoned, deserted, helpless, lost, adrift
IDIOM high and dry

strange ADJECTIVE
❶ *A strange thing happened last night.*
• unusual, odd, peculiar, funny, abnormal, curious, mysterious, weird, bizarre
OPPOSITES ordinary, normal
❷ *I find it hard to get to sleep in a strange bed.*
• unfamiliar, unknown, new, alien
OPPOSITE familiar

stranger NOUN
Actually, I'm a stranger here myself.
• newcomer, outsider, visitor, foreigner

strangle VERB
The victim had been strangled.
• throttle, choke

strap NOUN
The trunk was fastened with leather straps.
• belt, band, tie, thong

strategy NOUN
The school has a strategy to deal with bullying.
• plan, policy, procedure, approach, scheme, programme

stray VERB
Don't stray too far from the shore.
• wander off, drift, roam

streak NOUN
❶ *There was a streak of bright light in the sky.*
• band, line, stripe, strip, slash
❷ *She had left streaks of mud on the floor.*
• smear, stain, mark
❸ *There is a streak of vanity in his character.*
• element, trace, strain, vein

streak VERB
❶ *His face was streaked with tears.*
• smear, smudge, stain, mark, line
❷ *A group of motorbikes streaked past.*
• rush, speed, dash, fly, hurtle, flash, tear, zoom

stream NOUN
❶ *They drank from a clear mountain stream.*
• brook, rivulet
(North American & Australian) creek
(Scottish) burn
❷ *A stream of water poured through the hole.*
• flow, gush, jet, flood, rush, torrent, cataract, cascade
❸ *The museum has a steady stream of visitors.*
• series, string, line, succession

stream VERB
❶ *Water streamed down the basement walls.*
• pour, flow, run, gush, spill, cascade
❷ *Thousands of fans streamed through the gates.*
• swarm, surge, pile, pour, flood

street NOUN
see road

strength NOUN
❶ *Hercules was known for his enormous strength.*
• power, might, muscle, brawn, force, vigour
❷ *We need to test the strength of the roof.*
• toughness, sturdiness, robustness, firmness, solidity, resilience
❸ *The real strength of the team is in defence.*
• strong point, asset, advantage, forte, speciality
OPPOSITE weakness

strengthen VERB
❶ *Regular exercise strengthens your muscles.*
• make stronger, build up
❷ *Steel is used to strengthen concrete.*
• fortify, reinforce, stiffen, harden, toughen
OPPOSITE weaken

strenuous ADJECTIVE
❶ *The doctor told him to avoid strenuous exercise.*
• hard, tough, difficult, demanding, tiring, taxing, exhausting, gruelling
OPPOSITE easy
❷ *We are making strenuous efforts to save energy.*
• determined, strong, intense, vigorous, energetic, resolute
OPPOSITE feeble

stress NOUN
❶ *There are different ways of coping with the stress of exams.*
• strain, pressure, tension, worry, anxiety

❷ My piano teacher puts great stress on the need to practise.
• emphasis, importance, weight

stress VERB
He stressed the need for absolute secrecy.
• emphasize, draw attention to, highlight, underline

stretch VERB
❶ He stretched the rubber band until it snapped.
• extend, draw out, pull out, elongate, lengthen, expand
❷ She stretched her arms wide.
• extend, open out, reach out, straighten, spread out
❸ The sand dunes stretch for miles.
• continue, extend, go on

stretch NOUN
❶ It is a beautiful stretch of countryside.
• area, expanse, tract, sweep
❷ This is a dangerous stretch of the river.
• section, length, piece
❸ He had a brief stretch in the army.
• spell, period, time, stint

strict ADJECTIVE
❶ The sisters were brought up in a strict household.
• harsh, severe, stern, firm, rigid, authoritarian
OPPOSITE lenient
❷ He left strict instructions in his will.
• precise, exact, careful, meticulous
OPPOSITES vague, loose
❸ Please treat this in strict confidence.
• absolute, complete, total, utter

stride VERB
She strode across the hall to greet us.
• march, step, pace

stride NOUN
He took a stride towards the door.
• pace, step, tread

strike VERB
❶ He struck his head on the low ceiling.
• hit, knock, bang, bash, bump, beat, thump
(informal) wallop, whack

❷ The driver lost control and struck a lamp post.
• collide with, crash into, bang into, run into, hit
❸ The enemy could strike at any time.
• attack, pounce
❹ The clock struck midnight.
• chime, ring out, sound

striking ADJECTIVE
❶ Her eyes were her most striking feature.
• impressive, stunning, spectacular, outstanding, extraordinary, remarkable, astonishing, memorable, breathtaking
OPPOSITE unremarkable
❷ The resemblance between them is striking.
• conspicuous, noticeable, marked, obvious, strong, prominent, unmistakable
OPPOSITE inconspicuous

string NOUN
❶ The label was tied on with string.
• rope, cord, twine
❷ They have received a string of complaints.
• series, succession, chain, sequence, run

string VERB
Lights were strung from tree to tree.
• hang, suspend, sling, thread, loop

stringy ADJECTIVE
The meat is very stringy.
• chewy, fibrous, tough
OPPOSITE tender

strip VERB
❶ Deer had stripped the bark off the trees.
• peel, remove, scrape
OPPOSITES cover, wrap
❷ He stripped and got into the bath.
• get undressed, undress
(formal) disrobe
OPPOSITE dress

strip NOUN
Tear the paper into narrow strips.
• band, length, ribbon, piece, bit

stripe *NOUN*
The tablecloth had a pattern of blue and white stripes.
• line, strip, band, bar

strive *VERB*
We strive to do the best we can.
• try hard, aim, attempt, endeavour

stroke *NOUN*
❶ He split the log with a single stroke.
• blow, hit, action, movement, motion
❷ She rubbed out a few pencil strokes.
• line, mark

stroke *VERB*
Cats like to be stroked under the chin.
• pat, caress, fondle, pet, touch, rub

stroll *VERB*
After lunch, we strolled along the beach.
• walk slowly, amble, saunter

strong *ADJECTIVE*

OVERUSED WORD

❶ **A strong person, strong body:**

➤ powerful   ➤ brawny
➤ muscular   ➤ burly
➤ well-built   ➤ strapping
➤ beefy   ➤ athletic

(*literary*) mighty

Swimmers need to develop powerful shoulder muscles.

OPPOSITES weak, puny

❷ **Strong material:**

➤ robust   ➤ durable
➤ sturdy   ➤ long-lasting
➤ tough   ➤ stout
➤ hard-wearing   ➤ substantial
➤ heavy-duty

The drumsticks are made from hard-wearing maple.

OPPOSITES fragile, flimsy

❸ **A strong light, strong colour:**

➤ bright   ➤ brilliant

➤ dazzling   ➤ intense
➤ glaring

He looked nervous under the glaring camera lights.

❹ **A strong flavour, strong smell:**

➤ intense   ➤ piquant
➤ pronounced   ➤ tangy
➤ overpowering   ➤ concentrated
➤ pungent   ➤ undiluted

There was the pungent smell of burning rubber.

OPPOSITES faint, mild

❺ **A strong argument, strong case:**

➤ convincing   ➤ sound
➤ persuasive   ➤ solid
➤ effective   ➤ valid
➤ forceful   ➤ cogent
➤ compelling

The police have solid evidence of his guilt.

OPPOSITES weak, feeble, flimsy

❻ **A strong interest, strong supporter:**

➤ enthusiastic   ➤ fervent
➤ keen   ➤ avid
➤ eager   ➤ zealous
➤ passionate

I've been an avid fan of the band for years.

OPPOSITES slight, casual

struck
past tense see **strike**

structure *NOUN*
❶ The new dam is a massive concrete structure.
• building, construction, edifice
❷ Can you explain the structure of the poem?
• design, plan, framework, shape, form, arrangement, organization

struggle VERB
❶ *We struggled to get free.*
• wrestle, tussle, fight, battle, grapple
❷ *She struggled over the wet rocks.*
• stagger, stumble, labour, flounder
❸ *I struggled to make sense of the letter.*
• try hard, strive, strain, make every effort

struggle NOUN
❶ *There were some signs of a struggle.*
• fight, tussle, scuffle, brawl, clash, conflict
❷ *The book is about the struggle to get the vote for women.*
• campaign, battle, crusade, drive, push
❸ *I found the language a struggle at first.*
• effort, exertion, problem, difficulty

stubborn ADJECTIVE
My sister can be stubborn when she wants to be.
• obstinate, headstrong, strong-willed, wilful, uncooperative, inflexible, pig-headed
OPPOSITE compliant

stuck ADJECTIVE
❶ *The bottom drawer is stuck.*
• jammed, immovable, wedged
❷ *I'm completely stuck on the last question.*
• baffled, beaten, stumped, at a loss

stuck-up ADJECTIVE
(*informal*)
Our neighbours are really stuck-up.
• arrogant, conceited, haughty, proud, snobbish, superior
• (*informal*) snooty, toffee-nosed
OPPOSITE humble

stud VERB
➤ **studded with**
The lid of the chest was studded with jewels.
• inlaid with, dotted with, encrusted with

student NOUN
❶ *His children are students at the local school.*
• pupil, schoolboy, schoolgirl
❷ *She is a medical student.*
• undergraduate
– A person who has been awarded a university degree is a **graduate**.
– A student who is studying for a second degree is a **postgraduate**.

studious ADJECTIVE
He is a quiet, studious boy.
• hard-working, diligent, scholarly, academic, bookish
(*informal*) swotty

study VERB
❶ *She spent a year abroad studying French.*
• learn about, read, be taught
❷ *Scientists are studying the effects of climate change.*
• research, investigate, examine, analyse, survey, review
❸ *He has to study for his exams.*
• revise, cram
(*informal*) swot
❹ *She studied his face for a moment.*
• examine, inspect, scrutinize, look closely at, peer at

study NOUN
❶ *He got his degree after four long years of study.*
• learning, education, schooling, tuition, research
❷ *A new study of reading habits has been published.*
• investigation, examination, analysis, review, survey, enquiry (into)
❸ *Darwin used this room as his study.*
• workroom, office, studio
Words which mean 'the scientific study' of a subject often end with -logy or -ology, for example *cosmology*, *criminology* and *mineralogy*.

stuff NOUN
❶ *What's this stuff at the bottom of the glass?*
• matter, substance, material

❷ *The cupboard is crammed full of stuff.*
• things, odds and ends, bits and pieces, paraphernalia
❸ *(informal) Where can I put my stuff?*
• belongings, possessions, things
(informal) gear

stuff VERB
❶ *The cushions are stuffed with foam rubber.*
• fill, pad, upholster
❷ *I quickly stuffed all the papers into a drawer.*
• shove, push, thrust, force, squeeze, jam, pack, cram, ram

stuffy ADJECTIVE
❶ *Open a window – it's stuffy in here.*
• airless, close, humid, stifling, musty, unventilated
OPPOSITE airy
❷ *I find the writing style a bit stuffy.*
• pompous, starchy, stodgy, staid, old-fashioned, dull, dreary
OPPOSITES lively, fresh

stumble VERB
❶ *He stumbled backwards and fell over a chair.*
• trip, lose your footing, stagger, totter, flounder, lurch
❷ *She stumbled over her opening lines.*
• stammer, stutter, falter, hesitate
➤ **stumble across something**
I stumbled across some old photos.
• come across, find, unearth, discover, happen on, chance upon

stump VERB
We were all stumped by the last question.
• baffle, bewilder, puzzle, perplex, mystify
(informal) flummox

stun VERB
❶ *The pilot was alive but stunned.*
• daze, make unconscious, knock out, knock senseless
❷ *The whole town was stunned by the news.*
• amaze, astonish, astound, shock, stagger, stupefy, bewilder, dumbfound

stunning ADJECTIVE
Here are some stunning images of the Earth from space.
• spectacular, breathtaking, glorious, magnificent, gorgeous, superb, sublime, awesome

stunt NOUN
The acrobats performed breathtaking stunts.
• feat, exploit, act, trick

stupid ADJECTIVE
❶ *He is not as stupid as he looks.*
• dense, dim, dim-witted, brainless, unintelligent, slow, dopey, dull, simple, feeble-minded, half-witted
(informal) thick
OPPOSITE intelligent
❷ *It was a stupid idea anyway.*
• foolish, silly, idiotic, senseless, mindless, foolhardy, unwise, mad, crazy, hare-brained
(informal) daft
OPPOSITE sensible

sturdy ADJECTIVE
❶ *He was tall and sturdy for his age.*
• well-built, strapping, muscular, strong, robust, brawny, burly, powerful, solid
OPPOSITES weak, puny
❷ *She bought a pair of sturdy walking boots.*
• robust, strong, tough, stout, hard-wearing, durable, substantial
OPPOSITE flimsy

stutter VERB
He tends to stutter when he's nervous.
• stammer, stumble, falter

style NOUN
❶ *What style of shoes are you looking for?*
• design, pattern, fashion
❷ *The book is written in an informal style.*
• manner, tone, way, wording
❸ *She always dresses with great style.*
• elegance, stylishness, taste, sophistication, flair

stylish ADJECTIVE
He always manages to look stylish.
• fashionable, elegant, chic, smart, sophisticated, tasteful, dapper (*informal*) trendy, natty, snazzy
OPPOSITES unfashionable, dowdy

subdue VERB
❶ *The army quickly subdued all opposition.*
• conquer, defeat, overcome, overpower, quell, suppress, crush, vanquish
❷ *She struggled to subdue her true feelings.*
• suppress, restrain, repress, check, hold back, curb, control

subject NOUN
❶ *She has strong views on the subject.*
• matter, issue, question, point, theme, topic, concern
❷ *What is your favourite subject at school?*
• area, field, discipline, topic
❸ *His passport shows that he is a British subject.*
• citizen, national

subject VERB
➤ subject someone to
They subjected him to hours of questioning.
• put through, force to undergo, expose to, lay open to

submerge VERB
❶ *The submarine had no time to submerge.*
• go under water, go down, sink, dive, plunge
OPPOSITE surface
❷ *The village was now partly submerged.*
• flood, engulf, immerse, inundate, swallow up, swamp

submit VERB
❶ *He was finally forced to submit to his opponent.*
• surrender, give in, yield, capitulate
❷ *Submit your plans to the committee.*
• put forward, hand in, present, enter, offer, propose

subordinate ADJECTIVE
It was not easy for her to accept a subordinate role.
• lesser, lower, inferior, junior
OPPOSITES superior, higher

subscribe VERB
➤ subscribe to something
How do you subscribe to the mailing list?
• become a member of, sign up to, enlist in
OPPOSITE unsubscribe

subsequent ADJECTIVE
Subsequent events proved that she was right.
• following, later, succeeding, ensuing, next
OPPOSITE previous

subside VERB
❶ *One side of the old cottage has started to subside.*
• sink, settle, give way, collapse
❷ *The flood waters will eventually subside.*
• recede, ebb, go down, fall, decline
❸ *The pain should subside in a day or two.*
• decrease, diminish, lessen, ease, die down, dwindle

substance NOUN
❶ *A diamond is the hardest substance on Earth.*
• material, matter, stuff
❷ *What was the substance of the report?*
• content, subject matter, essence, gist

substantial ADJECTIVE
❶ *We have made substantial changes to the script.*
• considerable, significant, sizeable, important, major, appreciable, generous, worthwhile
OPPOSITES minor, insignificant
❷ *The farmhouse is a substantial building.*
• strong, sturdy, solid, robust, stout, hefty, durable, sound, well-built
OPPOSITE flimsy

A B C D E F G H I J K L M N O P Q R S T U V W X Y Z

substitute *NOUN*
He came on as a substitute in extra time.
• replacement, reserve, standby, stand-in
(*informal*) sub
– Someone who can take the place of an actor is an **understudy**.

substitute *VERB*
You can substitute honey for sugar in this recipe.
• exchange, swap, switch
You can also say: *'Honey can take the place of sugar.'* or *'You can replace sugar with honey.'*

subtle *ADJECTIVE*
❶ *The walls are a subtle shade of grey.*
• faint, delicate, soft, gentle, pale, mild, subdued, muted
OPPOSITES strong, bright
❷ *She noticed a subtle change in the atmosphere.*
• slight, gradual, negligible, minute, fine
OPPOSITE pronounced
❸ *I tried to give her a subtle hint.*
• gentle, tactful, indirect
OPPOSITE obvious

subtract *VERB*
Subtract this number from your final score.
• take away, deduct, remove
OPPOSITE add

suburbs *PLURAL NOUN*
They live in the suburbs of Melbourne.
• outskirts, outer areas, fringes, suburbia

succeed *VERB*
❶ *You have to work hard if you want to succeed.*
• be successful, do well, prosper, flourish, thrive
(*informal*) make it
❷ *No one thought the plan would succeed.*
• be effective, work out, turn out well
(*informal*) come off
OPPOSITE fail
❸ *Edward VII succeeded Queen Victoria.*
• come after, follow, replace,

take over from
OPPOSITE precede

success *NOUN*
❶ *She talked about her success as an author.*
• achievement, attainment, fame
❷ *The team has had an incredible run of success.*
• victory, win, triumph
❸ *The success of the mission depends on us.*
• effectiveness, successful outcome
OPPOSITE failure
❹ *The show was a runaway success.*
• hit, best-seller, winner
(*informal*) smash, smash hit

successful *ADJECTIVE*
❶ *He owns a successful chain of restaurants.*
• thriving, flourishing, booming, prosperous, profitable, popular
❷ *A trophy is awarded to the successful team.*
• winning, victorious, triumphant
OPPOSITE unsuccessful

succession *NOUN*
He received a succession of mysterious emails.
• series, sequence, run, string, chain, trail

successive *ADJECTIVE*
We are aiming for a third successive win.
• consecutive, uninterrupted, in succession, in a row, running

suck *VERB*
❶ *A sponge will suck up water.*
• soak up, draw up, absorb
❷ *The canoe was sucked into the whirlpool.*
• pull in, draw in
OPPOSITE push out

sudden *ADJECTIVE*
❶ *She felt a sudden urge to burst into song.*
• unexpected, unforeseen, impulsive, rash, quick
OPPOSITE expected

489

❷ *The bus came to a sudden halt.*
• abrupt, sharp, rapid, swift
OPPOSITE gradual

suffer VERB
❶ *I hate to see animals suffer.*
• be in pain, hurt, be in distress
❷ *The team suffered a humiliating defeat.*
• experience, undergo, go through, be subjected to, endure, face
❸ *She's not sleeping and her work is suffering.*
• be damaged, be impaired, diminish, decline, dip
➤ **suffer from something**
He suffers from a severe nut allergy.
• be afflicted by, be troubled with, have

suffering NOUN
The people endured great suffering during the war.
• hardship, deprivation, misery, anguish, pain, distress, affliction, trauma

sufficient ADJECTIVE
Make sure you get sufficient sleep.
• enough, adequate, ample, plenty of
OPPOSITE insufficient

suffocate VERB
Most of the casualties were suffocated by smoke.
• choke, asphyxiate, stifle, smother

suggest VERB
❶ *Viewers were asked to suggest a name for the show.*
• propose, put forward, nominate, recommend, advocate, advise
❷ *Her smile suggested that she agreed with me.*
• indicate, signify, show, imply, hint

suggestion NOUN
❶ *Does anyone have an alternative suggestion?*
• proposal, plan, idea, proposition, recommendation
❷ *There was a suggestion of a sob*

in her voice.
• hint, sign, indication, trace, suspicion, implication

suit VERB
❶ *Which date would suit you best?*
• be convenient for, be suitable for, please, satisfy
OPPOSITE displease
❷ *That colour really suits you.*
• look good on, become, flatter

suitable ADJECTIVE
❶ *Please wear clothes suitable for wet weather.*
• appropriate, apt, fitting, fit, suited (to), right
OPPOSITE unsuitable
❷ *Would tomorrow morning be a suitable time to meet?*
• convenient, acceptable, satisfactory
OPPOSITE inconvenient

sulk VERB
She was still sulking and wouldn't join in.
• be sullen, mope, brood, pout

sulky ADJECTIVE
He was turning into a sulky teenager.
• moody, sullen, brooding, moping, grumpy

sullen ADJECTIVE
The rest of us ate in sullen silence.
• sulky, moody, bad-tempered, surly, sour
OPPOSITES cheerful, good-tempered

sum NOUN
❶ *She can do complicated sums in her head.*
• calculation, addition, problem
❷ *What is the sum of the remaining numbers?*
• total, tally, aggregate
❸ *They lost a large sum of money.*
• amount, quantity

sum VERB
➤ **sum up**
Let me sum up the situation as I see it.
• summarize, outline, review
(*informal*) recap

summarize VERB
Can you summarize the main points of the story?
• sum up, outline, review, condense, abridge
IDIOM put in a nutshell

summary NOUN
Give a brief summary of your idea.
• synopsis, precis, abstract, outline, rundown

summit NOUN
The summit of the mountain was shrouded in mist.
• top, peak, crown, cap, tip
OPPOSITE base

summon VERB
❶ *The king summoned his knights from far and wide.*
• call for, send for, ask for, bid to come
❷ *I finally summoned the courage to phone.*
• gather, rally, muster

sun NOUN
Lizards bask in the sun to get warm.
• sunshine, sunlight
– To sit or lie in the sun is to **sunbathe**.
– A word meaning 'to do with the sun' is **solar**.

sunlight NOUN
These plants need a lot of sunlight.
• daylight, sun, sunshine
– Rays of light from the sun are **sunbeams**.

sunny ADJECTIVE
❶ *It was a beautiful sunny day.*
• bright, clear, cloudless, fine
OPPOSITES dull, overcast
❷ *We sat in a sunny spot in the garden.*
• sunlit, sun-baked, sun-drenched
OPPOSITE shady
❸ *She has a naturally sunny nature.*
• cheerful, happy, bright, joyful, merry, jolly
(*informal*) upbeat
OPPOSITES sad, melancholy

sunrise NOUN
They left at sunrise.
• dawn, daybreak, first light
(*literary*) break of day
OPPOSITE sunset

sunset NOUN
At sunset the cliffs are tinted red and gold.
• nightfall, dusk, twilight, close of day
(*North American*) sundown
OPPOSITE sunrise

superb ADJECTIVE
The Brazilian scored a superb late goal.
• excellent, outstanding, exceptional, tremendous, marvellous, wonderful, fine, superior, superlative, top-notch
(*informal*) brilliant, fantastic, terrific, fabulous, sensational, super
OPPOSITES bad, terrible

superficial ADJECTIVE
❶ *Don't worry, it's only a superficial scratch.*
• on the surface, shallow, slight
OPPOSITE deep
❷ *The programme gives a rather superficial view of the subject.*
• cursory, casual, lightweight, shallow, frivolous, trivial
OPPOSITES thorough, profound

superfluous ADJECTIVE
Get rid of any superfluous words.
• excess, unnecessary, redundant, surplus, spare, unwanted
OPPOSITE necessary

superior ADJECTIVE
❶ *A soldier should salute a superior officer.*
• senior, higher-ranking
OPPOSITES inferior, junior
❷ *They make chocolates of superior quality.*
• first-class, first-rate, top, top-notch, choice, select, finest, best
OPPOSITES inferior, substandard
❸ *I don't like his superior attitude.*
• arrogant, haughty, snobbish, self-important

a b c d e f g h i j k l m n o p q r s t u v w x y z

A
B
C
D
E
F
G
H
I
J
K
L
M
N
O
P
Q
R
S
T
U
V
W
X
Y
Z

(*informal*) snooty, stuck-up
IDIOM high and mighty

supernatural ADJECTIVE
*The old man claimed to have
supernatural powers.*
• magic, magical, miraculous, mystical,
paranormal, occult
OPPOSITE natural

supervise VERB
*Young children must be supervised by an
adult in the park.*
• oversee, superintend, watch over, be
in charge of, be responsible for, direct,
manage
IDIOM keep an eye on
– To supervise candidates in an exam is
to **invigilate**.

supple ADJECTIVE
❶ *These shoes are made of supple
leather.*
• flexible, pliable, soft
OPPOSITES stiff, rigid
❷ *Regular exercise helps to keep your
body supple.*
• agile, nimble, flexible, lithe

supplementary ADJECTIVE
*There is a supplementary charge for
postage.*
• additional, extra

supply VERB
❶ *The art shop can supply you with
paints.*
• provide, furnish, equip
– To supply someone with weapons is to
arm them.
❷ *They grow enough food to supply their
needs.*
• satisfy, meet, fulfil, cater for

supply NOUN
*We keep a supply of paper in the
cupboard.*
• quantity, stock, store, reserve, cache,
hoard
➤ **supplies**
I bought some supplies for the trip.
• provisions, stores, rations, food,
necessities

support VERB
❶ *Timber beams support the roof.*
• hold up, prop up, buttress, reinforce
❷ *How much weight will the bridge
support?*
• bear, carry, stand
❸ *Not many people supported this idea.*
• back, favour, advocate, champion,
promote, endorse
❹ *His friends supported him when he
was in trouble.*
• help, aid, assist, stand by, rally round
❺ *She has two children to support.*
• provide for, maintain, keep
❻ *He supports several local charities.*
• donate to, contribute to, give to
❼ *Which football team do you support?*
• be a supporter of, follow

support NOUN
❶ *She thanked her family for their
support.*
• backing, encouragement, aid, help,
assistance
❷ *The stadium was built with support
from local businesses.*
• donations, contributions, sponsorship,
subsidy, funds
❸ *The shelves rest on wooden supports.*
• prop, brace, bracket, strut, upright,
post
– A support built against a wall is a
buttress.
– A support put under a board to make a
table is a **trestle**.

supporter NOUN
❶ *The home supporters went wild.*
• fan, follower
❷ *He is a well-known supporter of
animal rights.*
• champion, advocate, backer, defender,
upholder

suppose VERB
❶ *I suppose you're wondering why I'm
here.*
• expect, presume, assume, guess
IDIOMS I take it, I dare say
❷ *Suppose you could travel back in time.*
• imagine, pretend, let's say

> **be supposed to do something**
Traditionally, ghosts are not supposed to speak.
• be meant to, be expected to, be due to, ought to, should

suppress VERB
❶ *The army soon suppressed the rebellion.*
• crush, quash, quell, curb, put down, stamp out, crack down on
❷ *She could not suppress a smile.*
• check, hold back, stifle, restrain, repress, bottle up, contain
– To suppress ideas for political or moral reasons is to **censor** them.

supreme ADJECTIVE
❶ *He is the supreme commander of the armed forces.*
• highest, superior, chief, head, top, principal, foremost, prime
❷ *With a supreme effort, she managed not to laugh.*
• extreme, enormous, very great, exceptional, extraordinary, remarkable

sure ADJECTIVE
❶ *Are you sure this is the right address?*
• certain, positive, confident, definite, convinced, satisfied
OPPOSITES unsure, uncertain
❷ *She's sure to find out eventually.*
• bound, likely, certain
OPPOSITE unlikely
❸ *He was pacing the floor, a sure sign he was nervous.*
• clear, definite, certain, reliable, undeniable, unambiguous
OPPOSITES unclear, doubtful

surface NOUN
❶ *The surface of Mars is barren and rocky.*
• exterior, outside, top
OPPOSITES inside, interior
❷ *A cube has six surfaces.*
• face, side, facet

surface VERB
❶ *The submarine slowly surfaced.*
• rise to the surface, come up, emerge
(*informal*) pop up

❷ *The road is surfaced with cobbles.*
• cover, pave, coat

surge VERB
❶ *Huge waves surged over the sea wall.*
• rise, roll, heave, billow, sweep, burst
❷ *Without warning, the crowd surged forward.*
• rush, push, sweep

surge NOUN
❶ *I felt a surge of panic.*
• rush, wave, upsurge, outpouring, onrush
❷ *There has been an unexpected surge in sales.*
• rise, increase, growth, escalation

surly ADJECTIVE
The landlord muttered a surly greeting.
• bad-tempered, unfriendly, sullen, sulky, grumpy

surpass VERB
This trip has surpassed all my expectations.
• beat, better, exceed, do better than, improve on, outdo, outshine, eclipse

surplus NOUN
We have a surplus of tomatoes from our garden.
• excess, surfeit, glut, oversupply
OPPOSITES shortage, dearth

surplus ADJECTIVE
The body stores surplus food as fat.
• excess, superfluous, spare, unneeded, unwanted, leftover

surprise NOUN
❶ *The news came as a complete surprise.*
• revelation, shock
(*informal*) bombshell, eye-opener
IDIOM bolt from the blue
❷ *To my surprise, I passed the audition.*
• amazement, astonishment, bewilderment, disbelief

surprised ADJECTIVE
They seemed genuinely surprised to see me.
• amazed, astonished, astounded, taken

a
b
c
d
e
f
g
h
i
j
k
l
m
n
o
p
q
r
s
t
u
v
w
x
y
z

A
B
C
D
E
F
G
H
I
J
K
L
M
N
O
P
Q
R
S
T
U
V
W
X
Y
Z

aback, startled, stunned, dumbfounded
(*informal*) flabbergasted

surprising ADJECTIVE
*Our experiment produced a surprising
result.*
• unexpected, unforeseen,
extraordinary, astonishing, remarkable,
incredible, staggering, startling
OPPOSITES expected, predictable

surrender VERB
❶ *After months of fighting, the rebels
were forced to surrender.*
• admit defeat, give in, yield, submit,
capitulate
❷ *He was asked to surrender his
passport to the authorities.*
• give, hand over, relinquish

surround VERB
❶ *The garden is surrounded by a stone
wall.*
• enclose, fence in, wall in
❷ *Armed police have surrounded the
building.*
• encircle, ring, hem in, besiege

surroundings PLURAL NOUN
The hotel is set in beautiful surroundings.
• environment, setting, location, habitat

survey NOUN
❶ *We did a survey of local leisure
facilities.*
• review, enquiry, investigation, study,
poll
– A survey to count the population of an
area is a **census**.
❷ *They got a detailed survey of the
house before buying it.*
• inspection, examination

survey VERB
❶ *She stood at the door, surveying the
mess.*
• view, look over, look at, gaze at, scan,
observe, contemplate
❷ *The team will survey the Antarctic
coastline.*
• inspect, examine, explore, scrutinize,
study, map out

survive VERB
❶ *They had enough water to survive
until help came.*
• stay alive, live, last, keep going, carry
on, hold out, pull through
OPPOSITE die
❷ *Only two people survived the crash.*
• live through, withstand, come
through, endure, weather
❸ *Few of the ancient traditions survive.*
• remain, continue, persist, endure,
abide
❹ *She survived her husband by ten
years.*
• outlive, outlast

suspect VERB
❶ *No one could possibly suspect him.*
• doubt, mistrust, have suspicions
about, have misgivings about, have
qualms about
❷ *I suspect we may never know the
truth.*
• have a feeling, think, imagine,
presume, guess, sense, fancy

suspend VERB
❶ *A lamp was suspended from the
ceiling.*
• hang, dangle, sling, swing
❷ *Play was suspended until the
next day.*
• adjourn, break off, discontinue,
interrupt

suspense NOUN
*The suspense will have you on the
edge of your seat.*
• tension, uncertainty, anticipation,
expectancy, drama, excitement

suspicion NOUN
❶ *Something she said aroused my
suspicions.*
• distrust, doubt, misgiving, qualm,
reservation
❷ *I had a suspicion that something was
wrong.*
• feeling, hunch, inkling, intuition,
impression, notion

suspicious ADJECTIVE
❶ *The two men became deeply suspicious of each other.*
• doubtful, distrustful, mistrustful, unsure, uneasy, wary
OPPOSITE trusting
❷ *There's something suspicious about this email.*
• questionable, suspect, dubious, irregular, funny, shady
(informal) fishy

sustain VERB
❶ *Squirrels store nuts to sustain them through the winter.*
• keep going, nurture, nourish, provide for
❷ *Somehow the film manages to sustain your interest.*
• maintain, preserve, keep up, hold onto, retain, prolong
❸ *The driver sustained only minor injuries.*
• suffer, receive, experience, undergo

swagger VERB
The lead guitarist swaggered about on stage.
• strut, parade

swallow VERB
The bread was so dry that it was hard to swallow.
• gulp down
➤ **swallow something up**
The summit was soon swallowed up by clouds.
• envelop, engulf, cover over, absorb

swam
past tense see swim

swamp NOUN
The area around the lake used to be a swamp.
• marsh, bog, mire, fen, quicksand, quagmire

swamp VERB
❶ *Their boat was swamped by heavy waves.*
• flood, engulf, inundate, deluge, submerge

❷ *Our phone lines have been swamped with calls.*
• overwhelm, bombard, inundate, deluge, snow under

swan NOUN
In the sky was a flock of migrating swans.
– A male swan is a **cob**.
– A female swan is a **pen**.
– A young swan is a **cygnet**.
SEE ALSO bird

swap or **swop** *(informal)* VERB
We swapped seats so I could sit by the window.
• exchange, switch, trade, substitute
– To exchange goods for other goods without using money is to **barter**.

swarm VERB
Fans and photographers swarmed around her.
• crowd, flock, mob, throng, cluster
➤ **swarm with**
The city centre was swarming with tourists.
• be overrun by, teem with, be inundated with, be crawling with

sway VERB
The branches were swaying in the breeze.
• move to and fro, swing, wave, rock, undulate

swear VERB
❶ *Do you swear never to tell anyone?*
• promise, pledge, vow, give your word, take an oath
❷ *He muttered and swore under his breath.*
• curse, blaspheme, use bad language

sweat NOUN
A bead of sweat trickled down her nose.
• perspiration

sweat VERB
I began to sweat in the heat of the bus.
• perspire

sweaty ADJECTIVE
When I'm nervous, my palms get sweaty.
• sweating, perspiring, clammy, sticky, moist

sweep VERB
❶ *She was sweeping the steps with a broom.*
• brush, clean, dust
❷ *He was in danger of being swept out to sea.*
• carry, pull, drag, tow
❸ *Another bus swept past them.*
• speed, sail, shoot, zoom, glide, breeze
➤ **sweep something away**
The floods swept away roads and bridges.
• carry off, clear away, remove, get rid of

sweet ADJECTIVE
❶ *Would you prefer sweet or salty popcorn?*
• sugary, sugared, sweetened, syrupy
OPPOSITES sour, savoury
❷ *The sweet smell of roses filled the room.*
• fragrant, aromatic, perfumed, pleasant
OPPOSITE foul
❸ *I could hear the sweet sound of a harp.*
• mellow, melodious, soft, pleasant, soothing, tuneful
OPPOSITES harsh, ugly
❹ *Baby elephants are so sweet!*
• charming, delightful, lovable, adorable, endearing, cuddly
(*informal*) cute

sweet NOUN
❶ *He bought a packet of sweets.*
• (*North American*) candy
– Sweets in general are **confectionery**.
❷ *There is apple pie for sweet.*
• dessert, pudding
(*informal*) afters

swell VERB
❶ *My ankle was starting to swell.*
• expand, enlarge, bulge, inflate, puff up, fill out, balloon, billow
OPPOSITE shrink

❷ *Over time the population of the city swelled to ten million.*
• grow, increase, expand, enlarge, rise, escalate, mushroom
OPPOSITE shrink

swelling NOUN
There was a painful swelling on the horse's leg.
• inflammation, lump, bump, growth, tumour

swerve VERB
The car swerved to avoid a pedestrian.
• turn aside, veer, dodge, swing

swift ADJECTIVE
❶ *He drew out his sword in one swift movement.*
• fast, quick, rapid, speedy, brisk, lively
OPPOSITES slow, unhurried
❷ *Her reply was swift and to the point.*
• prompt, quick, immediate, instant, speedy, snappy
OPPOSITES slow, tardy

swim VERB
We swam in the sea every day.
• go swimming, bathe, take a dip

| ⊗ | WORD WEB |

Common swimming strokes:

➤ backstroke
➤ breaststroke
➤ butterfly
➤ dog paddle or doggy paddle
➤ freestyle
➤ front crawl
➤ sidestroke

swindle VERB
They were swindled out of their life savings.
• cheat, trick, dupe, fleece
(*informal*) con, diddle

swing VERB
❶ *The inn sign swung and creaked in the wind.*
• sway, move to and fro, flap, rock, swivel, pivot, oscillate
❷ *She swung her bag over her shoulder and walked away.*
• sling, hang, suspend, string
❸ *He swung round when I called his name.*
• turn, twist, veer, swerve, deviate

swipe VERB
❶ *The crocodile nearly swiped us with its tail.*
• slash, lash, hit, strike, swing at
❷ (*informal*) *Who swiped my pen?*
• steal, snatch
(*informal*) make off with, nick, pinch

swirl VERB
The water was now swirling around their feet.
• whirl, spin, twirl, churn, eddy

switch VERB
❶ *How do you switch off your phone?*
• turn
❷ *This is the story of two men who switch identities.*
• exchange, swap, change, shift

swivel VERB
She swivelled round in her chair.
• spin, turn, twirl, pivot, revolve, rotate

swollen ADJECTIVE
My feet were swollen from walking all day.
• inflamed, bloated, puffed up, puffy

swoop VERB
❶ *The owl swooped down to catch a mouse.*
• dive, plunge, plummet, pounce, descend
❷ *Police swooped on the house in the early hours.*
• raid, attack, storm

sword NOUN
He raised his shield and drew his sword.
• blade, foil, rapier, sabre

– Fighting with swords is **fencing** or **swordsmanship**.

swore
past tense see **swear**

symbol NOUN
❶ *The dove is a symbol of peace.*
• sign, emblem, image, representation
❷ *The Red Cross symbol was painted on the side of the vehicle.*
• emblem, insignia, badge, crest, logo
❸ *The stone was covered in strange symbols.*
• character, letter, mark
– The symbols used in ancient Egyptian writing were **hieroglyphics**.

symbolize VERB
What does the rose symbolize in the poem?
• represent, stand for, signify, indicate, mean, denote

sympathetic ADJECTIVE
He gave me a sympathetic smile.
• understanding, compassionate, concerned, caring, comforting, kind, supportive
OPPOSITE unsympathetic

sympathize VERB
➤ sympathize with
You could at least sympathize with me!
• feel sorry for, feel for, commiserate with

sympathy NOUN
It's hard to feel sympathy for any of the characters.
• compassion, understanding, concern, fellow-feeling

synthetic ADJECTIVE
Nylon is a synthetic material.
• artificial, man-made, manufactured, imitation
OPPOSITE natural

system NOUN
❶ *The city needs a better transport system.*
• network, organization, structure,

framework, arrangement
(*informal*) set-up
❷ *I don't understand the new
cataloguing system.*
• method, procedure, process, scheme,
technique, routine

systematic *ADJECTIVE*
*Police began a systematic search of the
crime scene.*
• methodical, orderly, structured,
organized, logical, scientific
OPPOSITE unsystematic

table *NOUN*
Here is the full table of results.
• chart, plan, list

tablet *NOUN*
❶ *The doctor prescribed some tablets for the pain.*
• pill, capsule, pellet
❷ *There was a stone tablet above the entrance to the tomb.*
• slab, plaque

tack *VERB*
❶ *The carpet needs to be tacked down.*
• nail, pin
❷ *She tacked up the hem of her skirt.*
• sew, stitch
➤ **tack something on**
A small conservatory has been tacked onto the house.
• add, attach, append, join on

tackle *VERB*
❶ *Firefighters came to tackle the blaze.*
• deal with, attend to, handle, manage, grapple with, cope with
❷ *You can only tackle a player with the ball.*
• challenge, intercept, take on

tackle *NOUN*
❶ *He kept his fishing tackle in a special case.*
• gear, equipment, apparatus, kit
❷ *The player was sent off for a late tackle.*
• challenge, interception

tactful *ADJECTIVE*
I tried to think of a tactful way to say no.
• subtle, discreet, delicate, diplomatic, sensitive, thoughtful
OPPOSITE tactless

tactics *PLURAL NOUN*
The team changed tactics at half-time.
• strategy, moves, manoeuvres, plan of action

tag *NOUN*
I'll just remove the price tag.
• label, sticker, ticket, tab

tag *VERB*
Every item is tagged with a barcode.
• label, mark, identify, flag
➤ **tag along with someone**
My sister tagged along with us for a while.
• accompany, follow, go with, join
➤ **tag something on**
He tagged on a PS at the end of his letter.
• add, attach, append, join on, tack on

tail *NOUN*
You'll have to join the tail of the queue.
• end, back, rear
OPPOSITES front, head

tail *VERB*
(informal) They tailed the suspect to this address.
• follow, pursue, track, trail, shadow, stalk
➤ **tail off**
Audiences slowly began to tail off.
• decrease, decline, lessen, diminish, dwindle, wane

taint *VERB*
He was forever after tainted with suspicion.
• tarnish, stain, sully, blot, blight, damage, spoil

take *VERB*
❶ *She took her sister's hand.*
• clutch, clasp, take hold of, grasp, grip, seize, snatch, grab
❷ *Many prisoners were taken.*
• capture, seize, detain
❸ *He took an envelope from his pocket.*
• remove, withdraw, pull, extract
❹ *Has someone taken my calculator?*
• steal
(informal) swipe, make off with, pinch, nick

⑤ *I'll take you upstairs to your room.*
• conduct, escort, lead, accompany, guide, show, usher

⑥ *Would you like me to take your luggage?*
• carry, convey, bring, bear, transport, ferry

⑦ *Take any seat you like.*
• pick, choose, select

⑧ *Each cable car can take eight passengers.*
• hold, contain, accommodate, have room for

⑨ *I can't take much more of this.*
• bear, put up with, stand, endure, tolerate, suffer, stomach

⑩ *It'll take decades for the forest to recover.*
• need, require

⑪ *Let me take you name and phone number.*
• make a note of, record, register, write down, jot down

⑫ *Take the total sum from the original number.*
• subtract, take away, deduct, discount

➤ take after someone
Do you think she takes after her mother?
• resemble, look like, remind someone of

➤ take someone in
No one was taken in by his story.
• fool, deceive, trick, cheat, dupe, hoodwink

➤ take something in
I was too tired to take it all in.
• understand, comprehend, grasp, absorb, follow

➤ take off
① *Our plane took off on time.*
• lift off, blast off, depart

② *Her business has really taken off.*
• succeed, do well, catch on, become popular, prosper

➤ take something off
Please take off your coats.
• remove, strip off, peel off

➤ take part in something
Everyone has to take part in the show.
• participate in, be involved in, join in

➤ take place
Where exactly did the accident take place?
• happen, occur, come about

➤ take to something
How are you taking to life in the city?
• like, cope with, get on with

➤ take something up
① *I have recently taken up tap dancing.*
• begin to do, start learning

② *This desk takes up a lot of space.*
• use up, fill up, occupy, require

③ *I decided to take up their offer.*
• accept, agree to, say yes to

tale NOUN
It is a tale of love and betrayal.
• story, narrative, account, legend, fable, saga
(*informal*) yarn

talent NOUN
She shows a real talent for drawing.
• gift, ability, aptitude, skill, flair, knack, forte
– Unusually great talent is **genius**.

talented ADJECTIVE
He's a very talented actor.
• gifted, able, accomplished, capable, skilled, skilful, brilliant, expert
– Someone who is talented in several ways is said to be **versatile**.
OPPOSITES inept, talentless

talk VERB
① *When do babies start learning to talk?*
• speak, say things, communicate, express yourself

② *You two must have a lot to talk about.*
• discuss, converse, chat, chatter, gossip
(*informal*) natter

③ *The prisoner refused to talk.*
• give information, confess
SEE ALSO say

talk NOUN
① *I need to have a talk with you soon.*
• conversation, discussion, chat
– Talk between characters in a play, film or novel is **dialogue**.

② *There is a talk on Egyptian art at lunchtime.*
• lecture, presentation, speech, address
③ *There was talk of witchcraft in the village.*
• rumour, gossip

talkative ADJECTIVE
You're not very talkative this morning.
• chatty, communicative, vocal, forthcoming, loquacious, garrulous
OPPOSITE taciturn

tall ADJECTIVE
① *She is tall for her age.*
• big, giant, towering
– Someone who is awkwardly tall and thin is **lanky** or **gangling**.
OPPOSITE short
② *Singapore has many tall buildings.*
• high, lofty, towering, soaring, giant
– Buildings with many floors are **high-rise** or **multi-storey** buildings.
OPPOSITE low

tally VERB
➤ **tally with**
This doesn't tally with your previous answer.
• agree with, correspond with, match

tame ADJECTIVE
① *These guinea pigs are tame and do not bite.*
• domesticated, broken in, docile, gentle, manageable, trained
OPPOSITE wild
② *The film seems very tame nowadays.*
• dull, unexciting, unadventurous, boring, bland, humdrum
OPPOSITES exciting, adventurous

tame VERB
He was an expert at taming wild horses.
• domesticate, break in, subdue, master

tamper VERB
➤ **tamper with something**
Someone has been tampering with the lock.
• meddle with, tinker with, fiddle about with, interfere with, doctor

tang NOUN
You can taste the tang of lemon in the soup.
• sharpness, zest, zing

tangle VERB
① *The tree roots were tangled into a solid mass.*
• entangle, twist, knot, jumble, muddle
– Tangled hair is **dishevelled** or **matted** hair.
② *Dolphins can get tangled in fishing nets.*
• catch, trap, ensnare

tangle NOUN
Underneath the desk was a tangle of computer cables.
• muddle, jumble, knot, twist, confusion

tap NOUN
① *Turn the tap to the off position.*
• valve, stopcock
② *I thought I heard a tap on the window.*
• knock, rap, pat, strike

tap VERB
He tapped three times on the door.
• knock, strike, rap, pat, drum

tape NOUN
The parcel was tied up with tape.
• band, ribbon, braid, binding, string

target NOUN
① *His target was to swim thirty lengths.*
• goal, aim, objective, intention, purpose, hope, ambition
② *She was the target of a hate campaign.*
• object, victim, butt, focus

tarnish VERB
① *The mirror had tarnished with age.*
• discolour, corrode, rust
② *The scandal tarnished his reputation.*
• stain, taint, sully, blot, blacken, spoil, mar, damage

tart NOUN
I had a slice of lemon tart.
• flan, pie, pastry

a
b
c
d
e
f
g
h
i
j
k
l
m
n
o
p
q
r
s
t
u
v
w
x
y
z

tart ADJECTIVE
❶ *Cranberries have a tart flavour.*
• sharp, sour, acid, tangy
OPPOSITE sweet
❷ *She gave me a tart reply.*
• sarcastic, biting, cutting, caustic

task NOUN
❶ *The robot can carry out simple tasks.*
• job, chore, errand, exercise
❷ *Your task is to design a logo for the company.*
• assignment, mission, duty, undertaking

taste NOUN
❶ *I love the taste of ginger.*
• flavour, savour
❷ *Would you like a taste of my pudding?*
• mouthful, sample, bite, bit, morsel, nibble
❸ *She dresses with impeccable taste.*
• style, elegance, discrimination, judgement
❹ *He has always had a taste for travel.*
• liking, love, fondness, desire, inclination

Ⓦ WRITING TIPS

DESCRIBING TASTE
Pleasant:

> ➤ appetizing
> ➤ delectable
> ➤ delicious
> ➤ flavoursome
> ➤ luscious
> ➤ *(informal)* moreish
> ➤ mouth-watering

> ➤ palatable
> ➤ *(informal)* scrumptious
> ➤ succulent
> ➤ tasty
> ➤ tempting
> ➤ *(informal)* yummy

Unpleasant:

> ➤ disgusting
> ➤ foul
> ➤ inedible
> ➤ insipid
> ➤ nauseating
> ➤ nauseous

> ➤ rancid
> ➤ revolting
> ➤ sickening
> ➤ unappetizing
> ➤ uneatable
> ➤ unpalatable

Other:

> ➤ acidic
> ➤ acrid
> ➤ bitter
> ➤ bland
> ➤ burnt
> ➤ fiery
> ➤ flavourless
> ➤ fresh
> ➤ fruity
> ➤ hot
> ➤ juicy
> ➤ mellow
> ➤ metallic
> ➤ mild
> ➤ nutty
> ➤ peppery
> ➤ piquant
> ➤ pungent

> ➤ refreshing
> ➤ salty
> ➤ savoury
> ➤ sharp
> ➤ smoky
> ➤ sour
> ➤ spicy
> ➤ strong
> ➤ sugary
> ➤ sweet
> ➤ syrupy
> ➤ tangy
> ➤ tart
> ➤ tasteless
> ➤ vinegary
> ➤ yeasty
> ➤ zesty

taste VERB
❶ *Taste the sauce before adding salt.*
• sample, try, test, sip, savour
❷ *Can you taste any difference in flavour?*
• perceive, distinguish, discern, make out

tasteful ADJECTIVE
The room was decorated in a plain and tasteful style.
• refined, stylish, elegant, chic, smart, cultured, artistic
OPPOSITES tasteless, vulgar

tasteless ADJECTIVE
❶ *He apologized for telling a tasteless joke.*
• crude, tactless, indelicate, inappropriate, in bad taste
❷ *The fish was overcooked and tasteless.*
• flavourless, bland, insipid
OPPOSITE flavoursome

tasty ADJECTIVE
That pie was very tasty.
• delicious, appetizing, flavoursome
OPPOSITES flavourless, unappetizing

tattered ADJECTIVE
Some of the blankets were worn and tattered.
• ragged, ripped, torn, frayed, tatty, threadbare
OPPOSITE smart

taught
past tense see **teach**

taunt VERB
Two sets of rival fans taunted each other.
• jeer at, jibe, insult, sneer at, scoff at, make fun of, tease, mock, ridicule

taunt NOUN
He had to ignore the taunts of the crowd.
• jeer, jibe, insult, sneer

taut ADJECTIVE
Make sure the rope is taut.
• tight, tense, stretched
OPPOSITE slack

teach VERB
My dad is teaching me to play the guitar.
• educate, instruct, tutor, coach, train, school

teacher NOUN
She is a qualified dance teacher.
• tutor, instructor, trainer, coach
– A teacher at a college or university is a **lecturer**.
– In the past, a woman who taught children in a private household was a **governess**.

team NOUN
❶ *She's in the school hockey team.*
• side, squad, line-up
❷ *They were rescued by a mountain rescue team.*
• group, force, unit, crew, detail

tear VERB
❶ *The wind tore a hole in our tent.*
• rip, split, slit, gash, rupture, shred
❷ *A white van came tearing round the corner.*
• race, dash, rush, hurry, sprint, speed

tear NOUN
There was a tear in one of the sails.
• rip, split, slit, gash, rent, rupture, hole, opening, gap

tease VERB
I knew she was only teasing me.
• taunt, make fun of, poke fun at, mock, ridicule, laugh at
IDIOM *(informal)* pull someone's leg

technical ADJECTIVE
❶ *She is good with anything technical.*
• technological, scientific, high-tech
❷ *The manual was full of technical terms.*
• specialist, specialized, advanced

technique NOUN
❶ *He is trained in survival techniques.*
• method, procedure, approach, means, system
❷ *Her piano playing shows good technique.*
• skill, expertise, proficiency, artistry, ability

tedious ADJECTIVE
I found the opening chapter slow and tedious.
• boring, dull, dreary, tiresome, monotonous, unexciting, uninteresting
OPPOSITE exciting

teem VERB
➤ **teem with**
The pond teems with fish.
• be full of, be bursting with, swarm with, be overrun by, be crawling with, be infested with

teenager NOUN
The website is mainly aimed at teenagers.
• adolescent, youth, young person
(informal) teen

telephone VERB
see **phone**

tell VERB
❶ *I have something important to tell you.*
• say to, make known to, communicate

to, report to, announce to, reveal to, notify, inform

② *The film tells the story of a young shepherd.*
• relate, narrate, recount, describe

③ *The police told everyone to stand back.*
• order, command, direct, instruct

④ *Can you tell where we are yet?*
• make out, recognize, identify, determine, perceive

⑤ *It's impossible to tell one character from another.*
• distinguish, differentiate

➤ **tell someone off**
(*informal*) *We were told off for being late.*
• scold, reprimand, reproach
(*informal*) tick off

temper NOUN
① *The chef is always flying into a temper.*
• rage, fury, tantrum, fit of anger

② *He managed to keep an even temper.*
• mood, humour, state of mind

➤ **lose your temper**
She loses her temper at the slightest thing.
• get angry, fly into a rage
IDIOMS (*informal*) blow a fuse, blow your top, flip your lid, fly off the handle, hit the roof

temperature NOUN

WORD WEB

Units for measuring temperature:

➤ degrees Celsius   ➤ degrees
➤ degrees   Fahrenheit
   centigrade

– A **thermometer** is a device for measuring temperature.

– A **thermostat** is a device for keeping temperature steady.

temple NOUN
For places of religious worship see **religion**.

temporary ADJECTIVE
① *That will do for a temporary repair.*
• interim, provisional, makeshift

② *He suffered a temporary loss of hearing.*
• short-lived, momentary, passing, fleeting
OPPOSITE permanent

tempt VERB
Can I tempt you to try a spoonful?
• coax, entice, persuade, attract, lure
OPPOSITES discourage, deter

temptation NOUN
I resisted the temptation to laugh.
• urge, impulse, inclination, desire

tempting ADJECTIVE
It was a tempting offer.
• enticing, attractive, appealing, inviting, beguiling
OPPOSITES off-putting, uninviting

tend VERB
① *She tends to have a nap in the afternoon.*
• be inclined, be liable, be likely, be apt, be prone

② *He used to help his father tend the crops.*
• take care of, look after, cultivate, manage

③ *Volunteers tended the wounded in makeshift hospitals.*
• nurse, attend to, care for, minister to

tendency NOUN
He has a tendency to exaggerate.
• inclination, leaning, predisposition, propensity

tender ADJECTIVE
① *Cook the meat until it is tender.*
• soft, succulent, juicy
OPPOSITE tough

② *Frost may damage tender plants.*
• delicate, fragile, sensitive
OPPOSITES hardy, strong

③ *My gums are still a bit tender.*
• painful, sensitive, sore

④ *She turned to me with a tender smile.*
• affectionate, kind, loving, caring,

warm-hearted, compassionate,
sympathetic
OPPOSITE uncaring

tennis NOUN

WORD WEB

Terms used in tennis:

➤ ace	➤ match point
➤ advantage	➤ net
➤ backhand	➤ racket or
➤ ballboy or	racquet
ballgirl	➤ serve
➤ break point	➤ service
➤ court	➤ set
➤ deuce	➤ singles
➤ double fault	➤ slice
➤ doubles	➤ smash
➤ drop shot	➤ tie-break or
➤ foot fault	tie-breaker
➤ forehand	➤ umpire
➤ lob	➤ volley
➤ love	

For tips on writing about sport see
sport.

tense ADJECTIVE
❶ Every muscle in my body was tense.
• taut, tight, strained, stretched
❷ Do you feel tense before a big match?
• anxious, nervous, apprehensive, edgy,
on edge, jumpy, keyed up, worked up
(informal) uptight, jittery, twitchy
OPPOSITE relaxed
❸ The film ends with an incredibly tense
car chase.
• nerve-racking, nail-biting, stressful,
fraught

tension NOUN
❶ Can you check the tension on the
ropes?
• tightness, tautness
❷ The tension in the room was
unbearable.
• anxiety, nervousness, apprehension,
suspense, worry, stress, strain

tent NOUN
We slept overnight in a tent.
– A large tent used for a party or other
event is a **marquee**.
– To set up a tent is to **pitch** it and to
take down a tent is to **strike** it.

tepid ADJECTIVE
The water should be tepid, not hot.
• lukewarm, hand-hot

term NOUN
❶ He served a long term in prison.
• period, time, spell, stretch, stint, run
❷ The book includes a glossary of
technical terms.
• word, expression, phrase, name

terrible ADJECTIVE
❶ We heard there had been a terrible
accident.
• horrible, dreadful, appalling, shocking,
horrific, horrendous, ghastly, atrocious
OPPOSITE minor
❷ The first half of the show was terrible!
• very bad, awful, dreadful, appalling,
dire, abysmal
(informal) rubbish, lousy, pathetic
OPPOSITE excellent

terribly ADVERB
❶ He was missing his parents terribly.
• very badly, severely, intensely
OPPOSITE slightly
❷ I'm terribly sorry about this.
• very, extremely, awfully

terrific (informal) ADJECTIVE
❶ There was a terrific flash of lightning.
• very great, tremendous, mighty, huge,
enormous, massive, immense, colossal,
gigantic
❷ She's a terrific tennis player.
• very good, excellent, first-class, first-
rate, superb, marvellous, wonderful
(informal) brilliant, fantastic, fabulous

terrify VERB
The dogs were terrified by the thunder.
• frighten, scare, horrify, petrify, panic,
alarm

a
b
c
d
e
f
g
h
i
j
k
l
m
n
o
p
q
r
s
t
u
v
w
x
y
z

territory NOUN
We were now deep in enemy territory.
• land, area, ground, terrain, country, district, region, sector, zone
– A territory which is part of a country is a **province**.

terror NOUN
They ran away screaming in terror.
• fear, fright, horror, dread, panic, alarm

test NOUN
❶ *We had a maths test today.*
• exam, examination, assessment, appraisal, evaluation
– A test for a job as an actor or a singer is an **audition**.
❷ *This is a new test for allergies.*
• trial, experiment, check, investigation, examination

test VERB
❶ *Mum needs to have her eyes tested.*
• examine, check, evaluate, assess, screen
❷ *Pilots have been testing the new aircraft.*
• try out, experiment with, trial, sample
IDIOM put something through its paces

text NOUN
❶ *It is easy to add text to your web pages.*
• words, wording, content, script
❷ *For centuries scholars have studied these ancient texts.*
• work, book, piece of writing

textiles PLURAL NOUN
All their clothes are made from natural textiles.
• fabrics, materials, cloths

WORD WEB

Some textile arts:

➤ appliqué	➤ lacemaking
➤ crochet	➤ needlepoint
➤ dyeing	➤ needlework
➤ embroidery	➤ patchwork
➤ felting	➤ quilting
➤ knitting	➤ sewing

➤ spinning	➤ weaving
➤ tapestry	

For types of textiles see **fabric**.

texture NOUN
Silk has a smooth texture.
• feel, touch, consistency, quality, surface

W WRITING TIPS

DESCRIBING TEXTURE
Rough or hard:

➤ brittle	➤ gravelly
➤ bumpy	➤ lumpy
➤ coarse	➤ ruffled
➤ crumbly	➤ sandy
➤ firm	➤ scaly
➤ grainy	➤ wrinkled

Smooth or soft:

➤ creamy	➤ glassy
➤ downy	➤ light
➤ feathery	➤ silky
➤ fine	➤ velvety

Wet or sticky:

➤ (informal) gloopy	➤ runny
➤ glutinous	➤ slimy
➤ moist	➤ viscous
	➤ watery

Other:

➤ chalky	➤ pulpy
➤ chewy	➤ rubbery
➤ doughy	➤ soupy
➤ elastic	➤ spongy
➤ fibrous	➤ springy
➤ flaky	➤ (informal) squidgy
➤ greasy	➤ stretchy
➤ leathery	➤ stringy
➤ oily	➤ waxy
➤ papery	
➤ powdery	

thank VERB
How can I ever thank you enough?
• say thank you to, express your gratitude to, show your appreciation to

thankful ADJECTIVE
We were thankful to be home at last.
• grateful, appreciative, glad, pleased, relieved

thanks PLURAL NOUN
Please accept this token of my thanks.
• gratitude, appreciation
➤ **thanks to**
People are living longer thanks to better healthcare.
• because of, as a result of, owing to, due to, on account of

thaw VERB
❶ *Polar ice caps are thawing at a faster rate than ever.*
• melt, dissolve, liquefy
❷ *Leave frozen food to thaw before cooking.*
• defrost, unfreeze
OPPOSITE freeze

theatre NOUN
see **drama**

theft NOUN
She reported the theft of jewels from her hotel room.
• robbery, stealing
SEE ALSO **stealing**

theme NOUN
What is the theme of the poem?
• subject, topic, idea, argument, gist, thread

theory NOUN
❶ *Do you have any theories about the murder?*
• hypothesis, explanation, suggestion, view, belief, contention, speculation, idea, notion
❷ *He is studying musical theory.*
• principles, concepts, rules, laws

therapy NOUN
Acupuncture is an ancient therapy.
• treatment, remedy

thick ADJECTIVE
❶ *The tree has thick roots.*
• stout, chunky, heavy, solid, bulky,

hefty, substantial
OPPOSITES thin, slender
❷ *The stone walls are more than a metre thick.*
• wide, broad, deep
❸ *There was a thick layer of mist.*
• dense, close, compact, opaque, impenetrable
OPPOSITES thin, light
❹ *He spoke with a thick Polish accent.*
• heavy, noticeable
OPPOSITE slight
❺ *Beat the mixture into a thick paste.*
• stiff, firm, heavy
OPPOSITES thin, runny
❻ *(informal) Maybe I'm just being thick.*
• stupid, unintelligent, brainless, dense, dim
OPPOSITE intelligent

thief NOUN
Thieves broke in and stole valuable equipment.
• robber, burglar
– Someone who steals from people in the street is a **pickpocket**.
– Someone who steals small goods from a shop is a **shoplifter**.

thin ADJECTIVE
❶ *He was a thin little boy with a freckled face.*
• lean, slim, slender, skinny, bony, gaunt, spare, slight
– Someone who is thin and tall is **lanky**.
– Someone who is thin but strong is **wiry**.
– Thin arms or legs are **spindly**.
OPPOSITES fat, plump, stout
❷ *Her cloak was made of thin material.*
• fine, lightweight, light, delicate, flimsy, wispy, sheer
OPPOSITES thick, heavy
❸ *Draw a thin line underneath.*
• narrow, fine
OPPOSITES thick, broad
❹ *Add water to make a thin paste.*
• runny, watery, sloppy
OPPOSITES firm, stiff

thin VERB
You can thin the paint with a little water.
• dilute, water down, weaken

A
B
C
D
E
F
G
H
I
J
K
L
M
N
O
P
Q
R
S
T
U
V
W
X
Y
Z

> **thin out**
Towards evening the crowd began to thin out.
• disperse, scatter, break up, dissipate

thing NOUN
❶ *Magpies are attracted by shiny things.*
• object, article, item
❷ *She had a lot of things to think about.*
• matter, affair, detail, point, factor
❸ *Odd things keep happening to me.*
• event, happening, occurrence, incident
❹ *I have only one thing left to do.*
• job, task, act, action
> **things**
Put your things in one of the lockers.
• belongings, possessions
(*informal*) stuff, gear

think VERB
❶ *Stop to think before you do anything rash.*
• consider, contemplate, reflect, deliberate, meditate, ponder
– To think hard about something is to **concentrate** on it.
❷ *Do you think this is a good idea?*
• believe, feel, consider, judge, conclude, be of the opinion
❸ *When do you think you'll be ready?*
• reckon, suppose, imagine, estimate, guess, expect, anticipate
> **think about something**
I've thought about what you said.
• consider, reflect on, ponder on, muse on, mull over
– To keep thinking anxiously about something is to **brood on** it.
> **think something up**
They thought up a good plan.
• invent, make up, conceive, concoct, devise, dream up

thirsty ADJECTIVE
Exercise always makes me thirsty.
• dry, parched
– Someone who has lost a lot of water from their body is **dehydrated**.

thorn NOUN
Rose stems have thorns on them.
• prickle, spike, spine, needle, barb

thorny ADJECTIVE
❶ *He scratched his arm on the thorny branches.*
• prickly, spiky, spiny, bristly
❷ *This is quite a thorny issue for a lot of people.*
• difficult, complicated, complex, hard, tricky, perplexing

thorough ADJECTIVE
❶ *The police made a thorough search of the crime scene.*
• comprehensive, full, rigorous, detailed, close, in-depth, exhaustive, careful, meticulous, systematic, methodical, painstaking
OPPOSITES superficial, cursory
❷ *He's making a thorough nuisance of himself.*
• complete, total, utter, perfect, proper, absolute, downright, out-and-out

thought NOUN
❶ *I've given some thought to the problem.*
• consideration, deliberation, study
❷ *She was lost in thought for a moment.*
• thinking, contemplation, reflection, meditation
❸ *Look, I've just had a thought.*
• idea, notion, belief, view, opinion, theory, conclusion

thoughtful ADJECTIVE
❶ *He looked thoughtful for a moment.*
• pensive, reflective, contemplative, meditative, absorbed, preoccupied
OPPOSITES blank, vacant
❷ *She added some thoughtful comments in the margin.*
• well-thought-out, careful, conscientious, thorough
OPPOSITE careless
❸ *It was thoughtful of you to write.*
• considerate, kind, caring, compassionate, sympathetic, understanding
OPPOSITE thoughtless

thoughtless ADJECTIVE
It was thoughtless of me to say that.
• inconsiderate, insensitive, uncaring,

unthinking, negligent, ill-considered, rash
OPPOSITE thoughtful

thrash VERB
❶ The owner was reported for thrashing his dog.
• hit, beat, strike, whip, flog
❷ The visitors thrashed the home side.
• beat, defeat, trounce
(informal) hammer
❸ The crocodile thrashed its tail.
• swish, flail, toss, jerk, twitch

thread NOUN
❶ There is a loose thread hanging from your cuff.
• strand, fibre
❷ Do you sell embroidery thread?
• cotton, yarn, wool, silk
❸ I'm afraid I've lost the thread of this conversation.
• theme, drift, direction, train, tenor

threat NOUN
❶ She made a threat about taking revenge.
• warning, ultimatum
❷ The oil spill poses a threat to wildlife.
• danger, menace, hazard, risk

threaten VERB
❶ They tried to threaten him into paying.
• menace, intimidate, terrorize, bully, browbeat
❷ Uncontrolled logging is threatening the forests.
• endanger, jeopardize, put at risk
❸ The hazy sky threatened rain.
• warn of, indicate, signal, forecast

three NOUN
People arrived in groups of two or three.
– A group of three people is a **threesome** or **trio**.
– A series of three related books, plays or films is a **trilogy**.
– To multiply a number by three is to **triple** it.

threw
past tense see **throw**

thrifty ADJECTIVE
She has always been thrifty with her money.
• careful, economical, frugal, prudent, sparing
OPPOSITE extravagant

thrill NOUN
I love the thrill of riding on a roller coaster.
• excitement, stimulation, sensation, tingle
(informal) buzz, kick

thrill VERB
The thought of seeing a real shark thrilled him.
• excite, exhilarate, stir, rouse, stimulate, electrify
IDIOM (informal) give you a buzz
OPPOSITE bore

thrilled ADJECTIVE
She was thrilled to see her name in print.
• delighted, pleased, excited, overjoyed, ecstatic

thrilling ADJECTIVE
The movie starts off with a thrilling car chase.
• exciting, stirring, stimulating, electrifying, exhilarating, action-packed, gripping, riveting

thrive VERB
Crops thrive in this climate.
• do well, flourish, prosper, succeed, boom
OPPOSITE decline

thriving ADJECTIVE
The region has a thriving tourist industry.
• flourishing, successful, prosperous, booming, healthy, profitable
OPPOSITE declining

throb VERB
He felt his heart throbbing in his chest.
• beat, pound, pulse, pulsate, thump

a
b
c
d
e
f
g
h
i
j
k
l
m
n
o
p
q
r
s
t
u
v
w
x
y
z

throb NOUN

We could hear the incessant throb of the music next door.
• beat, pulse, pulsation, pounding, thumping

throng NOUN

Throngs of onlookers turned out to watch.
• crowd, swarm, horde, mass, drove

throng VERB

Spectators thronged into the piazza.
• swarm, flock, stream, crowd
➤ **thronged with**
In summer Venice is thronged with tourists.
• crowded with, packed with, full of, swarming with

throttle VERB

This stiff collar is throttling me!
• strangle, choke, suffocate

throw VERB

❶ *We threw scraps of food to the birds.*
• fling, toss, sling, cast, pitch, hurl, heave
(*informal*) bung, chuck
❷ *Her question threw me for a second.*
• disconcert, unsettle, unnerve, put off, rattle
(*informal*) faze
❸ *They threw a surprise party for her.*
• hold, host, put on, arrange, organize
➤ **throw something away or out**
I'm throwing out a lot of my old stuff.
• get rid of, dispose of, discard, scrap, dump
(*informal*) ditch, bin

thrust VERB

❶ *A woman thrust a leaflet into my hands.*
• shove, push, force
❷ *The man thrust at me with his spear.*
• lunge, jab, prod, stab, poke

thump VERB

❶ *He stood up and thumped his fist on the table.*
• bang, bash, pound, hit, strike, knock, hammer, punch
(*informal*) whack
❷ *My heart was thumping.*
• throb, pound, pulse, hammer

thunder NOUN

We heard thunder in the distance.
– A burst of thunder is a **clap**, **crack**, **peal** or **roll** of thunder.
SEE ALSO **weather**

thunder VERB

❶ *Waves thundered against the rocks.*
• boom, roar, rumble, pound
❷ *'What do you want?' a voice thundered.*
• shout, roar, bellow, bark, boom

thunderous ADJECTIVE

The speech was greeted with thunderous applause.
• deafening, resounding, tumultuous, loud, booming
OPPOSITE quiet

tick VERB

A clock was ticking in the background.
• click, make a tick, beat
➤ **tick someone off**
(*informal*) *She ticked him off for being late.*
• reprimand, reproach, scold
(*informal*) tell off

ticket NOUN

❶ *We won free cinema tickets.*
• pass, permit, token, voucher, coupon
❷ *What does it say on the price ticket?*
• label, tag, sticker, tab

tide NOUN

Lots of seaweed gets washed up by the tide.
• current
– An incoming tide is a **flow tide** and an outgoing tide is an **ebb tide**.
– The tide is fully in at **high tide** and fully out at **low tide**.

tidy *ADJECTIVE*
I like to keep my room tidy.
• neat, orderly, uncluttered, trim, spruce, in good order
IDIOM spick and span
OPPOSITES untidy, messy

tie *VERB*
❶ *He was tying string around the parcel.*
• bind, fasten, hitch, strap, loop, knot, lace, truss
– To tie up a boat is to **moor** it.
– To tie up an animal is to **tether** it.
OPPOSITE untie
❷ *The top two players tied with each other.*
• draw, be equal, be level

tie *NOUN*
❶ *The final score was a tie.*
• draw, dead heat
❷ *They still maintain close family ties.*
• bond, connection, link, association, relationship

tier *NOUN*
The seats are arranged in tiers.
• row, line, rank, level, layer, storey

tight *ADJECTIVE*
❶ *The lid was too tight to unscrew.*
• firm, fast, secure
– If something is so tight that air cannot get through, it is **airtight**.
– If something is so tight that water cannot get through, it is **watertight**.
OPPOSITE loose
❷ *These jeans are quite tight.*
• close-fitting, snug, figure-hugging
OPPOSITES loose, roomy
❸ *Make sure that the ropes are tight.*
• taut, tense, stretched, rigid
OPPOSITE slack
❹ *We had to squeeze into a tight space.*
• cramped, confined, compact, limited, small, narrow, poky
OPPOSITE spacious
❺ *He can be very tight with his money.*
• mean, stingy, miserly, tight-fisted
OPPOSITE generous

tighten *VERB*
❶ *She tightened her grip on the rail.*
• increase, strengthen, harden, stiffen
❷ *You need to tighten the ropes.*
• pull tighter, stretch, make taut, make tense
OPPOSITE loosen

till *VERB*
Farmers use tractors to till the land.
• cultivate, farm, plough, dig, work

tilt *VERB*
He tilted his head to one side.
• lean, incline, tip, slope, slant, angle
– When a ship tilts to one side, it **lists**.

timber *NOUN*
❶ *He bought some timber to build a shed.*
• wood, (*North American*) lumber
❷ *I could hear the timbers of the ship creaking.*
• beam, plank, board, spar

time *NOUN*
❶ *Autumn is my favourite time of the year.*
• phase, season, period
❷ *He spent a short time living in China.*
• period, while, term, spell, stretch
❸ *Shakespeare lived in the time of Elizabeth I.*
• era, age, days, epoch, period
❹ *Is this a good time to talk?*
• moment, occasion, opportunity
❺ *Try to keep time with the music.*
• tempo, beat, rhythm
➤ **on time**
Please try to be on time.
• punctual, prompt

 WORD WEB

Units for measuring time:

➤ second
➤ minute
➤ hour
➤ day
➤ week
➤ fortnight
➤ month
➤ quarter
➤ year
➤ decade
➤ century
➤ millennium

a b c d e f g h i j k l m n o p q r s **t** u v w x y z

Devices used to measure time:

- ➤ calendar
- ➤ clock
- ➤ hourglass
- ➤ metronome
- ➤ pocket watch
- ➤ stopwatch
- ➤ sundial
- ➤ timer
- ➤ watch
- ➤ wristwatch

timetable NOUN
I have a busy timetable this week.
• schedule, programme, rota, diary

timid ADJECTIVE
He spoke in a timid little voice.
• shy, bashful, modest, nervous, fearful, shrinking, retiring, sheepish
OPPOSITES brave, confident

tinge VERB
❶ *The clouds were tinged with gold.*
• colour, stain, tint, wash, flush
❷ *Our relief was tinged with sadness.*
• flavour, colour, touch

tinge NOUN
❶ *The walls are white with just a tinge of blue.*
• tint, colour, shade, hue, tone
❷ *There was a tinge of sadness in her voice.*
• trace, note, touch, suggestion, hint, streak

tingle VERB
My ears were tingling with the cold.
• prickle, sting

tingle NOUN
❶ *She felt a tingle in her toes.*
• prickling, stinging
IDIOM pins and needles
❷ *He felt a tingle of excitement.*
• thrill, sensation, quiver, shiver

tinker VERB
He was outside, tinkering with his bike.
• fiddle, play about, dabble, meddle, tamper

tint NOUN
The paper was white with a faint tint of blue.
• shade, tone, colour, hue, tinge

tiny ADJECTIVE
On the leaf was a tiny yellow tree frog.
• very small, minute, minuscule, miniature, mini, microscopic, diminutive (*informal*) teeny, titchy
OPPOSITES huge, giant

tip NOUN
❶ *The arrow had a poisoned tip.*
• end, point, nib
❷ *The tip of the mountain was covered in snow.*
• peak, top, summit, cap, crown, pinnacle
❸ *Here are some tips on how to draw faces.*
• hint, suggestion, pointer, piece of advice
❹ *We took a load of rubbish to the tip.*
• dump, rubbish dump

tip VERB
❶ *Tip your head back to stop a nosebleed.*
• lean, tilt, incline, slope, slant, angle
– When a ship tips slightly to one side, it **lists**.
❷ *She tipped everything onto the counter.*
• empty, turn out, dump, unload
➤ **tip over**
The surfboard tipped over on top of him.
• overturn, roll over, keel over, capsize
➤ **tip something over**
I tipped the jug over by accident.
• knock over, overturn, topple, upset, upend

tire VERB
My legs were beginning to tire.
• get tired, weaken, flag, droop
OPPOSITES revive, strengthen
➤ **tire someone out**
The long walk home had tired her out.
• exhaust, wear out, drain, weary
OPPOSITES refresh, invigorate

A B C D E F G H I J K L M N O P Q R S T U V W X Y Z

tired ADJECTIVE
We were all feeling tired after such a long day.
• exhausted, fatigued, weary, worn out, listless, sleepy, drowsy
(*informal*) all in, whacked, bushed, dead beat
OPPOSITES energetic, refreshed
➤ **be tired of something**
I'm tired of waiting.
• be bored with, be fed up with, be sick of, be weary of, have had enough of

tiring ADJECTIVE
Digging the garden is tiring work.
• exhausting, taxing, demanding, arduous, strenuous, laborious, gruelling, wearying
OPPOSITE refreshing

title NOUN
❶ *You need a good title for your story.*
• name, heading
– The title above a newspaper story is a **headline**.
– A title or description next to a picture is a **caption**.
❷ *She won two Olympic titles.*
• championship, crown
❸ *What is your preferred title?*
• form of address, designation, rank

together ADVERB
❶ *We wrote the song together.*
• jointly, as a group, in collaboration, with each other, side by side
OPPOSITES independently, separately
❷ *Let's sing the first verse together.*
• simultaneously, at the same time, all at once, in chorus, in unison

toil VERB
❶ *They had been toiling in the fields all day.*
• work hard, labour, sweat, slave
(*informal*) grind, slog
❷ *Every morning he toiled up the hill.*
• struggle, trudge, plod

toilet NOUN
They have a downstairs toilet.
• lavatory, WC, bathroom

(*informal*) loo
– A toilet in a camp or barracks is a **latrine**.

token NOUN
❶ *You can exchange this token for a free drink.*
• voucher, coupon, ticket, counter
❷ *Please accept this gift as a small token of our gratitude.*
• sign, symbol, mark, expression, indication, proof, demonstration

told
past tense see tell

tolerant ADJECTIVE
Do you think that people are more tolerant nowadays?
• open-minded, broad-minded, easy-going, lenient, sympathetic, understanding, indulgent, forbearing
OPPOSITE intolerant

tolerate VERB
❶ *I will not tolerate bad manners.*
• accept, permit, allow, put up with
❷ *Some species can tolerate extreme temperatures.*
• bear, endure, stand, abide, suffer, stomach

tomb NOUN
They discovered the tomb of an Egyptian pharaoh.
• burial chamber, crypt, grave, mausoleum, sepulchre, vault
– An underground passage containing several tombs is a **catacomb**.

tone NOUN
❶ *There was an angry tone to his voice.*
• note, sound, quality, intonation
❷ *The room is painted in dark earthy tones.*
• colour, hue, shade, tint
❸ *Eerie music sets the right tone for the film.*
• feeling, mood, atmosphere, character, spirit

took
past tense see take

a b c d e f g h i j k l m n o p q r s t u v w x y z

tool NOUN

The shed is full of gardening tools.
• implement, utensil, device, gadget, instrument, appliance, contraption (*informal*) gizmo

tooth NOUN

WORD WEB

Types of teeth:

> canine (tooth)   > premolar
> incisor   > wisdom tooth
> molar

- Upper canine teeth are sometimes known as **eye teeth**.
- A child's first set of teeth are its **milk teeth** or **baby teeth**.
- The canine teeth of a wild animal are its **fangs**.
- The long pointed teeth of an elephant or walrus are its **tusks**.

Common dental problems:

> cavity   > tooth decay or
> plaque   caries
> tartar

SEE ALSO **dentist**

top NOUN

❶ *They climbed to the top of the hill.*
• peak, summit, tip, crown, crest, head, height
OPPOSITES bottom, base
❷ *The desk top was covered with papers.*
• surface
❸ *Remember to screw the top back on.*
• lid, cap, cover, stopper

top ADJECTIVE

❶ *Their office is on the top floor.*
• highest, topmost, uppermost, upper
OPPOSITES bottom, lowest
❷ *We set off at top speed.*
• greatest, maximum, utmost
OPPOSITES minimum, lowest
❸ *He is one of Europe's top chefs.*
• leading, foremost, finest, best, principal, superior
OPPOSITE minor

top VERB

❶ *The cake was topped with icing.*
• cover, decorate, garnish, crown
❷ *She is hoping to top her personal best.*
• beat, better, exceed, outdo, surpass

topic NOUN

What was the topic of the conversation?
• subject, theme, issue, matter, question, talking point

topical ADJECTIVE

Each week the programme discusses topical news items.
• current, recent, contemporary, up to date, up to the minute

topple VERB

❶ *His chair suddenly toppled backwards.*
• fall, tumble, tip over, keel over, overbalance
❷ *High winds toppled trees and brought down power lines.*
• knock down, bring down, push over, overturn, upset, upend
❸ *They plotted in secret to topple the president.*
• overthrow, bring down, remove from office, oust, unseat

tore

past tense see **tear**

torment VERB

❶ *He was tormented by bad dreams.*
• afflict, torture, plague, haunt, distress, harrow, rack
❷ *Stop tormenting the poor animal.*
• tease, taunt, harass, pester, bully
– To torment someone continually is to **persecute** or **victimize** them.

torrent NOUN

❶ *A torrent of water flowed down the hill.*
• flood, gush, rush, stream, spate, cascade
❷ *We were caught in a torrent of rain.*
• downpour, deluge, cloudburst
❸ *It all came out in a torrent of words.*
• outpouring, outburst, stream, flood, tide, barrage

torrential *ADJECTIVE*
The rain was torrential all day.
• heavy, violent, severe, driving, lashing

toss *VERB*
❶ *He tossed a pebble into the pond.*
• throw, hurl, fling, cast, pitch, lob, sling
(*informal*) chuck
❷ *We'll toss a coin to decide.*
• flip, spin
❸ *The little boat was tossing about in the waves.*
• pitch, lurch, bob, roll, rock, heave
❹ *She tossed and turned, unable to get to sleep.*
• thrash about, flail, writhe

total *ADJECTIVE*
❶ *What was your total score?*
• complete, whole, full, entire, overall, combined
OPPOSITE partial
❷ *The party was a total disaster.*
• complete, utter, absolute, thorough, sheer, downright, out-and-out

total *NOUN*
A total of 5 million viewers tuned in.
• sum, whole, entirety

total *VERB*
So far the donations total 2000 euros.
• add up to, amount to, come to, make

totally *ADVERB*
I totally agree with you.
• completely, wholly, entirely, fully, utterly, absolutely, thoroughly
OPPOSITE partly

totter *VERB*
The little girl tottered across the floor.
• stagger, teeter, stumble, reel, wobble

touch *VERB*
❶ *She gently touched him on the shoulder.*
• feel, handle, stroke, fondle, caress, pat, pet
❷ *The car just touched the gatepost.*
• brush, graze, skim, contact
❸ *Nothing in the room had been touched.*
• move, disturb, interfere with, meddle

with, tamper with
❹ *Temperatures can touch 45 degrees in summer.*
• reach, rise to, attain
(*informal*) hit
❺ *I was deeply touched by her letter.*
• affect, move, stir
➤ **touch on something**
You touched on the subject of money.
• refer to, mention, raise, broach

touch *NOUN*
❶ *I felt a light touch on my arm.*
• pat, stroke, tap, caress, contact
❷ *There's a touch of frost in the air.*
• hint, trace, suggestion, tinge
❸ *She has added her own touch to the songs.*
• style, feel, quality
❹ *Are you still in touch with the family?*
• contact, communication, correspondence

touching *ADJECTIVE*
The film ends with a touching final scene.
• moving, affecting, emotional, poignant, heart-warming, tear-jerking

touchy *ADJECTIVE*
He's very touchy about his weight.
• easily offended, sensitive, irritable

tough *ADJECTIVE*
❶ *You'll need tough shoes for the climb.*
• strong, sturdy, robust, durable, resilient, hard-wearing, stout, substantial
OPPOSITE flimsy
❷ *She's tougher than she looks.*
• strong, resilient, determined, robust, rugged, hardened
OPPOSITE weak
❸ *The team struggled against tough opposition.*
• strong, stiff, powerful, resistant, determined, stubborn
OPPOSITES weak, feeble
❹ *Don't be too tough on her.*
• firm, strict, severe, stern, hard-hitting
OPPOSITES soft, lenient
❺ *The meat was overcooked and tough.*
• chewy, leathery, rubbery
OPPOSITE tender

❻ *The first part of the climb is the toughest.*
• demanding, strenuous, arduous, laborious, gruelling, taxing, exhausting
OPPOSITE easy
❼ *That's a tough question to answer.*
• difficult, hard, tricky, puzzling, baffling, knotty, thorny
OPPOSITES easy, straightforward

tour NOUN
We went on a sightseeing tour of the city.
• trip, excursion, visit, journey, expedition, outing, jaunt

tourist NOUN
The cathedral was full of tourists.
• sightseer, holidaymaker, traveller, visitor

tournament NOUN
We reached the finals of the basketball tournament.
• championship, competition, contest, series

tow VERB
Horses used to tow barges along the river.
• pull, haul, tug, drag, draw

tower NOUN
The abbey has a small tower.
– A small tower on a castle or other building is a **turret**.
– A church tower is a **steeple**.
– The pointed structure on a steeple is a **spire**.
– The part of a tower with a bell is a **belfry**.
– The tall tower of a mosque is a **minaret**.

tower VERB
➤ **tower above or over something**
The monument towers above the landscape.
• rise above, stand above, dominate, loom over, overshadow

town NOUN
They live in a seaside town near Melbourne.
– A town with its own local council is a **borough**.
– A large and important town is a **city**.
– Several towns that merge into each other are a **conurbation**.
– The people who live in a town are the **townspeople**.
– A word meaning 'to do with a town or city' is **urban**.

toxic ADJECTIVE
The flask contains a toxic gas.
• poisonous, deadly, lethal, harmful
OPPOSITE harmless

toy NOUN
He found a box full of old toys.
• game, plaything

trace NOUN
❶ *He vanished without a trace.*
• evidence, sign, mark, indication, hint, clue, track, trail
❷ *They found traces of blood on the carpet.*
• vestige, remnant, spot, speck, drop, touch

trace VERB
The police have been trying to trace her.
• track down, discover, find, uncover, unearth

track NOUN
❶ *They followed the bear's tracks for miles.*
• footprint, footmark, trail, scent, spoor
❷ *A rough track leads past the farm.*
• path, pathway, footpath, trail
❸ *The race is a single lap around the track.*
• racetrack, circuit, course
❹ *They are laying the track for the new tram system.*
• line, rails

track VERB
Astronomers are tracking the comet's path.
• follow, trace, trail, pursue, shadow, stalk

> **track someone down**
It took years to track everyone down.
• find, discover, trace, hunt down, sniff out, run to ground

tract NOUN
They had to cross a vast tract of desert.
• area, expanse, stretch

trade NOUN
❶ *The trade in antiques has been booming recently.*
• business, dealing, buying and selling, commerce, market
❷ *He took up the same trade as his father.*
• occupation, profession, work, career, business, craft

trade VERB
> **trade in something**
The company trades in second-hand computers.
• deal in, do business in, buy and sell

tradition NOUN
The Moon Festival is a Chinese tradition.
• custom, convention, practice, habit, ritual, observance, institution

traditional ADJECTIVE
❶ *The Maya have preserved their traditional way of life.*
• long-established, time-honoured, age-old, customary, habitual, ritual
OPPOSITE non-traditional
❷ *The dancers wore traditional costumes.*
• folk, ethnic, national, regional, historical
❸ *They chose to have a traditional wedding.*
• conventional, orthodox, regular, standard, classic
OPPOSITE unorthodox

tragedy NOUN
❶ *'Romeo and Juliet' is a tragedy by Shakespeare.*
OPPOSITE comedy
❷ *The accident at sea was a real tragedy.*
• disaster, catastrophe, calamity, misfortune

tragic ADJECTIVE
❶ *He died in a tragic accident.*
• disastrous, catastrophic, calamitous, terrible, horrendous, appalling, dreadful, unfortunate, unlucky
❷ *It is a tragic story of doomed love.*
• sad, unhappy, sorrowful, mournful, pitiful, heart-rending, wretched, pathetic
OPPOSITES light-hearted, comic

trail NOUN
❶ *Scientists have been following the trail left by the comet.*
• track, stream, wake
❷ *There is a bike trail through the woods.*
• path, pathway, track, route
> **on the trail of someone**
Police have been on the trail of the thieves.
• on the track of, on the hunt for, in pursuit of, following the scent of

trail VERB
❶ *Plain-clothes officers are trailing the suspect.*
• follow, track, chase, pursue, shadow, stalk
(*informal*) tail
❷ *She trailed her suitcase behind her.*
• pull, tow, drag, draw, haul
❸ *A few walkers trailed behind the others.*
• fall behind, lag, straggle
OPPOSITE lead
> **trail away or off**
Her voice began to trail away.
• fade, grow faint, peter out, dwindle

train NOUN
It was an unusual train of events.
• sequence, series, string, chain, succession

train VERB
❶ *All members of the crew had to be trained to scuba-dive.*
• coach, instruct, teach, tutor, school, drill

❷ *They are training hard for the Olympics.*
• practise, exercise, get into shape
(*informal*) work out

❸ *He trained his gun on the bridge.*
• aim, point, direct, target, focus, level

trainer NOUN
She is a professional voice trainer.
• coach, instructor, teacher, tutor

tramp NOUN
❶ *I had to sleep rough like a tramp.*
• homeless person, vagrant, down-and-out

❷ *We went for a tramp through the woods.*
• trek, walk, hike, ramble

❸ *I could hear the tramp of marching feet.*
• tread, stamp, march, plod

tramp VERB
They tramped across the muddy field.
• trudge, trek, traipse, stamp, march, plod

trample VERB
Don't trample the flowers!
• tread on, stamp on, walk over, crush, flatten, squash

trance NOUN
The fortune-teller went into a trance.
• daze, stupor, reverie, hypnotic state

tranquil ADJECTIVE
❶ *They led a tranquil life in the country.*
• calm, peaceful, quiet, restful, sedate, relaxing
(*informal*) laid-back
OPPOSITES busy, hectic
❷ *Her face now wore a tranquil expression.*
• still, calm, placid, serene, undisturbed, unruffled

transfer VERB
Some paintings were transferred to the new gallery.
• move, remove, shift, relocate, convey, hand over

transform VERB
They transformed the attic into an office.
• convert, turn, change, alter, adapt, modify, rework

translate VERB
The book has been translated into 36 languages.
• interpret, convert, put, render, reword
– A person who translates a foreign language is a **translator**.
– A person who translates what someone is saying into another language is an **interpreter**.
– An expert in languages is a **linguist**.

transmit VERB
❶ *He was secretly transmitting messages in code.*
• send, communicate, relay, convey, dispatch
– To transmit a programme on radio or TV is to **broadcast** it.
OPPOSITE receive
❷ *Can the disease be transmitted to humans?*
• pass on, spread, carry

transparent ADJECTIVE
The insect's wings are almost transparent.
• clear
(*informal*) see-through
– Something which is not fully transparent, but allows light to shine through, is **translucent**.

transport VERB
Oil is transported in huge tanker ships.
• carry, convey, transfer, ship, ferry, move, shift, take, bear

transport NOUN
For types of transport see **aircraft, boat, vehicle**.

trap NOUN
❶ *The animal was caught in a trap.*
• snare, net
❷ *The last question might be a trap.*
• trick, deception, ruse, ploy

trap VERB
❶ *Sea creatures can get trapped in plastic bags.*
• catch, snare, ensnare, capture, corner
❷ *She was trapped into admitting she had lied.*
• trick, dupe, deceive, fool

trash (*informal*) NOUN
Sometimes I just feel like reading trash.
• rubbish, drivel, nonsense

travel VERB
I usually travel to school by bus.
• go, journey, move along, proceed, progress
– When birds travel from one country to another they **migrate**.
– When people travel to another country to live there they **emigrate**.

traveller NOUN
A busload of weary travellers arrived at the hotel.
• passenger, commuter, tourist, holidaymaker, backpacker
– A person who travels to a religious place is a **pilgrim**.
– A person who travels illegally on a ship or plane is a **stowaway**.
– A person who likes travelling round the world is a **globetrotter**.

treacherous ADJECTIVE
❶ *He was told about a treacherous plot to kill him.*
• disloyal, traitorous, unfaithful, untrustworthy, double-crossing
– A treacherous act is **treachery** or **betrayal**.
– A treacherous person is a **traitor**.
(OPPOSITE) loyal
❷ *The roads are often treacherous in winter.*
• dangerous, hazardous, perilous, unsafe, risky
(OPPOSITE) safe

tread VERB
Please tread carefully.
• step, walk, proceed

➤ **tread on**
Don't tread on the wet cement!
• step on, walk on, stamp on, trample, crush, flatten, squash

treasure NOUN
Divers are searching for sunken treasure.
• riches, valuables, wealth, fortune
– A store of treasure is a **cache** or **hoard**.

treasure VERB
I will always treasure the memory.
• cherish, prize, value, hold dear, set store by

treat VERB
❶ *They treated me as part of the family.*
• behave towards, act towards
❷ *We are treating the case as murder.*
• regard, view, look on, consider
❸ *This question is treated in more detail in the next chapter.*
• deal with, discuss, explore, handle, tackle
❹ *Two people are being treated for minor injuries.*
• tend, nurse, attend to
❺ *Let me treat you to lunch.*
• pay for, stand, buy, offer

treatment NOUN
❶ *The hospital is for the treatment of sick animals.*
• care, nursing, healing
❷ *This is a new treatment for asthma.*
• remedy, therapy, medication
– Emergency treatment at the scene of an accident is **first aid**.
❸ *Old documents need careful treatment.*
• handling, care, management, use

treaty NOUN
The two sides signed a peace treaty.
• agreement, pact, contract, settlement

a
b
c
d
e
f
g
h
i
j
k
l
m
n
o
p
q
r
s
t
u
v
w
x
y
z

tree NOUN

WORD WEB

Some varieties of tree:

➤ alder	➤ juniper
➤ almond	➤ larch
➤ apple	➤ lime
➤ ash	➤ maple or acer
➤ aspen	➤ monkey puzzle
➤ baobab	➤ oak
➤ banyan	➤ olive
➤ bay or laurel	➤ palm
➤ beech	➤ pear
➤ birch	➤ pine
➤ cedar	➤ plane
➤ cherry	➤ plum
➤ chestnut	➤ poplar
➤ cypress	➤ redwood
➤ elder	➤ rowan or
➤ elm	mountain ash
➤ eucalyptus	➤ rubber tree
➤ fir	➤ silver birch
➤ flame tree	➤ spruce
➤ fruit tree	➤ sycamore
➤ hawthorn	➤ tamarind
➤ hazel	➤ willow
➤ holly	➤ yew
➤ jujube	

- Trees which lose their leaves in winter are **deciduous**.
- Trees which have leaves all year round are **evergreen**.
- Trees which grow cones are **conifers**.
- A young tree is a **sapling**.
- An area covered with trees is a **wooded** area or **woodland**.
- A large area covered with trees and undergrowth is a **forest**.
- A small group of trees is a **copse** or **coppice**.
- An area planted with fruit trees is an **orchard**.

tremble VERB

The poor dog was trembling with cold.
• shake, shiver, quake, quiver, shudder

tremendous ADJECTIVE
❶ *There was a tremendous explosion.*
• very great, huge, enormous, massive, immense, colossal, mighty
(*informal*) terrific
❷ *Winning the cup would be a tremendous achievement.*
• marvellous, magnificent, wonderful, superb, stupendous, extraordinary, outstanding
(*informal*) brilliant, fantastic, terrific

tremor NOUN
There was a tremor in her voice.
• trembling, shaking, quavering, quivering, vibration, wobble

trend NOUN
❶ *There is a general trend towards healthier eating.*
• tendency, movement, shift, leaning, inclination, drift
❷ *Have you seen the latest trend in footwear?*
• fashion, style, craze, fad, vogue

trial NOUN
❶ *The film is about a murder trial.*
• case, hearing, lawsuit
– A military trial is a **court martial**.
❷ *Scientists are conducting trials on a new vaccine.*
• test, experiment, check, evaluation

tribe NOUN
Boudicca was queen of the Iceni tribe.
• people, ethnic group, clan

trick NOUN
❶ *Let's play a trick on her!*
• joke, practical joke, prank
❷ *It is a trick to get your log-in details.*
• deception, ruse, fraud, hoax, ploy
(*informal*) con, scam

trick VERB
He tricked them into believing he was a police officer.
• deceive, dupe, fool, hoodwink, cheat, swindle
(*informal*) con

trickle VERB
The sweat trickled down his nose.
• dribble, drip, leak, seep, ooze
OPPOSITE gush

trickle NOUN
The water flow had slowed to a trickle.
• dribble, drip
OPPOSITE gush

tricky ADJECTIVE
❶ *I found myself in a tricky situation.*
• difficult, awkward, problematic,
complicated, delicate, ticklish
OPPOSITES simple, straightforward
❷ *I wouldn't trust her—she's tricky.*
• crafty, cunning, sly, wily, devious

trigger VERB
*The smoke must have triggered her
asthma attack.*
• set off, start, activate, cause, provoke,
spark

trim ADJECTIVE
He likes to keep his garden trim.
• neat, orderly, tidy, well kept, smart,
spruce
OPPOSITE untidy

trim VERB
❶ *He was at the mirror trimming his
beard.*
• cut, clip, shorten, crop, prune, pare,
neaten, tidy
❷ *The gown was trimmed with fur.*
• edge, fringe, decorate, adorn,
embellish

trip VERB
She tripped on the loose carpet.
• catch your foot, stumble, fall, slip,
stagger

trip NOUN
We went on a trip to the seaside.
• journey, visit, outing, excursion,
expedition, jaunt, break

triumph NOUN
*The season ended in triumph for the
team.*
• victory, success, win, conquest

triumphant ADJECTIVE
❶ *He took a photo of the triumphant
team.*
• winning, victorious, conquering,
successful
OPPOSITE unsuccessful
❷ *A triumphant look spread across her
face.*
• elated, exultant, joyful, gleeful,
jubilant

trivial ADJECTIVE
Don't worry about trivial details.
• unimportant, insignificant, minor,
slight, trifling, negligible, petty,
frivolous
OPPOSITES important, significant

troop NOUN
A troop of tourists crossed the square.
• group, band, party, body,
company

troop VERB
We all trooped into the main hall.
• walk, march, proceed, stream, file

troops PLURAL NOUN
see army

trophy NOUN
*She has won several international
tennis trophies.*
• cup, prize, award, medal

trouble NOUN
❶ *He and his family may be in
trouble.*
• difficulty, hardship, suffering,
unhappiness, distress, misfortune, pain,
sadness, sorrow, worry
❷ *There were reports of trouble outside
the ground.*
• disorder, unrest, disturbance,
commotion, fighting, violence
❸ *The trouble with this computer is that
it's very slow.*
• problem, difficulty, disadvantage,
drawback
❹ *Please don't go to any trouble.*
• bother, inconvenience, effort,
pains

A
B
C
D
E
F
G
H
I
J
K
L
M
N
O
P
Q
R
S
T
U
V
W
X
Y
Z

trouble VERB
❶ *Something must be troubling her.*
• distress, upset, bother, worry, concern, pain, torment, perturb
IDIOM prey on your mind
❷ *I don't want to trouble them at this hour.*
• disturb, bother, inconvenience, impose on, put out

troublesome ADJECTIVE
❶ *Do you find the heat troublesome?*
• annoying, irritating, trying, tiresome, bothersome, inconvenient, nagging
❷ *The boys have been troublesome all day.*
• difficult, awkward, unruly, unmanageable, disobedient, uncooperative

trousers PLURAL NOUN
see clothes

truce NOUN
The two sides agreed on a truce.
• ceasefire, armistice, peace

true ADJECTIVE
❶ *The film is based on a true story.*
• real, factual, actual, historical
OPPOSITES fictional, made-up
❷ *What if the rumours are true?*
• accurate, correct, right, undeniable
OPPOSITES untrue, false
❸ *The play aims to present a true picture of war.*
• genuine, real, faithful, authentic, accurate, proper, exact
OPPOSITES false, misleading
❹ *You've always been a true friend to me.*
• faithful, loyal, constant, devoted, sincere, trustworthy, reliable, dependable
OPPOSITE disloyal

trunk NOUN
❶ *He kept his things in an old travelling trunk.*
• chest, case, box, crate, suitcase, coffer

❷ *The trunk of a palm tree can bend in the wind.*
• stem, stock
❸ *Try to keep your trunk straight.*
• torso, body, frame

trust VERB
❶ *I've never really trusted her.*
• be sure of, have confidence in, have faith in, believe in
❷ *Can I trust you to keep a secret?*
• rely on, depend on, count on, bank on
❸ *I trust you are well.*
• hope, assume, presume, take it

trust NOUN
❶ *His supporters began to lose trust in him.*
• belief, confidence, faith
❷ *I'm putting the documents in your trust.*
• responsibility, safe-keeping, hands

trustworthy ADJECTIVE
She was the only trustworthy member of the crew.
• reliable, dependable, loyal, true, honourable, responsible
OPPOSITE untrustworthy

truth NOUN
❶ *They finally accepted the truth of his story.*
• accuracy, correctness, truthfulness, reliability, validity, authenticity
(*formal*) veracity
OPPOSITES inaccuracy, falseness
❷ *The truth slowly began to dawn on him.*
• facts, reality
OPPOSITES lies, falsehood

truthful ADJECTIVE
❶ *I've not been entirely truthful with you.*
• honest, frank, sincere, straight, straightforward
OPPOSITE dishonest
❷ *Please give a truthful answer.*
• accurate, correct, true, proper, faithful, genuine
OPPOSITES untrue, false

try *VERB*
❶ *I'm trying to improve my technique.*
• attempt, endeavour, make an effort, aim, strive
❷ *Would you like to try a larger size?*
• test, try out, sample, evaluate, experiment with
(*informal*) check out

try *NOUN*
❶ *We may not succeed, but it's still worth a try.*
• attempt, effort, go
(*informal*) shot, bash, crack, stab
❷ *Have a try of this smoothie.*
• test, trial, sample, taste

trying *ADJECTIVE*
❶ *It's been a very trying day.*
• difficult, demanding, stressful, frustrating, fraught
OPPOSITE relaxing
❷ *My sister can be trying at times.*
• annoying, irritating, tiresome, maddening, exasperating, infuriating

tub *NOUN*
We shared a large tub of popcorn.
• pot, drum, carton, jar, barrel, cask, vat

tube *NOUN*
Roll the paper into a tube.
• cylinder, pipe
– A flexible tube for water is a **hose**.

tuck *VERB*
He tucked his shirt into his jeans.
• push, insert, slip, stick, stuff

tuft *NOUN*
The goat was munching on a few tufts of grass.
• clump, bunch, wisp

tug *VERB*
❶ *I tugged the rope to test it.*
• pull, jerk, pluck, wrench
(*informal*) yank
❷ *We tugged the sledge up the hill.*
• drag, pull, tow, haul, lug, draw, heave

tumble *VERB*
❶ *The whole bridge collapsed and tumbled into the river.*
• topple, fall, drop, pitch, plummet, plunge, crash
❷ *I tumbled into bed and fell straight asleep.*
• dive, flop, sink, slump, stumble
❸ *Her long hair tumbled down her back.*
• flow, fall, cascade

tumult *NOUN*
His voice could not be heard above the tumult.
• uproar, clamour, commotion, din, racket, rumpus, hubbub

tune *NOUN*
I am learning a new tune on the guitar.
• melody, song, air, theme

tunnel *NOUN*
The prisoners dug a tunnel under the wall.
– A tunnel dug by rabbits is a **burrow** and a system of burrows is a **warren**.
– A tunnel beneath a road is a **subway** or **underpass**.

tunnel *VERB*
Moles tunnel in search of earthworms.
• burrow, dig, mine, bore, excavate

turmoil *NOUN*
Her mind was in a state of turmoil.
• chaos, upheaval, uproar, disorder, unrest, commotion, disturbance, mayhem
OPPOSITES peace, order

turn *VERB*
❶ *The Earth turns on its axis once every 24 hours.*
• go round, revolve, rotate, roll, spin, swivel, pivot, twirl, whirl
❷ *Turn left at the end of the street.*
• change direction, change course, wheel round
– To turn unexpectedly is to **swerve** or **veer** off course.
– To turn and go back in the direction you came from is to **do a U-turn**.

❸ *He suddenly turned pale.*
• become, go, grow
❹ *They turned the attic into a spare room.*
• convert, adapt, change, alter, modify, transform
➤ **turn something down**
I turned down the offer of a lift.
• decline, refuse, reject, spurn, rebuff
➤ **turn something off**
Please turn off the computer when you leave.
• switch off, put off, shut down, deactivate
➤ **turn something on**
How do you turn on your phone?
• switch on, put on, start up, activate
➤ **turn out**
❶ *Everything turned out well in the end.*
• end up, come out, work out, happen
(*informal*) pan out
❷ *The photo turned out to be a fake.*
• prove, be found
➤ **turn up**
Some friends turned up unexpectedly.
• arrive, appear, drop in
(*informal*) show up
➤ **turn something up**
Can you turn up the volume?
• increase, raise, amplify, intensify

turn NOUN
❶ *Give the handle several turns.*
• spin, rotation, revolution, twist, swivel
❷ *We came to a turn in the road.*
• bend, corner, curve, angle, junction, turning
– A sharp turn in a road is a **hairpin bend.**
❸ *Whose turn is it to do the washing up?*
• time, go, stint, slot, try, chance, opportunity
(*informal*) shot
❹ *My sister and I are doing a comedy turn in the show.*
• act, performance, scene, sketch
❺ (*informal*) *You gave me quite a turn there!*
• fright, scare, shock, start, surprise

tutor NOUN
She is a professional singing tutor.
• teacher, instructor, trainer, coach

twig NOUN
They gathered twigs to make a fire.
• stick, stalk, stem, shoot

twin NOUN
❶ *Two of my cousins are twins.*
– Twins who look alike are **identical twins** and twins who do not look alike are **unidentical twins.**
❷ *Venus was once thought to be a twin of the Earth.*
• double, duplicate, look-alike, match, clone

twinkle VERB
The city lights twinkled in the distance.
• sparkle, glitter, shine, glisten, glimmer, glint, gleam, flicker, wink

twirl VERB
❶ *He paced up and down, twirling his umbrella.*
• twiddle, twist
❷ *A few skaters twirled on the ice rink.*
• spin, turn, whirl, revolve, rotate, pirouette

twist VERB
❶ *Twist the handle to open the door.*
• turn, rotate, revolve, swivel
– To twist off a lid or cap is to **unscrew** it.
❷ *The road twists through the hills.*
• wind, weave, curve, zigzag
❸ *He twisted and turned in his sleep.*
• toss, writhe, wriggle
❹ *Heat can twist metal out of shape.*
• bend, buckle, warp, crumple, mangle, distort
❺ *She twisted her hair into a knot.*
• wind, loop, coil, curl, entwine

twist NOUN
❶ *Give the handle a sharp twist.*
• turn, spin, rotation, revolution, swivel
❷ *The plot is full of unexpected twists.*
• turning, surprise, revelation, upset

twisted ADJECTIVE
The trunk of the tree was twisted with age.
• gnarled, warped, buckled, misshapen, deformed

twitch VERB
One of the upstairs curtains twitched.
• jerk, quiver, tremble, shudder, start

two NOUN
The chairs come in a set of two.
– Two people or things which belong
together are a **couple** or a **pair**.
– Two musicians playing or singing
together are a **duo**.
– A piece of music for two players or
singers is a **duet**.
– To multiply a number by two is to
double it.
SEE ALSO **double, dual**

type NOUN
❶ *What type of music do you like to
listen to?*
• kind, sort, variety, category, class,
genre, species

❷ *The footnotes are printed in small
type.*
• print, typeface, font, lettering, letters,
characters

typical ADJECTIVE
❶ *It began as just a typical day.*
• normal, usual, standard, ordinary,
average, unremarkable,
run-of-the-mill
OPPOSITES unusual, remarkable
❷ *Special effects like this are a typical
feature of action movies.*
• characteristic, representative,
classic
OPPOSITE uncharacteristic

a
b
c
d
e
f
g
h
i
j
k
l
m
n
o
p
q
r
s
t
u
v
w
x
y
z

A
B
C
D
E
F
G
H
I
J
K
L
M
N
O
P
Q
R
S
T
U
V
W
X
Y
Z

Uu

ugly ADJECTIVE
❶ *The view is ruined by an ugly tower block.*
• unattractive, unsightly, hideous, ghastly, monstrous, grotesque, repulsive
OPPOSITES beautiful, attractive
❷ *The crowd was in an ugly mood.*
• unfriendly, hostile, menacing, threatening, angry, dangerous, unpleasant
OPPOSITE friendly

ultimate ADJECTIVE
My ultimate goal is to be a writer.
• eventual, final, concluding
OPPOSITE initial

umpire NOUN
see referee

un- PREFIX
To find synonyms for words beginning with un- which are not listed below, try looking up the word to which un- has been added, then add un-, in- or not to its synonyms. For example, to find synonyms for unacceptable, look up acceptable and then work out the synonyms, unsatisfactory, inadequate, not good enough, etc.

unable ADJECTIVE
➤ **unable to**
I was tied down and unable to move.
• incapable of, powerless to, unequipped to, unfit for

unanimous ADJECTIVE
❶ *The judges came to a unanimous decision.*
• united, undivided, joint, collective
– *A decision where most but not all people agree is a* **majority** *decision.*
❷ *Critics have been unanimous in their praise.*
• in agreement, united, in accord, of one mind

unattractive ADJECTIVE
see ugly

unavoidable ADJECTIVE
The accident was unavoidable.
• inevitable, bound to happen, certain, predictable

unaware ADJECTIVE
➤ **unaware of**
They were unaware of the dangers that lay ahead.
• ignorant of, oblivious to, unconscious of, uninformed about
IDIOM in the dark about

unbearable ADJECTIVE
The stench in the cave was unbearable.
• unendurable, intolerable, impossible to bear

unbelievable ADJECTIVE
❶ *I found the plot frankly unbelievable.*
• unconvincing, unlikely, far-fetched, improbable, incredible
❷ *She scored an unbelievable goal.*
• amazing, astonishing, extraordinary, remarkable, sensational, phenomenal, staggering, stunning

unbroken ADJECTIVE
❶ *She sat in the one unbroken chair.*
• undamaged, unscathed, intact, whole, sound
OPPOSITES broken, damaged
❷ *There was a minute of unbroken silence.*
• uninterrupted, continuous, non-stop
OPPOSITE discontinuous
❸ *His Olympic record is still unbroken.*
• unbeaten, undefeated, unsurpassed

uncanny ADJECTIVE
❶ *Moonlight helped to create an uncanny atmosphere.*
• eerie, weird, ghostly, unearthly, other-worldly, unreal, freakish
(informal) creepy, spooky
❷ *He bears an uncanny resemblance to Elvis Presley.*
• striking, remarkable, extraordinary, incredible

uncertain ADJECTIVE

❶ *I was uncertain what to do next.*
• unsure, doubtful, unclear, undecided, in two minds, in a quandary
OPPOSITES certain, positive
❷ *The future of the festival is still uncertain.*
• indefinite, unknown, undecided, debatable, unpredictable, insecure
IDIOM touch and go
OPPOSITES definite, secure

unclean ADJECTIVE
see **dirty**

unclear ADJECTIVE

❶ *The instructions were unclear.*
• vague, obscure, ambiguous, imprecise, opaque, cryptic
❷ *I'm unclear about what you want me to do.*
• uncertain, unsure, doubtful

uncomfortable ADJECTIVE

❶ *The bed I had to sleep in was uncomfortable.*
• hard, lumpy, stiff, cramped, restrictive
OPPOSITE comfortable
❷ *She felt uncomfortable talking about herself.*
• awkward, uneasy, embarrassed, nervous, tense
OPPOSITES at ease, relaxed

uncommon ADJECTIVE

It's not uncommon to see dolphins here.
• unusual, rare, strange, abnormal, atypical, exceptional, unfamiliar, unexpected

unconscious ADJECTIVE

❶ *He was knocked unconscious by the fall.*
• senseless, knocked out
IDIOMS out cold, out for the count
– Someone who is unconscious for an operation is **anaesthetized**.
– Someone who is unconscious because of an accident or illness is **in a coma**.
OPPOSITE conscious

❷ *It was an unconscious slip of the tongue.*
• accidental, unintended, unintentional
OPPOSITES deliberate, intentional
➤ **unconscious of**
She was unconscious of causing any offence.
• unaware of, ignorant of, oblivious to
OPPOSITE aware of

uncover VERB

❶ *Archaeologists have uncovered a second tomb.*
• unearth, dig up, excavate, expose, reveal, disclose, unveil, lay bare
❷ *She finally uncovered the truth about her family's past.*
• discover, detect, come across, stumble on, chance on
OPPOSITES cover up, hide

undergo VERB

Guide dogs undergo rigorous training.
• go through, submit to, be subjected to, experience, put up with, face, endure

underground ADJECTIVE

❶ *He found himself in an underground cavern.*
• subterranean, sunken, buried
❷ *They were members of an underground resistance movement.*
• secret, undercover, covert, clandestine
IDIOM cloak-and-dagger

undermine VERB

Losing the race could undermine her confidence.
• weaken, lessen, diminish, reduce, impair, damage, shake
OPPOSITES support, boost

understand VERB

❶ *Can you understand what he's saying?*
• comprehend, make sense of, grasp, follow, make out, take in, interpret, work out, fathom
IDIOM make head or tail of
– To understand something in code is to **decode** or **decipher** it.

❷ *You don't understand how hard it is for me.*
• realize, appreciate, recognize, be aware of, be conscious of
❸ *I understand they're moving to Sydney.*
• believe, gather, hear, take it

understandable *ADJECTIVE*
❶ *The instructions are quite understandable.*
• comprehensible, intelligible, straightforward, clear, plain, lucid
❷ *It's understandable that you feel upset.*
• natural, reasonable, justifiable, normal, not surprising, to be expected

understanding *NOUN*
❶ *The robot has limited powers of understanding.*
• intelligence, intellect, sense, judgement
❷ *Coins can contribute to our understanding of the past.*
• comprehension, knowledge, grasp, mastery, appreciation, awareness
OPPOSITE ignorance
❸ *It is my understanding that the software is free.*
• belief, view, perception, impression
❹ *Sufferers need to be treated with understanding.*
• sympathy, compassion, consideration, tolerance
OPPOSITE indifference
❺ *The two sides reached an understanding.*
• agreement, deal, settlement, arrangement, accord

understanding *ADJECTIVE*
Thanks for being so understanding.
• sympathetic, compassionate, caring, kind, thoughtful, helpful, tolerant, forgiving

undertake *VERB*
❶ *He is asked to undertake a long and dangerous journey.*
• take on, accept, be responsible for, embark on, set about, tackle, attempt

❷ *They undertook to pay all the costs.*
• agree, consent, promise, pledge, guarantee, commit yourself

underwear *NOUN*
The drawer was full of underwear.
• underclothes, underclothing, undergarments
(*informal*) undies
– Women's underclothes are sometimes called **lingerie**.

undo *VERB*
❶ *She undid the laces on her boots.*
• unfasten, untie, unbutton, unhook, unlace, loosen, release
– To undo stitching is to **unpick** it.
❷ *I slowly undid the packaging.*
• open, unwrap, unfold, unwind, unroll, unfurl
❸ *They say nothing can undo the curse.*
• reverse, negate, cancel, wipe out, annul

undoubtedly *ADVERB*
She is undoubtedly our best player.
• definitely, certainly, unquestionably, undeniably, indubitably, without a doubt, doubtless, clearly

undress *VERB*
You can undress in the changing room.
• get undressed, take off your clothes, strip
OPPOSITES dress, get dressed

unearth *VERB*
❶ *We unearthed some Roman coins in our back garden.*
• dig up, excavate, uncover, turn up
❷ *She unearthed some old letters in a drawer.*
• find, discover, come across, hit upon, track down

uneasy *ADJECTIVE*
❶ *Something about her made me feel uneasy.*
• anxious, nervous, worried, apprehensive, troubled, unsettled, tense, on edge
OPPOSITE confident

❷ *There was an uneasy silence.*
• uncomfortable, awkward,
embarrassing, tense, strained
OPPOSITE comfortable

unemployed ADJECTIVE
*Since the factory closed, he has been
unemployed.*
• out of work, jobless, redundant
(*informal*) on the dole
OPPOSITES employed, working, in work

uneven ADJECTIVE
❶ *The ground was very uneven in places.*
• rough, bumpy, lumpy, rutted
OPPOSITE smooth
❷ *Their performance has been uneven
this season.*
• erratic, inconsistent, irregular, variable,
unpredictable, erratic, patchy
OPPOSITE consistent
❸ *It was a very uneven contest.*
• one-sided, unbalanced, unequal,
unfair
OPPOSITE balanced

unexpected ADJECTIVE
Her reaction was totally unexpected.
• surprising, unforeseen, unpredictable,
unplanned
OPPOSITE expected

unfair ADJECTIVE
❶ *People protested that the tax was
unfair.*
• unjust, unreasonable, discriminatory,
one-sided, biased
OPPOSITES fair, just
❷ *I felt that her comments were unfair.*
• undeserved, unmerited, uncalled-for,
unjustified, out of order
OPPOSITES fair, deserved

unfaithful ADJECTIVE
see disloyal

unfamiliar ADJECTIVE
*We looked out on an unfamiliar
landscape.*
• strange, unusual, curious, novel, alien

➤ **unfamiliar with**
*They were unfamiliar with the local
customs.*
• unaccustomed to, unused to,
unaware of

unfit ADJECTIVE
❶ *He is too unfit to play tennis these
days.*
• out of condition, out of shape,
unhealthy
OPPOSITE fit
❷ *The water is unfit to drink.*
• unsuitable, unsuited, unsatisfactory,
inappropriate, ill-equipped

unfortunate ADJECTIVE
❶ *The unfortunate couple had lost all
their possessions.*
• unlucky, poor, pitiful, wretched,
unhappy, hapless, ill-fated
OPPOSITES fortunate, lucky
❷ *The team got off to an unfortunate
start.*
• unwelcome, unfavourable,
unpromising, inauspicious, dismal, bad
OPPOSITES good, favourable
❸ *Sorry, that was an unfortunate choice
of words.*
• regrettable, unhappy, inappropriate,
unsuitable, unwise

unfortunately ADVERB
*Unfortunately I cannot come to your
party.*
• unluckily, unhappily, regrettably, sadly,
alas

unfriendly ADJECTIVE
He is likely to get an unfriendly reception.
• unwelcoming, inhospitable,
unsympathetic, impolite, uncivil,
hostile, cold, cool, aloof, stand-offish,
unsociable, unneighbourly
OPPOSITES friendly, amiable

ungrateful ADJECTIVE
I don't want to seem ungrateful.
• unappreciative, unthankful
OPPOSITE grateful

unhappy ADJECTIVE

❶ *He was desperately unhappy away from home.*
• sad, miserable, depressed, downhearted, despondent, gloomy, glum, downcast, forlorn, dejected, woeful, crestfallen
IDIOMS (*informal*) down in the dumps, down in the mouth
OPPOSITES happy, cheerful

❷ *I'm still unhappy with my score.*
• dissatisfied, displeased, discontented, disappointed
OPPOSITES satisfied, pleased

❸ *It was just an unhappy coincidence.*
• unfortunate, unlucky, ill-fated
OPPOSITE lucky

unhealthy ADJECTIVE

❶ *He had been an unhealthy child.*
• sickly, infirm, unwell, poorly, weak, delicate, feeble, frail
OPPOSITES healthy, strong

❷ *She eats an unhealthy diet of junk food.*
• unwholesome, harmful, unhygienic
OPPOSITES healthy, wholesome

unhelpful ADJECTIVE

The receptionist was most unhelpful.
• uncooperative, unfriendly, disobliging
OPPOSITE helpful

unidentified ADJECTIVE

An unidentified aircraft was spotted at night.
• unknown, unrecognized, unspecified, unnamed, nameless, anonymous
OPPOSITE named

uniform NOUN

He changed into his police uniform.
• costume, outfit, livery, regalia
(*informal*) get-up

uniform ADJECTIVE

❶ *The air is kept at a uniform temperature.*
• consistent, regular, even, stable, steady, unvarying, unchanging
OPPOSITE varying

❷ *Pearls are rarely uniform in size.*
• identical, equal, the same, matching, consistent
OPPOSITE different

unify VERB

The new president promised to unify the country.
• unite, bring together, integrate, combine, join, merge, amalgamate
OPPOSITE separate

unimportant ADJECTIVE

Don't worry about unimportant details.
• insignificant, minor, trivial, trifling, secondary, irrelevant, slight, small, negligible, petty
OPPOSITES important, major

uninhabited ADJECTIVE

The island has been uninhabited for decades.
• unoccupied, empty, deserted, abandoned
OPPOSITES inhabited, populated

uninteresting ADJECTIVE

The journey home was fairly uninteresting.
• dull, boring, unexciting, tedious, dreary, banal, humdrum
OPPOSITES interesting, exciting

union NOUN

The city was formed by the union of two neighbouring towns.
• uniting, joining, integration, merger, amalgamation, fusion, combination
– A union of two rivers is a **confluence**.
– A union of two countries is their **unification**.

unique ADJECTIVE

Each person's fingerprints are unique.
• distinctive, different, individual, special, peculiar
(*informal*) one-off

unit NOUN

The shelves are built from separate units.
• piece, part, bit, section, segment, element, component, module

unite VERB
❶ *Their marriage united the two kingdoms.*
• combine, join, bring together, merge, unify, integrate, amalgamate
OPPOSITE separate
❷ *Local residents united to fight the plan.*
• collaborate, cooperate, come together, join together, join forces
– To unite to do something bad is to **conspire**.
OPPOSITE compete

universal ADJECTIVE
The idea met with universal agreement.
• general, common, widespread, global, worldwide, international

universe NOUN
Are we really alone in the universe?
• cosmos, space, infinity
SEE ALSO space

unjust ADJECTIVE
see **unfair**

unkind ADJECTIVE
What an unkind thing to say!
• unpleasant, unfriendly, unsympathetic, inconsiderate, uncaring, hard-hearted, mean, harsh, cruel, thoughtless, heartless, unfeeling, callous, uncharitable, nasty
OPPOSITES kind, sympathetic

unknown ADJECTIVE
❶ *The letter was in an unknown hand.*
• unidentified, unrecognized
OPPOSITE known
❷ *The author of the story is unknown.*
• anonymous, nameless, unnamed, unspecified
OPPOSITE named
❸ *We were now entering unknown territory.*
• unfamiliar, alien, foreign, undiscovered, unexplored, uncharted
OPPOSITE familiar

❹ *The main part is played by an unknown actor.*
• little known, unheard of, obscure
OPPOSITE famous

unlike ADJECTIVE
The landscape was unlike anything I had ever seen.
• different from, distinct from, dissimilar to
OPPOSITE similar to

unlikely ADJECTIVE
❶ *It is difficult to believe such an unlikely explanation.*
• unbelievable, unconvincing, improbable, implausible, incredible, dubious, far-fetched
OPPOSITE likely
❷ *It is unlikely that he will win.*
• doubtful, improbable, dubious
OPPOSITE likely

unlucky ADJECTIVE
❶ *Some people say that 13 is an unlucky number.*
• unfavourable, inauspicious, ill-omened, ill-starred, jinxed
❷ *She was unlucky not to get a medal.*
• unfortunate, luckless, hapless
OPPOSITE lucky

unmarried ADJECTIVE
He was the only unmarried man in the room.
• single, unwed
– If your marriage has been legally ended, you are **divorced**.
– An unmarried man is a **bachelor**.
– An old-fashioned word for an unmarried woman is a **spinster**.

unmistakable ADJECTIVE
There was an unmistakable smell of burning.
• distinct, distinctive, clear, obvious, plain, telltale

unnatural ADJECTIVE
❶ *An unnatural silence filled the room.*
• unusual, abnormal, uncommon, exceptional, irregular, odd, strange, weird, bizarre

❷ *Some of the acting was a bit unnatural.*
• stiff, stilted, unrealistic, forced, affected, self-conscious
❸ *His hair was an unnatural shade of yellow.*
• artificial, synthetic, man-made, manufactured
OPPOSITE natural

unnecessary ADJECTIVE
You can free up space by deleting unnecessary files.
• inessential, non-essential, unwanted, excessive, superfluous, surplus, extra, redundant, uncalled for, expendable
OPPOSITE necessary

unoccupied ADJECTIVE
❶ *The building itself was unoccupied.*
• empty, uninhabited, deserted, unused, vacant
OPPOSITES occupied, inhabited
❷ *The seat next to me was unoccupied.*
• vacant, free, available
OPPOSITES taken, occupied

unpleasant ADJECTIVE
❶ *He is a thoroughly unpleasant man.*
• unlikeable, disagreeable, objectionable, obnoxious, unfriendly, unkind, bad-tempered, nasty, malicious, spiteful, mean
❷ *The entire trip was an unpleasant experience.*
• uncomfortable, disagreeable, upsetting, distressing, awful, dreadful, horrible
❸ *What is that unpleasant smell?*
• disgusting, foul, repulsive, revolting, repellent, offensive
OPPOSITES pleasant, agreeable

unpopular ADJECTIVE
The new manager was unpopular at first.
• disliked, unwelcome, unloved, friendless, out of favour
OPPOSITE popular

unravel VERB
❶ *I unravelled the string and wound it into a ball.*
• disentangle, untangle, undo, untwist, separate out
❷ *No one has yet unravelled the mystery.*
• solve, clear up, puzzle out, work out, figure out, explain, clarify
IDIOM get to the bottom of

unreal ADJECTIVE
Everything seemed unreal, as if he was in a dream.
• dream-like, imaginary, make-believe, fictitious, fanciful
OPPOSITES real, realistic

unrest NOUN
A period of political unrest followed.
• disturbance, disorder, trouble, turmoil, dissent, strife, agitation, protest
OPPOSITES calm, order

unsafe ADJECTIVE
The coastal rocks are unsafe for climbing.
• dangerous, hazardous, risky, insecure, unsound, treacherous, perilous
OPPOSITE safe

unsatisfactory ADJECTIVE
The book comes to an unsatisfactory conclusion.
• disappointing, displeasing, inadequate, poor, weak, unacceptable, insufficient
OPPOSITE satisfactory

unscrupulous ADJECTIVE
The smugglers were cunning and unscrupulous.
• dishonest, unprincipled, disreputable, immoral, unethical, shameless

unseen ADJECTIVE
see **invisible**

unsettling ADJECTIVE
The silence was unsettling.
• disturbing, unnerving, disquieting, disconcerting, perturbing, troubling

A B C D E F G H I J K L M N O P Q R S T U V W X Y Z

unsightly ADJECTIVE
Litter makes the beach look unsightly.
• unattractive, ugly, unprepossessing, unappealing, hideous, grotesque

unsociable ADJECTIVE
Pandas are unsociable animals.
• unfriendly, unapproachable, reserved, withdrawn, retiring
OPPOSITES sociable, gregarious

unstable or **unsteady** ADJECTIVE
The table was a bit unsteady.
• shaky, wobbly, insecure, unbalanced, rickety
OPPOSITES stable, steady

unsuccessful ADJECTIVE
He led an unsuccessful expedition to the South Pole.
• failed, abortive, futile, ineffective, fruitless, unproductive
OPPOSITES successful, triumphant

unsuitable ADJECTIVE
The film is unsuitable for very young children.
• inappropriate, unfitting, unacceptable, ill-suited, out of place, out of keeping
OPPOSITES suitable, appropriate

unsure ADJECTIVE
She seemed unsure of what to say or do.
• uncertain, unclear, undecided, doubtful, in two minds, in a quandary
OPPOSITES certain, clear

untidy ADJECTIVE
❶ *The garden is looking a bit untidy.*
• messy, disorderly, cluttered, jumbled, tangled, chaotic
(informal) higgledy-piggledy, topsy-turvy
OPPOSITES tidy, orderly, well kept
❷ *His hair always looks untidy.*
• dishevelled, bedraggled, rumpled, unkempt, scruffy, slovenly
❸ *Her work was untidy and full of mistakes.*
• careless, disorganized, slapdash
(informal) sloppy

untrue ADJECTIVE
Almost every part of the story is untrue.
• false, incorrect, inaccurate, erroneous, wrong
OPPOSITES true, accurate

unusual ADJECTIVE
❶ *The weather is unusual for this time of year.*
• abnormal, out of the ordinary, exceptional, remarkable, extraordinary, odd, peculiar, singular, strange, unexpected, irregular, unheard-of
OPPOSITES normal, typical
❷ *Ebenezer is an unusual name.*
• uncommon, rare, unfamiliar, unconventional, unorthodox
OPPOSITE common

unwell ADJECTIVE
see ill

unwilling ADJECTIVE
He was unwilling to fight the old man.
• reluctant, hesitant, disinclined, loath, resistant
OPPOSITES willing, eager

unwise ADJECTIVE
It would be unwise to ignore the warning signs.
• foolish, foolhardy, ill-advised, senseless, stupid, silly
OPPOSITES wise, sensible

upheaval NOUN
I can't face the upheaval of moving house again.
• disruption, disturbance, upset, disorder, commotion, turmoil

uphill ADJECTIVE
❶ *The first half of the race is uphill.*
• upward, ascending, rising, climbing
OPPOSITE downhill
❷ *We are all facing an uphill struggle.*
• hard, difficult, tough, strenuous, laborious, arduous, exhausting, gruelling, taxing

a
b
c
d
e
f
g
h
i
j
k
l
m
n
o
p
q
r
s
t
u
v
w
x
y
z

A B C D E F G H I J K L M N O P Q R S T U V W X Y Z

upkeep NOUN
Which department is responsible for the upkeep of cycle paths?
• care, maintenance, servicing, running

upper ADJECTIVE
My bedroom is on the upper floor.
• higher, upstairs, top
OPPOSITE lower

upright ADJECTIVE
❶ *The car seat should be in an upright position.*
• erect, perpendicular, vertical
OPPOSITE horizontal
❷ *He is an upright member of the local community.*
• honest, honourable, respectable, reputable, law-abiding, virtuous, upstanding, principled, worthy
OPPOSITES disreputable, dishonest

uproar NOUN
The meeting ended in uproar.
• chaos, disorder, commotion, confusion, turmoil, pandemonium, mayhem, rumpus, furore

upset VERB
❶ *He must have said something to upset her.*
• distress, trouble, disturb, unsettle, disconcert, displease, offend, dismay, perturb, fluster, bother
❷ *Their arrival upset all our plans.*
• disrupt, interfere with, interrupt, affect, throw out, mess up
❸ *She upset a pot of soup.*
• knock over, tip over, overturn, topple, spill

upset ADJECTIVE
You sounded upset on the phone.
• worried, troubled, bothered, disturbed, agitated, unhappy, disappointed

upset NOUN
❶ *He is off school with a stomach upset.*
• illness, ailment, disorder
(*informal*) bug
❷ *There has been a major upset in the quarter-finals.*
• shock, surprise, upheaval, setback
IDIOM turn-up for the books

upside-down ADJECTIVE
❶ *A convex lens projects an image that is upside-down.*
• inverted, upturned, wrong way up
(*informal*) topsy-turvy
❷ (*informal*) *Suddenly her whole life was upside-down.*
• in disarray, in disorder, in a muddle, chaotic, disorderly, jumbled up
(*informal*) higgledy-piggledy
OPPOSITE orderly

up to date or **up-to-date** ADJECTIVE
❶ *Her clothes are always up to date.*
• fashionable, stylish, contemporary, modern
(*informal*) trendy, hip
OPPOSITE old-fashioned
❷ *The spacecraft uses the most up-to-date technology.*
• new, recent, current, the latest, advanced, cutting-edge, state-of the art, up-to-the-minute
OPPOSITES out of date, out-of-date
❸ *Keep up to date with all the celebrity gossip.*
• informed, acquainted, in touch
IDIOMS in the picture, up to speed
OPPOSITE out of touch
You write up-to-date (with hyphens) immediately before a noun: *The website provides up-to-date information.*

upward ADJECTIVE
It was a steep upward climb.
• uphill, ascending, rising
OPPOSITE downward

urban ADJECTIVE
Most of the population live in urban areas.
• built-up, municipal, metropolitan
OPPOSITE rural

urge VERB
She urged him to reconsider his decision.
• advise, counsel, appeal to, beg, implore, plead with, press
– To urge someone to do something is also to **advocate** or **recommend** it.
OPPOSITE discourage

➤ urge someone on
The home crowd urged their team on.
• encourage, spur on, egg on

urge *NOUN*
I had a sudden urge to burst into song.
• impulse, compulsion, desire, wish, longing, yearning, craving, hankering, itch, yen

urgent *ADJECTIVE*
❶ *I have an urgent matter to discuss.*
• pressing, serious, critical, essential, important, top-priority
OPPOSITE unimportant
❷ *The stranger spoke in an urgent whisper.*
• anxious, insistent, earnest

usable *ADJECTIVE*
❶ *The lift is not usable today.*
• operating, working, functioning, functional
OPPOSITE unusable
❷ *Is this voucher still usable?*
• valid, acceptable
OPPOSITE invalid

use *VERB*
❶ *You may use a calculator to help you.*
• make use of, employ, utilize
– To use your knowledge is to **apply** it.
– To use people or things selfishly is to **exploit** them.
❷ *Can you show me how to use the photocopier?*
• operate, work, handle, manage
– To hold and use a weapon or tool is to **wield** it.
❸ *Please don't use all the hot water.*
• use up, go through, consume, exhaust, spend

use *NOUN*
❶ *Would these books be any use to you?*
• help, benefit, advantage, profit, value
❷ *Can you find a use for this crate?*
• function, purpose, point
❸ *This is not an efficient use of your time.*
• usage, application, employment, utilization

used *ADJECTIVE*
They sell used computers.
• second-hand, pre-owned, old, hand-me-down, cast-off
OPPOSITES new, unused
➤ used to
She is used to getting her own way.
• accustomed to, familiar with, experienced in, in the habit of, no stranger to
OPPOSITE unaccustomed to

useful *ADJECTIVE*
❶ *A webcam is useful for chatting online.*
• convenient, handy, practical, effective, efficient
❷ *The leaflet offers some useful advice.*
• good, helpful, valuable, worthwhile, constructive, productive, fruitful
OPPOSITES useless, unhelpful

useless *ADJECTIVE*
❶ *Most of her advice was completely useless.*
• worthless, unhelpful, pointless, futile, unprofitable, fruitless, impractical, unusable
IDIOM of no avail
OPPOSITES useful, helpful
❷ *(informal) I've always been useless at maths.*
• bad, poor, incompetent, incapable *(informal)* rubbish, hopeless
OPPOSITE good

user-friendly *ADJECTIVE*
She has written a user-friendly guide to punctuation.
• easy to use, straightforward, uncomplicated, understandable

usher *VERB*
We were ushered into the dining hall.
• escort, conduct, guide, lead, show, take

usual *ADJECTIVE*
❶ *I'll meet you at the usual time.*
• normal, customary, familiar, habitual, regular, standard

❷ *It's usual to knock before entering.*
• common, accepted, conventional, traditional
OPPOSITE unusual

usually *ADVERB*
I don't usually get up this early.
• normally, generally, ordinarily, customarily, habitually, as a rule

utensil *NOUN*
A rack of cooking utensils hung on the wall.
• tool, implement, device, gadget, instrument, appliance
(*informal*) gizmo

utmost *ADJECTIVE*
This message is of the utmost importance.
• highest, greatest, supreme, maximum, top, paramount

utter *VERB*
The girl could scarcely utter her name.
• say, speak, express, pronounce, articulate, voice, mouth, put into words

utter *ADJECTIVE*
The three of us stared in utter amazement.
• complete, total, absolute, thorough, sheer, downright, out-and-out

Vv

vacancy *NOUN*
They have a vacancy for a trainee journalist.
• opening, position, post, job, situation

vacant *ADJECTIVE*
❶ *The house next door is still vacant.*
• unoccupied, empty, uninhabited, deserted
OPPOSITE occupied
❷ *The assistant gave me a vacant stare.*
• blank, expressionless, emotionless, impassive, glazed, deadpan
OPPOSITE expressive

vague *ADJECTIVE*
❶ *The directions she gave were rather vague.*
• indefinite, imprecise, broad, general, ill-defined, unclear, woolly
OPPOSITES exact, detailed
❷ *I have only a vague memory of that day.*
• blurred, indistinct, obscure, dim, hazy, shadowy
OPPOSITES definite, clear

vain *ADJECTIVE*
❶ *He is rather vain about his looks.*
• arrogant, proud, conceited, haughty, self-satisfied, narcissistic
OPPOSITE modest
❷ *I made a vain attempt to tidy my room.*
• unsuccessful, ineffective, useless, pointless, futile, fruitless
OPPOSITE successful

valid *ADJECTIVE*
❶ *The ticket is valid for three months.*
• current, usable, legal, authorized, official, in effect
❷ *The author makes several valid points.*
• acceptable, reasonable, sound, legitimate, genuine, justifiable, cogent
OPPOSITE invalid

valley *NOUN*
The village lies in a deep valley.
• vale, dale, gorge, gully, pass, ravine, canyon
(*Scottish*) glen

valuable *ADJECTIVE*
❶ *I believe the necklace is very valuable.*
• expensive, costly, dear, high-priced, precious, priceless
OPPOSITE valueless
❷ *He gave us some valuable advice.*
• useful, helpful, good, beneficial, constructive, worthwhile, invaluable
OPPOSITE worthless
The word invaluable is not the opposite of valuable: a piece of *invaluable advice* is one that is extremely valuable.

value *NOUN*
❶ *The house has doubled in value since they bought it.*
• price, cost, worth
❷ *He stressed the value of taking regular exercise.*
• advantage, benefit, merit, use, usefulness, importance

value *VERB*
❶ *I have always valued her opinion.*
• esteem, respect, appreciate, have a good opinion of, think highly of
IDIOM set great store by
– To value something highly is to **prize** or **treasure** it.
❷ *The painting was valued at 6 million dollars.*
• price, cost, rate, evaluate, assess

van *NOUN*
see vehicle

vanish *VERB*
His smile vanished in an instant.
• disappear, go away, fade, dissolve, disperse
OPPOSITE appear

vanity *NOUN*
Her rejection of him was a blow to his vanity.
• arrogance, pride, conceit, self-esteem,

a b c d e f g h i j k l m n o p q r s t u v w x y z

A B C D E F G H I J K L M N O P Q R S T U V W X Y Z

self-importance
(*informal*) big-headedness

vapour NOUN
A thick vapour rose up from the beaker.
• gas, fumes, steam, smoke
– Vapour hanging in the air is **haze, fog,
mist** or **smog**.
– When something turns to vapour it
vaporizes.

variable ADJECTIVE
*The weather is variable at this time of
year.*
• changeable, fluctuating, erratic,
inconsistent, unpredictable, fluid, fickle,
unstable
OPPOSITE constant

variation NOUN
❶ *There have been slight variations in
temperature.*
• difference, change, fluctuation, shift
OPPOSITE uniformity
❷ *This recipe is a variation on a classic
dish.*
• alteration (of), modification (of),
deviation (from)

varied ADJECTIVE
She has varied interests.
• diverse, assorted, mixed,
miscellaneous, wide-ranging, disparate,
motley
OPPOSITE uniform

variety NOUN
❶ *The centre offers a variety of leisure
activities.*
• assortment, range, mixture, array,
miscellany
❷ *We stock over thirty varieties of pasta.*
• kind, sort, type, category, form, make,
model, brand
❸ *Try to add more variety to your
writing.*
• variation, diversity, change, difference

various ADJECTIVE
*The shoes are available in various
colours.*
• different, several, assorted, varying,
differing, a variety of, diverse, sundry

vary VERB
❶ *Try varying the volume on the
speakers.*
• change, modify, adjust, alter
❷ *The length of daylight varies with the
seasons.*
• change, alter, differ, fluctuate
❸ *Estimates vary widely.*
• differ, be dissimilar, disagree, diverge

vast ADJECTIVE
❶ *He has accumulated a vast fortune.*
• huge, great, immense, enormous,
massive, gigantic, colossal
OPPOSITE tiny
❷ *A vast stretch of water lay between
them and dry land.*
• broad, wide, extensive, sweeping

vault VERB
➤ vault over something
He vaulted over the fence and ran off.
• jump over, leap over, bound over,
spring over, clear, hurdle
vault NOUN
*The documents are stored in an
underground vault at night.*
• strongroom, treasury
– An underground part of a house is
a **basement** or **cellar**.
– A room underneath a church is
a **crypt**.

veer VERB
*Suddenly, the car veered sharply to the
left.*
• swerve, turn, swing, change direction,
change course

vegetable NOUN

WORD WEB

Leaf vegetables:

➤ Brussels sprout	➤ kale
➤ cabbage	➤ lettuce
➤ cauliflower	➤ mustard greens
➤ Chinese cabbage or Chinese leaf	➤ pak choi
	➤ spinach
➤ endive	➤ Swiss chard
➤ globe artichoke	➤ watercress

Root vegetables:

➤ beetroot	➤ radish
➤ carrot	➤ swede
➤ celeriac	➤ sweet potato
➤ daikon	➤ turnip
➤ parsnip	

Legumes or pulses:

➤ broad beans or fava beans	➤ lentils
➤ butter beans or lima beans	➤ mangetout or sugarsnap peas
➤ chickpeas	➤ mung beans
➤ French beans or green beans	➤ peas
➤ kidney beans	➤ runner beans
	➤ snow peas
	➤ soya beans

Other vegetables:

➤ asparagus	➤ marrow
➤ aubergine	➤ mushroom
➤ butternut squash	➤ okra
➤ broccoli	➤ onion
➤ cauliflower	➤ pepper
➤ celery	➤ potato
➤ courgette	➤ pumpkin
➤ cucumber	➤ shallot
➤ garlic	➤ spaghetti squash
➤ Jerusalem artichoke	➤ spring onions
➤ kohlrabi	➤ sweetcorn
➤ leek	➤ water chestnut
	➤ yam

vegetarian NOUN
Many but not all Buddhists are vegetarians.
– A person who doesn't eat any animal products is a **vegan**.
– An animal that feeds only on plants is a **herbivore**.
OPPOSITES carnivore, meat-eater

vegetation NOUN
The rainforest is filled with lush vegetation.
• foliage, greenery, growth, plants, undergrowth

vehicle NOUN

WORD WEB

Some types of vehicle:

➤ ambulance	➤ motorbike or motorcycle
➤ bicycle	➤ people carrier
➤ bulldozer	➤ pick-up truck
➤ bus	➤ police car
➤ cab	➤ rickshaw
➤ cable car	➤ scooter
➤ car or (*old use*) motor car	➤ skidoo
➤ caravan	➤ sledge
➤ coach	➤ sleigh
➤ double-decker	➤ snowplough
➤ fire engine	➤ steamroller
➤ forklift truck	➤ tank
➤ four-wheel drive	➤ taxi
➤ hearse	➤ tractor
➤ HGV or heavy goods vehicle	➤ train
➤ horsebox	➤ tram
➤ jeep	➤ tricycle
➤ lorry	➤ trolleybus
➤ minibus	➤ truck
➤ minicab	➤ underground train
	➤ van

Old horse-drawn vehicles:

➤ carriage	➤ hansom cab
➤ cart	➤ stagecoach
➤ chariot	➤ trap
➤ gig	➤ wagon

For transport by air and sea see aircraft, boat.

veil VERB
Her face was partly veiled by a scarf.
• cover, conceal, hide, mask, shroud

vein NOUN
❶ *Blood pumps through your veins.*
• blood vessel
– Major blood vessels which carry blood from your heart to other parts of your body are **arteries**.
– Delicate hair-like blood vessels are **capillaries**.

② *The story is told in a light-hearted vein.*
• style, mood, manner, tone, character, spirit, humour

velocity NOUN
The asteroid is travelling at high velocity through space.
• speed, rate, rapidity, swiftness

vengeance NOUN
The duke swore vengeance on his enemies.
• revenge, retribution, retaliation
OPPOSITE forgiveness

venomous ADJECTIVE
The adder is Britain's only venomous snake.
• poisonous, toxic

vent NOUN
Hot air escapes through vents in the roof.
• outlet, opening, aperture, gap, hole, slit, duct

vent VERB
The crowd vented their frustration by booing.
• express, let out, give vent to, pour out, release, voice, air

venture NOUN
His first business venture was a disaster.
• enterprise, undertaking, project, scheme, operation, endeavour

venture VERB
We ventured out into the snow.
• set out, set forth, dare to go, emerge, journey

verdict NOUN
We are waiting for the verdict of the jury.
• decision, judgement, finding, conclusion, ruling

verge NOUN
There is a grassy verge alongside the road.
• side, edge, margin
– A stone or concrete edging beside a road is a **kerb**.

– The flat strip of road beside a motorway is the **hard shoulder**.
➤ **on the verge of**
Some species are now on the verge of extinction.
• on the edge of, on the point of, on the brink of, close to, approaching

verify VERB
An eyewitness verified his statement.
• confirm, prove, validate, support, back up, bear out, substantiate, corroborate

versatile ADJECTIVE
① *He's an extremely versatile musician.*
• resourceful, adaptable, flexible, multi-talented, all-round
② *Cotton is a very versatile fabric.*
• adaptable, multi-purpose, all-purpose

verse NOUN
① *The entire play is written in verse.*
• rhyme, poetry
② *I have learnt the first two verses of the poem.*
• stanza

version NOUN
① *Write your own version of the story.*
• account, description, report, statement
② *She starred in a film version of 'Wuthering Heights'.*
• adaptation, interpretation, rendering
– A version of something which was originally in another language is a **translation**.
③ *The new version of the game will be released in May.*
• design, model, form, variation, edition

vertical ADJECTIVE
Pull the lever back to its vertical position.
• upright, perpendicular, standing, erect
– A vertical drop is a **sheer** drop.
OPPOSITES horizontal, flat

very ADVERB
It was a very cold day.
• extremely, highly, exceedingly, especially, particularly, truly, remarkably, unusually, exceptionally, singularly, decidedly, really, intensely, acutely
(*informal*) terribly, awfully, seriously,

ultra, mega
OPPOSITES slightly, rather

vessel NOUN
❶ Small fishing vessels were bobbing about in the harbour.
• boat, ship, craft
❷ Archaeologists found clay vessels at the site.
• pot, dish, bowl, jar, jug, container, receptacle
❸ For blood vessels see **vein**.

veto VERB
They vetoed the proposal for a skatepark.
• reject, turn down, say no to, dismiss, disallow, ban, prohibit, forbid
OPPOSITE approve

vex VERB
Her behaviour vexed him a good deal.
• annoy, irritate, make you cross, anger, infuriate, exasperate

vibrate VERB
Every time a train went past the walls vibrated.
• shake, tremble, quiver, quake, shiver, shudder, judder, throb

vicious ADJECTIVE
❶ This was once the scene of a vicious murder.
• brutal, violent, savage, ferocious, bloodthirsty, cruel, callous, merciless, pitiless, ruthless, inhuman, barbaric, sadistic
❷ The dog looked extremely vicious.
• fierce, ferocious, violent, savage, wild

victim NOUN
Ambulances took the victims to hospital.
• casualty, sufferer
– Victims of an accident are also **the injured** or **the wounded**.
– A person who dies in an accident is a **fatality**.

victor NOUN
A Canadian crew came away as the victors.
• winner, champion, conqueror

victorious ADJECTIVE
The trophy was presented to the victorious team.
• winning, triumphant, successful, conquering, top
OPPOSITES defeated, losing

victory NOUN
He led his team to an unlikely victory.
• win, success, triumph, conquest
OPPOSITES defeat, loss

view NOUN
❶ There's a great view from the top floor.
• outlook, prospect, scene, scenery, vista, panorama
❷ She has strong views on the subject.
• opinion, thought, attitude, belief, conviction, sentiment, idea, notion
➤ **in view of**
In view of the circumstances, they gave us a refund.
• because of, as a result of, considering, taking account of

view VERB
❶ Both locals and tourists come to view the scenery.
• look at, see, observe, regard, gaze at, eye, scan, survey, inspect, examine, contemplate
❷ He viewed the newcomers with suspicion.
• think of, consider, regard, look on

viewer NOUN
The programme invites viewers to tweet their comments.
– People who view a performance are the **audience** or **spectators**.
– People who view something as they happen to pass by are **bystanders** or **onlookers**.

vigilant ADJECTIVE
You must be vigilant when cycling in traffic.
• alert, watchful, attentive, observant, wary, on the lookout, on your guard
OPPOSITE inattentive

541

a
b
c
d
e
f
g
h
i
j
k
l
m
n
o
p
q
r
s
t
u
v
w
x
y
z

vigorous ADJECTIVE
❶ She does an hour of vigorous exercise every week.
• active, brisk, energetic, lively, strenuous, forceful, powerful
OPPOSITES light, gentle
❷ He was a vigorous man in the prime of life.
• robust, strong, sturdy, healthy, fit
OPPOSITES feeble, weak

vigour NOUN
When they sighted land, they began to row with renewed vigour.
• energy, spirit, vitality, liveliness, enthusiasm, passion, dynamism, verve, gusto, zeal, zest
(informal) oomph, get-up-and-go

vile ADJECTIVE
❶ That medicine tastes vile.
• disgusting, repulsive, revolting, foul, horrible, loathsome, offensive, repellent, sickening, nauseating
OPPOSITE pleasant
❷ It was a vile act of cruelty.
• dreadful, despicable, appalling, abominable, contemptible, wicked, evil

villain NOUN
He is an actor who enjoys playing villains.
• rogue, scoundrel, wrongdoer, criminal
(informal) baddy, crook
OPPOSITE hero

violate VERB
The court decided that the company had violated environmental laws.
• break, infringe, contravene, disobey, flout, disregard, ignore

violation NOUN
This is a serious violation of the rules.
• breach, breaking, infringement, contravention, flouting

violence NOUN
❶ The film includes scenes of graphic violence.
• fighting, physical force, aggression, brutality, savagery, barbarity
OPPOSITES non-violence, pacifism

❷ The violence of the storm uprooted trees.
• force, power, strength, might, severity, intensity, ferocity, vehemence, fury, rage
OPPOSITES gentleness, mildness

violent ADJECTIVE
❶ There were violent protests in the streets.
• aggressive, fierce, ferocious, rough, brutal, vicious, savage
❷ The bridge was washed away in a violent storm.
• severe, strong, powerful, forceful, intense, raging, turbulent, tempestuous, wild
OPPOSITES gentle, mild

virtually ADVERB
Plastics can be made into virtually any shape.
• almost, nearly, practically, effectively, in effect, more or less, just about, as good as

virtue NOUN
❶ He led a life of virtue.
• goodness, morality, honesty, decency, integrity, righteousness, rectitude
OPPOSITE vice
❷ Your plan does have the virtue of simplicity.
• merit, advantage, benefit, strength, asset, good point
OPPOSITE failing

virtuous ADJECTIVE
She always felt virtuous after doing some exercise.
• good, worthy, upright, honourable, moral, just, pure, righteous, law-abiding
OPPOSITES wicked, immoral

visible ADJECTIVE
The house was barely visible from the main road.
• noticeable, observable, viewable, detectable, discernible, evident, obvious, apparent, manifest
OPPOSITE invisible

vision NOUN

❶ *I began to have problems with my vision.*
- eyesight, sight, eyes
– Words that mean 'to do with vision or eyes' are **visual** and **optical**.

❷ *In the story she is haunted by nightmarish visions.*
- apparition, dream, hallucination, phantom, mirage

❸ *He was a science fiction writer of great vision.*
- imagination, inspiration, creativity, inventiveness, foresight

visit VERB

❶ *We're planning to visit friends in Toronto.*
- call on, go to see, drop in on, look in on, stay with

❷ *They'll be visiting eight European cities.*
- stay in, stop over in, travel to, tour, explore

visit NOUN

❶ *It was our first visit to Disneyland.*
- trip, outing, excursion, tour

❷ *Some friends are coming for a short visit.*
- stay, call, stopover

visitor NOUN

❶ *We've got visitors coming this weekend.*
- guest, caller, company

❷ *The city welcomes millions of visitors each year.*
- tourist, holidaymaker, sightseer, traveller

visualize VERB

I'm trying to visualize him with a beard.
- imagine, picture, envisage, see, conjure up

vital ADJECTIVE

It is vital that we all stay together.
- essential, crucial, imperative, critical, all-important, necessary, indispensable
OPPOSITE unimportant

vitality NOUN

She is bursting with vitality and new ideas.
- energy, life, liveliness, spirit, vigour, vivacity, zest, dynamism, exuberance
(*informal*) get-up-and-go

vivid ADJECTIVE

❶ *He was an artist who loved to use vivid colours.*
- bright, colourful, strong, bold, intense, vibrant, rich, dazzling, brilliant, glowing
OPPOSITES dull, muted

❷ *She wrote a vivid account of her visit to China.*
- lively, clear, powerful, evocative, imaginative, dramatic, lifelike, realistic, graphic
OPPOSITES dull, lifeless

voice NOUN

❶ *Her voice broke with emotion.*
- speech, tone, way of speaking

❷ *He promised to listen to the voice of the people.*
- opinion, view, expression
For tips on describing voices see **sound**.

voice VERB

Local people voiced their objections to the plan.
- express, communicate, declare, state, articulate

volcano NOUN

WORD WEB

- Molten rock that builds up inside a volcano is called **magma**. When the molten rock reaches the surface it is called **lava**. Lava and ash pouring from a volcano is a **volcanic eruption**.

- A volcano that may erupt at any time is an **active** volcano. One that may not erupt for some time is a **dormant** volcano; and a volcano that can no longer erupt is an **extinct** volcano.

- The scientific study of volcanoes is **volcanology** or **vulcanology**.

volume NOUN
❶ *The volume of traffic over the bridge has increased.*
• amount, quantity, bulk, mass
❷ *How do you find the volume of the test tube?*
• capacity, size, dimensions
❸ *The novel was originally published in three volumes.*
• book, tome, publication

voluntary ADJECTIVE
❶ *Attendance on the course is purely voluntary.*
• optional, discretionary, by choice
OPPOSITE compulsory
❷ *She does voluntary work in a charity shop.*
• unpaid
OPPOSITE paid

volunteer VERB
I volunteered to do the washing-up.
• offer, come forward, be willing
OPPOSITE refuse

vomit VERB
Symptoms include fever and vomiting.
• be sick, heave, retch, spew
(*informal*) throw up, puke

vote VERB
Who did you vote for in the election?
• cast your vote
– To choose someone by voting is to **elect** them.

vote NOUN
❶ *The results of the vote will be known tomorrow.*
• ballot, poll, election, referendum
❷ *When did women finally get the vote?*
• right to vote, suffrage, franchise

voucher NOUN
You can exchange this voucher for a free drink.
• coupon, ticket, token

vow NOUN
They each took a solemn vow of secrecy.
• pledge, promise, oath, bond, word

vow VERB
He vowed never to reveal her identity.
• pledge, promise, swear, give your word, take an oath

voyage NOUN
The voyage lasted two weeks.
• journey, crossing, passage, trip, expedition, cruise

vulgar ADJECTIVE
❶ *The new colour scheme just looks vulgar to me.*
• tasteless, cheap, tawdry, crass, unrefined
(*informal*) tacky
OPPOSITE tasteful
❷ *The book sometimes uses vulgar language.*
• indecent, rude, offensive, coarse, crude
OPPOSITE decent

vulnerable ADJECTIVE
The cubs are vulnerable without their mother.
• unprotected, unguarded, defenceless, exposed, open to attack, at risk, in danger
OPPOSITES safe, protected
➤ **vulnerable to**
The town was vulnerable to attack from the north.
• in danger of, at risk from, exposed to, open to, susceptible to
OPPOSITES safe from, protected from

Ww

waddle *VERB*
A pair of geese came waddling towards us.
• toddle, totter, shuffle, shamble, wobble

wade *VERB*
❶ The river is too deep to wade across.
• paddle, wallow, splash
❷ She has piles of paperwork to wade through.
• plough, labour, work, toil

wag *VERB*
The dog was eagerly wagging its tail.
• move to and fro, wave, shake, swing, swish, waggle, wiggle

wage *NOUN*
How much is your weekly wage?
• earnings, income, pay, pay packet
– A fixed regular wage, usually for a year's work, is a **salary**.

wage *VERB*
The Greeks waged a long war against Troy.
• carry on, conduct, pursue, engage in, fight

wail *VERB*
All night long the wind wailed.
• howl, moan, cry, bawl, whine

wait *VERB*
I'll wait here until you get back.
• stay, stay put, remain, rest, stop, pause, linger
(*informal*) hang about, hang around, stick around, hold on

wait *NOUN*
There is a short wait between trains.
• interval, interlude, pause, delay, hold-up, lull, gap

wake or **waken** *VERB*
❶ She woke from a deep sleep.
• awake, awaken, wake up, stir, rise, come to, come round
❷ The doorbell woke me at 7.30.
• rouse, arouse, awaken, disturb

walk *VERB*
❶ Would you rather walk or take the bus?
• go on foot, travel on foot
❷ I offered to walk her home after the party.
• escort, accompany, guide, show, lead, take

OVERUSED WORD

❶ To walk slowly, casually:

➤ amble	➤ pace
➤ saunter	➤ step
➤ stroll	➤ tread

He sauntered down the lane, humming a tune.

❷ To walk quietly:

➤ creep	➤ stalk
➤ pad	➤ steal
➤ slink	➤ tiptoe
➤ prowl	➤ patter

I got up quietly and padded downstairs in my slippers.

❸ To walk heavily, loudly:

➤ stamp	➤ trudge
➤ pound	➤ traipse
➤ clump	➤ plod
➤ tramp	➤ wade

More police officers came clumping through the house.

❹ To walk smartly, proudly:

➤ march	➤ promenade
➤ stride	➤ swagger
➤ strut	➤ trot
➤ parade	

She imagined herself strutting down the catwalk in high heels.

a b c d e f g h i j k l m n o p q r s t u v w x y z

⑤ To walk unsteadily:

- ➤ stagger
- ➤ stumble
- ➤ shuffle
- ➤ shamble
- ➤ totter
- ➤ hobble
- ➤ toddle
- ➤ dodder
- ➤ lurch
- ➤ limp
- ➤ waddle
- ➤ lope

The creature shuffled off into the night.

⑥ To walk a long distance:

- ➤ hike
- ➤ trek
- ➤ ramble

They are planning to trek across the Himalayas.

⑦ To walk in a group:

- ➤ file
- ➤ troop
- ➤ march
- ➤ stream

We all trooped into the dining room for breakfast.

walk NOUN

❶ *We went for a walk in the country.*
• stroll, ramble, hike, trek, tramp, march, promenade
❷ *He was a tall man with a shambling walk.*
• gait, step, stride
❸ *There is a pleasant tree-lined walk alongside the canal.*
• path, trail, walkway, footpath, route

walker NOUN

The path is used by walkers and climbers.
• rambler, hiker
– Someone who walks along a street is a **pedestrian**.

wall NOUN

This is part of an ancient Roman wall.
• barricade, barrier, fortification, embankment
– A wall to hold back water is a **dam** or **dyke**.
– A low wall along the edge of a roof is a **parapet**.
– A wall built on top of a mound of earth is a **rampart**.

– A wall or fence made of sticks is a **stockade**.

wallow VERB

❶ *Hippos like to wallow in mud.*
• roll about, flounder, wade, lie, loll
❷ *He is wallowing in all the attention.*
• revel, take delight, bask, glory

wander VERB

❶ *A few goats wandered down from the hills.*
• roam, rove, range, ramble, meander, stroll
❷ *We must have wandered off the path.*
• stray, drift
❸ *Try not to wander too far from the topic.*
• digress, stray, drift, depart, deviate, get sidetracked

wane VERB

❶ *The afternoon light began to wane.*
• fade, fail, dim
OPPOSITE brighten
❷ *My enthusiasm was starting to wane.*
• decline, decrease, lessen, diminish, subside, weaken, dwindle
OPPOSITE strengthen

want VERB

❶ *He desperately wants to win a medal.*
• wish, desire, long, hope
❷ *She had always wanted a room of her own.*
• wish for, desire, fancy, crave, long for, yearn for, hanker after, pine for, hunger for, thirst for
IDIOMS set your heart on, be dying for
❸ *Your hair wants cutting.*
• need, require

want NOUN

❶ *You soon come to understand the wants of your pet.*
• demand, desire, wish, need, requirement
❷ *Livestock died from want of food and water.*
• lack, need, absence
❸ *Many families are still living in want.*
• poverty, hardship, need, deprivation, destitution

war NOUN
❶ *The war between the two countries lasted many years.*
• fighting, warfare, conflict, strife, hostilities
❷ *This is a victory in the war against drugs.*
• campaign, struggle, fight, effort

ward VERB
➤ **ward something off**
❶ *Use sunblock to ward off the sun's rays.*
• avert, block, check, deflect, turn aside, parry
❷ *Garlic is said to ward off vampires.*
• fend off, drive away, repel, keep away

warehouse NOUN
The goods were stored in a large warehouse.
• storeroom, depository, depot, store

wares PLURAL NOUN
They make a living selling their wares to tourists.
• goods, merchandise, produce, stock, commodities

warfare NOUN
A carved panel depicted scenes of warfare.
• fighting, combat, war, hostilities, conflict

warlike ADJECTIVE
'The War of the Worlds' portrays Martians as warlike.
• aggressive, violent, hostile, militant, belligerent
– Someone who seeks to start a war is a **warmonger**.
OPPOSITES peaceful, peace-loving

warm ADJECTIVE
❶ *It was a warm summer evening.*
• mild, balmy, sultry, summery
– A climate that is neither extremely hot nor extremely cold is **temperate**.
OPPOSITES cold, chilly
❷ *Use warm, not boiling, water.*
• tepid, lukewarm, hand-hot

❸ *She put on a warm coat and went out.*
• cosy, snug, thick, chunky, woolly, thermal
OPPOSITES thin, light
❹ *Let's give our guests a warm welcome.*
• friendly, welcoming, kind, hospitable, cordial, genial, amiable, sympathetic
OPPOSITES unfriendly, frosty

warm VERB
Come in and warm yourself by the fire.
• heat, make warmer, thaw out
OPPOSITE chill

warn VERB
I warned you it was dangerous to come here.
• advise, caution, counsel, alert, make someone aware
– To warn people of danger is to **raise the alarm**.

warning NOUN
❶ *There was no warning of the earthquake.*
• sign, signal, indication, advance notice (*informal*) tip-off
❷ *Perhaps the dream was a warning.*
• omen, portent, sign, premonition, foreboding
❸ *The referee let him off with a warning.*
• caution, reprimand

warp VERB
Heat may cause the plastic to warp.
• bend, buckle, twist, curl, bow, distort
OPPOSITE straighten

warrior NOUN
He wore the armour of a samurai warrior.
• fighter, soldier, combatant

wary ADJECTIVE
❶ *She took a wary step towards the creature.*
• cautious, careful, watchful, attentive, vigilant, on your guard
OPPOSITE reckless
❷ *Foxes are extremely wary of humans.*
• distrustful, suspicious, chary
OPPOSITE trusting

a
b
c
d
e
f
g
h
i
j
k
l
m
n
o
p
q
r
s
t
u
v
w
x
y
z

wash VERB

❶ *I washed quickly and went downstairs.*
• bathe, bath, shower
❷ *How often do you wash your hair?*
• clean, cleanse, shampoo
– To wash clothes is to **launder** them.
– To wash something in clean water is to **rinse**, **sluice** or **swill** it.
❸ *Wash the floor regularly with warm water.*
• mop, wipe, scrub, sponge
❹ *Waves washed over the deck.*
• flow, splash, lap, break, surge, roll
❺ *A huge wave washed him overboard.*
• carry, sweep

wash NOUN

❶ *It's time to give the dog a wash.*
• clean, bath
❷ *Put any used towels in the wash.*
• laundry, washing

waste VERB

Let's not waste any more time.
• squander, misuse, throw away, fritter away
OPPOSITE save

waste NOUN

A lot of household waste can be recycled.
• rubbish, refuse, litter, junk, garbage, trash
– Waste food is **leftovers**.
– Waste metal is **scrap**.

wasteful ADJECTIVE

We need to be less wasteful with our energy.
• extravagant, uneconomical, profligate, prodigal, lavish, spendthrift
OPPOSITES economical, thrifty

watch VERB

❶ *I could sit and watch the sea for hours.*
• look at, gaze at, stare at, peer at, view, eye, scan, scrutinize, contemplate
❷ *Watch how the goalkeeper reacts.*
• observe, note, take notice of, keep your eyes on, pay attention to, attend to, heed
❸ *Could you watch my bag for a minute?*
• keep an eye on, keep watch over, guard, mind, look after, safeguard,

supervise, tend
❹ *I got the feeling we were being watched.*
• spy on, monitor, track, tail, keep under surveillance
(*informal*) keep tabs on
➤ **watch out**
Watch out! There's a wave coming!
• be careful, pay attention, beware, take care, take heed

watch NOUN

I was keeping a close watch on the horizon.
• guard, lookout, eye, vigil

watchful ADJECTIVE

She kept a watchful eye on the door.
• alert, attentive, observant, vigilant, sharp-eyed, keen
OPPOSITE inattentive

water NOUN

How much of the Earth's surface is covered by water?
– Animals and plants which live in water are **aquatic**.
For areas of water see **landscape**.

water VERB

Please remember to water the plants.
• wet, irrigate, sprinkle, dampen, moisten, soak, drench
➤ **water something down**
❶ *Some paints need to be watered down.*
• dilute, thin out
❷ *The story has been watered down for the film version.*
• tone down, soften, tame, temper, moderate

watery ADJECTIVE

❶ *She gave me a bowl of watery, tasteless soup.*
• weak, thin, runny, diluted, watered down
❷ *Chopping onions makes my eyes watery.*
• tearful, wet, moist, damp

wave NOUN

❶ *We could hear the sound of waves breaking on the beach.*
• breaker, roller, billow

– A very small wave is a **ripple**.
– A huge wave caused by an earthquake is a **tidal wave** or **tsunami**.
– A number of white waves following each other is **surf**.
– The rise and fall of the sea is the **swell**.
– The top of a wave is the **crest** or **ridge**.
❷ *A wave of anger spread through the crowd.*
• surge, outbreak, flood, stream, rush, spate

wave VERB
❶ *The tall grass waved in the breeze.*
• sway, swing, shake, undulate, move to and fro, flap, flutter, ripple
❷ *He came in waving a newspaper in the air.*
• shake, brandish, flourish, twirl, wag, waggle, wiggle
❸ *She waved at us to go over.*
• beckon, gesture, signal, motion, indicate

waver VERB
❶ *For a second his voice wavered.*
• quiver, tremble, quaver, flicker, shake
❷ *Her new-found courage began to waver.*
• falter, give way, weaken, crumble
❸ *I wavered about whether to send the email.*
• hesitate, dither, vacillate, be uncertain, think twice
(*informal*) shilly-shally
IDIOM hum and haw

wavy ADJECTIVE
The quilt is stitched in a wavy pattern.
• curly, curling, rippling, winding, zigzag
OPPOSITE straight

way NOUN
❶ *He showed me the best way to make scrambled eggs.*
• method, procedure, process, system, technique
❷ *She is behaving in a very odd way.*
• manner, fashion, style, mode
❸ *Is this the right way to the castle?*
• direction, route, road, path
❹ *We've still got a long way to go.*
• distance, journey, length, stretch

❺ *In some ways, it's a good idea.*
• respect, particular, feature, detail, aspect
❻ *Things were in a bad way.*
• state, condition

weak ADJECTIVE
❶ *They were weak from hunger and thirst.*
• feeble, frail, sickly, infirm, puny, weedy
OPPOSITES strong, robust
❷ *He proved to be a weak leader.*
• ineffective, powerless, timid, meek, soft, faint-hearted, spineless, indecisive
OPPOSITE powerful
❸ *The footbridge was old and weak in places.*
• fragile, flimsy, rickety, shaky, unsound, unstable
OPPOSITES sound, sturdy
❹ *The story is spoiled by a weak ending.*
• poor, feeble, unsatisfactory, inadequate, unconvincing, implausible, lame
(*informal*) wishy-washy
❺ *The phone signal is weak here.*
• faint, low, dim, muted, faded, diluted, indistinct
OPPOSITES strong, clear

weaken VERB
❶ *Too much water will weaken the flavour.*
• reduce, lessen, diminish, sap, undermine
❷ *The storm had weakened overnight.*
• decrease, decline, fade, dwindle, die down, peter out, wane, ebb
OPPOSITE strengthen

weakness NOUN
❶ *Her illness left her with a feeling of weakness in her limbs.*
• feebleness, frailty, fragility, infirmity, instability
❷ *Our players have different strengths and weaknesses.*
• fault, flaw, defect, imperfection, shortcoming, weak point
OPPOSITE strength
❸ *I have a weakness for chocolate cake.*
• liking, fondness, taste, partiality,

a
b
c
d
e
f
g
h
i
j
k
l
m
n
o
p
q
r
s
t
u
v
w
x
y
z

penchant
(*informal*) soft spot

wealth NOUN
The family had acquired its wealth from oil.
• fortune, money, riches, affluence, prosperity
OPPOSITE poverty
➤ a wealth of
The website has a wealth of information on volcanoes.
• lots of, plenty of, a mine of, an abundance of, a profusion of
(*informal*) loads of, tons of

wealthy ADJECTIVE
He comes from a very wealthy family.
• rich, affluent, prosperous, moneyed, well-off, well-to-do
(*informal*) flush, loaded, well-heeled
OPPOSITES poor, impoverished

weapon NOUN

WORD WEB

Some types of weapon:

➤ bayonet	➤ machine gun
➤ blowpipe or blowgun	➤ missile
➤ bomb	➤ mortar
➤ club	➤ pistol
➤ cudgel	➤ revolver
➤ dagger	➤ rifle
➤ flick knife	➤ shell
➤ gun	➤ sword
➤ hand grenade	➤ taser
➤ harpoon	➤ torpedo
➤ machete	➤ truncheon

- Weapons in general are **weaponry** or **arms**.

- A collection or store of weapons is an **armoury** or **arsenal**.

Weapons used in the past:

➤ battering ram	➤ broadsword
➤ battleaxe	➤ cannon
➤ blunderbuss	➤ catapult
➤ bow and arrow	➤ crossbow
➤ cutlass	➤ sabre
➤ javelin	➤ scimitar
➤ lance	➤ spear
➤ longbow	➤ staff
➤ musket	➤ tomahawk
➤ pike	➤ trident

wear VERB
❶ *What are you wearing to the party?*
• dress in, be dressed in, be clothed in, have on, sport
❷ *She wore a frown all evening.*
• have on, bear, exhibit, display, put on, assume
❸ *The rug in the hallway is starting to wear.*
• become worn, wear away, wear out, fray
❹ *These boots have worn well.*
• last, endure, survive
➤ wear off
The effects of the potion are wearing off.
• fade, lessen, diminish, ease, subside, die down, dwindle
➤ wear someone out
All this talking has worn me out.
• exhaust, tire out, fatigue, weary, drain
(*informal*) do in

wear NOUN
❶ *Everyone was in formal evening wear.*
• dress, clothes, attire
(*informal*) gear, get-up
❷ *I've had a lot of wear out of this jacket.*
• use, service
(*informal*) mileage

weary ADJECTIVE
We all felt weary after a hard day.
• tired, worn out, exhausted, fatigued, flagging, drained, spent
(*informal*) all in, bushed
IDIOM ready to drop

weather NOUN
The weather should be fine tomorrow.
• conditions, outlook, elements
- The regular weather conditions of a particular area is the **climate**.
- The study of weather patterns in order to forecast the weather is **meteorology**.

Ⓦ WRITING TIPS

DESCRIBING THE WEATHER
Weather conditions:

- blizzard
- breeze
- cloudburst
- cyclone
- deluge
- downpour
- drizzle
- drought
- fog
- frost
- gale
- hail
- haze
- heatwave
- hurricane
- mist
- monsoon
- rainstorm
- shower
- sleet
- smog
- snowstorm
- squall
- storm
- sunshine
- thunderstorm
- tornado
- torrent
- tsunami
- typhoon

Cloudy:

- dull
- grey
- overcast
- sunless

Cold:

- arctic
- bitter
- chilly
- crisp
- freezing
- frosty
- icy
- (*informal*) nippy
- (*informal*) perishing
- raw
- snowy
- wintry

Hot:

- baking
- close
- humid
- muggy
- roasting
- sizzling
- sticky
- sultry
- sweltering
- torrid

Stormy:

- rough
- squally
- tempestuous
- thundery
- turbulent
- violent
- wild

Sunny:

- balmy
- bright

- cloudless
- dry
- fair
- fine
- mild
- summery
- sunshiny

Wet:

- damp
- drizzly
- lashing
- pouring
- rainy
- showery
- spitting
- teeming
- torrential

Windy:

- blowy
- blustery
- breezy
- gusty

Other:

- adverse
- changeable
- hostile
- inclement
- temperate
- foggy
- misty
- springlike
- autumnal

weather *VERB*
They had weathered many dangers together.
• survive, withstand, endure, come through, pull through

weave *VERB*
❶ *She has woven a thrilling tale.*
• construct, fabricate, put together, create, invent, spin
❷ *A cyclist weaved his way through the traffic.*
• wind, wend, thread, zigzag, dodge, twist and turn

web *NOUN*
A web of tunnels lay under the castle.
• network, labyrinth, complex, lattice, mesh

wedding *NOUN*
She was a bridesmaid at her aunt's wedding.
• marriage, union
(*formal*) nuptials

wedge VERB
❶ *The door was wedged open with a shoe.*
• jam, stick
❷ *A large man wedged himself into the seat next to me.*
• force, shove, push, cram, ram, stuff

weep VERB
She began to weep.
• cry, sob, shed tears
– To weep noisily is to **bawl** or **blubber**.
– To weep in an annoying way is to **snivel** or **whimper**.

weigh VERB
➤ **weigh someone down**
❶ *The streets were full of shoppers weighed down with bags.*
• load, burden, lumber
❷ *Many troubles were weighing him down.*
• bother, worry, trouble, distress, burden, depress
(IDIOM) prey on your mind
➤ **weigh something up**
She carefully weighed up the evidence.
• consider, assess, evaluate, examine, study, ponder, mull over

weight NOUN
❶ *We need to measure your height and weight.*
• heaviness
For weights and measures see measure.
❷ *Take care when lifting heavy weights.*
• load, mass, burden
❸ *His name still carries a lot of weight.*
• influence, authority, power, pull, sway
(informal) clout

weighty ADJECTIVE
❶ *The shelf was filled with weighty volumes.*
• heavy, substantial, bulky, cumbersome
(OPPOSITES) light, slim
❷ *They had weighty matters to discuss.*
• important, serious, grave, significant
(OPPOSITES) unimportant, trivial

weird ADJECTIVE
❶ *My sister has a weird taste in clothes.*
• strange, odd, peculiar, bizarre, curious, quirky, eccentric, outlandish, unconventional, unorthodox, idiosyncratic
(informal) wacky, way-out
(OPPOSITE) conventional
❷ *Weird noises have been heard in the tower at midnight.*
• eerie, uncanny, unnatural, unearthly, other-worldly, mysterious, ghostly, surreal
(informal) spooky, creepy
(OPPOSITE) natural

welcome NOUN
We were not expecting a warm welcome.
• greeting, reception

welcome ADJECTIVE
❶ *She makes a welcome addition to the cast.*
• pleasing, agreeable, desirable, acceptable, favourable, gratifying
(OPPOSITE) unwelcome
❷ *You're welcome to use my laptop.*
• allowed, permitted, free
(OPPOSITE) forbidden

welcome VERB
❶ *The elderly butler welcomed us at the door.*
• greet, receive, meet, usher in
❷ *I welcomed the chance to be alone for a while.*
• appreciate, be glad of, be grateful for, embrace

welfare NOUN
You are responsible for the welfare of your pet.
• well-being, health, comfort, security, good, benefit, interests

well ADVERB
❶ *The whole team played well on Saturday.*
• ably, skilfully, competently, effectively, efficiently, admirably, excellently, marvellously, wonderfully
(OPPOSITE) badly
❷ *Stir the mixture well and leave to cool.*
• thoroughly, carefully, rigorously,

properly, effectively, completely
❸ *Those colours go well together.*
• agreeably, pleasantly, harmoniously, suitably, fittingly, happily, nicely
❹ *I used to know her quite well.*
• closely, intimately, personally

well ADJECTIVE
❶ *She looks surprisingly well for her age.*
• healthy, fit, strong, sound, robust, vigorous, lively, hearty
(OPPOSITES) unwell, poorly
❷ *All was not well in the kitchen.*
• right, fine, all right, in order, satisfactory, as it should be
(*informal*) OK or okay

well-known ADJECTIVE
The new store will be opened by a well-known TV personality.
• famous, celebrated, prominent, notable, renowned, distinguished, eminent
(OPPOSITES) unknown, obscure

went
past tense see **go**

west NOUN, ADJECTIVE & ADVERB
Mumbai is in the west of India.
– The parts of a country or continent in the west are the **western** parts.
– To travel towards the west is to travel **westward** or **westwards**.
– A wind from the west is a **westerly** wind.

wet ADJECTIVE
❶ *All our clothes were wet and covered with mud.*
• damp, soaked, soaking, drenched, dripping, sopping, wringing wet
(OPPOSITE) dry
❷ *The pitch was too wet to play on.*
• waterlogged, saturated, sodden, soggy, squelchy, muddy, boggy
❸ *The paint was still wet.*
• sticky, tacky, runny
❹ *It was cold and wet all afternoon.*
• rainy, showery, drizzly, dank, pouring, teeming

wet VERB
Wet the paper with a damp sponge.
• dampen, moisten, soak, water, douse
– To wet something thoroughly is to **saturate** or **drench** it.
(OPPOSITE) dry

wheel NOUN
– A small wheel under a piece of furniture is a **caster**.
– The centre of a wheel is the **hub**.
– The outer edge of a wheel is the **rim**.

wheel VERB
❶ *A pair of seagulls wheeled overhead.*
• circle, orbit
❷ *Suddenly the whole herd wheeled to the right.*
• swing round, turn, veer, swerve

whereabouts NOUN
His whereabouts remain unknown.
• location, position, site, situation

whiff NOUN
I caught a whiff of perfume as she passed.
• smell, scent, aroma

while NOUN
You may need to wait a while for the next train.
• time, period, interval, spell, stretch

whimper VERB & NOUN
I heard a little whimper in the dark.
• cry, moan, whine

whine VERB
❶ *The dogs growled and whined all night long.*
• cry, whimper, wail, howl
❷ *What is he whining about now?*
• complain, protest, grumble, grouse, carp
(*informal*) gripe, moan, whinge

whip VERB
❶ *Slaves were whipped for minor offences.*
• beat, flog, lash, thrash, scourge
(*old use*) scourge
❷ *Whip the eggs in a separate bowl.*
• whisk, beat

❸ *She whipped a piece of paper out of her pocket.*
• pull, whisk, pluck, take

whirl VERB
❶ *Dead leaves whirled in the autumn wind.*
• turn, twirl, spin, circle, spiral, reel, revolve, rotate, pirouette
❷ *Her mind whirled with new questions.*
• spin, reel, swim

whisk VERB
Whisk the oil and vinegar together.
• beat, whip, mix, stir

whisper VERB
What are you two whispering about?
• murmur, mutter, mumble
OPPOSITE shout

white ADJECTIVE & NOUN
❶ *I took out a sheet of plain white paper.*
• snow-white, off-white, whitish, ivory, pearl
– To make something white or pale is to **bleach** it.
– When someone turns white with fear they **blanch** or **turn pale**.
❷ *Her hair had turned white.*
• hoary, silvery, snowy, platinum

whole ADJECTIVE
❶ *Have you read the whole trilogy?*
• complete, entire, full, total, unabbreviated, unabridged
OPPOSITE incomplete
❷ *The skeleton appears to be whole.*
• in one piece, intact, unbroken, undamaged, perfect
OPPOSITES broken, in pieces

wholehearted ADJECTIVE
I would like to express my wholehearted support.
• unconditional, unqualified, unreserved, full, complete, total
OPPOSITE half-hearted

wholesome ADJECTIVE
We had a wholesome breakfast of porridge and fruit.
• healthy, nutritious, nourishing
OPPOSITE unhealthy

wholly ADVERB
I'm not wholly convinced by this story.
• completely, totally, fully, entirely, utterly, thoroughly, absolutely, one hundred per cent
OPPOSITE partly

wicked ADJECTIVE
❶ *In the story she meets a wicked witch.*
• cruel, vicious, villainous, evil, detestable, mean, corrupt, immoral, sinful
OPPOSITES good, virtuous
❷ *They hatched a wicked plan to take over the world.*
• evil, fiendish, diabolical, malicious, malevolent, monstrous, nefarious, vile, base
❸ *He gave me a wicked grin.*
• mischievous, playful, cheeky, impish, roguish

wide ADJECTIVE
❶ *The hotel is by a wide stretch of sandy beach.*
• broad, expansive, extensive, vast, spacious, spread out
OPPOSITE narrow
❷ *She has a wide knowledge of classical music.*
• comprehensive, extensive, vast, wide-ranging, encyclopedic
OPPOSITE limited

widely ADVERB
The story of Robin Hood is widely known.
• commonly, generally, far and wide

widen VERB
The river widens as it nears the bay.
• broaden, open out, spread out, expand, extend, enlarge

widespread ADJECTIVE
❶ *Overnight storms have caused widespread flooding.*
• extensive, wholesale
OPPOSITE limited
❷ *The campaign has attracted widespread support.*
• general, common, universal, global, worldwide, ubiquitous, prevalent
OPPOSITE uncommon

width NOUN
What is the width of the left-hand margin?
• breadth, thickness, span
– The distance across a circle is its **diameter**.

wield VERB
❶ *A woman approached us wielding a clipboard.*
• brandish, flourish, hold, wave
❷ *He stills wields influence over his fans.*
• exert, exercise, command, hold, maintain

wife NOUN
Which goddess was the wife of Zeus?
• spouse, partner, consort, bride
IDIOMS other half, better half

wild ADJECTIVE
❶ *They came across a herd of wild horses.*
• undomesticated, untamed, feral
OPPOSITE tame
❷ *The hedgerow was full of wild flowers.*
• natural, uncultivated
OPPOSITE cultivated
❸ *To the west is a wild and mountainous region.*
• rough, rugged, uncultivated, uninhabited, desolate
OPPOSITE cultivated
❹ *It was a night of wild celebrations.*
• riotous, rowdy, disorderly, unruly, boisterous, noisy, uncontrollable, hysterical
OPPOSITES calm, restrained

❺ *The weather looks wild outside.*
• stormy, windy, blustery, gusty, turbulent, tempestuous
OPPOSITE calm
❻ *Take a wild guess.*
• unplanned, random, haphazard, arbitrary

wilful ADJECTIVE
❶ *She was wilful as a child.*
• obstinate, stubborn, strong-willed, headstrong, pig-headed, uncooperative, recalcitrant
OPPOSITE amenable
❷ *He was charged with wilful damage to property.*
• deliberate, intentional, planned, conscious, premeditated
OPPOSITE accidental

will NOUN
❶ *He had a strong will to succeed.*
• determination, drive, resolve, willpower, tenacity, commitment
❷ *She was forced to marry against her will.*
• wish, desire, inclination, preference

willing ADJECTIVE
❶ *Are you willing to help?*
• ready, prepared, inclined, disposed, happy, glad, pleased
OPPOSITE unwilling
❷ *I need a couple of willing volunteers.*
• enthusiastic, helpful, cooperative, obliging
OPPOSITES reluctant, grudging

wilt VERB
❶ *Without water the leaves will start to wilt.*
• become limp, droop, flop, sag
❷ *Both players seemed to wilt in the heat.*
• flag, droop, become listless
OPPOSITES revive, perk up

wily ADJECTIVE
Yet again he was outwitted by his wily opponent.
• clever, crafty, cunning, shrewd, scheming, artful, sly, devious

win VERB

❶ *Which team do you think will win?*
• come first, be victorious, succeed, triumph, prevail, come out on top
OPPOSITE lose

❷ *Last year we won first prize.*
• get, receive, gain, obtain, achieve, secure
(*informal*) pick up, walk away with, land, bag

win NOUN

This was a famous win over their old rivals.
• victory, triumph, conquest
OPPOSITE defeat

wind NOUN

The whole island was buffeted by strong winds.
– A gentle wind is a **breath**, **breeze** or **draught**.
– A violent wind is a **cyclone**, **gale**, **hurricane** or **tornado**.
– A sudden unexpected wind is a **blast**, **gust**, **puff** or **squall**.

wind VERB

❶ *A path winds up the hill.*
• bend, curve, twist and turn, zigzag, weave, meander, snake

❷ *She wound a bandage round her finger.*
• wrap, roll, coil, curl, loop, twine
OPPOSITE unwind

window NOUN

– The glass in a window is the **pane**.
– A semicircular window above a door is a **fanlight**.
– A window in a roof is a **skylight**.
– A decorative window with panels of coloured glass is a **stained-glass window**.
– A person whose job is to fit glass in windows is a **glazier**.

windy ADJECTIVE

❶ *It was a windy day in autumn.*
• breezy, blowy, blustery, gusty, wild, squally
OPPOSITES calm, still

❷ *We stood on a windy hilltop.*
• windswept, exposed, draughty
OPPOSITE sheltered

wink VERB

❶ *My friend winked at me and smiled.*
– To shut and open both eyes quickly is to **blink**.
– To flutter your eyelashes is to **bat** them.

❷ *The lights winked on and off.*
• flicker, flash, sparkle, twinkle

winner NOUN

The winner was presented with a silver cup.
• victor, prizewinner, champion, conqueror
(*informal*) champ
OPPOSITE loser

winning ADJECTIVE

❶ *For the second time he was on the winning team.*
• victorious, triumphant, successful, conquering, top-scoring, champion
OPPOSITE losing

❷ *She has a winning smile.*
• engaging, charming, appealing, attractive, endearing, captivating, disarming

wintry ADJECTIVE

I looked out on a wintry landscape.
• snowy, frosty, icy, freezing, cold

wipe VERB

I wiped the table with a damp cloth.
• clean, rub, polish, mop, swab, sponge
➤ **wipe something out**
The dinosaurs were wiped out 65 million years ago.
• destroy, annihilate, exterminate, kill off, get rid of

wire NOUN

Under the desk was a tangle of computer wires.
• cable, lead, flex
– A system of wires is **wiring**.

wisdom NOUN

She's a woman of great wisdom.
• sense, judgement, understanding,

intelligence, sagacity, common sense, insight, reason

wise ADJECTIVE
❶ *The soothsayer was very old and wise.*
• intelligent, learned, knowledgeable, knowing, perceptive, rational, thoughtful, sensible, sagacious
❷ *I think you made a wise decision.*
• good, right, sound, sensible, astute, shrewd
OPPOSITE foolish

wish VERB
You can make as many copies as you wish.
• want, desire, please, choose, see fit

wish NOUN
She had a lifelong wish to travel into space.
• desire, want, longing, yearning, hankering, craving, urge, fancy, hope, ambition
(*informal*) yen

wisp NOUN
She blew a wisp of hair away from her face.
• shred, strand, lock

wistful ADJECTIVE
She gave a wistful sigh as she read the letter.
• sad, melancholy, thoughtful, pensive, nostalgic

wit NOUN
❶ *No one had the wit to ask for help.*
• intelligence, cleverness, sharpness, shrewdness, astuteness, brains, sense, judgement
❷ *The film script sparkles with wit.*
• humour, comedy, jokes, witticisms
❸ *Uncle Charlie is a bit of a wit.*
• joker, comedian, comic
(*informal*) wag

witch NOUN
They say the family was cursed by a witch's spell.
• sorceress, enchantress
– A group of witches is a **coven**.

witchcraft NOUN
Thousands of women were accused of witchcraft.
• sorcery, wizardry, enchantment, black magic, necromancy

withdraw VERB
❶ *She withdrew a handkerchief from her pocket.*
• remove, extract, take out, pull out
OPPOSITE insert
❷ *They could still withdraw their offer.*
• take back, cancel, retract
OPPOSITES make, present
❸ *A number of riders withdrew from the race.*
• pull out, back out, drop out
OPPOSITE enter
❹ *The rebels withdrew to the hills.*
• retreat, draw back, pull back, fall back, retire, adjourn
OPPOSITE advance
❺ *Troops are being withdrawn from the city.*
• call back, pull back, recall
OPPOSITE send in

wither VERB
Crops were withering in the fields.
• shrivel, dry up, shrink, wilt, droop, go limp, sag, flop
OPPOSITE flourish

withhold VERB
He was accused of withholding vital information.
• keep back, hold back, hold onto, retain, keep secret
(*informal*) sit on
OPPOSITES release, make available

withstand VERB
The bridge is designed to withstand high winds.
• endure, stand up to, tolerate, bear, cope with, survive, resist, brave, weather

witness NOUN
Police have appealed for witnesses to the accident.
• observer, onlooker, eyewitness, bystander, spectator, viewer

A
B
C
D
E
F
G
H
I
J
K
L
M
N
O
P
Q
R
S
T
U
V
W
X
Y
Z

witty ADJECTIVE
I tried to think of a witty reply.
• humorous, amusing, comic, funny, entertaining, clever, droll
OPPOSITE dull

wizard NOUN
❶ *The whole kingdom was under the wizard's spell.*
• magician, sorcerer, enchanter, warlock
❷ *I thought you were a wizard with computers.*
• expert, genius, ace, master, maestro
(*informal*) whizz

wobble VERB
❶ *The front wheel was wobbling all over the place.*
• waver, sway, rock, totter, teeter, jiggle
❷ *My voice wobbles when I'm nervous.*
• shake, tremble, quake, quiver, waver, vibrate

wobbly ADJECTIVE
❶ *The baby giraffe was a bit wobbly on its legs.*
• shaky, tottering, unsteady
OPPOSITE steady
❷ *My shopping trolley had a wobbly wheel.*
• loose, rickety, rocky, unstable, unsteady
(*informal*) wonky

woman NOUN
This event is for women only.
• lady, female
– A woman whose husband has died is a **widow**.
– An old-fashioned word for an unmarried woman is a **spinster**.
– Words used in the past for a young unmarried woman are **maid**, **maiden** and **damsel**.

won
past tense see win

wonder NOUN
❶ *We were speechless with wonder.*
• admiration, awe, amazement, astonishment, reverence

❷ *It is one of the wonders of modern science.*
• marvel, miracle, phenomenon, sensation

wonder VERB
I wonder why he left in such a hurry.
• be curious about, ask yourself, ponder, think about
➤ **wonder at**
You can only wonder at the skill of the craftsmen.
• marvel at, admire, be amazed at, be astonished by

wonderful ADJECTIVE
❶ *It's wonderful what smartphones can do now.*
• amazing, astonishing, astounding, incredible, remarkable, extraordinary, marvellous, miraculous, phenomenal
❷ *We had a wonderful evening.*
• excellent, splendid, great, superb, delightful
(*informal*) brilliant, fantastic, terrific, fabulous, super

wood NOUN
❶ *The little cabin was made from wood.*
• timber, logs, planks
❷ *We followed a nature trail through the wood.*
• woodland, forest, trees, grove, copse, thicket

wooden ADJECTIVE
❶ *We sat down on a wooden bench.*
• wood, timber
❷ *The acting was a bit wooden at times.*
• stiff, stilted, unnatural, awkward, lifeless, unemotional, expressionless
OPPOSITE expressive

woolly ADJECTIVE
❶ *He wore a woolly hat with ear flaps.*
• wool, woollen
– Clothes made of wool, such as hats and scarves, are **woollens**.
❷ *Seal pups are born with a woolly coat.*
• thick, fleecy, shaggy, fuzzy, hairy
❸ *This is not just a woolly idea.*
• vague, confused, unclear, unfocused, hazy

word NOUN

① *What's another word for 'chuckle'?*
• expression, term
– The words used in a particular subject or language are its **vocabulary**.
② *I'll have a word with her about it.*
• talk, conversation, discussion, chat
③ *Do you have any words of advice?*
• remark, comment, statement, observation
④ *You gave me your word.*
• promise, assurance, guarantee, pledge, vow
⑤ *There has been no word since they left.*
• news, message, information, report, communication

word VERB
Be careful how you word the email.
• express, phrase, put into words

wording NOUN
I found the wording confusing at first.
• phrasing, choice of words, expression, language, terminology

wore
past tense see wear

work NOUN

① *It is hard work pedalling uphill.*
• effort, labour, toil, exertion, slog (informal) graft, grind
② *I've got a lot of work to do this weekend.*
• tasks, assignments, duties, chores, jobs, homework, housework
③ *What kind of work does she do?*
• occupation, job, employment, profession, business, trade, vocation
For types of work see occupation.
④ *Do you have a copy of the complete works of Shakespeare?*
• writing, composition, piece, text

work VERB
① *You've been working at the computer all day.*
• labour, toil, exert yourself, slave, slog (informal) beaver away
② *I used to work in a florist's on Saturdays.*
• be employed, have a job, go to work

③ *My watch has stopped working.*
• function, go, run, operate
④ *This camera is very easy to work.*
• operate, use, control, handle, run
➤ **work out**
① *He works out several times a week.*
• exercise, train
② *Things didn't quite work out as planned.*
• turn out, happen, emerge, develop
➤ **work something out**
See if you can work out the formula.
• figure out, puzzle out, calculate, determine, solve, decipher, unravel

worker NOUN
The factory employs around 200 workers.
• employee
– All the workers in a business are the **staff** or **workforce**.

world NOUN
① *Antarctica is a remote part of the world.*
• earth, globe, planet
② *He felt that the world was against him.*
• everyone, humankind, mankind, humanity
③ *Scientists are searching for life on other worlds.*
• planet
④ *She knows a lot about the world of sport.*
• sphere, realm, domain, field, arena, society, circle

worldwide ADJECTIVE
The award brought him worldwide celebrity.
• global, international, universal
OPPOSITE local

worried ADJECTIVE
She seemed worried about something.
• anxious, troubled, apprehensive, uneasy, disturbed, concerned, bothered, tense, nervous, fretful, agitated, upset
OPPOSITES unconcerned, carefree

a b c d e f g h i j k l m n o p q r s t u v w x y z

A
B
C
D
E
F
G
H
I
J
K
L
M
N
O
P
Q
R
S
T
U
V
W
X
Y
Z

worry VERB
❶ *Please tell me what's worrying you.*
• trouble, bother, distress, concern, upset, unsettle, disturb, make you anxious
IDIOM prey on your mind
❷ *There's no need to worry.*
• be anxious, be troubled, be concerned, brood, fret, agonize, lose sleep (over)

worry NOUN
❶ *She has a permanent look of worry on her face.*
• anxiety, distress, uneasiness, apprehension, vexation, disquiet, agitation
❷ *Money has always been a worry for them.*
• trouble, concern, burden, care, problem, trial
(*informal*) headache, hassle

worsen VERB
❶ *Anxiety can worsen an asthma attack.*
• make worse, aggravate, intensify, exacerbate, add to
OPPOSITES alleviate, relieve
❷ *Her condition worsened overnight.*
• get worse, deteriorate, degenerate, decline
IDIOM go downhill
OPPOSITES improve, get better

worship VERB
❶ *The Greeks worshipped many gods and goddesses.*
• pray to, glorify, praise, venerate, pay homage to
SEE ALSO religion
❷ *He used to worship his older brother.*
• adore, be devoted to, look up to, love, revere, idolize, esteem

worth NOUN
❶ *He had to sell the painting for a fraction of its true worth.*
• value, price, cost
❷ *How much worth do you place on friendship?*
• importance, significance, value, merit

worthless ADJECTIVE
It's nothing but a worthless piece of junk.
• useless, unusable, valueless, of no value
OPPOSITES valuable, useful

worthwhile ADJECTIVE
❶ *It may be worthwhile to get a second opinion.*
• useful, valuable, beneficial, advantageous, rewarding, profitable, fruitful
OPPOSITE pointless
❷ *They are raising money for a worthwhile cause.*
• good, deserving, admirable, commendable, respectable, worthy

worthy ADJECTIVE
The money we raise is going to a worthy cause.
• good, deserving, praiseworthy, admirable, commendable, respectable
OPPOSITE unworthy

wound NOUN
❶ *He is being treated in hospital for a head wound.*
• injury, cut, gash, graze, scratch, laceration
❷ *It was a serious wound to her pride.*
• insult, blow, affront, slight, offence, injury, hurt

wound VERB
❶ *Four people were wounded in the blast.*
• injure, hurt, harm
❷ *At first, he was wounded by her words.*
• hurt, insult, affront, slight, offend, pain, grieve

wrap VERB
❶ *I wrapped the presents in shiny gold paper.*
• cover, pack, package, enclose, encase
❷ *We wrapped ourselves in warm blankets.*
• enfold, swathe, bundle
– To wrap water pipes is to **insulate** or **lag** them.

❸ *Her death is still wrapped in mystery.*
• cloak, envelop, shroud, surround

wreathe VERB
❶ *The tree was wreathed in fairy lights.*
• festoon, garland, drape, deck, ornament, adorn, decorate
❷ *Mount Fuji is often wreathed in clouds.*
• encircle, envelop, swathe, shroud, surround

wreck VERB
❶ *His bike was wrecked in the crash.*
• demolish, destroy, crush, smash, shatter, crumple
(*informal*) write off
❷ *This could wreck my chances of seeing her again.*
• ruin, spoil, put a stop to, shatter, dash, scotch
(*informal*) scupper, put paid to

wreck NOUN
Divers discovered the wreck of an old Spanish galleon.
• remains, ruins, wreckage

wreckage NOUN
Wreckage from the aircraft was scattered for miles.
• debris, fragments, pieces, remains

wrench VERB
The wind wrenched the door off its hinges.
• pull, tug, prise, jerk, twist, force
(*informal*) yank

wrench NOUN
❶ *With a wrench he tore himself free.*
• jerk, jolt, pull, tug, twist
(*informal*) yank
❷ *It was a wrench leaving their old home.*
• pain, pang, trauma

wrestle VERB
❶ *They wrestled the suspect to the ground.*
• grapple, tussle, fight, battle
❷ *He'd been wrestling with the problem for weeks.*
• struggle, grapple, agonize (over)

wretched ADJECTIVE
❶ *She was left feeling wretched and alone.*
• miserable, unhappy, desolate, depressed, dejected, downcast, forlorn, woeful
❷ *They were forced to live in wretched conditions.*
• squalid, sordid, pitiful, bleak, harsh, grim, miserable
❸ *This wretched computer has frozen again!*
• annoying, maddening, exasperating, useless

wriggle VERB
She managed to wriggle through a gap in the fence.
• squirm, writhe, wiggle, twist, worm your way
➤ **wriggle out of something**
He tried to wriggle out of doing his fair share.
• avoid, shirk, escape, dodge, duck

wring VERB
❶ *She wrung the water out of her hair.*
• press, squeeze, twist
❷ *The actor paced up and down wringing his hands.*
• clasp, grip, wrench, twist, squeeze
➤ **wringing wet**
These towels are wringing wet.
• soaked, drenched, soaking, dripping, sopping, saturated

wrinkle NOUN
Her tiny hands were laced with wrinkles.
• crease, fold, crinkle, pucker, furrow, line, groove, ridge
– Wrinkles at the corners of a person's eyes are **crow's feet**.

wrinkle VERB
He wrinkled his nose in disgust.
• pucker, crease, crinkle, gather, crumple, furrow, rumple, scrunch up
OPPOSITE smooth

write VERB
❶ *He wrote the answer on a piece of paper.*
• jot down, note, print, scrawl, scribble

– To write words or letters on a hard surface is to **inscribe** it.
– To write your signature on something is to **autograph** it.

❷ *She wrote a diary of her experiences.*
• compile, compose, set down, draw up, pen

– To write a rough version of a story is to **draft** it.
– To write something hurriedly is to **dash it off.**

❸ *I've been meaning to write to you.*
• correspond (with)

IDIOM (*informal*) drop someone a line

writer NOUN

WORD WEB

People who write:

➤ author
➤ biographer
➤ blogger
➤ composer
➤ correspondent
➤ dramatist or playwright
➤ journalist or reporter
➤ novelist
➤ poet
➤ scribe
➤ scriptwriter or screenwriter
➤ speech-writer

writhe VERB

The snake writhed and tried to escape.
• thrash about, twist, squirm, wriggle

writing NOUN

❶ *The writing is very difficult to read.*
• handwriting, script, lettering, print

– Writing that is engraved or carved is an **inscription.**
– Untidy writing is a **scrawl** or **scribble.**
– The art of beautiful handwriting is **calligraphy.**

❷ *I am reading an anthology of crime writing.*
• literature, works, stories, publications, books

wrong ADJECTIVE

❶ *These calculations are all wrong.*
• incorrect, mistaken, inaccurate, erroneous
(*informal*) out
OPPOSITES right, correct

❷ *Do you think it would be wrong to keep the money?*
• bad, dishonest, irresponsible, immoral, unfair, unjust, corrupt, criminal, wicked, sinful
OPPOSITE right

❸ *I must have said something wrong.*
• inappropriate, unsuitable, improper, unwise, ill-advised, ill-considered
OPPOSITES right, appropriate

❹ *There's something wrong with the TV.*
• faulty, defective, amiss, awry, not right, out of order
➤ go wrong
Everything started to go horribly wrong.
• fail, backfire
(*informal*) flop, go pear-shaped
OPPOSITES go right, succeed

wrong ADVERB

Have I spelled your name wrong?
• incorrectly, inaccurately, mistakenly, erroneously
OPPOSITES correctly, properly

wrong NOUN

❶ *I'm sure you know the difference between right and wrong.*
• dishonesty, immorality, injustice, corruption, evil, wickedness, villainy

❷ *It is important to admit the wrongs of the past.*
• misdeed, injustice, offence, injury, crime, sin, transgression

wrongly ADVERB

He was wrongly accused of stealing.
• falsely, mistakenly, erroneously, incorrectly, inaccurately, in error
OPPOSITES correctly, accurately

wrote

past tense see write

yank *(informal) VERB & NOUN*
Don't yank on the horse's reins.
• tug, jerk, pull, wrench

yard *NOUN*
A pony stood in the middle of the yard.
• court, courtyard, enclosure

yearly *ADJECTIVE*
The village holds a yearly festival in mid-July.
• annual

yearn *VERB*
➤ yearn for something
I yearned for some peace and quiet.
• long for, crave, wish for, desire, hunger for, pine for, hanker after
(informal) be dying for

yell *VERB*
He yelled at them to stop.
• shout, call out, cry out, bawl, bellow, roar, howl

yell *NOUN*
She let out a loud yell of surprise.
• shout, cry, bawl, bellow, roar, howl

yellow *ADJECTIVE & NOUN*

WORD WEB

Some shades of yellow:

➤ amber	➤ lemon
➤ buttery	➤ mustard
➤ cream	➤ straw
➤ gold	➤ tawny
➤ golden	➤ yellow ochre

– Yellow hair is **blonde** or **fair** hair.

For tips on describing colours see **colour**.

yelp *VERB & NOUN*
One of the guards let out a yelp of pain.
• cry, howl, yowl

yield *VERB*
❶ *The King stubbornly refused to yield.*
• give in, give way, back down, surrender, admit defeat, concede, capitulate, submit
(informal) cave in
❷ *These trees yield plenty of apples every year.*
• bear, produce, grow, supply, generate

yield *NOUN*
We had a poor yield of potatoes this year.
• crop, harvest, produce, return

young *ADJECTIVE*
❶ *The play is aimed at a young audience.*
• youthful, juvenile
OPPOSITES older, mature
❷ *This game is a bit young for teenagers.*
• childish, babyish, immature, infantile
OPPOSITES adult, grown-up

young *PLURAL NOUN*
All mammals feed their young on milk.
• offspring, children, young ones, family, progeny
– A group of young birds that hatch together is a **brood**.
– A group of young animals that are born together is a **litter**.

youth *NOUN*
❶ *She spent much of her youth abroad.*
• childhood, boyhood or girlhood, adolescence, teens
❷ *The fight was started by a group of youths.*
• adolescent, youngster, juvenile, teenager, young adult
❸ *My grandad says he does not understand the youth of today.*
• young people, the younger generation

youthful *ADJECTIVE*
She still has a youthful look about her.
• young, youngish, vigorous, sprightly, young-looking

a b c d e f g h i j k l m n o p q r s t u v w x y z

Zz

zeal NOUN
She plays the leading role with zeal.
• energy, vigour, enthusiasm, spirit, passion, verve, gusto

zero NOUN
Four minus four makes zero.
• nought, nothing
– A score of zero in football is **nil**. In cricket it is a **duck** and in tennis it is **love**.

zest NOUN
After his recovery he had a renewed zest for life.
• enthusiasm, eagerness, vitality, energy, vigour, passion

zigzag VERB
The road zigzags along the coast.
• wind, twist, weave, meander, snake

zodiac NOUN

WORD WEB

Signs of the zodiac:

➤ Aquarius (or the Water-carrier)
➤ Aries (or the Ram)
➤ Cancer (or the Crab)
➤ Capricorn (or the Goat)
➤ Gemini (or the Twins)
➤ Leo (or the Lion)
➤ Libra (or the Scales)
➤ Pisces (or the Fish)
➤ Sagittarius (or the Archer)
➤ Scorpio (or the Scorpion)
➤ Taurus (or the Bull)
➤ Virgo (or the Virgin)

– An astrological forecast based on signs of the zodiac is a **horoscope**.

– Another word for a sign of the zodiac is a **star sign**.

– The study of the signs of the zodiac is **astrology**.

zone NOUN
The whole state was declared a disaster zone.
• area, district, region, sector, locality, territory, vicinity, neighbourhood

zoo NOUN
The zoo is enlarging its gorilla enclosure.
• zoological gardens, wildlife reserve, safari park
– A small zoo is a **menagerie**.

zoom VERB
❶ *A motorbike zoomed past us on the right.*
• speed, race, tear, dash, streak, whizz, rush, hurtle, fly
❷ *The camera zoomed in on a member of the audience.*
• focus, close
– A photograph taken at close range is a **close-up**.

Young Writer's Toolkit

Get started

Punctuation

Punctuation marks are used to make meaning clear. Even a slight change in punctuation can change the meaning of a sentence. Punctuation can also help you to create different effects in your writing.

full stop

A **full stop** comes at the end of a sentence. The first word in a sentence starts with a capital letter.

Short sentences can make writing seem dramatic and add pace and longer sentences are often descriptive. Be careful not to use too many short simple sentences. It can make your writing seem childish.

➤ *The door slammed shut. We were trapped.*
➤ *The house looked as though it hadn't been lived in for years, with its peeling paint and broken windows.*

question mark

A **question mark** is used at the end of a sentence to show that it is a question. If you are writing dialogue, remember the question mark goes inside the inverted commas.

➤ *Where are you?*
➤ *'Do you like football?' she asked.*

An **exclamation mark** is used to show that a sentence is about something urgent or surprising or to show a strong emotion such as delight or anger.

An exclamation mark can also show that a sentence is a **command** or **instruction**.

Even in informal writing, only one **exclamation mark** is needed.

> ➤ *What a lovely present!*
> ➤ *I can't believe you just said that!*
> ➤ *Run!*

comma

A **comma** is used to separate items in a list:

> ➤ *Javed wanted to visit Spain, Italy, Greece and Portugal.*

A **comma** is often used before a **coordinating conjunction** such as *or*, *and* or *but* in a **multi-clause** sentence. It introduces a pause and helps clarify meaning.

> ➤ *We're just waiting for Cheri, and then we'll set off.*

Commas are used after a **subordinate clause** or **adverb** or **adverbial** at the start of a sentence:

> ➤ *When he realized how much money I had spent, my dad went mad!*
> ➤ *Suddenly, I saw how much trouble I was in.*

Commas make a difference to the meaning of a sentence.

In the examples below, the sentence with the commas means that all zombies attack people and all will be prosecuted. The sentence without commas means that only some zombies always attack people and only those will be prosecuted.

> ➤ *Zombies who always attack people will be prosecuted.*
> ➤ *Zombies, who always attack people, will be prosecuted.*

colon

A **colon** can be used to introduce a list. A **colon** also introduces examples or explanations.

> ➤ *They came in four colours: red, blue, yellow and green.*
> ➤ *Athletes need to eat a lot of high-protein snacks: eggs and fish are popular choices.*

semicolon

A **semicolon** joins two sentences or main clauses which are of equal importance.

> ➤ *The film was brilliant; we had a great time.*

apostrophe

An **apostrophe** is used to show that letters are missing in words. These are called **contractions**. When writing formally, such as in exams, or for essays and letters, do not use contractions. However dialogue which shows the words that people say often uses contractions.

> ➤ *I can't = I cannot*
> ➤ *I don't = I do not*

An **apostrophe** also shows that something belongs to someone. If you are unsure of where to put the apostrophe, try to reword your sentence so that an apostrophe is not needed.

> ➤ *the murderer's fingerprints*
> ➤ *the children's shoes*
> ➤ *Where is Charles's coat?*

dash

A **dash** is often used in informal writing to show that sentences are linked or to introduce items in a list.

> ➤ *Jogging takes it out of you – especially if you aren't used to it.*
> ➤ *There are three of us – me, Sarah and Ali.*

brackets, commas or dashes

These can all be used to separate words or phrases that have been added as an explanation or afterthought.

- ➤ *I looked up (squinting because of the sun) and saw the birds flying.*
- ➤ *I looked up, squinting because of the sun, and saw the birds flying.*
- ➤ *I looked up – squinting because of the sun – and saw the birds flying.*

ellipsis

An **ellipsis** is three dots which show that a word has been missed out or that a sentence is not finished. It can add a feeling of suspense.

- ➤ *Suddenly, the door opened . . .*

An ellipsis can be used to show that words have been missed out of a long quote. This is useful in essays as it can save you a time.

- ➤ *From the lines, 'I picked him up . . . with just a toothbrush and the good earth for a bed' we learn that the hitchhiker is a drifter.*

hyphen

A **hyphen** joins words together and is important for making meaning clear.

They are useful if you create new words of your own.

- ➤ *my great-aunt*
- ➤ *a yellow-spotted, jelly-eating dinosaur*

inverted commas

When writing the exact words that someone has said, use **inverted commas** around the words. Be careful to always put the punctuation of the words that are spoken *inside* the inverted commas.

- ➤ *'Can I talk to you now, please?' she whispered.*

Sentences

A **sentence** may be a **single-clause** or a **multi-clause** sentence.
You can often change a piece of writing by making a few changes to
the structure of your sentences.

- Try to **vary the length** and type of sentences that you use. If you use
  too many of the same length and type, the reader can lose interest.

- Sometimes, **reordering** your sentence can give extra meaning and
  emphasis to a particular word or phrase.

  ➤ *The noises began on the stroke of midnight.*
  ➤ *On the stroke of midnight, the noises began.*

- Be careful not to join **two main clauses** with a **comma**. This creates
  a run-on sentence. You can fix it by making them into two sentences
  with a full stop and capital letter.

  ➤ *Humans could not breathe on Mars, the atmosphere is too thin.*
  ➤ *Humans could not breathe on Mars. The atmosphere is too thin.*

Paragraphs

A **paragraph** covers a single topic or idea. If you find you are starting a
new point in your argument, or are moving on to a new scene in your
story, it is time to start a new paragraph.

- In non-fiction writing, it helps to have a topic sentence which sums
  up the point of the paragraph.

- **Conjunctions** and **adverbs** can link ideas and paragraphs in your
  writing.

- You can use them to:

  ✔ sum up (*therefore*)

  ✔ add information (*in addition, also*)

  ✔ present points in order (*first, next, later, lastly*)

Formal language

Formal language is the language used in most of the writing you do at school.

- ✔ notes, letters or emails to a teacher
- ✔ exams
- ✔ official letters and emails
- ✔ essays or reports

When writing **formally**:

- ✔ write in complete sentences
- ✔ avoid contractions like *don't* and *I'm* (use *do not* and *I am*)
- ✔ avoid informal words and phrases, such as *thanks* (use *thank you* instead)
- ✔ in a letter or email, begin with *Dear* and end with *Yours sincerely*
- ✔ call the person you are writing to by their family name or title (if you do not know their name, call them *Sir* or *Madam*).

Informal language

Informal language is the language we use in everyday situations.

- ✔ letters, emails and messages to family and friends
- ✔ notes
- ✔ shopping lists and to-do lists

Informal language in writing is likely to include:

- ✔ some words in capital letters for emphasis
- ✔ lots of exclamation marks for emphasis
- ✔ abbreviations such as **LOL**
- ✔ contractions such as *didn't* or *wasn't*.

✓ Be creative

Try using descriptive words

Have a look at the **WRITING TIPS** panels in this thesaurus. There are lots of ways to describe things in your writing and these will give you some inspiration.

For example, look up the word **light** to find words for describing light. Does the light *glare*, or *flicker* or *glow*? Is it *muted*, *luminous* or *bright*?

W WRITING TIPS

DESCRIBING LIGHT
Effects of light:

➤ beam	➤ glitter
➤ blaze	➤ glow
➤ burn	➤ lustre
➤ dazzle	➤ radiance
➤ flame	➤ ray
➤ flare	➤ reflection
➤ flash	➤ shaft
➤ flicker	➤ shimmer
➤ glare	➤ shine
➤ gleam	➤ sparkle
➤ glimmer	➤ twinkle
➤ glint	➤ wink
➤ glisten	

Adjectives:

➤ bright	➤ diffused
➤ brilliant	➤ dim
➤ dappled	➤ harsh

Avoid overused words

Words like *bad*, *big* and *nice* are very useful but they become very boring and repetitive when used too often.

Using more specific words helps bring your writing to life in the mind of your reader.

You can look up the **OVERUSED WORD** panels in this thesaurus to help you. For example, look up the word **big**. Something might be *mammoth* or *whopping*, a room might be *roomy* and a decision might be *important* or *weighty* or *momentous*.

⬛ OVERUSED WORD

❶ Big in size, scale:

➤ large	➤ giant
➤ huge	➤ colossal
➤ great	➤ mammoth
➤ massive	➤ monstrous
➤ immense	➤ monumental
➤ enormous	➤ titanic
➤ gigantic	

(*informal*) whopping, mega
(*literary*) gargantuan
Our class made a **giant** *model of a human ear.*

OPPOSITES small, little, tiny

❷ Big in area, distance:

➤ vast	➤ considerable
➤ immense	➤ sweeping
➤ expansive	

Some day spaceships will be able to travel **vast** *distances.*

Try using accurate words

Using **accurate words** can make your writing factual and realistic. There are **WORD WEB** panels in this thesaurus which give you topic words and these will help you to be more precise.

For example, at **aircraft** you will find different types of aircraft such as *biplane, helicopter, glider, seaplane* or *spy plane*. You will also find names for the parts of an aircraft such as *fuselage, flight deck* or *rudder*.

> ### ✷ WORD WEB
>
> Some types of aircraft:
>
> | | |
> |---|---|
> | ➤ aeroplane (*North American* airplane) | ➤ hang-glider |
> | ➤ airliner | ➤ hot-air balloon |
> | ➤ air ambulance | ➤ jet |
> | ➤ airship | ➤ jumbo jet |
> | ➤ biplane | ➤ microlight |
> | ➤ bomber | ➤ monoplane |
> | ➤ delta wing | ➤ seaplane |
> | ➤ fighter | ➤ spy plane |
> | ➤ glider | ➤ (*historical*) Zeppelin |
>
> Parts of an aircraft:
>
> | | |
> |---|---|
> | ➤ cabin | ➤ passenger cabin |
> | ➤ cargo hold | ➤ propeller |
> | ➤ cockpit | ➤ rotor |
> | ➤ engine | ➤ rudder |
> | ➤ fin | ➤ tail |
> | ➤ flap | ➤ tailplane |
> | ➤ flight deck | ➤ undercarriage |
> | ➤ fuselage | ➤ wing |
> | ➤ joystick | |

Use phrases and idioms

An **idiom** is a phrase that does not mean exactly the same as the words in it. For example, *to be in hot water* is an idiom which means to be in trouble (not to be in actual hot water).

Idioms can make your writing more lively and humorous, especially if you are writing in an informal style or if you are writing what characters say. But be careful not to use too many or the same ones repeatedly.

Look for the (IDIOMS) sign in this thesaurus!

blow your own trumpet	lose your rag
send you to sleep	think twice
prey on your mind	keep a lid on
dead to the world	give a hand to
over the moon	sweep under the carpet
full of beans	

Use metaphors and similes

Using metaphors and similes is a good way of putting pictures into your readers' imaginations and helping them to 'see' your characters and descriptions clearly.

A **metaphor** is where you describe something as if it *were* something.

> ➤ *The lawn was a carpet of daisies.*

A **simile** is where you describe something as being 'as' or 'like' something else. For example, someone might have *a face like a squashed pumpkin* or *skin as rough as the bark of a gum tree.*

similes using 'as'

as blind as a bat	as graceful as a swan
as bright as day	as hard as nails
as clear as a bell	as light as a feather
as cunning as a fox	as nutty as a fruitcake
as deep as the ocean	as pretty as a picture
as dry as a bone	as quiet as a mouse
as fit as a fiddle	as strong as an ox
as good as gold	

similes using 'like'

built like a tank	memory like an elephant's
chatter like a monkey	move like a snail
eat like a pig	run like a deer
eyes like a hawk	sing like a bird
fits like a glove	stand out like a sore thumb
fight like cat and dog	swim like a fish

Create new words

You can add to the words in your thesaurus by creating new words.
Try building a new word starting with a word that you know, or one
that you have found in this thesaurus, and adding one of these **suffixes**
(endings) to it:

-ish	reddish, tallish, hairyish
-less or *-free*	a treeless landscape, a chocolate-**free** zone
-like	crablike arms
-proof	a zombie-**proof** room

You can add different beginnings (**prefixes**) to a word to create a new one:

eco-	eco-friendly house
over-	over-plumaged bird
extra-	the **extra**-funny story prize
super-	superhero, supersize

You can also build **compounds** by joining two words together.

-feeling	seasick-**feeling** face
-looking	wrinkly-**looking** skin
-smelling	liquorice-**smelling** plants
-smeared	blueberry-**smeared** cheeks
-faced	lizard-**faced** creature
-haired	purple-**haired** girl

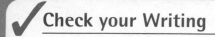

Check your Writing

British and North American spelling

There are differences in the way that certain words are spelled in
British and North American spelling.

The main differences are:

British English	North American English	example
-ence	-ense	defense
-ou-	-o-	mold
-our	-or	color
-s- or -z-	-z-	analyze, cozy

In British English, most verbs that end in *-ize* or *-ise* can be spelled
either way e.g. *recognize* or *recognise*. The ending *-ize* has been used
in British English since the 16th century. It is also the spelling used in
North America. It is a mistake to think that an *-ize* spelling is American.

There are some words that must always be spelled *-ise*.

words that are always spelled *-ise*		
advertise	devise	incise
comprise	enterprise	revise
compromise	exercise	supervise
despise	improvise	surprise

Here are some common words which have a different spelling in
British and North American English.

British English	North American English
analyse	analyze
armour	armor
behaviour	behavior
catalogue	catalog
centre	center